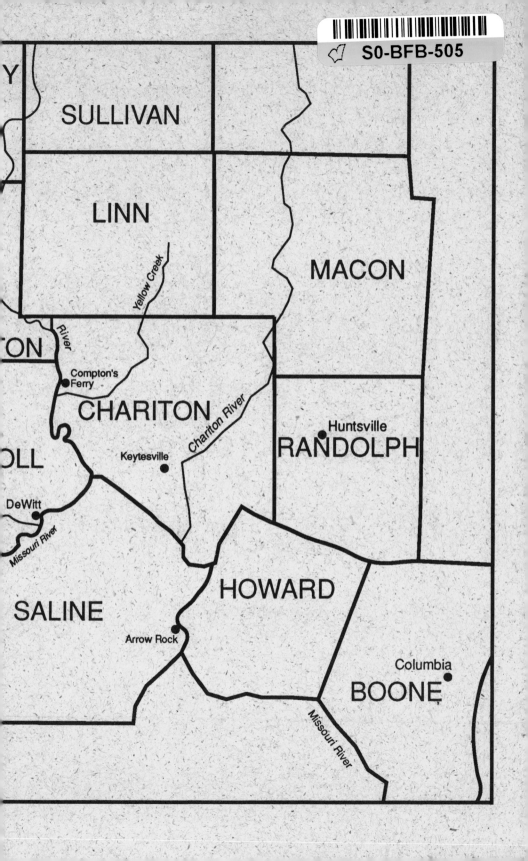

MORMON REDRESS PETITIONS

Documents of the 1833-1838 Missouri Conflict

RELIGIOUS STUDIES CENTER PUBLICATIONS

BOOK OF MORMON SYMPOSIUM SERIES

The Book of Mormon: The
Keystone Scripture
The Book of Mormon: First
Nephi, the Doctrinal
Foundation
The Book of Mormon: Second
Nephi, the Doctrinal Structure

The Book of Mormon: Jacob
Through Words of Mormon,
To Learn with Joy
The Book of Mormon: Mosiah,
Salvation Only Through Christ
The Book of Mormon: Alma,
The Testimony of the Word

MONOGRAPH SERIES

Nibley on the Timely and the
Timeless
Deity and Death
The Glory of God Is
Intelligence
Reflections on Mormonism
Literature of Belief
The Words of Joseph Smith
Book of Mormon Authorship
Mormons and Muslims
The Temple in Antiquity
Isaiah and the Prophets
Scriptures for the Modern World

The Joseph Smith Translation:
The Restoration of Plain and
Precious Things
Apocryphal Writings and the
Latter-day Saints
The Pearl of Great Price:
Revelations From God
The Lectures on Faith in
Historical Perspective
Mormon Redress Petitions:
Documents of the 1833–1838
Missouri Conflict

SPECIALIZED MONOGRAPH SERIES

Supporting Saints: Life Stories
of Nineteenth-Century
Mormons
The Call of Zion: The Story of
the First Welsh Mormon
Emigration
The Religion and Family
Connection: Social Science
Perspectives

Welsh Mormon Writings
from 1844 to 1862: A
Historical Bibliography
Peter and the Popes
John Lyon: The Life of a
Pioneer Poet
Latter-day Prophets
and the United States
Constitution

OCCASIONAL PAPERS SERIES

Excavations at Seila, Egypt

MORMON REDRESS PETITIONS

Documents of the 1833-1838 Missouri Conflict

Edited by Clark V. Johnson

Volume Sixteen
in the Religious Studies Center Monograph Series

Religious Studies Center
Brigham Young University
Provo, Utah

Library of Congress Catalog Card Number: 92–85092
ISBN 0–88494–850–1

First Printing, 1992

Distributed by BOOKCRAFT, INC.
Salt Lake City, Utah

Printed in the United States of America

This book is respectfully dedicated to my father, and to the men and women who wrote the documents presented. Their lives of integrity and dedication set an example for succeeding generations.

"He gave me 23 lashes with a cowhide and all this for my religeon for I am a member of the church of Jesus Christ of Latter day Saints."

Perry Keyes

The State of Missouri indebted to me
for a loss of property & damage sustained
under the exterminating order of Governor
Boggs of Missouri as follows —

One village lot worth one hundred dollars
One house on said lot worth one hundred dollars
also a Location of Land which cost me sixty
dollars — — — — —
expense and damage of moving from Davies
to Caldwell Co with my wife who was then
at the point of death — three hundred dollars
Expense and damage of being forc,d to flee from
Caldwell Co M° to the State of Illinois and also
of seeking a home among strangers two
hundred dollars. — — — — —

N.B. The above grievances & afflictions
I would not have suffered for the sum
of two thousand dollars

                            Harrison Burgess

State of Illinois
Pike County } ss May 18th 1839. Then personally
came before me Harrison Burgess

HARRISON BURGESS' PETITION

CONTENTS

ILLUSTRATIONS

BETWEEN PAGES 389–90

ACKNOWLEDGMENTS

No one puts a volume like this one together without the help of many other people. My debt to several people is significant. First, I am grateful to Paul C. Richards for his article in *BYU Studies* that drew my attention to the fact that a large group of petitions existed in the National Archives. Next I am grateful to James L. Kimball of the LDS Historical Department for showing me the important petitions held in the Church Archives.

I also express gratitude to the following for their help: the librarians of the Library of Congress, the National Archives, the Newberry Library of Chicago, the Illinois State Archives, the Chicago Historical Society, the Historical Department of The Church of Jesus Christ of Latter-day Saints, the Brigham Young University Harold B. Lee Library, and the Family History Library in Salt Lake City. I especially appreciate the county officers and clerks and the county genealogical and historical societies in Adams, Calhoun, Hancock, Jersey, Madison, McDonough, Morgan, Pike, Sangamon, and Scott Counties in Illinois, and Lee and Van Buren Counties in Iowa for opening their archives to me.

The individuals who have offered suggestions, typed, and read manuscripts are many, but among them I need to mention the following: Peggy Wahlquist Stout, Terry Wahlquist, Sabrina Vanderhoff, Ann Reed, Kaylene Porter Harding, Linda Haslam, Gladys Noyce, Brent Hall, Paul Damron, Richard Draper, Florian Thayne, James L. Kimball, Donald T. Schmidt, Leonard J. Arrington, Larry C. Porter, James B. Allen, Thomas G. Alexander, Ronald W. Walker, Cynthia Gardner, Rebecca H. Christensen, Charlotte Pollard, and Charles D. Tate, Jr.

I owe special recognition to Suzanne J. Woods and Stephanie S. Eliason of the BYU Religious Studies Center Publications Office. These two editors made major contributions to this book in checking my transcriptions of the petitions, organizing the manuscript, and preparing it for typesetting.

Finally, my special thanks go to my wife, Cheryl. Without her help and encouragement this work would have ground to a halt years ago.

INTRODUCTION

About a year after she was forced to leave Missouri, Philindia Myrick wrote:

> The mob came a ponus in the after part of the day with Mr Cumstock at thare hed and commens fireing on helpless men womens and children and thare was fifteen killed and was burried in one hole the next day and others wounded sum mortally and amung whom was my husband ~~instantly killed~~ Levi N. Myrick instantly killed and also a child of mine mortaly woun ded who died about 4 weeks after.

Philindia was among the 12,000–15,000 members of The Church of Jesus Christ of Latter-day Saints, nicknamed Mormons, who fled from Missouri after Governor Lilburn W. Boggs issued the Extermination Order, which required all Mormons to leave the state or be killed. The above passage is taken from an affidavit she filed on 10 January 1840 recounting her experience during the Haun's Mill massacre. Philindia Myrick's affidavit is representative of the almost 800 declarations made by some of those members of the Church who were driven from Missouri during the fall and winter of 1838–39.

The Mormon expulsion from Missouri is one of the most violent stories of religious persecution in U.S. frontier history. The collection of affidavits, or petitions for redress, provides a detailed account of the persecution of the Saints in Missouri as recorded by those who suffered there, but it also reflects the cultural, economic, social, and spiritual activities of the Saints who were present on the Missouri frontier in the 1830s.

Historical Background

Members of The Church of Jesus Christ of Latter-day Saints began settling western Missouri in 1831, at a time when small, utopian religious communities dotted the land west of the Allegheny Mountains. Their prophet-leader, Joseph Smith, dedicated several sites in Jackson County for the future use of the Church, and with determination the Saints began to build their homes (*HC* 1:191–202). But as early as April 1832, trouble arose between the Mormons and their Missouri neighbors. The Missourians felt their society was threatened by the continual influx of Mormons. Religious customs which united the Latter-day Saints socially, economically, and politically irritated the Missourians, and in 1833 mobs

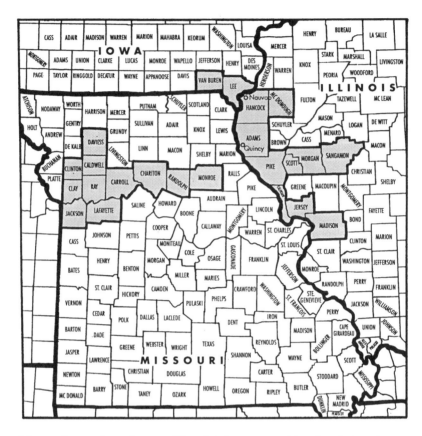

MISSOURI-ILLINOIS-IOWA COUNTIES. When the Mormons were driven from Jackson County in 1833, they settled in ten other counties in Missouri. In 1838, when they were forced to leave Missouri, they settled in Illinois and Iowa.

drove the Mormons from Jackson County. Most of the exiles settled in Clay County, but some moved north and east into the counties of Ray, Clinton, LaFayette, Carroll, Chariton, Randolph, Monroe, and into areas that later came to be known as Daviess and Caldwell counties. This brief respite lasted a few years, and the Mormons built homes and planted crops. Then in 1836, in response to continual Mormon immigration from the eastern states and agitation by Jackson County residents, mobs again began to gather against the Latter-day Saints.

In the years 1836–37, the citizens of Clay County undertook action to relocate the Saints in an unsettled part of Missouri (*Times and Seasons* 1:51). The Mormons moved to an area created for them by the Missouri legislature that became known as Caldwell County (Grant 22). Again they built homes and established farms and businesses; however, they knew little rest, for during the summer and fall of 1838, mobs once more came against them, and the violence escalated into the so-called Mormon War, which culminated in the expulsion of the Mormons from the state.

As an outgrowth of the Mormon War, Joseph Smith spent the winter of 1838–39 confined to jail in Liberty, Missouri. While imprisoned, he instructed the Saints to assemble all their grievances against Missouri, to organize a committee, and to present the information to the U.S. government (D&C 123:1–6). Joseph sent word to the Saints to prepare affidavits of their recent experiences with the design of securing redress from the federal government for the losses they had suffered in Missouri at the hands of mobocrats. In 1839, Church members commenced writing affidavits of their Missouri experiences and swearing to their authenticity before civil authorities, including justices of the peace, clerks of the court, clerks of the circuit court, clerks of county commissioner's courts, and notary publics in two counties in Iowa and ten counties in Illinois. Thus the Saints took every precaution to send sworn, legal documents authenticated by the seals of local government officials. They even sent documents authenticating the officials themselves. During the ensuing years the Mormons presented these documents to the federal government in an effort to obtain reparation for their sufferings in Missouri.

Appeals to Congress and Explanation of Organization

The petitions indicate that the Nauvoo Saints made at least three and probably four separate attempts to obtain redress from Congress (Richards 520, 522, 524; *HC* 4:250–51). These appeals are the basis for this book's organization—petitions have been grouped according to the appeal with which they were sent. Organizing the book in this way has necessitated

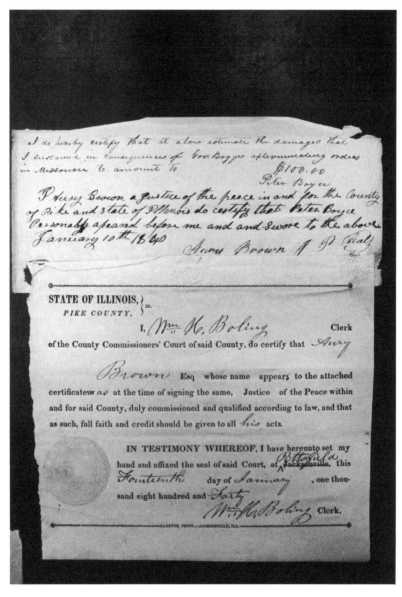

I do hereby certify that at a low estimate the damages that I sustained in consequence of Gov. Boggs exterminating orders in Missouri to amount To
$100.00
Peter Boyce

I Aury Brown a Justice of the peace in and for the County of Pike and state of Illinois do certify that Peter Boyce Personally appeared before me and and Swore to the above January 10th 1840
Aury Brown J P (Seal)

STATE OF ILLINOIS, } ss.
PIKE COUNTY,

I, *Wm. H. Boling* Clerk
of the County Commissioners' Court of said County, do certify that *Aury*
Brown Esq whose name appears to the attached certificates *as* at the time of signing the same, Justice of the Peace within and for said County, duly commissioned and qualified according to law, and that as such, full faith and credit should be given to all *his* acts.

IN TESTIMONY WHEREOF, I have hereunto set my hand and affixed the seal of said Court, at *Pittsfield* ~~Jacksonville,~~ this *Fourteenth* day of *January*, one thousand eight hundred and *Forty*
Wm. H. Boling Clerk.

GAZETTE PRINT....JACKSONVILLE, ILL.

CERTIFICATE OF OFFICE FOR AURY BROWN, JUSTICE OF THE PEACE. This certificate is an example of many that were sent to Contress to accredit the local officials who notorized the Mormons' petitions. *Photograph courtesy of LDS Historical Department.*

that judgments be made as to which appeal each petition belongs. These decisions were not always clear-cut, but the basis for them is explained below.

Church leaders made the first appeal beginning late in 1839 (Richards 520). Joseph Smith led the Mormon delegation, which originally consisted of Elias Higbee, Sidney Rigdon, and Orrin Porter Rockwell; Robert Foster later joined the group as a physician to Sidney Rigdon. The Prophet and Higbee were the first members of the delegation to reach Washington, D.C., arriving 28 November 1839. On the following day they met with President Martin Van Buren, who showed some sympathy, but offered no assistance. By 23 December 1839, Rigdon, Foster, and Rockwell had arrived in Washington, D.C. Together the five members of this delegation made every effort to place the Mormon cause before the U.S. Congress. Besides the introductory memorial signed by Joseph Smith, Sidney Rigdon, and Elias Smith, they presented 491 individual claims to Congress (*HC* 4:74). Nothing came from these attempts. Frustrated by their lack of success, Joseph, Porter Rockwell, and Dr. Foster left Washington late in February 1840 (*HC* 4:81). Rigdon and Higbee remained in Washington a few weeks more continuing the effort. However, nothing came of this final attempt, and Higbee returned to Nauvoo, followed shortly by Rigdon.

For purposes of organization, I have designated all petitions that are dated 1839 or 1840 and found in the LDS Historical Department's collection as part of the first appeal. This judgment is based on the fact that after the government failed to offer redress, Elias Higbee retrieved the petitions. It would make sense, therefore, that the petitions of the first appeal would be found in the Church's possession.

Documentation is scant on the Saints' next two attempts to obtain redress, one beginning in late 1840, and another beginning in early 1842. In fact, the petitions that are in the National Archives in Washington, D.C., were not known to exist until Paul Richards discovered them in the late 1960s or early 1970s (Richards 520). *History of the Church* records that in November 1840 Elias Higbee and Robert B. Thompson, acting under the direction of the Prophet, submitted a memorial and probably some individual claims to Congress (4:237). The location of the Higbee-Thompson memorial is not known, and no individual petitions were filed with Congressional documents of 1840 or 1841. A description of the missing memorial given by the Prophet Joseph Smith seems to indicate that the Higbee-Thompson memorial was essentially the same as the 1842 and 1839 memorials (*HC* 4:237). In 1842, another memorial, signed by Elias Higbee, Elias Smith, and John Taylor, was presented to Congress, probably as an introduction to more individual petitions (Richards 522–

23). In contrast to the first appeal, there is no record that the petitions of subsequent attempts were ever retrieved from Washington. Therefore, I have designated all of the individual petitions found in the National Archives, along with the memorial signed by Higbee, Smith, and Taylor, as the second appeal. This is done recognizing the fact that the individual petitions now held in the National Archives may have been sent in at different times.

The third appeal was quite different from the preceding appeals in that it did not include individual petitions, but instead was one summary petition signed by 3,419 people. It was prepared in Nauvoo in the late fall of 1843 (*HC* 6:88). Orson Pratt, Orson Hyde, and John E. Page presented the memorial to Congress during the winter and spring of 1844 (Page; *HC* 6:286). In spite of help from the Illinois Congressmen, this attempt also failed; Orson Hyde wrote on 9 June 1844 that Congress had rejected the petition (Hyde). He was also unsuccessful in getting help directly from President John Tyler. Finally, on 11 June 1844, Hyde wrote, "We are now thrown back upon our own resources. We have tried every department of Government to obtain our rights, but we cannot find them" (Hyde). This massive petition was never retrieved by the Saints, and was lost in the National Archives until it was discovered along with the petitions of the second appeal.

Some of the petitions included in this book are not grouped into any of the three main appeals. The first of these is the group of published accounts. These were published and circulated and must have been sent to Washington at some point since they are part of the National Archives Collection. They may have been sent along with an appeal, but since there is no record of such an appeal, and since they are unique in that they were published, they have been given their own part in this book. Another of these odd groups is made up of those petitions that were sworn before the Municipal Court of Nauvoo but never were sent to Congress. There are also a few petitions that were written after the third appeal: thirteen individual petitions are dated 1845. These seem to indicate that the Saints intended to make another, later appeal to the federal government, since they are similar to those petitions prepared in 1839 and 1840. Finally, there are those petitions which were not dated and could not be grouped with a specific appeal.

Collections and Locations of Petitions

The two main locations where original, handwritten petitions are found are the National Archives in Washington, D.C. and the LDS

Historical Department in Salt Lake City, Utah. (Copies of the original petitions from the National Archives are found in the BYU Archives.) There are a few other sources for the petitions in this collection, including the Journal History of the Church, the *History of the Church of Jesus Christ of Latter-day Saints*, the Joseph Smith Collection, and the Wilford C. Wood collection.

Most of the petitions were found in the Salt Lake collection, which includes 538 petitions (670 total documents); many were written in 1839 and 1840, but some were written as late as 1845.

There are 218 petitions in the National Archives. Most of these petitions are dated 1840. The National Archives' collection also includes some documents that are not petitions but are still related to the Missouri experience. These documents have been included in the final chapter of this book.

The *History of the Church* includes 40 petitions; the originals of most of these have been found in the Salt Lake Collection. The Journal History of the Church records 53 petitions, many of which are copies of petitions found in Salt Lake. The Joseph Smith Collection includes five petitions.

Just before publication of this book, another petition was discovered among the papers in the Wilford C. Wood collection. This collection consists of documents found in the cornerstone of the Nauvoo House in Nauvoo, Illinois. When Joseph Smith placed the printer's-copy of the Book of Mormon manuscript in the southeast cornerstone of the Nauvoo House, there were other documents also placed with it (Jessee 259–78). In 1882 Lewis C. Bidamon, husband of Emma Smith, removed the documents from the cornerstone when he tore down the east wing of the Nauvoo House. On 27 September 1882, it was reported that

> The stone was in the foundation . . . and in the center of it was a square cut chest, about 10x14 inches, and eight inches deep, covered with a stone lid, which fitted closely in a groove or shoulder at the top, and cemented around the edge with lead that had been melted and poured in the seam. On removing the lid, which was done with some difficulty, the chest was found to be filled with a number of written and printed documents, the most of them mouldy and more or less decayed (Jessee 265).

Among these was a fragment of a Missouri petition written by Lyman Wight.

It is difficult to determine the total petitions actually submitted to Congress. While in Washington, D.C. in 1840, Joseph Smith presented to Congress "about 491 claims against Missouri . . . leaving a multitude more of similar bills" (*HC* 4:74). This information was taken from a

FRAGMENT OF LYMAN WIGHT'S PETITION. This petition, discovered in the Wilford C. Wood Collection just prior to publication, is the only known petition not transcribed in this book. *Photograph courtesy of the Wilford C. Wood Foundation, Bountiful, Utah, and The Book of Mormon Critical Text Project, Royal Skousen, editor.*

register prepared for Joseph Smith by Thomas Bullock. The register is five pages long and contains the names and amounts each petitioner hoped to receive as compensation from the federal government. On the final page Bullock totals the dollar amount claimed by the Saints, $2,381,984.51, and writes in parentheses, "491 bills." This notation represents an error of 10 bills, for there are only 481 names listed on the register. The compilers of the Journal History of the Church also included a register of people who swore similar affidavits against the state of Missouri. This register is similar to the one prepared by Bullock, but it does not include the names of all the petitioners on the Bullock register. Its list of 482 names includes 11 names not on Bullock's list. Comparing the registers with the various petitions shows that there are 208 petitioners who are not listed on the registers and that 36 names are listed for which no petitions have been found.

These 36 lost petitions call attention to the fact that this collection is not complete. Still more significant is the fact that many more people suffered in Missouri than wrote petitions. As a group the petitions give an overview; they do not give a comprehensive account of the suffering or damages the Saints' sustained. It is estimated that 12,000–15,000 Saints were driven from Missouri. This collection represents petitions made by only 678.

This book contains 773 petitions written by 678 petitioners (121 people wrote two or more petitions). There are 49 petitions that are duplicated in one or more collections which fact accounts for the discrepancy between the number of documents in each collection and the total number of petitions in this study.

Contents of the Petitions

Although all of the Missouri Redress Petitions relate to the Mormon experience in Missouri, their contents are quite varied. The earliest event described in the petitions is the 1833 mobbing in Jackson County; the latest is the 1838 persecution caused by Governor Lilburn W. Boggs's Extermination Order. A few petitions are general narratives of the Mormon experience in Missouri, while most are accounts of individual losses and personal suffering. The general narrative petitions include Parley P. Pratt's and John P. Greene's published accounts, the introductory petitions that were sent with the first and second appeal, the scroll petition of the third appeal, and the six testimonies given before the Municipal Court of Nauvoo in 1843. Even among the individual petitions the contents differ. The affidavits of the first appeal contain simple bills or statements of

property loss. The petitions of the second appeal describe the suffering and personal atrocitites perpetrated upon individual Latter-day Saints by the mobs.

In addition, the petitions give insights about the petitioners themselves. Of the 678 petitioners who personally filed affidavits, 70 were women and 607 were men. At least 25 men and 10 women were illiterate, making their mark instead of signing their names. Twenty-five witnessed the Haun's Mill massacre or arrived shortly after the event; 8 claimed personal knowledge of the events and sufferings at DeWitt; 5 were at the Gallatin election; 3 described the events at Crooked River; and 23 were at Adam-ondi-Ahman. An astounding 106 men and 3 women claimed that they were taken prisoner by the Missouri militia or mobs.

These documents range from a few lines, such as the petition sworn by Stephen Blackman, to long narratives, such as the petition prepared by Joseph Smith. The detail in them varies tremendously; Stephen Blackman's is very concise:

> State of Missouri Dr to Stephen Blackman For damage and loss of property by burning and being driven from the State $150 For damage by loss of Son there is no earthly consideration can compensate

> Stephen Blackman

Then there are petitioners who give elaborate accounts of the losses they suffered in Missouri. Nahum Curtis is very specific:

May 13th 1839

> An account that I Nahum Curtiss have against the State of Missouri in Consequence of Mobocracy

To expenses moveing from the State of Michigan to the state of Missouri	$50.00
To Eight weeks that it took me to go with my family from Michigan to Missouri at $1 per day	48.00
To Eight weeks time each for my Two boys	96.00
To Loss on Land which I sustained in consequence of being driven from Missouri	1520.00
To Loss of time for myself and son in time of waring against the Mob six months each at one dollar per Day each	312.00
To Loss on Corn potatoes & oates and hay	150.00
To Loss of ploughs	5.00
To Loss on Cattle and Hogs	55.00

To one horse Taken by the Militia	50.00
To Loss of wagon in Consequence of mob Stealing it from me	20.00
To Expenses Moving from Missouri to Illinois	25.00
To waggon & team Moveing me to Illinois	40.00
To Money & property given to help the poor	50.00
To teams to help the poor out of the state of Missouri to Keep them from being killed by mob	40.00
	$2,461.00

I Shall not put any price upon my sufferings as your honorable body will Consider that I was a fellow Sufferer with the Rest and when you Judge what others ought to have you will consider that I had ought to have an equal porportion with the Rest

Nahum Curtis.

Of the 678 petitioners, 98 make no monetary claim against Missouri. The remaining 576 (85 percent) claim a total of $2,275,789, for an average of $3,761 per person. Simons Curtis claimed the smallest amount, 63 cents, while Edmund Nelson claimed $5,000 for loss of property and $500,000 for lost of liberty. Claims in land total $197,911; claims for improvements and property, defined as livestock, houses, personal property, etc., come to $197,127; and non-specific claims total $92,339. This last figure does not include Joseph and Hyrum Smith's claims for $100,000 each, with no breakdown of expenditures. Their claims are made more reasonable by the fact that the Prophet Joseph paid more than $50,000.00 in lawyer's fees while in Missouri (*HC* 3:327).

Some 232 petitioners state that they had purchased a combined total of 6,501 acres of land and asked for $55,046, making the average claim for land $237.27. This is less than $9 per acre, which was not high for land in Missouri in 1839. In their 1839 petition, Joseph Smith, Sidney Rigdon, and Elias Higbee state that land cost from $10 per acre for undeveloped prairie land to $425 per acre, depending on the location and improvements. Some of the land purchased by the Saints was called "congress land," which could originally be bought at $1.25 per acre; however, some paid between $5 and $415 per acre for congress land and received preemption certificates which gave them the right to purchase the land when the federal government placed it on the market. In the meantime, they settled the land, tilled the ground, and built houses and barns, thus increasing the value of their property. The petitions indicate that most of the Mormons owned at least one town lot and forty acres. A few owned eighty acres.

Only a very few owned several hundred acres, and they had lived in Missouri for several years.

Many of the petitioners indicate that they lived (and owned land) in more than one county during their sojourn in Missouri. The petitions show 119 Latter-day Saints owned land in Jackson County. Once they were driven from Jackson, they dispersed in every direction: 125 purchasing property in Clay County, 91 in Daviess, 25 in Ray, 19 in Carroll, 13 in Clinton, 7 in LaFayette, and 4 in Livingston counties. Van Buren, Randolph, and Chariton counties each had 3 land-holding Mormon families. An analysis of all of the petitions indicates that Mormon immigration did not cease even though there was persecution. By the summer of 1838, there were 4,900 people living in Caldwell County (Allen and Leonard 107). Among them were 290 petitioners who owned property.

Probably the reason the Mormons owned so little property overall was their recent arrival in Missouri. Of the 176 petitioners who indicate the year they arrived in Missouri, 58 had come between 1831 and 1836, and 126 had entered the state between 1837 and 1838. One claimant arrived as late as 1839. Thus, the majority of the petitioners arrived in Missouri just in time to be expelled; several indicate that they were detained by mobs while on their way to settle in Far West.

In spite of the fact that the Latter-day Saints owned relatively little land, much of it was taken from them. Albern Allen's 1840 petition is typical of many who claim they lost lands in Missouri. His affidavit indicates that he was foced to sign over his property to the Missouri militia at Far West. Like most of the Mormons in Caldwell County, Allen did not possess the deed to the land he farmed. Rather, he had been issued a preemption certificate, also called a duplicate, which he was forced to sign over to the mobbers. Allen claims he lost eighty acres. His petition is one of the few that defines his property in the precise terms used in the county records:

> N.E 1/4 of S. W. 1/4 of Section 32 Township No 56 Range 28 North of the base line and west of the 5th princepal Meridean also the NW. 1/4 of the South E 1/4 of Section 32 Township 56 Range 29 North of the base line of the 5th principal Meridian.

Most striking about the petitions are the testimonies of personal suffering that they contain. At least 73 petitions note that the mobs whipped, beat, and abused members of The Church of Jesus Christ of Latter-day Saints. Charles Hulett describes the beating of his son. Perry Keyes relates that thirty men beat his father "with there gunns and ramrods." He also describes how a mob attacked him while he was on the prairie hunting horses:

> Controll and one of his men by the name of Yocum held me while one of the others by the name of John Youngs whipped me he gave me 23 lashes with a cowhide and all this for my religeon for I am a member of the church of Jesus Christ of Latter day Saints commonly called Mormons

Keyes says they whipped him "untill I was scarsely able to stand," and adds that a mob also whipped Barnet Cole and Lyman Leonard.

Smith Humphrey writes that he had purchased a farm near the town of DeWitt in the summer of 1838 and planned on settling there permanently. He states that he was an eyewitness to much that happened there. Humphrey notes that on 19 August 1838 he was taken prisoner by a force of about one hundred men commanded by a Colonel Jones. During the time he was a prisoner, the mob declared that they were going to "drive them [*Mormons*] from that Co[*unty*]." Humphrey further swears that in the first days of October of the same year, he arose early one morning and found that his "Stables had been Set on fire by some unknown hand during the night." He wrote that he was then

> met by a party of 12 armed men commanded by Capt Hiram Standly who took me a prisoner back to my own house & there com pelled me to remove my goods from my house by their help in the presence of my self & family Set fire to & burned my two blocks of houses.

When his family was driven from his home, his wife was "sick with the ague." The mobbers forced them to move into town where they remained until 11 October 1838. According to Humphrey, the mob laid siege to DeWitt, fired into the town, and harassed the citizens "by night & by day." The people of DeWitt petitioned local county officers for help, but received none. Finally, sick and starving, they abandoned DeWitt and moved to Caldwell County, where they arrived 13 October 1838. Humphrey writes that "one woman died on the road."

Truman Brace describes his experience with a mob of fifty men who caught him hauling a load of wood on the prairies: "One of them named J Young asked me if I believed the book of Mormon; I told them that 'I did.'" They then demanded that Brace leave the county, whereupon he "told them I had neither teams or means to take me and my family away." Young threatened to shoot him, but others in the mob prevailed. Young, "then took an axe gad which I held in my hand and commenced beating me with the same. I suppose I received about fifty strokes." This whipping apparently occurred not far from Brace's home since his wife and daughter witnessed his plight and "entreated the mob to spare [*his*] life." Brace then made his way into his house, but the mob followed him and the abuse continued.

Tarlton Lewis had been converted to the Church about two years before he moved to Missouri in the fall of 1837. He located himself within one mile of Haun's Mill and was wounded at that massacre. Of his experience at the mill he writes:

> I looked and saw a number of armed men rushing out of the woods on Horseback at the distance of of twenty or thirty rods off Their number I judged to be between two hundred and two hundred and fifty. Two of our brethren made signs and cried for quarter, but their entreaties were not heeded The company began to fire upon us instantly.

Lewis and other men took shelter in the nearby blacksmith shop. The women and children fled to the woods or crossed the mill race where they found shelter in the brush and trees on the far side. The blacksmith shop, instead of being a shelter, soon became a death trap. Lewis writes, "I staid there until six or eight had fallen around me being Shot down by balls, which came through the Cracks. Six of us left the shop about the same time and were the last that left it." Of those six who fled the blacksmith shop, Lewis writes that they were "all either killed or wounded. . . . I was shot through the shoulder." The day following the massacre, the survivors, mostly women, buried their dead. Lewis states that "there were fifteen killed," and "ten or eleven men two boys and one woman Wounded." He further testifies that the mobbers continued their harassment of the survivors as they repeatedly visited the settlement during the weeks that followed:

> While I was confined with my wound; companies of Six or Eight came to my house three or four times Enquiring for arms and threatning to take me a prisoner and carry me off. Twice they Examined my wounds to see if I were able to be moved but concluded that I was not.

Nathan Knight, also a victim of the Haun's Mill incident, estimates the mob forces at 300 men, all mounted on horses. He heard the men commanded "to halt and form a line of Battle," and says the men "immediately commensed firing as they came into line." Knight swears that the mobbers frequently screamed out, "'kill all' 'Spare none' 'give no quarters.'" He describes the plight of the women and children as "wholly destitute of any presence of mind," saying that they were "screaming murder &c &c." With bullets "flying in every direction," he "saw many of his friends lay bleeding in their gore."[1] He further testifies that "he cried for quarters" to which the mobbers replied, "We have no time to quarter you, but god damn you we will halve you presently." Though

---

[1] Knight's petition is written in the third person.

severely wounded, Knight saved his own life by rising to his feet and "through their thickest fire made his way several rods over a hill" and secreted himself in a thicket. For six weeks he hung between life and death, and although he lived, he remained a cripple the rest of his life.

One of the most descriptive petitions regarding personal abuse suffered at the hands of mobocrats is sworn by William Seely, who states that he moved his family to the state of Missouri in March of 1838. He purchased congress land in Daviess County. On 10 October 1838, a mob came to his home and forced him to sign away his property and move to Caldwell County, Missouri. On 24 October 1838 he went to Bunkham's Strip to see a "Mr. Pinkham on business." Seely wrote that while at Pinkham's,

> He was Surprised & made prisoner by Some armed men. he was Stripped and Searched to see if he had any arms, by which he lost a Jack-knife the only weapon, offensive or defensive which he had about him; the armed men he believes were fifteen in number, two of whom Caught him by the Collar, thrust him out of doors, dragged him over a pannel of fence so vehemently as to do him bodily injury while at the same time a third one facilitated ~~my~~ his Course by the application of his foot to the rear of ~~my~~ his body—When over he was asked if he was a mormon, ~~for~~ to which he replied that he was.[2]

At this point his captors compelled him to march with them. Soon they joined Captain Samuel Bogart's company consisting of about seventy men. According to Seely, the "Question then arose What Shall we do with the prisoner, many Said at once, 'put him to death.'" This was the cry of those "volunteers who joined Bogart's Company, many of whom were men not Liable to duty by Law but who volunteered to give a martial Covering to the bloody deeds which they sought to perpetrate."

The following day, when Seely's friends came to his rescue, Seely says that Bogart's men fired upon the approaching Mormons and that "one man fell." The mobbers then forced Seely to stand

> in front of Bogart's Company So as to be Exposed to the fire of both sides, about 12 feet from Bogarts line. At the word "fire" by Bogart this affiant attempted to Escape but was Shot in the left Shoulder by some one of Bogarts men, which prostrated him to the Earth, and he was supposed to be dead, but his friends took him and Carried him to ~~his place~~ his family, where after four months tedious Confinement he in a measure recovered of his wounds.

---

[2]Seely's petition is also written in the third person.

Mormon women also suffered greatly at the hands of the mob. Several women wrote testimonials concerning the deaths of their husbands. Christiana Benner states, "My Husband was killed at Hauns mill By a mob who Robed me of my Goods and land and have left me Destitute of a companion or means of Support."

Although no women testify that they were raped, some write of the personal abuse they suffered. Ruth Naper, who survived the Haun's Mill massacre, writes concerning an attempted assault upon her:

> One night one of them [*mobbers*] came to my bed and laid his hand upon me which so frightened me that I made quite a noise and crept over the back side of my children, and he offered on no further insult at the time.

Elijah Reed witnessed the attempted abuse of a Mrs. Jimison (also spelled Jameson). To escape from the mob, Reed had fled to the Jimison's home where the following experience occurred 28 October 1838:

> In the night of of the that day a Company of men Came to the House & Demanded admittence & threatened to Breake Down the Door Mr J got up and opened the Door meantime I hid under the Bed the men Came in and said they were Soldiers & he [Jimmison] must go with them his wife asked where they said to the Malitia Camp above Richmond he Dressed himself & he & one of the men went for a horse at the Stable when they had got a little from the house the man Fired a gun & said the D——d rascal had ran from him he then returned to the house & they began to abus[e] Mrs Jimm[is]on wanting to sleep with her But she begged & cried For them to Desist & they Did so I lay under the Bed During this time they soon left the house & we supposed they had killed him.

Two of the general narrative petitions report that Mormon women were raped by the mob. Hyrum Smith states that one woman had been raped repeatedly by mobbers. Parley P. Pratt says that he knew of one or two women who had been raped, but would not give names for "delicacy forbids . . . mentioning the names."

Even though these petitions do not always specify monetary losses, they provide detailed accounts of the gruesome events that drove the Mormons from county to county in Missouri and finally from the state.

Taken as a group, these petitions give a panorama of the Mormon persecution in Missouri. At the same time, they describe the feelings, circumstances, and losses of the Latter-day Saints who composed the general Church membership and help us to evaluate Mormon life on the Missouri frontier.

In the past, scholars have argued that the Mormons were driven from Missouri because of the political, cultural, economic, social, and religious differences between themselves and the Missourians. Those scholars base their conclusions on documents written by some of the citizens of Jackson and Clay counties, when they demanded that the Mormons leave their counties (Bushman 11). But the petitions gathered here indicate that religious differences were the prime cause of LDS troubles, as time and time again mobbers asked the petitioners if they were followers of Joseph Smith, members of The Church of Jesus Christ of Latter-day Saints, or believers in the Book of Mormon before continuing with abuses.

Although this book has not attempted to examine both sides of the Mormon persecutions in Missouri, it has presented legally sworn documents which graphically substantiate the suffering and abuse committed by one people upon another, largely because of differences in religious belief. Simply stated, the Mormon Redress Petitions tell the story of a people wrongfully deprived of their rights as free men and women under both the constitution of the state of Missouri and the Constitution of the United States of America.

EDITORIAL PROCEDURES

Because the affidavits transcribed in this book were written by nearly 700 different authors, format and style vary tremendously from one petition to another. Although our main objective has been to be as true as possible to the handwritten originals, reproducing so many old documents written by so many different people called for more standardizations and approximations than were first expected.

The following list explains the specific editorial decisions we made. They apply to the book as a whole, but relate most directly to the handwritten, individual petitions, found in Chapters 4, 6, 9, and 10.

1.   Original spelling and capitalization have been maintained.

2.   Familiar marks of punctuation have been preserved even when they were used in unfamiliar ways. But unfamiliar marks of punctuation have been modified or deleted: a double period is transcribed as a single period.

3.   The spacing of the original petitions has been noted only when it seemed significant. When a large space seemed to indicate a paragraph break, a paragraph break has been made in its place. When a large space seemed to indicate a break between sentences, a bracketed period, [.], has been inserted in its place. When a large space seemed to represent a blank, as for an unknown name, then a long dash, ———, has been substituted in its place.

4.   Original paragraphing has been maintained, but indentation has been standardized. Due to software constraints, a few paragraph breaks had to be made where a petitioner did not indicate any. These breaks have been marked with the paragraph symbol, ¶.

5.   Abbreviations have been maintained, but punctuation has been altered to follow modern conventions. Petitioners had several ways of punctuating an abbreviated word—raising the final letter to a superscript, underlining a portion of the abbreviated word, etc. These obsolete marks of punctuation have all been omitted and replaced with a period.

6.   Superscripts have been lowered: 3rd to 3rd.

7.   Scribbles and marginal notes have, for the most part, been ignored. If they were deemed significant, they were described in a footnote. Navigational helps from the original petitions, such as page numbers or phrases like "continued on next page" have been omitted.

8. Words or letters that were blotted out, rubbed out, or struck over have all been printed as strikeovers, ~~mob~~, and have been preserved when they corrected more than a slip of the pen. Occasionally a petitioner did such a thorough job of obscuring a mistake that it was not possible to read the original mistake. In these instances, the struckover word or letter is treated as indecipherable.

9. Whenever possible, conjectural readings—Roman type inside brackets [Missouri]—have been given in places where words or letters are not clear and where words or letters are obscured or missing due to obvious damage to the original petition, such as a hole or tear in the paper.

10. An indecipherable letter has been indicated by a bracketed dot, [·], where each dot represents one indecipherable letter. An indecipherable word has been represented by a bracketed dash, [———], where each dash represents one indecipherable word.

11. Editorial insertions—italicized type inside brackets [*Missouri*]— were used only when it was necessary to prevent confusion. When petitioners wrote off the edge of the paper, the words or letters that were presumably written off the edge have been supplied as editorial insertions.

12. The original documents consist of two distinct parts—the petition proper and the notarization. The petition was defined as everything before the author's final signature and only that part was transcribed. Rather than transcribe the notarization information word for word, it was summarized and printed at the end of each petition, set in italic type inside brackets: [*Sworn to before C. M. Woods, C.C.C., Adams Co., IL, 16 Sep 1839*]. More information on the officials who notarized the petitions is found in the Appendix.

13. With the exception of tables, no attempt was made to reproduce the original format of the handwritten petitions. Original line-end hyphens have not been reproduced; instead, the words they divided have been joined. Likewise, the placement of signatures and headings has been standardized. Certain ornamental symbols, like braces, have been omitted.

14. When the petitioner listed claims in a table format, that format has been maintained. The printed tables are identical in content, but not in every other respect to the infinitely variable, handwritten tables; they are close approximations.

15. All monetary figures within tables have been printed numerically, using modern conventions. Dollar signs have been maintained or inserted only before the first amount, any subtotal amount, and the total amount in each table, and all other dollar signs have been omitted. Monetary figures not found in tables have not been modernized except that commas were transcribed as decimals.

16. A number of the petitioners could not write and made their marks in place of a signature. These marks have all been standardized and printed as a bold, slightly enlarged "X" between the given and surname. We deleted the words "his" or "her" and "mark" written above or below the "X" (see Plate 1).

17. No expertise in handwriting analysis was claimed and no attempt was made to analyze in detail the handwriting of the petitions. However, footnotes mark points at which a change was very obvious.

18. The original, handwritten documents were used whenever possible for transcriptions. When these were not available, secondary sources like *History of the Church of Jesus Christ of Latter-day Saints*, a seven volume work written by Joseph Smith, or Journal History of The Church of Jesus Christ of Latter-day Saints, a chronological record kept by the LDS Historical Department, dating from the organization of the Church to the present day, were utilized.

The book has been organized keeping the location of each original in mind. When a document's placement does not make its source obvious, the source of the transcription is given at the beginning of the petition in the upper right hand corner; additional sources are given in a footnote. A few standard abbreviations have been used throughout the book. The letters *NA* indicate the National Archives. *SL* designates those petitions that are found in Salt Lake in the Missouri Petition collection of LDS Historical Department. A few documents are part of the Joseph Smith Collection—abbreviated *JSC*—in the LDS Historical Department. The letters HC stand for *History of the Church* and *JH* indicates Journal History of the Church.

Note: The petitioners often used the word *do* in their bills of damage. We believe this to be an abbreviation of the word *ditto*. The petitioners also commonly wrote the letters *Dr* near the beginning of their petitions. This is probably an abbreviation of the word *Debtor*. The letters *SS* also appear in many petitions. The meaning of these letters might be *Sworn and subscribed*.

Part I

Published Accounts of Mormon Persecution

Introduction to Part I

The documents in Part I illustrate the efforts of Church leaders to take the Mormon cause to the American public. Both documents were originally published as pamphlets, presumably intended for distribution; however, eventually they were sent to Washington, D.C., for they now are found among the other petitions in the National Archives.

John P. Greene's *Facts Relative to the Expulsion of the Mormons or Latter-Day Saints, from the State of Missouri, under the "Exterminating Order"* is a collection of letters, minutes, public statements, and sworn affidavits, composed by Latter-day Saints and non-Mormons alike, which give evidence for the injustice the Mormons suffered in Missouri. These statements had been published previously in Illinois newspapers by a committee in Quincy, Illinois, which was determined to help the Latter-day Saints. With the encouragement of the Quincy committee, Greene presented the Mormon cause to the Democratic Association in Cincinnati, Ohio, which not only listened to him, but also helped him to publish the documents he had gathered. The pamphlet was initially published in Cincinnati in 1839.

Parley P. Pratt's *History of the Late Persecution Inflicted by the State of Missouri Upon the Mormons* is a narrative history of the Church in Missouri from its settlement in 1831 to its exodus in the spring of 1839. This document was "Entered, according to the Act of Congress, in the year 1839 . . . in the Clerk's Office of the District Court of the United States for the District of Michigan." Since it was later sworn to before a justice of the peace, it must have been intended for presentation to the federal government. In content it is an personal document in which Pratt details his observations and experiences with the Missouri mobs and militia. In addition, he talks graphically about his arrest, his trial, his incarceration, and the atrocities perpetrated upon the Saints by vindictive state and local leaders. It was initially published in Detroit, Michigan, in 1839.

Chapter 1

John P. Greene's Expulsion of the Mormons

FACTS

RELATIVE TO THE

EXPULSION OF THE MORMONS

OR

LATTER DAY SAINTS

FROM THE STATE OF MISSOURI,

UNDER THE

"EXTERMINATING ORDER."

BY JOHN P. GREENE,
AN AUTHORISED REPRESENTATIVE OF THE MORMONS.

CINCINNATI:
PRINTED BY R. P. BROOKS.
....
1839.

PREFACE.

"Better far sleep with the dead, than live with the oppressed."

TO CITIZENS AND CHRISTIANS OF THE UNITED STATES.

Friends and Brethren,—Your attention is earnestly requested to the following pamphlet.

It is no plea for Mormons. It is no defence of their creed, character or conduct. The Mormons are willing, for the present, that you should think evil of them, if it seems to you best. Their acts and purposes are known to God; and must sooner or later be known to men. They claim only the right of not being condemned unheard.

But whatever your opinion may be of them, individually or collectively, they know that you are ignorant of events which concern *every Freeman* of these States. They feel that it is their duty, as citizens and men, to expose to you the injustice they have received from the People, Authorities, Executive, and Legislature of Missouri, and therefore they present to your consideration a collection of facts, relative to their late *violent expulsion under Gov. Boggs' "exterminating order,"* from the properties they had purchased, the fields they had improved, the homes they had built. This pamphlet is not a detailed history of their persecution, but a simple sketch of its leading incidents, as given in a Memorial to the Legislature of Missouri by an *appointed committee* of their brethren; to which are added statements under oath and explanatory illustrations. The Editor of the pamphlet is John P. Greene, the authorised messenger of the Mormons, whose claims to confidence may be estimated from the following letter:—

QUINCY, (Illinois,) May 8th, 1839.

To all whom it may concern,

THE undersigned, citizens of Quincy, Illinois, take great pleasure in recommending to the favorable notice of the public, the bearer of this, John P. Greene. Mr. Greene is connected with the Church of "Mormons," or "Latter Day Saints," and makes a tour to the east for the purpose of raising means to relieve the sufferings of this unfortunate people; stripped as they have been of their all, and now scattered throughout this part of our state. We say to the charitable and benevolent, you need have no fears but your contributions in aid of humanity will be properly applied, if intrusted to the hands of Mr. Greene. He is authorised by his Church to act in the premises, and we most cordially bear testimony to his piety and worth as a citizen.

Very Respectfully, Your's.

> SAMUEL HOLMES, *Merchant,*
> I. N. MORRIS, *Att'y. at Law and Ed. of Argus,*
> THOMAS CARLIN, *Governor State of Illinois,*
> RICHARD M. YOUNG, *U. S. Senator,*
> L. V. RALSTON, *M.D.,*
> SAMUEL LEECH, *Receiver of Public Moneys,*
> HIRAM ROGERS, *M.D.,*
> J. T. HOLMES, *Merchant,*
> NICHOLAS WREN, *County Clerk,*
> C. M. WOODS, *Clk. Circuit Court, Adams Co. Ill.*

Mr. Greene's objects are two-fold. First, he wishes to make as widely known as possible to the Citizens and Christians of the United States the wrongs, which Mobocracy and Intolerance have inflicted; and secondly, to collect contributions for the relief of the destitute.

The views of the Mormons may be more fully understood from the two following letters:

To the Editors of the Argus.

GENTLEMEN—Observing in the last weeks Whig, a communication over the names of Messrs. Rigdon and J. and H. Smith, in relation to the letters of Mr. Lyman Wight, which have lately appeared in that paper, and believing that the sentiments therein expressed, are in unison with those entertained by the body, of which we form a part, and feeling desirous to give publicity to the same, we should esteem it a favor if you would give it a place in your columns, and by so doing, you will oblige,

Yours, Respectfully,   JOHN P. GREENE,
                                                  REYNOLDS CAHOON,
                                                  R. B. THOMPSON.

———

COMMERCE, May 17th, 1839.

To the Editors of the Quincy Whig.

GENTLEMEN—Some letters in your paper have appeared over the signature of Lyman Wight, in relation to our affairs with Missouri. We consider that it is Mr. Wight's privilege to express his opinion in relation to political or religious matters, and we profess no authority in the case

7

whatever; but we have thought, and do still think, that it is not doing our cause justice, to make a political question of it in any manner whatever. We have not at any time thought, that there was any political party as such, chargeable with the Missouri barbarities, neither any religious society as such.

They were committed by a mob, composed of all parties, regardless of all differences of opinion, either political or religious.

The determined stand in this State, and by the people of Quincy in particular, made against the lawless outrages of the Missouri mobbers, by all parties in politics and religion, have entitled them equally to our thanks and our profoundest regard; and such, gentlemen, we hope they will always receive from us. *Favors of this kind ought to be engraven on the rock to last forever.*

We wish to say to the public through your paper, that we disclaim any intention of making a political question of our difficulties with Missouri, believing that we are not justified in so doing. We ask the aid of all parties, both in politics and religion, to have justice done us to obtain redress of our grievances.

We think, gentlemen, in so saying we have the feelings of our people generally, however individuals may differ, and we wish you to consider the letters of Mr. Weight, as the feelings and views of an individual, but not of the society as such. We are satisfied that our people, as a body, disclaim all such sentiments, and feel themselves equally bound to both parties, in this State, as far as kindness is concerned, and good will; and also believe, that all political parties in Missouri are equally guilty. Should this note meet the public eye through the medium of your paper, it will much oblige your humble servants,   SIDNEY RIDGON,
JOSEPH SMITH, Jr.,
HIRAM SMITH.

Fellow Citizens and Brethren! Turn not a deaf ear to this cry of the oppressed! The Mormons are outlawed, exiled, robbed;—they ask of your justice and your charity that you befriend them. They have suffered these outrages from *Mob violence*; they bid you beware, lest licentiousness unreproved bring ruin to your own privileges. Law has been trampled down, and Liberty of Conscience violated, and all Rights of Citizenship and Brotherhood outraged by the house-burnings, field-wastings, insults, whippings, murders, which they have suffered; and in the name of Humanity and of Heaven, they pray you to utter the indignant condemnation merited by such crimes.

FACTS

RELATIVE TO THE

EXPULSION OF THE MORMONS

FROM THE STATE OF MISSOURI.

————

From the Quincy (Illinois) Argus, March 16, 1839.

THE MORMONS, OR LATTER DAY SAINTS.

We give in to-day's paper the details of the recent bloody tragedy acted in Missouri—the details of a scene of terror and blood unparalleled in the annals of modern, and under the circumstances of the case, in ancient history—a tragedy of so deep, and fearful, and absorbing interest, that the very life-blood of the heart is chilled at the simple contemplation. We are prompted to ask ourselves if it be really *true*, that we are living in an enlightened, a humane and civilized age—in an age and quarter of the world boasting of its progress in every thing good, and great, and honorable, and virtuous, and high-minded—in a country of which, as American citizens, we could be proud—whether we are living under a *Constitution and Laws*, or have not rather returned to the *ruthless* times of the *stern Atilla*—to the times of the fiery Hun, when the sword and flame ravaged the fair fields of Italy and Europe, and the darkest passions held full revel in all the revolting scenes of unchecked brutality, and unbridled desire?

We have no language sufficiently strong for the expression of our indignation and shame at the recent transaction in a sister State—and that State MISSOURI—a State of which we had long been proud, alike for her men and history, but now so *fallen*, that we could wish her star stricken out from the bright constellation of the Union. We say we know of no language sufficiently strong for the expression of our shame and abhorrence of her recent conduct. She has written her own character in *letters of* [b]*lood*—and stained it by acts of merciless cruelty and brutality that the waters of ages cannot efface. It will be observed that an organized mob aided by many of the civil and military officers of Missouri, with Gov. Boggs at their head, have been the prominent actors in this business, incited too, it appears, against the Mormons by political hatred, and by the additional motives of plunder and revenge. They have but too well put in execution their threats of extermination and expulsion, and fully wreaked their vengeance on a body of industrious and enterprising men, who had never wronged, nor wished to wrong them, but on the contrary had ever comported themselves as good and honest citizens, living under the same laws and having the same right with themselves to *the sacred immunities of life, liberty, and property.*

Proceedings in the town of Quincy for the purpose of affording relief to the people usually denominated "The Latter Day Saints."

At a meeting of the Democratic Association, held on Saturday evening the 23rd ultimo, Mr. Lindsay introduced a resolution setting forth, that the people called "The Latter Day Saints," were many of them in a situation requiring the aid of the citizens of Quincy, and recommending that measures be adopted for their relief; which resolution was adopted, and a committee consisting of eight persons appointed by the chair—of which committee J. W. Whitney was chairman. The Association then adjourned to meet on Wednesday evening then next, after instructing the committee to procure the Congregational meeting-house as a place of meeting, and to invite as many of the people to attend the meeting as should choose to do so, in whose behalf the meeting was to be held, and also all others, citizens of the town. The committee not being able to obtain the meeting-house, procured the court house for that purpose.

WEDNESDAY, FEB. 27th, 1839, ⎫
6 o'clock, P.M. ⎭

The members of the Democratic Association, and the citizens of Quincy generally, assembled in the court house to take into consideration, the state and condition of the people called "The Latter Day Saints," and organized the meeting by appointing Gen. Leach chairman, and James D. Morgan secretary.

Mr. Whitney from the committee appointed at a former meeting, submitted the following report.

The select committee, to whom the subject was referred of inquiring into and reporting the situation of the persons who have recently arrived here from Missouri, and whether their circumstances are such, as that they would need the aid of the citizens of Quincy and its vicinity, to be guided by what they might deem the principles of an expanded benevolence, have attended to the duties assigned them and have concluded on the following

REPORT:

The first idea that occurred to your committee was to obtain correctly the facts of the case, for without them the committee could come to no conclusions, as to what it might be proper for us to do. Without them, they could form no basis upon which the committee might recommend to this association what would be proper for us to do, or what measures to adopt. The committee, soon after their appointment, sent invitations to Mr. Rigdon, and several others, to meet the committee and give them a statement of the facts, and to disclose their situation. Those individuals accordingly met the committee and entered into a free conversation and disclosure of the facts of their situation, and after some time spent therein, the committee concluded to adjourn and report to this meeting, but not without first requesting those individuals to draw up and send us, in writing, a condensed statement of the facts relative to the subjects in charge of your committee, which those individuals engaged to do, and which the committee request may be taken as part of their report. That statement is herewith lettered A.

The committee believed that our duties at this time, and on this occasion, are all included within the limits of an expanded benevolence and humanity, and which are guided and directed by that charity which never faileth. From the facts already disclosed, independent of the statement furnished to the committee, we feel it our duty to recommend to this association that they adopt the following resolutions:

Resolved, That the strangers recently arrived here from the State of Missouri, known by the name of "The Latter Day Saints," are entitled to our sympathy and kindest regard, and that we recommend to the citizens of Quincy to extend to them all the kindness in their power to bestow, as persons who are in affliction.

Resolved, That a numerous committee be raised, composed of some individuals in every quarter of the town and its vicinity, whose duty it shall be to explain to our misguided fellow-citizens, if any such there be, who are disposed to excite prejudices and circulate unfounded rumors; and particularly to explain to them, that these people have no design to lower the wages of the laboring class, but to procure something to save them from starving.

Resolved, That a standing committee be raised, and be composed of individuals who shall immediately inform Mr. Rigdon and others, as many as they may think proper, of their appointment; and who shall be authorised to obtain information from time to time, and should they be of opinion that any individuals, either from destitution or sickness, or if they find them houseless, that they appeal directly and promptly to the citizens of Quincy to furnish them with the means to relieve all such cases.

Resolved, That the committee last aforesaid, be instructed to use their utmost endeavors to obtain employment for all these people who are able and willing to labor, and also to afford them all needful, suitable, and proper encouragement.

Resolved, That we recommend to all the citizens of Quincy, that in all their intercourse with the strangers, that they use and observe a becoming decorum and delicacy, and be particularly careful not to indulge in any conversation or expressions calculated to wound their feelings, or in any way to reflect upon those, who, by every law of humanity, are entitled to our sympathy and commisseration.

All which is submitted. 　　　　　　　　　　　J. W. WHITNEY, *Ch'n.*

Quincy, February 27, 1839.

A.

This, gentlemen, is a brief outline of the difficulties that we have labored under, in consequence of the repeated persecutions that have been heaped upon us; and as the Governor's exterminating order has not been rescinded, we, as a people, were obliged to leave the State, and with it, our lands, corn, wheat, pork &c., that we had provided for ourselves and families, together with our fodder, which we had collected for our cattle, horses, &c.,—those of them that we have been able to preserve from the wreck of that desolation which has spread itself over Davies and Caldwell counties.

In consequence of our brethren's being obliged to leave the State, and as a sympathy and friendly spirit has been manifested by the citizens of Quincy, numbers of our brethren, glad to obtain an asylum from the hand of persecution, have come to this place.

We cannot but express our feelings of gratitude to the inhabitants of this place for the friendly feelings which have been manifested, and the benevolent hand which has been stretched out to a poor, oppressed, injured, and persecuted people; and as you, gentlemen of the Democratic Association, have felt interested in our welfare, and have desired to be put in possession of a knowledge of our situation, our present wants, and what would be most conducive to our present good, together with what led to those difficulties, we thought that those documents[1] would furnish you with as correct information of our difficulties and what led to them, as any that we are in possession of.

If we should say what our present wants are, it would be beyond all calculations, as we have been robbed of our corn, wheat, horses, cattle, cows, hogs, wearing apparel, houses and homes, and indeed, of all that renders life tolerable. We do not, we cannot expect to be placed in the situation that we once were, nor are we capable, of ourselves, of supplying

---

[1] Here John P. Greene has a footnote which reads, "See the Memorial on page 10, and the order of Extermination and Gen. Clark's address in the Appendix." The Memorial is on page 15 in this publication; the appendix is contained in this chapter.

the many wants of those of our poor brethren, who are daily crowding here and looking to us for relief, in consequence of our property as well as theirs being in the hands of a ruthless and desolating mob.

It is impossible to give an exact account of the widows, and those that are entirely destitute, as there are so many coming here daily; but, from enquiry, the probable amount will be something near twenty, besides numbers of others who are able-bodied men, both able and willing to work, to obtain a subsistence, yet owing to their peculiar situation, are destitute of means to supply the immediate wants that the necessities of their families call for. We would not propose, gentlemen, what you shall do, but after making these statements, shall leave it to your own judgment and generosity.

As to what we think would be the best means to promote our permanent good, we think that to give us employment, rent us farms and allow us the protection and privileges of other citizens, would raise us from a state of dependance, liberate us from the iron grasp of poverty, put us in possession of a competency and deliver us from the ruinous effects of persecution, despotism and tyranny.

Written in behalf of a committee of "The Latter Day Saints."

E. HIGBEE, Pres.

J. P. GREENE, Clerk
To the Quincy Democratic Association.

Mr. Rigdon then made a statement of the wrongs received by the Mormons, from a portion of the people of Missouri, and of their present suffering condition.

On motion of Mr. Bushnell, the report and resolutions were laid upon the table, till to-morrow evening.

On motion of Mr. Bushnell, the meeting adjourned to meet at this place on to-morrow evening, at seven o'clock.

THURSDAY Evening, Feb. 28.

Met pursuant to adjournment.

The meeting was called to order by the chairman.

On motion of Mr. Morris, a committee of three was appointed to take up a collection; Messrs. J. T. Holmes, Whitney, and Morris, was appointed.

The committee subsequently reported that $48 25 cents had been collected.

On motion, the amount was paid over to the committee on behalf of the Mormons.

On motion of Mr. Holmes, a committee of three, consisting of S. Holmes, Bushnell, and Morris, were appointed to draw up subscription papers and circulate them among the citizens, for the purpose of receiving contributions in clothing and provisions.

On motion, 6 were added to that committee.

On motion of J. T. Holmes, J. D. Morgan was appointed a committee to wait upon the Quincy Greys, for the purpose of receiving subscriptions.

Mr. Morgan subsequently reported that twenty dollars had been subscribed by that company.

The following resolutions were then offered by Mr. J. T. Holmes:

Resolved, That we regard the rights of conscience as natural and inalienable, and the most sacred guaranteed by the constitution of our free government.

Resolved, That we regard the acts of all mobs as flagrant violations of law, and those who compose them, individually responsible, both to the laws of God or man for every depredation committed upon the property, rights, or life of any citizen.

Resolved, That the inhabitants upon the Western Frontier of the State of Missouri in their late persecutions of the class of people denominated Mormons, have violated the sacred rights of conscience, and every law of justice and humanity.

Resolved, That the Gov. of Missouri, in refusing protection to this class of people when pressed upon by an heartless mob, and turning upon them a band of unprincipled Militia, with orders encouraging their extermination, has brought a lasting disgrace upon the State over which he presides.

The resolutions were supported in a spirited manner by Messrs. Holmes, Morris and Whitney.

On motion the resolutions were adopted.

On motion the meeting then adjourned.

SAM'L. LEACH, Ch'n.

J. D. MORGAN, Sec'y.

COPY OF A MEMORIAL TO THE LEGISLATURE OF MISSOURI.

To the Honorable Legislature of the State of Missouri, in Senate and House of Representatives convened.

We, the undersigned petitioners, inhabitants of Caldwell county, Missouri, in consequence of the late calamity that has come upon us, taken in connection with former afflictions, feel it a duty we owe to ourselves and our country, to lay our case before your honorable body for consideration.

It is a well known fact, that a society of our people commenced settling in Jackson county, Missouri, in the summer of 1831, where they, according to their ability, purchased lands and settled upon them with the intention and expectation of becoming permanent citizens in common with others.

Soon after the settlement began, persecution began, and as the society increased persecution also increased, until the society at last was compelled to leave the county. And although an account of these persecutions has been published to the world, yet we feel that it will not be improper to notice a few of the most prominent items in this memorial.

On the 20th of July 1833, a mob convened at Independence, a committee of which called upon a few of the men of our church there, and stated to them that the store, printing office, and indeed all other mechanic shops must be closed forthwith, and the society leave the county immediately. These propositions were so unexpected, that a certain time was asked for to consider on the subject before an answer should be returned, which was refused, and our men being individually interrogated, each one answered that he could not consent to comply with their propositions. One of the mob replied that he was sorry, for the work of destruction would commence immediately. In a short time, the printing office, which was a two-story brick building, was assailed by the mob and soon thrown down, and with it much valuable property destroyed. Next they went to the store for the same purpose, but Mr. Gilbert, one of the owners, agreeing to close it, they abandoned their design. Their next move was their dragging of Bishop Patridge from his house and family to the public square, where, surrounded by hundreds, they partially stripped him of his clothes, and tarred and feathered him from head to foot. A man by the name of Allan was also tarred at the same time. This was Saturday, and the mob agreed to meet the following Tuesday, to accomplish their purpose of driving or massacreing the society.[2] (A) Tuesday came, and the mob came also, bearing with them a red flag in token of blood. Some two or three of the principal men of the society offered their lives, if that would appease the wrath of the mob, so that the rest of the society might dwell in peace upon their lands. The answer was, that unless the society would leave "en masse," every man should die for himself. Being in a defenceless situation, to save a general massacre, it was agreed that one half of the society should leave the county by the first of the next January, and the remainder by the first of the following April. A treaty was entered into and ratified, and all

---

[2] Here John P. Greene has a footnote which reads, "Vdie appendix."

things went on smoothly for *a while.* But some time in October (B) the wrath of the mob began again to be kindled, insomuch, that they shot at some of our people, whipped others, and threw down their houses, and committed many other depredations; indeed the society of saints were harrassed for some time both day and night—their houses were brickbatted and broken open—women and children insulted, &c. The store house of A. S. Gilbert & Co. was broken open, ransacked, and some of the goods strewed in the streets. These abuses, with many others of a very aggravated nature, so stirred up the indignant feelings of our people, that a party of them, say about 30, met a company of the mob of about double their number, when a battle took place in which some two or three of the mob and one of our people were killed. (C) This raised as it were the whole county in arms, and nothing would satisfy them but an immediate surrender of the arms of our people, and they forthwith to leave the county—Fifty-one guns were given up, which have never been returned or paid for to this day. The next day parties of the mob, from 30 to 70, headed by priests, (D) went from house to house, threatening women and children with death if they were not off before they returned. This so alarmed them, that they fled in different directions; some took shelter in the woods, while others wandered in the prairies till their feet bled. In the mean time the weather being very cold, their sufferings in other respects were very great. (E)

The society made their escape to Clay county as fast as they possibly could, where the people received them kindly, and administered to their wants. After the society had left Jackson county, their buildings, amounting to about two hundred, were either burned or otherwise destroyed, and much of their crops, as well as furniture, stock, etc., which, if properly estimated, would make a large sum, for which they have not as yet received any remuneration. (F) The society remained in Clay county nearly three years; when, at the suggestion of the people there, they removed to that section of country known now as Caldwell county. Here the people purchased out most of the former inhabitants, and also entered much of the wild land. Many soon owned a number of eighties, while there was scarcely a man that did not secure to himself at least a forty. Here we were permitted to enjoy peace for a season, but as our society increased in numbers, and settlements were made in Davies and Carrol counties, the mob spirit spread itself again. (G.) For months previous to our giving up our arms to Gen. Lucas' army, we heard little else than rumors of mobs, collecting in different places, and threatening our people. It is well known that the *people of our* church who had located themselves at De Wit, had to give up to a mob and leave the place, notwithstanding the militia were called out for their protection. From De Wit the mob went towards Davies county, and while on their way there they took two of *our men* prisoners and made them ride upon the cannon, and told them that they would drive the Mormons from Davies to Caldwell and from Caldwell to hell, and that they would give them no quarter only at the cannon's mouth. (H) The threats of the mob induced some of our people to go to Davies to help to protect their brethren who had settled at Diahman, on Grand river.

The mob soon fled from Davies county: and after they were dispersed and the cannon taken, during which time no blood was shed, the people of Caldwell returned to their homes in hopes of enjoying peace and quiet; but in this they were disappointed, for a large mob was soon found to be collecting on the Grindstone, from ten to fifteen miles off, under the command of C. Gillman, a scouting party of which, came within four miles of Far West, and drove off stock belonging to our people, in open day light. About this time word came to Far West that a party of the mob had come into Caldwell county to the south of Far West—that they were taking horses and cattle—burning houses, and ordering the inhabitants to leave their homes immediately—and that they had then actually in their possession three men prisoners. This report reached Far West in the evening and was confirmed about midnight. A company of about sixty men went forth under the command of David W. Patten, to disperse the mob, as they supposed. A battle was the result, in which Captain Patten and two of his men were killed, and others wounded. Bogart, it appears, had but one killed and others wounded. Notwithstanding the unlawful acts committed by Captain Bogart's men previous to the battle, it is now asserted and claimed that he was regularly ordered out as a militia captain, to preserve the peace along the line of Ray and Caldwell counties. That battle was fought four or five days previous to the arrival of Gen. Lucas and his army. About the time of the battle with Captain Bogart, a number of our people who were living near Honn's mill, on Shoal Creek, about twenty miles below Far West, together with a number of emigrants who had been stopped there in consequence of the excitement, made an agreement with the mob which was about there, that neither party would molest the other, but dwell in peace. Shortly after this agreement was made, a mob party of from two to three hundred, many of whom are supposed to be from Chariton county, some from Davies, and also those who had agreed to dwell in peace, came upon our people there, whose number in men was about forty, at a time they little expected any such thing, and without any ceremony, notwithstanding they begged for quarters, shot them down as they would tigers or panthers. Some few made their escape by fleeing. Eighteen were killed, and a number more severely wounded. (I)

This tragedy was conducted in the most brutal and savage manner. An old man, after the massacre was partially over, threw himself into their hands and begged for quarters, when he was instantly shot down; that not killing him, they took an old corn cutter and literally mangled him to pieces. (J) A lad of ten years of age, after being shot down, also begged to be spared, when one of them placed the muzzle of his gun to his head and blew out his brains. The slaughter of these people not satisfying the mob, they then proceeded to mob and plunder the people. The scene that presented itself after the massacre, to the widows and orphans of the killed, is beyond description. It was truly a time of weeping, of mourning, and of lamentation. As yet, we have not heard of any being arrested for these murders, notwithstanding there are men boasting about the country, that they did kill on that occasion more than one Mormon, whereas, all our people who were in the battle with Capt. Patten against Bogart, that can be found, have been arrested, and are now confined in jail to await their trial for murder.

(K) When Gen. Lucas arrived near Far West, and presented the governor's order, (L) we were greatly surprised, yet we felt willing to submit to the authorities of the State. We gave up our arms without reluctance; we were then made prisoners, and confined to the limits of the town for about a week, during which time the men from the country were not permitted to go to their families, many of whom were in a suffering condition for the want of food and fire-wood, the weather being very cold and stormy. Much property was destroyed by the troops in town, during their stay there: such as burning house-logs, rails, corn-cribs, boards &c., the using of corn and hay, the plundering of houses, the killing of cattle, sheep, and hogs, and also the taking of horses not their own, and all this without regard to owners, or asking leave of any one. In the mean time, men were abused, women insulted and abused by the troops, and all this, while we were kept prisoners. Whilst the town was guarded, we were called together by the order of Gen. Lucas, and a guard placed close around us, and in that situation, were compelled to sign a deed of trust for the purpose of making our individual property all holden, as they said, to pay all the debts of every individual belonging to the church, and also to pay for all damages the old inhabitants of Davies may have sustained in consequence of the late difficulties in that county. (M)

Gen. Clark was now arrived, and the first important move made by him was the collecting of our men together on the square, and selected out about fifty of them, whom he immediately marched into a house, and confined close; this was done without the aid of the Sheriff, or any legal process. The next day 46 of those taken, were driven like a parcel of menial slaves, off to Richmond, not knowing why they were taken, or what they were taken for. (N) After being confined in Richmond more than two weeks, about one half were liberated; the rest, after another week's confinement, were, most of them, required to appear at court, and have since been let to bail. Since Gen. Clark withdrew his troops from Far West, parties of armed men have gone through the county, driving off horses, sheep, and cattle, and also plundering houses. The barbarity of Gen. Lucas' troops ought not to be passed over in silence. They shot our cattle and hogs, merely for the sake of destroying them, leaving them for the ravens to eat. They took prisoner an aged man by the name of Tanner, and without any reason for it he was struck over the head with a gun, which laid his skull bare. Another man by the name of Carey was also taken prisoner by them, and without any provocation had his brains dashed out with a gun. He was laid in a wagon, and there permitted to remain, for the space of 24 hours, during which time no one was permitted to administer to him comfort or consolation, and after he was removed from that situation he lived but a few hours. (O) The destruction of property, at and about Far West, is very great. Many are stripped bare as it were, and others partially so; indeed, take us as a body, at this time, we are a poor and afflicted people, and if we are compelled to leave the State in the spring, many, yes, a large portion of our society, will have to be removed at the expense of the State, as those who otherwise might have helped them, are now debarred that privilege in consequence of the deed of trust we were compelled to sign, which deed so operates upon our real estate, that it will sell for but little or nothing at this time. (P) We have now made a brief statement of some of the most prominent features of the troubles that have befallen our people since their first settlement in this State, and we believe that these persecutions have come in consequence of our religious faith, and not for any immorality on our part. That instances have been of late, where individuals have trespassed upon the rights of others, and thereby broken the laws of the land, we will not pretend to deny, but yet we do believe that no crime can be substantiated against any of the people who have a standing in our church, of an earlier date than the difficulties in Davies county. And when it is considered that the rights of this people have been trampled upon from time to time, with impunity, and abuses heaped upon them almost innumerable, it ought, in some degree, to palliate for any infraction of the law, which may have been made on the part of our people.

The late order of Gov. Boggs, to drive us from this State, or exterminate us, is a thing so novel, unlawful, tyranical and oppressive, that we have been induced to draw up this memorial and present this statement of our case to your honourable body, praying that a law may be passed, rescinding the order of the Governor to drive us from the State, and also giving us the sanction of the Legislature to inherit our lands in peace—we ask an expression of the Legislature, disapproving the conduct of those who compelled us to sign a deed of trust, and also disapproving of any man or set of men, taking our property in consequence of that deed of trust, and appropriating it to the payment of debts not contracted by us, or for the payment of damages sustained in consequence of trespasses committed by others. We have no common stock, our property is individual property, and we feel willing to pay our debts as other individuals do, but we are not willing to be bound for other people's debts also.

The arms which were taken from us here, which we understand to be about 630, besides swords and pistols, we care not so much about, as we do the pay for them; only we are bound to do military duty, which we are willing to do, and which we think was sufficiently manifested by the raising of a volunteer company last fall, at Far West, when called upon by Gen. Parks, to raise troops for the frontier.

The arms given up by us, we consider were worth between twelve and fifteen thousand dollars, but we understand they have been greatly damaged since taken, and at this time, probably would not bring near their former value. And as they were, both here and in Jackson county, taken by the militia, and consequently by the authority of the State, we therefore ask your honourable body to cause an appropriation to be made by law, whereby we may be paid for them, or otherwise have them returned to us and the damages made good. The losses sustained by our people in leaving Jackson county, are so situated that it is impossible to obtain any compensation for them by law, because those who have sustained them are unable to prove those trespasses upon individuals. That the facts do exist,—that the buildings, crops, stock, furniture, rails, timber, &c. of the society, have been destroyed in Jackson county, is not doubted by those who are acquainted in this upper country, and since these trespasses cannot be proved upon individuals, we ask your honourable body to consider this case, and if, in your liberality and wisdom, you can conceive it to be proper to make an appropriation by law to these sufferers, many of whom are still pressed down with poverty in consequence of their losses, would be able to pay their debts, and also in some degree be relieved from poverty and woe, whilst the widows heart would be made to rejoice and the orphans tear measurable dried up, and the prayers of a grateful people ascended on high, with thanksgiving and praise, to the author of our existence, for that beneficent act. (Q) (R)

In laying our case before your honourable body, we say that we are willing, and ever have been to conform to the constitution and laws of the United States, and of this State. We ask in common with others, the protection of the laws. We ask for the privilege guaranteed to all free citizens of the United States and of this State to be extended to us, that we may be permitted to settle and live where we please, and worship God according to the dictates of our conscience without molestation. And while we ask for ourselves this privilege we are willing all others should enjoy the same.

We now lay our case at the feet of your legislature, and ask your honorable body to consider it, and do for us, after mature deliberation, that which your wisdom, patriotism, and philanthropy may dictate. And we, as in duty bound, will ever pray, &c.

> EDWARD PATRIDGE,
> HEBER C. KIMBALL,
> JOHN TAYLOR,
> THEODORE TURLEY,
> BRIGHAM YOUNG,
> ISAAC MORLEY,
> GEORGE W. HARRIS,
> JOHN MUNDOCK [*MURDOCK*],
> JOHN M. BURK.

A committee appointed by the citizens of Caldwell county to draft this memorial, and sign it in their behalf.

Far West, Caldwell co., Mo., Dec. 10, 1838.

APPENDIX.

DECLARATION.

The following statements of facts are made by me with a strong assurance of their correctness. Of many of the events described I was personally a witness; and the accounts of others I have received from men who were engaged in them, and in whose veracity I put entire confidence. Under oath, I should willingly declare, that to the best of my knowledge these notes contain the truth, and nothing but the truth.

JOHN P. GREENE.

A

On Tuesday, when the mob again assembled, they went to the houses of several of the leading Mormons; and, taking Isaac Morley, David Whitmer, and others, they told them to bid their families farewell, for they would never see them again. Then driving them at the point of the bayonet to the public square, they stripped and tarred and feathered them, amidst menaces and insults. The commanding officer then called twelve of his men, and ordering them to cock their guns and present them at the prisoners' breasts, and to be ready to fire when he gave the word,—he addressed the prisoners, threatening them with instant death, unless they denied the book of Mormon and confessed it to be a fraud; at the same time adding, that if they did so, they might enjoy the privileges of citizens. David Whitmer, hereupon, lifted up his hands and bore witness that the Book of Mormon was the Word of God. The mob then let them go.

B

A meeting of the people in Independence was held, and the mob entered into an agreement to drive the Mormons from the county or die. Very inflammatory language was used by Mr. Childs and Mr. Brazill. The latter of whom swore that he would expel them if he had to wade up to his neck in blood. It was the excitement produced by this meeting, and under these threatening circumstances, that the Mormons first placed themselves in an attitude of defence.

C

It is here to be particularly noted, that Lilburn W. Boggs, then Lieutenant Governor, was acting in concert with the militia officer, who headed this attack upon the Mormons, and assisted in making the treaty by which they pledged themselves to give up their guns and leave the county, on condition that they should be protected from all wrong and insult while so doing.

D

"Instigated by the press and pulpit, or, what is still worse, by the *personal examples of some of the clergy*, who actually marched with rifle in hand, at the head of parties of the mob, and afterwards published an excuse, in order to justify the mob in such awful wickedness;—(among other clergymen, who were personally engaged in such conduct, I would identify the *Rev. Isaac McCoy*, a noted missionary to the Indians.") P. P. PRATT.

E

Horrible to relate, several women thus driven from their homes *gave birth to children in the woods and on the prairies*, destitute of beds or clothing, having escaped in fright. It is stated, on the authority of Solomon Hancock, an eye-witness, that he, with the assistance of two or three others, protected 120 women and children, for the space of 8 or 10 days, who were obliged to keep themselves hid from their pursuers, while they were hourly expecting to be massacred—and who finally escaped into Clay county, by finding a circuitous route to the ferry.

F

Several persons, who returned for the purpose of securing the remnants of their property, were caught, and cruelly beaten. A Mr. Leonard was so beaten, that from head to foot he was left perfectly raw, and for months was unable to lie upon his back. Another was tied up and whipped in such an inhuman manner, that his bowels gushed, out and he died on the spot. The mob in Jackson county were not satisfied with their injuries. They often crossed the river and insulted, outraged, and plundered their victims—until such commotion was produced, that the inhabitants of Clay county were compelled to hold a meeting and invite the Mormons to seek another home.

G

After their removal into Caldwell and Davies counties, the Mormons were allowed to enjoy comparative quiet. The circumstances attending their settlement in Caldwell county were as follows: As it was found that difficulty arose when they were residing in other communities, it seemed better that they should live apart. Petitions were, in consequence, sent into the Legislature, and by them granted, that a county should be set off for their good; and Caldwell county was assigned to them as a place of residence. *Here they were allowed to organize the government for the county. Of the officers then* appointed, two of the judges, thirteen magistrates, and all the military officers, and the county clerk, were Mormons. These steps were taken, be it carefully observed, by the advice of the State Legislature; and the officers were appointed in the manner directed by law. The county town of Caldwell was Far West.

Early in August, at the State election in Davies county, at the town of Gallatin, after the polls were opened, Mr. Wm. Peniston, candidate for Representative to the State Legislature, stood upon the head of a barrel, and harangued the people. His speech was made up of attack and threats upon the Mormons, during which, with most degrading epithets, he accused them of being horse-thieves and robbers, and swore that they should not vote in that county. This language, as might naturally be expected, produced some feeling of indignation among the Mormons, who were present. Thereupon, a Mormon, Mr. Samuel Brown, replied to those near him, that the assertions were untrue, and that he intended to exercise his rights as a citizen; he was immediately struck at by R. Weldin, who threatened him for his impertinence, and, as he was attempting to repeat the blow, was caught by the arm by another Mormon, whose name was Durfee. Eight or ten men with clubs and staves fell upon Durfee, knocked him down, and a general engagement ensued, in which clubs, bricks, and dirks, were freely used. Finding the Mormons resolute, a compromise was effected, and their rights of voting being granted, the election proceeded, was concluded in peace, and all returned in quiet to their homes.

Meanwhile the election had been going on in Caldwell county.

The day following the election, two or three successive messengers, who, be it observed, *were not Mormons*, rode into Far West, (the county town of Caldwell), and spread the report that there had been a battle in Gallatin, and that several of the Mormons had been killed, and their bodies refused their friends for burial, and left upon the ground. This, as afterwards appeared, was a mere deceit, to lure them into violence. The news created much excitement, and 75 or 100 individuals determined to go in small parties and separately, to Diahman, and inquire into the truth of the report, where, on arriving, they were informed of the real state of the case. Fearing, however, that farther trouble might grow out of the affair, and desirous, if possible, to prevent it, an individual went to Adam Black, justice of the peace, and proposed that an agreement should be entered into to keep the peace on both sides. Mr. Black acceded to the proposal, and requested that Messrs. Joseph Smith and Lyman Wight should come to his house, and confirm the contract. The paper was drawn up by Mr. Black, and signed by both parties, and the Mormons returned to Far West, the same day, rejoicing in the thought that the difficulty was settled, as they hoped much good from Mr. Black's influence. The news of this agreement having gone abroad, some citizens of Davies county were greatly dissatisfied that Mr. Black had taken it upon himself to enter into it without their authority—whereupon, Mr. Black, to appease them, went to Austin A. King, Circuit Judge, and obtained a writ for the apprehension of Smith and Wight, under the charge that they and others, with threats of violence, had compelled him to sign the agreement. They gave themselves up and were brought before Judge King to Gallatin; and although no charge against them was sustained, yet to pacify the mob, who had meantime collected in great numbers, they were put under *their own bonds although no security whatever was demanded, (Judge King thus showing that he thought nothing of the accusation)*, to appear at the next court term. It should be distinctly stated that Joseph Smith, being a resident of Caldwell county, could not have been taken under the writ, but voluntarily submitted himself to the court. After the examination they returned home. Meanwhile Wight was constantly threatened with violence.

The excitement continued to increase, until a mob of about three hundred armed men from Davies and other counties was collected, who made prisoners of some of the Mormons, shooting and driving away their cattle, and threatening to exterminate or expel them from the county unless they would deny their faith. The conduct of the rioters became so alarming, that it was found necessary for Maj. Gen. Atchison to call out the militia from Ray and Clay counties, under the command of Generals Doniphon and Parks.

In order that it may be fully understood what were the relative states of mind of the Mormons and the people of Davies county, at this time, reference may be made to a letter from Major George Woodward to his wife, which was seen and read by me, John P. Greene, to whom Mrs. Woodward showed it. It was dated Head Quarters, Davies county. He says, that after having been patrolling Davies county for the last two days, for the purpose of ascertaining where the fault lay, and who were under arms, he had found many of the people of Davies and other counties armed and apparently hostile to the Mormons; and that having visited the city of

Diahman, to his great astonishment, instead of block-houses and entrenchments and cannon, as had been reported by the citizens of Davies county, he had found a poor but industrious people, living in pole houses, *and no men under arms, but each engaged about his own business.* He continues he is surprised to see such violence of feeling existing against a people who seem so inoffensive.

Gen. Atchison stationed Gen. Parks, with his detachment, to remain in Davies county 30 days, to keep the peace, as he found it was impossible for the militia to control the mob. Meanwhile, the Mormons in Caldwell county were relieved from all apprehension, being satisfied that the troops would not be removed until the difficulties were settled. In these hopes, however, they were sadly disappointed. The mob finding themselves prevented from perpetrating farther outrages in Davies county, collected at De Wit, (where the Mormons had a small settlement,) with increased force, a reinforcement from Jackson county, with a six pounder, having joined them. Here they proceeded to burn houses, shoot cattle, destroy property, threaten lives, and even fire at Mormons. Gen. Parks, hearing of their new attacks, moved at once with his troops to De Wit. The mob, however, had now become so strong that they put him at defiance, and declared that *they were a mob*—that they would make no compromise except on the condition of the Mormons quitting the State, and that otherwise they would exterminate them. The leaders of this mob were Major Ashby, *a member of the Legislature*, and Sashiel Woods, *a presbyterian clergyman.* Meanwhile, Gen. Atchison, hearing of the situation of the Mormons, (who were now hemmed in by the mob between the Missouri and Grand rivers, near their junction,) went down to De Wit; and, by his advice, *they sent a petition to Gov. Boggs, requesting his protection, who returned for answer, that he could give them no assistance, but that they must fight their own battle for themselves.* The Mormons were therefore compelled, at great loss of property, to evacuate the place, and fly to Far West, in Caldwell county.

H

At this time, General Doniphon, with 200 men, on his way to Davies county, to intercept the mob, came to Far West, where he and his men encamped for the night. *He held consultation with the civil and military officers of Caldwell county, who, be it remembered, although Mormons, were still commissioned by the State,* and advised them to collect under arms and march to Davies county, to defend the Mormons there from the depredations of the mob. He also stated that Gen. Parks, with his men, were on the way for Davies county. In consequence of this advice, some of them did arm and march, while others remained under arms in Caldwell county.

And here we wish particularly to call attention to the fact, *that the Mormons in Caldwell were the regular State militia for that county, and were at this time acting under the legal authorities of the county.* To prove that they were distinctly regarded by the executive as the State militia, we relate the fact, that, sometime in September last, Gen. Parks being ordered to collect a body of troops out of his brigade, which should be ready to march to the frontier in case of aggression from Indians, called for a company of 60 men from Caldwell county; whereupon, 300 volunteers, (*all Mormons*,) presented themselves, from *whom* he selected his company of minute-men.

The Mormons (*the State militia acting under the authorities of the county,*) marched into Davies county and encamped for the night, where they were met the next morning by Gen. Parks. Nothing of importance occurred during the day; Gen. P. making all possible inquiries to learn the true situation of affairs. The night following, a party of the mob under the command of C. Gilliam, burned seven Mormon houses west of Grand river, turning the families, women and children, out of doors. The appearance in the camp the next morning of these poor people who had been obliged to wade the river and march through snow during the night, excited much indignation. They were carried before Gen. Parks, who, having examined them, *called upon Col. Wight and ordered him* to sent out his troops (the *militia*, although Mormons,) and disperse the mob. This was done. The mob were met and scattered *without a gun's being fired*, and their cannon taken. The mob left many houses burning, which they had set on fire before they had fled. These houses belonged to the Mormons, they having purchased the pre-emption rights from the people of Davies county. The mob fled into other counties, spreading the report that the Mormons were massacreing the people of Davies county, and burning their property. The troops (the Mormon *State militia*,) now marched back to Caldwell, hoping that as the mob had dispersed, there would be peace. But in this they were disappointed. On the very evening of their arrival, they learned that a large mob had collected to the south of Far West, in Ray county, under the command of Samuel Bogart, *a methodist clergyman.* The report was, that they were plundering and burning houses, taking the arms of Mormons, &c. About 12 o'clock an express came in bringing intelligence that Bogart had made three men prisoners, one of whom only was a Mormon; upon which alarm two or three hundred men collected upon the public square at Fort West. Elias Higbee, the *first judge* of the county now commanded the militia officers to go out and re-take the prisoners; and Capt. David W. Patten, with about 60 men (all Mormons) obeyed the order. As they were passing through a thin piece of woods, and had, without knowing it, approached near Bogart's encampment, the guard stationed there by the mob fired without giving any warning, killing one of Capt. Patten's men. The mob were routed; but before they fled they placed the Mormon prisoner in their front and shot him. He was wounded severely, though he afterwards recovered. The Mormon troops here took about 40 horses, deserted by the mob. One of the Mormons, who had been killed during the battle, and buried on the field, was afterwards dug up by the ruffians, and literally hacked to pieces with a sword. The remains were collected and buried, after they had gone, by his friends.

I

The following is a short history of my travels to the state of Missouri, and of a bloody tragedy acted at Honn's Mills, or Shoal creek, October 30th, 1838.

On the 6th day of July last, I started with my family from Kirtland, Ohio, for the State of Missouri, the county of Caldwell, in the upper part of the State, being the place of my destination. On the 13th of Oct. I crossed the Mississippi at Louisiana, at which place I heard vague reports of the disturbances in the upper country, but nothing that could be relied upon. I continued my course westward till I crossed Grand River, at a place called Compton's Ferry; at which place I heard, for the first time, that if I proceeded any farther on my journey, I would be in danger of being stopped by a body of armed men. I was not willing, however, while treading my native soil, and breathing republican air, to abandon my object; which was to locate myself and family in a fine healthy country, where we could enjoy the society of our friends and connexions. Consequently, I prosecuted my journey till I came to Whitney's mills, situated on Shoal-creek, in the eastern part of Caldwell county. After crossing the creek and going about three miles, we met a part of the mob, about 40 in number, armed with rifles, and mounted on horses, who informed us that we could go no farther west—threatening us with instant death if we proceeded any farther. I asked them the reason for this prohibition, to which they replied, that we were Mormons, and that every one who adhered to our religious faith would have to leave the State in ten days or *renounce* their religion. Accordingly, they drove us back to the mills above mentioned.

Here we tarried three days; and, on Friday, the 26th, we re-crossed the creek, and following up its banks, we succeeded in eluding the mob for the time being, and gained the residence of a friend in Myers' settlement. On Sunday, 28th Oct., we arrived, about 12 o'clock, at Honn's mills, where we found a number of our friends collected together, who were holding a council, and deliberating upon the best course for them to pursue, to defend themselves against the mob, who were collecting in the neighborhood, under the command of Col. Jennings, of Livingston, and threatening them with house-burning and killing. The decision of the council was, that our friends there should place themselves in an attitude of self-defence.

Accordingly, about 28 of our men armed themselves, and were in constant readiness for an attack of any small body of men that might come upon them. The same evening, for some reason, best known to themselves, the mob sent one of their number to enter into a treaty with our friends, which was accepted, on the condition of mutual forbearance on both sides, and that each party, as far as their influence extended, should exert themselves to prevent any farther hostilities upon either party.

At this time, however, there was another mob collecting on Grand river, at William Mann's, who were threatening us, consequently we remained under arms on Monday, the 29th, which passed away without molestation from any quarter. On Tuesday, the 30th, that bloody tragedy was acted; the scenes of which I shall never forget. More than three-fourths of the day had passed in tranquility, as smiling as the preceding one. I think there was no individual of our company that was apprised of the sudden and awful fate that hung over our heads like an overwhelming torrent, which was to change the prospects, the feelings, and circumstances, of about 30 families. The banks of Shoal-creek, on either side, teemed with children, sporting and playing, while their mothers were engaged in domestic employments, and their fathers employed in guarding the mills, and other property, while others were engaged in gathering in their crops for their winter consumption. The weather was very pleasant—the sun shone clear—all was tranquil; and no one expressed any apprehension of the awful crisis that was near us—even at our doors.

It was about 4 o'clock, while sitting in my cabin with my babe in my arms, and my wife standing by my side, the door being open, I cast my eyes on the opposite bank of Shoal-creek, and saw a large company of armed men, on horses, directing their course towards the mills with all possible speed. As they advanced through the scattering trees that stood on the edge of the prairie, they seemed to form themselves into a three-square position, forming a van-guard in front. At this moment, David Evans, seeing the superiority of their numbers, (their being 240 of them, according to their own account,) swung his hat, and cried for peace. This not being heeded, they continued to advance, and their leader, Mr. Comstock, fired a gun, which was followed by a solemn pause of ten or twelve seconds, when, all at once, they discharged about 100 rifles, aiming at a blacksmith shop into which our friends had fled for safety; and charging up to the shop, the cracks of which between the logs were sufficiently large to enable them to aim directly at the bodies of those who had there fled for refuge from the fire of their murderers. There were several families tented in rear of the shop, whose lives were exposed, and amidst a shower of bullets fled to the woods in different directions.

After standing and gazing on this bloody scene for a few minutes, and finding myself in the uttermost danger, the bullets having reached the house where I was living, I committed my family to the protection of Heaven, and leaving the house on the opposite side, I took a path which led up the hill, following in the trail of three of my brethren that had fled from the shop. While ascending the hill we were discovered by the mob, who immediately fired at us, and continued so to do till we reached the summit. In descending the hill I secreted myself in a thicket of bushes, where I lay till eight o'clock in the evening, at which time I heard a female voice calling my name in an undertone, telling me that the mob had gone, and there was no danger. I immediately left the thicket, and went to the house of Benjamin Lewis, where I found my family, (who had fled there,) in safety, and two of my friends, mortally wounded, one of whom died before morning.

Here we passed the painful night in deep and awful reflections on the scenes of the preceding evening. After day-light appeared, some four or five men, with myself, who had escaped with our lives from the horrid massacre, repaired as soon as possible to the mills, to learn the condition of our friends, whose fate we had but too truly anticipated.

When we arrived at the house of Mr. Honn, we found Mr. Merrick's body lying in rear of the house;—Mr. McBrides in front, literally mangled from head to foot. We were informed by Miss Rebecca Judd, who was an eye witness, that he was shot with his own gun, after he had given it up, and then cut to pieces with a corn cutter, by a Mr. Rogers, of Davies county, who keeps a ferry on Grand river, and who has since repeatedly boasted of this act of savage barbarity. Mr. York's body we found in the house, and after viewing these corpses, we immediately went to the blacksmith shop, where we found nine of our friends, eight of whom were already dead; the other, Mr. Cox, of Indiana, struggling in the agonies of death, who expired. We immediately prepared and carried them to the place of interment. This last office of kindness due to the relicts of departed friends, was not attended with the customary ceremonies, nor decency, for we were in jeopardy, every moment expecting to be fired upon by the mob, who, we supposed, were lying in ambush, waiting for the first opportunity to despatch the remaining few who were providentially preserved from the slaughter of the preceding day. However, we accomplished, without molestation, this painful task. The place of burying was a vault in the ground, formerly intended for a well, into which we threw the bodies of our friends promiscuously.

Among those slain I will mention Sardius Smith, son of Warren Smith, about 9 years old, who, through fear, had crawled under the bellows in the shop, where he remained till the massacre was over, when he was discovered by a Mr. Glaze of Carroll county, who presented his rifle near the boy's head and literally blowed off the upper part of it. Mr. Stanley of Carroll told me afterwards that Glaze boasted of this fiendlike murder and heroic deed all over the country.

The number killed and mortally wounded in this wanton slaughter was 18 or 19, whose names, as far as I recollect, were as follows: Thomas M'Bride, Levi Merrick, Elias Benner, Josiah Fuller, Benjamin Lewis, Alexander Campbell, Warren Smith, Sardius Smith, George Richards, Mr. Napier, Mr. Harmer, Mr. Cox, Mr. Abbott, Mr. York, Wm. Merrick,[3] (a boy 8 or 9 years old,) and three or four others, whose names I do not recollect, as they were strangers to me.

Among the wounded who recovered were Isaac Laney, Nathan K. Knight, Mr. Yokum, two brothers by the name of Myers, Tarlton Lewis, Mr. Honn, and several others. Miss Mary Stedwell while fleeing was shot through the hand, and, fainting, fell over a log, into which they shot upwards of twenty balls.

To finish their work of destruction this band of murderers composed of men from Davies, Livingston, Ray, Carroll and Chariton counties, led by some of the principal men of that section of the upper country, (among whom I am informed were Mr. Ashby from Chariton, member of the State Legislature, Col. Jennings of Livingston county, Thomas O. Bryon, Clerk of Livingston co., Mr. Whitney, Dr. Randall, and many others,) proceeded to rob the houses, waggons and tents, of bedding and clothing, drove off horses and waggons, leaving widows and orphans destitute of the necessaries of life, and even stripped the clothing from the bodies of the slain!

According to their own account, they fired *seven* rounds in this awful butchery, making upwards of sixteen hundred shots at a little company of men, about thirty in number.

I hereby certify the above to be a true statement of facts according to the best of my knowledge.

JOSEPH YOUNG.

---

[3]The boy Young refers here is Charles Merrick, according to other accounts of the Haun's Mill massacre.

STATE OF ILLINOIS, } ss.
COUNTY OF ADAMS }

I hereby certify that Joseph Young this day came before me and made oath in due form of law that the statements contained in the foregoing sheets are true according to the best of his knowledge and belief. In testimony whereof I have hereunto set my hand and affixed the Seal of the Circuit Court at Quincy this fourth day of June in the year of our Lord one thousand eight hundred and thirty-nine.

C. M. WOODS,
Clerk Circuit Court Adams co. Ill.

J

A younger brother of the boy here killed, aged eight, was shot through the hip. The little fellow himself states, that seeing his father and brother both killed, he thought they would shoot him again if he stirred, and so feigned himself dead, and lay perfectly still, till he heard his mother call him after dark.

K

It must be constantly recollected, that the Mormons in Caldwell county considered themselves, as they really were, the *regular State Militia*, acting under the command of county officers and by the advice of Generals Doniphon and Parks, for the purpose of putting down a mob. *They had never opposed or thought of opposing the authorities of the State, or of any county.* They had in every instance agreed to keep the peace against lawless violence, *as citizens*, not as Mormons. They were naturally surprised when the State Executive, by whom their officers were commissioned, sent other militia officers to command their surrender. It was not against the State, but for the State, not against Law, but to maintain Law, that they had armed. "The Mormon War," of which so much has been said, was then simply and truly an attempt to put down the very mob, against whom the militia of other counties has been called out; and Gov. Boggs might with equal justice have arrested any other militia officers as these officers of the Mormon militia. This two-fold relation of the Mormons,— first, of militia to preserve order under State authority, and second, of friends to those whom they were called to defend, must be carefully born in mind. And now let a few facts be detailed of the surrender to Gen. Lucas.

The first knowledge the Mormons of Far West and Caldwell received that the other militia of the State were called out against them, was the appearance of 3000 armed men within half a mile of their town. Ignorant of whom these people might be and of what their purposes were, the

Mormons sent out a flag of truce to inquire the cause of their appearance. The answer returned was, that they wanted three individuals named, who were then in Far West, two of which were not members of the church, and that for the Mormons themselves *they intended to exterminate them, or drive them from the State.* It was still, however, not stated who they were, nor was any authority shown under which they were acting. In this state of ignorance and uncertainty the Mormons passed the night and the following day, naturally supposing that this was another mob, and keeping up a guard therefore against surprisal. These suspicions were confirmed by the facts, that *the party under Gilliam had been seen to join them,* and that various Mormons had been taken prisoners, and especially by the cruel murder of Mr. Carey. The next day after the arrival of these troops, Joseph Smith jr., Lyman Wight, Sidney Rigdon and Parley P. Pratt, Caleb Baldwin and Alexander McRae, were by the deceit and stratagem of Col. George M. Hinkle, *himself commander* of the Mormons, betrayed and made prisoners. It was at this time that the Mormons first received information of the Governor's order, and immediately held consultation to know what should be done. *They determined at once and without hesitation to follow the rule, they had always as good citizens observed, of obeying the authorities of the State,* and resolved to surrender, although but a few hours previous, *supposing the men thus collected to be a mob,* they had sworn to stand by each other till death, and never yield to lawless force. As soon as it was known that these troops were a body lawfully acting under the executive order, there was but one desire, and that was to give themselves up. Meanwhile a court martial was held in Gen. Lucas' camp, for the trial of the prisoners already alluded to, who were all condemned to be shot the next morning at 8 o'clock. The execution of this sentence was prevented by the remonstrance of Gen. Doniphon against such cold blooded murder, and by his threats of withdrawing with his troops. Gen. Atchison, it should be stated, had in great indignation withdrawn from the army while at Richmond, as soon as the Gov's. exterminating order had been received.

Hinkle's treachery will be easily understood. Fearing himself a conflict, he had entered into treaty with the officers of the troops, and had promised to deliver up the leading Mormons. This he did as stated in Lyman Wight's memorial, by fraudulently putting them in the enemies power, under pretence of holding a conference. The treaty which he entered into, was not fully understood in the other particulars. But the Mormons had but one course, and that was to surrender; this they did on the following morning. They were marched into a hollow square under Major Bronson, Hinkle having withdrawn himself, and there grounding their arms, they yielded themselves prisoners of war.

L

Copy of a Military Order by the Governor of Missouri.

HEAD QUARTERS, MILITIA, ⎱
CITY OF JEFFERSON, Oct. 27, 1838. ⎰

SIR:—Since the order of the morning to you, directing you to cause four hundred mounted men to be raised within your division, I have received by Amos Rees, Esq. and Wiley E. Williams Esq., one of my aids, information of the most appaling character, which changes the whole face of things, and places the Mormons in the attitude of an open and avowed defiance of the laws, and of having made open war upon the people of this State. Your orders are, therefore, to hasten your operations and endeavour to reach Richmond, in Ray county, with all possible speed. The Mormons must be treated as enemies, and must be exterminated or driven from the State, if necessary, for the public good. Their outrages are beyond all description. If you can increase your force, you are authorised to do so to any extent you may think necessary. I have just issued orders to Maj. Gen. Wallock, of Marion county, to raise 500 men and to march them to the northern part of Davies, and there unite with Gen. Doniphon, of Clay, who has been ordered with 500 men to proceed to the same point, for the purpose of intercepting the retreat of the Mormons to the North. They have been directed to communicate with you by express. You can also communicate with them if you find it necessary. Instead, therefore, of proceeding, as at first directed, to re-instate the citizens of Davies in their homes, you will proceed immediately to Richmond, and there operate against the Mormons. Brig. Gen. Parks, of Ray, has been ordered to have four hundred men of his brigade in readiness to join you at Richmond. The whole force will be placed under your command.

L. W. BOGGS, Gov.
And Commander-in-chief.

To Gen. Clark.

M

The following address, was delivered at Far West, by Maj. Gen. Clark, to the Mormons, after they had surrendered their arms, and themselves prisoners of war:

"*Gentlemen*—You whose names are not attached to this list of names, will now have the privilege of going to your fields to obtain corn for your families, wood, &c. Those that are now taken, will go from thence to prison—be tried, and receive the due demerit of their crimes—but you are now at liberty, all but such as charges may be hereafter preferred against. It now devolves upon you to fulfil the treaty that you have entered into, the leading items of which I now lay before you. The first of these you have already complied with, which is, that you deliver up your leading men to be tried according to law. Second, that you deliver up your arms—this has been attended to. The third is, that you sign over your properties to defray the expenses of the war—this you have also done. Another thing remains for you to comply with, that is that you leave the State forthwith, and whatever your feelings concerning this affair— whatever your innocence, it is nothing to me. Gen. Lucas, who is equal in authority with me, has made this treaty with you. I am determined to see it executed. The orders of the Governor to me, were, that you should be exterminated, and not allowed to continue in the State, and had your leader not been given up and the treaty complied with before this, you and your families would have been destroyed, and your houses in ashes.

There is a discretionary power vested in my hands which I shall try to exercise for a season.—I did not say that you shall go now, but you must not think of staying here another season or of putting in crops; for the moment you do, the citizens will be upon you. I am determined to see the Governor's Message fulfilled, but shall not come upon you immediately— do not think that I shall act as I have done any more—but if I have to come again, because the treaty which you have made here shall be broken, you need not expect any mercy, but extermination—for I am determined the Governor's order shall be executed. As for your leaders, do not once think—do not imagine for a moment—do not let it enter your mind, that they will be delivered, or that you will see their faces again, for their fate is fixed, their die is cast—their doom is sealed.

I am sorry, gentlemen, to see so great a number of apparently intelligent men found in the situation that you are;—and, oh! that I could invoke the spirit of the unknown God to rest upon you, and deliver you from that awful chain of superstition, and liberate you from those fetters of fanaticism with which you are bound. I would advise you to scatter abroad and never again organize with Bishops, Presidents, &c., lest you excite the jealousies of the people, and subject yourselves to the same calamities that have now come upon you. You have always been the aggressors—you have brought upon yourselves these difficulties by being disaffected, and not being subject to rule—and my advice is that you become as other citizens, lest by a recurrence of these events you bring upon yourselves irretrievable ruin.

N

Copy of Mittimus sent by Judge King with Joseph Smith Jr. and others, to the keeper of Liberty Jail, in Clay County, Missouri.

STATE OF MISSOURI, ⎱
RAY COUNTY. ⎰

To the keeper of the Jail of Clay County, greeting.

WHEREAS Joseph Smith Jr., Hiram Smith, Lyman Wight, Alexander McRae and Caleb Baldwin, as also Sidney Rigdon, have been brought before me, Austin A. King, Judge of the Fifth Judicial Circuit in the State of Missouri, and charged with the offence of treason against the State of Missouri, and the said defendants on their examination before me being held to answer further to said charge, the said Joseph Smith Jun., Hiram Smith, Lyman Wight, Alexander McRae and Caleb Baldwin, to answer in the County of Davies, and the said Sidney Rigdon, to answer further in the County of Caldwell for said charge of treason, and there being no Jail in said Counties, these are, therefore, to command that you receive the said Joseph Smith Jun., Hiram Smith, Lyman Wight, Alexander McRae, Caleb Baldwin and Sidney Rigdon, into your custody in the Jail of said County of Clay, there to remain until they be delivered therefrom by due course of law. Given under my hand and seal the 29th day of November, 1838.

AUSTIN A. KING,

STATE OF MISSOURI, ⎱ SS.
County of Clay ⎰ .

I, Samuel Hadly, Sheriff of Clay County, do hereby certify that the above is a true copy of the mittimus to me directed in the cases therein named.

SAMUEL HADLY, *Jailor,*
BY SAMUEL TILLERY, *Dep'y Jailor,*
Clay County, Missouri.

Copy of Caleb Baldwin's Petition,

STATE OF MISSOURI, ⎱ SS.
LIBERTY, CLAY CO., *March* 15, 1839. ⎰

To the honorable Judge Tompkins, or either of the Judges of the Supreme Court of Missouri.

Your petitioner Caleb Baldwin, begs leave to represent to your honor, that sometime in the month of Nov. he was taken prisoner in Far

West by Gen. Clark, and marched to Richmond under a strong guard without any charges being preferred against him, and brought before the honorable Austin A. King, and underwent a partial examination *exparte* in its nature, under the high hand of oppression, and was not allowed the privilege of being examined before the Court then sitting, neither had he the privilege of introducing any testimony before said Court.

Your petitioner would further state, that the said Austin A. King while acting in his official capacity as a committing magistrate, did tell your petitioner that there was no law for him your petitioner, and that he could not stay in the state. Yet your petitioner was held by a strong guard by the said Austin A. King, and after a long examination the said King committed your petitioner to the Jail of Clay County, together with the others of your petitioners, where he has been restrained of his liberty near four months, for the crime of treason against the State, without the least shadow of testimony against him to that amount, or any testimony that was sufficient to have held a man in confinement a single moment. And your petitioner can show before your Honor that he has never committed treason against the State of Missouri, nor any other crime, but has always held himself in readiness to submit to every shadow of law. And now Sir, these are charges too heavy to be borne with submission. And the family of your petitioner has been driven out of the State since his confinement, without any means for their support. And how Sir, in the name of the great God I adjure you, to grant me the State writ of Habeas Corpus, directed to some proper officer, and bring your petitioner before your Honor that he may be discharged according to law. And your petitioner as in duty bound will ever pray.

CALEB BALDWIN.

STATE OF MISSOURI, ⎱
Liberty, Clay Co., ⎰
March 15th, 1839.

Personally came before me Caleb Baldwin, and made oath that the foregoing matters and facts contained in the above are true, to the best of his knowledge.

CALEB BALDWIN.

March 15th 1839

Sworn to before me Abraham Shafer, a Justice of the Peace within and for Clay County in the State of Missouri, *this 15th day of March* 1839.

ABRAHAM SHAFER, J. P.

Copy of Lyman Wight's Petition.
To the Honorable Judges of the Supreme Court for the State
of Missouri.

I petition to you, gentlemen, or either of you, for a writ of Habeas Corpus to bring me before your honors, there to investigate and lay before you the situation and circumstances of your petitioner, who is now falsely imprisoned in the Clay County Jail, Mo. Your petitioner begs leave of your honors here to set forth some of the most prominent points which have led to this false imprisonment. Your petitioner deposeth and saith, that he was a lawful citizen of Davies County, and that some time in the month of August last, whilst peaceably at work on his farm, he was threatened day by day by the citizens of Davies county that if he did not deny his religion they would either exterminate him or drive him from the county. Your petitioner verily believed that it was the threats of some few foul perpetrators until some time in the month of August, when they not only met from that county, but from other counties, with an armed force of rising 300 rank and file, and before the militia could be raised under General's Atchison and Doniphon, they had marched within two and a half miles of your petitioners house, who was assisted by a small number of the same Church to which he belonged. Gen's. Atchison and Doniphon succeeded in dispersing this lawless band—but no sooner was this done than they commenced gathering in Carroll County, where they succeeded in driving from seventy to a hundred families, commonly called Mormons, from that county. The first news your petitioner got of this extraordinary transaction was by the way of the militia under Col. Dunn, who informed your petitioner that this same band, about 400 strong, well armed and prepared for war, with a field piece, a six pounder, was then within fourteen miles of your petitioners house; the advice from the general officers and judges was, that the people called Mormons should stand in their own defence until the militia could be called out to quell this lawless band, who had threatened to exterminate the Mormons, or drive them from Davies county. This advice was adhered to by the Mormons; they met the enemy, and without the firing of a gun, or the shedding of blood, took the cannon from them. This band becoming enraged, divided into small squads and fell upon individual Mormons, turned them out of doors, and burned their houses; and, as many of these marauders were from different counties, they burned many of the other citizens houses, supposing them to belong to the Mormons. Your petitioner declares and says, that through the whole transaction he was not away from home, his wife being very much out of health. This scene being exaggerated by the many false representations called forth a large body of militia; your petitioner, on the 29th day of

October, went to the Far West, Caldwell county, where, on his arri[v]al, he found a large body of militia encamped near that place; he was informed by George M. Hinkle that the officers desired to see him; your petitioner replied, he could not be detained for his wife was sick. Hinkle replied, I should not be detained long. Accordingly I went—met General's Lucas, Doniphon, and Wilson, when Hinkle observed, "here is the prisoners I agreed to deliver you." Gen. Lucas then drew his sword and ordered us into the camp; from thence your petitioner was moved to Jackson county under a strong guard, and from thence to Ray county where he was put in irons; here for the first time he was made acquainted with the charges against him, and then delivered over to Austin A. King, Judge of the Fifth Judicial Court, who sat in the capacity of Conservator of the Peace: he put your petitioner on trial with some fifty or sixty others under a strong armed force, thence calling on renegado Mormons for testimony; and when their testimony was found insufficient to prove to the court that they had not fully and fairly denied the faith, and become wilfully malicious against the prisoners, they were put on trial themselves. This, together with the exterminating order of the Governor, so intimidated the witnesses that some have since acknowledged that they swore for the time being to save their lives. Your petitioner was kept two weeks in irons; in the meantime there was an armed force continually harassing the Mormons in Caldwell and Davies counties, taking prisoners, promising protection to those who would swear against the present prisoners and those that would not should be put on trial. After a scare of this kind for fifteen days, your petitioner was informed that he could produce his testimony; no sooner were their names given than they were driven by an armed force to the extremity of leaving the State, or hiding up, so that they could not be found, and this to save their lives, as their arms were taken from them, and they threatened with extermination if they did not leave the State; therefore your petitioner was obliged to submit to the evidence, false and exparte as it was in its nature, and abide the decision of the Judge, who pronounced your petitioner to be guilty of Treason, ordered him to be conveyed to the above named Jail, where he has laid in close confinement for near four months. Your petitioner begs leave to state a few facts to your honors concerning his family in the meanwhile. On the 3rd day of November his wife was put to bed with a son, whilst Cornelius C. Gilliam, with 100 painted men, surrounded the house, screeching and howling in the attitude of the Delaware Indians, he (Gilliam) calling himself after the Delaware Chief, and it was with the utmost difficulty that the militia could keep them out of the house. In this situation your petitioners' family remained, threatened day by day to leave the county or be exterminated;—accordingly when her babe was eight days old, she was informed she could stay no longer; that she must not only leave the county, but the State—that she need not flatter herself that she would ever see her husband again, for if they could not find law to kill him, they would kill him without law. She was stripped of her beds and bedding, and of her household furniture, then placed in an open wagon with six helpless children to make the best shift she could to get out of the State. The last news your petitioner received from her she was on the bank of the Mississippi river in a tent, depending on the charity of the people for her support; this being the fifth time that your petitioner and family have been unlawfully driven from their house and home since they arrived in the State of Missouri, which was on the sixth day of Sept. 1831.

Your petitioner further states, that there is a slight probability of there being a Court in Davies county at the next Term, as there is no place to hold it, therefore your petitioner begs leave to say to your honors that his health is fast declining, and as the life of your petitioner and family depends upon his liberty, he will therefore earnestly pray your honors to receive his petition and forthwith issue a writ of Habeas Corpus, directed to the Sheriff of Clay county, Mo., commanding him to bring the body of your petitioner before your honors, so that his case may be heard and fairly investigated. And your petitioner pledges himself to prove the above named items, together with many more, too numerous to mention in this petition. As your petitioner considers himself innocent of any crime, he will therefore the more earnestly pray your honors to receive his petition and grant him the writ, &c.   LYMAN WIGHT.

STATE OF MISSOURI, ⎫
    Clay County. ⎭

Personally appeared before me, Lyman Wight, and maketh oath and saith, that the facts stated in the foregoing petition are true, as far as stated from his own knowledge, and as far as stated from the information of others he believes to be true. Given under my hand this 15th day of March, A. D. 1839.   LYMAN WIGHT.

Subscribed and sworn to before me, Abraham Shafer, a Justice of the Peace within and for Clay county, in the State of Missouri, this 15th day of March 1839.   ABRAHAM SHAFER, J.P.

Copy of Joseph Smith, Jr's Petition.

To the Honorable Judge Tompkins, or either of the
Judges of the Supreme Court for the State of Missouri.

Your petitioners, Alanson Ripley, Heber C. Kemble, Joseph B.
Noble, William Huntington, and Joseph Smith, junior, beg leave respectfully to represent to your honor, that Joseph Smith, junior, is now
unlawfully confined and restrained of his liberty, in Liberty jail, Clay
county, (Missouri;) that he has been restrained of his liberty near five
months. Your petitioners claim that the whole transaction which has been
the cause of his confinement is unlawful from the first to the last. He was
taken from his home by a fraud being practised upon him by a man by
the name of George M. Hinkle, and one or two others, thereby, your
petitioners respectfully show, that he was forced, contrary to his wishes,
and without knowing the cause, into the camp which was commanded by
General Lucas, of Jackson county, and from thence to Ray county, sleeping
on the ground, and suffering many insults and injuries, and deprivations,
which were calculated in in their nature to break down the spirits and
constitution of the most robust and hardy of mankind. He was put in chains
immediately on his being landed at Richmond, and there underwent a long
and tedious exparte examination; not only was it exparte, but your petitioners
solemnly declare that it was a mock examination; that there was not the least
shadow of honor, or justice, or law, administered toward him, but sheer
prejudice, and the spirit of persecution and malice, and prepossession against
him on account of his religion; that the whole examination was an inquisitory
examination. Your petitioners show that the said Joseph Smith, junior, was
deprived of the privileges of being examined before the court, as the law
directs; that the witnesses on the part of the State were taken by force of arms,
threatened with extermination or immediate death, and were brought without
subpœna or warrant, under this awful and glaring anticipation of being
exterminated if they did not swear something against him to please the mob,
or his persecutors; and those witnesses were compelled to swear at the muzzle
of the gun, and that some of them have acknowledged since, which your
petitioners do testify, and are able to prove, that they did swear false, and that
they did it in order to save their lives. And your petitioners testify that all the
testimony that had any tendency or bearing or criminality against said Joseph
Smith, junior, is false. We are personally acquainted with the circumstances,
and being with him most of the time, and being present at the times spoken
of by them, therefore we know that their testimony was false, and if he could
have had a fair and impartial and lawful examination before that court, and
could have been allowed the privilege of introducing his witnesses, he could
have disproved every thing that was against him; but the court suffered them

to be intimidated—some of them in the presence of the court, and they were driven also, and hunted, and some of them entirely driven out of the State. And thus he was not able to have a fair trial; that the spirit of the court was tyrannical and overbearing, and the whole transaction of his treatment during the examination was calculated to convince your petitioners that it was a religious persecution, prescribing him in the liberty of conscience, which is guaranteed to him by the Constitution of the United States, and the State of Missouri; that a long catalogue of garbled testimony was permitted by the court, purporting to be the religious sentiment of the said Joseph Smith, junior, which testimony was false, and your petitioners know that it was false, and can prove also, that it was false; because the witnesses testified that these sentiments were promulgated on certain days, and in the presence of large congregations; and your petitioners can prove by those congregations, that the said Joseph Smith, junior, did not promulge such ridiculous and absurd sentiments for his religion, as was testified of, and admitted before the Honorable Austin A. King; and, at the same time, those things had no bearing on the case, that the said Joseph Smith, junior, was pretended to be charged with; and, after the examination, the said prisoner was committed to the jail for treason against the State of Missouri; whereas, the said Joseph Smith, junior, did not levy war against the State of Missouri, neither did he commit any covert acts; neither did he aid or abet an enemy against the State of Missouri during the time that he is charged with having done so; and, farther, your petitioners have yet to learn that the State has an enemy; neither is the proof evident, nor the presumption great, in its most indignant form, upon the face of the testimony on the part of the State, exparte as it is in its nature, that the said prisoner has committed the slightest degree of treason, or any other act of transgression against the laws of the State of Missouri; and yet said prisoner has been committed to Liberty jail, Clay county, (Mo.,) for treason.

He has continually offered bail to any amount that could be required, notwithstanding your petitioners alledge that he ought to have been acquitted. Your petitioners also alledge that the commitment was an illegal commitment, for the law requires that a copy of the testimony should be put in the hands of the jailor, which was not done. Your petitioners alledge that the prisoner has been denied the privilege of the law in a writ of Habeas Corpus, by the judges of this county. Whether they have prejudged the case of the prisoner, or whether they are not willing to administer law and justice to the prisoner, or that they are intimidated by the high office of Judge King, who only acted in the case of the prisoners as a committing magistrate, a conservator of the peace, or by the threats of a lawless mob, your petitioners are not able to say but it is a fact that they do not come forward boldly and administer the law to the relief of the prisoner; and, farther, your petitioners alledge that immediately after the prisoner was taken, his family was frightened and driven out of their house, and that, too, by the witnesses on the part of the State, and plundered of their goods; that the prisoner was robbed of a very fine horse, saddle, and bridle, and other property of considerable amount; that they, (the witnesses,) in connection with the mob, have finally succeeded, by vile threatening and foul abuse, in driving the family of the prisoner out of the State, with little or no means, and without a protector, and their very subsistence depends on the liberty of the prisoner. And your petitioners alledge that he is not guilty of any crime whereby he should be restrained of his liberty, from a personal knowledge, having been with him, and being personally acquainted with the whole of the difficulties between the Mormons and their persecutors; and, that he has never acted, at any time only in his own defence, and that, too, on his own ground, property, and possessions; that the prisoner has never commanded any military company, nor held any military authority, neither any other office, real or pretended, in the State of Missouri, except that of a religious teacher; that he never has bore arms in the military rank, and in all such cases has acted as a private character, and as an individual.

How, then, your petitioners would ask, can it be possible, that the prisoner has committed treason. The prisoner has had nothing to do in Davies county, only on his own business as an individual. The testimony of Doctor Avard concerning a council held at James Sloan's, was false. Your petitioners do solemnly declare, that there was no such council; that your petitioners were with the prisoner, and there was no such vote nor conversation as Doctor Avard swore to; that Doctor Avard also swore false concerning a constitution, as he said, was introduced among the Danites; that the prisoner had nothing to do with burning in Davies county; that the prisoner made public proclamation against such things; that the prisoner did oppose Doctor Avard and George M. Hinkle against vile measures with the mob, but was threatened by them if he did not let them alone; that the prisoner did not have any thing to do with what is called Bogart's battle, for he knew nothing of it until it was over—that he was at home, in the bosom of his own family during the time of that whole transaction; and, in fine, your petitioners allege that he is held in confinement without cause, and under an unlawful and tyrannical oppression, and that his health, and constitution, and life, depends on being liberated from his confinement.

Your petitioners aver that they can disprove every item of testimony that has any tendency of criminality against the prisoner, for they know it themselves, and can bring many others also to prove the same. Therefore, your petitioners pray your honor to grant to him the State's writ of habeas corpus, directed to the jailor of Clay county, (Mo.,) commanding him forthwith to bring before you the body of the prisoner, so that his case may be heard before your honor, and the situation of the prisoner be considered and adjusted according to law and justice, as it shall be presented before your honor, and as in duty bound, your petitioners will ever pray.

And, farther, your petitioners testify that the said Joseph Smith, junior, did make a public proclamation in Far West, in favor of the militia of the State of Missouri, and of its laws, and, also, of the constitution of the United States; that he has ever been a warm friend to his country, and did use all his influence for peace; that he is a peaceable and quiet citizen, and is not worthy of death, of stripes, bonds, or imprisonment.

The abovementioned speech was delivered on the day before the surrender of Far West.

> ALANSON RIPLEY,
> HEBER C. KIMBALL,
> WILLIAM HUNTINGTON,
> JOSEPH B. NOBLE,
> JOSEPH SMITH, jun.,

STATE OF MISSOURI, } ss.
    County of Clay,

This day personally appeared before me, Abraham Shafer, a Justice of the Peace within and for the aforesaid county—Alanson Ripley, Heber C. Kimball, Wm. Huntington, Joseph B. Noble, and Joseph Smith, jun., who, being duly sworn, doth depose and say that the matters and things set forth in the foregoing petition, upon their own knowledge, are true in substance and in fact, and so far as set forth upon the information of others, they believe to be true.

> ALANSON RIPLEY,
> HEBER C. KIMBALL,
> WILLIAM HUNTINGTON,
> JOSEPH B. NOBLE,
> JOSEPH SMITH, jun.

Sworn and subscribed to before me, this 15th day of March, 1839.

> ABRAHAM SHAFER, J.P.

We, the undersigned, being many of us personally acquainted with the said Joseph Smith, jun., and the circumstances connected with his imprisonment, do concur in the petition and testimony of the abovenamed individuals, as most of the transactions therein mentioned we know from personal knowledge, to be correctly set forth, and from information of others, believe the remainder to be true.

> AMASA LYMAN,
> H. G. SHERWOOD,
> JAMES NEWBERY,
> CYRUS DANIELS,
> ERASTUS SNOW,
> ELIAS SMITH.

Copy of Alexander McRea's petition.
To the Honorable Judge Tompkins, of the Supreme Court
for the State of Missouri.

Your petitioner, Alexander McRae, would beg leave respectfully to represent to your honor, that he has been confined and restrained of his liberty near five months, part of the time in chains; that your petitioner alleges his confinement to be unlawful and unjust, for the following reasons: In the first place, your petitioner is confined on the charge of treason against the State, which crime, according to the Constitution of the State, as well as of the United States, can consist only in levying war and committing overt acts, or in adhering to the enemies of the same, which your petitioner declares he has never done, for he has yet to learn that the State has an enemy; that your petitioner on the examination was not allowed the privileges of the law in being examined before the Court; that he was threatened and intimidated and was not allowed the liberty of speech and the rights of conscience; that the examination on the part of the Court was tyrannical and overbearing towards your petitioner, such as was not lawful and warrantable in a free government; that the witnesses of your petitioner were intimidated by an armed force that had been for a length of time harassing and driving the Mormons from their homes and possessions, and this fact was known by the Court, and yet the Court employed this same armed force as a pretended guard to guard your petitioner, and suffered them to practice many abuses upon the witnesses of your petitioner, and participated largely himself in the same spirit of persecution; therefore, the witnesses of your petitioner were driven out of the place and some of them out of the State. Your petitioner solemnly declares that he never witnessed a more partial, and unjust, and unlawful transaction than was practised upon your petitioner; that the whole transaction was nothing more nor less than a spirit of persecution against your petitioner. Your petitioner heard the Court say that there was no law for the Mormons, and that they could not stay in the State. Your petitioner declares that there is no evidence against him whereby he should be restrained of his liberty; that the family of your petitioner have been robbed of their property and driven out of the State since your petitioner has been confined, and that they are now destitute of the necessaries of life, and that they consist of a weakly woman and two small children, the oldest only three years of age, and that your petitioner's health is declining in consequence of his confinement.—Your petitioner therefore prays your honor to grant to him the State writ of *habeas corpus*, directed to the Jailor of Clay county, (Mo.) commanding him forthwith to bring before you the body of your petitioner, so that his case may be heard, and that your honor dispose of the case of your petitioner as you may deem just and proper, and as in duty bound he will ever pray, &c.   ALEXANDER McRAE.

STATE OF MISSOURI,   }
Clay County,   }

Personally appeared before me, Alexander McRae, and maketh oath and saith that the facts stated in the foregoing petition are true as far as stated from his own knowledge, and as far as stated from the information of others he believes to be true. Given under my hand this 15th day of March, A.D. 1839.   ALEXANDER McRAE.

Sworn and subscribed to before me, Abraham Shafer, a Justice of the Peace within and for Clay county, in the State of Missouri, this 15th day of March, 1839.   ABRAHAM SHAFER, J.P.

Copy of Hiram Smith's Petition.
To the honorable Judge Tompkins, or either of the Judges of the
Supreme Court for the State of Missouri.

Your petitioner, Hiram Smith, would beg leave respectfully to represent to your Honor, that he has been confined and restrained of his liberty near five months, some part of the time in chains, that some time in the month of last October there was an armed force under the command of Gen. Lucas, who encamped in the vicinity of Far West in Caldwell County, when and where your humble petitioner was taken from his own house, and from the bosom of his family, and was driven by force of arms into the camp of Gen. Lucas, from thence was under a strong guard carried to Jackson County, and thence to Richmond, Ray County, where without the issuing any precept or warrant by any judicial officer, or without any specific charge alleged against him your humble petitioner, and there he was brought before Austin A. King Judge of the Fifth Judicial District of the State, when after a lengthy examination *exparte* in its nature, for he does aver, that he had ample testimony to have disproved all the testimony that was brought him, but was prevented from so doing by the great excitement which all that time displayed itself in Ray County, and that too in such a manner as to intimidate the witnesses, which prevented them from giving in their testimony. Many of them were threatened with violence, and were pursued and driven out of the County, and some even out of the State; under such circumstances Judge King committed your petitioner for treason against the State, and removed him or caused him to be removed to the Jail of Clay County, Mo., and where he has been kept in close confinement up to this date. Your petitioner positively declares, that he knew nothing personally of the difficulties in Davies County; all he knew of them was by report. Your petitioner declares that about the middle of October, he learnt by a small company of Militia under the command of Gen. Doniphon of Clay County, that a large armed force having a cannon with them, were coming to Davies County to exterminate the people called Mormons from the County, your petitioner having much property there, he went by himself to take care of it and to secure it from being destroyed; and after he had preserved his property he returned to his home in Far West, in Caldwell County. Your petitioner also declares, that the burning of houses and plundering in Davies County, he had no hand in, and knew nothing of it, only by report. Your petitioner also states that he had no knowledge of any Council at any time in Davies County, as stated in testimony. Your petitioner also states, that he has made no speech neither in public nor private nor any thing in any wise whereby the most wicked and prejudiced person on the earth could interpret it into treason, in Davies County or in any other. Your petitioner also states, that he never has aided in a civil nor in a military capacity; he never has borne arms nor done military service at any time, in all his lifetime up to this date, but has been lawfully exempt from all such service; the family of your petitioner has been robbed of all their substance for their support, both of food, raiment and household furniture, and have been driven from the State with constant threatenings of death, if they did not leave the State, by a lawless banditti that was let loose upon the Mormon people without restraint, whilst your petitioner is restrained of his liberty, without scarcely the least shadow of testimony of evil against him, whilst his family has been driven from their home, and even from the State, and all their property and effects for support taken from them by a mob, or this lawless banditti before mentioned, which facts are notorious to the most part of the people in this part or region of country. Your petitioner states that his health is fast declining in consequence of his confinement. Your petitioner states that one term of the Court has passed by since your petitioner has been deprived of his liberty, yet no charge has been preferred against him. Your petitioner thinks the proceedings are unlawful in this whole transaction with your petitioner, therefore, your petitioner prays your Honor to grant to him a

State's writ of Habeas Corpus, directed to the Jailor or Sheriff of Clay county, Mo., commanding him forthwith to bring before you the body of your petitioner, so that this case may be heard before your Honor, and the situation of your petitioner may be considered and adjusted according to law and justice, as it shall be presented before your Honor, and as we are in duty bound will ever pray.

15th March, 1839   HIRAM SMITH.

STATE OF MISSOURI, ⎫
CLAY COUNTY. ⎭

Personally appeared before me Hiram Smith and maketh oath and saith, that the facts stated in this foregoing petition are true as far as stated from his own knowledge, of others he believes to be true, given under my hand this 15th day of March A. D. 1839.

HIRAM SMITH.

Sworn to before me, Abraham Shafer, a Justice of the Peace for Clay county, Missouri, this 15th day of March, 1839.

ABRAHAM SHAFER, J.P.

STATE OF MISSOURI. ⎫ ss.
COUNTY OF CLAY, ⎭

This day personally appeared before me, Abraham Shafer, a Justice of the Peace within and for the county of Clay aforesaid, Alanson Ripley, Heber C. Kimball, William Huntington, Joseph B. Noble and Hiram Smith, who being duly sworn do depose and say, that the matters and things set forth in the foregoing petition, upon their own knowledge are true in substance and in fact, and so far as set forth upon the information of others they believe to be true.

ALANSON RIPLEY,
HEBER C. KIMBALL,
WM. HUNTINGTON,
JOSEPH B. NOBLE.

Sworn and subscribed to, this 15th day of March, 1839, before me

ABRAHAM SHAFER, J.P.

O

Messrs. Editors: At the request of my friends, or at least those in whom I have confided as friends, I have written an account of my troubles and losses in the State of Missouri. I went to Missouri to procure land for myself and children. I entered two hundred acres of land and settled on it with the intention of living in peace with all men; and we lived in peace and harmony until the fourth of November, when a worthless mob came and scattered all our joys. It was Sunday, late in the afternoon, they came to one of my buildings (which was evacuated, but part of my goods were in it,) and burned it with its contents to the ground, except a few articles which they carried off. They then came to my son-in-law's, where he was at home with his wife and child, and ordered him from his own house and home. They next came to my house to order me from my own house and land. My son-in-law started to come to my house to see what they intended to do to me and my family—the ruffians ordered him back—he would not go back, but told them he had disturbed no one, had violated no law, and always reverenced and supported the government of the United States—he therefore contended that he had a right to go where he pleased. One of them spoke and said, "you are a d—d liar," and got down from his horse and struck him with a rock. My son-in-law then went up to him and threw him down, a second one then broke a club over him, and the third one presented a gun and fired at him, but we do not know whether the ball hit him or not, as he was so shamefully bruised with a gun which they broke over him that the doctors could not tell whether the ball had entered his scull or not. When they were murdering him in this awful manner, oh! it makes my heart lament to think of it, his wife with uplifted hands and streaming eyes begged of them to spare his life, but they took no notice of her lamentations, and regarded her as a mere reptile beneath their feet, and continued to beat him over the head with a gun until they bursted the brains from his scull. After thus inhumanly mangling him they mounted their horses and bawled out at us to begone by early breakfast time the next morning or they would kill every one of us. When his wife had recovered and come to herself, in the agony of her soul she exclaimed, oh my father, my companion is killed,—yes, replied these ruffians, with horrible oaths, your companion is killed, and we will kill more of your companions. These barbarous villains then rode off laughing at our distress. After some ten or fifteen minutes we raised him up and gave him some water, which caused him to revive a little; we then took him to the house and laid him down and began to make preparations for starting. It was then dark, and in getting ready to start we all happened to be out of the house except my little grand-daughter, who on seeing her father in this miserable condition, left her seat and sat down by him, and wept as if she participated in his misery; she was only three years old. It was about one hour in the night when we got ready to start—although the moon shone bright it was a dreary night to us. I was at the stable when the mob came in sight; two of my daughters came to me, and although most distracted, prevailed on me not to go near them or say a word or we should all be murdered. In this wretched condition we moved off, leaving our houses, homes, and property to be filched and destroyed by a lawless set of demons in human form. We went four miles from home that night, carrying my son-in-law, whose misery was past description. In the morning we went back for our cows and other property, but the mob who had augmented and collected on the spot refused to let us have our cows, but said if we would come back and say nothing we might have part of our household goods, but the rest of our property they intended to keep to pay the destruction of property in Davies county; so they kept the whole and divided it among themselves. When the news came back that we could get nothing, it was distressing to us all, for we left in such a confused state that we took nothing for ourselves or horses. We took neither bread nor meat, or even a fowl, or any necessary article of the kind, although we had plenty that we had left. The mob then burned my three houses, my stable and crib, which contained about 100 bushels of corn, the rest was in the field. There were many of them I did not know, but six of them that I did know I will mention, viz: Benjamin Clark, Jesse Clark, Atherton Wethers, Peliman Ellis, John Gardner, of Chariton county, and John Hase, of Elk township. Thus I, an old man, almost three-score years old, and a cripple, with a set of helpless women and my son-in-law, spent that night and the next day until noon alone in the wilderness. At that time my other son-in-law, with his wife and three small children came to us as we were crossing the creek in Macon county. A melancholy sight it was for them to behold their father, mother, and sisters, driven from home wandering in the desert, and the still more heartrending sight was to see their kinsman thus brutally slaughtered, weltering in his own blood and destitute of any place to lay his mangled body, except on the ground in the howling wilderness.

PETER WIMMER.

Messrs. Editors: The undersigned, residents of Adams county, Ill., in presenting the above, think it our duty to say, that the said Mr. Wimmer has lived close by us for about two months, and we can consider him in no other way than an honest and industrious citizen. He wishes us to say that he is willing to testify to the above, yea, and even more than is stated; his family also say the same. Now Messrs. Editor, there are two questions which naturally present themselves to us; the first is, why were these people thus barbarously treated and driven from their homes? All the answer we can give is, it was *pretended* that they were Mormons. The truth of the case appears to be this, two of the family, both females, believe in most of the doctrines held by the Latter Day Saints, or Mormons, but they did not assemble with the Mormons, either in a religious, defensive or warlike capacity. The second question is, upon what pretext do these wretches seize to shield them from justice? (That they were in every sense of the word a *mob* is apparent, as they had no officers and were not organised in any way except this, the men who were most inhuman and desperate should be their leaders.) The answer is, Executive order, yes, *Executive order*—the more than savage order of extermination, as given by Gov. Boggs. That Boggs did give such orders is apparent from the address of Maj. Gen. Clark, at Far West. The General says, "the orders of the Governor to me were, that you (*Mormons*) should be *exterminated* and not allowed to remain in the State," etc. Now, that under this brutal order all manner of misconduct and barbarity has been condescended to, is a point that we think requires no proof, except what is before the public. The conclusion is, then, that the Executive is responsible, and ought to be held accountable for the great loss of property and lives.

S. J. COMFORT,
D. A. MILLER.

P

The gross injustice of the deed of trust by which the Mormons signed over their property "to defray the expenses of the war," as Gen. Clark says, or "to pay the debts of every individual belonging to the church," as Bishop Partridge expresses it, can be fully understood at a glance. It was an enormous and wholesale robbery. Let us consider the circumstances. A mob attacks the Mormons in Davies county, disperses their families, kills their cattle, burns their houses, murders them, and when the Mormon militia, *called out legally, like other militia, to restore peace*, attacks this mob, the cry is raised of a Mormon war; and this legal militia, armed *against* the mob, is forced to surrender to militia supported *by* the mob. And, then it is demanded that they should pay for the ruin, and attendant expenses, which the confusion of this mob had caused, when it was the Mormons themselves who had been plundered, and in every way persecuted. The State was, in all common justice, bound to make them restitution for the losses they had suffered; and, instead, by force they wrung from them their all.

But again—with what plausibility could it be demanded, that the property of every Mormon should be given up in order that the debts of every other Mormon should be paid? *They held no common property* except the fund in the hands of the Bishop *for the support of the poor*. No man was in any way bound for another's debt. Each was independent in his possessions. Here, again, was an indiscriminate, illegal plunder of the poor people of the State.

But we cannot estimate the full injustice done until we consider the *forced* sales of property after their surrender. Be it remembered, that they were ordered to leave the State within a certain time, under threat of extermination, and that this was the winter season; be it remembered, too, that after they had given up their arms, they were wholly defenseless against attack, and were thus daily subject to every insult and outrage which abandoned villains could inflict. Let one picture to himself their condition, when thus threatened and abused, and we shall see at once how glad they were to escape at any cost or sacrifice. Caldwell county, its age considered, was the best cultivated in the State, and presented, in every way, the most promising appearance. The owners of this whole county were, with but the few exceptions of individuals who were not Mormons, forcibly dispossessed of the improvements they themselves had made. They were compelled to sell their property for what they could get, or, rather, let us say, for what their persecutors were willing to give them.

Q

Some facts relative to the removal of the Mormons and their present condition should be stated. The Mormons were so perfectly aware of the flagrant wrong of Gov. Boggs' exterminating order, and of the treaty by which they were subsequently deprived of their property, that they sent in a memorial to the legislature, demanding justice at their hands. A committee was appointed to examine into their case, and visit Caldwell and Davies counties. This was in December. The committee, however, did nothing, and another was appointed who were equally negligent of their duty. Meanwhile the Mormon question was constantly agitated in the house. These debates may be seen by a reference to the Missouri Republican. It was in January that the Mormons became satisfied, that they could expect no justice at the hands of the Missouri Legislature; and it may be well here to make it known that the farther consideration of their memorial was laid upon the table until July, *thus securing their expulsion from the state under the exterminating order and Clark's treaty.* There was but one course now open for the Mormons, and that was to make their escape with the utmost expedition. This they effected as best they could; and it will be easy to conceive, what were the sufferings of these helpless people, oftentimes women and children, whose natural protectors were in prison or had fled away, in the midst of the cold of winter. Many were stripped of clothing and bedding. Many sold all their household stuff to pay the immediate expenses of their journey. Many without cattle, horses, or waggons, had no means of conveyance. In this situation it was thought proper to make some general effort for the removal of the helpless families—a contribution was raised from among the Mormons who had means, and a committee appointed for its expenditure. It was through this charity among themselves that the destitute were enabled to remove to the State of Illinois; where at Quincy they were kindly received and provided for, to the lasting honor of the citizens of that place. The condition of these outcast strangers was wretched indeed. Their numbers were so great that many could find no shelter.

In the months of Feb. and March there were at one time 130 families and upwards upon the west back of the Mississippi, unable to cross on account of the running ice, many of them entirely destitute of food and only scantily supplied from the east side of the river, by those who with great difficulty succeeded in conveying them provision. Their only shelter was the bed clothing from which they could make tents, and many had not even this. In this miserable situation many women gave birth to children. The Mormons who were already in Quincy, formed a committee among themselves, to aid to the best of their power the committee of Far West in giving assistance to their suffering brethren. They received them as they came, sent forward all who had means and strength into the interior, provided the poor and sick with lodgings, fuel, food and clothing. *This committee were necessarily obliged to incur debts to a large amount in this work of charity, for which they are now personally liable, and for which surely the benevolent minded will not allow them to suffer.* Contributions should be raised and forwarded to these abused brethren. The citizens of Quincy have generously done what was in their power. Who will not be ready to help the distressed? There are many there now and in the vicinity who are dependant upon charity, and their brother Mormons, scattered abroad and spoiled, are not in the condition to give them the aid which, at another time, they would according to the principles of their church readily afford. Hundreds of others equally destitute have sought a home in Iowa.

R

COMMERCE, Ill., April 12, 1839.

Messrs. Editors:—Inclosed I send you a communication from Gov. Lucas of Iowa Territory.—If you think the publication thereof will in any way promote the cause of justice, by vindicating the slandered reputation of the people called "Mormons," from the ridiculous falsehoods which the malice, cupidity, and envy of their murderers in Missouri have endeavoured to heap upon them, you are respectfully solicited to publish it in the "Argus." The testimony of Gov. Lucas, as to the good moral character of these people, I think will have its deserved influence upon the people of Illinois, in encouraging our citizens in their humane and benevolent exertions to relieve this distressed people, who are now wandering in our neighbourhoods without comfortable food, raiment, or a shelter from the pelting storm.

I am, gentlemen,
very respectfully,
Your ob't serv't.,
I. GALLAND.

EXECUTIVE OFFICE, Iowa, }
Burlington, March, 1839. }

DEAR SIR:—On my return to this city, after a few weeks absence in the interior of the Territory, I received your letter of the 25th ult., in which you give a short account of the sufferings of *the people called Mormons*, and ask "whether they could be permitted to purchase lands and settle upon them in the Territory of Iowa, and there *worship Almighty God* according to the dictates of their own consciences, secure from oppression," &c.

In answer to your inquiry, I would say that I know of no authority that can constitutionally deprive them of this right. They are citizens of the United States, and are entitled to all the rights and privileges of other citizens. The 2nd section of the 4th article of the Constitution of the United States (which all are solemnly bound to support,) declares that "the citizens of each state shall be entitled to all the privileges and immunities of citizens in the several states;" this privilege extends in full force to the Territories of the United States. The first amendment to this constitution of the U.S. declares that "Congress shall make no law respecting an establishment of religion or prohibiting the free exercise thereof."

The Ordinance of Congress of the 13th July, 1787, for the government of the Territory northwest of the river Ohio, secures to the citizens of said Territory and the citizens of the States thereafter to be formed therein, certain privileges which were, by the late act of Congress organizing the Territory of Iowa, extended to the citizens of this Territory. The first fundamental article in that ordinance, which is declared to be forever unalterable, except by common consent, reads as follows, to wit: "No person demeaning himself in a peaceable and orderly manner shall ever be molested on account of his mode of worship or religious sentiments in said Territory." These principles I trust will ever be adhered to in the Territory of Iowa. They make no distinction between religious sects. They extend equal privileges and protection to all; each must rest upon its own merits and will prosper in proportion to the purity of its principles, and the fruit of holiness and piety produced thereby.

With regard to the peculiar people mentioned in your letter, I know but little. They had a community in the northern part of Ohio for several years, and I have no recollection of ever having heard in that State of any complaint against them for violating the laws of the country. Their religious opinions I conceive has nothing to do with our political transactions. They are citizens of the United States, and are entitled to the same political rights and legal protection that other citizens are entitled to.

The foregoing are briefly my views on the subject of your inquiries.

With sincere respect,

I am your obedient servant,

ROBERT LUCAS.

Isaac Galland, Esq., of Commerce, Illinois.

PUBLIC MEETING.

At a meeting of the citizens held in the chapel of the Cincinnati College, on the evening of June 17th, for the purpose of affording John P. Greene, the representative of the Mormon people, an opportunity to set forth the claims of that sect to the sympathies and charities of the American people, relative to their recent persecutions and sufferings in the State of Missouri, Wm. Greene was called to the chair, and N. Allen appointed secretary.

After Mr. Greene had made his statement, the meeting was addressed by the Hon. Thomas Morris, who offered the following resolutions, which were then unanimously adopted:

Resolved, That we have heard with sensations of the deepest regret the tale of wrong and suffering, inflicted on the people called Mormons, while resident citizens of Missouri, by an armed mob of the people of that State, who, it appears to us, acted under the advice and orders of Governor Boggs, and whose conduct we believe to be an outrage upon every principle of justice, and all law, human and divine; alike disgraceful to the actors, and to the State which neglects to bring them to condign punishment.

Resolved, That we will cheerfully aid, by our means, the widows and fatherless, made so by the hand of ruthless violence, in this most unprincipled and disgraceful transaction, and we assure the surviving sufferers of our sincere sympathy in their distress, and will extend to them as far as in our power, that support which they so much need to alleviate their present wants, and to restore them to their just rights.

Resolved, That the story of wrongs done the Mormon people, which we have just heard, almost surpasses human credulity; and we believe they ought to be spread before the American people and the world, in the best authentic form that can be obtained.

Resolved, That a committee of four persons, (of whom the chairman of this meeting shall be one,) be appointed to collect all the facts in their power, and present them to a future meeting in the form of a preamble and resolutions.

Resolved, That all those who may think proper to contribute, may do so by handing over the same to the chairman of this meeting, who will keep a list of names, and the amount donated by each, and report the same to the next meeting.

Resolved, That the proceedings of this meeting be published in the City newspapers.

The meeting then adjourned to Monday evening next, to meet at the Cincinnati College. WM. GREENE, Chairman.

N. A LLEN, Secretary.

MORMON MEETING.

An adjourned meeting was held in the College Chapel, last evening, according to previous notice; Wm. Greene, Esq., in the chair.

Mr. J. P. Greene addressed the meeting, going over much the same ground as at his previous address. He told some additional facts, however, in relation to the conduct of the executive of Missouri, and showed some of the reverend clergy in that section in a light by no means enviable.

The chairman then submitted the preamble and resolutions below, on the passage of which an exciting debate took place. J. C. Vaughan, Esq., and Dr. M'Dowell opposing, and Rev. Mr. Channing and Dr. Weston in favour of their passage; the debate was short but spirited, and want of room only prevents us from giving a sketch of it. The preamble and resolutions were passed, and are as follows:

The committee appointed at a meeting of the citizens of Cincinnati, to consider the sufferings of the people called Mormons, beg leave to report the following preamble and resolutions:

WHEREAS, It is our duty as men and christians, to *befriend the oppressed every where*—a duty which becomes more urgent, when the injured have equal claims with ourselves to the protection of institutions, by which our own rights are guarded; and whereas, *freedom of conscience* is a sacred trust, which all men should solemnly respect; and this freedom is infringed whenever predjudice, bigotry, intolerance or popular caprice are allowed to persecute men for opinions, which the few or the many may judge absurd or noxious; and whereas, *civil liberty* is an inheritance, won by long struggle, and bequeathed to us, which we are in gratitude and in honour bound to transmit unimpaired; and this liberty is violated whenever the rights of any individual, however humble or hated, are trampled upon with impunity, and whenever mobs are permitted to attack the object of their dislike, under any pretext whatever of defending the property, reputation or morals of communities; and whereas the people called Mormons are *our fellow citizens*, and have a just title to all civil and religious privileges, till proved guilty and subject to penalty before legal tribunals; and whereas, Missouri mobs have cruelly persecuted these people, plundered their stores, stolen their cattle, wasted their fields, burnt their houses, driven them from their homes, abused their women, murdered their men, and a Missouri executive has unconstitutionally, and against all law, *exiled them under threats of extermination*, thus authorizing outrage and robbery, and a Missouri legislature has slighted the appeal for justice and refused restitution for the wrongs of 10,000 injured citizens; Therefore,

Resolved, That we are compelled as citizens, christians, and men, to express our indignation at this precedent given for religious persecution, lawless violence, and mob rule.

Resolved, That we commend the conduct of the citizens of Quincy, Illinois, in their generous defence and aid of the Mormons, and trust that their example will be followed by the expression of just censure of these social crimes through public meetings and the press.

Resolved, That we approve of the attempt of John P. Greene, to make known the history of his people's wrongs to the whole nation, through addresses and publications.

Resolved, That we consider the destitute, the aged, the widows, the orphans, among the Mormons, proper objects of charity, and that we will now take up a contribution for their relief.

WM. GREENE, *Chairman.*

N. ALLEN, *Secretary.*

Chapter 2

Parley P. Pratt's History of the Late Persecution

HISTORY

OF THE LATE

PERSECUTION

INFLICTED BY THE STATE OF MISSOURI UPON THE

MORMONS,

IN WHICH TEN THOUSAND AMERICAN CITIZENS WERE ROBBED,
PLUNDERED, AND DRIVEN FROM THE STATE, AND MANY OTHERS
IMPRISONED, MARTYRED, &C. FOR THEIR RELIGION, AND
ALL THIS BY MILITARY FORCE, BY ORDER OF THE EXECUTIVE

BY P. P. PRATT,

Minister of the Gospel.

WRITTEN DURING EIGHT MONTHS IMPRISONMENT IN THAT STATE

"Great is the truth, and it will prevail."

Price 25 cents per copy, or $16 per hundred.

DETROIT:

DAWSON & BATES, PRINTERS.

1839.

PERSECUTION OF THE MORMONS, &c.

The following is a copy of a declaration, which was signed by the mob at the commencement of their operations, in 1833; and, it may be considered as their articles of agreement in conspiring against the laws of the land; and the very foundation of that awful scene which has well nigh destroyed a flourishing society of many thousands, and involved the whole State in irretrievable ruin.

"We, the undersigned, citizens of Jackson county, believing that an important crisis is at hand, as regards our civil society, in consequence of a pretended religious sect of people, that have settled and are still settling in our county, styling themselves Mormons: and intending as we do to rid our society, peaceably if we can, forcibly if we must: and believing as we do, that the arm of the civil law does not afford us a guarantee, or at least a sufficient one, against the evils which are now inflicted upon us, and seem to be increasing by the said religious sect; deem it expedient and of the highest importance, to form ourselves into a company for the better and easier accomplishment of our purpose; a purpose which we deem it almost superfluous to say, is justified as well by the law of nature as by the law of self-preservation. It is now more than two years since the first of these fanatics or knaves, (for one or the other they undoubtedly are) made their first appearance amongst us; and pretending as they did, and now do, to hold personal communion and converse, face to face, with the most high God—to receive communications and revelations direct from Heaven—to heal the sick by laying on hands—and in short, to perform all the wonder-working miracles wraught by the inspired Apostles and prophets of old. We believe them deluded fanatics, or weak and designing knaves; and that they and their pretensions would soon pass away; but in this we were deceived. The arts of a few designing leaders amongst them have thus far succeeded in holding them together as a society, and since the arrival of the first of them, they have been daily increasing in numbers, and if they had been respectable citizens in society, and thus deluded, they would have been entitled to our pity rather than our contempt and hatred. But from their appearance, from their manners, and from their conduct since their coming among us, we have every reason to fear, that with very few exceptions, they were of the very dregs of that society from whence they came—lazy, idle and vicious.

This we conceive is not an idle assertion, but a fact susceptible of proof; for, with the few exceptions above named, they brought into our county with them, little or no property, and left less behind them; and we infer, that those only, yoked themselves to the Mormon car, who had nothing earthly or heavenly to loose by the change; and we fear that if some of the leaders among them, had paid the forfeit due to crime, instead of being chosen embassadors of the Most High, would have been inmates of solitary cells. But their conduct here, stamps their characters in their true colors. More than a year since it was ascertained that they had been tampering with our slaves, and endeavoring to sow dissentions and to raise seditions amongst them. Of this, their Mormon leaders were informed; and said that they would deal with any of their members who should again in like case offend. But how specious are appearances. In a late number of the Star, published in Independence, by the leaders of this sect, there is an article inviting free negroes and mulattoes from other States, to become Mormons, and remove and settle among us. This exhibits them in still more odious colors. It manifests a desire on the part of their society to inflict on our society, an injury that they knew would be to us insupportable, and one of the surest means of driving us from the county; for it would require none of the supernatural gifts that they pretend to, to see that the introduction of such a cast among us, would corrupt our blacks, and instigate them to bloodshed.

"They openly blaspheme the most High God, and cast contempt upon His Holy Religion, by pretending to receive Revelations direct from Heaven—by pretending to speak in unknown tongues by direct inspiration—and by divers pretences derogatory of God and religion, and to the utter subversion of human reason. They declare openly that their God hath given them this county of land, and that sooner or later, they must and will have possession of our lands for an inheritance; and in fine they have conducted themselves on many other occasions in such a manner, that we believe it a duty we owe to ourselves, to our wives and children, and to the cause of public morals, to remove them from among us. We are not prepared to give up our pleasant places and goodly possessions to them; or to receive into the bosom of our families as fit companions for our wives and daughters, the degraded free negroes and mulattoes, who are now invited to settle among us. Under such a state of things, even our beautiful county would cease to be a desirable residence, and our situ[ation][1] intolerable. We therefore agree, that after ti[mely] warning, and upon receiving an adequate compens[a]tion for what little property they cannot take with them, they refuse to leave us in peace as they found us, we agree to use such means as may be sufficient to remove them. And to that end, we severally pledge to each other, our lives, our bodily powers, fortunes,

---

[1] The brackets appearing here and in the fourth paragraph following indicate a conjectural reading where the edge of the original page is torn.

and sacred honors! We will meet at the Court House in the town of Independence, on Saturday next, to consult of ulterior movements."

Hundreds of signatures were signed to the foregoing, among which were the following, viz: Henry Chiles, Attorney, Russel Hicks, Attorney, Hugh L. Brazeale, Attorney, Henry Westen, J. P., John Smith, J. P., John Cook, J. P., Lewis Franklin, jailor, Thomas Pitcher, Lt. Col. Militia, and Constable, Samuel C. Owens, County Clerk, D. Lucas, Colonel of Militia, and Judge of County Court, Jones H. Flornay, P.M., Moses Willson.

Before I proceed with the history, I will briefly notice a few items of the foregoing bond of conspiracy, for I consider most of it as too barefaced to need any comment. In the first place I would enquire whether our belief as set forth in this declaration, as to gifts, miracles, Revelations and tongues, is not the same that all the Apostles and disciples taught, believed and practiced, and the doctrine of the New Testament?

2ndly, I would enquire when the New Testament religion ceased, and a law revealed or instituted, which made blasphemy of the belief and practice of it? or what holy religion the Jackson mob were speaking of, which was thrown into contempt by the revival of the New Testament religion?

3rdly, They complain of our Society being very poor, as to property; but have they never read in the New Testament that God had chosen the poor in this [wor]ld, rich in faith, and heirs of the kingdom of God? [an]d when did poverty become a crime known to the [la]w?

4thly, Concerning free negroes and mulattoes.—Do not the laws of Missouri provide abundantly for the removal from the state of all free negroes and mulattoes? (except certain priviledged ones;) and also for the punishment of those who introduce or harbor them? The statement concerning our invitation to them to become Mormons, and remove to this state, and settle among us, is a wicked fabrication, as no such thing was ever published in the Star, or any where else, by our people, nor any thing in the shadow of it; and we challenge the people of Jackson, or any other people, to produce such a publication from us.

In fact, one half dozen negroes or mulattoes, never have belonged to our Society, in any part of the world, from its first organization to this day, 1839.

5thly, As to crime or vice, we solemly appeal to all the records of the courts of Jackson county, and challenge the county to produce the name of any individual of our Society on the list of indictments, from the time of our first settlement in the county, to the time of our expulsion, a period of more than two years.

6thly, As it respects the ridiculous report of our threatening that we would have their lands for a possession, it is too simple to require a notice, as the laws of the country guarantee to every man his rights, and abundantly protect him in their full enjoyment. And we hereby declare, that we settled no lands, only such as our money purchased, and that no such thing ever entered our hearts, as possessing any inheritance in any other way. And

7thly, We ask what public morals were in danger of being corrupted, where officers of the peace could openly violate their several oaths in the most awful manner, and join with hundreds of others in murder, treason, robbery, house burning, stealing, etc.

But to proceed with my history. Pursuant to the last clause of the bond, the mob met at the court house, on the 20th of July, and proceeded immediately to demolish the brick printing office and dwelling house of W. W. Phelps & Co., and destroyed or took possession of the press, type, books and property of the establishment; at the same time turning Mrs. Phelps and children out of doors, after which they proceeded to personal violence by a wanton assault and battery upon the Bishop of the Church, Mr. Edward Partridge, and a Mr. Allen, whom they tarred and feathered, and variously abused. They then compelled Messrs. Gilbert Whitney & Co. to close their store and pack their goods, after which they adjourned to meet again on the 23rd of July; on which day they again met, to the number of several hundred, armed with fire-arms, dirks and sticks, with red flags hoisted, and as they entered town, threatening death and destruction to the Mormons. On this day six individuals of the Church signed an agreement to leave the county, one half by the first of January, and the other half by the first of April, 1834; hoping thereby to preserve the lives of their brethren, and their property. After this the mob dispersed, threatening destruction to the Mormons on the next New-Years' day if they were not off by that time.

After this, an express was sent to the Governor of the State, stating the facts of the outrages, and praying for some relief and protection. But none was afforded, only some advice for us to prosecute the offenders, which was accordingly undertaken. But this so enraged the mob that they began to make preparations to come out by night and re-commence depredations. Having passed through the most aggravating insults and injuries without making the least resistance, a general enquiry prevailed at this time throughout the Church, as to the propriety of self-defence. Some claimed the right of defending themselves, their families and property, from destruction; while others doubted the propriety of self defence; and as the agreement of the 23d of July, between the two parties had been published to the world, wherein it was set forth, that the Mormons were not to leave until the 1st of January and 1st of April, 1834. It was believed by many of the Mormons that the leaders of the mob would not suffer so bare-faced a violation of the agreement before the time therein set forth; but Thursday night, the 31st of October, gave them abundant proof that no pledge, verbal or written, was longer to be regarded; for, on that night, between forty and fifty, many of whom were armed with guns, proceeded against a branch of the Church, about eight miles west of town, and unroofed and partly demolished ten dwelling houses; and in the midst of the shrieks and screams of women and children, whipt and beat, in a savage manner, several of the men; and with their horrid threats, frightened women and children into the wilderness. Such of the men as could escape, fled for their lives; for very few of them had arms, neither were they embodied; and they were threatened with death if they made any resistence. Such, therefore, as could not escape by flight, received a pelting by rocks, and a beating by guns and whips.

On Friday, the first of November, women and children sallied forth from their gloomy retreats, to contemplate, with heart-rending anguish, the ravages of a ruthless mob, in the mangled bodies of their husbands, and in the destruction of their houses and furniture. Houseless, and unprotected by the arm of civil law in Jackson county—the dreary month of November staring them in the face, and loudly proclaiming a more inclement season at hand—the continual threats of the mob, that they would drive every Mormon from the county—and the inability of many to remove because of their poverty, caused an anguish of heart indescribable.

These outrages were committed about two miles from my residence; news reached me before daylight the same morning, and I immediately repaired to the place, and was filled with anguish at the awful sight of houses in ruins, and furniture destroyed and strewed about the streets; women, in different directions, were weeping and mourning, while some of the men were covered with blood from the blows they had received from the enemy; others were endeavoring to collect the fragments of their scattered furniture, beds, &c.

I endeavored to collect together as many men as possible, and after consultation, we concluded to embody for defence. Accordingly we collected some sixty men, armed ourselves as well as we could, and took shelter the next evening in a log house. We set a guard, and sent out spies through the different parts of the settlement to watch the movements of the mob; but some time in the night two of the enemy advanced to our guard, being armed with guns and pistols, and while they were conversing I walked near them, and one of them struck me over the head, with all his might, with his gun. I staggered back, the blood streaming down my face, but I did not fall. As I had command of our party, I ordered our men to disarm the two ruffians and secure them, which was done; and this probably prevented a general attack of the mob that night. The next morning they were let go in peace.

The same night (Friday) a party in Independence commenced stoning houses, breaking down doors and windows, destroying furniture, &c. This night the brick part of a dwelling house belonging to A. S. Gilbert, was partly demolished, and the windows of his dwelling broken in, while a gentleman lay sick in his house.

The same night the doors of the house of Messrs. Gilbert and Whitney were split open, and the goods strewed in the street, to which fact upwards of twenty witnesses can attest.

After midnight a party of our men marched for the store, &c. and when the mob saw them approach they fled. But one of their number, a Richard M'Carty, was caught in the act of throwing rocks in at the door, while the goods lay strung around him in the street. He was immediately taken before Samuel Weston, Esq. and a warrant requested, that said M'Carty might be secured; but his justiceship refused to do any thing in the case, and M'Carty was then liberated.

The same night many of their houses had poles and rails thrust through the shutters and sash, into the rooms of defenceless women and children, from whence their husbands and fathers had been driven by the acts of the mob which were made by ten or twenty men upon one house at a time. On Saturday, the 2d November, all the families of these people who lived in Independence, moved out of town about one half mile west, and embodied for the preservation of themselves and property. Saturday night a party of the mob made an attack upon a settlement about six miles west of town. Here they tore the roof from a dwelling, broke open another house, found the owner, Mr. David Bennet, sick in bed; him they beat inhumanly, and swore they would blow his brains out, and discharging a pistol, the ball cut a deep gash across the top of his head. In this skirmish one of their men was shot in the thigh.

On Sunday evening, about sunset, myself and a Mr. Marsh set out on horseback to visit the Circuit Judge at Lexington, a distance of some forty miles. We were under the necessity of going the most private paths across the country, in order to avoid our enemies; but we had a most faithful pilot, who knew every crook and turn of the country. We had rode but a few miles, when it became so extremely dark that we could not see each other. Our pilot dismounted several times and felt his way; but at length we came to a halt, and lay down upon the ground until it broke away and became some lighter, and then we were enabled to go on; but the rain began to fall in torrents, and continued all the latter part of the night; we soon became completely drenched, and every thread about us perfectly wet; but still we dare not stop for any refreshment or shelter until day dawned, when we found ourselves forty miles from home, and at the door of a friend, where we breakfasted and refreshed ourselves.

We then repaired to Lexington and made oath, before Judge Riland, of the outrages committed upon us, but were refused a warrant; the Judge advising us to fight and kill the mob whenever they came upon us. We then returned to the place where we breakfasted; and, night coming on, we retired to bed.—Having been without sleep for the three previous nights, and much of the time drenched in rain, together with the severe wound I had received, I was well nigh exhausted. No sooner had sleep enfolded me in her kind embrace, than a vision opened before me:

I found myself in Jackson county, heard the roar of fire-arms, and saw the killed and wounded lying in their blood. At this I awoke from my slumber; and awaking brother Marsh and the family with whom we tarried, I told them what I had seen and heard in my dream, and observed to them that I was sure that a battle had just ensued. Next morning we arose and pursued our journey homeward, with feelings of anxiety and amazement which cannot be described.

Every officer of the peace had abandoned us to our fate, and it seemed as if there was no way but for men, women and children to be exterminated. But as we rode on, ruminating upon these things, a man met us, from Independence, who told us that there was a battle raging when he left, and how it had terminated he knew not.

This only heightened our feelings of anxiety and suspense. We were every moment drawing nearer to where a moment would decide whether we were to find our friends alive and victorious, or whether they were slain, and we in the hands of a worse than savage enemy.

On coming within four miles of Independence, we ventured to enquire the distance, at a certain house. This we did in order to pass as strangers, and also in hopes to learn some news.

The man seemed frightened, and enquired where we were from? We replied, "From Lexington."— Said he, "Have you heard what has happened?"

We replied that we had understood there was some difficulty respecting the Mormons, but of all the particulars we had not been informed. "Why!" said he, "The Mormons have riz and have killed six men." At this we seemed much surprised, and enquired if the government would not put down such an insurrection? We then passed on, and as soon as we were out of sight, we left the road and rode into the woods. Taking a circuitous route through thickets of hazel, interwoven with grape-vine, &c., and after some difficulty and entanglement, we came in sight of Independence, and advanced towards it, wishing to pass through, in order to get to a camp of our men near a half mile west of town. But seeing parties of armed men advancing towards us, we wheeled about and retreated a distance, and turned again to the woods, and struck around on the side of the town, through the wilderness, towards the tents of our brethren, rushing our horses with the greatest speed; thus we avoided being taken, and arrived safe. But what was our astonishment when we found our brethren without arms, having surrendered them to their enemies. The truth of the matter was this: on Monday eve, while I lay sleeping at our friend's, near Lexington, the same eve that I dreamed of the battle, the mob again advanced upon the settlement where they had first destroyed the ten houses, and commenced an attack upon houses and property, and threatening women and children with immediate destruction. While some 60 of the mob were thus engaged, about 30 of our men marched near them, and a battle ensued, in which the mob were entirely routed, leaving two of their number dead on the field, together with a number of horses. Several were severely wounded on both sides, and one young man of the Church died the next day, his name was Barber.

One of the enemy who fell, was an Attorney by the name of Brazeale, he had been heard a short time before to say, that he would wade to his knees in blood or drive the Mormons from the county.

The same night runners were despatched in every directio[n], under pretence of calling out the militia; spreading as they went, every rumor calculated to excite the unwary; such as, that the Mormons had taken Independence, and the Indians had surrounded it, being allied together, &c. The same eve, November 4th, the said McCarty, who had been detected in breaking open the store of Gilbert & Co., was suffered to take out a warrant and arrest the said Gilbert, and others of the Church, for a pretended assault and false imprisonment of said McCarty.

Late in the eve, while the court were proceeding with the trial in the court house, a gentleman unconnected with the court, perceiving the prisoners to be without councel and in eminent danger, advised said Gilbert and his brethren to move for jail as the only alternative to save life; for the north door was already barred, and a mob thronged the house with a determination to beat and kill; accordingly Gilbert and four others were committed to jail, the dungeon of which must have been a pallace compared to a court room where dignity and mercy were strangers, and naught but the wrath of man in horrid threats stifled the ears of the prisoners. The same night, Gilbert, Morley and Carrill, were liberated from jail, that they might have an interview with their brethren, and try to persuade them to leave the county; and on their return to jail, about 2 o'clock on Tuesday morning, in custody of the sheriff, an armed force of six or seven men, stood near the jail and hailed; they were answered by the sheriff, who gave his name and the names of his prisoners, crying, "don't fire, don't fire, the prisoners are in my charge," &c. They however fired one or two guns, when Morley and Carill retreated; Gilbert stood, with several guns pointed at him. Two, more desperate than the rest, attempted to shoot, but one of their guns flashed, and the other missed fire. Gilbert was then knocked down by Thomas Wilson. About this time a few of the inhabitants arrived, and Gilbert again entered jail; from which he and three others were liberated about sunrise, without further prosecution of the trial. The same morning, November 5th, the town began to be crowded with armed men from every quarter, and it was said the militia had been called out, under the sanction of Lieut. Gov. Boggs, and that one Col. Pitcher had the command. Among this militia, (so called) were embodied the most conspicuous characters of the mob. Very early on the same morning, several branches of the Church on hearing of the outrages in Independence, volunteered, and united their forces, and marched towards town to defend their brethren. When within one mile of town, they halted, and were soon informed that the militia were called out for their protection. But in this they placed little confidence; for the body congregated had every appearance of a county mob, which subsequent events soon verified. On application to Col. Pitcher, it was found that there was no alternative but for the Church to leave the county forthwith; and to deliver up certain men to be tried for murder said to have been committed by them in the battle the previous evening. The arms of this people were also demanded by the Colonel, and among the committee appointed to receive their arms, was several of the most unrelenting of the old mob committee of July; who had directed in the demolishing of the printing office &c., viz: Henry Chiles, Abner Staples, and Lewis Franklin.

Rather than have submitted to these outrageous requirements, the Saints would willingly have shed their blood; but they knew that if they resisted this mob, the lies of the designing, and the prejudice of the ignorant would construe their resistance into a violation of law, and thus bring certain destruction upon them: therefore they surrendered their arms to the number of 50, and agreed to leave the county forthwith. The men who were demanded as prisoners, were also surrendered and imprisoned; but were dismissed in a day or two without trial. A few hours after the surrender, we arrived at the camp of our brethren near Independence, on our return from Lexington, as stated in the foregoing, and when we found that the struggle was over, and our liberties completely trampled under foot, I retired into the woods and kneeled down, and wept before the Lord.

The sun was then setting, and 12 miles separated me from my family; but I determined to reach home that night. My horse being weary, I started on foot, and walked through the wilderness in the midst of darkness, avoiding the road, lest I should fall into the hands of the enemy. I arrived home about the middle of the night; spent a few hours with my family, and arose again before day, and fled to the wilderness, as the mob were driving our people, and hunting them in every direction. After walking a few miles, I found a brother by the name of Lowry, who was moving from the county in a covered waggon, he having a permit from the mob to pass in safety.

This man concealed me in his waggon, and thus we passed in safety, although frequently meeting armed men, who were pursuing our brethren. When night again overtook us, we were on the bank of the Missouri River, which divided between Jackson and Clay counties. Here we encamped for the night, as we could not cross the ferry till morning. I left the camp and ascended the tall bluff, and finding a cavity of a rock, I slept therein. But before morning, I was joined by Mr. Morley and several others, who fled for their lives, and brought news that the mob were driving, and probably butchering men, women and children. On hearing this news, we tried to pray, but we could say but little. Next morning we crossed over the river, and found ourselves once more in a land of peace. While I thus made my escape, companies of ruffians were ranging the county in every direction, bursting into houses without fear, knowing that the arms were secured, frightening women and children, and threatening to kill them if they didn't flee immediately. At the head of one of these companies appeared the Rev. Mr. McCoy, (a noted Missionary to the Indians) with a gun upon his shoulder, ordering the Mormons to leave immediately, and surrender every thing in the shape of arms. Other pretended preachers of the Gospel took part in the persecution; calling the Mormons the common enemy of mankind, and exulting in their afflictions. On Tuesday and Wednesday nights, the 5th and 6th of November, women and children fled in every direction, before a merciless mob. One party of about a hundred and fifty women and children, fled to the prairie, where they wandered for several days, mostly without food, and nothing but the open firmament for their shelter. Other parties fled towards the Missouri. During this dispersion of women and children, parties of the mob were hunting men, firing upon some, tying up and whipping others; and some they pursued upon horses for several miles.

Thursday, November 7th, the shore began to be lined on both sides of the ferry, with men, women, children, goods, waggons, boxes, chests, provisions, &c., while the ferrymen were very busily employed in crossing them over; and when night again closed upon us, the wilderness had much the appearance of a camp meeting. Hundreds of people were seen in every direction. Some in tents and some in the open air around their fires, while the rain descended in torrents. Husbands were enquiring for wives, and women for their husbands; parents for children, and children for parents.

Some had had the good fortune to escape with their family, household goods, and some provisions; while others knew not the fate of their friends, and had lost all their goods. The scene was indescribable, and I am sure would have melted the hearts of any people upon earth, except our blind oppressors, and a prejudiced and ignorant community. Next day, our company still increased, and we were chiefly engaged in felling small cotton wood trees, and erecting them into temporary cabins, so when night again came on, we had the appearance of a village of wigwams, and the night being clear, we began to enjoy some degree of comfort.

About 2 o'clock the next morn, we were aroused from our slumbers by the cry of "Arise, and behold the signs in the Heavens." We arose, and to our great astonishment, all Heaven seemed enwraped in a splendid fireworks, as if every star in the broad expanse, had been suddenly hurled from its course, and sent lawless through the wilds of ether. I can give the reader no better idea of this scene, than by an allusion to the shooting of a bright meteor, with a long train of light following its course, such as most of us have seen in a bright starlight night. Now suppose that thousands of such meteors with their fiery trains, were to run lawless through the Heavens for hours together, this would be a scene such as our eyes beheld on that memorable morning; and the scene only closed by giving place to the superior light and splendor of the king of day. No sooner was this scene beheld by some of our camp than the news reached every tent, and aroused every one from their slumbers; every eye was lifted towards the Heavens, and every heart was filled with joy at this majestic display of signs and wonders, showing the near approach of the coming of the Son of God.

In fact we looked up and lifted up o[u]r heads rejoicing, knowing that our redemption drew near. It is a singular coincidence that this wonder should happen at the very time of our dispersion. And let others think as they may, I take it as a special manifestation, to fulfil the scriptures, and to rouse our drooping spirits, by a fresh memorial, reminding us of a coming Messiah, for the redemption of those who look for him; and to the destruction of their oppressors.

After a few days, I sent a lad with a horse for my wife, who escaped in safety, by riding 15 miles on horseback; leaving all our goods, which, however, I afterwards obtained, at the risk of my life. But all my provisions for the winter were destroyed or plundered; and my grain left growing on the ground, for our enemies to harvest. My house was afterwards burned, and my apple trees, rails and improvements destroyed or plundered. In short, every member of the society was driven from the county, and fields of corn were plundered and destroyed. Stacks of wheat were burned—household goods plundered, and improvements and every kind of property lost, and at length no less than TWO HUNDRED AND THREE HOUSES BURNED, according to the estimate of their own people in Jackson.

The Saints who fled, took refuge in the neighboring counties—mostly in Clay county, which received them with some degree of kindness. Those who fled to the county of Van Buren, were again driven, and compelled to flee; and those who fled to Lafayette county, were soon expelled, or the most part of them, and had to move wherever they could find protection.

When the news of these outrages reached the Governor of the state, courts of enquiry, both civil and military, were ordered by him; but nothing effectual was ever done to restore our rights, or to protect us in the least. It is true the attorney general, with a military escort and our witnesses, went to Jackson county and demanded indictments, but the court and jurors refused to do any thing in the case, and the military and witnesses were mobbed out of the county, and thus that matter ended. The governor also ordered them to restore our arms which they had taken from us, but they were never restored; and even our lands in that county were robbed of their timber, and either occupied by our enemies for years, or left desolate.

Soon after Jackson county had rebelled against the laws and constitution, several of the adjoining counties followed her example by justifying her proceedings, and by opposing the saints in settling among them; and soon this rebellion became general in the upper country. The counties of Clay, Ray, Clinton, and various others, held public meetings, the tenor of which was, to deprive the members of our society of the common rights of citizenship, and to drive them from among them, and force them to settle only in such places as the mob should dictate; and even at that time some of their proceedings went so far as to publicly threaten to drive the whole Society from the state. The excuses they offered for these outrages, were, 1st, The Society were principally guilty of being eastern or northern people. 2nd, They were guilty of some slight variations, in manners and language, from the other citizens of the state. 3rd, Their religious principles differed in some important particulars from most other societies. 4th, They were guilty of emigrating rapidly from the different states, and of purchasing large quantities of land, and of being more enterprising and industrious than some of their neighbors. 5th, Some of our Society were guilty of poverty, especially those who had been driven from time to time from their possessions, and robbed of their all. And lastly, they were said to be guilty of believing in the present government administration of Indian affairs, viz; that the land west of the Mississippi, which government has deeded in fee simple to the emigrating tribes, was destined by Providence for their permanent homes. All these crimes were charged home upon our Society, in the public proceedings of the several counties; and were deemed sufficient to justify their unlawful proceedings against us. The reader may smile at this statement, but the public journals published in that country, in 1835, actually printed charges and declarations against us of the tenor of the foregoing. By these wicked proceedings our people were once more compelled to remove, at a great sacrifice of property, and were at last permitted to settle in the north of Ray county; where, by the next legislature, they were organized into the counties of Caldwell and Daviess. Here they again exerted the utmost industry and enterprise, and these wild regions soon presented a more flourishing aspect than the oldest counties of the upper country. In the mean time a majority of the state so far countenanced these outrages, that they actually elected Lilburn W. Boggs, one of the old mobbers of Jackson county, who had assisted in the treason, murder, house-burning, plundering, robbery, and driving out of twelve hundred citizens, in 1833, for governor of the state, and placed him in the executive chair, instead of a solitary cell in the state penetentiary, as his crimes justly deserved. This movement may be said to have put an end to liberty, law, and government, in that state. About this time, also, Colonel Lucas, whose name was attached to the written circular of the first conspiracy in Jackson county, was advanced to the office of Major General, instead of being hung for treason. Moses Wilson, one of the head leaders of the mob, was advanced to the office of Brigadier General; and Thomas Wilson, another of the Jackson county mob, was elected a Captain of the Militia.

The reader will recollect that in a former part of this history, these Wilsons are represented as acting a most forward part in all the murders, house-burning, robbing and driving; and that Thomas Wilson, in particular, went so far as to fire upon certain prisoners, and to knock down one while in care of an officer, who was committing them to jail. These crimes, which in a country of laws would have hanged them or imprisoned them for life, so far exalted them in the eyes of their associates, that their worthy deeds proved a step stone to office. They all very readily received their commissions from their accomplice, Governor Boggs; and thus corruption, rebellion, and conspiracy had spread on every side, being fostered and encouraged by a large majority of the state; and thus the treason became general.

In the mean time our Society had greatly increased by a rapid emigration, and having long felt the withering hand of oppression from so corrupt an administration, they had endeavored to organize themselves, both civil and military, in the counties where they composed the majority, by electing such officers as they thought would stand for equal rights, and for the laws and constitution of the country. And in this way they hoped to withstand the storm which had so long beat upon them, and whose black clouds now seemed lowering in awful gloom, and preparing to burst, with overwhelming fury, upon all who dare to stand for liberty and law.

On the Fourth of July, 1838, many thous[a]nds of our people assembled at the city of Far West, the county seat of Caldwell, erected a liberty pole, and hoisted the bold eagle, with its stars and stripes, upon the top of the same. Under the colors of our country we laid the corner stone of a house of worship, and had an address delivered by Elder Rigdon, in which was painted, in lively colors, the oppression which we had long suffered from the hand of our enemies; and in this discourse we claimed and declared our constitutional rights, as American citizens, and manifested a determination to do our utmost endeavors, from that time forth, to resist all oppression, and to maintain our rights and freedom according to the holy principles of liberty, as guaranteed to every person by the constitution and laws of our government. This declaration was received with shouts of hosannah to God and the Lamb, and with many and long cheers by the assembled thousands, who were determined to yield their rights no more, except compelled by a superior power.

But in a day or two after these transactions, the thunder rolled in awful majesty over the city of Far West, and the arrows of lightning fell from the clouds and shivered the liberty pole from top to bottom; thus manifesting to many that there was an end to liberty and law in that state, and that our little city strove in vain to maintain the liberties of a country which was ruled by wickedness and rebellion. It seemed to portend the awful fate which awaited that devoted city, and the county and people around.—Soon after these things, the war clouds began again to lower, with dark and threatening aspect. The rebellious party in the counties around had long watched our increasing power and prosperity with greedy and avaricious eyes, and they had already boasted that as soon as we had made some fine improvements, and a plentiful crop, they would drive us from the state, and again enrich themselves with the spoils. Accordingly, at an election held in Daviess co., the robbers undertook to drive our people from the poll box, and threatened to kill whoever should attempt to vote. But some were determined to enjoy their right or die; they therefore went forward to vote, but were seized by the opposing party and attacked, and thus a fight commenced. But some of our people knocked down several of the robbers, and thus cleared the ground and maintained their rights, though vastly unequal in numbers. The news of this affair soon spread far and wide, and caused the people to rally, some for liberty and some to support the robbers in their daring outrages. About one hundred and fifty of those who were on the side of liberty, marched to the spot next day, and went to the residence of the leaders in this outrage, and soon an agreement was signed for peace. But this was of short duration, for the conspirators were stirred up throughout the whole State, being alarmed for fear the Mormons, as they called them, should become so formidable as to maintain their rights and liberties, insomuch that they could no more drive and plunder them. About this time, meetings were held by the robbers in Carroll, Saline, and other counties, in which they openly declared their treasonable and murderous intentions of driving the citizens who belonged to our society from their counties, and if possible, from the State. Resolutions to this effect were published in the journals of Upper Missouri, and this without a single remark of disapprobation. Nay more, this murderous gang when assembled and painted like Indian warriors, and when openly committing murder, robbery, and house burning, were denominated citizens, white people, &c., in most of the papers of the State, while our society who stood firm in the cause of liberty and law, were denominated Mormons, in contradistinction to the appelation of citizens, whites, &c, as if we had been some savage tribe, or some colored race of foreigners. The robbers soon assembled, to the number of several hundred, under arms, and rendezvoused in Daviess county, being composed of individuals from many of the counties around. Here they commenced firing upon our citizens, and taking prisoners. Our people made no resistance, except to assemble on their own ground for defence. They also made oath before the Circuit Judge, A. A. King, to the above outrages.—One thousand men were then ordered into service, under the command of Major General Atchison, and Brigadier Generals Parks and Doniphan. These were soon mustered and marched through Caldwell, and took their stand in Daviess county, where most of them remained thirty days. The robbers were somewhat awed by these prompt measures, so that they did not proceed farther at that time in Daviess, but they proceeded to De Witt, a small town in Carroll county, which was mostly settled by our people.— Here they laid siege for several days, and subsisted by plunder and robbery, watching every opportunity to fire upon our citizens. At this time they had one field piece, and were headed by a Presbyterian priest by the name of Sashel Woods, who, it is said, tended prayer, night and morning, at the head of the gang. In this siege they say that they killed a number of our people. They also turned one Smith Humphrey and his wife and children out of doors when sick, and set fire to their house, and burned it to ashes before their eyes. At length they succeeded in driving every citizen from the place, to the sacrifice of every thing which they could not take with them.

This event happened during a cold, bad spell of weather, in October, and as many of the citizens were sickly, and worn down by fatigue and war, and robbed of shelter and of every thing comfortable, they came near perishing; some of them did perish before they arrived in Caldwell, a distance of some sixty miles. Here they were hospitably taken in by their brethren. Even two or three families often crowded into one small house. The militia under General Parks made some show of trying to prevent these outrages, but at length General Parks informed our people that his forces were so small, and many of them so much in favor of the rebellion, that it was useless to look any longer to them for protection.—Several messages were also sent to the Governor, but he was utterly deaf to every thing which called for the protection of our society, or any of the citizens who belonged to it. But on the contrary, he hearkened to the insinuations of the robbers; and actually presumed to give orders for the raising of several thousand volunteers from the middle counties of the State, to march against the Mormons, as he termed them. This force was soon on their march with the Governor at their head; but when he had come near the Upper Country, he was officially notified that the Mormons were not in a state of insurrection, but were misrepresented by the robbers. His Excellency then disbanded his forces and sneaked back to Jefferson City to wait till the robbers should drive the Mormons to some act which might be considered illegal, which would give him some pretext for driving them from the State.

After the evacuation of Dewitt, when our people were officially notified that they must protect themselves, and expect no more protection from any department of the State Government, they assembled in the city of Far West, to the number of near one thousand men, and resolved to defend their rights to the last; calling upon every person who could bear arms to come forward in the support of our houses, our homes, our wives and children, and the cause of our country and our God. In the mean time the robbers elated with success, and emboldened by the negligence of every department of the State Government, were increasing in numbers daily, and were on their march for Daviess, with their artillery and military stores, declaring that they would now drive the citizens from Daviess and from Caldwell counties, which were settled mostly by our people.—In this march they took a number of the citizens prisoners, among whom was Amasa Lyman, a minister of the Gospel, and an excellent citizen of Caldwell county. They kept him a number of days, while his wife and children mourned his absence, and they held frequent consultations to kill him, but at length he was set at liberty. Our forces assembled in Daviess county to the number of several hundred, to protect their homes; and at length a detachment of about one hundred men, under the command of Col. D. W. Patten, met the robbers, and took from them their artillery, which consisted of one six pounder, and some powder and balls also, were taken from the enemy. All this was done without bloodshed, as the robbers buried their cannon in the earth and fled at the first news of the approach of our army. While the army were busily engaged in searching the camp of the robbers to find their field piece, a young lad saw some swine rooting in the middle of the highway, and he at length discovered some projecting part of the cannon, which had been uncovered by the swine, and he exclaimed, "here is the cannon." At this, the soldiers gathered round, and soon raised the monster from its untimely grave. It was taken in triumph to the city of Diahman, and there on the heights of Daviess, amid rejoicing thous[a]nds, it uttered its voice in favor of liberty and law, and told the sad tale for some twenty miles around, that the robbers had lost their God of war, notwithstanding the pious prayers of priest Wood. On another occasion the Robbers were transporting a waggon load of arms and ammunition from Ray county to Daviess, through Caldwell county, but in Caldwell they providentially broke the[i]r waggon. In the mean time our sheriff got wind of the movements, and went with a company of Caldwell militia, and took the arms and ammunition and brought them in triumph to the city of Far West, where they helped to arm the patriotic citizens for defence. About the time of the taking of the cannon, a small party of our men, under the command of the brave Lieut. B. went out through Daviess among those who pretended great friendship for the laws, but were secretly aiding the robbers. This party pretended to be men from the Platt who had come down to assist the robbers against the citizens, or Mormons as they were called. Under this disguise their horses and themselves were fed free of cost, and welcomed every where to all they could eat and drink, and many furnished them rifles, and ammunition, together with coats, blankets, &c., wishing them success. Sometimes they would offer to pay for their entertainment, but their zealous hosts refused to take pay, and wished that their horses could eat a thousand bushels of grain, for they were more than welcome.

In this way our troops were supplied with considerable armament, and their secret enemies were discovered and detected in their wicked plottings. During this time the robbers were busily engaged in burning and plundering houses, and driving women and children from their homes, to perish with hunger and cold, while they were robbed of every thing they possessed, and their houses burned to ashes. Hundreds were thus compelled to flee to the cities and strongholds; women and children came in by night and by day; and some of them in the midst of a tremendous snow storm, in which they came near perishing; but those who fled were kindly received into the houses of their brethren, and thus their lives were spared, but only to witness a more dreadful scene at hand. It is said that some of our troops, exasperated to the highest degree, retalliated in some instances by plundering and burning houses, and bringing the spoil to feed the hungry and clothe the naked, whose provisions and clothing had been robbed from them; and upon the whole, I am rather inclined to believe it was the case; for human nature cannot endure all things.

Soon after these things had transpired in Daviess county, Caldwell was threatened from every quarter; and her citizens assembled in Far West, many of them moving their wives and children, goods, provisions, and even houses into the city; leaving their lands desolate, in order that they might be embodied and prepared to defend themselves and families to the last. Our Colonel and his other commissioned officers, had the troops paraded night and morning on the public square, and ordered them to be always ready in case of alarm. When we were dismissed at eve, we were ordered to sleep in our clothes, and be ready at a moments warning, to run together at any hour of the night. During this state of alarm, the drum was beat, and guns fired, one night, about midnight. I ran to the public square, where many had already collected together, and the news was that the south part of our county, adjoining Ray, was attacked by a mob, who were plundering houses, threatening women and children, and taking peaceable citizens prisoners; and telling families to be gone by the next morning or they would burn their houses over their heads. With this information, Captain Killian (to whom Col. Hincle had committed the command of the troops in Far West, when he himself was not present) sent out a detachment under the command of Captain Durphey, aided by the brave D. W. Patten. This company, consisting of about sixty men, was sent to see what the matter was on the lines; and who was committing depredations, and if necessary, to protect or move in the families and property; and if possible, effect the release of the prisoners.

This company was soon under way, having to ride some ten or twelve miles mostly through extensive prairies. It was October, the night was dark, and as we moved briskly on, (being forbidden to speak a loud word,) no sound was heard but the rumbling of our horses hoofs over the wide extended and lonely plains. While the distant plains, far and wide, were illuminated by blazing fires; and immense columns of smoke were seen rising in awful majesty, as if the world was on fire. This scene of grandeur can only be comprehended by those who are acquainted with the scenes of prairie burning. As the fire sweeps over millions of acres of dry grass in the fall season, and leaves a smooth black surface, divested of all vegetation. The thousand meteors blazing in the distance like the camp fires of some war host, throw a fitful gleem of light upon the distant sky, which many might mistake for the Aurora Borealis. This scene added to the silence of midnight—the rumbling sound of the prancing steeds—the glistening of armor—and the unknown destiny of the expedition—all combined to impress the mind with deep and solemn thoughts; and to throw a romantic vision over the imagination, which is not often experienced, except in the poet's dream, or the wild imagery of sleeping fancy. In this solemn procession we moved on for some two hours, when it was supposed that we were in the neighborhood of danger. We were then ordered to dismount and leave our horses in care of part of the company, while the others should proceed on foot along the principal highway, to see what discoveries could be made. This precaution was for fear we might be suddenly attacked, in which case we could do better on foot than on horse back. We had not proceeded far when as we entered the wilderness, we were suddenly fired upon by an unknown enemy, in ambush. First one solitary gun, as was supposed, from some out post of the enemy, brought one of our number to the ground, where he lay groaning while the rest of the troop had to pass directly by his dying body. It was dawn of day in the eastern horizon, but darkness still hovered over the awful scene. When our men saw that they were ambushed and attacked, they found it too late to retreat, and orders were issued to form along in the brush, and under the cover of trees, which was instantly done, while the enemy, though unseen, were pouring in a deadly fire upon our whole line. We soon returned the fire, and charging upon the enemy, the whole wilderness seemed for a few moments as if wrapped in a blaze of lightning; and overwhelmed with the sharp crack of peals of thunder. The enemy were soon driven from their ambush and completely routed. Having a creek immediately in their rear, many were seen forcing their retreat through the stream, and up to their arms in water. The firing now ceased, and the whole battle ground resounded with the watchword, God and Liberty. Our forces which had been thrown into some disorder, were instantly formed, and their pieces reloaded, while here and there over the battle ground, lay the dead and wounded. The enemy had left their horses, saddles, camp and baggage, in the confusion of their flight, which fell into our hands. Their baggage waggon was immediately harnessed to a couple of horses, and the wounded were picked up and laid in it upon blankets, while every man saddled and mounted a horse, and we commenced our retreat to the place where we had left our horses and guard, a distance of more than a mile; here we halted, and laid our wounded upon blankets, on the ground, while we made arrangements in the wagon for them to ride more comfortably. —There were about six of our men badly wounded, among whom was the brave D. W. Patten, a ball having entered the lower part of his body. It was an awful sight to see them pale and helpless, and hear their groans. We had as yet lost but one man, who was left dead on the ground; his name was Gideon Carter. The enemy had one killed and four wounded, as we afterwards learned. We ascertained from the prisoners whom we had rescued, and one whom we had taken, that the enemy consisted of one

Captain Bogart and his company, who together with some volunteers from different neighborhoods, mounted about 60 men. Our party engaged, was from forty to fifty in number, at the time of the engagement. There were three of our fellow citizens prisoners in their camp. Two of these ran away and escaped at the commencement of the firing, and the other was shot through the body in trying to run to our lines, but fortunately he recovered, and is now a witness against them.

Having now arranged every thing to the best advantage for the wounded, we moved on slowly towards Far West. When we came within fiive miles of the city, our express had reached there with the news of the battle, and we were met by a surgeon and others for our relief, and among others the wife of the pale and dying Patten.

Our wounded were now taken into a house, and their wounds dressed; and as Mrs. Patten entered the room and cast her eyes on the pale and ghastly features of her husband, she burst into tears, exclaiming O God! O my husband! how pale you look! He was still able to speak, but he died that evening in the triumphs of faith; having laid down his life as a martyr in the cause of his country and his God. The young Obanian, who was shot through the body by the first fire of the enemy's sentinel, also died about the same time. Thus three brave men had fallen; and their blood cries against their enemies for vengeance. The others I believe recovered of their wounds. Having conveyed the wounded to this place of hospitality, we hastened home to Far West, and delivered the horses and spoils of the enemy to Col. Hincle, the commanding officer of the Regiment. These several defeats of the mob in Daviess and Caldwell, checked, for a time, their ruinnous ravages. They saw that it was impossible to conquer a people who were fighting for their homes, and their wives and children, unless they could come against them with some show of authority, for it was a well known fact, that the Mormons never resisted authority, however abused; therefore their next exertion was to spread lies and falsehoods of the most alarming character; such as that the Mormons were in a state of rebellion against the Government, and that they were about to burn Richmond, &c. This flame was greatly assisted by several in high authority who deserted from the Church, and fell away to the robbers because of fear, and also for the sake of power and gain. These deserters became far more false, hardened and blood-thirsty, than those who had never known the way of righteousness, insomuch that they were filled with all manner of lying and murders, and plundering. The Governor who had long sought some opportunity to destroy us, and drive us from the State, now issued an order for General Clark to raise several thousand men, and march against the Mormons, and drive them from the State, or exterminate them if necessary, etc. While General Clark was mustering his forces for this murderous and treasonable enterprize, Major General Lucas, and Brigadier General Wilson, the old leaders of the Jackson county conspiracy, being nearer the scene of action, and wishing to immortalize their names, put themselves at the head of the old Jackson county robbers, together with the late forces of the robbers who had all the while been embodied against us, and turning the brave and humane General Atchison out of the command, took the lead of all the assembled forces of the upper country, consisting of three or four thousand men, and with this formidable force, commenced their march directly for the city of Far West, where they arrived, while General Clark and his forces were several days march in the rear. In the mean time, the Governor's Order, and all these military movements, were kept an entire secret from the Mormons, and even the mail was withheld from Far West, thus cutting off all intelligence. We had only heard that companies of armed men were seen in the south part of the county: and we had sent a white flag and a guard of one hundred and fifty men, to make inquiries. But while they were absent on this business, an alarm came in to town that the whole county to the South of us was filled with hostile troops, who were murdering, plundering, and taking peaceable citizens prisoners, in their own houses, etc. On receiving this intelligence, every man flew to arms, for the protection of our city. It was now towards evening, and we had heard nothing of our white flag, and the hundred and fifty men who went South in the morning. While we stood in our armor, gazing to the South in anxious suspense, we discovered an army advancing on horse back, over the hills, at two miles distance from the town. We at first supposed it might be our little company of a hundred and fifty returning to us, but we soon saw that there were thousands of men, with a long train of baggage waggons; we then were in hopes that it might be some friendly troops sent for our protection; and then we thought it might be a troop of the robbers coming to destroy us. At all events, there was no time to be lost, for although our force then present did not exceed five hundred men, yet we didn't intend that they should enter the town without giving some account of themselves.—We accordingly marched out upon the plains on the South of the city, and formed in battle array, extending our line of foot something like a half mile, while a small company of horse was posted on our right wing on a commanding eminence, and another small company in the rear of our main body, intended as a kind of reserve. By this time the sun was near setting, and the advance of the unknown army had come within plain view, at less than one mile distant. On seeing our forces presenting a small but formidable front, they came to a halt, and formed along the borders of the wilderness. And in a few moments both parties sent out a white flag, which met between the two armies; when our messenger demanded who they were, and what was their intentions? The answer was, that they wanted three persons out of the city before they massacred the rest.—This was a very alarming and unexpected answer. But they were soon prevailed upon to suspend hostilities till morning, when we were in hopes of some further and more satisfactory information. The hostile army under the command of Lucas, then commenced their encampment for the night, and our little army continued to stand to their arms for fear of some treachery. Our company of a hundred and fifty soon returned, informing us that they had been hemmed in through the day, and only escaped from their superior knowledge of the ground.—We also sent an express to Daviess county, and by morning were reinforced by quite a number of troops, with Colonel Wight at their head. In the mean time, the painted robbers and murderers under the command of one Gillum, came pouring in from the west, to strengthen the enemy, and another company of murderers came in from Carrel county, and were taken into the ranks of Lucas, after murdering some twenty of our citizens at Haun's mill, of which I will give a particular account hereafter. Thus both parties were considerably reinforced during the night.¶

In the mean time our people, being determined, if attacked, to defend their homes, and wives and children to the last, spent the night in throwing up a temporary breastwork of building timber, logs, rails, &c., and by morning our south side of the city was fortified with a breastwork, and also a considerable part of the east and west sides; the whole line of fortification extending a mile and a half. This nights labor may seem incredible; but it happened that a great quantity of building materials had been accumulated near the spot where were thrown up the breastworks: and this proved an excellent material for the work. The next day, towards evening, we were informed that the Governor had ordered this force against us, with orders to exterminate us or drive us from the State. As soon as these facts were ascertained, we determined not to resist any thing in the shape of authority, however tyrannical or unconstitutional might be the proceedings against us; therefore we had nothing more to do but to submit to be massacred or driven at the option of our persecutors. Colonel Hinkle waited on Messrs. J. Smith, S. Rigdon, Hiram Smith, L. Wight, George Robinson and myself, with a polite request from General Lucas, that we would surrender ourselves as prisoners, and repair to his camp, and remain over night, with assurances that as soon as peaceable arrangements could be entered into next morning, we should be released. With this request we readily complied, as soon as we were assured by the pledge of the honor of the principal officers, that our lives should be safe; we accordingly walked near a mile voluntarily, towards the camp of the enemy; who, when they saw us coming, came out to meet us by thousands, with general Lucas at their head. When the haughty General rode up to us, and scarcely passing a compliment, gave orders to his troops to surround us, which they did very abruptly, and we were marched into camp surrounded by thousands of savage looking beings, many of whom were painted like Indian warriors. These all set up a constant yell, like so many blood hounds let loose on their prey, as if they had achieved one of the most miraculous victories which ever dignified the annals of the world.— In camp we were placed under a strong guard, and before morning, A. Lyman and several others were added to our number. We hardly got an interview with the General that evening; he maintained a most haughty and unsociable reserve; but a hint was given us that the general officers held a secret council which they dignified a Court Martial, in which without being heard, or even brought before them, we were all sentenced to be shot; and the day and hour appointed, as we learned afterwards by General Donaphan, who was one of the council, but who was so violently opposed to this cool blooded murder, that he assured them he would revolt and withdraw his whole brigade, if they persisted in so dreadful a proceeding, his remonstrance and a few others so alarmed the haughty murderer and his accomplices that they dare not put the decree in execution; and thus through a merciful providence of God, our lives were spared through that dreadful night, which was spent by us on the ground in the open air, and amid the most horrid imprecations, threats and insults, that ever was witnessed, even in the abodes of the damned. News reached us by their own troops before morning, that they had murdered one prisoner on their march the day they entered Caldwell, by knocking out his brains, and also, that several of our citizens were then lying here and there unburied, whom they had shot down and murdered in cold blood, and also that several females had bee[n] ravished, and much robbery committed, besides the beef and corn which was taken from us to support three or four thousand men and horses for several days. No pen need undertake to describe our feelings while there confined; not knowing the fate of our wives and children, and our brethren and sisters, and seeing no way for our lives to be saved except by the miraculous power of God. But notwithstanding all earthly hopes were gone, still we felt a calmness indescribable, and a secret whispering, portending that our work was not yet done, and therefore our enemies would be restrained from taking our lives. While in this situation, Wm. E. McLellin, (who had once been intimate with me as a fellow laborer in the Gospel, having deserted from the Church) came to me, (being one of the soldiers against us) and observed, well Parley, you have now got where you are certain never to escape; how do you feel as to the course you have taken in religion? I replied that I had taken that course which I should take if I had my life to live over again. He seemed thoughtful for a moment, and then replied, well Parley, I think if I were you, I would die as I had lived: at any rate, I see no possibility of escape for you and your friends. This little interview gave us to understand that our doom was fixed in the minds of the people.

Next morning General Lucas demanded the Caldwell militia to give up their arms, which was done, to the number of upwards of five hundred. The rest of the troops having fled during the night. After the troops had surrendered, the city of Far West was surrounded by the robbers, and all the men detained as prisoners, none being permitted to pass out of the city, although their families were starving for want of sustenance. The mills and provisions being some distance from the city. The brutal mob were now turned loose to ravage, steel, plunder and murder without restraint. Houses were rifled, and women ravished, and goods taken as they pleased. On the third morning after our imprisonment, we were placed in a waggon, in order for removal, and many of the more desperate then crowded round, and cocking their rifles, swore they would blow us through. Some guns were snapped, but happily missed fire; and the rest were in a small degree restrained by the officers, and we still lived. We were now marched to Far West, and each one was permitted to go with a guard and take a final leave of our families, in order to depart as prisoners, to Jackson county, a distance of some 60 miles. This was the most trying scene of all. I went to my house, being guarded by two or three soldiers. The rain was pouring down without, and on entering my little cottage, there lay my wife, sick of a fever, with which she had been for sometime confined. At her breast was an infant three months old, and by her side a little girl of six years of age. These constituted my household, no other person belonged to my family. On the foot of the same bed lay a woman in travail, who had been driven from her house in the night, and had taken momentary shelter in my little hut of ten feet square, (my larger house having been torn down.) I stepped to the bed, she burst into tears, I spake a few words of comfort, telling her to try to live for my sake, and her little babes, and expressing a hope that we should meet again, though years might separate us. She promised to try to live, and though an age should separate us, we would live for each other. I then kissed her and the little babes, and departed. Till now I had refrained from weeping, but to be forced from so helpless a family, who were destitute of provisions and fuel; in a bleak prairie with none to assist them, and exposed to a lawless banditti, who were utter strangers to humanity, and this at the approach of winter, was more than nature could well bear; I went to General Wilson in tears, and stated the circumstances of my sick, heart-broken and destitute family, in terms which would have moved any heart which had a latent spark of humanity yet remaining. But I was only answered with an exulting laugh, and a taunt of triumph, from this hardened murderer.

As I returned from my house towards the main body of the army who were to conduct us, I halted with the guard at the door of Hiram Smith, and heard the sobs and groans of his wife, at his parting words. She was about to be confined in child-birth when he left her to accompany us. As we returned to the waggon we saw S. Rigdon taking leave of his wife and daughters, who stood at a little distance in tears of anguish inexpressible; whilst in the waggon sat Joseph Smith; while his aged father and venerable mother came up, overwhelmed in tears, and took us all by the hand.

In the mean time, hundreds of the brethren crowded around us, anxious to take a parting look, or a silent shake of the hand, for feelings were too intense to allow of speech. In the midst of these scenes, orders were given, and we moved slowly on, surrounded by a brigade of Jackson and Van Buren county troops. After marching about 12 miles, we encamped for the night on Crooked River. Here General Wilson began to treat us more kindly; he became very sociable, conversing freely on the subject of his former murders and robberies, committed against us in Jackson. He did not pretend to deny any thing, but spoke upon the whole as frank as if he had been giving the history of some thing done in ages past, with which we were not personally concerned. He also informed us that he had been exhorted by many to hang us on the way to Jackson, but he should not suffer us to be injured. Indeed, it was now evident that he was proud of his prey, and felt highly enthusiastic in having the honor of returning in triumph to the town of Independence, with the exhibition of his prisoners, whom his superstition had magnified into Noble or Royal personages; who would be gazed upon as Kings, or as something supernatural.

Next morning we were on our march, and in the after part of the day, we came to the Missouri River, which separated between Jackson county and us.—Here the brigade was halted, and the prisoners taken to a public house, where we were permitted to shave our beards and change our linen, after which we partook of an excellent dinner at the expense of the General. This done, we were hurried to the ferry, and across the river with the utmost haste; when but few of the troops had passed, this movement was soon explained to us. The truth was, General Clark had sent an express to take us from General Wilson, and prevent us from going to Jackson, as both armies were competitors for the honor of possessing the wonderful, or in their estimation, Royal Prisoners. Clark and his troops from a distance, who had not arrived in the city of Far West till after our departure, was desirous of seeing the strange men, whom it was said had turned the world upside down; and was desirous of the honor of possessing such a wonderful trophy of victory, or of putting us to death himself. And on the other hand, Wilson, Lucas and their troops, were determined to exhibit us in triumph through the streets of Independence. Therefore when demanded by General Clark's express, they refused to surrender us, and hurried us across the ferry with all possible despatch; after which, marching about a mile, we camped in the wilderness for the night, with about fifty troops for our guard, the remainder not crossing the ferry till next morning.

Next morning being Sunday, we were visited by some gentlemen and ladies. One of the women came up and very candidly enquired of the troops, which of the prisoners was the Lord whom the Mormons worshipped? One of the guard pointed to Mr. Smith, with a significant smile, and said this is he. The woman then turning to Mr. S., enquired whether he professed to be the Lord and Saviour? Do not smile gentle reader, at the ignorance of these poor innocent creatures, who are thus kept under, and made to believe such absurdities by their men, and by their lying Priests. Mr. S. replied, that he professed to be nothing but a man, and a minister of salvation sent by Jesus Christ to preach the Gospel. This answer so surprised the woman, that she began to enquire into our doctrine; and Mr. Smith preached a discourse both to her and her companions, and to the wondering soldiers, who listened with almost breathless attention, while he set forth the doctrine of faith in Jesus Christ, and repentance and baptism for remission of sins, with the promise of the Holy Ghost, as recorded in the second chapter of the Acts of the Apostles.—The woman was satisfied, and praised God in the hearing of the soldiers, and went away praying aloud that God would protect and deliver us. Thus was fulfilled a prophesy which had been spoken publicly by Mr. Smith, a few months previous; for he had prophesied that a sermon should be preached in Jackson county, by one of our Elders, before the close of 1838.

About 10 o'clock the brigade had all crossed the ferry and come up with us. We were then marched forward in our carriages, while the troops were formed in our front and rear, with quite a martial appearance. As we went through the settlements, hundreds of men, women, and children flocked to see us, and our general oft halted the whole brigade to introduce us to the ladies and gentlemen, pointing out each of his prisoners by name. We were oft shaken by the hand; and, in the ladies at least, there often appeared some feelings of sympathy. In this way we proceeded until we arrived at Independence. It was now past noon, and in the midst of a great rain. But hundreds crowded to witness the procession, and to gaze at us as we were paraded in martial triumph through all the principal streets—our carriages moving in the centre, while the brigade on horseback were formed in front and rear, and the bugles sounded a blast of triumphant joy.

This ceremony being finished, a vacant house was prepared for our reception, into which we were ushered through the crowd of spectators who thronged every avenue. The troops were then disbanded, and each returned to the bosom of his family, where, amid the joys of domestic felicity, they rested from the fatigues of war. In the mean time we were kept under a small guard, and were treated with the greatest hospitality and politeness, while thousands flocked to see us day after day. We spent most of our time in preaching and conversation, explanatory of our doctrines and practice, which removed mountains of prejudice, and enlisted the populace in our favor, notwithstanding their old hatred and wickedness toward our Society.

We were soon at liberty to walk the streets without a guard; and soon we were removed from our house of confinement to a respectable hotel, where we were entertained in the best style of which the place was capable. We had no longer any guard; we went out and came in when we pleased, a certain keeper being appointed merely to look to us; with him we walked out of town and visited the desolate lands which belonged to our Society, and the place which, seven years before, we had dedicated and consecrated for the building of a temple, it being a beautiful rise of ground, about half a mile west of Independence. When we saw it last it was a wilderness, but now our enemies had robbed it of every stick of timber, and it presented a beautiful rolling field of pasture, being covered with grass. Oh, how many feelings did this spot awaken in our bosoms! Here we had often bowed the knee in prayer to Jehovah in by-gone years; and here we had assembled with hundreds of happy saints, in the solemn meeting, and offered our prayers, and songs, and sacraments, in our humble dwellings; but now all was solemn and lonely desolation; not a vestage remained to mark the place where stood our former dwellings; they had long since been consumed by fire, or removed to the village and converted to the use of our enemies. While at Independence we were once or twice invited to dine with Gen. Wilson, and others, which we did, with much apparent politeness and attention on their part, and much cheerfulness and good feeling on our own.

After about a week spent in this way, during which I was at one time alone in the wilderness, more than a mile from town, we were at length (after repeated demands) sent to General Clark, at Richmond. This place was on the same side of Missouri that Far West was, and about thirty miles distant. Generals Lucas and Wilson had tried in vain to get a guard to accompany us; none would volunteer, and when drafted, they would not obey orders; for, in truth, they wished us to go at liberty. At last a colonel and two or three officers started with us, with their swords and pistols, which was more to protect us than to keep us from escaping. On this journey some of us rode in carriages, and some on horseback. Sometimes we were sixty or eighty rods in front or rear of our guard, who, by the by, were three sheets in the wind, in the whiskey line, having a bottle in their pockets; but knowing that we were not guilty of any crime, we did not wish to escape by flight. At night, having crossed the ferry, we put up at a private house. Here our guards all went to bed and to sleep, leaving us their pistols to defend ourselves in case of any attack from without, as we were in a very hostile neighborhood.

Next morn we rode a few miles, and were met by an express from Gen. Clark, at Richmond, consisting of Col. Price and a company of soldiers, who immediately surrounded us with poised pieces, in regular military order, as if we had been Bonaparte and his body guards, on a march from St. Helena; thinking, perhaps, that if we should escape, the United States and all Europe would be immediately overthrown. In this way we were escorted to Richmond, the head quarters of Maj. Gen. Clark and his army, which was composed of three or four thousand men. Here, as usual, we had to endure the gaze of the curious, as if we had been a caravan of exhibiting animals. We were conducted, with some military parade, into a block house, and immediately put in chains; besides a strong guard, who stood over us night and day, with presented rifles and pistols. We were soon introduced to Gen. Clark, who seemed more haughty, unfeeling, and reserved, than even Lucas or Wilson.

We enquired of the general what were his intentions concerning us. I stated to him that we had now been captives for many days, and we knew not wherefore; nor whether we were considered prisoners of war, or prisoners of civil process, or prisoners of hope; at the same time remarking that all was wrapt in mystery; for, as citizens of the United States, and of Missouri, in time of peace, we could not be considered as prisoners of war; and without civil process, we were not holden by civil authority; and as to being prisoners of hope, there was but little chance to hope from present appearances. He replied, that we were taken in order to be tried. "Tried? by what authority?" I enquired. "By court martial," said he.—"What!" said I, "ministers of the gospel, who sustain no office or rank in military affairs, and who are not even subject by law to military duty, to be tried by court martial, and this in time of peace, and in a republic where the constitution guarantees to every citizen the right of trial by jury?" "Yes," said he, "this is according to the treaty stipulations entered into at Far West, at the time of the surrender, and as agreed to by Col. Hinkle, your commanding officer." "Col. Hinkle, our commanding officer?" enquired I; "what has he to do with our civil rights? he was only the colonel of the Caldwell militia." "Why," said the general, "was he not the commanding officer of the fortress of Far West, the head quarters of Mormon forces?"

I replied that "we had no fortress, nor Mormon forces, but were part of the militia of the state of Missouri;" at which the general seemed surprised, and the conversation ended.

We were astonished above measure at proceedings so utterly ignorant and devoid of all law or justice. Here was a Major General, selected by the governor of Missouri, and sent to banish or exterminate a religious society. And then to crown the whole with inconceivable absurdity, this officer and his staff considered the state of Missouri a separate independent government, having a right to treat with a foreign nation, a right which belongs only to the United States, and not to any one state in the Union. And then, to cap the climax, he considers the Mormons a nation distinct from all other governments; and, in fact, enters into a treaty with the colonel of one of the regiments of their own state militia, which was at that time under his immediate command, as a part of his own forces. Thus Col. Hinkle is converted into a foreign minister, an envoy extraordinary, in behalf of the Mormon empire, to enter into treaty stipulations with his Missouri Majesty's forces, under Generals Lucas, Wilson, and Clark. The city of Far West, the capitol of Mormonia, is the Ghent where this treaty of peace is ratified. After which the standing army of Mormonia stack their arms, which are carried in triumph to Richmond. The royal family and other nobles are surrendered in this treaty to be tried by court martial and punished, and the inhabitants of the fallen empire, like those of Poland, are to be banished to Illinois instead of Siberia. But this banishment (more cruel than that of Poland by the Russians) is to include every man, woman, and child of the whole empire, with the exception of a few who are retained in prison, and their women and children sent off from their homes and firesides to wander alone. And at the same time a deed of trust is drawn up, and all the Mormons are compelled, on pain of death, to sign away their houses, lands, and property, for the disposal of their conquerors.

We found, on our arrival at Richmond, that all these things had actually taken place; and in addition to all the rest of these unheared of outrages, eighteen of our citizens had been shot dead at Hauns' Mill, in Caldwell county, and many others wounded, all this without making any resistance. The circumstances of this massacre were as follows: some two hundred robbers, on hearing of the governor's order for extermination, rushed suddenly upon some of our Society, who, on seeing them approach, took shelter in a log building which had been occupied as a blacksmith shop. On seeing their enemies approach in a hostile manner, they cried for quarter, but were instantly fired upon, and when most of them had fallen, and were lying in heaps, in the agonies of death, the murderers put their guns through the crevices between the logs, and shot the dead and dying thro' and through, as a token of bravery, and also to glut their bloodthirsty disposition.

A little boy had crawled under the bellows in hopes to escape; but, on being discovered, he was instantly shot. Another little boy, of nine years of age, whose father (Warren Smith) had just fell dead, cried out to the enemy to spare his life; but they replied, "Kill him—God damn it, kill him—he is the son of a damned Mormon!" At this they shot his head all open, and laid him sprawling by his father; thus leaving Mrs. Smith to mourn the loss of husband and child both at once. This was a worthy family, from Ohio, who had long been near neighbors to me; and better neighbors I never had. About the same time, an old soldier of the revolution, by the name of McBride, came up to them and begged for his life; but they hewed him in pieces with some old pieces of a sythe. The women fled, but were fired upon; and one young lady (Mary Steadwell, from Ohio, who was a worthy lady, and had been a member of my family,) was shot in the hand while fleeing, and fell behind a log in time to save her life, just as a shower of balls struck it.

The robbers then loaded themselves with household plunder and departed. These particulars are as we have learned them; but being confined in prison, we lack much information on the subject of the Hauns' Mill massacre, which will doubtless be given in the writings of others. Now to return to the subject as we left it at Richmond.

I must not forget to state that when we arrived at Richmond as prisoners, there were some fifty others, mostly heads of families, who had been marched from Caldwell on foot, and were now penned up in a cold, open, unfinished court house; in which situation they remained for some weeks, while their families were suffering every thing but death. The next morning after my dialogue with Gen. Clark, he again entered our prison and informed us that he had concluded to deliver us over to the civil authorities for an examining trial. I then asked him why he did not do away the unlawful decree of banishment, which was first ordered by Gen. Lucas, in compliance with the governor's order, compelling all our people to leave the state by the next spring? He replied that he approved of all the proceedings of Gen. Lucas, and should not alter them. I make this statement, because many writers have commended Clark for his heroic, merciful, and prudent conduct towards our Society, and have endeavored to make it appear that Clark was not to be blamed for any of the measures of Lucas.

The court of enquiry now commenced, before Judge A. A. King. This continued from the 11th to the 28th of November, during which we were kept most of the time in chains, and our brethren, some fifty in number, were penned up in the open, unfinished court house.

It was a very severe spell of snow and winter weather, and we suffered much. During this time Elder Rigdon was taken very sick, from hardship and exposure, and finally lost his reason; but still he was kept in our miserable, noisy, and cold room, and compelled to sleep on the floor with a chain and padlock round his ankle, and fastened to six others; and here he endured the constant noise and confusion of an unruly guard, who were changed every few hours, and who were frequently composed of the most noisy, foul-mouthed, vulgar, disgraceful, indecent rabble, that ever defiled the earth. While he lay in this situation, his son-in-law, George Robi[n]son, the only male member of his numerous family, was chained by his side; and thus Mrs. Rigdon and her daughters were left entirely destitute and unprotected. One of his daughters, Mrs. Robi[n]son, a young and delicate female, with her little infant, came down to see her husband, and to comfort and take care of her father in his sickness. When she first entered the room, amid the clank of chains and the bristle of weapons, and cast her eyes on her sick and dejected parent, and sorrow worn husband, she was speechless, and only gave vent to her feelings in a flood of tears. This faithful lady, with her little infant, continued by the bed of her father till he recovered from his sickness, and till his fevered and disordered mind assumed its wonted powers of intellect.

In this mock court of enquiry, the judge could not be prevailed on to examine the conduct of the murderers, robbers, and plunderers, who had desolated our Society. Nor would he receive testimony except against us. And by the deserters and apostates who wished to save their own lives and property at the expense of others; and by those who had murdered and plundered us from time to time, he obtained abundance of testimony, much of which was entirely false. Our Church organization was converted, by such testimony, into a temporal kingdom, which was to fill the whole earth, and subdue all other kingdoms. Much was enquired by the judge (who, by-the-by, was a Methodist,) concerning the prophesy of Daniel— "In the days of these kings shall the God of Heaven set up a kingdom, which shall break in pieces all other kingdoms, and stand forever," &c. "And the kingdom, and the greatness of the kingdom, under the whole Heaven, shall be given to the saints of the Most High," &c.—These texts, and many others, were enquired into with all the eagerness and apparent alarm which characterized a Herod of old, who feared a rival in the person of King Jesus, and who, after enquiring dilligently into the prophesies concerning the birth of Christ, and on learning that Bethlehem was the honored place designated by the Jewish oricles for the birth place of Messiah, and on learning from the wise men of the east that he was the already born, sent forth a cruel order for the extermination of the children of Bethlehem, from two years old and under. In this way Herod thought to falsify the oricles of God—to destroy the King of the Jews, and maintain his own usurpation of power. But, lo! he was disappointed. The angel of the Lord had caused the father and mother and infant to flee into Egypt. So this cruel judge decreed the destruction of the Church and Kingdom of God, in the last days. But we shall see, in the sequel, that those whose destruction was firmly decreed (by Gov. Boggs, the modern Herod, and his wicked coadjutors,) fled into Illinois, instead of Egypt; for the predictions of Daniel and others must be fulfilled now, as well as those predictions concerning Christ were fulfilled, in spite of judges and governors.

Much enquiry was also had concerning our sending Missionaries to all nations to preach the Gospel. And after all these enquiries, our religion was converted by false testimony and by false coloring, into treason against the State of Missouri; and like the Pharisees of old, all these modern ignoramuses seemed to think, "if we let them thus alone all men will believe on them, and the Mormons will come and take away our place and nation." Here let me remark, that it is, and ever has been, the firm and expressed belief of our society, that Religion is one thing, and Politics another, and that the laws of all governments should be respected, and obeyed, so long as their administration protects the lives and property of their citizens, until the end of the world, when Christ will reign as King of kings and Lord of Lords. But if self-defence and opposition to tyranny and oppression amounts to treason, then I for one, am a treasoner with every feeling of my heart; for had I the power, I would restore the supremacy of the laws and Constitution, which have been violated by the authorities of Missouri. Justice should be administered to the guilty Governor, Generals, Judges, and others who have murdered, plundered and driven us; and those who have suffered should be restored to their rights and to their possessions, and the damages should be paid them. Mark the saying, I am opposed to the unlawful proceedings of the highest authorities of Missouri, and would glory in laying down my life in opposing such abominations.

But to return to my narrative: At the close of the Court of Inquiry, some twenty or thirty were dismissed, among whom were A. Lyman, one of our number who had been with us in our captivity, and in our chains: and some twenty others were let to bail; and Messrs. Joseph Smith, Jr., Hiram Smith, Sidney Rigdon, Lyman Wight, Caleb Baldwin and Alexander McRay, were committed to the jail of Clay county, on the charge of treason. And Messrs. Morris Phelps, Luman Gibbs, Darwin Chase, Norman Shearer, and myself, were committed to the jail of Richmond, being accused of defending ourselves in the battle with Bogart and his company.

This done, the civil and military authorities dispersed, and the troubled waters became a little more tranquil. As our people were compelled by the memorable treaty of Far West, to leave the State by the following spring, they now commenced moving by hundreds and by thousands, to the State of Illinois, where they were received in the most humane and friendly manner by the authorities, and by the citizens in general. Mean time, bands of murderers, thieves and robbers, were roaming unrestrained among our unarmed and defenceless citizens; committing all manner of plunder, and driving off cattle, sheep and horses—abusing and insulting women, etc.

My wife and children soon came to me in prison, and spent most of the winter with me in the dark, cold and filthy dungeon, where myself and fellow prisoners were constantly insulted and abused by our dastardly guards, who often threatened to shoot, hang us, &c.

The State Legislature were soon in session, and from this body, so high in responsibility, we had hoped for some redress or protection. But what was our astonishment, when after much noisy debate on the subject, they refused to investigate the matter, and actually became partakers of the same crimes by passing a law appropriating $200,000 for the payment of the troops engaged in this unlawful, unconstitutional and treasonable enterprise. This last act of unheard of outrage, sealed with eternal infamy, the character of the State of Missouri, and established her downfall, to rise no more. She will be looked upon by her sister States as a star fallen from Heaven, and a ruined and degraded outcast from the federal union. While the whole civilized world will detest and abhor her, as the most infamous of tyrants. Nay, tyranny itself will blush to hear her deeds mentioned in the annals of history; and the most cruel persecutors of the christians or reformers, in Pagan or Papal Rome, will startle with astonishment from their long slumbers, and with a shudder of the deepest horror, and a frown of the most indignant contempt, they will look upon her unheard of deeds of blind infatuation, and inconscienable absurdity. The spirits of the ancient martyrs will hail their brethren of the Church of latter-day Saints, as greater sufferers than themselves, and the blood of ancient and modern Saints, will mingle together in cries for vengeance, upon those who are drunken with their blood, till justice will delay no longer to execute his long suspended mission of vengeance upon the earth.

These disgraceful proceedings of the legislature were warmly opposed by a large minority of the House, among whom were D. R. Atchison, of Clay county, and all the members from St. Louis, and Messrs. Rollins and Gordon, from Boon, and by various other members from other counties, but the mob majority carried the day, for the guilty wretches feared an investigation, knowing that it would endanger their lives and liberties.

Many of the State journals have tried to hide the iniquity of the State, by throwing a covering of lies over her atrocious deeds. But can they hide the Governor's cruel order for extermination or banishment? Can they conceal the facts of the disgraceful treaty of the Generals, with their own officers and men, at the city of Far West? Can they conceal the fact that ten or eleven thousand men, women and children, have been banished from the State without trial or condemnation. And this at an expense of two hundred thousand dollars, and this sum appropriated by the State Legislature, in order to pay the troops for this act of lawless outrage? Can they conceal the fact that we have been imprisoned for many months, while our families, friends and witnesses have been driven away? Can they conceal the blood of the murdered husbands, and fathers; or stifle the cries of the widow and fatherless? Nay!—The rocks and mountains may cover them in unknown depths—the awful abyss of the fathomless deep may swallow them up—and still their horrid deeds will stand forth in the broad light of day, for the wondering gaze of angels and of men! They cannot be hid.

But to return—Mr. Smith, and his fellow prisoners in Clay county, applied for a writ of habeas corpus, and were brought before the county Judges, and their cases examined as to why they were in confinement. At this trial, Mr. Rigdon was let to bail under bonds of two thousand dollars, and the rest were about to be dismissed, but the mob was so violent as to threaten the lives of the Judges if they let them go. Therefore they were detained. In April, having been confined near six months, they were taken to Daviess county, to be tried by a band of robbers, under the name of Grand Jury. Here a bill was soon found against them for high treason, and various other offences. Their venue was then changed, and they were sent towards Columbia, Boon county, for trial. This was some 120 miles down the country, towards Illinois. On their way to this place, they all made their escape from the sheriff and three guards. Some say that the guards got beastly drunk and let them escape. Others, that they were bought for the paltry sum of $250, but be this as it may, they escaped unhurt, and arrived safe in Illinois, where they were kindly received, and welcomed by the Governor, and by the community, as men who had escaped from a long and terrible persecution. And there they have now been for some months, and that publicly, without any attempt on the part of the State of Missouri to retake them, although they are but just over the line. Why does the State thus neglect them?—The answer is, that they are now ashamed of their own conduct, and glad to drop the subject and let it slumber where it is.

On the seventeenth of March, (as the time drew near for all of the Society to leave the State) my wife took leave of the prison, and with a broken heart returned to Far West, in order to get passage with some of the brethren, for Illinois. She tarryed in Far West about a month, and all the Society had gone from the State, but a few of the poor, and widows, and a committee who tarryed behind to assist them in removing. About the middle of April, a gang of robbors entered Far West armed, and ordered my wife and the committee, and the others, to be gone by such a day, or they would murder them. Thus my wife was driven away, according to the previous orders of the Governor, while I was still detained in a filthy dungeon. My family were conveyed to Quincy, Illinois, distance one hundred and eighty miles, by David W. Rogers, of New York, who is a descendant of the celebrated martyr, John Rogers, of Smithfield, England.

On the 26th of April, 1839, the last of the Society departed from Far West. Thus had a whole people consisting of about 10 or 11 thousand souls, been driven from houses and lands, and reduced to poverty, and had removed to another State during one short winter, and part of a spring. The sacrifice of property was immense, probably amounting to several millions, and one of the most flourishing counties of the State, and part of several others, were reduced to desolation, or inhabited by gangs of robbers.

On the 24th of April, our cases were had before the Grand Jury of the county of Ray; and Darwin Chase and Norman Shearer were dismissed, after being imprisoned near six months. This release happened just as Mr. Shearer came to visit his son for the last time before he left the country. He came into the prison to see us, and not knowing of the intended release, he took an affectionate leave of us and of his son, who seemed to weep with heart-broken anguish. But while he yet lingered in town, his son was called before the court, and with Mr. Chase, was told that they might go at liberty. The father and son then embraced each other, almost overcome with joy, and depa[r]ted. At the same time my brother Orson Pratt, whom I had not before seen for a year, came from Illinois to see me, but was only permitted to visit me for a few moments, and then was ordered to depart. Mrs. Phelps, who had waited in prison for some days, in hopes that the court would release her husband, now parted with him, overwhelmed with sorrow and tears, and with her infant, moved slowly away, to remove alone to Illinois, and leave her husband behind. Thus our families wander in a strange land, without our protection, being robbed of house and home. O God! Who can e[n]dure the thought? Come out in justice, O Lord! and restore us to our mourning families.

Our number in prison was now reduced to four.— One having been added about the middle of April. His name was King Follett; he was dragged from his distressed family just as they were leaving the State. Thus of all the prisoners (which were taken at an expense of two hundred thousand dollars) only two of the original ones, who belonged to the Church, now remained, (Mr. Gibbs having denied the faith, to try to save his life,) these were Morris Phelps and myself. All who were let to bail were banished the State, together with those who bailed them. Thus none are like to have a trial by law, but ourselves, and we are without friends or witnesses in the State. After the Grand Jury had found a bill against us for defending ourselves in the battle with Bogart's company, we were kept in prison at Richmond for about a month, we then took a change of venue, and were ordered to be sent to Columbia, Boon county, for trial. On the 22d of May we were handcuffed together, two and two, with irons round the wrist of each, and in this fix we were taken from prison and placed in a carriage. The people of Richmond gathered around us to see us depart; but none seemed to feel for us except two persons. One of these, (General Parks' Lady) bowed to us through the window, and looked as if touched with pity. The other was a Mr. Huggins; merchant of Richmond, who bowed with some feeling as we passed. We now took leave of Richmond, accompanied by sheriff Brown, and four guards, with drawn pistols, and moved on towards Columbia. No tongue can describe our sensations as we came forth from a most filthy dungeon, where we had been confined for near seven months, and began to breathe the free air, and to change the scenery, and look abroad upon the face of the earth. There was a sweetness in the air and a perfume from the earth, which none could so fully sense, except such as have been for a long time confined in tainted air. It had been thundering and raining for some days, and the thunder storm lasted with but short cessations from the time we started, till we arrived at the place of destination, which was five days. The small streams were swollen so as to be very difficult crossing them. On the second day we came to a creek which was several rods over, with a strong current, and very deep. It was towards evening, and far from any house, and we had had no refreshment through the day. Here we halted, and knew not what to do; we waited awhile for the water to fall, but it fell but slowly. All hands were hungry and impatient, and a lowery night seemed to threaten that the creek would rise before morning by the falling of additional rains. In this dilemma, some counciled one thing, and some another.— Some said, go back some miles to a house, and tarry till morning. Others said camp here for the night.— Others said swim the river, and leave the carriage and baggage till morning, and some advised to attempt to drive some miles around the head of the stream. At last I proposed to the sheriff that if he would take off my irons I would go into the water to bathe; and by that means ascertain the depth and bottom; this he consented to do, after some hesitation. I then plunged into the stream, and swam across and attempted to wade back; I found it to be a hard bottom, and the water about up to my chin; but a very stiff current. After this, Mr. Brown, the sheriff, undertook to cross on his horse; but just as his horse neared the opposite shore, he sprung sidewise, to gain a bank, and Mr. Brown was thrown off his horse and buried in the stream. He could not swim, but sprang out, hallowing and flouncing in a manner that caused much merriment to the company. This accident decided the fate of the day. Being now completely wet, he resolved to effect the crossing of the whole company, bag and baggage. Accordingly several stripped off their cloths and mounted on the bare backs of the horses; and, taking their clothing, saddles, and arms, together with our trunk and bedding upon their shoulders, they bore them across in safety, without wetting. This was done by riding backwards and forwards, across the stream, several times. In this sport and labor, prisoners, guards, and all, mingled in mutual exertion. All was now safe but the carriage. Mr. Phelps then proposed to swim that across, by hitching two horses before it; and he mounted on one of their backs, while myself and one of the guards swam by the side of the carriage to keep it from upsetting by the force of the current. And thus, Paul like, we all got safe to land. Every thing was soon replaced; and ourselves in the carriage, and our suite on horseback, we moved swiftly on, and at dark arrived at a house of entertainment, amid a terrible thunder storm. Next morning we proceeded on, but in a few miles came to another swimming stream; but after some consultation, it was thought best to go around the head of the stream. We accordingly took our back track for a half mile, and then striking to the north in the open prairie, without any track, we rode some seven miles around, crossed the head of the stream, and returned to the road which we had left; this day we crossed the Missouri at a place called Arrow Rock, being named from the circumstance of the natives coming there from all quarters to get a kind of hard rock from the bluff to make arrow points. In this journey we had slept each night on our backs, on the floor; being all four of us ironed together, with hand and ankle irons made for the purpose. This being done, the windows and doors were all fastened, and then five guards with their loaded pistols staid in the room, and one at a time set up and watched during the night. This cruelty was inflicted on us, more to gratify a wicked disposition, than any thing else; for it was in vain for us to have tried to escape, without any irons being put on us, and had we wished to escape, we had a tolerable good opportunity at the creek.

When we arrived within four miles of Columbia, the bridge had been destroyed from over a large and rapid river; and here we were some hours in crossing over, in a tottleish canoe, having to leave our carriage, together with our bedding, clothing, our trunk of clothing, books, papers, &c., but all came to us in safety after two days. After we had all crossed the river, our guards having swam their horses, mounted them, and we proceeded towards Columbia, the prisoners walking on foot, two being fastened together by the wrists.

After walking two or three miles, Mr. Brown hired a carriage, and we rode into Columbia. It was about sun-set on Sunday evening, and as the carriage and our armed attendants drove through the streets, we were gazed upon with astonishment by hundreds of spectators, who thronged the streets, and looked out at the windows, doors, &c., anxious to get a glimpse of the strange beings called Mormons. On our arrival we were immediately hurried to the prison, without going to a tavern for refreshment, although we had travelled a long summer day without any thing to eat. When unloosed from our fetters, we were ushered immediately from the carriage into the jail, and the next moment a huge trap-door was opened, and down we went into a most dismal dungeon, which was full of cobwebs and filth above, below, and all around the walls, having stood empty for near two years. Here was neither beds, nor chairs, nor water, nor food, nor friends, nor any one on whom we might call, even for a drink of cold water; for Brown and all others had withdrawn to go where they could refresh themselves. When thrust into this dungeon, we were nearly ready to faint with hunger, and thirst, and weariness. We walked the room for a few moments, and then sank down upon the floor in despondency, and wished to die; for, like Elijah of old, if the Lord had enquired, "What dost thou here?" we could have replied, "Lord, they have killed thy prophets, and thrown down thine altars, and have driven out all thy saints from the land, and we only are left to tell thee; and they seek our lives, to take them away; and now, therefore, let us die."[2]

[*Sworn to before John Johnson, 15 Jan 1840.*]

---

[2]Parley P. Pratt and Morris Phelps left Columbia, Missouri prison in July 1839. King Follett escaped with Pratt and Phelps, but was apprehended again. Luman Gibbs, who had turned against the others, remained in prison (*HC* 3:399–402).

Part II

The First Appeal to Congress

Introduction to Part II

In 1839 the leaders of The Church of Jesus Christ of Latter-day Saints began their first appeal for redress from the federal government for their losses in Missouri. Part II consists of the documents of this first appeal which include a general introductory petition, referred to as a memorial, and many individual petitions. The Prophet Joseph Smith himself led the Mormon delegation which consisted of Elias Higbee, Sidney Rigdon, and Orrin Porter Rockwell. They left Nauvoo on 29 October 1839 and traveled to Quincy, Illinois, where they stayed an extra day because Sidney Rigdon had become ill. In Quincy they were joined by Robert Foster, a medical doctor who consented to travel with them to nurse Rigdon (*HC* 4:19–20). By the time they reached Columbus, Ohio, Rigdon had become so ill that Joseph Smith and Elias Higbee left him there with Rockwell and Foster and continued on to Washington, D.C. (*HC* 4:21).

Joseph Smith and Elias Higbee arrived in Washington on Thursday, 28 November 1839. The following day they met with President Martin Van Buren. After he had read one of their letters of introduction he said, "with a kind of half frown, . . . What can I do? I can do nothing for you! If I do anything, I shall come in contact with the whole state of Missouri" (*HC* 4:40). However, he promised to reconsider the matter.

Most histories show that Joseph had only one interview with the President during his visit to Washington. Yet it is possible that he had a second meeting with President Van Buren, for on Thursday, 6 February 1840, Joseph recorded, "It was with great reluctance he [Van Buren] listened to our message, which, when he had heard, he said: 'Gentleman, your cause is just, but I can do nothing for you;' and 'If I take up for you I shall lose the vote of Missouri'" (*HC* 4:80).

Rigdon, Rockwell, and Foster joined the Prophet and Higbee on 23 December 1839. From that time through 6 February 1840 the members of the delegation tried to present the Mormon cause before the U.S. Congress. Instead of allowing the Mormons to present their petitions directly to Congress, the Senate voted to refer the matter to the Senate Judiciary Committee. The Prophet Joseph Smith recorded that besides the memorial signed by himself, Sidney Rigdon, and Elias Higbee, they presented 491 individual claims to Congress "leaving a multitude more of similar bills hereafter to be presented" (*HC* 4:74).

Frustrated, Joseph, Porter Rockwell, and Dr. Foster left for Nauvoo on 20 February 1840 (*HC* 4:81). Elias Higbee and Sidney Rigdon remained in Washington a few weeks longer, but met with little success.

On 9 March 1840, Higbee wrote to the Prophet Joseph Smith that Senator Richard M. Young of Illinois had made a last attempt to help the Saints; Higbee reported that he and Rigdon would return to Nauvoo when he received the final report from the Senate Judiciary Committee (*HC* 4:94).

As Higbee had expected, the Committee determined that the federal government could not intervene in a state's right "to redress the wrongs of its own citizens" (*HC* 4:92). On 24 March 1840, Higbee wrote that he had withdrawn "the accompanying papers" (presumably the petitions) and would return to Nauvoo immediately (*HC* 4:98–99).

Today the individual petitions that Higbee withdrew are housed in the LDS Historical Department. However, the memorial that was sent with this First Appeal remained in Washington, D.C., and is found in the National Archives.

Chapter 3

The First Memorial

To the honorable the Senate and House of Representatives of the United States of America in Congress assembled:

Your Memorialists, Joseph Smith, Junr., Sidney Rigdon, and Elias Higbee, would most respectfully represent, that they have been delegated by their brethren and fellow citizens, the "Latter Day Saints" (commonly called <u>Mormons</u>) to prepare and present to your Honorable bodies, a statement of their wrongs, and a prayer for their relief, which they now have the honor to submit to the consideration of the Congress of the United States.

This memorial Showeth:—That in the Summer of the year 1831, a portion of the sect above-named commenced a settlement in the County of Jackson in the State of Missouri: The individuals making that settlement had emigrated from almost every State in the Union, to that lovely spot in the "<u>Far West</u>," in the hope of improving their condition; of building homes for themselves and posterity; and of erecting Temples where they and theirs might worship their creator, according to the dictates of their own consciences. Though they had wandered far from the homes of their childhood, still they had been taught to believe, that a citizen born in any one State in this great Republic, might remove to another and enjoy all the rights and immunities guarantied to the citizens of the State of his adoption; that wherever waved the American flag, beneath its stars and Stripes, an American Citizen might look for protection and justice—liberty in person, and in conscience.

They bought farms, built houses, erected churches; some tilled the earth, others bought and sold merchandise; and others again toiled in the occupation of the mechanic. They were industrious and moral; they prospered; and though often persecuted and vilified for their difference in religious opinions, from their ~~other~~ fellow citizens, still they were happy. They saw their society incresing in numbers; their farms teemed with plenty; and they fondly looked forward to a future big with hope. That there was prejudice existing against them they knew; that slanders were propogated against them they deplored; yet they felt that these things were unmerited and unjust; that time and an upright conduct would outgrow them in this enlightened age of the world. While this summer of peace and happiness and hope beamed upon them, and shone over the infant settlement of the "Saints," the dark cloud that bore in its bosom the thunderbolt of their destruction was gathering fast around them, pregnant with prejudice, oppression and ~~destruction~~ final expulsion or extermination. On the 20th of July 1833 around their peaceful vilage, a mob gathered to the surprise and terror of the quiet, unoffending Mormons; why, they knew not. They had broken no law; they had harmed no man in deed or thought. Why then were they thus threatened and abused? Soon a Committee from the mob called upon the leading "Saints" of the place, and issued forth the mandate that the stores, the printing office, and the work shops must all be closed; and that forthwith every Mormon must leave the county. The message was so terrible, so unexpected, the "Saints" asked time for deliberation, for consultation; which being refused, the Brethren were severally asked "Are you willing to abandon your homes?" the reply was such as became freemen living in a free country: "We will not go": which determination being made known to the Committee of the Mob; one of them replied: "he was sorry, as the work of destruction must now begin." No sooner said than done. The printing office, a two story brick building, was assailed by the Mob, and torn down, and with all its valuable furniture and materials litterally destroyed. They next proceeded to the principal store with a like purpose; its owner in part, Mr Gilbert, agreed to close it, and they delayed their purpose of destruction. They then proceeded to the dwelling of Mr Partridge, the beloved Bishop of the Church; they dragged him from his family to the public square, and when surrounded by hundreds of spectators, they partially stripped him of his clothes, and in the most unfeeling manner, covered him with tar and feathers from head to foot. Another by the name of Allen, was treated in a similar manner, at the same time. The mob then dispersed, with an agreement to meet again on the following Tuesday; the above outrages having been committed on Saturday. Tuesday came, and with it came the Mob, bearing a red flag in token of blood. They proceeded to the houses of Isaac Morley and others of the leading men, seized them, and told them to bid their families farewell; ~~that~~ as they would never see them again. They were then driven at the point of the bayonet to the Jail, and there, amid the jeers and insults of the crowd were thrust into prison, to be kept as hostages and for immolation, in case any of the mob should be killed while depredating upon the persons and property of the "Saints". At this awful and critical juncture some two or three of the Mormons offered to surrender up themselves as victims, if that would satisfy the fury of the mob; and purchase peace and security for their unoffending brethren, their helpless wives, and innocent children. The reply of the mob was—"the Mormons must leave the county en masse" or every man shall be put to death" The Mormons terrified and defenceless, were ~~thus~~ in this manner reduced to the necessity of entering into an agreement to leave the county; one half by the first of January—the other half by the first of April next ensuing. This treaty being made and ratified, the mob dispersed.¶

Again for a time, the persecuted Mormons enjoyed a respite from their relentless persecutors, but their repose was of short duration. Some time in the month of October a meeting was held at Independence, at which it was determined to remove the Mormons or die. Inflammatory speeches of the most violent character were made to excite the populace; and one of the speakers went so far in his denunciations as to swear "that he would remove the Mormons from the County, if he had to wade to his neck in blood". Up to this time, the Mormons had faithfully observed the forced treaty stipulations on their part; and were guilty of no offence against either the laws of the land or of society; but were peaceably following the routine of their daily duties. Shortly after the meeting above referred to, another persecution commenced, with increased sufferings on the part of the devoted Mormons. Some of their people were shot at; others were whipped without mercy; their houses assailed with brickbats; the doors broken open; and thrown down; their women grossly insulted; and their weeping daughters brutally abused before their mother's eyes. Thus were they for many days and weeks without offence and without resistance, by night and by day, harrassed, insulted and oppressed. But there is a point beyond which human endurance ceases to be a virtue; when the worm, ~~when~~ if trampled upon, will in the agony of its distress turn upon ~~on~~ its oppressor. A company of about thirty Mormons fell in with twice that number of the Mob, engaged in the destruction of their property; when a battle ensued in which, one Mormon was killed, and two or three of the mob. We here regret to say, that acting in concert with the officer who commanded the Mob, was Lilbourn Boggs, at that time Lieutenant Governor of the State of Missouri. When the news of this battle was spread abroad, the public mind became much inflamed against our people; the militia collected in arms from various quarters, and in great numbers; and being excited to fury by the false accounts which had been circulated against us; they demanded an immediate surrender of all our arms, and gave a peremptory order that we should quit the County without further delay. Compelled by overpowering numbers, the Mormons submitted, and surrendered up fifty-one guns which have never been returned or accounted for. The next day, parties of the mob went from house to house threatening the women and children with death, if they did not immediately leave their homes. Imagination cannot permit, nor tongue express, the terror and consternation which now pervaded the Mormon Community. The weather was intensely cold; the women and children horror stricken and defenceless, abandoned their homes, and fled for safety in every direction; very many of them without the necessary articles of clothing to protect them from the peltings of the pitiless storm and piercing cold to which they were exposed. Women gave birth to infants in the woods, and on the bleak bosoms of the prairies houseless and unsheltered; —at that critical and trying time without any of the necessaries usual on such occasions, without their husbands, and without Physicians or midwives or any other assistance except as they could assist each other. One hundred and twenty women and children, for ten successive days with only three or four men to aid them, concealed themselves in the recesses of the forest, in hourly expectation of massacre, until they found an opportunity of escaping into Clay County.

The Society of Mormons, after these disturbances, removed to the County of Clay, where they were kindly received by their brethren and the inhabitants, who administered to their necessities in the most charitable manner. In the mean time the houses of the Mormons, in the county of Jackson which they had abandoned, numbering about two hundred, were burned down, or otherwise demolished by the mob who destroyed at the same time, much of their crops, furniture, and stock. The damage done to the property of the Mormons by the mob in the county of Jackson under the circumstances above related, as near as they can ascertain, would amount to the sum of One Hundred and Twenty thousand Dollars. The number of Mormons thus disfranchised and driven from their houses and homes in the County of Jackson amounted to about Twelve hundred souls. For the property thus destroyed, no remuneration has been made. After the expulsion of the Mormons from the county of Jackson, in the manner above stated, they removed to and settled in the County of Clay. They there purchased farms from some of the citizens, and entered other lands at the land office—wild lands, offered for sale by the General Government. The most of them again became freeholders, owning each an eighty acre tract ~~of land~~ or more of land. The Mormons now lived peaceably in the County of Clay for about three years, and during all that time increased gradually in numbers by emigration, and in wealth by their industry, and diligent attention in their several occupations. After they had resided in that County for the time above mentioned, the citizens not connected with their society, began to look upon them with suspicion and alarm. Reports were again circulated against them; public meetings were held in the Counties of Clay and Jackson, at which violent resolutions were passed against their people, and rumors of mobs began again to spread alarm and dismay among the unoffending Mormons. At this critical juncture, the Mormons being desirous of avoiding if possible, further conflict, with their neighbours and fellow citizens; and anxious to preserve the peace and harmony of the Society around them as well as their own safety, deputed a Committee of their leading men to propose terms of peace. An interview took place between them and a Committee of citizens not connected with their, society, at which it was agreed, that the Mormons should leave the County of Clay, and that the citizens of Clay County should purchase their lands. These terms were complied with, and the Mormons now removed to, and took up their abode in the County of Caldwell where they once more reorganized a settlement; but not without very heavy pecuniary losses and other inconveniences, as the citizens of Clay County never paid them for their lands, with the exception of a very small part of the purchase money to some, while others have not as yet, and perhaps never will, receive a single farthing. The Mormons by this removal sacrificed much of money and of feeling; but the sacrifice was made upon the altar of duty as christians, rather than again to affording a pretext for the disturbance of the peace of the community.

Your Memorialists would humbly beg leave here to give what they beleive to be a just and unvarnished explanation of the causes which have led to the bitter prejudices and persecutions against their Society as above related, without malice and without exaggeration; with the Christian desire of rendering fair and impartial justice to all concerned. That there have been some unworthy members among them, they will not deny; but they aver at the same time, that taken as a community, they have been and are as moral, as upright, and as observant of the laws of God and of the land as any body of people in the world of the same number. Why then this prejudice, and never ending persecution? An answer they think will be found in the facts: That they were a body of people, distinct from their fellow citizens, in religious opinions, in their habits, and in their associations; and withal sufficiently numerous to make their political and moral power a matter of anxiety and dread to the political and religious parties by which they were surrounded. Which prejudices arose, not from what the Mormons had done, but from the fear of what they might do, if they should see proper to exercise this power. In addition to this, the Mormons had either purchased of the settlers or the General Government, or held by Pre-emption rights, what were regarded the best lands in that region of the Country. The tide of speculation during this period of time ran high; and the cupidity of many was thus unlawfully aroused to possess themselves of these lands, and add to their wealth by driving the mormons from the country, and taking forcible possession of them; or constraining them to sell through fear and coercion at prices merely nominal and of their own fixing.

After the removal of the Mormons from Clay County, they settled in the county of Caldwell; your memorialists do not deem it necessary for their purpose to detail the history of the progress of the settlements and anxieties of the mormons from the time they settled in Caldwell County in the year 1836 until the fall of the year 1838. They would, however, aver that during all that time they deported themselves as good citizens; obeying the laws of the land, and performing the moral & religious duties enjoined by their faith. That, there may have been some faithless ones among the faithful, is very possible. Nay they will not deny, but that there may have been some who were a scandal to their brethren. But what society your memorialists would ask, has not some unworthy members in it? Where the sect, religious, moral or political; Where the community; in which there cannot be found some of its members who trample under foot both the laws of God and of their fellow man? They sincerely believe that the mormon community have as few such persons as any other association, religious, moral, or political. Within the above last mentioned period, and under all these difficulties, the mormons continued to increase in wealth and in numbers, until in the fall of the year 1838, they numbered as near as they can estimate, about 15,000 souls.

They now held by purchases from the Government, of the settlers, and by pre-emption, almost all the lands in the County of Caldwell and a portion of the lands of in Daviess & Carroll Counties. The County of Caldwell was settled almost entirely by mormons; and mormons were rapidly filling up the counties of Daviess and Carroll. When they first commenced settling in those counties, there were but few settlements, and the lands were for the most part wild and uncultivated. In the fall of 1838 large well improved farms had been made and stocked; lands had risen in value; and in some instances had been sold for from $10 to $25 per acre. The improvement and settlements had been such that it was a common remark that the county of Caldwell would soon be the wealthiest in the state. Thus stood the affairs of the society in the fall of 1838 when the storm of persecution again commenced and raged over their devoted heads. The mob again commenced its devastations, and drove the mormons forth; houseless, homeless, and pennyless upon the charities of the world; which to them, thank God, had been in times of trial and distress like Angels visits; but not few nor far between. This last persecution had its origin at an election which was held in the county of Daviess on the first monday in August 1838. A mormon went to the polls to vote, when one of the mob standing by, opposed his voting; contending that a mormon had no more right to vote than a negro. One angry word brought on another until unfortunately blows ensued. They are happy nevertheless to state that the mormon was not the aggressor; having acted as they believe entirely on the defensive. Others joined in the assault; not one or two, but many against the mormon. His brethren seeing him thus assailed by numbers and exposed to great bodily injury, interfered to rescue him from his periolous situation, when others of the mob came and joined in the affray; being determined, as they said, "that the mormons should not vote". A general riot now commenced; the mormons being determined to exercise the right of voting as citizens of the county; and the mob being equally determined that they should not —victory in this instance decided on the side of right. Rumor reached the mormons of Caldwell County the next day, that two of their brethren had been killed in this affray; and that a refusal had been made to surrender their bodies for burial. Not knowing at the time that this rumor was without foundation, much excitement prevailed, and several of the mormons started for Daviess County with a view of finding, if possible, for their brethren, whom they supposed to have been murdered, a decent burial. They arrived next morning among the citizens and found great excitement prevailing. They had held a public meeting and resolved to drive all the mormons from the Country. Individuals began again to threaten the mormons as a body, and to swear that they should all leave the country in three days. The mormons also heard that a large mob was collecting against them, headed by Adam Black one of the Judges of the County court of Daviess County. Under these circumstances and with a view to allay this excitement some of the brethren called on Judge Black and enquired whether the report they had heard was true. Upon his denying the truth of it, they requested him to give that denial in writing which he freely did; which writing they published with a view to calm the public mind, and to allay the existing excitement. Having done this, they rested in quiet for some time, hoping that these efforts would produce the desired effect. Their surprise under these circumstances can be easily imagined, when a short time after this, they learned that this same Judge Black had gone before Judge King and made affidavit that he was forced to sign that instrument by an armed band of mormons; and thereupon procured a warrant for the apprehension of Joseph Smith Jr and Lyman Wight which was placed in the hands of the Sheriff to be executed. It was also reported that the accused individuals had refused to be taken, and that an armed party of citizens was collecting to come and take them by force. Your memorialists aver that the Sheriff had never made any effort either to take them or serve the process, and that Smith and Wight, so far from opposing resistance, did not know that a writ had been issued against them until they learned that such was the case by the report above related. In the mean time the rumor had spread over the whole country, that the mormons were compelling individuals to sign certain instruments in writing, that they (the mormons) were not resisting the process of the law. The public mind had now become much inflamed and the mob began to collect from all quarters, and in large numbers, with the pretext of assisting the Sheriff to execute the process.

And let it be here observed, in passing, that Judge Adam Black had before that time sold the improvement and pre-emption claim on which he then resided to the mormons; had received his pay for the same; that through his instrumentality the mormons were broken up and driven off; and that he now unlawfully retains both their money and the improvements. As soon as the report of their intended resistance reached Smith & Wight, they determined immediately to go ~~in pursuit of~~ to the ~~Sheriff~~ Judge who issued the warrant against them, and before the mob proceeded to extremities, ~~to~~ and submit themselves to the law. They both surrendered themselves accordingly to Judge King who had issued the process, underwent a trial, and in the absence of any just accusations against them, were acquitted and dis-charged. They hoped that this voluntary submission of theirs to the law, and their successful vindication of themselves against the charges prefered against them would allay the excitement of the community; but not so. The long desired opportunity had arrived of consummating the extermination of the mormons or their expulsion from the country, by giving to their ~~proceedings~~ persecutions the color and form of legal proceedings; and it could not be forborne. The mob which had assembled with the pretext of assisting the officers of the law in the execution of their duty, did not disperse on the acquittal of Smith and Wight, as was expected; but continued embodied in their encampments in the form of a military force; and committing from time to time one depredation after another upon the property of the mormons. The mormons, in this extremity, appealed ~~for succour~~ [——] to the laws of the land, and to the officers of the law for protection against their infractions. After much delay the militia under Generals Atchison, Donaphan, and Parkes were sent to their relief. They arrived on the 13th of Sept. and encamped between the mob and the mormons. These officers made no attempt to disperse the mob, and excused themselves by saying, "that the sympathies of their men were in their favor". After remaining in this situation for several days, these officers at length adopted the following expedient of settling the existing difficulties, and restoring peace. They mustered the mob and enrolled them with their troops, and then disbanded the whole together, with orders to return to their several homes. The officers then returned home, with the exception of Genl. Parks, who remained for their protection with his men. The mormons then made an agreement with the citizens of Daviess County, to buy out their lands and pre-emption rights; and appointed a committee to make the purchases, with instructions to buy until they purchased to the amount of $25,000.

While these purchases were making some of the sellers were heard to say, "that as soon as they had sold out to the mormons, and received their pay, they would drive them off, and keep both lands and money". The mob, when disbanded by the Generals in Daviess County as aforesaid, instead of repairing to their homes, as commanded, proceeded in a body to the adjoining County of Carroll and encamped around the mormon village, Dewitt. They sent to the County of Jackson and procured a piece of cannon and invested the village so closely, that no person could leave the town in safety. When they did so, they were fired upon by the mob. The Horses of the mormons were taken, their cattle and Hogs either killed or taken and driven away, and the citizens of the village amounting to about seventy families reduced to the greatest extremity by sickness and a want of the necessary supplies of food to support exhausted nature.

Thus situated, they applied to Governor Boggs for protection and relief: but neither protection nor relief came. Being thus abandoned to their fate by the Executive authority, no alternative was left them, but to seek protection by flight, and the abandonment of their houses and homes to the ravages of the mob. Accordingly on the evening of the 11th of October 1838 they invested families fled from Dewitt, and made their way to the counties of Daviess & Caldwell, leaving many of their effects behind them; in the possession of their besiegers.

Your memorialists will not undertake to draw a picture of the horrors and sufferings of that flight, when shared alike by women and children as well as men. Let a case or two suffice. One lady, who had given birth to an infant just before the flight commenced died on the road, and was buried without a coffin. Many others were sick, from starvation and fatigue, and being deprived of medical aid and sustenance, died upon the road. The remnant of this little band of sufferers arrived at in Daviess and Caldwell Counties at length, and found temporary relief from their troubles, among their friends and brethren in these counties; but it was of short duration. After the abandonment of Dewitt and the flight of the mormons from Carroll County, one Asahel Woods addressed the mob, and advised them to take their cannon and march to the County of Daviess and drive the mormons also from that County and seize upon their lands and property saying by way of encouragement; that "the mormons could get no benefit of the law, as they had recently seen that no attention had been paid to their applications for protection". They then commenced their march from Carroll to Daviess County with their cannon. On their way they seized two mormons, made them ride on the cannon, and taunted them as they went along with their threats, "that they were going to drive the mormons from Daviess to Caldwell, and from Caldwell to Hell; and that they should find no quarters but at the cannon's mouth". The mob at this time was reported to number about 400 strong. The mormons in their distresses, in pursuance of the laws of Missouri, made application to Judge King, the circuit Judge of that circuit, for protection; and for the aid of the officers of the law to protect the Magistracy in the performance of their duty. Judge King as they have been informed and believe made a requisition on Major General Atchison to call out the militia to protect the mormons against the mob. General Atchison thereupon issued orders to Brigadiers Parks & Donaphon. In pursuance of these orders issued on the 18th of October 1838 General Donaphan arrived at "Far West," a mormon village in the county of Caldwell, with a small detachment of militia. After he had been at "Far West" two days only, he disbanded his troops, alledging to the mormons as his reason for so doing, that his men had feelings in common with the mob; and that he could not rely upon them. In a short time afterwards, General Parks arrived at "Far West" and also disbanded his detachment. During this period the mob was marching slowly making its way, from Carroll to Daviess County. General Donaphan while at "Far West" directed the mormons to raise a company to protect themselves; telling them, that one Cornelius Gilliam was raising a mob to destroy their town; and advised them to place outguards to watch the movements of the mob. He also directed them to raise a company of mormons and send them to Daviess County to aid their brethren there, against the like depredations; as a mob was marching down upon them from Carroll County. This the mormons did. They had mustered a company of about sixty men who had proceeded to Diamon, when General Parks arrived at "Far West" as aforesaid. Having learned that General Donaphan had disbanded his men he (Gen Parks) expressed great diss-atisfaction that he should have done so. The evening on which General Parks disbanded his men as before related, he proceeded to Diamond in order to learn what the mob were doing; and if possible to protect the mormons. When General Parks arrived in Daviess County, he found that the mob had already commenced their work of destruction, which was on the 20th of October 1838. They commenced by burning the house of a man who had gone to Tennessee on business, and left his wife at home with two small children. When the house was burned down the wife sought refuge with her children in the hay-mow and had to walk three miles before she could find a shelter. She carried her two children all that distance and had to wade Grand River which was at the time, about three feet deep. The mob on the same evening burned seven other houses and destroyed all the mormon property that came in their way. The next morning Colonel Lyman Wight an officer of the militia, and a member of the mormon society, enquired of General Parks what was to be done, as he now saw the course the mob was determined to pursue. General Parks replied, that he (Wight) should take a company of men and if necessary give the mob battle, and that he would be responsible for the ~~act~~ consequences; saying, they would have no peace with the mob until they had given them a scourging.¶

On the next morning in obedience to this order David W. Patten, a mormon officer, was despatched with one hundred men under his command in the direction of the mob, which was advancing from Carroll county, with orders to protect the citizens from injury, and to collect and bring into "Far West" such of the mormons as were scattered through that part of the county; and that if the mob interfered to prevent the execution of his orders, he should fight them. The company under the command of Patten, was the same in part that had gone from "Far West" by the orders of Gen. Donaphon to protect the citizens of Daviess County. As Patten advanced in the direction of the mob, they retreated before him, leaving their cannon on the way, which fell into the hands of Patten and his men. The mob being thus dispersed, Patten returned with his ~~men~~ company to Daviess county; and in a few days afterwards came back to "Far West". It was now supposed that all difficulties were at an end, and that the mormons would be suffered to rest in peace. But contrary to this expectation, on the evening of the 23d of October messengers arrived at "Far West" and informed the ~~citizens~~ mormons that a body of armed men had made its appearance in the south part of the county; and that they were burning houses, destroying property, and threatening the mormons with death, "un__less they left the county the next morning by 10 oclock, or renounced their religion.__" About midnight another messenger came with news of like import. Patten again collected about sixty mormon men and proceeded to the scene of the disturbance, to protect, if possible, the lives and property of the mormons from the threatened destruction. On his arrival in the neighborhood, where the first ravage had been committed, he found that the mob had gone to another part of the county, and were continuing to perpetrate acts of plunder and outrage both against the persons and property of the mormons. He marched a short distance further, when he unexpectedly came upon the encampment of the mob. The sentinels of the mob instantly fired upon him and killed one of his men. They continued their fire until Patten ordered a charge, when, after a few fires the mob were dispersed and fled in all directions. But poor Patten was killed and one of his men also fell by his side to rise no more. After this fight and the dispersion of the mob, Patten's company again returned to "Far West" but without their leader. The report of these proceedings created much excitement; and the citizens, through false and exaggerated statements, were made to believe that the mormons were actually in rebellion against the laws of the country. So cruel and so unprovoked, had been the persecutions against them; and those entrusted with the power of the civil and military authority having failed to exercise either for their protection; the mormons saw no alternatives, but that which the laws of nature gave, of self defence; and so far, on this occasion, they exerted it. About this time, the Governor of the state, issued ~~an~~ the bloody order to General Clark to raise several thousand men, "<u>to march them against the mormons and drive them from the state, or</u> ~~to~~ <u>exterminate them</u>. Major General Lucas & Brigadier Genl. Wilson collected three or four thousand men, and with this formidable force, commenced their march against the mormons, and arrived at "Far West" without molestation, and without seeing an enemy on the way. In their rear marched Gen. Clark with the residue of the army. The mormons were taken by surprize, not having heard of these immense warlike preparations until the enemy was upon them. And so far from expecting an armed force acting under state authority against them, they still had hoped, that the Governor would in pity, send a sufficient force in time to protect their lives and property from the ravages of the mob. When this formidable army first made its appearance upon their borders, the mormons intent on peace sent a white flag several miles in advance of their village to meet them, to ascertain for what purpose so large an armed force was marching against them, and what the mormons were to expect under such appaling circumstances. They gave us no satisfactory answer, but continued their march without explanation upon our peaceful village. Immediately on their arrival at "Far West" a man came from their camp, bearing a white flag, and demanded the surrender of three persons from the mormons, before, as he said, "<u>they massacred the rest</u>." These persons refused to go. As soon as this messenger returned back to the camp with our answer, Gen. Donaphon immediately marched his whole Brigade upon our village in battle array. The mormons of "Far West" thereupon formed ~~a~~ their "forlorn hope" in line of battle immediately in front of Donaphon's army. Donaphon now perceiving that blows were to be received as well as given, and that the fight was ~~now~~ no longer, on one side only; first ordered a halt, and then commenced a hasty retreat. Fortunately night came on, and separated the parties without collision. On the next day towards evening, the Mormons were officially informed, that the Governor of the State had sent this immense force against them with positive orders, "<u>either to exterminate, or to drive them from the state</u>".

As soon as the mormons learned that this order had the sanction of the Governor of the state, and had been officially promulgated; they determined to make no further resistance in defence of their rights as citizens; but to submit themselves to the authorities of the state however tyrannical and unjust the exercise of such authority might be. The commanders of the missouri militia before "Far West" now sent a messenger into the town requesting an interview at their encampment with five of the principal persons among the mormons, pledging their honor for their safe return to their brethren, and families, on the following morning at eight oclock. This interview the mormons supposed was intended as an overture of peace; and as the pledge of a safe conduct was given; Lyman Wight, George W Robinson, Joseph Smith Junr., Parley Pratt, and Sidney Rigdon started for the Camp of the ~~Militia~~ besiegers. Before they arrived at the Camp of the Governor's Troops under this invitation, they were surrounded on all sides by the invading army; and by an order from Gen. Lucas placed under a strong guard and marched in triumph into camp, when they were told that they were "prisoners of war." A court martial was held that night, without a hearing on the part of the mormon delegates, and in the absence of all testimony, these men, who had thus trusted their lives to the honor of the Governor's officers, were condemned to be shot next morning. The execution of this bloody sentence was only prevented by the manly protest of Gen. Donaphon. He denounced the act as cold blooded murder, and immediately withdrew his Brigade from the scene, where this horrible outrage was to be perpetrated. This noble stand taken by General Donaphon arrested the murder of the prisoners. It is here worthy of remark, and we repeat it more in sorrow than in anger, that seventeen preachers of the Gospel were on this court marshal, and horrible to relate were in favor of this merciless sentence. The next morning, the Prisoners were marched under a strong guard to ~~the~~ Independence, the seat of Justice of Jackson County, where they were detained for a week or two, and then marched to Richmond where General Clark was encamped with his troops. Here a court of ~~inquiry~~ Examination was held before Judge King which continued from the 11th to the 28th of November; during which time, these five prisoners were confined in chains with about fifty other mormon prisoners taken at "Far West;" and were penned up in an open unfinished court House[.] In this mock court of inquiry the prisoners were deprived of all testimony, by an armed force stationed at the Court House; they being advised by their attorneys, not to attempt to bring any persons as witnesses in their behalf, as they would certainly be in danger of either losing their lives or of being immediately driven from the County. The proceeding was of course exparte, and no ~~testimony~~ witnesses examined except those against the~~m; and that of a most~~ prisoners; consisting of individuals much prejudiced ~~character~~ against the Mormons. ~~In this inquiry~~ During this investigation a great many questions were asked relative to our religious opinions. The conclusion of the examining court, was, to commit the prisoners once more to jail on a charge of treason against the state. They do not deem it necessary to detail their sufferings while in prison. The horrors of a gloomy dungeon for four long months, shut up in darkness; exposed to the want of every comfort; and for much of the time to the damp and chilling cold of winter, can better be imagined than described. In the following April the prisoners were brought out from their prison and ~~sent~~ ordered to the County of Daviess for trial. They were there formally indicted for Treason, and a change of venue awarded to Boon County. The prisoners were accordingly sent under an armed escort to the County of Boon; and while on their way suffered to escape; when they fled for safety to the state of Illinois. That they were purposely suffered to escape, cannot be questioned. The truth is, that many of their persecutors, of whom the Governor was most conspicuous at this time, had become ashamed of their conduct against the mormons, and resorted to this subterfuge, as the best means of getting out of the scrape, ~~and consequently~~ by giving the prisoners this opportunity to escape. In proof of this assertion, the prisoners have ever since been living publicly in the state of Illinois, on the border of Missouri; and the Executive of Missouri has as yet made no demand upon the Executive of Illinois for their surrender, as is his duty, if they are considered fugitives from justice. Can it be supposed that the people of Missouri would thus tamely submit to the commission of Treason against the State, by a portion of their citizens and make no effort to punish the guilty, when they were thus known to be living publicly in an adjoining sister state? Is not this ~~presumptive~~ fact evidence of the innocence of the Mormons, and of the guilt of their accusers and persecutors?

But to return to the military operations of Gen. Lucas before the town of "Far West;" we need only say, that the exterminating order of Governor Boggs was carried into full effect. Immediately after the above named individuals were taken and treated as prisoners of war; all the mormons in "Far West," above five hundred in number, surrendered up their arms to the invaders without further resistance. The mormons now fled in all directions; women and children marked their footsteps on the frozen ground with blood, it being dead of winter, as they fled from the state of misssouri and from the merciless hands of their pursuers. The order of the Governor admitted of no discretion, and all were driven from the State, who were not destroyed. Fifteen thousand souls, between the time of the sacking of "Far West" and the following spring, abandoned their homes, and their property, and fled in terror from the country. The mormons being thus broken up, and ruined; in want of every necessary of life; ~~and~~ with broken and bleeding hearts, sought refuge in the state of Illinois, where most of them now reside. Your memorialists will not trespass further upon your time, by the relation of individual cases of suffering and distress. They would fill volumes and many of the pages would be stained with the blood of innocent women and children. But what shall they say of the conduct of many of the Missouri Militia? Alas! What ~~should~~ can be said in extenuation, when humanity would shudder and hide herself in shame, if one half only of the House burnings, destruction of property, robbery, rapes, and murder, should be told? One instance only, will they mention, of the many trying scenes of blood and rapine that were then & there transacted. Two hundred of the Governor's militia came suddenly upon some mormon families emigrating to the state of Missouri, who had not yet reached the body of the society; and were encamped at Haun's Mill in Caldwell County. The mormons took refuge in an old log house which had been used as a blacksmith shop. On seeing the milita approach, they cried for quarter; but in vain! They were instantly fired upon, when eighteen of their number fell dead upon the spot. Their murderers then advanced & putting the muzzles of their guns between the logs, fired indiscriminately upon men and children—the living, dying & the dead. One little boy, whose father (Warren Smith) had just been killed, cried piteously to the militia to spare his life. The reply was "<u>kill him</u>," "<u>kill him</u>," (with an oath) "<u>he is the son of a damned mormon</u>." He was accordingly shot in the head and fell dead by the side of his father. Just before this little boy was shot, an old man by the name of McBride, a soldier of the revolution, hearing his cries for mercy, came up and begged them to spare his life. But instead of listening to his entreaties they hewed him to pieces with an old scythe. They then loaded themselves with plunder and departed from this appaling scene of blood and carnage.

Your memorialists have thus, in dis-charge of the duty confided to them by their Brethren, given a brief outline of the history of their wrongs and persecutions in Missouri. All which they can prove, and aver to be true.

The mormons have not provoked these outrages. They have not either as a body, or as individuals, knowingly violated the laws of Missouri, or of the United States. Their only offence consists in a difference in religious sentiment; and that they have sometimes; but rarely, resorted to the laws of self defence. The above statements will show, that the Mormons have on all occasions submitted to the laws of the land, and yielded obedience to its authority in every instance; and often at the hazard of both life and property. Whenever they have opposed resistance to the mob, it was only in self defence; and not even then without the authority and sanction of the officers of the law. And what are the wrongs of which they complain? The mormons numbering fifteen thousand souls have been driven from their homes in Missouri; property to the value of two millions of dollars has been taken from them or destroyed; some of their brethren have been murdered; some wounded and others beaten with stripes; the chastity of their wives and daughters inhumanly violated; all driven forth as wanderers, and many, very many, broken hearts and pennyless. The loss of property they do not so much deplore, as the mental and bodily sufferings to which they have been subjected; and thus far without redress. They are human beings, possessed of human feelings, and human sympathies. Their agony of soul for their suffering women and children was the bitterest drop in the cup of their sorrows. For these wrongs and sufferings, the mormons, as American citizens, ask; is there no redress? If so; how and where shall they seek and obtain it? The constitution, you are sworn to support, alike guarrantees to every citizen, the humblest in society, the enjoyment of life, liberty and property. It promises to all, religious freedom; the right to all, of worshipping Almighty God, beneath their own vine and fig tree, according to the dictates of their own consciences. It guarrantees alike, to all the citizens of the several states, the right to become citizens of any one of the states; and to enjoy upon their removal, all the rights and immunities of the citizens of the state of their adoption. Yet, of all these rights and immunities, the mormons have been deprived. They have, without a just cause; without the form of trial; been deprived of life, liberty, and property. They have been persecuted from place to place for their religious opinions. They have been driven from the State of Missouri at the point of the bayonet and treated worse than a foreign enemy; they have been beaten with stripes as slaves; and threatened with destruction if they should ever venture to return; Those, who should have protected them, have become their most relentless persecutors; and what are ~~they~~ the mormons to do? It is the theory of our Constitution and laws, that, for the violation of every legal right, there is provided a legal remedy. What then we would respectfully ask, is the remedy for these violations of right in the persons & property of the mormons? Shall they apply to the Legislature of the State of missouri for redress? They have done so. They have petitioned, and their petitions have been treated with silence and contempt. Shall they apply to the Federal Courts in missouri? They are not permitted to go there; and their juries would be made up of citizens of that state with all their prejudices against them; ~~And~~ But if they could apply to the courts of missouri; whom shall they sue? The final order for their ~~destruction~~ expulsion and extermination, it is true, was ~~granted~~ issued by the executive of the state; but is he amenable? and if so, is he not wholly irresponsible, so far as indemnity is concerned? Will not the great mass of our persecutors justify themselves under that order? For ourselves we see no redress, unless it be awarded by the Congress of the United States. And here we make our solemn, last appeal, as American citizens—as christians, and as men. To your decision, favorable or otherwise, we will submit; and if it should unfortunately be against us, we will return to our brethren in silence, and without a murmur;

in the full belief, if our grievances do not admit of remedy, that it is not the fault of your honourable Bodies, and that as christians it is our duty to bear them with patience; until the Great Disposer of all human events shall in his own good time remove us from these persecutions to that promised land, "where the wicked cease from troubling, and the weary are at rest"

And your memorialists as in duty bound will ever pray &c

Washington City January 27th A.D. 1840.   Joseph Smith Jr.
                                                          Sidney Rigdon
                                                          Elias Higbee

[*Not sworn.*]

Chapter 4

Individual Affidavits from the LDS Historical Department

A—F

ABBOT, Rufus

Illenois Quincy May th11 1839—
a bill of Damages a gains the State of Missorie in conciquence of the Goviners Exterminatin order—

first for ~~being Driven~~ moving in to the State	$100.00
for Being Driven from Jackson County	500.00
for Loss of propperty Destroyed By mobs and under Rated	1,200.00
for being Driven from the State and Being Broke up	400.00
	$2,200.00

I Certify the a bove a count to be Just and true a cording to the Best of m[y] Knowledg—

Rufus Abbot

[Sworn to before C. M. Woods, C.C.C., Adams Co., IL, 11 May 1839.]

ADAMS, Arza

Illinois Quincy June 1st 1839
A bill of damages and debt a gainst the State of Missouri in Concequence of the Governor refusing protection and his exterminating order

first Mooving into the state	$300.00
Being drivin from Dewit	200.00
Loss of property and time in the state	250.00

Mooving out of the state   250.00
                                                          $1,000.00

    I Certify that the above account is Just and true according to the best of my knowlege

                      Arza Adams

[Sworn to before C. M. Woods, C.C.C., Adams Co., IL, 1 Jun 1839.]

ALEXANDER, Randolph

    State of Missouri Dr. to damages

to mooving to sd. State distance 500 miles	$70.00
to loss of time Caused by Bogs's exterminating order 5 months	100.00
to being driven from the State	500.00
to loss in Cattle, hogs household and furnitur	50.00
to loss in land and town lots	900.00
[Total]	$1,770.00

    The above traspired in the years 1838, &, 1839

    I do hereby Certify that the above Account is Just and true to the best of my knowledege

                      Randolph Alexander

[Sworn to before C. M. Woods, C.C.C., Adams Co., IL, 11 May 1839.]

ALLEMAN, John

State of Illinois ADam County may the 24th AD 1839
    A Bill of damage against the state of missouri by me John Alleman

To moving from the state of Pennsylvania to the state of missouri with the intention of being asettler of said state	
to moving to said state with two waggons Expense	$150.00
to loss time	100.00
to moving from the state of missouri by the Exterminating orders of the govener of the state of missouri	100.00
	$350.00

                      John Alleman

[Sworn to before C. M. Woods, C.C.C., Adams Co., IL, 25 May 1839.]

ALLEN, Albern

In The years of Our Lord 1838 and 1839—
The State of Missouri To Albern Allen Dr—as follows (to wit)

To loss of time on the account of the Govenors Orders	
To leave the State	$150.00
" on account of the same in Land	600.00
" " " " in Stock	100.00
" " " " Beef and Pork	50.00
Farming utensils	20.00
Moving on the account of the Governors exterminating Orders	400.00
	$1,320.00

Albern Allen

[Sworn to before W. Laughlin, J.P., Adams Co., IL, 11 May 1839.]

ALLEN, Anna

May the 6 1839
Anna Alle left kirklen Ohio [·] are

1838 expensese to be mooved to Mo with 3 children	$100.00
Settled in davis county dreven from there to far west and lose of property	100.00
and then dreven out of the s[t]ate and expense	300.00
lose of time	50.00
	$550.00

I certify that the amount that is on the last acount on the other page $550 is just a cord ing to the best of my knolage

Anna Allen

[Sworn to before C. M. Woods, C.C.C., Adams Co., IL, 7 May 1839.]

ALLEN, Elihu

Illinois Quincy may 18th 1839
A bill of Damage a gainst the State of Missouri for Being Driven from the S[t]ate unlafully

123

first for mooveing in to the State	$400.00
for propperty Lost in the State	300.00
for mob Damage	200.00
for mooveing out of the State	100.00
	$1,000.00

I certify the a bove a count to Be Just and true a cording to the Best of my Knowledg

Elihu Allen

[Sworn to before C. M. Woods, C.C.C., Adams Co., IL, 18 May 1839.]

ALLEN, Joseph S.

Ilinois May th 9 1839

A Bill of my damages in Missourie in the Spring of 1834 I mouved into Clay Co and in the Summer of 1836 a mob arose and Compld our pople to leve the Co and they thretened my life I moved my famley to Colwell County I having to leve my house and improvements and shop and timber I Charge one hundred and fifty Dollers and in the Summer and fall of 1838 a mob arose and threatened Life and burnt Some houses and I had a house in Davis Co and timber in Colwell Co ~~of~~ for a house my ~~house~~ timber in Colwell Co ~~and~~ I charge thirty five Dollers and my house in Davis and Crop in Colwell I C[h]arge one hundred and twenty Dollers I was taken a prisner and my arms ~~and~~ taken from me and I was kept from my famley and buisness a week for my arms I C[h]arge thirty five Dollers and the order of the Govener was to drive us from the S[t]eate or kill us for imprisment and the loss of property and the expence of moveing being exposed to the inclemence of the wether I Charge two hindred Dollers

Joseph S Allen

I certify the a bove Charges to Be true and Just acording to the Best of my Knowledg

Joseph S Allen

[Sworn to before C. M. Woods, C.C.C., Adams Co., IL, 9 May 1839.]

ALLEN, Nelson

May the 14 1839

A Bill of losses by Being driven from the State of Missouri

For the loss on the sale of my land	$475.00

For the loss of five acres of corn	40.00
For the loss of time and exspence of moveing From missouri to illinois	40.00
For the loss of one cow 16 dollars one fat hog 9 dol	25.00
For the loss of one rifle 16 dollars one grindstone 1 dollars	17.00
By being depive of the use of my horse for three Months and a half which the mob took from me	12.00
	$609.00

N. B. This account is made For the years 1838 & 1839.

Nelson Allen

[Sworn to before W. Laughlin, J.P., Adams Co., IL, 14 May 1839.]

ALLEN, Rufus

This may Certify that I mooved from the State of New york in the year of 1838 and was driven out of the state of Missourie in 1839 by the governors Exterminatures orders for this I Charge the State of Missourie damages on Land & Crops & stolen property nameley one waggon & one gun to the amount of one hundred and fifty dolars & damages for tine and expence of mooveing out of the State of Missourie a distance of two hundred & seventy miles eighty dollars for the rigt of Citizenship two hundred dollars

Rufus Allen

I Certify that the above account is true according to the best of my Knolwledge

Rufus Allen

[Sworn to before C. M. Woods, C.C.C., Adams Co., IL, 7 May 1839.]

ALLRED, Reuben W.

May 1839

state of Missouri Dr to Reuben W Allred for driveing me from my house and home and destroing my property and my Citizenship and time and expences and sofourth and Whole a mount 600 Dollars

Reuben W Allred

125

I sertify that the Within statement to be true

Reuben W Allred

[Sworn to before C. M. Woods, C.C.C., Adams Co., IL, 6 May 1839.]

ALRED, Isac

Quincy Ill May 1839
    State of Missouri to Isaac Allred Sen Dr.

to the nesesity of removing from Clay to Calwell Co in consequence of the non protection of Law in said state During 1836	$ 600.00
to being deprived of my citisonship in said state by the non protection of Law and the Govners Exterminating order of 1838	1,000.00
to Loss on land	1,000.00
to Loss on Grain and Cost of removing from said State	200.00
to Exsposur of myself & family's heath	500.00
~~$3,800.00~~	$3,300.00

    I certify the a bove acount to Be Just and true a cording to the Best of my Knowledg

Isac Alred

[Sworn to before C. M. Woods, C.C.C., Adams Co., IL, 18 May 1839.]

ANNIS, John C.

    A Bill of damages done by A Ruth less Mob of Jackson County liberty and Colwell County in Eighteen hundred and 34,36,39 Damages done by mobs in layfeatte County Damage by driving out of layfeatte and loosing all my Crops and thretning lives three hundred Dollars Dr. And in Clay County 1836 Drove out of that County to Colwell Damages two hunded Dollars and from Colwell to illenois in Eighteen hundred thirty nine the Mobs drove of my Cattle and killed my hogs and forsed property from my family and Jeneral Clark drawd us up and thretned us with immediate death if we did not Sign a way all our property and lands and Evry thing that we had to pay the Expence of the war I had about four hundred acres of land and by the Mob I have had to Sacrifise it with my hous hold property in part and had to Suffer the Cold and hunger and fatigue And thretning of our lives and taking a way Armes and Equipments

three Rifles at Twenty dollars Each and three Swords at five dollars Each
and Sevn pistols 25 dollars and loss of property to the amount of four
thousand Dollars and Caused us Sickness and trouble

quincy Ilenois Apreel 9 1839   [*Subtotal*] $5,600.00

John C. Annis

loss of labour 5 years and loss of Caracter and Citizen Ship	5,000.00
for the Share of five years	500.00[1]
	$15,600.00

J C Annis

    I certify the within a count to Be Just and True a cording to the Best
of my Knowldg—

John C Annis

[*Sworn to before C. M. Woods, C.C.C., Adams Co., IL, 3 Jun 1839.*]

ARCHER, John

Mooved from Indianna to Clay County Missouri May ~~the~~ 1835, expence of mooing 25 dollars driven from Clay to Cldwell loss damages and expence of mooving	$100.00
loss and sacraffice of property	300.00
loss of 8 months time	160.00
expence and damages of mooving from Caldwell County Missouri	200.00
	$810.00

    I certify that the above to be a trew coppy acording to the best of my
knoledg

John Archer

[*Sworn to before C. M. Woods, C.C.C., Adams Co., IL, 6 May 1839.*]

AVERY, Daniel[2]

Lee County I.T. March the 5 1840

---

[1] The petitioner probably meant to write $5,000.00 here. On the back of the petition he
wrote a second chart and listed $5,000.00, not $500.00, as the charge for this item.

[2] Also found in *HC* 4:60–61 and in JH 5 Mar 1840.

I Daniel Avry Do here by Certify that the following Scenes transpired in the State of Missouri to my personal Knowledg

first in the year 1838 Some time in the fall I was cald on By the martial Law of the State of Missouri to aid and asist to Resque women and children from the hands of a mob from the waters of Grand River whos husbands and Fathers had ben Driven off we found the house invested By the mob Som of which was in the house thretnig the lives of the women and children if they did not Leave theire propperty and Efects ameditly and follow theire Husband, and father, one family Lost a child while in this Situation for the want of care the women being compeld By thes monsters to provide and cook theire food this company of mob was commanded by James welden

I allso Saw a bout Seventy familie Driven from Dewit by a mob command by Seshel Wood I helpt Bury one woman the first Knight whoo had ben confind in child Bed a Knight or two before and could not indure the Suffering. the next Sene I Saw I was peasibly traviling the road aman ~~was~~ By the Name of Patison Obanion was shot Dead at my feete we advaned alittel further when two men were Kild and Several wounded I after Learnd that this Gang of mobers was commanded By Samuel Bogart. in conciquence of Being persued out of the State By this laules mob I was not an Ey witness to the many thousand wicked acts commited By the Goveners Exterminating ~~order~~ malitia

Daniel Avery

[Sworn to before D. W. Kilbourn, J.P., Lee Co., IA, 21 Mar 1840.][3]

BABCOCK, Dolphus

Illenois Quincy May th14 1839

a bill of Damages against the State of Mysorie in Conciquence of the Govners Exterminating order—

first, for mooving to the State	$125.00
for propperty lost in the State	1,280.00
for leaving the State by mob	10.00
	$1,415.00

---

[3] The official and date are partially obscured by a torn page in the original, and so this information is conjectural.

I certify the above to be Just and true acording to the Best of my Knowledge

Dolphus Babcock

[Sworn to before C. M. Woods, C.C.C., Adams Co., IL, 14 May 1839.]

BADLAM, Alexander

Quincy ill Nov 2nd 1839

This is to Certify that in Consequence of the late diffeculty between the Church of Latter day Saints and a portion of the Inhabitants of the Upper part of the State of Missouri I have been Compelled to Leave the State of Missouri in a time and under circumstances as it Regarded Myself and family were the most Painful and afflicting Residing as I did in the County of Daviss at the time the Malitia Entered it and being obliged to Move to Caldwell County in a Severe Snow Storm Myself Sick and a part of My family also. driven from my home to Seek a Shelter among those who would not Suffer thier fellow beings to perish while they were able to afford Relief I had no team of my own as they had been sacrificed in the time of the Mob and Lost on the Parriries for the want of care which Could not be afforded on account of the Mob I feel that My Loss is very great because it was all I had If I Should Set the damage at the Sum of five hundred dollars I think it would be less than my Real Loss

Alexander Badlam

[Not sworn.]

BAGGS, Cinthia

May the 6 1839

Cinthia Baggs left Washington Illinois ~~and~~ April the 12 1836 Movd out May the 6 1839 She has 6 children

the expense for being mooveing to Mo	$50.00
i was driven from Clay to Calwell Count damage Sustained	500.00
Drereven from crooked rivr to far west 200.00 and then dreven from the State and Damage and expenses to Ill	400.00
	$1,150.00

i certify that the above is a trew statement acording to the best of my knowlage

Cinhiy **X** Baggs

[Sworn to before C. M. Woods, C.C.C., Adams Co., IL, 7 May 1839.]

BAGLEY, Eli

A bill of damages against the State of Missouri.

1837. For mooveing out and in the State of Mo.		$100.00
For the loss of property and labour		500.00
		$600.00

deprived of Citizenship in Caldwell County Mo. 1837 by a lawless Mob. and lost of all by an exterminating order of the Governor.

I do hereby Certify that the above bill of accompts are Correct according to the best of my knowledge.

Eli Bagley

[Sworn to before C. M. Woods, C.C.C., Adams Co., IL, 6 May 1839.]

BAKER, Jesse

Illenois Quincy May thll 1839
a bill of Damages Sustaned in the State of Missorie

for mooveing into the State	$100.00
fo propperty lost in the State	150.00
for mooveing out of the State and loss of propprety	500.00

I certify the a bove to Be Just and true a cording to the Best of my knowledg—

Jesse Baker

[Sworn to before C. M. Woods, C.C.C., Adams Co., IL, 11 May 1839.]

BALDWIN, Caleb

May 12, 1839 Caleb Baldwin VS The State of Missouri
In damagees from the time I left the State Ohio, in Mooveing to Missouri With my family into Jackson and thare Labouring and making

improvement and suffering Much violence by the Mob with Every A buse that Could be heaped uppon me and my family for which I file A bill of damage Against the State of Missouri for the sum of $2000.00

 2nd Being driven from Jackson County in to Clay County After trying to defend Ourselves Against Mobs, and some of Our Bretheren Kild. and others whiped All most to death we succeeded in getting a cross the Missouri river into Clay, where the people used us well for A time After which thay like other Mobs soon rose up to drive us from that place With Much Cruelty. and succeeded for which we suffered much loss and distress, for this I file abill for damages Against the State of Missouri for the amount of   200.00

 3rd for being taken prisioner and fals imprisionment for A time of six months or Nearly so and part of the time in Chains, without any Just Charges Being preferd Against me of Any Nature in the mean time my family driven out of the State in the Cold inclement Season to wander on the broad praraias threw the upper Missouri without proper Means and Suffering much fear because of the Lawles Mobers and deprived of their right of Citizenship for which I Clame damages to the
A mount of   10,000.00

 I certify the foregoing to be true According to the best of my understanding—

Caleb Baldwin

[*Sworn to before C. M. Woods, C.C.C., Adams Co., IL, 4 Jun 1839.*]

BALDWIN, Nathan B.

State of Illinois Morgan County SS
 This day Personally appeared before Me Horatio G. Rew an acting Justice of the Peace Within and for the Cunty of Morgan aforesaid Nathan B. Baldwin and on Oath Says he Belongs to the ~~Denomination or Order of Men Called Mormons~~ Church of Jesus Christ of Latter day Saints that was a resident of Davis County in the State of Missourie dureing the Late Dificulties between Missourians And ~~Mormons~~ latter Day Saints during the ~~Summer and~~ autumn of 1838 That dureing the dificulties aforesaid he Was arrestedby a body of armed Men Citizens of Missourie dureing a Serious Illness in consequence of Which he Was unable to protect or defend his person or Property from Which arrest he Was Soon released the Persons So arresting him violently Seizing upon and carraing away his arms of defence consisting of Two Rifle Gunns one of Which Said Deponant Says Was Worth Twenty Dollars and the other Ten Dollars and

that the Same or Either of them have not been returned to him Said Deponant. he Said Deponant further Sais that in the Early part of the month of November AD 1838 he together with all other ~~Mormons~~ latter Day Saint in Said County of Davis in the State of Missourie aforesaid Were Orderd by Brigadir Genl Willson by and With the consent and Sanction of the Executive of the State of Missourie to Leave the County of Davis Within the Limit of ten days there after in Which order they Were permitted to pass the then approching Winter in the County of Caldwell or to pass immediately out of the State of Missouri & further this deponant says that in consequence of the Preemptory orders aforesaid he was Compelled to depart from Said County of Davis Leaving a two Heorse Waggon Worth fifty Dollars and that he has not been permitted to return for or in anyway to come into possession of Said Waggon Since he further Says that he Sustained a Loss of One Hundred and Thirty Eight Days at a Value of Two Dollars pr day including Currant Expences for the time being and a further Loss of fifty dollars by Way of Expences and unavoidable Sacrefices on property on leaving the County of Davis and State of Missourie in obediance to the premptory orders aforesaid all of Which Losses So by him Sustained this deponant Says amount to the Sum of Four hundred and Six Dollars And further Said Deponant Says that the Authorities of the State of Missourie Neglect and refuse to Make reparation for Losses and Damages So Sustained as afore Said. Wherefore the Said Deponant Prays the Interposition of Congress to aid and assist him in obtaining redress of his Losses and Injuries Sustained as aforesaid all of Which is by Said Deponant Respectfully Submitted

Nathan B. Baldwin

[*Sworn to before H. G. Rew, J.P., Morgan Co., IL, 14 Jan 1840.*]

BALLARD, Philip

Quincy May the 5th 1839
    The state of Missouri Dr To Philip Ballard
    A Bill of damages viz

To Loss in sale of land	$65.00
To Loss of time by being thrown out of business	80.00
To sundry small losses and removal	60.00

    I do hereby Certify that the above bill of damage is just and true according to the best of my knowledge

Philip Ballard

[*Sworn to before C. M. Woods, C.C.C., Adams Co., IL, 6 May 1839.*]

BATES, Archibald

Illenois May the 7 1839

A bill of Damagees and loss against The State of missorie in consequence of the govorners orders

By being Driven from clay county and Also Deprived of live ing the platte Country one thousand dollars

And also Driven from Davis county Out of the State with the loss of an Improve ment worth two hundrd Dollars

one horse and two cows one thousand Dollars

I do here By certify that the a bove a count is true and Just a cording to the Best of my knowledge

Archibald Bates

[Sworn to before C. M. Woods, C.C.C., Adams Co., IL, 7 May 1839.]

BATSON, William

A bill of danages tha I hold against Missouri for moveing to Missouri, for being driven from Jackson Co. Mo. in the year 1833 for the loss of propety for the loss of Lands for the loss of health, for being driven from Clay Co. Mo. from my land for being drivin from Coldwell Co. Mo. from my Land and the loss of property and health and Sitizen Ship $10000.00

this May the 6th A.D. 1839   William Batson

I certify this to be a true copy of damages to the best of my knowledge

William Batson

[Sworn to before C. M. Woods, C.C.C., Adams Co., IL, 6 May 1839.]

BEEBE, Calvin

I do hearby Certify that in the year eighteen hundrd thirty one and in the Month of Septtember I removed to Jackson, County Misouri with my family I expended four hundred dollars in puchaseing wild lands for a residence in that County I built a dwelling house on what is calld the big Blue River I builded a Double house anhalf a Mile from indipendance the County ceat of said County Made a handsome improvement in the yeare eighteen hundred and thirty three I was driven from said County by Mob force leaving betwen thirty and forty hogs Much of My house hold furniture for want of opertunity to get it a way also two hundred Bushels

of Irish & Sweet potatoes togeather with turnip and other garden sauce
with Much Difficulty I Disposed of eight acres of Corn at less than half
price I removed a cross the Misouri River to Clay County I was admited
in to a stable or rather a hovel it being verry small and in the fall seasen
and coald I took aviolent Coald and feover ensued which confined me till
the next March and thus the sufferings of my self and family with sickness
Coald and hunger was more than I can Describe with my penn not being
pemited to return to that County I disposed of my lands their at perhaps
one tenth of the real value the buildings being Destroyd by fire and the fen
cing removed from the land and all the timber of value Caried away and
I Certify that two thousand dollars at least would be my loss in that County
by an un humane Mob with out envy Shadow of reason or Cause in the
Spring followin from my sickess I hired a small piece of ground which I
ocupied three seasons the latter part of this time I builded a house for a
dwelling on Congress land being Destitute of means to purchase Said land
at this time their was threatnings against the latter day Saints to which I
belonged Many abusively beat and their property Destroyd as the example
had been in Jackson County I still improved the place which I builded my
house on untill I was Compeld by force to leave that County my loss I
sustaned in that County I Certify at least to be five hundred dollars by
Mobs who held many Special offices from, that place I retreated to
Caldwell County with the rest of my friends except my Father who had
Suffered the loss of one thousand dollars I think payd out for lands
principally in Jacson Co he came to my house in Clay Co Sick and died
destitute of Comfertable Clothes I buried him in the wilderness in a day
of deep Trouble and sorrogh his faith in his relgeon was his Comfort to
his end after moving to Caldwell I had prosperity I remoed from that
County to Clinton Co agoining But their seemed to be Consideable warmth
against our people Settling in that County I therefore went to Davis County
and purchased a verry handsome improvement on the bank of grand River
it Contained twolog Buildings and ten acres in Cutivation the land not yet
in market I hired a good log house built on it which Cost me one hundred
and fifty dollars the house was finished for a store hous and filed with
goods or Merchantdise for which I received rent and in the fall of eighteen
hundred and thirty eight the store house was taken away by the Mob party
and the improvement ocupied by the same Caricters By force and this all
Justified by the athority of the and thus I lost my place which I certify was
five hundred dollars loss to me My place in Clinton County or farm
Contained one hundred and Seventy four acres of land with a small
improvement which Cost me eight hundred dollars I increased the improvement to forty acres and for the Second time I put out many frute trees
and black lo[ores] in the Month of oct eighteen hundred thirty eight their

came an army under the command ColonelNed Gillom they took up quarters on my farm they ware all mounted Riflemen with their faces painted black and red they would be a hegeous sight in a Civil Country I was made a prisner of war in my own house the Colonel Said to me I must go and help burn far west and Drive the shepticks from the Country or suffr the tared part of two days one knight and Consumed three acres of My Corn one stack of hay one fat Beef two hundred pounds of Cheese— Robed my bee house and chickens and he stated his orders was from Govener L Bogs and thus from my house to far west they proceded their March the next March following I was Notified to leave the State by Companes Detached for that purpose after a hard Strugle I Sold My place for two hundred dollars less than the first Cost I then left the State I now resid in the town of Montrose Le County Iowa Teritory and my loss by the last procedings of the mob of Misouri is two thousand dollars Making in all five thousand dollars and now not with standing all the Charges profered against the people caled the Mormans I can say for one that no Court of record will produce a stain a gainst my Carecter Oct 28 1839

Calvin Beebe

Territory of Iowa Lee County SS
Personally appeared before me D. W. Kilbourn a justice of the peace in For the County aforesaid Calvin Beebe who being duly sworn according to law deposeth and saith, that the statements within set forth are correct & true.

Calvin Beebe

[Sworn to before D. W. Kilbourn, J.P., Lee Co., IA, 28 Oct 1839.]

BEHUNIN, Isaac

Damiges which Isaac Behunin Receivd in lossing of property By the unlawful Acts of the Citizens of the State of Missourie total loss Seven hundred and Seventy five dollars $775.00

Quincy Illenois May the 31 1839
I here by certify that the above is a tru account according to the Best of my Reccollection

saac Behunin

[Sworn to before C. M. Woods, C.C.C., Adams Co., IL, 31 May 1839.]

BEHYMER, Jonethan

Illenois Quincy May the 20 1839
    a bill of Damage a gainst the State of Missouri for Being Driven from the State

first for mooving to the State	$200.00
for loss of propperty in the State	1,200.00
for mooveing from the State	50.00
	$1,450.00

    I Do crtify the abov to Be Just and true a cording to the Best of my knowldg

                                                            Jonethan Behymer

[*Sworn to before C. M. Woods, C.C.C., Adams Co., IL, 20 May 1839.*]

BENNER, Christiana

Illenois Quincy May 30th 1839
    A bill of Damages a gainst the state of Missourie for Being unlawfully Driven

first for mooveing to the State	$100.00
for property Lost in the State	5,000.00
for mooveing from the State	50.00

    My Husband was kiled at Hauns mill By a mob who Robed me of my Goods and land and have left me Destitute of a companion or means of Support
    I certify the a bove to Be true and Just acording to the Best of my knowledg

                                                            Christiana Benner

[*Sworn to before C. M. Woods, C.C.C., Adams Co., IL, 31 May 1839.*]

BENNER, Henry

State of Illinois adams County may the 24 AD 1839
    A Bill of damage against the state of missouri by Henry Benner

To moving from the state of Ohio to the state of missouri
    with the intention of being a Settler of said state

to moving to said state	$275.00
to loss on building mill in said state	100.00
to loss time and moving from said state in Consequence of the goveners exterminating Orders	175.00
	$550.00

Henry Benner

[Sworn to before C. M. Woods, C.C.C., Adams Co., IL, 25 May 1839.]

BENNET, David

The State of Missourie Dr. to David Bennet

For mooving from the State of Ohio to the State of Missourie in 1832	$150.00
for being driven from jackson County to Vanburun County in 1833	50.00
For being orderd from Vanburun I mooved back to jackson County in 1833	
for being driven from jackson County to Clay County in 1833. for the loss of twenty three acres of land with ten acres of Improvement and two houses Wheat and Corn & other articles to tedious to mention	700.00
to one Rifle	25.00
for being Shot and beat so that I have not got over it yet loss of health & time	5,000.00
For being driven from Clay County and State of Missourie to the State of Illenois in 1839	350.00
Total	$6,275.00

I do hereby Certify that the above accompt is a just and an accurate accompt according to the best of my knowledge May 17th 1839 Adams County Illenois

David Bennet

[Sworn to before C. M. Woods, C.C.C., Adams Co., IL, 18 May 1839.]

BERNELL, Jacinth

Quincy Illinois January 10th AD 1840

I Jacinth Brunell do hereby Certify that I was a resident of Caldwell County Missouri, and that I owned lands there, had made a comfortable dwelling, and was well fixed to live, But by the Exterminating Order of Govenor Boggs was Driven from my lands without Cause, and with out Compensation to my great loss, of property as wel as my Citizenship, Loss of goods house hold furniture 300 Dollars and in lands &C 339 Dollars making in all 639 Dollars all of which I have not recieved any Compensation for, and now appeal to the honerable Boddy of the United States for redress of my wrongs as it cannot be had in that state, and I certify the above to be a true statement of facts to the best of my Judgment

Jacinth **X** Bernell

[Sworn to before C. M. Woods, C.C.C., Adams Co., IL, 10 Jan 1840.]

BETT, Henry H.

May the 6 1839
   Henery H Bett Moved from Daler County Indiany Sept the 5 1837

to the expnse of mooveing and driving 11 head of cattle	$200.00
Settled in davis County lose of property by having to lave the county and one horse Stole and 3 head of sheap	500.00
then haveing to lave the State and the expense of mooveing with a wife and 9 children	800.00
to the lose of time and one yooke of cattle	300.00
acount	$1,800.00

   i Certify that the above acount to be trew acording to the best of my knolage

Henry H Bett

[Sworn to before C. M. Woods, C.C.C., Adams Co., IL, 6 May 1839.]

BIDWELL, Robert W.

May 21st 1839
   An account that I Robert W. Bidwell have a gainst the State of Missouri in consequence of Mobocracy

for moveing into the State of Missouri	$125.00
Damages sustained in the State of Do.	600.00

for moveing myself and family and others to Illenois from
Missouri   150.00

$875.00

    as it Respects my Sufferings they are Somewhat Similar to the Rest of those who had to Suffer in the State of Missouri therefore you are at Liberty to allow me what your honorable Body shall Deem to Be my Due

Robt. W Bidwell

    I Do Certify that the above is Just and true according to the Best of My Knowlege

Robt W Bidwell

[Sworn to before C. M. Woods, C.C.C., Adams Co., IL, 21 May 1839.]

BILLINGS, Titus

    A Brief a count of the suffering and loss of propperty of myself and Family by the people of upper Missouri—

    In the Spring of 1832 I started with my Family together with many others for the purpose of finding a permenent home together with other Settlers of that State—

    we moved from Kirtland Ohio we started from that place March th 24 & arived in Jackson Co Mo in May & settled on 34 Acres of Land within a half a mile of Independence I built a house & Barn which cost 200 Dollars & got my liveing mostly by teaming for the People of the County and always had a good understanding amongs them but in the Summer and fall of 1832 & knowing that many of my Bretheren was a comeing to this County & not haveing a chance for raiseing a crop that season I thought best to cut a quantity of [——] hay which ammounted to 24 tons Weight which was hauled 6 miles & was worth 5 Dollars per ton this hay was put into a large stack very long & put upon a farm belonging to Gov Boogs rented by Bishop Partrige and the Inhabitants of that place supposed the hay to belong to ~~Bishop Partridge~~ him this was set on fire and burnt to ashes between sundown & dark this was in Oct it was a year afterwards before I found out the Person that set it on fire there was a man by the name of James Allen asked me if I suspected who set it on fire I told him not he said he knew he was presant when it was done a man by the name of Franklin told him he was a going to commence driveing the Mormons that Evening & would commence by burning Partriges Haystack & wanted him to go & assist him this he said he would be gratified too when called upon and when called upon failed to appear and the act was thrown upon me which was 30 Dollars the next was driveing me from Jackson Co and burning my house and Barn & destoying my improvements with four Acres of Wheet we was driven from that Co in Nov. 1833—we went into Clay Co & there being so many of our People that we [had] to settle in places that was sickly my Family was all taken sick & were not able to help ourselves and lost one year. after liveing 3 seasons in Clay Co we were then compelled to leave that Co in the Spring of 1837—we then moved to Caldwell Co, there I entered 120—Acres of land fenced & broke 15 Acres built me a house which cost me one hundred Dollars besides another piece of land I bought containing 20 Acres of timber land which cost one hundred Dollars I also bought a village Lot which cost forty Dollars all which I have ben driven from together with my farming tools household furniture Provisions &c, &c,—and now driven from the State of Missouri with my Family amidts the blasts of a cold and chilling winter and that too by an unmer[*ci*]full mob after liveing in Missouri 7 years and never have had a writ served upon me not broken the law in one instance and now I say that these things have come upon ~~me~~ us on acount of the religion which we profess takeing all these things into consideration the loss of my Property cannot be less than two thousand Dollar

May the 23 1839   Titus Billings

[*Sworn to before C. M. Woods, C.C.C., Adams Co., IL, 24 May 1839.*]

BINGHAM, James R.

The State of Missouri Dr
    to James R Bingham for loss of property Sustained by him in Davies County Mo in the years 1838 & 1839

to Eighty acres of Land in ——— Township held by deed with Houses thereon	$800.00
these houses were burnt by the men under Command of Cornelius Gillam the fire applied by Robert Gillam	
to nine hundred bushels of Corn at 25 cts pr bu.	125.00
to one Stack of hay	20.00
to one Stack of Corn fodder	6.25
to one acre of Flax	20.00
to 2 ploughs	19.50
to 1 hoe $1.50 to three axes at $2.50 each	9.00
to 2 bee Stands at $3.00 each	6.00

to 2 pair of trace Chains at $3.00 pr pair	6.00
to 1 waggon $35.00 one ox 25.00	65.00
to 3 cows at $25.00 each	75.00
to 55 hogs at $3.00	165.00
Thirty buckskins at $1.00 each	30.00
to one Gun eight dollars	8.00
to one Do forty dollars	40.00
to loss of time ~~myself 7 months~~	
to loss of time myself and 3 sons and oxen and waggon	
7 months each	364.00
to one Sword	3.00
to Saddle bridle and bed cover	14.00

The State of Missouri Dr.

James R. Bingham for loss Sustained by the Mob in Jackson County Mo in 1833

to loss of time myself thre Sons Horses and waggon 7	
months each	364.00
to three hundred head of Hogs	600.00
to farm and crop	200.00
to to ~~geese~~ household funiture and farming utensils	50.00
to being deprived of citizensip in the State of Missouri	10,000.00

P.S we were Citizens in Said State twenty six years previous to Govenor Boggs order to leave the State

[*Sworn to before W. Oglesby, J.P., Adams Co., IL, 11 May 1839.*]

BIRD, Benjamin F.

The S[t]ate of Mosura Dr to Benjm F Bird

1838	To money and time Expende in moveing from	
	N Y State to mosura	$130.00
	to hors and wagon and harnes taken by the mob	
	returne after ten day	20.00
1839	Damag in the sail of 160 akers of Land	500.00
	To Damag and not haveing the Libertey that the	
	Laws of the Land garentee to Everey Sivelisd	
	Citiso[n] and being Driven ought of the State	
	by Mob	6,000.00

To Damag money Spent and time Lost in Moving
out of the State   100.00
                                                  $6,750.00

                                              Benjm F Bird

    I certify the a bove acount to Be Just and true a cording to the Best of my Knowldg

                                              Benjm F. Bird

[Sworn to before C. M. Woods, C.C.C., Adams Co., IL, 13 May 1839.]

BIRD, Phineas R.

1838	The State of Masura Dr To Phineas R Bird	
	To mooving in the state one hundred and twenty	$120.00
	To bilding one hous in Davis and drove out by the Mob and abusedby the mob	225.00
	To four hundred Dollars Cash lost by being Drove from Davis Countey	400.00
	To gun taken lock lost and gun damag	8.25
1839	To moving out of the sState and being deprived of living in the State of Masura	8,000.00
	To money Spent and time Lost in Moveing out of the State	100.00
		$8,853.25

Clayton May 11 AD 1839

[Sworn to before J. Douglas, J.P., Adams Co., IL, 11 May 1839.]

BIRDENO, Zebiah

Illenois adams county may 11th 1839
    my bill of Damage against State of missouri in 1838

to wit—for Right for Preemtio and improvement with crop of corn pottatoes turnips and other vegitables on the place two hundred Dollars	$200.00
three bee stand one plough tumb full of honey	21.00
Loss of hogs twenty Dollars	20.00
house hold furniture four Dollars	4.00

time Lost for one boy five months Sixty five Dol	65.00
traveling Expences six Dollars	6.00
total sum three hundred and Sixteen Dol	$316.00

Zebiah Birden[o]

[Sworn to before W. Oglesby, J.P., Adams Co., IL, 11 May 1839.]

BLACKMAN, Stephen

State of Missouri Dr. to Stephen Blackman

For damage and loss of property by burning and being driven from the State $150.00

For damage by loss of Sun there is no earthly consideration can compensate

Stephen Blackman

I certefy the within to be correct

May 6th 1839 Stephen Blackman

[Sworn to before C. M. Woods, C.C.C., Adams Co., IL, 6 May 1839.]

BLOOD, Roswell

Illenois Quincy May 14th 1839

A bill against State of Mo for being Driven Loss of propperty &c—

first for mooving in to th State	$25.00
for loss of propperty in the State in concequence of the mob	100.00
for mooveing from the State Loss of time and Expence	50.00
	$175.00

I certify the a bove a count to Be Just and true acording to the Best of my Knowledg

Roswell Blood

[Sworn to before C. M. Woods, C.C.C., Adams Co., IL, 15 May 1839.]

BOSLEY, Edmund

Illenois May 7th 1839
    a bill of Damages and Debt a guinst the State of Missouri Sustained in Conciquence of Goveners Exterminating order

first for mooving from Newyork State to Davisse County Mo Distance 12 Hundred mils family consiting 6 persons Charge	$300.00
money paid out for premption lands	300.00
improoveing and Crops on the ground left	500.00
from Davis to far West Driven	300.00
Sacrafis of propperty and being Driven from the Far West out of the State I charge	1,000.00
	$2,400.00

    I Do Hereby crtify that the a bove a count is Just and true a cording to the Best of my knowledg

                               Edmund Bosley

[*Sworn to before C. M. Woods, C.C.C., Adams Co., IL, 7 May 1839.*]

BRACE, Truman

April the 20 1839
    to the assemBly of states know ye by these presents that i Truman Brace have boare long & suferd much by the mobbers of mesoura for the which i think i am intitled to damage pertickulars first driven from Jackson county after being thretned with deth & weiglaid & shot at being under the necessaty of a lookout by knight & by day by the which my famaly which consisted of wife & six children suferd much by my absence through feer & for want of my assistance we ware not alloued to cross the river into clay the ferry being garded on the other sid nu[m]bers of us ware ableged to flee to the south & leve our crops for the mob
    whire we suferd cold & fategue in fine i wisht for dett but itt f[l]ed from me on my flight into the wilderness i found some eight o ten children belonging to our people wandring on the frozen porary with bair feet much bluddy tired out this is the begining of our suferings 5 ~~houses~~ [——] ~~bilded~~ & [——] ~~ableged to~~ [——] i have ben driven from clay County to colwell from colwell or from mesoura to ilenoy i have made [——] 5 houses on the account of the mob

two of them ware burnd by the mob i have made four fields from whil i have ben driven & am r[e]dust to the necessaty of working out by days for my support in my old age

i have lost by the mobbers of missoura two horses one steer one yo sheap two guns four pistoles much household furnature tgether with eigt years time for the which i have nothing to show & have not much but mi hands to help myself my children are gone & scatred from me by reson of the mobers of misoughry which otherwais mite have ben a consolation & of gret worth to me in my declining life. i have seen one bef meet devided into twelve parts that all mite have a shair i have seen eightteen mak a meel on two perary chickens with the ac[——] in of a small pone of bred together with a few frozen potatoes i could relate many potickelars which are of seris consideration but am about to leve the subJect lest it shold be in vain becaus of the hardness of the harte of this generation i will relate one pertickular that trancepired in Jackson county as i was crosing a small perary with a teem to hall some wood with an ax on my shoulder and a gad in my hand i was surrouned by forty eight men on hors back all well armed with rifles & pistels & knives forst from me the ox gad with the which gave me some forty or fifty blows then forst the ax from me & steping two three paces backword threw the ax aming at my head regardliss of [——] one felloue missing his ame indaingerd theis one lives ~~assist at~~ which in[r]aged the furry of the mobbers on the wich one on horsback riding behind me gave me a blow with his rifle on my head ara whide wap then prezented & they gave me 39 bloes as they say the like i would not unde[r]go for twice th some of one hundred thousand dollars for loss of reputation & damage Myself & famaly i demand one hundred thousad dollars of the state of masoura & am determd never to relinqish the clame nor give it up til paid or satisfaction given made otherwais

Truman Brace

In the revalutionary war my father Was ingaged fiting for liberty which is all that i clame according to the constitucion & that i am determid hace i am redust so that my tax is small but i am shure to havet to pay & little or much it goes to support you Judgee & law givers you miletary forces from which i demand protection so i remane a well wisher to my country my name is above riten

[Sworn to before C. M. Woods, C.C.C., Adams Co., IL, 13 (no month given) 1839.]

BROWN, Alanson

Illenois Quincy May 16th 1839
    a bill of Damage a gainst the State Of Missouri for Being Driven
from the State By a mob

first for mooving in to the state	$100.00
for loss of propperty in the state	500.00
for mooveing out of the state Loss of time Damag &c	500.00

    I certify the above acount to Be Just and true a cording to the Best
of my Knowleg—

Alanson Brown

[Sworn to before C. M. Woods, C.C.C., Adams Co., IL, 16 May 1839.]

BRUNSON, Seymour

    Seymour Brunsons Account against the State of Missouri
    For the loss of time and expences in mooving from the State of Ohio
to the State of Mo Caldwell County $200.00
    For the loss of time and property by the Mob an when driven from
the State and the unevoidable expences of mooving out of the State

500.00

    Expence of Sickness and nursing inconciquence of being driven in
the inclement Season   400.00

    with the doctors bill total amount $1,100.00

Seymour Brunson

    I certify the above account to be just and true according to the best
of my Knowledge

Seymour Brunson

[Sworn to before C. M. Woods, C.C.C., Adams Co., IL, 8 May 1839.]

BRUNSON, Seymour

    Account against the state of Missouri for actual survace rendered by
my Self and Company being Called uppon by judge King the Circuit judge.
to gow and rescue and bring the three following named families from the

mob whoo had without cause or provication driven there husbands from
home and threatned there lives if they returned   Asael A. Lathrops
                                                         Phineas Youngs
                                                      and A. W. Jacksons

   upon this expedition I was gon 12 days inconcequence of the moove-
ments of the mob which rendered it impracticalele to return Sooner for the
Safety of anomber of family depended uppon our Staying a few days at a
little place Called Adam Ondi aman nomber of privats 35 all mounted men
wages one dollar and fifty cents perday and fifty cents perday for expences
                                                                    $240.00
   three baggage waggons to moove the families with with thre drivers
and teems three dollars per day   108.00
   and allso for the arms and aquipments of my Company whoo ware
Called uppon to Stand as minute men for the term of 3 year to defend the
State in unison with others from Savage barbarity Called out by the order
of Lilburn W Boggs and dis armed by his exterminating order without
acquasition or notification number of Rifles guns 50 worth 20 dollars a
piece   1,000.00
   and one hundred pistils worth twelve dollars a pair   1,200.00
   sixty two swords worth Six dollars a piece   372.00
   General Lucus was the Executive officer of the Exterminating order
of the Governer and Succeeded by General Clark
total amount $3,020.00

                                                      Seymour Brunson
                                                Captain of the 2nd Company
                                                59 Reg 2nd Brig 3rd division
                                                      Missoure Malittia

   I certify the above account to just and true according to the best of
my Knowledge
                                                      Seymour Brunson
                                                            Captain

[*Sworn to before C. M. Woods, C.C.C., Adams Co., IL, 8 May 1839.*]

BURGES, William

   Damages Sustained on Account of Being Driven from the State of
Mosouria Deprivation of Citazenship in the State &c

expenses of Moving into the State $125.00

Damages Sustaing in the State	600.00
Expences of moving out of the State	100.00
	$825.00

William Burges

[Sworn to before C. M. Woods, C.C.C., Adams Co., IL, 23 May 1839.]

BURGESS, Harrison

The State of Missouri indebted to me for a loss of Property & damage sustained under the exterminating order of Governor Boggs of Missouri as follows—

One Village Lot worth one hundred dollars One house on said lot worth one hundred dollars also a Location of Land which cost me sixty dollars expense and damage of moving from Davies to Caldwell Co with my wife who was then at the point of death three hundred dollars

Expense and damage of being forcd to flee from Caldwell Co. Mo. to the State of Illinois and also of seeking a home among strangers two hundred dollars

N B The above grievances & afflictions I would not have suffered for the sum of two thousand dollars

Harrison Burgess

[Sworn to before D. B. Bush, J.P., Pike Co., IL, 18 May 1839.]

BURK, John M.[4]

I here by Certify that General John Clark and his aid at their arrival at far West in Caldwell Co Misorie came to my Tavern stand and without my Liave Pitched their Markees in my yard and did take my wood and hay to furnish the same and did bring their horses in also and without my Leave take hay for them and did take Posession of my house and use it for a council house and did place a strong around it so as to hinder any person from going in or out and I myself was not premited to go in and for all this have received no remuneration and was not even permited to pass out of town to water Travelers horses with out a permit the above took place in the first part of Nov 1838 I also Certify that Caleb Baldwin, Lyman Wight,

---

[4] Also found in *HC* 4:56 and in JH 6 Jan 1840.

Hyrum Smith, Joseph Smith Jun., and Mr. Mcray in Clay Co. Mo did apply for a writ of Habeus corpus and Did not get it

John M. Burk

[*Sworn to before D. W. Kilbourn, J.P., Lee Co., IA, 6 Jan 1840.*]

BURKET, George

The State of Mosura Dr to 1839 George Bergat
May 9th to damage for driving me from Jackson co and Not having the privelage of possesing his house But was drivin out by the force of arms therefore

I charge the State of Mosura the amount of	$1,000.00
also for loss of Wheat and corn	200.00
also for loss of potatoes and flax and Hogs	300.00
also for loss of time and money Expended in moving out of the county	350.00
also for driving myself and famieley from my Home in Caldwell Co by the force of arms Contrary to law	1,500.00
To money paid for land	900.00
for time, cost and money Expended in moving out of the State contrary to law	500.00
for loss of corn and Wheat and potatoes and household furniture and farming utensals	500.00
To one gun and Sword and pestales	50.00
	$5,300.00

George Burket

[*Sworn to before C. M. Woods, C.C.C., Adams Co., IL, 13 May 1839.*]

BUTLER, Charity

A bill of damages Sustained by the Misourians in beeing driven from sd. state in the year 1838 & 9
this 14th May 1839
State of Mo dr to Charity Butler

to thre acrs of corn & two acrs of Oats	$60.00
to seven hundred bundles of corn fodder	7.00

to hay sheep and other articles	100.00
Expences of Mooveing Privations &c	2,000.00

I certify the above to be true

Charity Butler

[*Sworn to before C. M. Woods, C.C.C., Adams Co., IL, 13 May 1839.*]

BUTLER, J. L.

State of Mo Dr To J. L. Butler fo[rm] Damages & losses By being driven from sd state

expences Mooveing to Mo	$50.00
~~loss on land Mooving & being driven from state~~	
240 acrs land	2,400.00
to 3 yoke of oxen	225.00
crop of corn in Davies Co foder and hogs, s[ack] of Millstones	200.00
for plow & other farming tools	40.00
for mooveing from Mo to Ill	20.00
exposure of health of family	10,000.00
Defamation of Caracter & for citizenship	10,000.00

I certify the above to be true This the 6th May 1839

J L Butler

[*Sworn to before C. M. Woods, C.C.C., Adams Co., IL, 6 May 1839.*]

BUTLER, Ormond

By this it may be under Stood that I the under Signer was driven from Jackson County five years ago last November, with my famaly with out Shelter my house burnt my corn and other crops Destroyed and my Cows taken by the mob and never got them I have had no abiding place cince and now from Colwell County from my land from my house and home by a lawles mob, our travels our sufferings them may tell that has tried it five years and upward I therefoer State my damage at two thousan Dollar

Adams County Ellenoys april the 16th 1839   Ormond Butler

I certify the with in to Be true and Just acording to th Best of my knowledg

Ormond Butler

[*Sworn to before C. M. Woods, C.C.C., Adams Co., IL, 17 May 1839.*]

BUTTERFIELD, Josiah

State of Mo. Dr. to Josiah Butterfield

To expences of journey & time in moveing from Ohio to Mo. in the summer of 1838	$200.00
Loss of time while in the State of Mo. six months at 35 dollars per month	210.00
To Loss of horse & waggon taken by the mob & malitia	100.00
To one musket taken by the malitia in Daviss Co.	8.00
To loss of furniture at Richmond landing	16.00
For being driven out of Daviss Co. in the month of November and being thereby exposed to the inclemency of the weather which has caused the sickness of my wife during the winter from which She has not yet recovered	1,000.00
For being driven out of the State of Mo. by the authorities there of & being deprived of citizenship	2,000.00
To loss on a Note due me in consequence of being driven out of the State of Mo.	240.00
	$3,774.00

I hereby certify that the above account is true and just according to the best of my knowledge

Quincy Ill. May 7th 1839   Josiah Butterfield

In addition to the above I was taken prisner from my dwelling without any cause & shamefuly treated by the malitia in Daviss Co. Mo.

[*Sworn to before C. M. Woods, C.C.C., Adams Co., IL, 10 May 1839.*]

CAHOON, Reynolds

Quincy May 6th 1839

I Reynalds Cahoon do Certify to the following Losses Vis 1stly the loss of 12 acres of Corn distroyed by the throwing down of my enclosures

& turned in Cattle and hogs into it and destroyed the Same & threatened the life of any man that Should attempt to come near to Save it Also being deprived of a block Building made for the yuse & Benefit of My family Valued at $200.00
the Loss of Furnature & Clothing &c   50.00
1 Rifle 1 Shot gun   15.00
the above named Corn is considered to be worth   120.00

On or about the 8th of November 1838 I was Called upon by GEneral Parks of Richmond Ray Co to Call the people together Comonly called Mormons or Latter day Saints to come together with their guns Also Recd orders from Brigadir General Wilson I complied with his request We were paraded in Military order then General Wilson told us we were prisioners of War and must give up our guns and leave the County in ten days, Also leave the State in the Course of the Winter General Wilson took from us 143 guns besides Several Swords & pistols and after they got our guns there was a Company under the Command of Gillham Commenced plundering and ~~took~~ takeing horses also taking Store goods as neer as I relect 200$ worth & 50 horses Not withstanding many was fastened with Staples & Locks to trees by the help of pries and &c they Loosed them

Reynolds Cahoon

[*Not sworn.*]

CAHOON, William F.[5]

I hereby Certify That in the year of 1838 I was Residing in Davis County Missouri and while from home I was taken Prisoner in Far West by the Millitia and kept under gard for Six or Eight days in which time I was fourst to Sign a deed of trust after which time I was permitted to return home to my Family in Davis County and finding my Family Surounded by an Armed fource with the rest of My Nabours who was much frightened and the orders from the Millitia was to leave the County within ten days in which time my house was broken open & maney goods taken out by the Millitia—And we was not permitted to go from place to place without a pass from the gineruel an on leaving the County I received a pass as follows—I permit Wm. F Cahoone To pass from Davice to Colwell County & there remaine During the winter and thence to pass out of the State of Missouri Sign Nov 10th 1838 Reeves or Brig Ginral in which time both me and my family Suffred much on account of Could & hunger

---

[5] Also found in *HC* 4:52–53 and in JH 8 Jan 1840.

because we was not permitted to go out Side of the Guard to obtain wood and provision and according to orders of the millitia in the Spring following I took my family & left the State with the loss of much propperty and trouble

Wm. F Cahoon

[Sworn to before D. W. Kilbourn, J.P., Lee Co., IA, 3 Jan 1840.]

CALKINS, Lemira

A Bill of damages that I have Sustained by the inhabitants of the State of Missoura by being driven from my home and my property destroyed by a mob I was residing in the territory North of Clinton. uppon a place which I had bought the preemtion a Rite of a quarter Section of land there being on the Same a good log house a Stable Corn Crib and about Seven Acres under improvement I had a good Crop of Corn and potatoes and other vegetables of which I never received but litle benifit when I left home I went to bury a little Grand Child a bout forty miles not knowing there was any trouble the Same day we buryed the Child the Mob Got my waggon and I Could not return home this was on the 23 of October and was never able to go back till the middle of December and then found my house Robbed and plundered of every thing

Some of my Neighbors Gave up what few articles they had taken but the most part I never Could find which I Shall Charge the moderate Sum of forty dollars I was threatened to be mobed out of the place while trying to find my lost Goods by William Martin one Green and Clayton Robinson. for my Corn potatoes garden Sauce hemp one hundred dollars

for being driven from my home[6] and what I have had to Suffer by the Same In Cold in Storms with frozen feet and all the privation I have had to undergo and Still do and will have to for the want of a home one thosand dollars is but a Small Compensation but that is the least I Can Charge for personal abuse Received from William Martin and his wife the Said Green Clayton Robinson and Jeremiah Prior and his wife one thousand dollars and if I Could be placed back again with the Same prospect as before I Could not be hired for the Sum of ten thousand dollars [to] under go the Same Change

Lemira Calkins
A widow

---

[6]Written in the margin of this petition is the following: "I Lived on Grand River at the three forks LC"

I Certify the above Bill to be a Just estimate of damages as far as I am able to give it acording to the Best of my Judgement and abilites

Lemira Calkins

[Sworn to before C. M. Woods, C.C.C., Adams Co., IL, 8 May 1839.]

CALKINS, Lucy

May 7th 1839
A bill of damag & losses
drove from jackson County in 1833 insulted & abused & having to flee into the wilderness by the threats of unresoneble men
also having to leave Clay County under the same prinsipals
$500.00
and last of all dispeld from the state and deprived of all privileges leaveing house & home & having to infer the inconveinences of moveing in the inclemmon season of the year

house and lot in far west	900.00
Wood land one hundred dolars	100.00
plow land	50.00
damage of mooveing and leaveing housess furniture for which I have to suffer for the want of the same	500.00

I certify that the a bov acount is Just and true acording to the best of my Knowledg

Lucy Calkins

[Sworn to before C. M. Woods, C.C.C., Adams Co., IL, 7 May 1839.]

CARN, Daniel

Adams County Illinois May 4th 1839
A bill of Damages against the State of Missouri in the year 1837. I with my famley Moved to that State and Expended $75 Dollars and paid for Land $540 Dollars and then paid $58 Dollars for improveingit besides my own Labour and allso paid $540 Dollars for for houses and Lots $1015 Dollars in Cash and Received on the hole $130 Dollars and also Lost on house furnature $300 Dollars and then hade to Leave all my Liveing and Came away all most with out aney thing I also was falseley imprecent for the Space of 24 Days and treated verry Mean for which I Shall Charge $500 Dollars
for which the hole amount of my bill is $2810 Dollars

I Certify the above to be Just and true

Daniel Carn

[Sworn to before C. M. Woods, C.C.C., Adams Co., IL, 18 May 1839.]

CARROLL, James

May 13th 1839

An account that I James Carroll have against the state of Missouri in Consequence of Mobocracy

Expence of Money going to Masouri	$24.00
Expence of Time 5 weeks going to Misouri at one Dollar pr Day	30.00
To Loss of Waggon on the Road going to Missoure	25.00
To the Loss of Two Mares in the state of Missouri	100.00
To Money Cheated out of by Different persons in the State of Missouri	40.00
To expence of Moveing from Caldwell to Ray Co	2.00
To Expence of Moveing from Ray to Clay County	4.00
To Expence of Moveing from Clay to Caldwell Co	5.00
To Six months Lost time in Missouri on the account of the Rageing of the Mob at thirty Dollars pr Month	180.00
To Expence of Moveing from caldwell to the State of Illinois	10.00
	$420.00

As to the Sufferings of myself and family through The Means of Mobocracy it is out of My power to Relate and therefore I Cannot tell what amount I had ought to have but will Leave your honorable Body to Judge when I Relate that we were forced from our homes to Remain in an open frame in the Cold weather when the Snow fell in torrents and would Blow upon us in the Night and we with our Little ones would have to Crawl out of our Beds while the were Coverd frequently with Snow that would blow in to the prarrie from the north and we had to endure it while the Cruel hearted Mob at Beholding our situation would Laugh and Desired in there hearts to put an end to our Existance therefore I Leave it with yow to Decide what I should have or whether I should have any thing or not

James Carrolle

The State of Illinois Hancock County
Personally appeared before the subscriber an acting Justice of the peace in and for said County the within named James Carroll and deposeth and saith that the withon account is Just and true.

James Carroll

[*Sworn to before A. Smith, J.P., Hancock Co., IL, 14 May 1839.*]

CARSON, George

Illenois Quincy may the 20 183[9]
a bill of Damages a gainst the State of Missouri for Being Driven from the State By a mob—

first for mooveing in to the State	$150.00
for propperty Lost in the State	200.00
for leaving the State and Loss of propprty	1000.00
	$1350.00

I certify the a bove a count to Be Just and true a cording to the Best of my Knowledg

George Carson

[*Sworn to before C. M. Woods, C.C.C., Adams Co., IL, 18 May 1839.*]

CARTER, Simeon[7]

I Simeon Carter Certify that I have been a resident of the State of Mesouri for Six years & upwards & that I have Suferd many things bye a Lawles mob both me & my family having been Driven from place to place & Sufferd the loss of much propity & finally our expultion out of the State, I further Certify that I belong to the Church of the Latter day Saints Commonly Cauled Mormons. & I Certify that in the year Eighteen hundred & thirty Eight both me & my People Sufferd much bye the People of the State of Mesouri. & I further Certify that in this Same year in the month of ~~October~~ November between the first & Six ware Sorounded bye a Soalgery of the State of Mesouri in the city of Farwest in Caldweel Co. M.S. both me & manny of my Mormon Brethren & ware Compeled bye this Solgerry which ware armed with all the implements of war to Shed blood bye a publick Declaration of an entire extermination to Sign a way

---

[7] Also found in *HC* 4:49–50 and in JH 2 Jan 1840.

our all our propity personal & real Estate & to leave the State of Mo. immediately I Certify I had at that time one hundred & Sixty two acres of Land, the Same which I held the Certificates for. I further Certify that I was oblged to give up my Duplicates to help me to a Small Some to Carry me out of the State I further Certify not

Simeon Carter

[*Sworn to before D. W. Kilbourn, J.P., Lee Co., IA, 2 Jan 1840.*]

CARY, Nancy

Quncy May 6 1839 Illenois
a List of Damages and propperty Lost By being Driven from the State of Missorie

in mooving from Kirtland Ohio to the Missorie to Far West three months Journing Spent fifty Dollars in foure weeks from the time we arived at far west my Husband was taken prisinor by the army cald out for the purpos of puting in to Exicution the Goviners exterminating order I think there were twenty five Hundred of this Hellish cruel Band when a man By the Name of ———Donihue Struck him with the britch of his gun and broke his Skull he lived two Days which time he was Deprived of ade or comfort from me or any other person

one Hors taken by this hellish cruel band	$65.00
thre Rifles valid	60.00
for mecanical tools Sundra articls of Hous Hold and farmin impliments	100.00
for Expences of leaving the State	50.00

the loss of my companion Deprivation of CitizenShip there is no Earthly Concderaton will Satisfy me

Nancy Cary

[*Sworn to before C. M. Woods, C.C.C., Adams Co., IL, 6 May 1839.*]

CASE, Francis C.

Quincy Illinois May the 16th 1839
damages due to Francis Case in concequence of of the exterminateing order of the State of Missouri Govener Boggs which is twelve hundred and fifty dollars

I here by certify that the above is a true account according to the best of my recollection

Francis C. Case

[Sworn to before C. M. Woods, C.C.C., Adams Co., IL, 16 May 1839.]

CASPER, Thomas D.[8]

Quincy Illinois March 16, 1840
This is to certify that I Thomas D. Casper was a resident of the State of Missouri the year 1838, I was not a member of the Church of Morrmons or Latter day Saints But witnessed the following acts of distress as I was on business I enquired for Perry Moppin and learned that he with Samuel Snowden Esqr. had gone after Mr Willson a Mormon and had threatened and sworn to take his life if he did not tell his name and they swore they had the tools to take his life if he had not told them his name further they agreed that the Mormons should leave the Country of Missouri except they would deny the faith or their religion And I heard Anthony Mc Custion say that he would head a mob in any caase to prevent the Lawyers from attending to any case of their the Mormons aggreivences and he was a Postmaster and I saw saw two men that said they had been at Houns Mill at the Murder and one by the name of Wilhite and the other Moppin stated that he had slain three Mormons and I—Thomas D. Casper witnessed other things too tedious to mention and Solomly Swear before God and men that what is here written is a true statement of facts relative to the suffering of the mormons in the State of Missouri

Thomas D Casper

[Sworn to before W. Tainter, who signed for C. M. Woods, C.C.C., Adams Co., IL, 16 Mar 1840.]

CATHCART, Daniel

State of Missouri Dr To Daniel Cathcart

For damages Sustaind by loss of propperty in Davis Co
by being driven from the state $200.00
Sickness by exposure   500.00

Daniel Cathcart

---

[8] Also found in *HC* 4:63–64 and in JH 16 Mar 1840.

I certify the within to be correct

May 6th 1839   Daniel Cathcart

[*Sworn to before C. M. Woods, C.C.C., Adams Co., IL, 6 May 1839.*]

CHAMBERLIN, Solomon

State of Missouri Dr to Solomon Chamberlin

1833   I was driven from Jackson Co Mo with the loss
           of my inheritence and left my crops on the
           ground two houses burned and the loss of
           some cattle I was there between 2 and 3 years
           and the loss that I susstaind I should Say was
           not less than $2,000.00
       we were in clay between 2 and 3 years we was
           driven or rejected from Clay Co I lost 3 houses
           and my improvement and the loss that I
           sustained there I should say was not less than   400.00
       I was one of the first that setled at farwest I
           owned a house and lot in far west and 5 miles
           north of there I owned a timber lot and had a
           deed ofit and had it under fence and a good
           large hewed house and other buildings about
           40 miles north west of far west I had another
           place and was living on it at the time the
           troubles Commenced we had I suppose 8
           hundred bushels of corn on the ground and a
           barn full of other things accordingly of whict I
           never got so mitch as [——] a horse feed
       here I was robed of all most all my house hold
           furniture and all my farming eutentials the mob
           took possession of my house and crops a bout
           this time the troops came from far west to
           Diamon and 2 or 3 days before their arrival we
           went in to Diamon and the night we surrenderd
           the mob stole 2 [——] elegant mares and one
           very valuable mule from me 7 miles north of
           the before mentioned place I held a clame on
           one mile I was one of the first t square and
           built a house on it for all the before

mentioned houses lands crops etc I receivd
but $25 to this day I shoud think that all these
losses would not be less than   13,000.00

the loss of ~~my~~ Some of my blood that [———] was shed by the mob I have not reckened

Solomon Chamberlin

[*Not sworn.*]

CHAMPLIN, William L.

May the 9th 1839 Illenois Quinsey
An account against the State of Missouri for debt and damage Sustained in Consequence of the Exterminating Order

damage and removal	$75.00
Loss of Property	30.00
	$105.00

I Certify the above account to be Just and true according to the best of my Knowledge

Wm L Champlin

[*Sworn to before C. M. Woods, C.C.C., Adams Co., IL, 9 May 1839.*]

CHAPMAN, Isaac B.

May the 9 1839
I Isaac B Chapman Make acharge against the state of the missouri

1 for mooveing to the missouri and time and mony	$100.00
2 [———] the loss of property one house and lot and field of corn	100.50
Loss of time being under arms in my own defence and mooveing out of the state	200.00
Damage and suffereges being driven from my house and holme to suff[er] the cold and pierceing winter	1,000.00
Deprived of Citse Ship	3,000.00
~~Total~~	
the amount	$4,400.50

Isaac B. Chapman

I hearby sertify the above acount to be correct acording to the best of my Knoledg

Isaac B. Chapman

[Sworn to before C. M. Woods, C.C.C., Adams Co., IL, 10 May 1839.]

CHASE, Darwin

The State of Missouri To Darwin Chase Dr

Daniges in hogs & Sheep	$40.00
being Driven from Jackson County and loss of property	100.00
for abuse being clubed in the highway by Mr. ~~Crocket~~	
Cockrel	100.00
loss on lands in Clay County	200.00
loss of time	50.00
loss in lands & town property in Caldwell County	500.00
loss of time untill imprisiond	50.00
then for false imprisionment & being detaind in jail five months & 24 dayes in Ray County one half of the time in the dungeon	585.00
for being driven out of the State contrary to law ecquaty Justice & the Constitution of the United States	1,000.00
	$2,625.00

I hereby certify the above to be a true coppy of my Dameges & losses Sustaind in the State of Mo.

Quiny Ill May the 7th 1839   Darwin Chase

[Sworn to before C. M. Woods, C.C.C., Adams Co., IL, 7 May 1839.]

CHASE, Eli

A Bill Ill. Feb 27th 1839

of loss & dameges which I sustained[.] after locating my self in Jackson Co. Mo. April 6th 1832 with many others of my friends after wearing out an unwholsom life of about Twenty months[.] after receiveing many abuses threatnings & persecutions by the citizens of said Co. on account of our Religion. In 1833 I was under the necessity of leaving the Co. not knowing where to go you may depend we had to scatter in haste[.] a distresed time indeed I in Co with several others (as it was the shortest cut out of the Co) made our way to South Grand Riv. in Vanburen Co.

immediately after building Cabins we Received orders to leave that Co. forth with we went to Clay Co. I lived there about two years from thence was driven to the waters of Grand Riv. North. after living there two years I had to leave the State. as equal Rights cannot be had in Mo. as there is no Law for us in Mo.

I appeal to the General Goverment for redress sum it all up together agrievences with loss & damages I sustained in being driven unlawfully by the people of Mo. from place to place for the seven last years agreeable to my calculation would amount to no less than twenty thousand dollars

I therefore Claim the same to be my right And petition for the same at the feet of the President

Yours with Res.
Eli Chase

[*Not sworn.*]

CHASE, Eli

The State of Mo. to Eli Chase Dr

damages in loss of & use of property & time in being driven from Jackson Co.	$1,000.00
Do. being driven from Clay Co.	500.00
Do. Being driven from Caldwell Co. loss of land and property &c &c	2,000.00
Do. Being wounded hunted threatend persecuted driven out of the state	500.00

I hereby certify the above to be a true copy to the best of my Knowledge

Quincy Ills May 15th 1839   Eli Chase

[*Sworn to before C. M. Woods, C.C.C., Adams Co., IL, 16 May 1839.*]

CHASE, Stephen

My loss and Damages which I Consider I Sustained in Consequence of my Religion. being Persicuted and Driven by a Ruthless mob in Jackson Co. Mo. and in Clay Co. likewise also in Coldwell Co. &c. &c. is at the least calculation Twenty five thousand Dollars Given under my hand in

Adams Co. Ill. this First Day of March 1839   Stephen Chase

[*Not sworn.*]

CHASE, Stephen

May 5the 1839

A Bill of Damage in part of what I Received in the State of Missouri for my Religion by a Class of unreasonable unlawful ungodly men—Viz. In Jackson Co. in Sd State & in Consequence of being Drove from my Land and home. had to leave much of my Personal Property. th and lying out of the use of it these Eight years I think the Damage at the least Calculation $500.00

Do. In Clay Co Damages for being Drove from there and the loss in a Contract in land and lying out of business I think to be 200.00 800.00

Do. In Caldwell Co. being Drove from my house and Lands with the loss of my Crops my Cattle Sheep Hay and the most part of my household Furniture Farming tools &c. 200.00

Total of Damiges Receved one Thousand five hundred Dollars

Stephen Chase

[Sworn to before C. M. Woods, C.C.C., Adams Co., IL, 17 May 1839.]

CHIDESTER, John M.

The State of Missourie To John M Chidester Dr

Damages for preventing use of Moveing in to Jackson Co and threatning my life	$500.00
damage for haveing to leave Clay Co and for loss of property and expence of Mooveing and loss of time	550.00
damage for Chains and Cropr	250.00
damage for Cow and hogs	60.00
damage for time and other property in Davis	200.00
for haveing to leave the state expences and trouble of Mooveing and also being insulted and threatend by James Brown and others time after time	1,100.00
	$2,660.00

I hereby certify the above to be a true Copy of my of my Damages & losses sus tained in the State of Mo.
Quincy Ill May 8th 1839 John M Chidester

[Sworn to before C. M. Woods, C.C.C., Adams Co., IL, 17 May 1839.]

CHILD, Alfred B.

Account of Damages done myself and Family by being Driven from the State of Missorie by order of Govenor Boggs

Expens of Moving into the State	$150.00
Loss of time and property of myself and Family	100.00
one horse Crib of Corn Loss on Land	120.00
Removing out of the State	150.00
	$520.00

The above is justly estimated according to the best of my knowledge

Alfred B. Child

[Sworn to before C. M. Woods, C.C.C., Adams Co., IL, 11 May 1839.]

CHILES, Nathaniel

Quincy Ill May the 15th 1839

Damages sestane in being driven from the State of Missouri

Deprivation of land	$40.00
ten acres of corn 10 per	100.00
loss of time and property and being Driven from the State	500.00
	$640.00

I Certify the above to be true according the best of my knowledge

Nathaniel Chiles

[Sworn to before C. M. Woods, C.C.C., Adams Co., IL, 15 May 1839.]

CLAPPER, Christian

Illenois adams County May 24th 1839

An Account which I hold Christian Clapper hold against the State of Missouri in Consaquance of the goveners Exterminag orders

for thime and Expance of moveing to Missouri	$200.00
Loss in sale of Land and grain	350.00
to hogs and other property	100.00
to moveing Expances from Mssouri to this place	100.00
	$750.00

Christian Clapper

[Sworn to before C. M. Woods, C.C.C., Adams Co., IL, 25 May 1839.]

CLAPPER, Jacob

may 24 1839 State of Illinois adams County
A Bill of Damage against the State of missouri by me Jacob Clapper

to moving from the state of Ohio to the state of missouri
with the Intention of Being a Setler of Said State

to Expense moving to Said State	$100.00
to hogs and other property	75.00
to Loss in sale of land	200.00
to Loss in grain	200.00
to moving from Said State in Consequence of the govenors Exterminating orders	75.00
	$650.00

Jacob Clapper

[Sworn to before C. M. Woods, C.C.C., Adams Co., IL, 25 May 1839.]

CLAPPER, Mary

Illinois Adams County May 24 1839
An acount which I Mary Clapper hold a gainst the State of Missouri in Conceqence of the govner Extermating order

Moving Ex[pp]ence and time to Missouri	$10.00
to loss of one horse	45.00
to los in Sale of land	45.00
to mving Exspense from said State	27.50
	$127.50

Mary **X** Clapper

[Sworn to before C. M. Woods, C.C.C., Adams Co., IL, 25 May 1839.]

CLARK, Hiram
FELSAW, William

Quinca May 6 1839

To Damiges for being Compeld to leave the State of Masoura by the athorities of the Same	$500.00

Also for fears of Self & family being Exterminated from of the fase of the Earth while in the Staet	500.00
To Damage for having to leave our buisness from time to time to garde our Selves & famileys from being murdered by the mob of Mosouri In the fall of 1838	400.00
To Expens of mooving too & from the State of Masouri	500.00
To 3 Guns taken from us	45.00
	$1,945.00

We certify this to be a true acount acording to The bes of our knoledge

Hiram Clark
Wm. Felsaw

[Sworn to before C. M. Woods, C.C.C., Adams Co., IL, 6 Apr 1839.]

CLARK, Isaac

Illenois Columbus March the 13 1840
　　This Certifies that I Isac Clark was Driven from the State of Missouri By a mob to my Loss of propperty as follows

first for mooveing to the State	$100.00
for Loss of propperty in the State	150.00
for mooveing fromth State	100.00

　　This Driveing was by mob and the Goviners Exterminateing malitia in winter of 1839—

Isaac Clark

[Sworn to before W. Oglesby, J.P., Adams Co., IL, 13 Mar 1840.]

CLARK, John W.

Quinsey April 31 1839
　　A bill of lost property sustain in consequence of mobery and order of Governer Boggs in the State of Missorie

Forty acres of land cost $130.00 and sold for $20 loss	$110.00
One acre of land and improvements thare on in the City Farwest cost $445.00 could not sell it for nothing loss	445.00
Fifty bushels of corn	20.00
A part of a horse harness	5.00

loss of time in consequens of having to stand under arms
   agains mobs and not having a chance to labor and
   moving out of the State   100.00
expence money in moving to and from the State   100.00
total amount of loss $780.00

     I hereby certafy the above to be a true bill of my loss acording to the
best of my reckolection

                                          John W Clark

[Sworn to before C. M. Woods, C.C.C., Adams Co., IL, 7 May 1839.]

CLARK, Joseph[9]

Quincy Illinois March 16th 1840
     I Joseph Clark Certify that I was a citizen of the State of Missouri in
1838 and when peasibly travling the Highway I was Shot at Twice by
Goviner Boges Exterminating ~~order~~ malitia Commanded By majer
Generel John Clark

                                        Joseph Clark

*[Sworn to before W. Tainter, who signed for C. M. Woods, C.C.C., Adams
Co., IL, 16 Mar 1840.]*

CLARK, Lorenzo

Illenois Quincy June 1st 1839
     A bill of damages and debt Against the State of Missouri in Conce-
quence of the Governor refusing Protection and His Exterminating order

First mooveing into the State	$300.00
Being driven from Dewit	200.00
Loss of Property and time in the State	250.00
Mooving out of the State	250.00
	$1,000.00

     I Certify that the above acount is Just and true acording to the Best
of my knowledge

                                       Lorenzo Clark

[Sworn to before C. M. Woods, C.C.C., Adams Co., IL, 1 Jun 1839.]

---

[9] Also found in *HC* 4:63 and in JH 16 Mar 1840.

CLARK, Rodmon, Jr.

Illenois Quncy M[a]y the 11 1839
    A bill of Damages a gainst the State of Missorie

first for mooveing to the State	$400.00
for propperty Lost in the State By mob	200.00
from being Driven from the State and loss of propperty	200.00

    I certify the a bove a count to Be Just and True a cording to the best of my Knowledg

Rodmon Clark Jr

[*Sworn to before C. M. Woods, C.C.C., Adams Co., IL, 11 May 1839.*]

CLARK, Timothy B.

Illenois Quncy May 18th 1839
    a bill of Damages a gainst the State of Missouri acuird in conciquence of the Goviners Exterminating order

for mooveing in to the State loss of propperty time and expence	$200.00
for Loss on Landed propperty in the State being mobed off	2,000.00
Loss of crops and cattle and Horses	300.00
for leaving the State loss of time and Expences	100.00
	$2,600.00

    I Certify the a bove to Be Just and true a cording to the Best of my Knowledg

Timothy B Clark

[*Sworn to before C. M. Woods, C.C.C., Adams Co., IL, 17 May 1839.*]

CLARK, Timothy B.[10]

Montrose Lee Co Iowa Ter Jany 7th 1840
    This is to Certify that I was at work on my Farm on the last of October 1838 when an armed Company under Genl Lucas came and took myself

---

[10] Also found in *HC* 4:58 and in JH 7 Jan 1840.

and my three Sons prisoners, and threw down my fences and opened my gates and left them open and left my Crops to be destroyed and while I was a prisoner they declared that they had made clean work in destroying the Crops as they passed through the Country and they took from me two yoke of Oxen and three Horses and two Wagons and compelled me and my Sons to drive them loaded with produce of my own farm, to supply their Army,

I had in possession at the time Four hundred and Eighty Acres of Land and rising of an hunderd Acres Improved with a small Orchard and Nursery the necessary buildings of a farm &c And in consequence of my Imprisonment my fences remained down and most of my crops were destroyed. And further this deponent saith not

Timothy B Clark

[Sworn to before D. W. Kilbourn, J.P., Lee Co., IA, 7 Jan 1840.]

CLEAVELAND, Isaac

Illenois Quncy may the 7 1839
    A Bill of Damage and Debt against the State of Missorie in [——] Conciquence of the Goviners orders

First for tine and money in moving from the State of the	
ohio to the State of Missorie	$100.00
time lost in the war	100.00
Dammage in property	50.00
time and exspense in moving from the State	100.00
	$350.00

I certfy the a bove a count to Be true and correct a cording to the Best of my Knowledg

Isaac Cleaveland

[Sworn to before C. M. Woods, C.C.C., Adams Co., IL, 20 May 1839.]

COLBY, Alanson

Quincy Illinois May the 18th 1839
    Danages Received in being driven from the state of Missouri

time & Expense of mooving to the state	$50.00
time & loss of property in state	100.00

time & Expense in mooving from the state   <u>50.00</u>
                                             $200.00

I Certify the above to be accordind to the best of my Knowledge

Alanson Colby

[Sworn to before C. M. Woods, C.C.C., Adams Co., IL, 18 May 1839.]

COLE, Owen[11]

Quincy Illinois March 17th 1840.

    This is to Certify that I Owen—Cole was a resident of Colwell County State of Missouri and whil residing at my dwelling house the Malitia under Governor Bogs and by his orders ~~they~~ plundered my house and shot me through my thigh my damage sustained by the Malitia by being driven from the State, besides my wound, was five hundred Dollars. These Militia men were Quartered on the lands of the People caled Mormons contrary to the Laws and Constitution of the State

    I hereby Certify this to be a true statement

Owen Cole

[Sworn to before W. Tainter, who signed for C. M. Woods, C.C.C., Adams Co., IL, 17 Mar 1840.]

CORY, Uzal

Quincey the 16 of May 1839

A bill of damages a ganste the State of Mosuria to the loss no my land	$400.00
to abuse dun by Antoney Mecristin	200.00
to loss of time and money spent in moving	100.00
To being compeld to leave the State of Muria by orders of the guvener	500.00
[*Total*]	$1,200.00

    this may Sertefy this is a trew State ments of fackes a cording to the best of my noleage

Uzal Cory

[Sworn to before C. M. Woods, C.C.C., Adams Co., IL, 16 May 1839.]

---

[11] Also found in *HC* 4:64 and in JH 17 Mar 1840.

COX, Frederick W.

May 12th 1839 Adams County Ill.
     An account of loss and damage Recd. on account of the the orders of the Governor of Missouri

in Land selling and unsold	$500.00
farming utensils and other articles	150.00
in going to and from the state	150.00
damage exposure and sufferings	1000.00

I Certify the above to be true according to the best of my knowledge

Frederick W Cox

[*Sworn to before C. M. Woods, C.C.C., Adams Co., IL, 18 May 1839.*]

CRANDAL, John W.

John W. Crandall being duly sworn according to law doth depose and say that he moved to Jackson County Missouri August July 1832 and that after living there about 15 months he was driven by the mob from the County and comppelld to abandon all his porperty consisting of a house and his crop of grain hay &c he then settled in Caldwell County that when the authorities of the State commenced the war of extirmination against the Mormons he was taken prisoner and detained 3 days and nights and at that time was furnished with a pass by General Lucas and directed to leave the State which he did on the 12th day of December 1838 to his damage $5000

John W Crandal

[*Sworn to before R. Humphrys, N.P., Van Buren Co., IA, 9 Mar 1840.*]

CRANDALL, Patrick

I Patrick Crandall do solemnly Swear that the Damage Sustained by me Patric Crandall in the Year of our Lord Eighteen Hundred and thirty three in the County of Jackson and State of Missouri By A mob that Rose against the Church of Latter day Saints in Loss of Crops and other property to my Damage five hundred Dollars from that time untill the Year 1839
     Loss of property By me sustained fifteen Hundred Dollars in Clay and Davis Counties.

In the Fall of 1838 I and others ware Compelled by Jan. Parks and Wilson to [—— —— —— —— ——] leave the State

Patrick **X** Crandall

[Sworn to before W. Stanley, J.P., Van Buren Co., IA, 13 Mar 1840.]

CRANDEL, Simeon

this is to Cirtify that I moveed from Ohio to missouri in the year Eighteen hundred thirty two with the itention to Settle for life accordingly I Settle on a peace of land and Commenced improveing the Same my Expencis Coming in to the Country was one hundred Dollars my improvements of eight acres ~~houses~~ of Corn and house and one Cow be Sides Some furniture for whitch I Charge two hundred and fifty dollars from thence I moved to vanburen and built one house for whitch I Charge fifty Dollars from thence I moved to Clay and built one house for whitch I Cha[r]ge twelve dollars from thence I moved to Davis County leaveing Eleven acres of wheat on the ground for whitch I Cha[r]ge Sixty dollars in davis County I built two houses and I improved twenty acres of land for whitch I Cha[r]ge three hundred dollars besides ten acres of Corn and ten acres of wheat on the ground for whitch I Cha[r]ge two hundred and twenty five dollars be Sides I lost Sixty hogs and Sixteen head of Cattle and Six Sheeps be Sides farmings utentials for which I Cha[r]ge three hundred Dollars be Sides twelve ton of hay for whitch I Cha[r]ge forty Eight dollars from thence I moved to Caldwell County there I built one house for which I Ch[ar]ge fifty dollars

from thence I moved to quincy illinoi for whitch I Cha[r]ge fifty dollars ~~from~~ my lost of time from the year Eighteen hundred thirty two to the present time together with my family Consisting of Eight Children wandering about from place to place I Shall leave to the Consideration of the goverment of this our united States

Simeon Crandle

I certify the above to be Just and true acording to the best of my Knowledge

Simeo Crandel

[Sworn to before C. M. Woods, C.C.C., Adams Co., IL, 13 May 1839.]

CRANDELL, Benjamin

Aloss of Property in Jackson Ct. Mo. in 1833

To land 30 acrs at $10 pr. acr.	$310.00
To Corn wheete potatoas & 6 tun of hay	97.50
32 hogs $3.00 pr hog	96.00
10 calves at $3.00 pr. Calf	30.00
100 Dollars cash expended in going up	100.00
[*Subtotal*]	$633.50
Loss in Clay Ct. Mo., to one cow $20.00 and a number of hogs $15	35.00
Loss in Davisse Ct. Mo. in 1838 & 1839—to One qr. sect. and intitled to a preemption wright	800.00
two cows and one sheep	44.00
15 hogs at $3.00 pr hog	45.00
9 tuns of hay at $5.00 pr tun	45.00
6 acr. of corn at $8 pr. acr. 48 brls. at $200.00 pr. br.	96.00
5 acrs. wheet $50.00 20 bus buck wheete & potatoas	70.00
garden stuff & turnips	17.50
One Cary plow $15.00 three chears & 2 bedsteeds	18.00
One wheele $2.00 one bake oven lost & a kittel	4.00
one citty lot in Adamondiahmon	200.00
one Rifel in Jackson Ct $20.00	20.00
1 [Rifle] in Davis Ct $14.00	14.00
expences from Jackson up	125.00
12 months loss of time worth	140.00
	$2,307.00

Benjamin Crandal

I certy th above to Be true and Just a cording to the Best of my aknowledg

Benjamin Crandell

[*Sworn to before C. M. Woods, C.C.C., Adams Co., IL, 11 May 1839.*]

CRANDELL, Thomas

the los of property in Jack Son County in the State of missouri

to Seven acres and half of Corn	$70.00

to potatoes 36 bushels	18.00
two cows	30.00
Six calves	18.00
Twelve hogs	25.00

the los of property in Colwell County in the State of missouri

ten hogs	30.00
five acres of wheat	25.00
housen furniture	25.00
Eighty acres of land	400.00
one year of tim lost	220.00
Expenses	250.00
the loss of helth and famley Suffering	500.00

Thomas Crandell

I certify the a bove a count to Be true and Just acording to the Best of my Knowledg

Thomas Crandell

[*Sworn to before C. M. Woods, C.C.C., Adams Co., IL, 11 May 1839.*]

CRANDLE, Daniel

the loss of property and tim and expenses and Sufferege in Jack Son County and davis County in the State of missouri
the Sum of three $300.00

I certify the a bove to Be True and Correct acording to the Best of my knowledge

Daniel Crandle

[*Sworn to before C. M. Woods, C.C.C., Adams Co., IL, 11 May 1839.*]

CRANDLE, Jacob

the loss of property in Jack Son County in the State of missouri all So the loss of propety in Colwell County in the Same S[t]ate the loss of time expenSes and Sufferages to the amount of $300

I certify the a bove to Be true and Just acording to the Best of my Knowledge

Jacob Crandle

[*Sworn to before C. M. Woods, C.C.C., Adams Co., IL, 11 May 1839.*]

CRIHFIELD, Absalom

Aprile the 13th 1839

Abill or damages A gainst the State of Mis souri for driveing from Jackson county and Destroiing Crops Corn potatoes wheat Burning Buildings and So forth Seven hun dred Dollars for Driveing from Cald well County Destroying and taken property and Driveing from the State Seven hun dred Dollars

laid in By Absalom Crihfield

I certify the above acount to Be true and Just acording to the Best of my Knowledg

Absalom Crihfield

[*Sworn to before C. M. Woods, C.C.C., Adams Co., IL, 10 May 1839.*]

CURTIS, Enos

State of Missouri Dr

to Moveing from Pennsylvania Tioga County Rutland Township to Missouri time and expence	$300.00
to being Driven from Clay County to Coldwell having my Crop to move the loss of time and Expence	150.00
to the Loss of propperty having my house plundered of Clothing and furnature	200.00
to the loss of Corn potatoes and other Loss	100.00
to the loss of Cattle and hogs	50.00
to the Loss of Land	408.00
to the loss of four Musketts	40.00
to the loss of time of four hands by the mob	100.00
to two bee Stands	8.00
to the Loss of time and Expence of moveing being Driven out from Missouri	500.00

I Do Certify the a bove a count to Be Just and true a cording to the Best of my Knowledg

Enos Curtis

[Sworn to before C. M. Woods, C.C.C., Adams Co., IL, 8 May 1839.]

CURTIS, Jeremiah

May 13th 1839

An account That I Jeremiah Curtiss have against the State of Missouri in consequence of Mobocracy

Expences on the Road from Michigan to the state of Missouri	$80.00
To three months time moveing to the State of Missouri from the State of Michigan at one Dollar per Day	78.00
Loss of Six months time Dureing the war against an unlawful Set of Mobbers at one Dollar pr Day	156.00
Loss on Land	120.00
Expences in Cash moveing to Illinois from Missouri	10.00
Expences of Team to move us from Misouri to the State of Illinois	30.00
Loss of time Comeing to Illinois one month at One Dollar pr Day	26.00
	$500.00

Was I to under take to Charge for my sufferings I would not know how to commence for the fact is being Drove from my home and for Suffering as I have Done with my fellow Sufferers is inexpressible therefore I will Leave it with your honorable Body to Decide and allow me accordingly

State of Illinois Hancock County

Personally appeared before the subscriber an acting Justice of the peace in and for said County. Jeremiah Curtiss and made oath that the above account is Just and true

Jeremiah Curtis

[Sworn to before A. Smith, J.P., Hancock Co., IL, 14 May 1839.]

CURTIS, Jeremiah

Handcock Co State of Illinois

This may Certify that I Jeremah Curtis moved to Missouri in the year 1835 in June 1837 the people met in mass Judge Bird Sat as Chairman they pasd a Resolution that all of the Mormons Should leave the County of Clay the Spring following I left Clay and Settled in Calwell Coun[ty] Bought Land of Goverment built a house Commenced farming lived thereon untill the autum of 1838 when hostilities Commenced between the Inhabitants and the Mormons I moved my family to Farwest five miles— the Soon appeard in great numbers they Succeded in Setting a Guard around the town they finally Capitulated by giving up Six of our leaders and Sign away our property both real and personal which we did at the point of the bayonet being Surrounded by a Strong guard—We was nextly orderd to give up our arms this we did being Surrounded by a Strong guard our arms was thrown into an open waggon in the rain taken to Richmond after four or five month[s] we had the priveledge of getting our arms by paying fifty Cents apiece and Swearing we must leave the State nextly we had orders to leave the State immediately but General Clark who had the Command Said of Clenency we might have untill the following Spring to leave the State in—accordingly I Sold my property at half price and in the winter moved to Illinois through Snow and frost to the great Injury of the health of myself and family while the troop was quartered in Farwest the destruction of property was immense they burnt up house logs and Rails they killed Cattle hogs and Sheep and destroyd a great quantity of Corn and after the troops left there on the Camp ground there was a great quantity of meat and Corn Wasted

Jeremiah Curtis

[*Sworn to before A. Monroe, J.P., Hancock Co., IL, 6 Jan 1840.*]

CURTIS, Joseph

Handcock Co and State of Illenois

This may Certify that I Joseph Curtis was at the Surrender of the mormons at Far west Surrendered my armes I afterwards was taken prisioner Marched to Richmond thirty miles Surrounded by a Strong guard after two days I was discharged without finding anny accusation against me—I was discharched with out any means for Sustanance untill I got home

The commander of the Guard was Lieutanant Lakey

Joseph Curtis

[*Sworn to before A. Monroe, J.P., Hancock Co., IL, 6 Jan 1840.*]

CURTIS, Moses

May 13th 1839
An account That I Moses Curtiss have against the State of Missouri in consequence of Mobocracy

To Loss of Time in consequence of The Mobbers of Missouri 6 months at one Dollar pr Day	$156.00
To the Loss of one sword	5.00
To expence of getting a gun that was taken by Mobbers	0.62 ½
To Two weeks Lost time teaming	12.00
To three weeks time moveing poor from Missouri	18.00
	$191.62 ½

I would wish to inform you that I was taken prisoner and had to suffer with my fellow creatures therefore when your honorable body says how much others ough to have for suffering Remember me and allow me accordingly
Your &c

Moses Curtiss

State of Illinois Handcock County
Personally appeared before the subscriber an acting Justice of the peace in and for said County Mosess Curtiss and made oath to the above account as being Just and true—

Moses Curtis

[*Sworn to before A. Smith, J.P., Hancock Co., IL, 14 May 1839.*]

CURTIS, Moses

Handcock Co State of Illinois
This may Certify that I Moses Curtis was at the Surrender at Farwest in the County of Calwell State of Missouri and under a Strong guard I was compell to give up my arms I was afterwards taken prisioner by Leutenant Lakey who mearched us to Richmond thirty miles after two days I was discharged without any charge being found against me and no means of Sustanance being found for my Support

Moses Curtis

[*Sworn to before A. Monroe, J.P., Hancock Co., IL, 6 Jan 1840.*]

CURTIS, Simons P.[12]

I Simons P Curtis a resident of Quincy Adams Co Ill certify that in the year 1838 I was a citizen of Coldwell Co Mo residing in the city of Far West also that I went in search of a lost steer and in passing by Capt Bogart's Camp while he was guarding the city I saw the hide and feet of said steer which I knew to be mine the flesh of which I suppose they applied to their own use I also certify that Wiley E Williams one of the Governors aids who was gunkeeper caused me to pay 37 1/2 cents to him I also paid 25 cents to a Justice of the Peace to qualify me to testify that the gun was mine

The said Wiley E Williams is said to be the one that carried the story to Gov Boggs which story was the cause of the exterminating order being issued as stated by the Gov in said order

Simons P Curtis

[Sworn to before C. M. Woods, C.C.C., Adams Co., IL, 19 Jan 1840.]

CURTISS, Jacob

May the 13th 1839

An account ~~of my~~ that I Jacob curtis have agains[t] the State of Missouri in consequence of Mobocracy

To Expences on the Road from the State of Michigan to Missouri	$75.00
To expence of team two months at one Dollar pr. Day	52.00
To my own time on the Road Driveing team to Missouri Two months at one Dollar pr Day	52.00
horse taken away by mob worth	40.00
Copper Kettle taken away by mob worth	5.00
Loss on Land	120.00
Loss of Time for myself and son Six months at one Dollar pr Day each	312.00
Expences of the team to move us from the State of Missouri to Illinois	30.00
Loss of time Comeing to Illinois ~~to Missouri~~ at one Dollar pr Day for one month	26.00
	$712.00

---

[12] Also found in JH 17 Mar 1840.

I with the Rest have Suffered but will have to Leave it with your honorable body to Decide according to your Judgment what I had ought to have as I have no Doubt you will give me in proportion with the rest of my fellow Creatures who where Driven out of Missouri by a Lawless Crew Liveing in Defyance to Law or gospel

Jacob Curtiss

[Sworn to before A. Smith, J.P., Hancock Co., IL, 14 May 1839.]

CURTISS, Lyman

May 13th 1839

An account That I Lyman Curtis have against the State of Missouri in consequence of Mobocracy

To Loss on horses & Waggon in going to Missouri from the State of Michigan	$55.00
To Expences on the Road to Missouri	12.00
To Loss of Six weeks Time going to Missouri at one Dollar per Day Makeing	36.00
To Moveing from Clay to Caldwell County	6.00
To Loss of time in Consequence of Mobocracy Amounting to Six Months at one Dollar per Day	156.00
To the Loss of a Sword Taken by the Millitia	6.00
To the Expences of Moveing from the State of Missouri To the State of Illinois	50.00
To Sixty Two & half cents paid for Redeeming my Gun that the mob took away from me	0.62 ½
	$321.62 ½

As to the Sufferings of Myself & family I cannot put any price upon it but will Leave it with your honorable Body to Decide as I was a fellow Sufferer with the Rest of my Brethren in consequence of an out Lawed Rebellious Set of Mobbers in the State of Missouri

Lyman Curtiss

[Sworn to before A. Smith, J.P., Hancock Co., IL, 14 May 1839.]

CURTISS, Nahum

May 13th 1839

An account that I Nahum Curtiss have against the State of Missouri in Consequence of Mobocracy

To Expences moveing from the State of Michigan to the state of Missouri	$50.00
To Eight weeks that it took me to go with my family from Michigan to Missouri at one Dollar pr Day	48.00
To Eight weeks time each for my Two boys	96.00
To Loss on Land which I sustained in consequence of being driven from Missouri	1,520.00
To Loss of time for myself and son in time of waring against the Mob six months each at one Dollar pr Day each	312.00
To Loss on Corn potatoes & oats and hay	150.00
To Loss on ploughs	5.00
To Loss on Cattle and Hogs	55.00
To one horse Taken by the Militia	50.00
To Loss on waggon in Consequence of Mob Stealing it from me	20.00
To Expences Moving from Missouri to Illinois	25.00
To waggon & team Moveing me to Illinois	40.00
To Money & property given to help the poor	50.00
To teams to help the poor out of the state of Missouri to Keep them from being killed by mob	40.00
	$2,461.00

I Shall not put any price upon my sufferings as your honorable body will Consider that I was a fellow Sufferer with the Rest and when you Judge what others others ought to have you will consider that I had ought to have an equal proportion with the Rest

Nahum Curtiss

[*Sworn to before A. Monroe, J.P., Hancock Co., IL, 14 May 1839.*]

CUTLER, Alpheus

A Bill of Damage Sustained By Alpheus Cutler in Consequence of the Unlawful Conduct of the Inhabitants thereof & the Unconstituional Decrees of the Governor

Damage on Land	$600.00
Do. Do. on Personal Property	400.00

Do. Do. for being obliged to remove with a large family & an old aged mother the Inconveniences & the Exposure to the weather & being thrown out of Business &c &c	350.00
Do. Do. Expences for Journey	100.00
	$1,450.00

Alpheus Cutler

I Do hereby Certify the within Statements to be true according to the Best of my knowledge

Alpheus Cutler

[*Sworn to before C. M. Woods, C.C.C., Adams Co., IL, 6 May 1839.*]

CUTLER, Thaddeus

May the 4, 1839
A bill of damages Sustained by the unlawful Procedings Of the mob in Missouri and the Unlawful and the Unconstitutional Decrees of the Govenors orders in the same

Damage for being compelled to leave the state and loss of personal Property loss of time &c	$500.00
Expenses of moveing	60.00
[*Total*]	$560.00

Thaddeus Cutler

I do here by certify the within statements to be True which I shall testify to.

Thaddeus Cutler

[*Sworn to before C. M. Woods, C.C.C., Adams Co., IL, 6 May 1839.*]

DAILY, Moses

The State of Missourie to ~~John Dai~~ Moses Daily Dr
To bill of damamages and loss of property in consequence of having Been unconstitutionally driven from the state

Bill of damages for moving to and from the State including loss of time eight hundred dollars	$800.00

For loss of property viz lands stock and produce
Twenty four hundred dollars   2,400.00

                                                        Moses Daily

I certify the above to be a Just and true account According to the best
of my knowledge

                                                        Moses Daily

. [*Sworn to before C. M. Woods, C.C.C., Adams Co., IL, 16 May 1839.*]

DALEY, John

the State of Missouri Dr. to John Daley for dammgees done in 1838
& in 1839—in—Causing me to Sell & leave my farm & land in Missouri
Colwell Co. Far west at thieer own price eight hundred & eighty acors of
land with a hous and rising of a hundred acors of improvement and a good
meddow of a 11 acors of timothy grass & a Young orchard planted out &
12 acors of good wheat on the Same Said land & farm was conciddard last
August to be worth five thousand dollars—all for which I had to take
$1475.00 or leave it & take nothing besides their taking $100.00 of my
property for nothing the property was hogs corn & oats also my expence
from Ohio to Missouri & from Missouri to Illinoise $450.00 four thousand
dollars dammagees at least would not would not make me whole

Quincy Addams Co. May 24th 1839   John Daley

[*Sworn to before C. M. Woods, C.C.C., Adams Co., IL, 25 May 1839.*]

DANIELS, Sheffield

I sheffield Daniels Removed my family from Ohio to the state of
misouri in 1837[.] And purchest Land and settled my family and Went to
work as a free sitison of the united states and lived in peas for twelv months
And more When a mob arose Drove me and my Family From my Peasable
Posesions

And the Loss of property three new bilding burnt and loss off crops
and other property $3,000.00

I heard mc gee say the mormons had better sell thair land or if tha
did not thay would destroy all theirr rails and fences and propety and you
must beoff amedately or you will [be] kiled he was at my house with 16
armed men i removed to vanburen County and built ahouse and was driven

183

from thence to Clay receiving no Compensation for which i charge
500.00

for beaing driven from Clay to Colwell County damage   2,000.00

for being forced to sine a deed of trust and giveing up my armes and imprisenment and beeing forsed to leave the state and sufering of my self and famely and being deprived of sitessonship   5,000.00

I Certify the within a count to Be True a cording to the Best of knowldg

Sheffield Daniels

[Sworn to before C. M. Woods, C.C.C., Adams Co., IL, 6 May 1839.]

DANIELS, Solomon

Illenois Quincy May 9th 1839

a cont of Debt and Damage a gainst the State of Missori which took place in conciqence of the Goviners Exterminating order first for mooveing to State $300.00

Driven from Jackson County in 1833 my Barn and wheat Burned and allso my House my fences De Stroyed and was Driven from the county Loss of property Damage   1,000.00

Sacrafis of propperty and Loss of time in Clay Co for three years when I was again Driven from that to Caldwell County   300.00

for propperty Destroyd in Caldwell   170.00

Loss of land in Caldwell Co   600.00

for Leaveing the State   500.00

I certify the a bove to Be a true acount a cording to the Best of my knowleedg

Solomon Daniels

[Sworn to before C. M. Woods, C.C.C., Adams Co., IL, 9 May 1839.]

DAVIS, Arce

Illinois Quincy May 11 1839

a bill of damages Sustained in the State of Missouri

for moveing into the state $150.00

for property lost in the state   80.00

for moveing out of the state   200.00

I certify the above to be just and true according to the best of my knowledge

Arce Davis

[Sworn to before C. M. Woods, C.C.C., Adams Co., IL, 11 May 1839.]

DAVIS, William

The State of Missourie Dr to William Davis

to mooving from the State of Indianna Sheby County to Missourie Clay County 600 miles 34 days	$102.00
For being driven from Clay County to Caldwell County in 1838 for loss of property and time and exposure of health	1,442.00
beside one Rifle worth twenty dollars	20.00
For 80 acres of Land in Clay County Fishing River Township 14 acres of improvement hewed log hous one thousand Dollars	1,000.00
to Forty acres of Land in Clinton Co.	200.00
to mooving from the State of Missourie to the State of Illenois in 1839. 21 days at three dollars per day Sixty three dollars	63.00
Total	$2,827.00

I do hereby Certify that the above accompt is a just and an acurate accompt according to the Best of my Knowledge

Adams Co Illinois May 18th 1839   William Davis

[Sworn to before C. M. Woods, C.C.C., Adams Co., IL, 18 May 1839.]

DAYTON, Hiram

Qunsey May 9th 1839

Amount of damages which I sustained by the mobs and Authorities of the state of Missorie in the year 1838 & 9

Loss of time in guarding my self and family against the mob and being prevented building a house to shelter the same	$60.00
The loss of three horses and two Cows	265.00

For the loss of one Daughter by death, and sickness, in my family for the want of winter	2,000.00
For being driven from the state by order of Govenor Boggs and deprived of my rights	2,000.00
For the loss of land and other property	600.00
	$[4],925.00

Hiram Dayton

I certify the above to be true to the best of my knowledg an recollection

Hiram Dayton

[*Sworn to before C. M. Woods, C.C.C., Adams Co., IL, 10 May 1839.*]

DEAM, Henry

Illenois Quincy May th 15 1839

a bill of Damages a gainst the State of Missouri for Being Driven from the State

for mooving in to the State	$50.00
for loss of time and having to leave the State	100.00
	$150.00

I certify the above to Be true and Just according to the Best of my knowledg

Henry Deam

[*Sworn to before C. M. Woods, C.C.C., Adams Co., IL, 15 May 1839.*]

DEMILL, Freeborn

A bill of damages against the state of Missouri

1833	Loss of time and labour in Jackson County Mo.	$500.00
	For improvements	300.00
1836,	Also for improvements &c in Clay Co. Mo.	300.00
	Also for lands and improvements in Caldwell ~~Clay~~ Co. Mo.	500.00
1839		

For the loss of time and mooveing out of the State into Illenoy & for two Rifles with expences 430.00

deprived of Citizenship in Jackson County Mo. 1833. by a
lawless mob. also in Clay County Mo. 1836 by the same
Mob. and last of all by an exterminateing orde the
Governor. 203.00

I hereby Certify that the above bill of accomps are Correct according
to the best of my knowledge—

Quincy May 6th 1839   Freeborn Demill

[*Sworn to before C. M. Woods, C.C.C., Adams Co., IL, 6 May 1839.*]

DIBBLE, Philo

this is to Cirtify that I moved from Ohio to missouri Jackson County
in the year Eighteen hundred thirty two with the intention of Settleing
Down for life accordingly I purchased land and improved twenty acres
and built one house for Coming into the Country my Expences was three
hundred Dollars for my house and improvement I Cha[r]ge three hundred
Dollars be Sides Sixty Dollars of furniture that was stole out taken out of
my house and twenty hogs for whitch I Cha[r]ge and two one hundred and
twenty Dollars be Sides five acres of Corn for whitch I Charge fifty Dollars
from thence I was Compeled to move to Clay County there I Entered forty
acres of land I improved fifteen acres and built two houses for whitch I
Cha[r]ge five hundred Dollars from thence I was Compeled to leave then
I moved to Caldell County there I entered nine Eightees of land and built
two houses and improved ten acres of the Same for whitch I Charge two
thousand Dollars be Sides Sevn Cows and four hogs and three acres of
Corn and five ton of hay and two houses for which I charge three hundred
Dollars From thence I for whitch I Chrge one hundred and forty one
Dollars be Sides one gun and a Sword and one Clock that was Smashed
Down I in my house for whitch I Charge fifty Dollars from thence I was
Compeled to leave the State forthwith on peril of my life then I moved to
quincy illinois for which it Cost me Sixty Dollars from the time I first
mooved into missouri to the presant tim having to leave my houses from
time to time in the Dead hours of the nights and flee in to the woods with
my litle family Consisting of five litle Children for Safty be Sides I was
Shot in the bowels with a ball and two buck Shots I was Examined by
Doctors they pronounceed me mortally wouded Disstroying my bodly
health I and having to wandering a bout from palce to palce being Exposed
to the inclemincy of the wether Causeing Sickness to prey upon ours
bodies and Disstroying our reputation and our freedom whitch is near and

Dear to us for whitch our forefathers bled now I ask the goverment of this our united States to pay me for the losses I have Susstained by not protecting me in my wrights ~~the~~ now I Shall leave it to your Consideration

Philo Dibble of Illinois

I certify the a bove to be Just and true acording to the best of my knowledg

Philo Dibble

[Sworn to before C. M. Woods, C.C.C., Adams Co., IL, 13 May 1839.]

DIMICK, Jefferson

Illinois Quincy May 18th 1839
    a bill of damages against the State of Missouri for being driven from the State unlawfully

first for moveing into the State	$150.00
for property lost in the State	25.00
for mob damage	100.00
for moveing out of the State	25.00
	$300.00

I Certify the above account to be just and true according to the best of my Knowledge

Jefferson Dimick

[Sworn to before C. M. Woods, C.C.C., Adams Co., IL, 18 May 1839.]

DOPP, Peter

Illenois Quincy May 28th 1839
    a bill of Damages a gainst the State of Missouri for Being unlawfully Driven from it

first for mooving into the State	$300.00
for propperty lost in the State	300.00
for mooveing out of the State	100.00
	$700.00

I certify the a bove acount to Be Just and true according to the Best of my Knowledg

Peter Dopp

[Sworn to before C. M. Woods, C.C.C., Adams Co., IL, 29 May 1839.]

DOWNEY, Calvin C.

Illenois May 31st 1839

A bill of Damages a gainst the State of Missouri for Being unlawfully Driven from it —

first for moveing in to the State	$200.00
for propperty Lost in the State	386.00
for mooveing out of the State Loss of time and Expence &c &c	50.00

I certify the a bove to Be Just and true a cording to the Best of my knowledg

Calvin C. Downey

[Sworn to before C. M. Woods, C.C.C., Adams Co., IL, 31 May 1839.]

DOWNEY, Harvey

Illenois Quincy May the 31st 1839

a bill of Damages against the State of Missouri for Being Driven from the State unlawfully—

first for mooveing in to the State	$200.00
for property Lost in the State	50.00
for mooving out of the State Loss of propperty and time Expen[s]e &c &c	40.00

I certify the a bove acount to Be Just and true acording to the Best of my knowledg

Harvey Downey

[Sworn to before C. M. Woods, C.C.C., Adams Co., IL, 31 May 1839.]

DRAPER, Ruth

Quincy May 5th

1838	The State of Missouria Dr To Ruth Draper	
	To a bill of damiges Viz	
	To Bedding Clothing and Chest taking by mob & Destroyd	$75.00

	To Expence of moving to Missouria from ohio	40.00
1839	To Expence of moving from Missouria to Illinois	30.00
	To Loss of time and Damiges Occasiond by Exterminating order	

I Do hearby Certify the above bill of Accaunty to be Correct According to my Best Reccollection

Ruth Draper

[Sworn to before C. M. Woods, C.C.C., Adams Co., IL, 6 May 1839.]

DRAPER, Thomas

this to sertify that i have lost my goods ~~by water~~ that i sent to richmond landding and being stoped on the road ~~and being~~ my Self and teams and drove back the loos of property and time and damage is two thousand Dollars

Thomas Draper

[Sworn to before E. Petty, J.P., Pike Co., IL, 18 May 1839.]

DRAPER, William, Jr.

Shoal Crick Colwell Co Nov 1st 1838
State of Missouri To William Draper Jr Dr

| To One yoke of Oxen killed by the Militia | $40.00 |
| To Damage sustained in purchaseing Lands in consequence of the Governors Exterminating order and Leavein the State | 500.00 |

State of Illinois County of Pike
I William Draper do solemnly swear that to the best of my Knowleaged and belief the above account as it is set forth is true and correct. So help me God.

Wm Draper Jun

[Sworn to before J. Clark, C.C.C., Pike Co., IL, 13 May 1839.]

DRURY, Joel

Quincy Illinoys May the [~~29th~~] 6th 1839
Debtor from the State of Missouri to Joel Drury for losses injury and abuse I was driven in Davis County [—— ——] with my wife and three children ~~when the~~ from my peaceable home when they were sick with the

chill fever and ague and myself both blind and lame from place to place in the cold weather of last November and from thence we had to flee for our lives 25 miles to Cauldwell County and from thence about 2 hundred miles to the State of Illinois where we are now encampet on a praerrie with a scanty alowence of bed clothes to shelter us from the storm and rain one hundred and 50 dollars for trouble damage and expence

Joel Drury

    I do Here By certify the within to Be a true Bill acording to the Best of my knowledge

Joel Drury

[Sworn to before C. M. Woods, C.C.C., Adams Co., IL, 7 May 1839.]

DUDLEY, Joseph

Quincy Illinois May 11th 1939
    A Bill of Damages and Debt against the State of Missouri

First for moving to the State	$25.00
Loss on Land	200.00
Loss on property	100.00
Expences of moving away	25.00

    I Certify the above account to be Just and true according to the best of my knoledge

Joseph Dudley

[Sworn to before C. M. Woods, C.C.C., Adams Co., IL, 11 May 1839.]

DUDLEY, Moses

    Debts and Damages against the State of Missourie

For moving in to the State	$40.00
For the Loss of property	70.00
For my time 4 months 25	100.00
For Bing Driven out of the State By orders of the Govenar	1,000.00

    This may Certify that the above is a tru Statement of facts according to the Best of my knowledge

Quincy May the 33 [22] 1839   Moses Dudley

[Sworn to before C. M. Woods, C.C.C., Adams Co., IL, 22 May 1839.]

DUDLEY, William

Illenois Quincy May 11th 1839
a bill of Damages against the Stad of Missori

first for mooveing in to the State	$100.00
for loss of propperty in the State	100.00
for mooveing out of the State Damag By mob	400.00

I certify the above acount to Be true and Just a cording to the best of my Knodlg

Wm Dudley

[*Sworn to before C. M. Woods, C.C.C., Adams Co., IL, 11 May 1839.*]

DUDLY, James

Illenois Quinsy May the 11 1839
a bill of Damage a gainst the State of Mo—

first for mooving to the State	$100.00
for Loss of propperty Lost in the State By mob	900.00
for mooving from the State and Loss of propperty by mob	100.00

I certify the abov acount to Be Just and true a cording to the Best of my knowledg

James Dudly

[*Sworn to before C.M. Woods, C.C.C., Adams Co., IL, 11 May 1839.*]

DUNCAN, Homer

May the 6th 1839
A charge against the state of Missouri for the loss of propperty occasioned by the Missouri mob

for plows and other farmind utentials	$50.00
one horse	75.00
thirty acres of corn	300.00
for sick ness and Loss of time	150.00
for preemption write	500.00
	$1,075.00

I certify the within account to be correct according to the best of my knowledge

Homer Duncan

[Sworn to before C. M. Woods, C.C.C., Adams Co., IL, 6 May 1839.]

DUNCAN, John

Losses of John Duncan by traveling to the State of Missouri and being Driven away by the people of that State

travil to and into the State 1500 miles at 8 [*dollars*] /100 [*miles*] =	$120.00
travel out of Said State 200 miles at Ditto,	16.00
Seven months time Lost much of it in perills and abuses in Caldwell and Davis Counties at 20 Dolls per month	140.00
	$276.00

the foregoing I Certify to be Just and true

Citty of Quincy Illinois May 13th 1839   John Duncan

[Sworn to before C. M. Woods, C.C.C., Adams Co., IL, 13 May 1839.]

DURFEE, Jabis

Ilanois May the 6 1839

State of Masoerie Dr for damages for being driving out of the state Exspences for mooveing from Ohio to the state two hundred dollars for 160 acres of land and im provements and crops lost in Jackson County Eight hundred dollars lost in Clay County Crops fifty dollars being driving from davis county for im provements and crop hogs and hens turkeys and mill and for loss of tim and tools one thousand dollars exspencis for mooveing out of the state by the govener order two hundred and fifty dollars to for three Rifles three swords and two pistols Sixty dollars the whole aCount $2,310.00

Jabis Durfee

I sirtify the above acount tobe a trew acount acroding to the best of my knollag

Jabis Durfee

[Sworn to before C. M. Woods, C.C.C., Adams Co., IL, 6 May 1839.]

DURFEY, James

May th 7 1839 Illenois

a bill of Debt and Damage a ganst the State of Missouri Sustained by the Goviners Exterminating order first

Mooving from the State of Ohio to Missouri With a family of 16 persons cost of mooving and time Expended $200.00

Lost in Jackson co Mo   42.00

time Lost in Defending my family and property a gainst a mob my Self and 3 boys 5 months for which I charge   750.00

Los of crops of hogs cattl Horses Sheepe ~~cattle Horses~~ hold furniture farming utentials &c   815.00

Loss on Land   2,120.00

for mooving out of the State   1,000.00

I Do Certify that the above a count is True and Just acording to the best of my Knowledg

James Durfey

[Sworn to before C. M. Woods, C.C.C., Adams Co., IL, 7 May 1839.]

DUSTIN, Peter

A bill of damages against the state of Missouri.

1831	For moveing to the State	$300.00
1833	For the loss of properity taken and two years labour in Jackson Co.	500.00
1836	For the loss of properity and three years labour in Clay County Mo.	500.00
1839	loss of properity in Land & Stock [——] in the County of Caldwell Mo.	200.00
	For mooveing from the State	100.00
		$1,600.00

deprived of citizenship in Jackson County Mo. 1833 by lawless mob, also in Clay County Mo. 1836 by the same mob, and last of all by an exterminating order of the governor.

I do hereby certify that the above bill of accompts are Correct according to the best of my knowledge.

Peter Dustin

[Sworn to before C. M. Woods, C.C.C., Adams Co., IL, 6 May 1839.]

DUZETT, Edward P.

Quincy Ill May 11th A.D. 1839
  A bill of damages against the State of Missouri

For moveing onto of the State	$25.00
loss of property by the mob	25.00
loss by moveing out of the State	25.00

I certify the above to be just and true to the best of my knowledge

Edward P. Duzett

[Sworn to before C. M. Woods, C.C.C., Adams Co., IL, 11 May 1839.]

DWELINGER, Rachael

Illenois quincy May th 7 1839
  a bill of Damages and Debt a gainst the State of Missorie in Concicuence of the Goviners Exterminating order

first for land in Jackson County Sold under value Loss not less than	$100.00
to Loss on land in fayett Coldwell Clay	820.00
one cow	15.00
Loss on H[o]gs Destroyed By mob	50.00
Loss of houshold furniture	25.00
for mooveing to the State	100.00
for mooving Being Driven from the State By an unlawful mob	500.00
	$1,610.00

I Do Here by Certify that the above acount is Just and true acording to the Bes of my Knowledg

Rachael Dwelinger

[Sworn to before C. M. Woods, C.C.C., Adams Co., IL, 7 May 1839.]

EAMES, Ruggles

Damage Sustained by me Ruggles Eames by being driven from Jackson County State of Missouri AD 1833 by a mob that Rose against the church of the latter day Saints and in AD 1839 Compelled to leave the State two thousand Dollars in Land cattle hogs and Other property

Ruggles Eames

[Sworn to before S. G. Jackson, J.P., Van Buren Co., IA, 12 Mar 1840.]

EGBERT, John

May the 9th 1839 Illinois Quinsey
    An account against the State of Missouri for debt and damage Sustained in consequence of the Exterminating Order—

in the year 1833 I was drove out of JackSon County to clay	
Improvement and crop	$100.00
Drove from Caldwell in 1839	
Loss on Land	600.00
Loss of stock	155.00
Damag & removal	200.00
	$1,055.00

I certify the above to be a Just and true account according to the best of my Knowledge

John Egbert

[Sworn to before C. M. Woods, C.C.C., Adams Co., IL, 9 May 1839.]

EKIEW, Moses

A bill of damages against the State of Missouri

For mooveing to the State	$20.00
For Corn, and fodder 250.00 for cattle 150.00 hogs 80.00	480.00
For house & furniture 100.00 Sundaries 20.00	120.00

deprived of Citizenship in Jackson County Mo. 1833. by a lawless mob. also in Clay County Mo. 1836. by the Same Mob. and last of all by an exterminateing order of the Governor.

I do hereby certify that the above bill of accompts are Correct according to best of my knowledge

Moses E[kiew]

[Sworn to before C. M. Woods, C.C.C., Adams Co., IL, 6 May 1839.]

EMETT, Phebee

A list of damages sustained from the sta[te] of Mo in being driven from sd. s[t]ate in the year 1838 & 9

to thirteen head of oxen and cows	$300.00
to being driven from Jackson Co & privations	1,000.00
to land 220 acrs	1,100.00
to one cow and two sheep and many other articles and privations of mooveing to this state	25,000.00

I crtify the above to be true

Adams Co Ill. May 14th 1839   Phebee Emett

[*Sworn to before C. M. Woods, C.C.C., Adams Co., IL, 13 May 1839.*]

ENGLISH, Lydia B.

May 10 1839
Loss & damage against the state of Missouri

Expence of moving to Missouri	$130.00
Loss in Jackson Co house & chair shop land & garden vegatables	1,500.00
My husband Wm Whiting being wounded by the Mob in Jackson Co the exposures & hardships were to much for his feeble constitution to bear he died in Oct following the pain & distress of his body as well as mind, likewise the distress of my family all sick at once the hardships & privations caused by such a violation of the laws of the Land, the disstress of mind, driven from home in the chily month of Nov to seek a home among strangers, no money can amply atone for such losses & crosses	5,000.00
My second husband deceased	
Moveing to Caldwell	35.00
Moveing to Illinois	130.00
Driven the third time from home in cold winter being exposed to cold rain and snow & all troubles	1,500.00
[*Total*]	$8,295.00

Lydia B English

I certify the within a count to Be Just and true acording to the Best of my Knowledge

Lydia B English

[*Sworn to before C. M. Woods, C.C.C., Adams Co., IL, 14 May 1839.*]

ETTLEMAN, Henry

Illinois Adams County May 24, 1839

an accounty w[hit]ch I Henry Ettleman hold a gainst the State of Missouri in Consuquence of the govner Extarminateing orters

for move ing to and from Said State	$350.00
the lose of in Sale in land	300.00
to lose in hoses and Stock and grain	200.00
to lose of rifle gun and other art[ice]ls	25.00
to the of time	150.00
	$1,125.00

Henry Ettleman

[*Sworn to before C. M. Woods, C.C.C., Adams Co., IL, 25 May 1839.*]

ETTLEMAN, Jacob

Illinois Adams County May 24 1839

An acount which I Jacob Ettleman hold Against the State of Missouri in Concequence of the govern Extermting order

for moving to Said State	$250.00
lose in State of land	500.00
lose in horses and Stock and grain and time	250.00
	$1,000.00

Jacob Ettleman

[*Sworn to before C. M. Woods, C.C.C., Adams Co., IL, 25 May 1839.*]

ETTLEMAN, Philip

AD 1839 24th Day of may A Dams County State of Illinois

A Bill of Damage against the State of missouri by me Phillip Ettleman to moving from the State of Ohio to the State of missouri with the intention of Being a Settler of that State ~~when~~ I went to the land office in Said State and entered land and paid for the same and had to leave Said State on the Exterminating Orders of the govener of Said State

the Loss in all amounting to $200.00

Philip Ettleman

[Sworn to before C. M. Woods, C.C.C., Adams Co., IL, 25 May 1839.]

EVANS, David

May the 9th 1839 Illinois Quinsey

An account against the State of Missouri for Debt and dammage Sustained in Consequence of the Exterminating Order

I was driven from Calewell County Mo in the Month of November 1838 from all I possessed

Land	$300.00
Damage with Loss and removal	100.00
	$400.00

I Certify the above account to be Just and true according to the best of my Knowledge

David Evans

[Sworn to before C. M. Woods, C.C.C., Adams Co., IL, 9 May 1839.]

EWELL, Pleasant

A Bill of Damage Sustained by Pleasant Ewell against the State of Missouri in Consequence of the Unlawfull Conduct of the Inhabitants thereof & the Unconstitutional Decrees of the Governors Orders

Damages on Land	$1,500.00
Do. Do. on Stock	200.00
Do. Do. Chattle Property	200.00
Do. Do. For being obliged to remove & the Inconvenencies & Exposure to weather & thrown out of Business &c	300.00
Do. Do. Expence for journey & ware & Tare	200.00
	$2,600.00

P. Ewell

I do hereby Certify that the within is true to the best of my knowledge

P. Ewell

[Sworn to before C. M. Woods, C.C.C., Adams Co., IL, 6 May 1839.]

FISHER, Edmund

Charges against Missouri.

1st for preventing my going into and Settleing in Jackson Co without jeopardiseing my life after Comeing one thousand miles for that express purpose, Mo. Dr. for the above $500.00

2d for preventing my going into Clay Co. and Settleing therein after moveing my Family one thousand miles for that express purpose being stopped by an armed force of about one hundred men Mo. Dr for the above. 1,000.00

3d for time lost by guarding against Mobs and otherwise occasioned by the Militia, about Seven months Mo. Dr. for the above 140.00

4th for one Rifle ~~and one~~ Mo. Dr. 15.00

5th for one Cow Mo. Dr for the above. 25.00

6th Mo. Dr. for one hog 3.00

7th for moveing from the state under Gov. Boggs exterminateing orders, Mo. Dr for the above 1,000.00

8th for injury done to the sale of property Mo. Dr for the above 250.00

9th for Slander and false imprisonment to great for me to say I therefore leave it for the Court to which this may Come

Missouri Dr to Edmund Fisher for all the above named Damages $2933.00

besides Slander and false imprisonment and several other abuses

Edmund Fisher

[Sworn to before C. M. Woods, C.C.C., Adams Co., IL, 25 May 1839.]

FISHER, Thomas J.

May the 7 1839 Illenois State Adams County

A bill of Debt & Damage against the state of Missourie Sustaind by the Governors order

first for moveing into the state 4 in family moving
    five hundred [——] miles $100.00

loss of crops furniture s[*t*]ock farming tools   100.00

loss of time inDefendin my family & property   180.00

Damage & moving from the state   1,000.00

      I Do Certify that above account is true & Just according to the best of my knowledge

                                        Thomas J **X** Fisher

[*Sworn to before C. M. Woods, C.C.C., Adams Co., IL, 7 May 1839.*]

FOLLETT, Louisa

State of Missouri Dr. to Louisa Follett

1833	To loss of improvemants on land and buldings	$100.00
	To loss of provision and wheat in the ground	50.00
	To loss of time and expence of mooving from Jackson Co. to Clay Co.	20.00
1835	To loss of property, time & expence by being driven from Clay Co. to Caldwell Co.	150.00
1838 &39	To loss in land and buildings not gitting the value of them on the account of being obliged by the Mob to leave the state	800.00
	To loss of outher property from the same caus such as stock, provisions, furniture &c	100.00
	To loss of time and expences by mooving from Missouri to Illenois, and being detained from business previous to removal by the unlawful procedings of the Mob	200.00
	To loss of the company, and being deprived of the assistance of my husband (King Follett) who is now, and has ben for a long time kept in prison as I think contireary to the Laws of the land	500.00
	To being deprived of rights of citizen ship in the state of Missouri, having ben driven by a mob under the order of Govener Boggs from that state to the state of Illenois	2,000.00
		$3,920.00

I certify the a bove account to Be Just and true a cording to the Best of m[y] knowledg

Louisa Follett

[*Sworn to before C. M. Woods, C.C.C., Adams Co., IL, 11 May 1839.*]

FOOT, Reuben

May the 5—1839—

A Bill of Losses By the exterminating order of the Governer of Missouri

For mving from the state of new york to the State of Missouri my time which was two months and my expences amounted to the some of fifty dollars for which I demand of the State of Missouri	$50.00
For the loss of my house which the mob burned for me I Demand of the State above mentioned	150.00
For the loss on the Sale of my land I demand	200.00
For the loss of two acres of corn I demand	23.00
For the Loss of Six months time caused by the mob	120.00
For the expences and inconveniencence of bying my provisions for my family and renting ground and aplace to live and also a new location I demand which trouble and expence was caused by the Goveners order I demand of the State of Missouri	500.00
For the expences of and Suffering of moveing from the State in the inclement Season of the year I demand	40.00
For the Loss of my hogs I demand	10.00
For the loss of my pach of turnups I demand	5.00
and also for Six days fals imprisonmend I demand	10.00
the whole Bill amountend to	$1,108.00

this is not all but being deprived of my wrights as a Citisan which my Forefathers Bled for I leave to the honor of those to whome this Bill may be presented to value as they see proper N.B. The above account is made For the years 1838 & 1839—

Reuben Foot

[*Sworn to before W. Laughlin, J. P., Adams Co., IL, 14 May 1839.*]

FOOT, Stephen

A Bill of Expence and damage Against the State of Missori For being driven by the Governors Order

to Expence Money Moveing from State of New York	$100.00
to team and time of driver Eleven Weeks	50.00
to false Imprisonment at Far west by Goverment Order Six days	12.00
to Loss of time and Expence of Moving From Missori to Illinois	50.00
	$212.00

BeSides my Right of Citzenship and home

Illenois May 10th 1839   Stephen Foot

I certify the above a count to Be Just and true a cording to the Best of my Knowledg

Stephen Foot

[*Sworn to before C. M. Woods, C.C.C., Adams Co., IL, 15 May 1839.*]

FOOT, Timothy B.

The following is an estimate of damageges Sustained by me in consequnce of being exiled from the State of Missourie by the unlawful procedings of govornor Boggs—

Time and expences Moving to the State	$225.00
loss in land	520.00
Stock	50.00
grain left and distryed	95.00
Time and expenses Moving out of the State	125.00
Being deprived of citizenship and personal abuse	500.00
	$1,515.00

Timothy B. Foot

State of Illenois Adams County

personally Came Timothy B. foot Befoure me the undersigned a Lawfull acting Justis of the peas in and for the County of adams and State of Illenois and after Being duely Swoorn Sayeth that the within Estimate of damages Sustaind By him B̶y̶ threw the unlawfull proceding of the governer of the State of Misorie Last winter agains the peopel Cald Latter Day Saints is a Just Estiamate of Land damages to the Best of his knoweldge and Belief

Timothy B. Foot

[*Sworn to before P. W. Martin, J.P., Adams Co., IL, 9 May 1839.*]

FOOT, Timothy B.[13]

This may certify that I Timothy B Foot formerly of Newyork arrived in Caldwell County State of Missourie in May 1837 I then and there Entered at the Lexington land Office Eighty acres in Section 32 Township 56 Range 28 and about one hundred and eleven acres in Section 5 Township 55 Range 28 on which I resided un[ti]ll about the first of Nov. 1838 when I with many of my neighbors werr arrested and made prisoners by a large body of armed men said they done it by order of Gov. Boggs was a prisoner some 2 or 3 days then received orders from Commanding Officer to leave the State immediately then by permission of the officer of the guard I went to my family which I removed as soon as possible into Ray Co. believeing that the Legislator (which was about to assemble) would take measures to restore piace and the citizens to their rights the winter passed away the Legislator adjourned without doing any thing then in consequence of repeated abuses that my family received and my life being threatened I concluded that it would be prudent to leave the State— Being without means to pay my debts and convey my family out of State I was obliged to Sell my land on the conditions proposed by the purchaser the sum recevd being less than half of the value I had to give a warrantee deed and deliver the Duplicates that I recievd at the Land office—Arrived April 5th 1839 in Adams Co. Illinois where I now reside

Jan. 14th 1840   Timothy B Foot

[*Sworn to before W. Laughlin, J.P., Adams Co., IL, 18 Jan 1840.*]

FOOTE, David

Quincy Illinois May 16th 1839

A bill of damages against the state of Missouri for being driven from that state by orders of the Governor

---

[13] Also found in JH 14 Jan 1840.

Expences in moving to that state	$120.00
Loss of property	280.00
For being driven from the state by orders of the Gov	200.00
and loss of time	100.00

I hereby certify that the above accounts are true and just according to the best of my knowledge

David Foote

[*Sworn to before C. M. Woods, C.C.C., Adams Co., IL, 16 May 1839.*]

FOOTE, Warren

Quincy Illinois May 16th 1839
A bill of damages against the state of Missouri for being driven from that state by orders of the gvernor

Expenc in moveng to that state	$50.00
Loss of time	200.00
For being driven from the state by the Govs. orders	250.00

I hereby certify that the above accounts are true and just according to the best of my knowledge

Warren Foote

[*Sworn to before C. M. Woods, C.C.C., Adams Co., IL, 16 May 1839.*]

FORBUSH, Rufus

Adams County Columbus May the 22 1839
this may cirty fy the true a count of the lose of property and time and exspences and sufferings that me and my famely did under go on the account of the mob in the missouri

two guns	$40.00
Los of time of two boys that are able to do mens work	240.00
my time	120.00
exspences	150.00

Rufus Forbush

I certify the within account to Be Just and true a cording to the Best of my Knowledge

Rufus Forbush

[Sworn to before C. M. Woods, C.C.C., Adams Co., IL, 22 May 1839.]

FORD, William

This may Certify that in Eighteen hundred and thirty sevn I mooved from ohio to Missourie in Caldwell County & in 1839 was driven out of the state of Missourie under the perril of my life and family and in Concequence of this I Charge the state of Missourie for damages on Loss of land and other property and time and Expence of mooveing out of the state of Missourie to the state of illenois the distance of two hudred and fifty miles three hundred dollars for damages I hav susstaned & five hundred dollars for being deprivd. of the right of Citizenship Makeing Eight hundred dollars

May the 6 1839   Wm. Ford

I Certify that the within is a true Copy of damagees according to the best of my Knowledge

Wm. Ford

[Sworn to before C. M. Woods, C.C.C., Adams Co., IL, 6 May 1839.]

FORESTER, Oliver

This is To Certify That I, have Traveled from the State of new York St. Laurence Countey, To the State of Missouria for The express purpose of Locating my Self being a young man Arived in Davis Countey State of Missouria made a location Acording to the Custom of that Country with the intention of Improving, it Soon as immidiatley, I, Lost my labour after I, arrived thair witch was five months & my Expences in Going to the State of Missouria, & in Returning a gain To the State of Illinois. My Damages, I mean to include all in one charge

To Damages Received by the Citizens of misouria $400.00

Oliver Forester

[Sworn to before C. M. Woods, C.C.C., Adams Co., IL, 17 May 1839.]

FORNEY, Fredrick

Illinois Adams County May 24 1839
    A Bill of Damage Lost by the Exterminating order of the governor of the State of Missouri viz

to Loss in Land	$74.00
to Loss in moving from the State of Missouri	50.00
To Loss in grain	20.00
T[o] Los Lost by me by not having Priveligs of Staying in the State	50.00
	$194.00

Fredrick **X** Forney

[Sworn to before C. M. Woods, C.C.C., Adams Co., IL, 25 May 1839.]

FORNEY, John

Illenois Quincy May the 11 1839
    a bill of Damag a gainst the State of missori for Being Driven from the State

first for mooving to the State	$100.00
for loss of land and other propperty in the Stat	500.00
for Being Driven from the State and Loss of other proppert	500.00
	$1,100.00

    I certify the above to Be true and Correct acording to the Best of my Knowledg

John Forney

[Sworn to before C. M. Woods, C.C.C., Adams Co., IL, 11 May 1839.]

FOSSETT, William M.

Quncy May 6th 1839
    A bill of Damiges against the State of missori

mooveing to the State	$600.00
two years labor	400.00
Loss of Land	100.00

mooveing from the State   40.00

Deprived of the wright of citizen Ship my life threatend and now with out house or home

I Here by Certify that the a bove acount of Debt and Damage is correct acording to the best of my knowledg

Wm. M Fossett

[*Sworn to before C. M. Woods, C.C.C., Adams Co., IL, 6 May 1839.*]

FOUTZ, Jacob[14]

Quincy Illinois March the 17th AD 1840

This is to cirtify that I was a citisen, resident of Caldwell County Missouri at the time of Govenor Boggs Exterminating Order was issued and that, I was quartered on by the Mob Militia, without my leave or consent, at different times, and at one time by William Mann, Hiram Cumstock, and Brother, who professed to be the captains, also Robert White, And that I was at the murder at hauns Mill, and was wounded

And that I was driven from the state, to my inconvenience, and deprived of my freedom, As well as to my loss of at least four hundred Dollars

Jacob Foutz

[*Sworn to before W. Tainter, who signed for C. M. Woods, C.C.C., Adams Co., IL, 16 Mar 1840.*]

FRAMPTON, David

Missouri Mob Dr.

1833 Dr. Jackson County mob to David Frampton for loss of time 6
    months & loss of improvement 7 acres & Crop corn & hogs by
    being Driven out by them Contrary to the Constitution of united
    States & Expences 200 Dollars—Clay county mob Dr for loss of
    time & 60 Dollars & poperty 30 dollars $200.00
                                                                       60.00
                                                                       30.00
State Mob 6 months los time 20   120.00
1 rifle 18 doll. 3 pistols 12 doll 1 Sword   ~~30.00~~ 33.00
1 month imprisond falsely   1,000.00

---

[14] Also found in *HC* 4:68–69 and in JH 17 Mar 1840.

During that time my 2 Sons David aged 15 years & Samuel aged 12 years was taken from my house to Clay County & my life threatend if I went into that County or for them money Could not hire such of mee & being Deprived of them & Willim also 19 years old   1,000.00

loss of Property in hogs & Corn & other grain   100.00

for beeing driven out of Said State by Governors Bogs order & from my land that I never got any Pay for 25 acres 200 Doll Expences 40 Doll

200.00

[*Subtotal*]   2740.00

40.00

$2780.00 $2,810.00

March 1839   David Frampton

[*Sworn to before C. M. Woods, C.C.C., Adams Co., IL, 30 Mar 1839.*]

FRAMPTON, David

Facts

At the time the people Called Mormons was driven out of Jackson County Missouri I went to Colonel Thomas pitcher & L. Bogg then lieutenant govornor to see if I & others Could have protection 2 weeks teling them I was affraid of some men the Govornor told me You had beter go T, Pitcher swore by God the mormons Should go Except 2 families that had denied the faith; & again when we was taken Prisonors by Governor Boggs Exterminating order I seen A horse taken by A part of Bogards men among Whom was Isaac & John Allen of fishingriver & would not give him up the Owner was Johanathan Hubble & one of the same Company his Sir name I do not know more than Odle raised his gun & Swore he had A damd notion to Shoot me Down I turn & walkd off, John Mar of Clay County told us that any of us that would Deny the faith & Jo Smith we might Stay the rest Must all go; General Clark Said all must go as soon as possible & not think of making another Crop or if You do Ill bring my army & Drive you away; Colonol Price Ordered his men if we Spake to any body out of the Court house where wee lay that they should Shoot us down after Keeping me & others about 4 weeks unlawfuly, dischargd us finding no accusation against us I Came home & to my astonishment my 2 sons David & Samuel was taken away & my life threatned if I attempted to get them or Come in Clay County

David Frampton

[*Sworn to before J. H. Holton, N.P. Adams Co., IL, 17 Mar 1840.*]

FRY, David

David Fry mooved from the State of indeanea to Mourie 2 of October 1837

to expences of mooveing to Mo	$30.00
dreven from Clinton Co to Colwell County from my home and effects	200.00
Dreven from colwell ~~to~~ out of the State of Mo	400.00
to the losele of time 8 months	240.00
to expenses from November to May	100.00
	$970.00

my famaly consists of 9

I certify that [t]he above a count to be trew [acor]ding to the best of knowalage

David Fry

[Sworn to before C. M. Woods, C.C.C., Adams Co., IL, 6 May 1839.]

FRY, William A.

Quincy may the 11 1839

this may Certify that I William A Fry Lived in the State of missurie for the term of three years and Lived in Peace with all mankind till a mob a rose to drive out all the mormans then I sufferd the fate of the rest of the the mormans so Cauld a mob Came to my house ten in number they demanded the guns got two then offering to kill us after they got our guns they thretend to burn our houses to the ground and all the familey in it we was orderd to Leave the County in six days or they would drive us to hell Los of Porperty Catle hogs Corn hay oats Potatoes house hold furnature Los of time Expence of moving out total Los of Porperty one thousand dollars after we had Left the County we was all taken Prisners and serchd on the high way mutch a buse was offerd to us all Small fire arms was held to my Brest while they Plunderd my wagon I went to general Allen and he orderd some of his offior[s] to give me a Pass found nothing a gainst me

William A. Fry

I certify the above acount to Be Just and true a cording to the best of my Knowledg

William A Fry

[Sworn to before C. M. Woods, C.C.C., Adams Co., IL, 11 May 1839.]

G—O

GARDNER, Morgan L.

Morgan L Gardner vs Against Missouri

In Damages from the time I left the State of Ohio and going to the State of Missouri—to Jackson County and being Driven from that place to Clay County and Sufering much Loss and Distress of mind Being an expenc and thrown out of employ $500.00

Having again to remove from Clay to Caldwell and Loss of property 100.00

Having to Leave my Famaly and flee for my Life and Sufering much in Consequ[ence] of Exposure and ill health Being gon Six months and the Loss of property 500.00

and Being Driven from the State of Missouri By Orders of the govenor 1,000.00

I Certify the Above to Be a true Statment of facts and maters acording to the Best of my Knowledge

Quincy Illinois May 7th 1839 Morgan L Gardner

[Sworn to before C. M. Woods, C.C.C., Adams Co., IL, 9 May 1839.]

GATES, George

Quincy Illinois May 18th 1839
loss of property in the state of Missouri

time & Expence in mooveing to State	$140.00
loss of property in the State	50.00
mooveing out of the State	25.00
	$215.00

I Certify the above to be true according the best of my knowledge

George Gates

[Sworn to before C. M. Woods, C.C.C., Adams Co., IL, 18 May 1839.]

GATES, Gipson

The State of Missouri Dr to Gipson Gates

For mooving from the State of Ohio to the State of Missouri in 1832	$290.00
For being Driven from Jackson County in 1833 for the loss of property time and health	2,500.00
to 40 acres of land	50.00
to 6 acres of Corn	50.00
to 2 acres of Wheat	10.00
to one Rifle	18.00
For being Driven in 1838 from Clay County to Caldwell for the loss of house hold furniture	375.00
For being driven out of the State of Missouri in AD 1839 time & expence of mooving	158.00
For 88 acres of land with 22 acres improvement in Clay Co Fishing River	775.00
Total	$4,286.00

I do hereby Certify that the above accompt is a just & accurate according to the best of my knowledge

Gipson Gates

[*Sworn to before C. M. Woods, C.C.C., Adams Co., IL, 10 May 1839.*]

GATES, Gipson[15]

I Gibson Gates do hereby Certify that I was residing in Jackson County Missouri in the fall of th e year of 1833 and had Been for the space of about one year I was at a meeting one day for worship when a man By the name of Masters came to us stateing that he was sent By the mob to inform us that if we would forsake our religion they were willing to Be our Brother[s] and to fight for us But if not said he our young men are ready and we can scarce constrain them from falling upon you and cuting you to piaces soon after this there came a large company of armed men to my place and withe much thretning and profane words ordered me to Be gone By the next day or they would kill me and my famlily in consequence of which thretning we quit our house in the month of Nov. leaving most

---

[15] Also found in *HC* 4:71 and in JH 20 Mar 1840.

of our effects suffering verry much with cold fatigue and hunger we took on the priarre and went southward twenty miles or more where we staye a few weeks But still Being theatened By the mob we removed to Clay County where we lived in peace untill the fall of 1838 whe[n] a mob arose against the people of the church of the Later day saints when I we were again obliged to leave our home seeke safety in an other place for a few weaks when we returned our house had Been Broken open and the lock of trunk Broken and the most valuable contents thereof taken away the most of our Beding and furniture was either stolen or destroyed and then orderd to leave the State

Gipson Gates

[Sworn to before D. W. Kilbourn, J.P., Lee Co., IA, 20 Mar 1840.]

GATES, Jacob

this is to certify that in the year one thousand Eight hundred and thirty four I left the State of Vt and located in the State of Missouri clay county purchased a farm lived two years when we ware compeled by the people of that county to leave it and removed to Coldwell County here I lived until the Spring of 1839 when I was driven from the State of Mo on the peril of my life and the life of my family I was imprison thretened and abused and in short great ware the sufferings of my family caused by the People of Missouri and as I have not been protected in my rites as a free born sitizon of Amarica I ask yes I clame at the hand of these United States an Appropriation equil to the amount of damages sustained which is as folows commensing in Clay Co. Mo. loss of propity and expence in removeing from Clay county $150.00 the loss in Caldwell County Mo. Land and Bildings $1000.00 fals imprisonment $1000.00 defimation $500.00 deprived of Sitison Ship $1000.00 expence of removeing to Illinois a distence of 250 miles five hundred dollars makeing in all four thousands one hundred and fifty dollars

Jacob Gates

I do hereby certify that the above list of accompt are Correct according to the best of my knowledg

Jacob Gates

[Sworn to before C. M. Woods, C.C.C., Adams Co., IL, 6 May 1839.]

GAYLORD, Liester

in the year 1838 and 1839
The amount of Property and time lost by being Driven and
    Deprived of my rites and Privileges to one house and
    Clearing one lot and Fensing the same $50.00
To the amount of lost time and expenses at Davis Co Mo
    and mooving From Davis to Caldwell Co. mo.   40.00
loss of time and expenses in and From Caldwell Co mo to
    illinois   150.00
Damage of arms   10.00

                                             Liester Gaylord

I Certify the within a count to Be correct a cording to the best of my knowledg

May the 6 1839 Quincy Illinois   Liester Gaylord

[Sworn to before C. M. Woods, C.C.C., Adams Co., IL, 6 May 1839.]

GEE, George W.

State of Missouri to George W. Gee Dr

to loss of time and expence for mooveing to the state of
    Mo. $100.00
to loss of property while in the State   219.75
to loss of time and expence for being complled to leave
    the State   187.50
total $507.25

I certify the above acct. to be true according to the best of my knowledge

                                             George W. Gee

[Sworn to before C. M. Woods, C.C.C., Adams Co., IL, 18 May 1839.]

GIFFORD, Alpheas

May
    I take this oppertunity to relate a scech of my Sufferings in missoui
i moved into jackson County march 1833 after labering through the

summer was driven from the county into clay to suffer with my sick famly without a hous afte living thare three years and a half and labering under meny disadvantags and suffering much through sickness and other fatigues on the acount of being driven Then we was driven from thier in to Caldwell After remaining thier one year and a half we was driven from the Staete into the state of elinois whear we now dwell and we are now destitute [o]f bedding Clothing and provision and all moste every comfert of life all this onthe account of being driven

a charge for actual losses by being driven from jackson County to hundred dollers from Clay to hundred and fifty dollers for losses in Caldwell three hundred dollers for the act of driveing from the state I charge ten thousand dollers for being deprived of liberty of living in the state of missouri nothing will satisfy but being and protected

Alpeus gifford

I certify the with in to be just and true a cording to the Best of my Knowldg

A[lp]heas Gifford

[*Sworn to before C. M. Woods, C.C.C., Adams Co., IL, 14 May 1839.*]

GILBERT, Mary Ann

May 13th 1839
the State of Missourie to Mary Ann Gilbert Dr. Occasioned by the Mob of Said State in the years 183[8] and 1839

to freight and loss of goods	$100.00
to loss of time and the expeses of moveing	300.00
to Suffering and being deprived of Citizenship	1,000.00

Mary Ann Gilbert

[*Sworn to before W. Oglesby, J.P., Adams Co., IL, 13 May 1839.*]

GODDARD, Stephen H.

To the highest orthorities of the United States I here present you a bill of damages against the State of Missouri Since the year 1837 Nov 1st

For the expense of moveing to that State and also the expense of returning from there with the exposure of health and many inconveniances on the account of being driven from there two hundred dollars $200.00

For being Compelled to leave my work in Clay County or deny my belief in the Scriptures[.] The loss of Clothing and other property which were Stolen from my house in Clay County about the time of the Battle on Crocked River one hundred and fifty dollars   150.00

For the danger myself and family were exposed to in the time of the Campaign in far-West with the Confiscation of of house and lands with other property eight hundred   800.00

For the privation of Citizenship one thousand dollars   1,000.00

Whole amount $2,150.00

Quincy Adams County Nov. 1st 1839   Stephen H. Goddard

[Sworn to before C. M. Woods, C.C.C., Adams Co., IL, 1 Nov 1839.]

GOFF, James

May the 6th 1839

I charge against the state of Missourie for the propperty lost on the account of the Mob in Mo

for fourteen acres of corn	$120.00
for twelve acres of corn	120.00
one cow and farming utintials	40.00
for loss of time	100.00
for fifty acres of land	150.00
house and lot	150.00
	$680.00

I certify the with in to be correct according to the best of my knowledge

James Goff

[Sworn to before C. M. Woods, C.C.C., Adams Co., IL, 6 May 1839.]

GOLDSMITH, Gilbert

quinsy may the 7 1839

Stait of masourie Dr to Gilbert goldsmith for damage for being driving out of the state by the govener order for to Exspencis mooveing to mosaurie from ohio $75.00

to loss of property in Jacksoncounty 1833   500.00

to for be ing driv ing from ray co by amob to [wit] Saniel Cleven ger,[16] and seanier, wm millsap, thomas keney, James allin ka[···] millsap, Abraham rhimer, All arm with pis tales and whips, and for the loss of property   75.00

In davis county in 1838. Loss of crops and improvements Hoghs and for loss of time   600.00

Exspencis for m ooveing to Ilanois and time   50.00
to one hors and 1 gun 1 sword   93.00
                                                                   $1,393.00

I sirtify the ab ove to be atrew acount acording to the best of my knowlag

Gilbert Goldsmith

[Sworn to before C. M. Woods, C.C.C., Adams Co., IL, 8 May 1839.]

GOLLAHER, William C.

Illenois May th 28 1839
    a bill of Damages a gainst the State of Missouri for Being unlaufully Driven from it

first for moove[ing] into the State $50.00
for Loss of propperty and time and Damage while in the
    State   800.00
for Loss of time and Damage of mooveing out of the
    State   150.00
[Total] $1,000.00

I certify the a bove a count to Be Just and true a cording to the Best of my Knowledg

William C. Gollaher

[Sworn to before C. M. Woods, C.C.C., Adams Co., IL, 29 May 1839.]

GOLLIHER, James

Quincy Ilenoy May 18th 1839

---

[16]It is unclear whether the "ger" is part of a name (Clevenger) or an abbreviated form of "Junior." The editor assumes "Junior" because it is followed by "and seanier" (senior).

Damage receivd by the inhabit[*ants*] of Missourie & expences in
Mooveing $1,000.00
    also expo[s]ed to the weather in which sickness followed & the loss
of one of my Children othr sickness also occasioned by the same

James Golliher

I certify the a bove to be true according to the best of my knowledge

J Golliher

[*Sworn to before C. M. Woods, C.C.C., Adams Co., IL, 18 May 1839.*]

GOULD, William

May 10th 1839
    State of Missouri Dr to the under signed for damage Sustained by
being driven out of the State. loss in sale of land one hundred and fifty
dollars. loss of time fifty dollars Expence of moveing fifty dollars
                                                                    $250.00

Clayton May 11: 1839   Wm. Gould

[*Sworn to before J. Douglas, J.P., Adams Co., IL, 11 May 1839.*]

GRAHAM, Carter

Illenois Quincy May 16th 1839
    a bill of Damages a gainst the State of Missouri for Being Driven
from the State

first for mooving to State	$175.00
for loss of propperty in the State	1,300.00
for Being Driven from the Sta	200.00

    I [c]ertify the a bove to Be Just and true a cording to the Best of my
Knowledg

Carter Graham

[*Sworn to before C. M. Woods, C.C.C., Adams Co., IL, 22 May 1839.*]

GRANT, Ezra F.

May the 10th 1839

State of Missouri Debt to the undersigned for damages sustained by being driven from the afore said state loss of time fifty dollars one rifle eighteen dollars and expence of moveing thirty dollars whole amount

$98.00

Ezra F. Grant

[*Sworn to before J. Douglas, J.P., Adams Co., IL, 11 May 1839.*]

GRAVES, Alvin C.

Nov 1833

State of Missourie Dr to Alvin C. Graves for being Driven from Jackson County to Clay and from Clay to Caldwell and from caldwell out of the state

Dr to being Driven from Jackson County being forsed to leave my land ~~and~~ of two hundred and forty acres with a good improvement of a house and about 30 acres under fence and tanyard with a bout one thousand Dollars worth of stock Ordered off by a mob headed by Gabrael Fitzhugh and the loss of my crop	$5,000.00
to being Driven from Clay County to Caldwell in 1836 and 1837	1,500.00
to being Driven from Caldwell in 1838 having to leave the state in the winter and the sufferings of my family	3,000.00
to being forsed to leave my farm of one hundred ten acres of land with ~~about~~ house and smokehouse and stable and a bout fifteen acres under fence	1,000.00
to my house and smokehouse being burned	500.00
to being deprived of citizanship	25,000.00
	$36,000.00

Alvin C Graves

I certify the above ~~to~~ acount to be correct acording to the best of my Knowledg

Alvin C. Graves

[*Sworn to before C. M. Woods, C.C.C., Adams Co., IL, 6 May 1839.*]

GRAYBILL, Michael

Illenois adams county May 11th 1839
    the following is my charge for Damage a gainst the State of missauri
Viz in 1838 and 1839

house taken seventy five Dollars	$75.00
one waggon and harness Sixty Dollars	60.00
five months time Lost my self and three boys three hundred and Sixty Dolls	360.00
in Land fifty Dollars	50.00
vegitables five Dollars	5.00
hogs twenty Dollars	20.00
five hundred and seventy Doll. total sum	$570.00

Michael Graybill

[*Sworn to before W. Oglesby, J.P., Adams Co., IL, 11 May 1839.*]

GREENE, Addison[17]

Quincy March 17 1840
    I Addison Greene do Certify that in the month of october one thousan Eight hundred & thirty Eight; when I was peacable walking the high rodes in Ray County State of Mosur[a] I was molested & taken a prisnor by ten armed men, who took from me one dobled Barrel fowling pice & a[···]ipags thetning to blowout my Brains & Swore that if ~~they~~ I was a Mormon they would hang me without further cerrimoney—
    Thay had previously been too my lodging & taken my horse Saddle & Bridle. all was then taken in to the woods about one Miled too Bogards Camp I was Kept a Prisnor untill the next morning when I was let go but have not obtained any part of my proprty what was worth about one hundred & fifty dollars.

A Greene

[*Sworn to before J. H. Holton, N.P., Adams Co., IL, 17 Mar 1840.*]

---

[17] Also found in *HC* 4:65 and in JH 17 Mar 1840.

GREENE, John P.[18]

Quincy March 17, 1840

I John P. Greene was in company with Severel of my neighbors wa[*l*]king the Rode in peace when one of oure company a young man by the name of Obanion was Shot down at my Side! being Shot by a company of mobbers. & Soon after this we ware fireed uppon a gain & two more ware Kiled & Several other woundd this was about the 25 day of oct. one thousan Eight hund[*red*] & thirty Eight in the State of Mosura. & I do hereeby Certify the above to bee true according to the best of my knowledge

John P. Greene

[*Sworn to before J. H. Holton, N.P., Adams Co., IL, 17 March 1840.*]

GROSBERRY, Zimri

Illinois Quincy May 15, 1839

A Bill of Damages against the State of Missouri

~~First~~ for being driven from the State	
First for loss of property in the State	$50.00
for moving out of the State	25.00
[*Total*]	$75.00

I certify the above account to be true and just according to the best of my knowledge

Zimri Grosberry

[*Sworn to before C. M. Woods, C.C.C., Adams Co., IL, 15 May 1839.*]

GROVER, Thomas

Illenois May the 7 1839

a bill of Damages and Debt a gainst the State of Missourie in conciquence of the Goviner order of Extermination

Damage By hogs and Cattle Being stolen	
by the missourians and also farming tools	$65.00

---

[18] Also found in *HC* 4:65 and in JH 17 Mar 1840.

also loss on a farm	900.00
also loss on two town lots	75.00
also loss on Grain	85.00
	$1,125.00

I Do here by certify that the a bove acount to Be Just and true a cording to the Best of my knowledg

Thomas Grover

[*Sworn to before C. M. Woods, C.C.C., Adams Co., IL, 7 May 1839.*]

GROVES, Elisha H.

Columbus Adams County Ill May 6: 1839

This is to cirtify of the Loss that I have met with in the State of Mosouri I removed into the County of Daves in the winter of 1837 have ing bought one hudred and Sixty Acres of Land which Cost me three hundred and Sixty Dollars on which I Done two hundred Dollars worth of Improvement in the mont of october 1838 the mob drove me from My place and Stold my Cattle hogs plows hoes Chanes Destroyed bees I removed into Diammon a town in the County of Daves Commeced by the Morman peopele whare my wife was brot to bed on the 7 of November without a Shelter to Cover from the Storm on the 11 of November I was Drove out of the County of Davis into Calwell Still without a shelter to Cover from the Storm a gain drove out of the State of Mosouri by the threats of the Mob which has destroyed my health and that of my famely

Expence in moveing	$30.00
Lost in my Possession	500.00
2 yoke of work Cattle	120.00
in hogs	50.00
in plows hoes Chanes bees	40.00
one Cow Corn fodder hay potatoes Cabig	50.00
Chickens	5.00
5 monts time with a tum	200.00

I am know a liveing neare Colubus in Aams Co Ill destitute of a home or menes to obtain the Comforts of Life

tun thousand Dollars would not be a Compsation for the abuse the Loss of health the Suffering and the Loss of Citisonship which I had for Six years in the State of Mosouri

I have here given a fare Statement of my Loss and Sufferings in the fall and winter of 1838 & 39

Elisha H Groves

I Certify the above account to be Just and true according to the best of my knowadge

Elisha H. Groves

[*Sworn to before C. M. Woods, C.C.C., Adams Co., IL, 22 May 1839.*]

GROVES, Elisha H.[19]

I Elisha H Groves of the town of Quincy and state of Illinois depose and saith that I was a resident of Davies County in the state of Missouri and that on the 16th day of November in the year of our Lord 1838 Judge Vinson Smith and others came to my house and ordered myself and famely Levi Taylr David Osborn & othes to Leave our possessions which we had bought of Government and payed our money for the same saying we must within three days leave the County or they would take our lives. for ther was no Law to save us after that time in consequence of ther procedings together with Govorner Boggs exterminating order we were compelld to Leave the state of Missouri Furthermore this deponent saith not. Given under my hand at Quincy the 17 day of March AD 1840

Elisha H. Groves

[*Sworn to before W. Tainter, who signed for C. M. Woods, C.C.C., Adams Co., IL, 16 Mar 1840.*]

HAMILTON, James B.

Illinois Quincy May 14 1839
    a bill of Damage a gainst the State of Missouri for Deprivation propperty time mooving an other Expences

first fo mooveing to the State	$40.00
for property lost in the State By a mob	500.00
for mooveing out of the State	150.00
	$690.00

---

[19] Also found in *HC* 4:68 and in JH 17 Mar 1840.

I certify the a bove a count to be Just and true a cording to the best of my knowledg.

James B. Hamilton

[Sworn to before C. M. Woods, C.C.C., Adams Co., IL, 15 May 1839.]

HANCOCK, Alvah

I Alvah Hancock do certify that I was driven from Jackson co from house & lands crops & stock by a mob In the year of our lord 1833 one thousand dollars

& being compeld to leave clay co & go to coldwell five hundred dollars

& being drove from colwell from ~~two~~ one forty acres with thre bildings & a good improvement And one fration peace with three bildings and a good stock of hogs & bees & cattle damage three thousand dollars.

full a mount four thousand five hundred dollars

Alvah Hancock

[Sworn to before D. H. Wells, J.P., Hancock, Co., IL, 14 Mar 1840.]

HANCOCK, Joseph

Nauvoo March 14th 1840

I Joseph Hancock of Hancock Co Illenois do certify that I was driven from my possesions in Caldwell and Clay Countys Mo Consisting of two eighty acors of land one in Clay the other in Caldwell Co, also a City lot in farwest together with Cattle horses hogs and grain to the amount of twelve hundread dollars $1,200.00

land 3,000.00

$4,200.00 Amount

Also I testefy that I hered many threats a gainst the mormons, one in perticular Archabold Moss swore he would kill any Mormon he Could see in any place whare he Could find him

my boy was robed of his rifle and I have not seen it since worth $16 dollars

Joseph **X** Hancock

[Sworn to before D. H. Wells, J.P., Hancock Co., IL, 14 Mar 1840.]

HANCOCK, Levi W.

Loss I have endured by the state of Missouri

Moveing from Ohio to Mo	$100.00
Loss in lands	500.00
Loss in buildings	100.00
Loss in hogs & other Creatuers	75.00
Loss in tooles & timber	100.00
Damage for being drove from the state in the stormy month of march cost and trouble & time which has bin the cause of considrable sickness and perhaps will bring death	1,000.00
whole amount	$1,875.00

May—19th—1838   Levi W Hancock

[*Not sworn.*]

HANCOCK, Levi W.

Nauvoo Hancock Co Illenois March 14th 1840

I Levi W Hancock do Certify that I was driven from my possessions in Missouri Consisting of forty acors of land three miles from farwest ten acors on the side of town which was to be run into lots also one City lot nere the Contemplated Church was to stand together with much looss property houses shop tools and lumber to work hogs sheep & poltry to the amount of

land	$2,000.00
buildings improvement and other losses	500.00
	$2,500.00

Levi W Hancock

[*Sworn to before D. H. Wells, J.P., Hancock Co., IL, 14 Mar 1840.*]

HANCOCK, Solomon

The State of Missouri to Solomon Hancock Dr. For damages in being driven from Jackson County in Novr. 1833 and loss of property and Time and other privations $500.00

And again from Caldwell County in the Sprind of 1839 loss of property &c   1,000.00

[*Sworn to before C. M. Woods, C.C.C., Adams Co., IL, 3 Jun 1839.*]

HANCOCK, Thomas

The State of Missouri to Thomas Hancock dr. For being driven from Caldwell County in the Spring of 1839 and loss of property Expense of moving and other privations $500.00

[Sworn to before C. M. Woods, C.C.C., Adams Co., IL, 3 Jun 1839.]

HARRIS, George W.

Quincy Illinois May 8th 1839
        The State of ~~Illinois~~ Missouri to Geo W Harris Dr

to one lot in Far West with hous and barn and frute trees on the Same	$1,000.00
to another lot in Far West unocupied	600.00
to a wood lot of forty acres Joining the City	1,000.00
to a lot of land in Adam on Diammon Joining Square	1,000.00
to three Sections of land that I improved on for my Self and famely in Daves County	3,000.00
to fals imprisonment for rising of thre weeks in an unfinished Coart hous with the windows broken out of about avery window and very Coald wether Say worse than laying out in the woods in the same kind of weather	3,000.00
	$9,600.00

Geo W Harris

[Not sworn.]

HARRIS, Moses

Missouri Dr. for damages
        first for moveing to Missouri $200.00
        for standing under arms against a mob 2 weeks and for being driven from my place in Coldwell Co. Mo. and the loss of property and the loss of health $3,000.00
        for not having the right as a sitizen of Missouri 3,000.00

this May the 6th AD. 1839   Moses Harris

I certify this to be a true copy of damages to the best of my knowledge

Moses Harris

[*Sworn to before C. M. Woods, C.C.C., Adams Co., IL, 6 May 1839.*]

HARTWELL, Reuben P.

quincy May 6th 1839
    A bill of damags sustained by Missouri Mob

to exspence money two and from Missouri	$150.00
to being hindered from buisness by mob	150.00
to damage done to waggon by Esq Black	10.00
to suffering through fear of extermination	300.00
to sacrifce of propperty	25.00
	$635.00

I hearby certify the above to be a true account acording to the best of my knowledge

Reuben P. Hartwell

[*Sworn to before C. M. Woods, C.C.C., Adams Co., IL, 6 May 1839.*]

HARVEY, John

Quincy Illinois May 11 1839
    A Bill of Damages and Dept in the State of Missouri

First For moving to the State	$50.00
Loss on Land	200.00
Losses on Grain	50.00
Expences of Moving Away	50.00

I Certify the above account to be Just and true according to the best of my knoledge

John Harvey

[*Sworn to before C. M. Woods, C.C.C., Adams Co., IL, 11 May 1839.*]

HARVEY, Johnathan L.

State of Missouri to Johnathan L. Harvey

October	Dr. to payment on land $80.00	$80.00
5th 1838	to one Rifle $20.00	20.00
	one heifer $8 50/100	8.50
	to damage & expense for being complled to	
	remove out of the state $50.00	50.00
	to hay & fodder $10.00	10.00
Apr 5th	to loss of time from August 5th to Aprail 5th	
1839	1839 25$ per month $200.00	200.00
	total	$440.50

I certify the above to be true according to the best of my knowledge

Johnathan L. Harvey

[Sworn to before C. M. Woods, C.C.C., Adams Co., IL, 18 May 1839.]

HAWK, William[20]

Montrose Lee co Iowa Jan 7 1840

I hereby certify that Some time in the month of Oct 1838 an armed force collected in the County of Carrol near Dewitt and in open day light drove a man by the name of [H]umphrey out of his house and set fire to it and burned it to ashes and then sent an express ordering all the Mormons to leave the place as Soon as the next day the next day they Sent another express ordering them to leave in six hours or they would be massacred upon the ground they also fired their guns at diffirent persons traveling the road near the town the mormons were at length compelled to leave their possessions and all removed to caldwell consisting of Seventy and perhaps one hundred families many of whome were in want of the Sustinance of life sick & Some died upon the way about two weeks after this another armed force invaded Farwest took my gun and compelled me to Sign away my property both personall and real and leave the State fourth with

Wm. Hawk

[Sworn to before D. W. Kilbourn, J.P., Lee Co., IA, 7 Jan 1840.]

---

[20] Also found in *HC* 4:58 and in JH 7 Jan 1840.

HAWLEY, Pierce

Pierce Hawley left Sangamon County Illinois to go to the State of Mos[ura] on the 4 of Sept 1837

i left I went with 34 head of cattle 69 head of Sheap 6 hosses 3 waggons arived in colwell county on the 20 of November [vying] to high wal[ers] expences	$255.50
purchesed 30 acros of land and lost of laber and land	250.00
Mooved to ray county to rent afarm the lose of the crop by being drove from the same	425.00
one man was whiped that i sent to gether my grane	
Sept 1838 i baught a lot in Duett for to moove there but was prevented by the mob i was take a prisner and forbced to moove then on the penelty of my life and had to loose my lot for i could not sel it the lot cost	100.00
Damage Sustained	100.00
Driven from ray county on the 24 of octtober by the mob to colwell count Damag for beng driveen with my wife and nine children	300.00
then haveing to leave the S[t]ate with my famaly in the wintir and the lose of propperty by suirepise by being compeld to sel my property at a redused prise	1,000.00
the mob stole 2 ho[r]ses one [acrage] 3 hogs which was worth	350.00
the lose of time from the the first of Octtober 1838 to the first of may 1839 with my self and famaly	500.00
	$3,280.50

I certify that the a bove acount to be just acording to the best of my knowlage

Pierce Hawley

[Sworn to before C. M. Woods, C.C.C., Adams Co., IL, 6 May 1839.]

HAWN, James

A bill of Damiges a gainst State of mysouri for being Driven Loss of propperty I Charge five Hundrd Dollars
Quincy may 18th 1839

I certify the a bove to Be Just and and true a cording to the Best of my Knowledg—

James Hawn

[Sworn to before C. M. Woods, C.C.C., Adams Co., IL, 17 May 1839.]

HAYSE, Thomas

Illanois Quincy May the 8th 1839
 a bill of Debt and damages against the state of missouri which accrued in consequence of the goviners order of Extermination

first Charge for expence in Moving to the state	$300.00
loss of time and property personal	100.00
and [beeind] Driven from house and Land and wife and Childern and state	1,000.00

 I hereby Certify the above to be just and true given under my hand the Day and date above written

Thomas Hayse

[Sworn to before C. M. Woods, C.C.C., Adams Co., IL, 8 May 1839.]

HEDLOCK, Reuben

May the 7 1839 Quincy Illenois
 a bill of Damiges and debt against the State of Missouri for being Driven from place to pl[ace] and at last by the order of the Goviner out of the State

for mooveing from the State of New York to Caldwell County Mo	$200.00
two Horses taken by the mob	150.00
Loss of landed propperty	230.00
Loss of furnitur and other propperty	25.00
for being Driven from the State	500.00
	$1,105.00

 I Do certify that the a bove acount is Just and true a cording to the best of my Knowledg

Reuben Hedlock

[Sworn to before C. M. Woods, C.C.C., Adams Co., IL, 7 May 1839.]

HENDRICKS, James

May th9 1839 Illenois Quincy
    A count against the State of Mo for Debt and Damage Sustaned in conciquence of the Exterminating order

first time and expence	$150.00
for Being Driven from Clay to caldwel	50.00
Loss on Land in Caldwell	1,120.00
Stole of houshold goods by the mob	61.00
Stolen one cow and other propprty	51.00
mooving from the State Saccrfis	1,000.00
	$2,432.00

I have also ben made a cripple for life having ben Shot By this Hellish Band
    I certify the a bove a count to Be Just and true a cording to the Best of my knowledg

James Hendricks

[Sworn to before C. M. Woods, C.C.C., Adams Co., IL, 9 May 1839.]

HENDRICKSON, Cornelius

Handcock Co and State of Illinois Warsaw illinois January 4 1840
    An estimation made of property and time of my Self and famlys loss in State of missouri by being Driven a bout by mob from place to place from The year 33 to year 38 and last of all driven from The State by orders of the governor which amounts To one thousand three hundred dollars

Cornelius Hendrickson

I do also testify that I was in far west Callwell County when the militia troops Came there demanded our arms which we gave up and then placed a Guard around us for many days and distroyed the Property Such as burnig house logs and rails and many other deprodations &c

Cornelius Hendrickson

NB I saw Joseph Smith Jr Sidney Rigdon limon white And fifty or Sixty others taken prisoners and led off &C

[Sworn to before A. Monroe, J.P., Hancock Co., IL, 6 Jan 1840.]

HERR, John P.

Quincy May the 7th 1839
    State of Missouri Dr for damages

For loss of property in Jackson County in 1833
by having to leave the County in consequence of a mob $50.00
for loss in Clay County in consequence of a mob in 1836   75.00
for loss of property and labour in Caldwell County, in
    consequence of the Govenors exterminating order in
    1838   500.00
for cittizenship distress and trouble
    What you please

                John P. Herr

    I hereby certify that the above is a true bill according to the best of my knowledge

                John P. Herr

[*Sworn to before C. M. Woods, C.C.C., Adams Co., IL, 7 May 1839.*]

HERRICK, Lemuel   SL

in the year 1834 in Jackson County Mo

to the Burning my house $150.00
to Burning my fence laying my impruvment wast[e]   150.00
to the desstrucktion of my Crops   100.00
to mooving from place to place for 8 weeks   100.00
to loss of propoty in Caldwell in 1838 to three horses stolen   100.00
to loss in my land   600.00
to loss in persnell property   200.00
to Mooving from Caldwell to Ilanoiss   100.00
                $1,500.00

    A Bill of damage done by the Mobbers of Missouri to me

                Lemuel Herrick

I certify the within acount to Be Just and true a cording to the Best of my Knowledg

Lemuel Herrick

[Sworn to before C. M. Woods, C.C.C., Adams Co., IL, 29 May 1839.]

HESS, Jacob

May the 11th 1839. Illinois Quinsey

An account against the State of Missouri for debt and Damage Sustained in Consequence of the Exterminating Order

Loss on Land	$175.00
Damage & Crop	108.00
Removal	30.00
	$313.00

I certify the above to be a true and Just account according to the best of my Knowledge

Jacob Hess

[Sworn to before C. M. Woods, C.C.C., Adams Co., IL, 11 May 1839.]

HEWITT, William

Illenois May the 7th 1839

A bill of Damages and Debt a gainst the State of Missouri in Conseqeunce of the Governors Extermnating order	
first for being Deprived of 160 acres of Land	$300.00
for 1 rifle gun	20.00
for the Loss of time in Defence	186.00
for being Driven from the State	500.00
	$906.00

I do hereby certify that the a bove a count is Just and true according to the Best of my knowledge

William Hewitt

[Sworn to before C. M. Woods, C.C.C., Adams Co., IL, 7 May 1839.]

HICKS, S.

This may Certify that in 1836 i moved from the State of michigan to missura and was Stoped on the rode in miss[ura] by a mob and in 1838 drove out of the State missura by the governor orders under the penelty of deth

lost mooving to the State of missura	$50.00
Lost in property in ray County	30.00
Lost in property in Caldwell County	200.00
Damages and expenses of moving to this place	50.00
~~Rites of CitizenShip moving to this place~~	

I Certify that the within is a true Copy of damages acording to the best of my Ability

May the 6 1839   S. Hicks

[Sworn to before C. M. Woods, C.C.C., Adams Co., IL, 6 May 1839.]

HIGBEE, Isaac

Quincy May the 6th 1839

A bill of damages against the state of Missouri for moving from the state of Ohio to Jackson Co. Missouri in 1833	$75.00
for the loss of property in land burning my house grain &c	500.00
loss of property in Clay County	300.00
for the loss of property ~~of~~ in Land and stock in caldwell County Mo. in 1838	500.00
for removing out of the state in concequence of the govenors exterminating order	50.00
for being deprived of citicenship in being driven from Jackson County and also from the state What you please	

I do hereby certify the above to be true

Isaac Higbee

[Not sworn.]

HIGBEE, John S.

A Bill of Damages Against the state of missouri

expences for moveing from ohio to Jackson Co. in:	$100.00
for being Driven from Jackson County in 1833 looseing my crop stock expence of moveing an loss of time	1,000.00
for being Driven from Clay County in 1836 for loss of property stock property	300.00
for Driveng from Caldwell County in 1838 loss of property expence of moving on account of the exterminating order by the govenor	1,000.00
for loss of citicenship	1,000.00
for false imprisonment 30 Days	600.00

I certify the above a counts to Be Just and true a cording to the Best of my Knowledg

John S. Higbee

[Sworn to before C. M. Woods, C.C.C., Adams Co., IL, 8 May 1839.]

HIGBEE, Sophia

Quincy May the 6th 1839

A bill of damages against the state of Missouri for moving from ohio to Jackson Co. Mo.	$75.00
for loss of property in improvements & stock in Jacson Co in 1833 in consequence of being driven by a mob	500.00
for losses in Clay Co. in consequence of being driven in 1836	300.00
for loss of property in Caldwell Co in labour and stock &c	200.00
for expence of moving out of the state	40.00

for being deprived of my citicenship in consequence of the govenors exterminating order in 1838 and being exposed in the ~~my~~ 73d year of my age and the loss of my husband since I came here no earthly consideration can compensate me

Sophia Higbee

I do hereby certify the above to be true according to the best of my knowledge

Sophia Higbee

[Sworn to before C. M. Woods, C.C.C., Adams Co., IL, 6 May 1839.]

HILL, Elisha

Handcock C State of Illenois

A Bill of Damages Sustaind by a mob in the state of Missouri during the years 1838 and 9 by being driven from the state

Sacrafised to go there in Sale of property	$100.00
Expence of moveing there	130.00
Sacrafised by the mob in the State	500.00
Expence of moveing from the State and lost time	170.00
To 1 rifle gun taken by the Malitia	25.00
Total nine hundred and twenty five Dollars	$925.00

Elisha Hill

[Sworn to before A. Monroe, J.P., Hancock Co., IL, 6 Jan 1840.]

HILLMAN, Sarah

Loss of property in Mo. by the mob

to one house and 40 acres of Land worth		$500.00
to one span of horses	do	100.00
to one house and city lot	do	100.00
to time and a gun that was taken		100.00

Sarah Hillman

[Not sworn.]

HOLBROOK, Chandler

Losses sustaind by moving into the State of missouri

April 14 1834, moved from the State of New York into missouri	70.00
In the year 1838 & 1839	

Losses time 3 month lost	80.00
A yong mare	80.00
Potatoes Turnips Buckwheat and Corn	80.00
Things stolen	40.00
six sheep	18.00
[*Subtotal*]	$368.00
Losses on Lands sustained moving from the State Defermation, False Imprisonment and the losses on Lands	700.00
	$1,068.00

Chandler Holbrook

I do hereby certif that the above bill of accounts are correct according to the best of my knowledge

Chandler Holbrook

[*Sworn to before C. M. Woods, C.C.C., Adams Co., IL, 6 May 1839.*]

HOLLINSHEAD, Thomas

This is a true Statement of the loss and damages which I have Sustained in the State of Missouri in the County of Carroll, being driven off from my purchased possessions in the Town of dewitt, for which I payed $400 Dollars and hold a lawful Deed on record in Carrolton in the above named County the above Circumstances took place in the month of October in year 1838 by a mob of the Citizens of Carroll and other adjacent Counties and after I had Complied So far as to leave my House, was afterward taken prisener by two of the mob, and plundered of my watch worth $20 Dollars and then lodged in the County Goal where I was detained 7 days; I was then let out with [s]trict orders to leave the County in 24 hours; this was done by the Clerk of that County and others: and afterwords ordered to leave the State with the others professing the Same religion as my Self

My Clame of property, and expenses disappointment and so forth I consider to be worth Eight hundred Dollars $800

Adams Co. Illinois May 6th 1839   Thomas Hollinshead

I here by Certify the within to be a true satement

Thos. Hollinshead

[*Sworn to before C. M. Woods, C.C.C., Adams Co., IL, 6 May 1839.*]

HOLMAN, David

Quincy Illinois May 18th 1839
    A Bill against the State of Missouri

for in the Stat	$50.00
for the Burning of my house	150.00
for Laws of time	200.00
and Cow	25.00
for Moveing from the State	25.00
[*Subtotal*]	$450.00
for Land	480.00
	$930.00

I Certify the above account to be Just and true acording to the best of my Knowlage

David Holman

[*Sworn to before C. M. Woods, C.C.C., Adams Co., IL, 18 May 1839.*]

HOLMAN, James S.

Quincy Illinois May 18 1839

loss of property in the state of Missouri	
damage in going to the state	$200.00
loss of property in the state	200.00
in coming out of the state	40.00

I Certify the above to be true according to the best of my knowledge

James S. Holman

[*Sworn to before C. M. Woods, C.C.C., Adams Co., IL, 18 May 1839.*]

HOLMAN, Joshua S.

A bill of damages against the State of Missouri in 1838 For moveing to the state and one year labour being A mecanick and haveing A large famely, Being on expense	$500.00
in 1839 For the losse property and labour and remooving from the state	300.00

for being deprived of Citersnship by being driven by A cruel mob. Make it your own case

Joshua S. Holman

I do hereby Certify that the a bove bill of damages and Losses were Sustained by me and are correct according to the best of my judgement and abilities

Joshua S Holman

[*Sworn to before C. M. Woods, C.C.C., Adams Co., IL, 6 May 1839.*]

HORR, Alvin

A bill of property Lost by reason of the mob of Missouri

fifteen ackers of corn and potatoes in fayette Co	$75.00
loss of time and expense	30.00
~~Credit for our right~~	~~10.00~~
Clay County to a house and nine ackers of improvement on a lease	100.00
to loss of time	30.00
to labour	9.00
~~Credit for wheat and corn~~	~~18.00~~
Davis County to one improvement	150.00
to eleven ackers of corn	88.00
to wheat potatoes turnips garden and pumpkins	25.00
by the loss of waggon farming tools and bees	50.00
loss of time and expenee of moving	88.00
to one rifle sword and pistol	25.00
~~Credit to loss of hogs~~	~~15.00 Credit in~~ [——]
Credit by one watch	10.00
by cash	29.00
	$685.00

I certify the above to be a true bill of my loss as pertains april 14—1839

Alvin Hor

I certify the Within a count to Be just and true a cording to the Best of my Knowledg

Alvin Horr

[Sworn to before C. M. Woods, C.C.C., Adams Co., IL, 1 Jun 1839.]

HULET, Charles

Illenois Quincy May th14 1839
    a bill of Damages against the State of Missouri for Bein Driven from the State

fo mooving to the State and expences	$1,500.00
Loss of propperty in the State	1,000.00
for leaveing the State by mobocracy	1,500.00
	$4,000.00

I certify the a bove acount to be Just and true a cording to the best of my Knowledg

Charles Hulet

[Sworn to before C. M. Woods, C.C.C., Adams Co., IL, 14 May 1839.]

HULET, Francis

This may Certify that I Francis Hewlet was Driven from my Land from my house and home and famaly exposed to Storm in the month of November and my Self whipt by a lawles mob, the disavantages I have Labourd under with loss of time and property for five years and upwards, and after Setling in peace in Colwell County am again driven from my land house and home in the month of march I therefoer State my Damage at two thousan Dollars.

April the 19th 1839 at Adams County Ellinois   Francis Hulet

I certify the within to Be a true acount acording to the Best of my knowledg

Francis Hulet

[Sworn to before C. M. Woods, C.C.C., Adams Co., IL, 21 May 1839.]

HULET, Sylvester

Illenois Quincy May 14th 1839
    a bill of Damage a gainst the State of Missouri for being Driven from the State and loss of propperty

first for mooving to State and Expence	$75.00
for the loss of propperty in Jackson co and oth[er] placs bein Driven from place to place	1,500.00
for leaving the State and Expences	1,000.00
	$2,325.00

I certify the above acount to be true and Just a cording to the best of my knowledg

Sylvester Hulet

[Sworn to before C. M. Woods, C.C.C., Adams Co., IL, 14 May 1839.]

HUMPHREY, Smith[21]

Illinois Adams co March 16th 1840
    I Smith Humphrey Certify that I was a Citizen of Mysouri in Eighteen Hundred and thirty Eight and Sometine in the Month of oct of the Same year I was fallen uppon by A mob Commanded By Hyrum Standly the[y] took my Goods out of my House and Said Stanley Set fire to my house and Burnt it Before my Eyse and orderd me to leave the place forth with I Remoovd from Dewitt to Caldwell County where I was a gain a Saild By Govener Bogs Exterminating malitia the[y] took me prisiner and Robd my waggon of foure Hundred Dollars in cash and one thousand Dollars worth of Goods and Drove me out of the State

Smith Humphrey

[Sworn to before W. Tainter, who signed for C. M. Woods, C.C.C., Adams Co., IL, 16 Mar 1840.]

HUNT, Jefferson

Illeenois quincy May the 11 1839
    a Bill of damage a gainst the State of Missur[i]

---

[21] Also found in JH 16 Mar 1840.

Los of Property while in the State Los of land	$1,000.00
Los of Cattle Sheep hogs house hold furnature	500.00
for Being drove out of the State	500.00

I do hear By Certify that the aBove is a Just and tru Bill according to the Best of my knowdge

Jefferson Hunt

[Sworn to before C. M. Woods, C.C.C., Adams Co., IL, 11 May 1839.]

HUNTINGTON, Dimick B.

Quincy Illenois may the 8th 1839

A Bill of Domage against the State of Missouri in Consequenc of the Governors Exterminateing Order

first for moveing to the State	$100.00
for Loss of Property in notes Land and Stock &c	4,200.00
for Loss of time in Defending my rights against a mob	500.00
for moveing from the State	1,000.00
	$5,800.00

I certify the above acount to Be Just and true a cording to the Best of my knowledg

Dimick B Huntington

[Sworn to before C. M. Woods, C.C.C., Adams Co., IL, 9 May 1839.]

HUNTINGTON, William

State of Missouri Dr. to Wm. Huntington

to moveing from state of New York to Missouri	$150.00
to Log house built in Davis County	50.00
to ten months time one month of the time acting as One of the committe in Davis county settling the business Of the church agreable to the order of General Willson in said time my Life was thretned from time to Time at Last driven out of the county by a ruthless Mob	100.00
to Being drove out of the state by order of Govenor Bogs— said damge I will not Estimate but will leave it for others	

Quincy May 7th 1839   Wm. Huntington

Amt estimated $1,650.00

I hereby certify that the above account is just and true according to the best of my knowledge

Wm. Huntington

[*Sworn to before C. M. Woods, C.C.C., Adams Co., IL, 7 May 1839.*]

HUNTSMAN, Jacob

Illenois Quincy May th11 1839
    a bill of Damage a gainst the State Missorie for Loss of time and propperty

for mooving in to the State	$50.00
for Loss of propperty in the State	200.00
for Leaving the State	25.00
	$725.00

I Certify the a bov to Be a Just a count a cording to the Best of m[y] Knowledg

Jacob huntsman

[*Sworn to before C. M. Woods, C.C.C., Adams Co., IL, 11 May 1839.*]

HUNTSMAN, James

Illenois Quincy May th 11 1839
    a bill of Damagees a gainst the State of missouri for Being Driven from it—

first for mooving to th State	$150.00
for loss of propperty in the State on Land and other propprty	1,000.00
for leaving th State and Being Broke up &c &c	100.00

I certify the a bove acount to Be Just and true a cording to the Best of my knowedg—

James Huntsman

[*Sworn to before C. M. Woods, C.C.C., Adams Co., IL, 11 May 1839.*]

HUNTSMAN, James W.

May the 9th 1839 Illinois Quinsey
        An account against the State of Missouri for debt & damage Sustained in consequence of the Exterminating Order

Damage and removeal $100.00

        I certify the above account to be Just and true according to the best of My Knowledge

                                                        James W. Huntsman

[Sworn to before C. M. Woods, C.C.C., Adams Co., IL, 9 May 1839.]

HUNTSMAN, John

Quincy Ill May 11th 1839
        A bill of damages a gainst the State of Missouri

For moveing in to the State $50.00
loss of property and moveing out of the State   150.00

        I certify the above to be just and true to the best of my knowledge

                                                        John Huntsman

[Sworn to before C. M. Woods, C.C.C., Adams Co., IL, 11 May 1839.]

HUNTSMAN, Lydia

Illenois Quincy may 11th 1839
        a bill of Damages a gainst the State of missourie for Being Driven from the State

first for mooving in to the State $20.00
for propperty Loss in the State of Mo   100.00
For mooving out of the State   20.00
                                                                     $140.00

        I certify th a bove to Be true and Just a cording to th Best of my knowledg

                                                        Lydia Huntsman

[Sworn to before C. M. Woods, C.C.C., Adams Co., IL, 11 May 1839.]

HUNTSMAN, Peter

Quincy Ill May 11th A.D. 1839

For moveing in to the State of Missouri	$100.00
For loss of property in lands &c	500.00
Damage by moveing out of the State	100.00

I certify the above to just and true according to best of my knowledge

Peter Huntsman

[Sworn to before C. M. Woods, C.C.C., Adams Co., IL, 11 May 1839.]

HURLBUTT, Simeon

May the 10th, 1839
Damages against State of Missouri

In moving to Missouri	$50.00
the Loss of my Clame in the State	650.00
in mooving to Caldwell Co	15.00
the Loss of grain and hay	75.50
my expences in moving to Illinois	30.00
the Loss on Land	800.00
Eight months loss of time	160.00
Damages in being driven and loss	1000.00
	$2780.50

Simeon Hurlbutt

I certify the a bove acount to Be true and Just acording to the Best of my knowledg

Simeon Hurlbutt

[Sworn to before C. M. Woods, C.C.C., Adams Co., IL, 14 May 1839.]

HUSTON, James

Adams County Illinois
A Bill of Damage Lost by the Exterminating order of the State of Missouri

To moving from the ohio to the State of Missouri	$300.00

Lost by a rifel gun and stopag on the way	40.00
Lost in Sale of Land	300.00
Lost by being Driven from my home & grain and other Articles	80.00
Loss in moving from Said State and the Expense is	100.00
	$820.00

May 24th 1839   Lost by me James Huston

[Sworn to before C. M. Woods, C.C.C., Adams Co., IL, 25 May 1839.]

JACKMAN, Levi

State of Missouri Dr to Levi Jackman

1833	To loss of buildings and improvemants	$150.00
	" loss of wheat on the ground	25.00
	" loss of time and expence of removing from Jackson Co. to Clay Co. having ben driven by the Mob	45.00
1836	To loss of buldings and auther property in Clay Co. and time and expence of removing to Coldwell Co. having ben driven by the mob	75.00
	extrey expence of obtaining provision	15.00
1838 & 39	To loss of land property in the city Far West	200.00
	To one rifle gun taken by the melitia from the gun smiths shop	15.00
	To loss on the value of Stock and auther property being obliged to sel it for les than its value on the account of having to leve the State by the order of Govener Boggs	50.00
	To loss of time of myself and boys and expence of removing from Caldwell Co. to the State of Illinois	150.00
	To damiages by being deprived of the rigts of Citezen Ship	1,000.00
	[Total]	$1,825.00

[Sworn to before A. Smith, J.P., Hancock Co., IL, 7 May 1839.]

JACKSON, Henry

A short account of my labours suffering & losses for the last seven years on the 26th of June 1832 myself and family started with my team for ~~Missoury~~ Jackson Co. Mo. Where we arrived Sept the 2d after ~~the~~ an expense of one hundred & fifty dollars I settled on 20 acres of Land builded an house cleared and fenced 6 acres all of which labor was worth one hundred dollars.

In the spring of 1833 I cultivated the above named six acres of ground a promising prospect presented itself to crown the labours of my hands, but much to my sorrow my fence was throne down almost every day; cattle & hogs turned in; untill my crop was destroyed; the loss of which is not less than 40 Dollars. Having labored with my hands for the support of my family & had obtained a hansome stock of Hogs amounting to 20 in all 7 of them would have weyed one hundred & fifty each; in all worth 30 d also a debt of 10 dollars 75 cts for labor which I lost—Then driven from the Co of Jackson by the force of arms, with my brethren the Latter Day Saints, I went with my family into Clay Co Mo here I had resort only to the labor of my hands, for our support, During the summer of 1834 I went to fort Levens Worth, where I labored at 13 dollors per month, until I collected means sufficient to buy 20 acres of land, situated on the state rode, 4 miles west of Liberty, where I built a house 18 by 30 with a petition wall: and cleared fenced and put into cultivation five acres of ground I remained here untill the fall of 1837 when I was forced to leave this place at the loss of 2 hundred dollars I sustained here leaveing me again only to the labor of my hands for the support of my family untill the spring of 1838 after living in the Co of Caldwell one year I removed to Randolph Co. Mo. where I rented a small farm and cultivated the same here my crop was again destroyed myself & family driven not only from home & [——] without any means of subsistance but from the state of Missouri having payed my taxes and worked the roads

Loosing again my crop worth 50 dollors together with Suffering by being driven amidst the stormy blasts of snow & rain in the month of March which So effected my Sight that I am not able to work which damage I Co-estimate at ~~the loss~~ no less than a maintainance for life after sustaining a loss of property to the amount of 590 dollars.

This 21 of May 1839   Henry Jackson

[Sworn to before C. M. Woods, C.C.C., Adams Co., IL, 24 May 1839.]

JACKSON, John

To Damage Sustaind by me John Jackson by being Driven from Jackson County and also from Caldwell County in the State of Missouri by Mob
    three thousand Dollars

John Jackson

[Sworn to before S. G. Jackson, J.P., Van Buren Co., IA, 6 Mar 1840.]

JACOBS, Henry

State of Missourie to Henry Jacobs Debtor to wit the following

to twenty acres of corn at fifty bushels per acre amounting to one thousand bushels at fifty cents per bushel	$500.00
Do. to two acres of oats at twenty five bush per acre amounting to fifty bushells at twenty five cents per bushells	12.50
Do. to one waggon	50.00
Do. to twenty eight hogs at two dollars and fifty cents per head	70.00
Do. to two guns	26.00
Do. to the possession of eighty acres of land and improvement on the same	150.00
Do. to personal abuse and being driven by the express order of the Govornor from the State of Missourie together with many difficultys attending the same being deprived of the rights of a free citisan of said Stait I shall charge the sum of	1,000.00
Do. to Sundry articles to wit—such as garden sauce farming tools house hold furniture &C for which I shall charge the sume of	75.00
Do. to the Loss of time seven months—also the expence of moveing from Missourie to the State of Illinois AD being in the month of Febuary and exposing my family at that inclemment seosen of the year I shall charge the State afore mentioned the sume of	200.00

I certify that the above Bill of damages to be according to the best of my Judgment

Quincy Illinois May the 8th 1839   Henry Jacobs

[Sworn to before C. M. Woods, C.C.C., Adams Co., IL, 8 May 1839.]

JOHNSON, Aaron

State of Missouri Dr to Aaron Johnson for Sundry damages and for the loss of property by mob and Malitia and for expences in moveing to and being driven from the State LoSes

expenes in moveing my family and furniture from Connectticut to Mssouri	$156.00
to eleven bushels of potatoes and about three tons of hay a load of Corn and a load of pumpkins which was consumed by the troops in far west Mo by Capt Kirk Patrick's Company which was Stationed as a gard near my residence in far west Mo the forepart of November in the year one Thousand Eight Hundred and thirty Eight	19.00
Do to one ax	2.00
Do to one fat cow	19.00
Some of the afore said Company of Capt Patrick's Cut a double harness in pieces and carried away the lines and neck straps; the names I Could not asertain damages	5.00
to one Sword	8.00
to loss on real estate	300.00
Expenses in removeing from the State	6.60

Being compelld to leave my home in mo and in consiquence of the loss of my property in mssouri not haveing means to be entertained like travellers but being exposed to the inclemency of the season without any Shelter save a covered waggon and a thin cotton tent from the Six of March untill the 20 of April the loss of health in consiquence thereof [——] is verry great in [—— —— —— —— ——] Being deprived of citizen ship in Mo the loss of time in Mo in consiquence of mob

Quincy Ill April 20 1839
    I do hereby certify that the above is a true Statement

Aaron Johnson

[*Sworn to before C. M. Woods, C.C.C., Adams Co., IL, 7 May 1839.*]

JOHNSON, Benjamin

Illenois Quincy May 18th 1839
    a bill of Damages a gainst the State of Missouri for being Driven from the State By a mob

first for mooving in to the State	$150.00
for propperty Lost in the State	200.00
for mooving out of the State	300.00

I certify the a bove to Be true and Just a cording to the Best of my Knowledg

Benjamin Johnson

[Sworn to before C. M. Woods, C.C.C., Adams Co., IL, 17 May 1839.]

JOHNSON, Edw.

State of Mis[o]uria To Edw. Johnson Dr

To Travling or Moving with my famely goods And Chattals from upper Canada on the intention of Being a setler & Cittizen in the Western part of of Misouria Wharein I was prevented By the Mob in Sharaton County Novr. 1838 & my famely sick

To 6 1/2 Days Travling With 3 Teems	$45.50
To Expences pr. Teem & Cattle said 6 1/2 Days	32.50
To ferrage pr. Detroit River	9.00
To Custom at the office of Detroit	28.50
To 8 Days Travling with 3 Waggons 160 miles	56.00
To Expences on the same	40.00
To 15 Days Travling with 3 Teems a $7 pr. Day	105.00
To the Expences on the Same	45.00
To ferrage over Mud Creek	3.00
To 10 Days Traveling with the afore said Teems	70.00
To Expences on the same	30.00
To ferrage on the Mississippy	9.50
To sundries viz Corn oats swine and other Articles to Tedious to Mention	130.00
To Loss on farm I was force to sele under val[u]e	250.00
To 2 Days Travling & ferrage across Mississippi	14.00
	$778.00

May the 24th 1839

Edw. Johnson

[Sworn to before C. M. Woods, C.C.C., Adams Co., IL, 24 May 1839.]

JOHNSON, Huntington

Huntington Johnson Bill of property los in Missouri in concequence of the mob & govener Bogs exterminating order

1 house & improvments on 1 acre of land in sitty farwest	$350.00
1 gun taken by the mob	15.00
Corn & hay & pumpkins	25.00
personal property	25.00
125 days lost time at 125 cts per day	156.25
the expence of moving out of the state	60.00
[*Subtotal*]	$631.25
the expense of moveing into the state	125.00
	$756.25

the abov is a true a count as far as I can recolect

Quincy May 7th AD 1839   Huntington Johnson

[*Sworn to before C. M. Woods, C.C.C., Adams Co., IL, 7 May 1839.*]

JOHNSON, Jacob

May the 9th 1839 Illenois Quinsey

An account against the State of Missouri for debt and damage Sustained in Consequence of the Exterminating Order—

I was driven from Jacckson County to Clay in the year 1833—for my improvement	$50.00
Wagon & Crop	50.00
[*Subtotal*]	$100.00
Driven from Caldwell 1839	
Loss on Land	200.00
Damage & removal	50.00
	$350.00

I certify the above to be a Just & true according to the best of my Knowledge

Jacob Johnson

[*Sworn to before C. M. Woods, C.C.C., Adams Co., IL, 9 May 1839.*]

JOHNSON, Jacob H.

May the 9th 1839 Illinois Quinsey
    an Account against the State of Missouri for debt and damage
Sustained in Consequence of the Exterminating Order—

Damage & removal $100

    I certify the above to be a Just and tru account according to the best
of my Knowledge

Jacob H X Johnson

[*Sworn to before C. M. Woods, C.C.C., Adams Co., IL, 9 May 1839.*]

JOHNSTON, Jesse W.[22]

Quincy Illinois March the 16 1840
    I Jesse W Johnston Certify that the following Circumstances took
place in the State of Missouri while I was a Resident of that State Viz. I
was takeen prisner By Goviner Bogs Exterminateing malitia I Saw one
man kild Belonging to the mormon Church and was forsed By them to
take Corn out of the fields of the mormon Church with out Care[.] this was
in the fall of 1838

Jesse W. Johnston

[*Sworn to before W. Tainter, who signed for C. M. Woods, C.C.C., Adams
Co., IL, 15 Mar 1840.*]

JONES, Benjamin

Quincy ~~May~~ Illinois May the 7 1839
    Debts and Damages against the State of Missourie for being Drivin
from that State By orders of the Govanor Expense of Moving into that
State $100.00
    the Loss of properity in Lands & Cattle Sheep and Crops and one
Rifle and two Pistols   500.00
    For fals Imprisoment when I was Inacunt and know proof found
agains me   1,000.00

---

[22] Also found in *HC* 4:64 and in JH 16 Mar 1840.

For my time while I was Standing in the Defense of my famaly and for the time of two Boyes imployed in the Same Bussness   100.00
And for Being Driven out of the State By orders of the Govanor
   1,000.00
This may Certify that this is a true Statment of facts acording to the Best of my Knowledge

Benjamin Jones

[*Sworn to before C. M. Woods, C.C.C., Adams Co., IL, 16 May 1839.*]

JONES, David

A bill of debt and damage against the State of missouri

the loss of one horse	~~$40.00~~ $30.00
house hold furniture	30.00
also sundary artacles	5.00
corn and foder	10.00
for beng driven from my farm my life thrtned my family exposd and driven to extreme poverty and expeld from jackson county	500.00
also being driven from clay county	500.00
also in caldwell county loss of cattle	50.00
also on the price of a wagon	15.00
loss of grain and foder	35.00
Sheep and hogs	10.00
~~land~~ provement on land	150.00
als[o] being orderd out of the State by order of the govaner to leave my house and home	5,000.00
totle amout	$6,335.00

I certify the above to bee a true a count a cording to the best of my knowledge

may the 14tnth 1839   David Jones

[*Sworn to before C. M. Woods, C.C.C., Adams Co., IL, 17 May 1839.*]

JONES, Stephen

Quincy Ill May 8th 1839
   A Charge of damages sustaind by Stephen Jones in Consequence of being driven at different times by mobs in the State of Missouri

the whole amount sumed together two hundred and fifteen Dollars

$215.00

I certify the above acount to Be Just and true acording to the Best of my Knowle[*dge*]

Quincy Ill May 8th 1839   Stephen Jones

[*Sworn to before C. M. Woods, C.C.C., Adams Co., IL, 15 May 1839.*]

JUDD, Arza, Jr.

Handcock County Illenois
   A bill of damages of property lost in the State of Missouri in consequence of a mob that arose in 1838

loss of property by moveing to the state	$600.00
expence of Moveing into the state	200.00
loss of property and time in the state	200.00
loss by moveing out of the state or expence	100.00

Arza Judd Jun

[*Sworn to before A. Monroe, J.P., Hancock Co. IL, 6 Jan 1840.*]

JUDD, Philo

I Philo Judd do solmly swear that having moved to the State of Missouri in the Year of our Lord 1832 and Settled in Jackson County in 1833 the Church of latter day Saints Being assailed by a mob I with some others ware fired upon by said mob with out Cause or provocation Killed one man that was with me and wounded several others I was compelled By said mob to leave said county to my Damage in loss of time and property five Hundred Dollars the Names of some of Said mob Ware Hugh L Brazeal James Campell James Mcgee and others to Numerous to mention
   In the Year of our Lord 1838 & 9—in Clay and Caldwell Counties A mob Raised against said Church that Compelled me to leave said State to my Damage in loss of property Fifteen Hundred Dollars

Philo **X** Judd

[*Sworn to before W. Stanley, J.P., Van Buren Co., IA, 12 Mar 1840.*]

KEIRNS, Elisabeth

Elisabeth keirns mooved from larance County Ohio May 3 1838

expenses	$100.00
i sent my buoy to davis to bild a house but the mod drove him from his work damage	100.00
the mob robed my house damage	100.00
driven out out of the State damage	500.00
expence by the way	50.00
	$850.00

Elizabeth keirns

I certify that the above acount to be just according to the best of my knolage

Elisabeth keirns

[*Sworn to before C. M. Woods, C.C.C., Adams Co., IL, 6 May 1840.*]

KELLER, Alva

I Alva Keller of Hancock County State of Illenois do Somomly Swear that the following is a correct accunt of the Losses and damages that I sustained in being driven by the Authorty of the State of Missourie to this place, to wit, Loss of one hundred and forty five acres of Land valued at Sixteen hundred Dollar

Damages in mooveing and Loss of my farming tools household furniture &c, together with the loss of twenty acres of wheat to the amount of Six hundred Dollars

May 9th 1839   Alva Keller

[*Sworn to before D. Prentis, J.P., Hancock Co., IL, 9 May 1839.*]

KELLEY, Charles

The State of Mo Dr to C Kelley

Moving Family from Kirtland Ohio to Caldwell County Missouri	$100.00
Improvement of 7 Acres of Land & Log Cabin in <u>Davies County Mo</u>	100.00

10 Acres of Land & Log Cabin	65.00
Moving from Missouri expences & Loss of Time	200.00
For loss of Corn potatoes &c	100.00

I do herby Certy the above to Be a true and Just account acording to the Best of my Knowledeg

Charles Kelley

[*Sworn to before C. M. Woods, C.C.C., Adams Co., IL, 8 May 1839.*]

KETCHAM, Joseph

Quincy May the 6 1839

acharge of damage against the state of Missouri expense of mooving from the state of ohio to Missouri in the year 1832	$75.00
for being driven out of Jackson and loss of property in the year 1833	100.00
for loss of property in being driven out of Clay county	50.00
for loss of property in being driven out of state of Missouri 1839	100.00
loss of property sustained by my Wife before marage	500.00

i am at this time driven intirely out of the state by the governers order without house or home

Joseph Ketcham

i surtify the above account to be correct according ot the best of my knowledg

Joseph Ketcham

[*Sworn to before C. M. Woods, C.C.C., Adams Co., IL, 6 May 1839.*]

KEYS, Perry

Damage Sustaned By A removal from the State Misourie in the Mormmon War

Expence of Mooving to Caldwell Co	$7.00
Loss of one yoke of oxen	75.00
13 Head of hogs @ 4.00	52.00
To farming utentials hous hold Furniture & 60	50.00

5 Acrs Corn in the field	40.00
Removal from Caldwell County To Quincy	9.00
5 Months Lost Time	100.00
Damages	500.00
	$833.00

Quincy Adams Co Ills May th 23d 1839   Perry **X** Keys

[*Sworn to before C. M. Woods, C.C.C., Adams Co., IL, 24 May 1839.*]

KILLIEN, John

Illenois Quincy May 8th 1839 —
        a bill of Debt and Damage a gainst the State of Missouri which occurd
in Conciquince of the Govners order of Extermination —

first for Land in Jackson County unlawfully taken from me	$400.00
Being Driven from Jackson County loss of time moneey Expended property losst	400.00
from Clay to Caldwell Expence of money Loss of propperty	100.00
Loss of Lands in Caldwell	1,600.00
Loss on personal Estat	450.00
Loss on premption in Davis	3,000.00
for time Lost and mooving from the State to Illenos	500.00

        I Crtify the a bove a count to Be Just and true a cording to the Best
of my Knowledg

John Killien

[*Sworn to before C. M. Woods, C.C.C., Adams Co., IL, 8 May 1839.*]

KING, Eleazer, Jr.

Illenois Quincy May th 15 1839
        Abill of Damage for being Driven from the State in Conciquence of
the mob

first for mooving in to the State	$100.00
for propprty Lost in the State	300.00

for mooving from the State By the order of the Goviner   <u>100.00</u>
                                                $500.00

I certify the a bove to Be true and Just a cording to the Best of my knowledg

Eleazer King Jr.

[Sworn to before C. M. Woods, C.C.C., Adams Co., IL, 15 May 1839.]

KING, Elezer

Illenois Quincy May the 15 1839
a bill of Damages a gainst the State of Missouri for Being Driven from the State &c &c

first for mooveing in to the State	$60.00
for Loss of propperty in the State	150.00
for mooveing out of the Statate and Loss in Being	
Bookein up	<u>200.00</u>
	$410.00

I crtify the a bove account to Be Just and true a cording to the Best of my knowledg

Elezer King

[Sworn to before C. M. Woods, C.C.C., Adams Co., IL, 15 May 1839.]

KING, John M.

Damages Sustained on Account of Being driven from the State of Mosouria

Expenses of Moving into the State	$100.00
damages and Losses Sustained in the State	350.00
Expenses of Moving out &c	<u>50.00</u>
	$500.00

John M King

[Sworn to before C. M. Woods, C.C.C., Adams Co., IL, 23 May 1839.]

KNIGHT, Joseph, Jr.

Quincy May 6th 1839

the loss of property sustain by oppression in the state of missuria driven from Jackson county the expence of moveing	$25.00
a mill burnt down	200.00
a house burnt	50.00
3 akers of land and 50 peech trees	50.00
hay and corn	25.00
the expence of moveing from clay county	50.00
the loss on land	25.00
moveing out of the state	100.00
loss onland and town property	470.00
the loss of time on the whole	100.00
mooveing to the State	100.00
	$10,140.0

I hereby Certify that the above bill of acounts are correct acording to the best of my knowledg

Joseph Knight Jr

I CErtify the within to be true

Joseph Knight

[*Sworn to before C. M. Woods, C.C.C., Adams Co., IL, 6 May 1839.*]

KNIGHT, Nathan K.[23]

Quinsey April 13th 1839

Mmount of property taken from Nahan K Knight by the Missorie Mob, together with Damages Claimed by him and also a statment of the conduct of the mob

Amount of Notes taken by the mob	$400.00
One cow shot	40.00
One horse taken and spoiled	80.00
a quantity of wearing apparrel taken	46.00

---

[23] Also found in JH 13 Apr 1839.

a quantity of bedding	60.00
one ax	4.00
one gun	10.00
one umbrella Bakoven leadinglines and rasor	7.77
For being shot through the lungs and finger	5,000.00
For being compelled to leave the state of Mo.	1,000.00

In October betwen the twentieth and twentysixth on Ray Co near Whitneys Mills I was stoped with several others whilst on my way to Far West and detained a bout a week and driven back, when we made our escape and by a circuitous rout arived at Hauns Mills in Calwell Co. Mo. on the thirtieth of October, the Mob fellupon us by surprise and commensed to massacre men women and children, until about twothirds of our men had fallen during which time we raised a standard of peace, and pled for quarters But could obtain none! But kill and destroy the whole; was their cry; altho their number was ten times greater than ours, Beein no prospect of quarters, those that Could made their escape, as I was the last mormon that remained on the ground except three boys hid in a blacksmith shop I Nathan K. Knight saw a Missourian cut down a mormon, with a corncutter and also saw them stripping the dying and heard the boys crying for mercy. I Bro Knight made ~~my~~ escape acrost the Mill dam after receiving ~~my~~ his wounds through ~~my~~ his longues and finger. After the Massacre was over I he was led to a house by a woman and whilst lying under ~~my~~ his wounds I he heard Mr Moppins say that he blew one of the boys brains out. After I recovered of my wounds so as to be able to walk out I was way laid and had two ball holes shot through my blanket after which I was carried to Far west and one day whilst walking the streets of Far West I was met by three Missurians who thretened to butcher ~~me~~ him and one of them by the name of Roggers drew a butch knife and said that he had not got his corncutter with him that he cut down McBride with but by J. I have got some thing that will do as well, but by chance I made my escape

Nathan K. X Knight

Noah Packard[24]

[Not sworn.]

---

[24]This petition was possibly written for Nathan K. Knight by Noah Packard because the petition appears to be written in the same hand as Packard's signature. However, it is also possible that Packard was signing as a witness attesting to Knight's petition.

KNIGHT, Newel

Illenois Quincy May th 15 1839
    a bill of Damages against th State of Mo for Being Driven from it

first for mooving in to the State	$175.00
for propperty lost in the State	1,500.00
for moving out of the State	100.00

    I certify the a bove to Be Just and true acording to the Best of my knowledg

Newel Knight

[Sworn to before C. M. Woods, C.C.C., Adams Co., IL, 15 May 1839.]

KNIGHT, Vinson

    State of Missouri Dr. To Vinson Knight

to improvements on lands and preemtion rights	$3,500.00
to Merchandise	4,000.00
to hogs	800.00
to Oxen & Cows	750.00
to Grist mill	500.00
to boat	100.00
to Household goods	150.00
to expence of moveing out of the State	200.00
	$10,000.00

    The above bille is losses which came in consequenc of being exterminated from the state of Missouri in the fall of 1838 Aand I certify that it is a tru bill as near as I can come at it

Oct. 29th 1839 Commerce   V Knight

[Not sworn.]

LAKE, Jabez

May the 10th 1839
    the State of Missouri To Jabez Lake Drt.
    Occasiond by the Mob in Said State in the year 1838 and 1839

To time lost 8 months at 20 Dolart per months	$160.00
to expence in moveing	20.00
to one ox yoke	3.00
to being Deprived of CittizanShip and to Suffring Self and family	1,000.00

Jabez Lake

[Sworn to before W. Oglesby, J.P., Adams Co., IL, 11 May 1839.]

LAKE, Samuel

May the 10th 1839
the State of Missouri to Samuel Lake Drt.
Occasiond by the Mob in Said State in the 1838 and 1839

to time seven Months	$140.00
to expences in Moving from Missouri	20.00
To debts due me	17.00
to Suffering Abuse an deprivement of Citizenship	5,000.00

Samuel Lake

[Sworn to before W. Oglesby, J.P., Adams Co., IL, 11 May 1839.]

LANE, Johnston F.

I here present you with a bill of damages against the State of Missouri.

In the first place the expences of moving there and having to leave and having by the authority of the Govoror to be deprived of Sitisonship, twelve hundred Dollars $1,200.00

and being exposed myself and family to the cold stormy wather of November 1838 and many other inconveniaces and suffirings   200.00

Quincy Adams County Ill. 1st November 1839   Johnston F Lane

[Sworn to before C. M. Woods, C.C.C., Adams Co., IL, 1 Nov 1839.]

LANE, William W.

Handcock Illinois January 6th 1840

A Bill of Damage a ganst the s[t]ate of Missoria by William W lane in conciquence of the order of the govner of the stat of Masuria to Ex pell

262

from the s[t]at[e] forth with all of the people called mormons for the loss of property against the s[t]at[e] affor said tha did forcible took my gun and detaind him worth $20 and Lost on stock and grain 30 dollars and moveing forom the state in the Month of feb uary Exspencis and sufferidgese Loss of time time one hundred and fifty dollars

I allso wasse presant when tha quartered on fair west the masarianss and took all of us mormons prisners

William W Lane

[*Sworn to before T. Crawford, J.P., Hancock Co., IL, 6 Jan 1840.*]

LATHROP, Asahel A.

A Bill of damages. loss of my family together with all of my Property loss of time and abuse of my own person by the inhabitants of the State of Missourie which I declare was without any cause or provication

firstly I was located in the territory North of Livingston County State aforesaid and was living in peace with all men a[s] I supposed verry unexpectedly to me I was warned to leave my place immediately or suffer Death my family at this time were sick one at least I was compelled to leave them with no one to administer to them but my Companion and she in a condition that she had ought to recieve the kindest of treatment but it was to the reverse of this for after I was compeled to leave my home my house was thronged with a company of armed men consisting of fourteen in number and they abusing my family in [many] allmost every form that Creturs in the shape of human Beeings could invent whilst in this situation one of my children Departed this Life and was buired by the Mob, my companion not being able to attend to the funeral rites on acount of fatigue and trouble which she had to experience by these monst ers and all this in my absense I was absent fifteen days before I could returne and when I did returne I found them in a soriful situation not one of the remaining ones able to wait uppon the other I was compelled to move them about sixty miles and after ariving there my Wife lived onely three days and in a short time the remainder of my family two in number followed which I have no reason to doubt was wholly occasioned by trouble and the want of care which they were deprived of by a Ruthless Mob

my property there consisted of a Claim on one quarter sextion
   of land forty acres under improvement with good buildings
Do. twenty one head of cattle
Do. seven head of horses
Do. twenty head of sheep

Do. five Hundred head of hogs together with farming tools
and many other things not mentioned in this
Do. another claim in the same region of country with a
dweling house on the same
the amount of Property loss of time Abuse of my own person
also thirty five acres of corne on the aforesaid place
the whole which I shall estimate at the modered sum of $30,000.00
Allso one house and lot situated in the Town of Far West
in Caldwell Co. State of Missourie valued at $500.00
Allso twenty acres of timbered land of which I have a Deed
laying in the sam[e] Town Co. and State valued $200.00

Written in Quincy St. of Illinois April 9th 1839   Asahel A Lathrop

I will now give the names of some of the mob that took possession
of my house and abused my family after forceing me to leave them under
the [——] thretnings of immediate death if I did not comply they allso
compelled my wife to [——] cook for them untill by being fatigue and
worne out she was confined to her bead when I returned to their assistance.
the name of the Captain of the mob that was at my house was

James Weldon
Howard Weldon—a Black of his
Calvin Hatfield
Standly Hatfield
Andy Hatfield
Samuel Low
Doct. William P Thompson one of the Justices of the Peace
A mister Scott a constable—a connextion of the said Thompson
William Cochran allso a constable and many others that I do not
recolect the people in the North part of Livingston county and the Territory
adjoining met at the House of the affore said Thompson it being the public
place of holding Courts and there adopted measures in regard to drivings
the Mormons from the affore said county and territory and from that band
I had orders to leave the place

Asahel A Lathrop

I certify the above instrument to be a Just estimate of damiges as far
as I am able to give it. for to come to the full amount language would fail
me to doe it

Asahel A. Lathrop

[Sworn to before C. M. Woods, C.C.C., Adams Co., IL, 8 May 1839.]

LATHROP, Asahel A.[25]

This is to certify that I Asahel A. Lathrop was a citisan of the State of Missourie at the time the difficulty originated betwene the People Called Mormans and the inhabitants of the affore said state and herein give a statement of the transactions that came under my observation according to the best of my recolextion. I setled in Missourie in the summer of 1838 in Caldwell County where I purchesed land and erected buildings the said land I now have a deed of and in the fall of 1838 I purchesed a claim on what is called the East fork of Grand River together with a large stock of cattle and horses sheep and hogs it being some sixty miles from the affore said County where I first located and moved on to the Latter place supposing that I was at peace with all men but I found by sad experience that I was surrounded by enimies for in the fall of 1838 whilst at home with my family I was notified by a man by the name of James Welden that the people of Livingston County had meet at the house of one Doct. William P. Thompson then living in the atached part of said County for the purpos of entering into measures respecting the people Called Mormons and the said Weldon was a member of the same and allso the afore said W. P. Thompson was a Justice of the Peace and they all Jointly agreeed to Drive every Mormon from the state and notified me that I must leave immediately or I would be in danger of loosing my life. at this time my family some of them were sick but after listning to the entreties of my Companion to flee for safty I committed them in to the hands of God and left them it being on Monday morning and in a short time after I left there came some time on fifteen men to my house and took possession of the same and Compelled my wife to Cook for the same and allso made free to take such things as they saw fit and whilst in this situation my child Died. which I have no reason to doubt was for the want of care which owing to the abuse she recieved and being deprived of rendering that care that she would had she been otherwise situated my boy was burried by the Mob my wife not being all[*owed*] to pay the last respects to her child. I went from my home into Davis county and applied to Austin A King and General Atchison for advise as they were acting officers in the State of Missourie and there was men called out to goe and liberate my family which I had been absent from some ten or fifteen days and on my return I found the remainder of my family confined to there beads not being able the one to assist the other and my house guarded by an armed force. I was compelled to remove my family in this situation on a head to a place of

---

safty this together with all the trouble and for the want of of care was the cause of the Death of the residue of my family as I have no doubt which consisted of a wife and two more children as they Died in a few days after the arival to my friends such was my situation that I was obliged to assist in making my own coffins.

I will give the names of some of the men that drove me from my home and abused my family they were as follows—those that I found at my house on my return Samuel Low, Calvin Hatfield Standly Hatfield Andy Hatfield and those that were leading men was James Weldon Doct. William P. Thompson a Justice of the peace and William Cochran and many others the names I do not recolect. and I have also seen men abused in varyus ways and that whilst they were considered Prisioners such as the mob cocking ther guns and swering that they would shoot with there guns to there face and the officers of the milita so called standing by without uttering a word and in there councils they have said if a Missourian should Kill a mormon he should draw a pention the same as a soldier of the Revolution I was also compelled to give up my gun and the terms was I must leave the affore said State of Missourie or be exterminated my property is yet remaining in said State whilst I am deprived of the controle of the same

Written this 17th day of March 1840   Asahel A. Lathrop

[Sworn to before D. W. Kilbourn, J.P., Lee Co., IA, 21 Mar 1840.]

LEANY, Isaac

State of Missouri Dr to Isaac Leany

to two shots through the breast $10,000.00	$20,000.00
to one shot through each hip $5,000	10,000.00
to two others one a cross each arm $500.00 each	1000.00
to one suit of clothing shot and cut in pieces	50.00
to one rifle gun firs rate and in good order $30.00	30.00
time lost six months at $25 each	150.00
sundies expences while wounded	500.00
sundries abuses and slanders	10,000.00
	$41,730.00

By the time this is considered the question will arise when and whear did this hapen and why not taken in fo concideration in the State; to this I will answer that on the 25th or 26th of October 1838 I was informed that a mob of about twenty men had invaded our neighbourhood came a pon the customers at Hawns mills and demanded their guns and offered many insults and hard threats such as murder and went so far as to snap their pieces at one man five times but could not make fire and he made his es cape and gave the alarm and the neighbours was called to gather for to hold a council to k[n]ow what was to be done for the best and after much deliberation David Evans was appointed captain of our company and David Evans Anthony Blackburne and Jacob Myers appointed a commit- tee to make atreaty of peace ~~of~~ piece with them and about this time thare came a mesenger to us from another company gathered at the house of Isaac McCrosky this Mesenger we recieved kindly he informed us that their company had gathered for self defence haveing heard the lies that the company of Nehemiah Cumstock had circulated after they retarned from their invasion at the mill but want to make peace withus and requested us to send three men to the house of Oliver Walker to make a treaty of peace with three men that they would send to the same place these men were to meet unarmed acording to agreement but fear made them send ten with rifles instead of three unarmed though they received our three with respect and civility Samuel Todd was their spokesman and said Evans ours a treaty was soon effected to the satisfaction of both parties they also agreed to send to Cumstock and request them to make a treaty withus as also but they were angry not only withus but with them for making a treaty with us but David Evauns sent them word that he would not fight them untill he offered them terms of peace and when they came on he remem- bered his promise for on the 30th of October ~~in the~~ they came on Captain gave orders to not fire and he advanced in front of our company ~~and for quarter~~ called for quarters till I suppose they fired between fifty and a hundred shots without making any answer when he returned we could do no better than fire a few rounds and Let our women and children made their escape seeing six or seven of our men at that time shot down and wellering in their blood some of us fired once some twice and some ran off with their guns loaded when such as was not wounded too bad made their escape by flight fifteen being slain on the ground such as was not dead when they took the ground was shot a seccond time all save one old man about 65 years old which was cut in pieces with an old sythe blade after surrendering him self prisoner of war I my self made my escape being shot as before descrbed I am aware that this is a hard story to credit but I have the scars to prove the fact which can be seen at any time

the names of the dead	wounded
Thomas McBride	Jacob Fouts
John York	Jacob Hawn

Benjamin Lewis
Josiah Fuller
Austin Hammer
Elias Benner
Waren Smith
Sardis Smith aged 12 years
Levi Merick
Wm Napier
Simon Cox
George Richards
John Lee
John Byers
Mr Campbell

Jacob Potts
Jacob Myres
George Myres
Wm Yocum
Tarlton Lewis
Nathan Night
Isaac Leany
Charles Jimison
Alma Smith aged about 9 years old
John Walker
Miss Mary Steadwell
mortally wounded
Hiram Abbot
Charles Merick a little boy

After the slaughter was over the mob robed the houses carrying of all that they could amounting to bedclothing wearing clothes two waggons about fifteen horses and returned to their camps in one or two days they returned camped at the mills whare they taried a bout three weeks robed the mills of a bout a hundred bushels of wheat and a bout as much corn and plundered the whole neighbourhood shot anumber of fat hogs stole what honey they could eat and send to their homes and in this time but about four or five men only was left in the neieighbourhood they all sick wounded or taken prisoners while the women was exposed to all manner of hardships having to do the milling and geting wood in the cold weather it is impossible to describe this scene of affliction I will only say that our suffering must have been beyond conception

Now to make the story as short as possible I will finish with giveing the names of some of those thieves murders and robers one of which was Wm Man Esq Nehemiah Cumstock Esq and Captain of one company of mob Jesse Maupin James Reynolds Stephen Reynolds who boasts of shooting Waren Smith the second time Mr Glase with a hair lip Hiram Cumstock Howard Maupin

I Do hereby certify that the within is a true statement

Isaac Leany

[*Sworn to before C. M. Woods, C.C.C., Adams Co., IL, 6 May 1839.*]

LEBARON, Alonzo

Quincy Illinois May 18th 1839
    Damages Received by the mob of Missouri

time & expence in going to the State	$25.00
time & property lost in the State	65.00
leaving the State and expense	10.00
	$90.00

I Certify the above to be true according to the best of my Knowledge

Alonzo LeBaron

[*Sworn to before C. M. Woods, C.C.C., Adams Co., IL, 18 May 1839.*]

LEE, Francis

May the 9th 1839 Illinois Quinsey
    an account against the State of Missouri for Debt and damage Sustained in Consequence of the Exterminating Order

Loss on land	$200.00
Damage & removal	100.00
	$300.00

I Certify the above to be a Just & true account according to the best of my Knowledge

Francis Lee

[*Sworn to before C. M. Woods, C.C.C., Adams Co., IL, 9 May 1839.*]

LEE, Permert

Illenois Quincy May 18th 1839
    A bill of Damages a gainst the State of Missouri for Being Driven from the State By a mob and loss of propperty in the State and mooveing from the State I charge five Hundrd Dollars
    I certify the a bove to Be true and Just a cording to the Best of my knowldg

Permert Lee

[*Sworn to before C. M. Woods, C.C.C., Adams Co., IL, 17 May 1839.*]

LEMMON, James

James Lemmon Loss by the mob in Dav[*iess*] In the year 1838 & 1839

To a Preemption ~~wright~~ with a right of Claim to a [——] on One qr. Sect at	$[——]²⁶
~~also to One baught of an other improvement Baught of an other~~ also One other improvement baught of an other man	[——]
6 acrs. of Corn at $80.00 and other Vigatabels	[——]
One cow at $20.00	20.00
to a number of hogs some port and some stocks	125.00
to ~~hay~~ two Stacks of hay worth	15.00
to flax 5.00 and expences and Loss of time	205.00
	$915.00

James Lemmon

I certify the above account to be true and Just according to the best of my Recollection

James Lemmon

[*Sworn to before C. M. Woods, C.C.C., Adams Co., IL, 11 May 1839.*]

LEMMON, John

A List of the Loss of John Lemmon Property, by the Mob in the countyes of, Jackson, Clay, and Davisse, In the years from 1833 up to this present date May 1839

In Jackson Cty June 1834 to 6 acrs. of wheete as good as common for that cuntry. say to average 40 bushell pr. acr. 240 bus. at $0.50 pr. bushell amt. to $120.00 Say $100.00 $100.00

A loss on an improvement on the Lost Rainge in Sd. County, concisting of a hewd. Log house 20 ft. squair comfourtabelly fixd. of 56 Appetrees set out some peachtrees & some Churrey trees plumbs &C with a first Rate gardain it Worth $50.00 together with other appurtancies worth in all at least $500.00 with a tital then say   2[2]5.00

Expencies and other losses in moving   25.00

[*Subtotal*] $[4]50.00

in Clay Ct. To a premption Right bought of Sollomon Kimsey said to be secuard. by his Br. Hiram Kimsey and gave me an Order to Hiram

---

²⁶Most of the numeric figures in this position are illegible because the page is torn.

for the same he Hiram said it was good & he would do so the first time he saw Esqr. Kuykendall for it must be don before a Justice of the peace & I knew no better for I had never examoned the law at that time about the matter he faild to comply with his promise but went & borrowed the money and entered the Land and was obligd to sell it for $400.00 to Refund the money when it was worth $1000.00 and cant be got now for two thosand then say in its situation then, worth to me   500.00

also a Loss by being oblegd. to leve Clay Ct. on a (40 acr.) tract ajoining it bought of the said Sollomon Kimsey at the same time of purchase and also a (20 acr.) entered by myself had to take $100.00 less then I had been Offered not on the account of the fall of Land for the same more then doubeld. itself in the course of One year then say in Justice

200.00

Expence of Moving to Daviss now cauld then Grand River $50.00 as I had to hire teems in the ded of winter I and my fammally & waggoners had like to freeze to Deth on One of the large peraroas not being able to Retch a house as their was no Road but the peraroah at that time on the Roret we went and I have never injoyed good helth since   50.00

together with menney other expences & loss of time at lest   50.00
[*Subtotal*] $800.00
[*Subtotal from above*]   450.00
                                                                  $1,250.00

and my wife at the same time not abel to git about and was thought & said by menney she would not live to git thair neather has she ever injoyd. good helth since

Davisse County in 1838 and 1839

To improvement imbraceing two (qr. Sect.) One in markit the other not and was intitaled to a preemption wright, but was prevented from proving it up, by the mob imbodying themselves for that and other like purposses. but Umberson Lyon a short time prior to this in conversation about the place Observd. that if he had a deed to the two quarter Sections that no mans $2000.00 two thousand Dollars could tutch it using his Own language after our surrender of arms at Fair West and I being a prisoner I wrote a line to Mr James Lyon & Umberson Lyon his sun informing them that I wishd. to sell them my place Crop hogs &C Wishing to pay them $100.00 that they had Loand me and that without being askd. for by me [——] at one time observing that I did not no but what I would have to borrow some, naming of a certain condition this is the way they came to offer it without being askd.— and looking on them as purrticular friends as they allways had expresd. it and thair acts had menefestd. the same— and in answer to my Line to them said they would do so and in seeing Umberson he told me that he or his Father on his Return home would go and enter it straightway & I should be well paid and they entered it but to their Disgrace he Refused to pay me (one god Dam cent) using their own base language and have collected the hundred Dollars since—they having a certifcate from the Regester of publick lands and in possesion of the other that is not in markit, then taking his Own expesions it must be worth $1600.00 but it is worth more to one or would be if I could injoy the wrights of a free cition—but say fifteen hundred as I am deturmend to be within bounds with everry thing $1,500.00

To 23 Porke hogs to average 200 lbs each pr. hog at $4.00 pr. (100)			184.00
35 Do Do 150 Do 3.50 Do			192.75
13 large brude Sows at $5.00 pr. Sow			65.00
50 odd young stock hogs say 50 worth $3.50 pr. hog			175.00
a large number of pigs and shots some weend. and some not, to say about 80 worth at least			100.00
20 acours of good corn averging 10 brls. pr. acr. at $2.00 pr. barl.			400.00
800 Binds of corn blads at 2 Cts. pr. bind			16.00
upwards of 100 bus. turnips $10.00 and 500 Cabbag at 2 Cts. pr. Cabg.			20.00
Irish potatoas Beets Parsnips &C worth at least			20.00
1 carey plow and 1 bassheere with a cotter with stocks worth 8.00 each			16.00
2 hows $2.00 One pair of hams $2.00 One two intch chissell $2.00			6.00
[*Subtotal*]			$3,944.75
3 Spring Calvs and One year Oald Steer			15.00
2 Large sheepe $8.00 one Rifel gun and One pistol			43.00
1 Bedsteed 2 sythes & hangings 1 Rake & pitchfork			10.00
1 acr. of good flax the most of it Ready for dresing			20.00
1 two years Oald filley $50.00 and One loome $6.00			56.00
5 Mounth loss of time pr. self and 4 Suns at $15.00 pr. mounth each			300.00
Expences through the 5 above months and gitting out of the State			113.00
[*Subtotal*]			$4,501.75
NB a mistake in carrying out the first itiem of			50.00
			$4,451.75

I Shall be Satisfyd. to git my Real Losses With Out Damages which would bee conciderable for my self and Famelly have Suffered Much and Continues to Do so for want of means to help Our selves too and in concequence of our healths being much impaird by exposure

John Lemmon

I certify the a bove a count to Be true and Just a cording to the Best of my Knowledg

John Lemmon

[*Sworn to before C. M. Woods, C.C.C., Adams Co., IL, 11 May 1839.*]

LEONARD, Abigail

on the night of 20 Feb 1834[27]

I Abagail Leonard depose and say that in the year eighteen hundred and thirtyfour in the Month of febuary or first of March in the County of Jackson and State of Missouri a company of men armed with whips and guns about fifty or sixty came to the house of my husband among them was John Youngs, Mr Yocom, Mr Cantrell, Mr Patterson, Mr Knowland, five of the number entered the house among them was John Youngs they ordered my husband to leave the house threatning to shoot him if he did not, he not complying with thier desires, one of the five took a chair, and struck him upon the head, knocking him down, and then draging him out of the house. I in the mean time beging of them to spare his life, when one of the number called to the others telling them to take me into the house for I would "overpower every Devil of them," three of the company then approached me and presenting thier guns declared with an oath if I did not go in they would blow me through, while this was transpiring Mr Patterson jumped upon my husband with his heels, my husband then got up they striping his clothes all from him excepting his pantaloons, then five or six attacked him with whips & gun sticks, and whipped him untill he could not stand but fell to the ground. I then went to them and took thier whips from them. I then called to Mrs Brace who resided in the same house with us to come out and help me carry my husband into the house. when carried in he was very much lacerated and bruised, and unable to lie upon a bed and was also unable to work for a number of months also at the same time and place Mr Josiah Sumner was taken from the house and came in very

---

[27] This date is not written in the same hand as the rest of the petition and may have been added later.

bloody and bruised from whipping; but I did not see him whiped, and further your deponent saith not

Abigail Leonard

[*Sworn to before H. Kimball, J.P. Hancock Co., IL, 11 Mar 1840.*]

LEWIS, David   JSC[28]

Settled with the rest we felt to rejoice we had neither Spyes nor guards out nor was aprehending danger, when about three hundred mounted men came in atack and fell upon us without Showing us any mercy what ever we never saw them until they was as near as one hundred & fifty yards of us we then amediately ran into ablacksmith Shop, they began fyering on us without asking us to Surrender without giving us the chance to Surrender when we called up on them to Spare our lives when men ran out & held up there handkerchiefs & hats for peace they Shot them down when they attempted to run they was Shot down & when they Stood Still they Shot them down threw the cracks in the Shop there was also a window in the end & another in the Side of the Shop, the Shop was neither chinked nor daubed So they had all chances to make a Speedy Slaughter of us, we Saw that they would Show us no murcy we then begun fyering at them but in this time our number was but few and the enemy mostly behind trees & logs So that there was but few of them killed or wounded, I think that I could venture to Say that neither ancient or modern times have ever witnessed Sutch a cenery of things as was thare witnessed, there was a few men women & children in consequence of threts & the abuse that they had received had guethered themselves toguether in defence of there own lives & there property when they was fell upon by a lawless band, without being Shown the least murcy without Spareing men women or children there was one woman Shot threw the hand othe[rs] had holes Shot threw there clothes, they continued there bloody works until 17 was killed and 15 wounded I must here remark that this woman that was wounded was not in the Shop but was in a tent & when they commenced fyering at hur She run & hid hurself behind a log & it is Said that there was 12 or 14 bullets Shot in the log that She was behind, the other women that was Shot threw there clothes ran out of the houses that was near the shop knowing that there husbands was in the Shop & Screamed for murcy but instead of haveing murcy Shown to there hus-

---

[28]The original, handwritten version of this petition is not found in the same LDS Historical Department collection which contains the other Missouri petitions, but instead is found in the Historical Department's Joseph Smith Collection.

bands & friend they had to make a quick retreat to Save there own lives, there was one Small boys branes was Shot out, there was too other little boys during the fray consealed themselves under the Bellas & those cruel harted retches after killing both of there fathers came & Stuck there guns threw a crack of the Shop & Shot them both One dy ed & the other recovered, they then came in to the Shop among those that was dyining & struggleing in there blood & them all that they could perceive life in they blown there branes out curseing them as loud as Screams could yell, there was too men that laid among the Slain that passed for dead men that escaped being Shot again one of them was wounded & the other was not, and after these cruel retches had found out that these men had escaped there notice I heard them Sware that if they ever got in another engagement tha they would enspect more closer by Sticking there k[n]ife in there toes, this barberous work commenced on TueSday evening about an hour by Sun, they kep on Shootin as long as they could find any to Shoot untill Sun down, it would be miraculous to tell how them escaped that did escape & also to tell how Some was Shot that did recover, how painful it is, when I think upon it my heart is filled & my eyes is ready to drip with tears to See my friend & near neighbors a falling around me, groaning & dying Struggleing in there blood, & to See the widows tears & to hear the orphants cry, to See the helpless babes a weeping Standing by, there was Thomas Mc bride a verry old man & justice of the [——] after he had gave up his gun & Surrendered himself a prisner he was Shot dow & after laying a little while he attempted to rise he was hewn down with an oald peace of a Sythe blade after a while he attempted to rise again he then was hacked down and hacked into peaces this was done by Jacob Roggers I had one brother killed & an other wounded I escaped myself but had Several holes Shot threw my clothes, the dead was thrown into a well about 8 or ten feet deep, because there was no one left that was able to burry them, this was too days before the Surrender at Far West, and the Second day after the masacre took place a large company of them came back and fyered there guns & blowed there bugle & frightened the neighbourhood, but did not kill any more, I had forgot to mention there Stealing & robing the houses on the day after the masacre, there was Several that was on there way to Far West from the east that in consequence of the way being guarded by the mob Stoped at the mill five of them was killed & after they was done Shooting the wounded over they then went into the houses & tents & robed the widows of there beds & clothing & left them to perish with the cold they als[o] took off those movers waggons & teams in order to hall off the goods that they had taken they took Several valuable horses they robed the women of there mantles & the men of there clothes, they Striped the boots off of the dead & Sold them, Steaven Runels boasted of Shooting the too little boys, Some of them thou[*ght*] it was not right others said a littl Sprout would be a big tree afte the mob had left the ground & it began to get dark I crep from my hideing place & went down near the mill & found my brother which was ga[*s*]peing & groaning in his blood I brought him to my house which was in a few hundred yards of the Shop he lived a few hours & dyed & while he was dying his wife loaned a young man his noble gildon to go to Far West to get assistance to burry the dead, the young man Started in haste & got in too or three miles of Far West & thare he met a company of men they ast him where he was from & where he was going he told them they then ast him where the militia was, he told them he did not know of any. they then told him to turnabout & go with them & they would Show him where they was, for they Said that there was 5 or 6 thosand out here a little piece, they then took him to ray county to Samuel McCristens & Stay all night. they thare robed him of a fine fur cap & threatened to take his over coat telling him that it was too fine for a mormon they thereatened to Shoot him & disputed among themselves who Should have the horse, in the morning Sashel Woods the Same that took his cap & threttened to take his coat & Shoot him Saddled up his horse & rode him round the lot & then Stoped & couneled with his company & then put his Saddle on an other horse and Samuel McCriStin Saddled up the horse & rode him off the young man told them that the horse belonged to a woman that hur husband was dying, this company then took the young man to Richmon & kep him a prisner this companys, names was as follows Sashel Woods Joseph Ewen Jacob Snordan Wiley Brewer John Hille and four more there names not recollected,

I Shall next proceede to give an account of the treatment that we had to endure after our friends was Slain, capt. Nehemiah Cumstock with 40, or 50 men came to the mills & located themselves for too or three weeks & took possession of the mille, dureing this time they lived on the best that the neighbourhood could afford, the industry of the mormons had procured to them Selves a plenty of that which was palatable & good, the capt & his company went from house to hous & plundered & Stold & burnt Some books they robed Some houses of every thing that belonged thare to, they, killed our hogs robe[*d*] beegams they ground the wheat that was in the mill & mad[*e*] use of it ther was ten widows in the neighbourhood, whoos husband they had killed & many helpless orphants whoo was dependent on gooing to these wicked retches for there meal & flower there was many exposed to the cold that was left destitute of meanes to Subsist on, there was many laying wounded & no one Scarcely to attend to there wants & there lives was day threattened, it was dreadfull to tell the awfullness of our Situation, & this abuse we received from men of our own coular & of our own nation & we now not but our four fathers have fought Side and Side for our liberty, they told all manner of lyes & falsehoods against us in order to justify the evil conduct that they done, if we had done any crime we never refused to have the law put in force against us but they new that we had not violated the law & new that takeing us to the law would not accomplish the object that they had in view, for they had not forgot the Spoil that they had gained by driveing the mormons from jackson county, it was our farmes & our Stock & our property that they wanted, I Stand in defyance of the State of Misourie to proove one acusation against us that they So cruely treated that was worthy of the notice of the law for there was many of us in consequence of Sickness had bin confined dureing all of the difficultys & there was five that was killed that had jus came to the country too days before they was killed. Now those wicked retches went from house to house on Search of gunes & other other things that they wanted I was at the house of Jacob Foutz who was laying wounded when capt comstock with a company came in with there faces painted black with a half moon painted under each eye they begun to question Mr. Foutz if he knew where Sutch & Sutch of his neighbours was he told them that he did not I then got up & Started out I was ammediately followed out by Some of his company they told me to not go away until the capt Seen me they then went in and Saw the capt & he came out & told me that I must begaune or on the act of Starting by Tuesday evening this was on Sunday evening or denounce mormonism or go to richmond & Stand a trial I ast him what it was I must deny, he Said I must deny Jo Smyths being a prophet, I told him as for going to richman & Standing a triel I did not regard Standing a trial according to law for any thing that I had done, but to be tried by a mob law I did not like it for they heaped the mormons all in a lump & what they had against one they had against all, & as for moveing I thought it quite a Short notice for aman to have to move in when the weather was So cold & had neither waggon or team I told him that my wife was Sick & I did not know how I Should go So Soon I told him that the road was Said to be guarded that none was allowed to pass must I be drove off by one company and another to kill me as I went I told him that I thought the conditions of the treaty was that we might Stay untill Spring, he said that, that was the first conclusion but that he just had received new orders from the General & that was that all mormons Should be driven out forthwith, I then ast him if the way was not guarded So I could not go Safely he Said that he would give me a ticket that would take me Safely I then went my way & we parted, on the next day I hapened at the mill where the capt & his company was he the[n] rote a pass & gave it to me which reads as follows, November the 13th 1838 this is to certify that David Lewis a mormon is permitted to leave and pass through the State of Misourie in an Eastward direction unmolested during good behaviour Nehemiah Comstock, Capt Militia

on the next day after I got my pass Hiram comstock the capts brother came with too or three others men to my house & brought with them a prisoner, they told me that thay had a prisner they ast me if I new him I told them that I had Saw him but did not know his name, they after asking Several questions, told me to go with them to there c[a]mp, I went down with them they told me that the prisner Said that he was well acquainted with me they then told me that I might considder my Self a prisner they then gave me plenty to eat & drink but kep me until next day & Set me at liberty

David Lewis

I was born Aprile the 10th 1814 in the State of Kentucky Simpson County & remained in the Same Stat & County untill Aprile the 22th 1837 I then went to the State of Missouri I there witnessed thos horred Senes of which I have Spoken, & my real losses, besides my difficulty troubles & vexations is not les than, 400 dollars all accasioned by those difficultys & those difficultys was accasioned by mobs

this March the 14th, 1839   David Lewis

[*Not sworn.*]

LEWIS, Nathan

Quiny May 28th 1839

This May Certify that I Nathan Lewis beeing a Mechanic And have bin drove out of the State of missouri by the hands of a mob And by the orders of the governer of that State now feeling the Loss of business and Property for this Cause I Present my Case to the Publick hopeing that I may get some redress for the losses that I hav sustain which losses is as near as I Can asertain is about the Sum of $552

Nathath Lewis

[*Sworn to before C. M. Woods, C.C.C., Adams Co., IL, 28 May 1839.*]

LITTLEFIELD, Rhoda

May the 6 1839

Rody littlefield lef Massachusetts County of middlesex April the 22 1838

to the expense of mooving to Mo	$100.00
to the lose of propperty in Davis County	20.00
driven out of the State and the expense by the way and lose of propperty and land	400.00
	$520.00

i certify that the above to be a trew statement acording to [t]he best of my knowlage

Rhoda Littlefield

[Sworn to before C. M. Woods, C.C.C., Adams Co., IL, 7 May 1839.]

LOVELESS, John

A Bill of Damage Sustained by John Lovless against the State of Missouri in Consequence of the unlawful Conduct of the Inhabitants in Jackson County in AD 1833 & again in the year A. D. 1838 in Caldwell & the Unconstitutional Decrees of this Governor

In the year A. D. 1833 the mob Came to my house in Jackson County & told me to Leave my house forth with or they would shut me & my family in the house & burn all togather we accordingly left the house taking only what we Could Carry on our Backs also Shooting at me & the Ball grazing my face so as to Draw Blood & otherwise abuseing me

Do. Do. Loss of Property on this occasion	$500.00
Do. in Caldwell in 1838 Do. on Land	500.00
Do Do. Personal Property	300.00
Do. For Being obliged to remove & the Inconveniences & Exposure to weather & thrown out of Business &C &C	500.00
Do. Do. Expences for Journey	$100.00
also for being taken Prisoner & being Confined	1900.00

for four Days & my life was threatened Seventimes During this time by a Mr Donahu who in my Presence Killed a Mr. Cary by Striking him with the ~~Britch~~ ofgun over the head & also abuseing the rest of the Prisners I also Saw Several Cattle & Hogs Shot Down By the Mob while I was a Prisner by them

I also Saw the Mob go into the ~~Brethrens~~ sitisens Houses which the ~~Brethren~~ Sitisens had left & Plundering of their Property &c &c

John Loveless

279

I Do herby certify that the above is atrustement are tru according to the best of my knowledge

John Loveless

[Sworn to before C. M. Woods, C.C.C., Adams Co., IL, 6 May 1839.]

LOWRY, John[29]

I Certify that I saw General John Clark and his aid at thir arrival of Far Wist Caldwell Co. Mo in the yard John M. Burk and gave orders [——] to their waters to pitch their Markees in his yard and to take of his wood for fire I also saw Capt. Samuel Bogart ~~eome~~ with his men come near my dwelling and Did pitch their Camp and took my house Logs with out my Leave and did burn them I also saw him with the horse of Joseph Smith Jun. in his possession

John Lowry

[Sworn to before D. W. Kilbourn, J.P., Lee Co., IA, 6 Jan 1840.]

LYMAN, George

Damages Sustained on Account of Being driven from the State of Mosouria

Expenses of Moving into the State	$75.00
damages and Losses Sustained in State	300.00
Expenses of Moving out &c	50.00
	$425.00

George Lyman

[Sworn to before C. M. Woods, C.C.C., Adams Co., IL, 23 May 1839.]

LYON, Aaron C.

Losses sustained by Mr Aaron C Lyon in the late affray in the state Missouri in property as followes

To loss on Land 400 Acres	$2000.00
" Do. " Cattle	100.00

---

[29] Also found in *HC* 4:56 and in JH 6 Jan 1840.

" "	Sheep	5.00
" "	200 hogs $1.00	200.00
" "	100 bushels of Corn 25 cts.	25.00
" "	20 Do. potatoes 37-1/2	7.50
" Loss on house hold goods &c		50.00
" on Farming tools "		30.00
" Loss of time " "		50.00
" " " 6 Tons of hay $3		18.00
[*Subtotal*]		$2,485.50
To 1 Town Lot in FarWest		100.00
to Loss on one horse		30.00
Amt		$2,615.50

I Windsor P Lyon do swear that the above losses were sustained by Aaron C Lyon in the County of Caldwell State of Missourie during the year AD 1838

Windsor P. Lyon

[*Sworn to before M. M. McGregor, J.P., Hancock Co., IL, 11 May 1839.*]

LYTLE, Andrew

Quncy Ill May 11th AD 1839
the bill of damages against the State of Missouri

For movning in to the State	$50.00
loss of property and Lost time by the mob	175.00
loss of ~~property~~ by moveing out of the State	25.00
[*Total*]	$250.00

I certify the above to be just and trou to the best of my knowledg

Andrew Lytle

[*Sworn to before C. M. Woods, C.C.C., Adams Co., IL, 11 May 1839.*]

MABAY, John

Illinois Quincy May 31 1839
A bill of Damages against the State of Missouri for Being unlawfully Driven from it

first for mooving in to the State	$100.00
for propperty Lost in the State	150.00
for mooving from the State Loss	
Loss of time Expences &c &c	25.00

I certify the a bove acount to Be Just and true a cording to the Best of my Knowledg

John Mabay

[*Sworn to before C. M. Woods, C.C.C., Adams Co., IL, 31 May 1839.*]

McBRIDE, Amos

Illenois Quincy May 29th 1839

a bill of Damages a gainst the State of Missouri for being driven from the State unlawfully

first for mooveing in to the State	$50.00
for propperty Lost in the State	75.00
for mooveing out of the State	40.00
	$165.00

I certify the a bove a count to Be true and Just acording to the Best of my Knowledge

Amos McBride

[*Sworn to before C. M. Woods, C.C.C., Adams Co., IL, 29 May 1839.*]

McBRIDE, Catharine

Quincy Illinois may 18th 1839

Damages Received by the Sitizons of Missouri in Consequence of being Driven from the State by the Governers Orders time and Expences

in going to and from the State	$100.00
loss of time & property in the State	200.00
	$300.00

this band also murdered my husband faling upon him in ahelpless Condition and Cuting him to peases with a sythe blaid I Certify the above to be true according to the best of my Knowledge

Catharine McBride

[*Sworn to before C. M. Woods, C.C.C., Adams Co., IL, 18 May 1839.*]

MACKLEY, Jermiah

May the 9th 1839 Illinois Quinsey

An account against the State of Missouri for debt and damage Sustained in Consequence of the Exterminating Order

80 Acres of Land Withe the Improvements	$500.00
Loss of Crop and other Property	400.00
	$900.00

I Certify the above account to be Just and true according to the best of My Knowledge

Jermiah Mackley

[Sworn to before C. M. Woods, C.C.C., Adams Co., IL, 15 May 1839.]

McMILLEN, James

Quincy Illinois may the 18th 1839

Damages Received by the mob of missouri and Caused to be

time & expense in mooving to the State of Missouri	$75.00
loss of property in the State	250.00
time & expense in mooving from the State	50.00
	$375.00

I Certify the above to be true according to the best of my knowledge

James McMillen

[Sworn to before C. M. Woods, C.C.C., Adams Co., IL, 18 May 1839.]

McRAE, Alexander

Quincy May 13th 1839.

A bill of debt and damage against the state of missouri in concequence of the governers exterminating order first for mooving into the state expinces from 25 to 30 Dollars for time in moving and use of Horse and waggon seven weeks at two Dollars and fifty cents per Day 122.50 after I moved to the state I bought a house and lot in the town of Far West for which I have not been able to get any thing at all. I concidder it worth at least 150 Dollars. how much it has cost me to come away I do not know I have been in Prison near six month without law or justice or unlawfully and my family was driven out while I was in prison all this I shall leave to the generosity of the authorities of the united states

Alexander McRae

I Cirtify that the above is just and true according to the best of my judgment

Alexander McRae

[*Sworn to before C. M. Woods, C.C.C., Adams Co., IL, 13 May 1839.*]

McVAY, John

May the 11th 1839 Illinois Quinsey
An account against the State of Missouri for debt and Damage Sustained in Consequence of the Exterminating Order

20 Acres of Land	$100.00
Damage	80.00
1 Gun	20.00
	$200.00

I certify the above to be a Just and true account according to the best of my Knowledge

John McVay

[*Sworn to before C. M. Woods, C.C.C., Adams Co., IL, 11 May 1839.*]

MAGINN, Ezekiel[30]

Quincy Illinois March 17th 1840
I Ezekiel Maginn Certify that I was a Citizen of the State of Missouri in the year of 1838 and was an Ey witness to the following facts first I Saw the malitia cald for By Govener Bogs Exterminateing order Enter the House of Lyman Wight and took from it Bed and Beding pillows and Dishes personly known to me to Be his propperty.

Ezekiel Maginn

[*Sworn to before C. M. Woods, C.C.C., Adams Co., IL, 17 Mar 1840.*]

---

[30] Also found in *HC* 4:64–65 and in JH 17 Mar 1840.

MANSFIELD, Matthew

Illinois Adams County May 10th 1839

This may Certify that I Matthew Mansfield removed to the State of Missouri in the month of August went as far as Chariton County ware I purchased Corn potatoes and cut hay for my cattle about the last of October I had Orders from Thomas Watson Col to leave that County in six days or we should have our house burned down over our head in three days ther came to the house at night eight or ten of the mob and demanded the guns the took one from me and one from an nother man then went of after saying the would give us a bufalo receit for then several of them known to some in the house Names Jams Parkes Bdiott Gentrey Young Watson I went in four days leaving the whole of my corn potatoes and hay with loss of time five hundred dolars when we ware on the road we met a nother company who stoped us and said the would take care of us the let us pas after serching our wagons and taken some books and papers and several articals from us and given us a pass for a Buse and Suffering self and family five hundred dollars is but little Compensation

Matthew Mansfield

[*Sworn to before C. M. Woods, C.C.C., Adams Co., IL, 11 May 1839.*]

MARTIN, William

May 13th 1839

the State of Missouri to william Martin Drt. Occasiond By the Mob of Said State in the year of 1838 and 1839

to ~~the~~ one horse	$75.00
To two Cows	25.00
To Loss on Crop	25.00
To of hogs	25.00
To loss of time 3 weeks	25.00
To expences of moveing and t[ax]es	100.00
To Suffering and being deprived of CittisonShip in the State of Missouri	1,000.00
	$1,275.00

William Martin

[*Sworn to before W. Oglesby, J.P., Adams Co., IL, 13 May 1839.*]

MAYNARD, Silas

State of Missori Dr To Silas Maynard

For Loss of House & Lot in City Far West	
" " " " in Caldwell County	$500.00
For Abuse for Self & Family ~~by Mob~~	150.00
For one Cow Taken by Mob	25.00
For one Rifle Taken by Mob	30.00
For Loss of Furniture	25.00
For being made prisoner unlawfully and kept Confined four weeks	100.00
For Moveing to the State Mo	100.00
For being driven from the St. M thereby deprived the right of Citizenship Contrary to Law & Constitution of the U.S.	500.00
	$1,430.00

I do hereby Certify the Above to be a just and true accompt according to my Judgement

Silas Maynard

[*Sworn to before C. M. Woods, C.C.C., Adams Co., IL, 8 May 1839.*]

MELIN, William R.

Illenois Quincy May th13 1839

A bill of Damagees against the State of Missourie for being Driven from the State in consequence of the Govinors Exterminating order

first for mooveing in to the State	$120.00
for mooveing out of the State and loss of time in concequence of the mob	50.00

I Do Certify the a bove a count to Be true and Just a cording to the Best of my Knowledg

William R. Melin

[*Sworn to before C. M. Woods, C.C.C., Adams Co., IL, 13 May 1839.*]

MERRILL, Thomas

March 1840 Quinsey Adams County Illinois
    A bill of Loss Sustained by Leaving the State of Missouri in the Year
of 1838 and 1839—in Consequence of the Exterminating Order

120 Acres of Land		$1000.00
Receivd payment on the Land	[*subtracted*]	350.00
[*Subtotal*]		$650.00
About 50 head of Hogs		50.00
7 do of Cattle		50.00
house furniture		60.00
farming tools		15.00
Corn Crop and potatoes		50.00
Damage		200.00

The above is a Correct Statement according to the best of my
Knowledge

Thomas Merrill

[*Sworn to before J. H. Holton, N.P., Adams Co., IL, 17 Mar 1840.*]

MIDDAGH, George

Handcock Co and state of Illenois
    A bill of damages a gainst the state of missauri in concequence of
being driven from the state in 1838

Loss of property by moveing to the state	$2,500.00
expence of moveing into the state	100.00
loss of time and property in the state	231.00
expence of moving out of the State	50.00

George Middagh

[*Sworn to before A. Monroe, J.P., Hancock Co., IL, 6 Jan 1840.*]

MIKESELL, G. W.

Illenois Quincy May 14th 1839
    A bill of Damagees a gainst the State of Missourie in concequence
of the Goveners Exterminating orDer

first for mooving in to the State for Damage Don and mooving
out of the State all Estimated at $850

I Certify the a bove acount to be Just and true a cording to the best
of my Knowledg

G. W. Mikesell

[*Sworn to before C. M. Woods, C.C.C., Adams Co., IL, 18 May 1839.*]

MIKESELL, Hiram W.

Illenois Quincy May the14 1839
a bill of Damage against the State of Missoriri for Beining Driven
out of the State
for comining to the State Loss of propperty and having to leave the
State &c for which I Charge $4000.00
I Certify the a bove to Be Just and true acording to the Best of my
Knowledg

Hiram W. Mikesell

[*Sworn to before C. M. Woods, C.C.C., Adams Co., IL, 18 May 1839.*]

MIKESELL, J. A.

Illenois Quincy May the 14th 1839
a bill a gainst the State of Missouri in Conciquen of the Govinors
order of Extermination and Being Driven from the State

first for mooving in to the state	$50.00
for propperty Lost in the State	1,000.00
for mooving out of the state	200.00
	$1,250.00

J. A. Mikesll

[*Sworn to before C. M. Woods, C.C.C., Adams Co., IL, 18 May 1839.*]

MIKESELL, John H.

Illenois Quincy may the 14th 1839
A bill of Damiges against the State of Missouri in conciquenc of the
Goviners order

first for mooveing into the State	$50.00
fo loss of propperty in the State	500.00
for mooveing out of the State	20.00
	$570.00

I Certify the a bove to be true and Just a cording to the best of my Knowledg

John H. Mikesel[*l*]

[Sworn to before C. M. Woods, C.C.C., Adams Co., IL, 18 May 1839.]

MILAM, William

Quincy Illenois may the 16the 1839

damages [——] due to William Milam in concequence of the extermination order of Bogs from from misourie Two thousand dollars

I here by certify that the above is a true account according to the best of my recollection

William Milam

[Sworn to before C. M. Woods, C.C.C., Adams Co., IL, 16 May 1839.]

MILES, Joel S.

Illinois Quincy may the 11 1839

a bill of Damage a gainst the State of Missorie sustained by a mob

for coming in to the State	$100.00
for loss of propperty and time in the State	1,000.00
for leaving the State	25.00
	$1,125.00

I c[er]tiffy the above to Be true and Just a cording to the Best of my knowledg

Joel S. Miles

[Sworn to before C. M. Woods, C.C.C., Adams Co., IL, 11 May 1839.]

MILLER, John

Illenois Quincy May the18 1839

A bill of Damages a gainst the State of Missouri for Being unlawfully Driven from the State

first for mooving to the State
Loss of time and Expence $60.00
fo loss of land and other propprty in the State 200.00
for mooving out of the State 60.00
$320.00

I Certify the above a count to Be true and Just a cording to the best of my Knowledg

John Miller

[Sworn to before C. M. Woods, C.C.C., Adams Co., IL, 18 May 1839.]

MILLER, William

Acount Against the State of missouri
one ox killed buy the mllitia worth thirty five dollars and for trave[*l*]ing from the State of Ohio to the mo. with a team and from there back to the State of Illenaise and time lost in the State of missouri buy reason of the mob and for improvements on land which amounts to five hundred dollars
and also being deprived of CitizenShip

William Miller

I Certify the a bove to Be true and Just acording to the Best of my Knowowledg

William Miller

[Sworn to before C. M. Woods, C.C.C., Adams Co., IL, 13 May 1839.]

MILLS, Elvira P.

A Bill of Loss and damages sustained in and by the state of Missouri.

Expense of moving to Jackson Co. Mo. May 1832 with
two yoke of oxen and one span of Horses and two
waggons $162.00
driven from Jackson and lost twenty acres of land worth
fifteen dollars per acre 300.00
Lost twenty seven bbb. corn at one dollar fifty cents per
bbb. 45.50
Do one gun 20.00

Do three cows at twenty dollars each	60.00
Do one yoke of oxen	80.00
Damag estimated at one thousand dollars	1,000.00
[*Subtotal*]	$1,667.50
for being driven from Jackson and Cla y1839, Amount of property lost on being being driven fron Caldwell out of the state	100.00
Damage estimated at	1,000.00
[*Subtotal*]	$1,100.00
[*Subtotal from above*]	$1,667.50
Whole amount	$2,767.50

Elvira P Mills

I Certify the a bove acount to Be Just and true a cording to the Best of my Knowldg

Elvira P Mills

[*Sworn to before C. M. Woods, C.C.C., Adams Co., IL, 14 May 1839.*]

MITCHELL, Isaac

qincy illionayes march the 16th 1840
    i issac mitchell doo [c]ertify that i had one mare Stolen wo[r]th one hundred dolares by gin parikes or hi[s] compny in the Stae of mosury davis county

isaac mitchell

[*Sworn to before W. Tainter, who signed for C. M. Woods, C.C.C., Adams Co., IL, 16 Mar 1840.*]

MORLEY, Isaac

Illenois Quincy May 28 1839
    A bill of Damage against the state of Missouri in Conciquence of the Goviners Exterminating order

$100.00

first for mooving into the state
for Damage in Jackson county Being Driven from the Same
    and for loss of propperty in 1833   500.00

for Being Driven from Clay Co to Caldwell Loss of propprty and time Being thrown out of Buisness	200.00
for Loss of propperty in Caldwell Co. and Being Driven from the State time and Expenes	2,000.00
	$2,800.00

I was allso imprisened in Jackson County falsly twelve Hours and Shot at By a mob in 1833

imprisened in Richmond Ray County 20 Days and have never had an acusition found against me in the State this was in 1838

I Certify the a bove a count to Be Just and true a cording to the Best of my knowledg

Isaac Morley

[Sworn to before C. M. Woods, C.C.C., Adams Co., IL, 28 May 1839.]

MORRIS, Jacob

May 18th 1839

An Account I Jacob Morris have against the State of Missouri in Consequence of Mobocracy

To Moveing from Indianna To Clay Co Missouri	$80.00
To 2 Teams moveing from indianna to Mo	96.00
To time formy self Comeing to Missouri 8 weeks	48.00
To Loss Sustained in Selling my place	650.00
To Loss on Cattle	25.00
To one house Burnt up by Militia	40.00
To 8 acres of wheat on the ground	32.00
To 200 bushel of Corn Los on it	25.00
To 30 Dollars Cheated out of	30.00
To one hundred Dollars Cheated out of	100.00
To Moveing expences from Missouri Back to Illinois	90.00
[*Subtotal*]	$1,216.00
To one gun and Pistol worth	31.00
	$1,247.00

I have Lost many things that I have not Charged for that are Too Tedious to Mention and as it Respects my Sufferings it is out of My power to Describe or put on any Amount as a compensation but I and my family have had to suffer in Consequence of Mobocracy therefore your honorable

Body are Left to Decide what amount I had ought to have Respectfully yours &C.,

Jacob Morris

[Sworn to before C. M. Woods, C.C.C., Adams Co., IL, 21 May 1839.]

MORRISON, Arthur

Arthur Morrison emigrated to Jackson County in the State of Missouri in the ~~fall~~ Winter of Eighteen hundred and thirty two Shortly after which time the persecution of the Saints began and still increased and grew untill I with the Body of the Church was compelled to leave My house and home property and evry thing I possessed to a ruthless banditty of Ruffians Who swore if I did not leave the County immediately with out dely the[y] would not spare life I also complied with there unreasonable requests and left in the dead of Winter not Knowing where to go to find a place to lay my head or a Shelter for my family yet notwithstanding the unhollowed persecution in that Section of Country I found a Situatio[n] in Clay County the most Heathenish Creature of the West could not forbear to give us a place after the expulsion from Jackson County after Seeing how we was and had been treated by the inhuman wretches therefore we found a place in Clay County for a little season untill we could right up and gete in tolerable circumstances once more but after residing there untill Some 3 year or about the year Eighteen hundred and thirty five the persecution in the aboved named County began to rear its head and still kep increasing untill it became irresistable and I ~~like~~ With the ballance of the Church of Latter day Saints Was compelled to leave house and home & property and ~~was~~ located my self in the County of Caldwell there I for the third time Suffered a loss with the rest of Said church Which is unparelled in the history of ancients or Moderns. There I commenced Merchandising and after I had been there Som 2 year or about the year Eighteen hundred and thirty Eight and Nine the persecu[tion] again began to Show its self in the above named County Mobs arose Stolle Robed Plundered and Murdered around in the outor parts of our County I being a Commissioned officer in that County and Subject to the command of the Colonel of Said County I was ordered out to defend his wrights and likewise did youse my bst expersions So to doo Shortly after which time the Elections ~~for~~ came and I being duly elected and Commissioned by Lilburn W. Boggs a County Judge from that time persecution began to prevail pretty universly and the State of Missouri and the Governor issued an order for anumbered thousand of Troops to be raised and immediately take up the line of March for Far West and he also issued another order which Was for the [e]xtermination of the Whole body or church of Latter day Saints they arrived and captured the place and give us our choice Either to leave or Be massacred and we of corse chose to leave the State. and there I left My all when Neatly stimated will amount to ten thousand I was also deprived of Citisen Ship which Gentleman I hope and trust you will realize is so near and dear to all therefore I most humbly trust you will restore at the riske of all yea it is only that which you are bound to define.

A Morrison

[*Sworn to before C. M. Woods, C.C.C., Adams Co., IL, 1 Nov 1839.*]

MORSE, Moses

Bill of articles lost and Damages occasioned by the Mob of Missouri in Davies & Caldwell County

1 on 80 acres of land in	$300.00
2 on improvement preemtion	200.00
3 on lot in fairwest	100.00
4 on lot in diammon	100.00
5 to two hundred bushels of corn	80.00
6 to one wagon stole by Mob	40.00
7 to one Cow $12 one log chane $4	16.00
8 to 3 Sheep $12 ten gallons honey $10	22.00
9 to seven head of hogs four dollars each	28.00
10 for being drove out of house and home	00
in the dead of winter and expences	00
to the state of illinois and loss of 5 months time and	
impaire of health in my family one $1000	1,000.00
[*Subtotal*]	$1,886.00
30 bushels of potatoes	
300 head of cabage	15.00
one gun	26.00
	$1,907.00

as for damages i care not all i crave your honerable body is a just recompence for my true loses yours with respect

House of Congress year 1839   Moses Morse

[*Sworn to before C. M. Woods, C.C.C., Adams Co., IL, 11 May 1839.*]

MOSIER, Frerick

Illenois Quincy may 20th 1839
      a bill of Damage a gainst the State of Missouri for propperty Lost &c

first for mooving into State	$60.00
for propperty Lost in the State	250.00
mooving from the State	20.00
	$320.00

      I certify the a bov to to Be true and Just a cording to the Best of my knowledg

                                                            Frerick Mosier

[Sworn to before C. M. Woods, C.C.C., Adams Co., IL, 20 May 1839.]

MYERS, George

May the 9th 1839 Illenois Quinsey
      An account against the State of Missouri for debt and damage Sustained in consequence of the Exterminating Order

Damage & removal	$150

      I certify the above account to be Just and true according to the best of my Knowledge

                                                            George Myers

[Sworn to before C. M. Woods, C.C.C., Adams Co., IL, 9 May 1839.]

MYERS, Jacob

May the 11th 1839 Illinois Quinsey
      An account against the State of Missouri for Debt and damage Sustained in Consequence of the Exterminating Order

465 Acres of Land	$1,030.00
Improvement	355.00
Damage & Remooval	240.00
	$1,625.00

I certify the above to be a Just and true account according to the best of my Knowledge

Jacob Myers

[Sworn to before C. M. Woods, C.C.C., Adams Co., IL, 11 May 1839.]

NAPER, Ruth

May the 6 1839

Ruth Naper left ~~the~~ Cok County Ill and went to Mo Sept the 1 1835 expensees of mooveng with 6 in a famaly $200.00

i settle n[eea]r hons mill and there my husban Wilian Naper was murderd and my house plundrd and left to behold the hored seane and i charge for the sume 500.00

then haveing to lave S[t]ate and expenses by the way 300.00

to the lose of time <u>150.00</u>

$950.00

I certify that the above to be a trew acount acording to the best of my knowlage

Ruth Naper

[Sworn to before C. M. Woods, C.C.C., Adams Co., IL, 7 May 1839.]

NEWBERY, Jams

Illinois May the 7 1839

a bill of Damages a gainst the state of Missouri which has occurd in Conciquenc of the goviners order of extermintion

first in mooveing from Ohio to Jackson Co Mo my family consisted of 12 persons $200.00

for Being Driven from thence to Clay Co 150.00

from Clay to Cald well after having Ben Driven from house to Hous 3 times in Clay for this a buse and Loss of propperty and time 500.00

loss of propperty and Being Driven from the State together with the Loss of labor 1,000.00

I Do here By Certify that the a bove acount is Just and true a cording to the Best of my Knowldg

Jams Newbery

[Sworn to before C. M. Woods, C.C.C., Adams Co., IL, 7 May 1839.]

NISWANGER, William

May the 11 1839
    State of Missouri Dr to Wm [N̶i̶s̶w̶a̶n̶g̶e̶r̶] Loss

Loss of property Lands and Cropes Do Dolla[r]	
to Loss of Sale of Land	$210.00
to the Loss on Cattle taken from me	20.[00]
to the Loss of planks and Lumber	25.00
to the Loss of hogs	15.25
to the Loss of Corn & Crop of wheate	50.37
to the Loss of Sundry Article	10.12
to the Loss of Eight Months Worke By the Mob and goviner Bogs	200.08
to the Exspence of Movinge from state and trouble	75.37½
	$61[3].41½

State of Missouri Dr to William Niswanger

[*Sworn to before C. M. Woods, C.C.C., Adams Co., IL, 11 May 1839.*]

OAKS, Almera

the damages done in davis County By Being drove By the mob By the orders of the gvernor to one house and lot and the loss of time of my sons and moveing to Caldwell County and the loss of property taken By the mob in davis County state missori Ad 1838—	$200.00
and the loss of time in Caldwell County State missouri and moveing from that to the state of illinois Ad 1839—	130.00

Almera Oaks

I Certify that the within is a true coppy of Damiges acording to the Best of m[y] Knowledg

Almera Oaks

[*Sworn to before C. M. Woods, C.C.C., Adams Co., IL, 6 May 1839.*]

O'BANIAN, Evins

Illinois Quincy May th11 1839
    a bill of Damages against the State of Missori

first for mooving in to the State	$200.00
for loss of propperty in the State	700.00
for Leaving the State and loss of propperty	300.00

I Certify the a bove a count to Be Just and true a cording to the Bes of my Knowledg

Evins Obanian

[*Sworn to before C. M. Woods, C.C.C., Adams Co., IL, 11 May 1839.*]

OLNEY, Oliver

Illenois Quincy May 11th 1839

A bill of Damages against the State of Missouri for being driven out of the State by the orders of Governor Bogs

Loss in price of land by leaving the State	$400.00
Loss of goods bedding Clothing Cloth Leather Castings	800.00
Loss of time in being harrsed by the Mob at Dewit Carl County and drove out to Cal Co	50.00
Also for being driven out of the State	100.00
Loss of Stock Hogs &c	200.00
Loss of time Colwell County an being hindred in going on with business	200.00

I do Hereby Certify that the a bove account is Just according to the best of My knowledge

Oliver Olney

[*Sworn to before C. M. Woods, C.C.C., Adams Co., IL, 11 May 1839.*]

OMSTED, Harvey

May 13th 1839

An account That I Hervy omsted have against the state of Missouri in Consequence of Mobocracy first the expences and time for moveing from Illinois to Jackson County State of Missouri	$50.00
For improvements in Jackson County Made on Congress Land	25.00
Lost 2 hundred Bushels of Corn at 25 cents pr Bushel	50.00

To fodder of 5 acres	10.00
To Ten bushels of Potatoes at 25 cets pr Bushel	2.50
To one Calf	3.00
To 32 acres of Deeded Land at 5 Dollars pr acre	160.00
To Expences of Crossing the River into Clay county	2.50
To Time taken to hunt a house and fencing it and moveing into it in Clay County	16.00
Expences of moveing from Clay to Ray County Mo	3.50
Expences of Moveing from Ray to Davis Co makeing 5 trips Takeing 20 Days at 3 1/2 Dollars pr Day	70.00
To improvement & Claim on Congress land in Davis Co	250.00
To Six hundred Bushels of Corn at 25 cents pr Bushel	150.00
To 15 bushel of potatoes at 50 cents pr Bushel	7.50
To 8 hundred Bundles of fodder at $1.25 cents per Hundred	10.00
To seven Tons of hay at 3 Dollars pr ton	21.00
To three Calves taken from me out of the field worth	11.00
Two ploughs taken out of the field worth	12.00
one horse	40.00
Eight head of hogs worth eight Dollars a piece	64.00
thirteen shoats worth 2 Dollars a piece	26.00
Building a house in Diahman worth	30.00
2 axes 1 Bedsted grubbing hoe and three hoes worth	9.00
2 Sheep worth 4 Dollars a piece	8.00
Moveing from Davis to Caldwel County	7.00
Expence of Building a house in Caldwell County	20.00
Expence of Moveing from caldwel County to the state of Illinois and the time it took to move	97.50
[*Subtotal*]	$1,254.50
To 4 acres of wheat at 10 Dollars pr acre	40.00
	$1,294.50

I Shall not attempt to put any amount on my sufferings as it is out of my power to Describe my feelings and I am inadaquate to the task but will Just Relate that I was one with my family that was Drove from Jackson County inthe time that the Mob Broke out against the people of god there and myself wife & Children were driven out in the Cold winter from our homes & possesions into Clay County where we had to hunt a Covering to keep us from the blasts of winter again we were Driven with our Children from Davis County out of the State of Missouri and in consequence of So long an exposure to the inclement weather it proved Almost to intolerable a burthen to be borne but after a long and serious fit of sickness in the State of Illinois She through the Mercy of god I hope will Recover but our Sufferings we cannot Relate in full therefore I shall leave it with your honorable Body to Determene what I Should have or whether I Should have any thing or not

Hervy Omsted

State of Illinois Hancock County

Personally appeared before the subscriber and acting justice of the peace in and for said county Harvey Omsted and deposeth and saith that the within account is just and true.

Harvey **X** Omsted

[Sworn to before A. Smith, J.P., Hancock Co., IL, 14 May 1839.]

ORMSBY, Gideon

June the 1st 1836

I here present you a bill of damagees against the State of Missouri that I have sustained since June 1836 to the present time

For being driven from Clay County and turned into the open Prairies to seek shelter and the exposier of health &c five hundred dollars

$500.00

Sept 1st 1838

For the loss of time in defending myself against a ruthless mobb The the loss of Seven acres of Corn handsomely cut and stooked up and twenty loads of pumpkins taken by the Militia and other property The sacrifice of Houses and lands being deprived of liberty and driven out of the State Estimated at five thousand dollars   5000.00

The Bill made out Quincy June 8th 1839   Gideon Ormsby

[Sworn to before C. M. Woods, C.C.C., Adams Co., IL, 31 May 1839.]

OSBORN, David et al.

To the Honl The Senate and the Honls The House of Representatives in Congress assembled at the city of Washington in the district of Columbia on the first monday of december A D. 1839—

A petition of certain individuals residing in the cty of Pike Illinois We would represent to your honorable body that a few years ago we emigrated to the state of Missouri and located confiding in the protection of said State and the general government, but contrary to the Constitution and laws of the United States, and the just expectations of your petitioners, were during the winter and spring past, forst to leave our hou[s]es and homes by the exterminating order of Governor Boggs of Missouri and under these precarious circumstances had to flee to our present places of abode for refuge—and our names with the amount of damages each person has sustained we have written below and we believe that said injuries were inflicted upon us virtually because we dared to worship God according to the dictates of our own consciences

Therefore your humble petitioners ask your honorable body to grant us a quantity of land either in this State or in the Ioway Territory equal to our losses as hereafter named—or take such other measures to remedy said injuries received by your petitioners as you in your wisdom shall deem expedient and as in duty bound you will ever pray—

Names of your Petitioner

David Osborn, for land, corn, &c	$400.00
Levi Gifford for house, & damages	500.00
Daniel Howe, for improvements, &c	400.00
Andrew Whitlock for property & 16 days false imprisonment	500.00
Silas Smith for property	1,200.00
Noah Rogers for land, and other property	1,960.00
Chandler Rogers for property & expences	1,250.00
Warner Hoopes for property & expence	250.00
Jonathan Hoopes for land and houses and other property	1,115.00
John Sweat for property, expences &c	200.00
Henry Stevenson for property, expences &c	340.00
James Allred for land and property	2,000.00
Hugh Snively for property & expences	430.00
Joseph S Carrelton	150.00
MB Welton property & expens	350.00
Martin C. Allred for land and property	200.00
James [Brown] for Property &c	250.00
Henry A Cleaveland for land, expences &c also for 3 months time lost in consequence of being wounded	2,000.00
Orren Rockwell for Land property &c	3,000.00
O. P. Rockwell for loss of property time and expences	2,000.00

Noble Rogers for Property & Expences   700.00

[Sworn to before W. H. Boling, C.C.C.C., Pike Co., IL, 22 May 1839.]

OSGOOD, Levi

Quincy Illinoys May the 6th 1839
   The State of Missouri Debtor for loss of debt one hundred 36 Dolars
and fifty cents [——] three chests of goods worth 55 dollars being driven
from Davis Co to caldwell Co and from thence to Illinoy Destitude of a
home and nearly blind for trouble damage and expense one hundred and
50 dollars

Leevi Osgood Wife and [—— ——] three Children

   I certify the a bove a count to Be corred and true a cording to the Best
of my Knowlledg

Levi Osgood

[Sworn to before C. M. Woods, C.C.C., Adams Co., IL, 7 May 1839.]

OUTHOUSE, John

   An account of losses damages &C—occasioned by the mob or the
orthorities of the State of Missouri, since 1836

Loss of time to the amount of	$500.00
Loss of Proporty to the amount of	135.00
Damage for burning two houses	100.00
Expense of travling and fategue	100.00
Loss of land and a comfortable home	1,000.00
Loss of a rifle gun	40.00
Loss of my right as a free citizen of U. S. A.	[——]

   I certify the a bove a count to Be Just and true acording to the Best
of my Knowledg

John Outhouse

[Sworn to before C. M. Woods, C.C.C., Adams Co., IL, 11 May 1839.]

OUTHOUSE, Turner

Quincy Ilenoy May 18th 1839

Damagees receivd by the Mob of Missourie &
   expences in mooveing $800.00

Turner Outhouse

I certefy the a bove to be true according to the best of my knowlege

T Outhouse

[Sworn to before C. M. Woods, C.C.C., Adams Co., IL, 18 May 1839.]

OVERTON, Mahala an

A Charge of damages sustaind by Mary Ann overton in Consequence of being driven by Mobs in the state of Missouri being sumed Amounts to ten thousand Dollars
    I certify the a bove acount to Be Just and true a cording to the Best of my knowledg

Mahala an Overton

[Sworn to before C. M. Woods, C.C.C., Adams Co., IL, 15 May 1839.]

OWEN, Ephraim

June 1838 the State of Missouri Dr

	Traveling Expences Removeing to the State	$50.00
	team Hire 2 Waggons 3 yoke of oxen and one	
	Span of Horses 32 days at $5.00 pr day	160.00
	wages paid to teamster	21.18
Oct	Loss of time incured by family removeing	100.00
1838	2 Waggons and one set of Harness	90.00
	Claim bought from Wm. Morgan of 80 acres	
	adjoining the Town of Diamon $10.00	
	praire Entrance money deducted	700.00
	Claim brought from Wm. Grant of 120 acres	1,080.00
	Same place and price	
	10 ton of Hay at 6 dollars pr ton	60.00

	1 Bureau Taken by A Black	45.00
	Spade chains Barrels Boxes &c & taken by Lee	20.00
	Cattle destroyed or driven off part of a drove	1,000.00
	Stone goods rights and credits first cost	2,000.00
~~Jan~~ 1	3 yoke of oxen	160.00
Nov 1838	Loss of time and traveling Expences in fleeing to Escape Imprisonment ~~and traveling expences~~	150.00
	Total	$5,636.18
	1 gun and sword 25.00 Loss of time Leaveing state 50.00	75.00
		$5,711.18

For being fired at by three Ruffians at once whilst while riding peaceably along the publick highway. For Authorities refusing to grant redress. For Imprisonment on a false charge Suffering abuse from a Lawles mob deprivation of citizenship &c are items for which a freeman can make no bill no money cannot purchase the Sacred privileges and immunities of a freeborn Son of America no verily as the Lord God Liveth, the Love of Liberty is So entwined about his heart that he would rather, yea much rather Shed the Last drop of his blood, and Lay down his life at the feet of a forreign or domestic foe; than to Surrender those Sacred rights.

I certify the foregoing to be Substantially true As I expect to answer before god at the great day. Given under my hand at Quincy May the 10th 1839

Ephraim Owen

[*Not sworn.*]

OWEN, Jedidiah [31]

to whom it may concern

This is to certify that on the day following on which the troops arrived at far west that two men of Said troops came to my house Broke open my trunk and took therefrom both mony and clothing and also a number of papers among which were deeds and notes ect and also a number of cooking utesils and in consequence of the cruel and unhuman treatment which I and others have received from those ~~men~~ troops we are reduced

[31] Also found in *HC* 4:56–57 and in JH 6 Jan 1840.

to a State of almost absolute Starvation and Daniel Avery and myself are appointed as a committee to go out and beg corn and meal or any thing we may obtain that can render them assistance or relieve them in their Suffering condition

Jedidiah Owen

[Sworn to before D. W. Kilbourn, J.P., Lee Co., IA, 6 Jan 1840.]

OWEN, Saly

Sally Owen i left Green County Indany may 1836 i mooved to Cay County Mo

expences to Mosuri	$30.00
damage sustained by being driven from Clay to colwell County	100.00
remooved to Clinten County	
driven from Clinton Co to ~~Colwell~~ davis Co damage by lose of propperty and land	1,500.00
Damage by being driven from davis to Colwell	100.00
to 120 acres of land in colwell	700.00
the exposure form davis to Colwell accured the death of my husban	
damage and expense by being driven out of the State of Mo by my self and 6 children	1,000.00
to the lause of time	200.00
	$3,500.00

i certify that the a buve a count to be a just ~~a count~~ acording to the best of my knolage

Saly **X** Owen

[Sworn to before C. M. Woods, C.C.C., Adams Co., IL, 6 May 1839.]

P—Z

PACKARD, Noah

Quinsey May 9th 1839
 Damages sustained in consequence of the unconstitutional orders of Govenor Boggs against the church of Christ of latterday saints in the state of Missorie in the year year eighteen hundred thirty eight
 For being Compelled to leave the state ~~of~~ $1,000.00 For being deprived of my Constitutional rights a boon of Heaven by our fathers; to high for computation, I shall therefore submit it to the Honorable President and Congress

Noah Packard

[Sworn to before C. M. Woods, C.C.C., Adams Co., IL, 16 May 1839.]

PACKER, Jonathan T.

May the 9th 1839 Illinois Quinsey
 An account against the State of Missouri for Debt and Dammage sustained inconsequence of the Exterminating Order—

Loss on land	$250.00
Damage & removal	50.00
	$300.00

 I certify the above to be a Just and true account to the best of my Knowledge

Jonathan T Packer

[Sworn to before C. M. Woods, C.C.C., Adams Co., IL, 9 May 1839.]

PAGE, Ebenezer

the loss of property and damage I have recieve in Mo to	
four acres of corn	$50.00
to loss of cattle	85.00
to time lost in campain and in prison	85.00
to-4 four acres of land and bild	200.00
to exspence of mooveing	75.00

to loss of furniture in the house	45.00
to tools chain	28.00

Ebenezer page

My wife sustain loss preveous to our merriag   200
I certefy the within to be true to the best of my knowlege

Ebenezer Page

[*Sworn to before C. M. Woods, C.C.C., Adams Co., IL, 6 May 1839.*]

PAGE, Rachel

State of Missouri Dr To Rachel Page For being driven three times from county to county and lastly from the state, and loss of property
$800

Rachel Page

I doe hereby certify the within statement to be true

Rachel Page

[*Sworn to before C. M. Woods, C.C.C., Adams Co., IL, 6 May 1839.*]

PARKER, Samuel

The State of Missouri To Samuel Parker dr in consequence of abuse receivd by the inhabitance haveing to arm myself and stand gard by day and by night in october and November in 1838 to defend my self and famely from a lawless mob being without a house for a shelter $100.00

being driven from davis to Caldwell County in the winter season to seeck shelter wheare their was none to be had   150.00

haveing to dispose of my property for jest what the mob would give me   250.00

being deprivd of sitizenship and expence of moveing from the State
300.00

meeting with an accident in consiquence of moveing by which I am in dainger of loosing one of my arms   1,000.00

to gun taken by the mob   15.00
$1,815.00

Quincy May 18th 1839   Samuel Parker

[*Sworn to before C. M. Woods, C.C.C., Adams Co., IL, 18 May 1839.*]

PARRISH, Ezra

Do A bill of Damage Sustained by Ezra Parrish against the State of Missouri in Consequence of the unlawful Conduct of the Inhabitants thereof & the unconstitutional Decrees of the Governor

Damage on Land	$400.00
Do. Do. on Personal Property	100.00
Do. Do. for being Obliged to remove & the Inconvencienses & the Exposure to the weather & being thrown out of Business &c &c	200.00
Do. Do. Expences for Journey	100.00
	$800.00

also for being obliged to flee into the woods & laying there for Three Days & Nights for fear of my life being taken as the Mob was seeking for me & also took my Rifle from me & otherwise abuseing Me

I also heard the Mob Say they would have Killed Elijah Reed if they Could find him

Ezra Parrish

I Do hereby Certify the within Statements to be true accoding to the Best of my knowledge

Ezra Parrish

[Sworn to before C. M. Woods, C.C.C., Adams Co., IL, 18 May 1839.]

PARSONS, Isaac

quincy may the 6 1839

damage against the state of Missouri for mooving out of the state of ohio into the state of Missouri in the year 1833	$100.00
for being for loss of property in being drivin out of lafyett County in the year 1834	50.00
loss of property in being driven out of Clay County 1837	100.00
loss in being driven out of state by the order of the governars order without house or hone at this time	150.00

Isaac Parsons

I Certify the with in to be true Copy of my damage acording to the best of my knollage

Isaac Parsons

[*Sworn to before C. M. Woods, C.C.C., Adams Co., IL, 6 May 1839.*]

PARSONS, Thorit

May 6th A.D. 1839 Quincy, Adams Co. Ill.
State of Missouri Dr.
for expences of moving from Ohio to Missouri $150.00
for being driven out of Lafayette Co.—loss of property and time $200.00
for being driven from Clay Co. to Caldwell Co. and loss of property and time $200.00
for being driven out of the State of Mo. loss of land hogs time and expenses of moving $500.00
for false imprisonment $1000.00

Thorit Parsons

I certify this to be a true copy of damages to the best of my knowledge

Thorit Parsons

[*Sworn to before C. M. Woods, C.C.C., Adams Co., IL, 6 May 1839.*]

PATTEN, Charles W.

May the 12th 1839
Onerable sirs bfor home this bill may Cum Clameing at your hand my Writes of sitisenship as wone of the free born suns of Collumby—in as much as I hav ben arested by an out brakeing mob in upper moseurey and driven thru from my hose With my famoley beaing Compelld to Leave a cumfetable living and Ceak aliving for my self and Famoley by deys workes under these Conciderations I feel to make out my bill of Damagues—and request of you my writes as you hav power to administer jestus to all men according to Law.

Damegues sustained in jackson County 1 hous	$40.00
1 hudred bushels of Corn	25.00
2 1/2 achers of wheat	25.00
to hay and foder	25.00

time lost 3 munths	75.00
Expens of mooving	25.00
Totel amount	$215.00

Damegues sustained in Clay C.O. 1 hous too munths time and expns of mooving	$100.00
Damegus sustained in Coldwell County 1 thousend bushels of Corn at	200.00
Hogs and Cattel and Sheap &C to to the amount of	100.00
Lost time five munths at thirty Dollers permunth a mounting to	150.00

these air sum of the out rages against me and my famoley besides beaing Compled to make the frosen ground our bed and the Canopies of the hevens our shelter from time to time tho meny out rages ware Committed against others much wise than a gainst us to my noledg—such as tare men from ther beds and jurkein by them out adores by the har of their heds beating them with Clubs and whips untill they ware unable to stand alone—their wives and ther Childron driven to the woods—at the our of midnight—thir their houses throne down—and in sum instentces life was not spared—

men torne from thr famoleis and Cast in to prisons bound in Chanes for munths beaing deprived of the priviledg of Law-intirely-grant to examon our Case and Cause that an in vestigation Should take plaCe that the ergresers Should be broat jestus

Expenses I Cured in leaving the State—fifty Dollers

the hole amount of actuel LawCes is seven hundred and fifteen Dollers

I Doo surtify that the above account is Correct acording to the best of my noledg

Charles W. Patten

[*Sworn to before C. M. Woods, C.C.C., Adams Co., IL, 18 May 1839.*]

PATTERSON, Jeremiah

A Bill of Damages against the State of Missouri in Consequence of the Gov. Exterminateing order

first in mooving to the state	$170.00
Loss on Land	160.00
Loss of time	270.00
Expences in mooving from the state	29.75

Being Compild to moove By the Gov. Exterminateing
order from the State   200.00
                                                      $829.75

    I Do hereby Certy the above to Be a true and Just account to the Best of my knowledge

Illenois May 8th 1839   Jeremiah Patterson

[Sworn to before C. M. Woods, C.C.C., Adams Co., IL, 8 May 1839.]

PEA, John

Illienois May the 28 1839
    a bill of Damages a gainst the State of Missouri for Being Driven from the Stat unlawfully

first for mooveing to the State	$100.00
for Loss of propperty Lost in the State Such as Land and oth[er] propperty	1000.00
for Leaveing the State Loss of time and Damage &c &c	500.00
	$1650.00

    I certify the above a count to Be true and Just a cording to the Best of my knowledg

John Pea

[Sworn to before C. M. Woods, C.C.C., Adams Co., IL, 28 May 1839.]

PECK, Ezekiel

Illenois Quincy May the 10 1839
    a count of Debt and Damage against the State of Missouri Which has accrd in Conciquence of the Goviners Exterminating order—

for mooveing from the State of New York to Missorie Jackson County	$200.00
Being Driven from Jackson	500.00
from Clay to Caldwell	50.00
for Bein Driven from the State and Loss of propperty	1000.00
Total	$1,750.00

I certify the a bove to Be true and Just a cording to the Best of knowledg

Ezekiel Peck

[*Sworn to before C. M. Woods, C.C.C., Adams Co., IL, 10 May 1839.*]

PECK, Hezekiah

Illinois Adams county March 14th 1840

A bill of Damage a gainst the State of Missouri for Being Driven from the State By a mob

for mooveing into the State	$500.00
for loss of propperty in the	1,500.00
for mooveing out of the State	100.00
Total	$2,100.00

I certify the a bove to Be true and correct acording to the Best of my knowledg

Hezekiah Peck

[*Sworn to before W. Tainter, who signed for C. M. Woods, C.C.C., Adams Co., IL, 16 Mar 1840.*]

PENICK, Fedrich M.

Bill of articles lost and damages accasioned by the mob of Missouri in davies and Caldwell Counties and Clay for loss of time and having to hall My crop from clay thirty miles in consequence of mob	$200.00
and for being drove out of house and home in the dead of winter and expences to illenois	1,000.00
loss on improvements in davis	200.00
on lot in diammon	100.00
one ax Stole by the mob	3.00
one hewing ax	4.00
Corn and other produce on the place	100.00
one Sadle	10.00
one gun and pistol	20.00
one grub hoe	1.50
two hoes	2.00

one pair of plow gears   3.00

Fedrich M. Penick

[*Sworn to before C. M. Woods, C.C.C., Adams Co., IL, 11 May 1839.*]

PERRY, Asahel

Illenois Quincy May the 11, 1839
the State of Mssori Dr for Loss opropperty and Damagees Don in concequence of Being Driven from the State By a mob

first for mooving to the State	$800.00
for loss of time and damages in the State	500.00
for loss of land priviledg	500.00
for Being Driven from the State	500.00
	$2,300.00

I Certify the above to Be a Just and true a count a cording to the Best of m[y] knowldg

Asahel Perry

[*Sworn to before C. M. Woods, C.C.C., Adams Co., IL, 11 May 1839.*]

PERRY, Hiram

Illenois Quincy May the 11 1839
a bill of Damages Sustand in Conciquene of the Goviners order of Extermination—

first for mooveing in to the State	$200.00
for Loss of propperty and Damages in the State	250.00
for being unlawfully Driven from the State loss of propperty &C	300.00
	$750.00

I Certify the above to Be a Just and true acording to the Best of my knowledg

Hiram Perry

[*Sworn to before C. M. Woods, C.C.C., Adams Co., IL, 11 May 1839.*]

PERRY, Isaac

Illenois Quincy May the 11th 1839
The state of Missori dr for Loss of property and damages don in conciquence of being driven from the state by mob

first for moving to the State	$200.00
for loss of time and damages in the state	300.00
for Beeing driven from the state	300.00

I Cirtify the above to Be a Just and true account according to the Best of my knowledge

Isaac Perry

[*Sworn to before C. M. Woods, C.C.C., Adams Co., IL, 11 May 1839.*]

PERRY, William

Amount of damages done me by the State of Missourie

Time and expenses in moving to the State	$200.00
Loss of property	195.00
Loss of time while in the State	150.00
Time and expenses in moving from the State	30.00

I certify the above to be a just and true Statement according to the best of my knowledge

William Perry

[*Sworn to before C. M. Woods, C.C.C., Adams Co., IL, 14 May 1839.*]

PETTEGREW, David [32]

This is to Certify that I David Pettegrew was a citizen of Jackson County Missouri and owned a good farm lay ing on the Blue River six miles west of Independance and lived in peace with the inhabitance untill the summer and faul of 1833 when the inhabatence began to threaten us with destruction I was at work in my field and a man by the name of Allen and otheers with him Came along and Cried out Mr Pettegrew you air at work as though you was determined to stay here but we determin that you shall lieve the County a mediately I replied that I was a free borne citizon

---

[32] Also found in *HC* 4:71–73 and in JH 20 Mar 1840.

of the united states and had done harme to no man I therefore Clame protection by the law of the land and that the law and Constitution of the land would not Suffer them to Commit so horrid a Crime they then replied that the old law and Constitution is wornout and we are about to make a new one I was at a meeting whare we had met for prair and aman by the name of Masters Came and desired an intervue with us he then stated that he was sent by the mob to us to inform us that if we would for sake our mormon and prophet religion and become of thair riligion tha the mob would be our brothers and would fight for us but if you will not we air reddy and will drive you from the county a few days after this a large mob Came to my house Commanded by General Moses Wilson and Hugh Brazil and Lewis Franklin and brook down my doore and burst in to my house armed with guns and Clubs and knifes some of them were painted red and black this was in the night and my family was much frightened tha threatened me with a meadiate deth if I did not leave the place after much abuce tha left us for the night but in a few days after they returned and drove me and my family in to the street not suffering us to take eny thing with us I saw that we must go or die we went south to Vanburan County in company with 80 or 90ty others in a short time after I returned to my farm and found my house plundered my grain and crop and stock and all my farm and farming tools laid wast and destroyed and shortly after my house was burned to ashes I Caled on Esqr Western of Independance and in quired of him if he Could in form me what all this mobing and riot ment in forming him ~~that~~ of the destruction and plundering of my house to which he gave me no satisfaction but in sulted me and treated me rufly Governor Boggs lived in the County and I have seen him passing through among us in our great destress and gave no aten tion to our destresses he was then Lieutenant Governor of the state on my return to my family in Vanburan County I was much abused by a man by the name of Brady he said he would kill me if I ever atempted to go to my farm or if he see me passing that way again I returned to my family and in a few days after a company of men Came where we lived and said tha would spill my blood if I did not leave the place amediately the leaders of this Company were John Cornet and Thomas Langly and Hezekiah Warden tha lived in Jackson County this was in the cold winter and our sufferings was grate I fled a cross the Missouri River to Clay County whare I lived theree years in which time I often heard Judge Cameran and others say that you mormons cannot guit your wrights in eny of the Courts of the upper countys and I had not the privolige of Voting as a free citizon I mooved to Caldwell County bought land and opened a good farm lived in peace untill the summer and fall of 1838 when mobes arose in the Countys around about and I with the rest was obliedged to take up armes in self defence for the cry was that mob law should prevail we stood against them untill the army Came and took us all prisioners of war I with the rest was obliedged to sign a deed of trust at the point of the sword I with sixty others was selected out and marched to Richmond in Ray County by the command of General Clark whare tha kept us a number of weeks pretending to try us as treasoners and murderers at length I obtained my liberty and returned to my family in Caldwell County and I found that thair was no safty thair for thair was no law but all a seen of robing and plundering and steeling tha wear about to take me agarn and I was obliedged to leave my family and flee to Ilinoise in about two munths my family arived having suffered much abuce and loss of helth and property

Soon after the arival of my family my son a young man died and I atribit his deth to the cruel barbarity of the mob of Missouri he being a prisoner among them and having suffered much because [——] of them my father was a soaldier and served in the revalutionary war under the grate Washington but I have not had protection on my own lands or I have not bin permited to see my farm in Jackson County Missouri in seven years

soaldiers ware stationed or quartered in diferent parts of Farwest and tha treated us [very] rufly and threatening to shoot us and making use of any thing they pleased such as burning house timbers and rails and garden fences and steeling and plundering what tha pleased

These deeds cover a part of the land I owned in Caldwell County Missouri

when I was at Richmond a prisoner before Judge King we sent for many witnesses and when tha came thay were taken and cast in to prison with us and we were not permited to have any witnesses the day I came out of prison tha compeled me to sign a wrighting which was [——] not true or remain in prison

David Pettegrew

[*Sworn to before D. W. Kilbourn, J.P., Lee Co., IL, 21 Mar 1840.*]

PICKARD, Jane

Illenois Quincy May the 11 1839
    a bill of Damages a gainst the State of Missouri

for Being Driven from place to [place] and mooing to the State first for which I Charge	$100.00
for Being Driven from Jacson Count and loss of propperty &c &c	150.00

for Being Driven from the State and Loss of propperty by
the mob   200.00

I certify the a bove to Be true and Just a cordg to the Bestof my
Knowledg

Jane Pickard

[*Sworn to before C. M. Woods, C.C.C., Adams Co., IL, 11 May 1839.*]

PIERCE, Isaac W.

State of Illinois Morgan County SS.

This day personally appeared before me Horatio G Rew and acting
Justice of the peace within and for the county of Morgan aforesaid Isaac
W Pierce and on oath Says he belongs to the ~~denomination or order of men
called mormons~~ Church of Jesus Christ of latter day Saints that was a
resident of Far West in Caldwell County in the state of Missouri during
the late difficulties between Missourians and ~~Mormons~~ latter day Saints
during the autumn of 1838 that during the difficulties aforesaid he together
with the rest of the men residents in Caldwell County aforesaid was arreted
by a body of armed men Citizens of Missouri from which arrest he was
[~~soon~~] released after being compelled to give up his arms of defence and
ordered by majer General Lucas to leave the state of Missouri aforesaid
by the first of the then coming March and being kept under guard about
ten days he said deponant further says that while he was kept under guard
he saw small detachments of the Missourians aforesaid going about the
town of Far West plundering individuals houses also driving off cattle and
taking Corn without liberty. this deponant further says that in consequence
of the preemptory orders aforesaid he sustained a loss of time and unavoidable Sacrifices on land and property of two hundred and fifty dollars
and a further loss of fifty dollars by expences on leaving the state of
Missouri in obediance to the premptory orders aforesaid all of which
losses so by him sustained this deponant says amount to the Sum of three
hundred dollars and further Said deponant Says that the authorities of the
state of Missouri neglect and refuse to make reparation for losses and
damages so sustaned as aforesaid therefore the said Deponant Prays the
interposion of Congress to aid and assist him in obtaining redress of his
losses and injuries sustained as aforesaid all of which is by said deponant
Respectfully Submitted

Isaac W Pierce

[*Sworn to before H. G. Rew, J.P., Morgan Co., IL, 15 Jan 1840.*]

PINKHAM, Nathan

Illinois Quincy May 18th 1839
    a bill of Damage a gainst the State for loss of propperty Being Driven from the State

firs for mooveing in to the State	$100.00
for loss of propperty in the State in Conciquence of mob	1,500.00
for mooveing out of the State	100.00
	$1,700.00

    I certify the above a count is Just and true Acording to Best my knowldg

Nathan Pinkham

[Sworn to before C. M. Woods, C.C.C., Adams Co., IL, 17 May 1839.]

POTTS, Jacob H.

Illinois giving may the 11 1839
    a bill of Damages and debt a gainst the State of Missori in Conciquence of the governors Exterminateing order

firs for land in Caldwell County Sold under value Loss and Less than	$400.00
loss on cows	15.00
the loss of one Sadle bridle & blanket	20.00
and amare taken at the Same time at haun[s] mill was gon ten weks 50 cts per day	35.00
one rid to death in the fray	60.00
and Loss of other property Sold under value not less than	50.00
the Loss of time for the Space of eight [mo]nths thirty dollarys per months	240.00
damaged by being wounded twice in the right Leg and Sufferiage by the Same	500.00
Expence of moveing from the state	100.00
[*Total*]	$1,420.00

    I Do Here by Certify that the above account is Just and true acording to the best of my Knowledge

Jacob H. Potts

[Sworn to before C. M. Woods, C.C.C., Adams Co., IL, 11 May 1839.]

POTTS, Jacob H.
STILTZ, Levi

AD 1840 Ill Adams County Columbus March the 12

I was asitizen of Missori for near three years where I selected a home and purchced the same with my own money in the Cunty of Caldwell it being the west half of the south east qr of Sec 13 T 26 R 56 contaiined eighty acres twenty acres of the same was in astate of cultivation four acres of it was in corn eight acres in wheat this being under afree govorment I expected to enjoy Equal rights with other men which my fore Fathers fought for but in concequence of A decree that went forth from the govornor I was deprived of that privilege and was forced to dis[pose] of it at a low rate and leave the state in February 1839 But previous to this in the month of Oct 1838 there was some excitement raised but the of it I know not but our lives were threatened in that neigborhood and we met together to council the matter over to now what was best for us to do and the council was adjourned till the next day then we met together again durring which time their number of late emigrants came and encamped at the same plac this being at Hauns Mill and in the evening about an hour and ahalf by sun their was alawless set of bandities say about two hundred and fifty men headed by Captain Cumstock and Ginings all on horse back they came up and commenced fireing on us with out uttering awor[d] our people began to call for quarters but none was giving the mob continued their fireing untill they had killed and wounded about 30 of our people 16 of them was killed and wounded so they died by 10 oclock the next day 1 boy in four week 1 young in 8 weeks and as as far as I know the rest remains alive yet and amongst the wounded I was one I received two wounds in my right leg which proved aserious injury to me I also had agood mare saddle bridle blanket and halter taken at the same time Levi Stiltz lost amare sadle and bridle Benjamin Lewis was killed and two horses taken from the widow Isaac Laney severely wounded William Yokkam badly wounded and his horse taken Jacob Haun was wounded and his critter taken he was the ow;ener of the mill and land where the fray took place Jacob Myers lived on the same place he was wounded and his criter taken Charles Jameson and Jacob Foutz was wounded

And amumber of other horses was taken from the late emigrants and their was eight of those killed two of them was little boys the names of those that was killed is Benjamin Lewis John York Austin Hamer Simon Cox John Lee Amos Mcbride Mr Merick and boy Mr Smith and boy Mr Canada Hiram Abbot Josiah Fuller Mr Naper the names of the other four I no not and the mob plundered many things that I have not mentioned waggons horses clothing bed clothing &c in testimony whereof I set my hand

Jacob H Potts

I also was asitize of Mo at the time above mentioned and had entered forty acres of land in the same neighborhood and was treated in the same manner as is above mentioned except being wounded I was at the mill at the same time above mentioned I had amare saddle and bridle taken after ward I was taken prisoner and my gun was taken from me and the same mob passed through the neighborhood painted plundering what eve they could get their hands on. I can testify that the above ritten is correct

Levi Stiltz

State of Illinois Adams County SS

this day personally Came before me the undersigned Justice of the peace within & for the County aforesaid Jacob H. Potts and Levi Stiltz & after being Duly sworn Deposeth and Sayeth that the foregoing statements are facts & that they are Correct & true to the best of their belief & farther these Deponats sayeth Not.

Jacob H. Potts
Levi Stiltz

[*Sworn to before W. Oglesby, J.P., Adams Co., IL, 13 Mar 1840.*]

POWEL, James et. al.[33]

Illinois Adams county March 11th 1840—

I James Powel Do certfy that I was a citizen of the State of Missouri in 1838 I Solomly Declere that while I was peacebly traveling to one of my nearest Neighbors I was assaulted By a company of men to the number of 5 Aurtheston Wrathey John Gardner Philomen Ellis Jesse Clark and Ariel Sanders first they threw a stone and took me Betwene the Showlders which very much Disanabled me they then Shot at me and Did not hit me one of them then Struck me with his gun and Broke my Skull a bout Six inches a part of my Brain Run out I have had fourteen pieces of Bone takeen out of my Skull my Sistim is So Redused that I have not Done a Days work Sence I know no Reason why they Should have Done so as I Did not Belong to the mormon Church Neither had I ever Heard one preach in this Situation I was forsed to leave the State forth with I was Carried

---

[33] Also found in *HC* 4:61–62 and in JH 11 Mar 1840.

three Days without haveing my head Drest when I arivd at Huntsville Doct Head offerd me asistance I Refer to him for futher testimony

James **X** Powel

Attest John Smith

we certify that the foregoing afidavet of James Powels is true and correct as we Stood By and Saw it with oure Eyse we allso herd then Say they would Kill the Mormons if they Did not Cleare out we card wounded man in oure waggon till he was out of Reach of the mob

Peter W Wimmer
Susan Wimmer
Ellen Wimmer

[Sworn to before W. Oglesby, J.P., Adams Co., IL, 12 Mar 1840.]

PRIOR, Abel

A memorandom of the Damage Done to me in Jackson County and else where Able Prior. November t[h]e 8 1833 A mob Came to my house headed by Stephen Cantril two by the name of Patterson the others not known by me they cocked a pistol at me and told me if I opend my mouth they would blow me through the same Day between fifty and sixty Came and gave the same order headed by Elder MC Coye A Baptist Pries[t] here I had 22 Acres of land with a house thereon and a good improvement of which I had to leave imediately or lose my life and fled into the wilderness not seeing a house until about Chrismas having my rist partly cut off at the time allso being about 63 years old the suferings were indiscribeable having Counted up my losses and Damages [——] I make out my bill against the mauraurders of Jackson county— $2000: Dollars

Charges against Clay County being forced to leave ther Count allso for loss of time and expence of moveing [——] 600 Dollars

Charges against Daviess County for Driveing from that County allso and loss of property and expence of moveing [——] $2000: Dollars

Abel Prior

I certify the above a count to Be Just and true acording to the Best of my knowledg

Abel Prior

[Sworn to before C. M. Woods, C.C.C., Adams Co., IL, 29 May 1839.]

PRIOR, Abel

Quincy Illinois January 8th AD 1840

I do hereby Certify that I removed with my family into Jackson County Missouri, in the year 1831, and owned a tract of land on which I made an improvement, and while peaseably employed at my own business I was assailed by a lawless Mob and driven from my home and compelled to leave the county, and then went into Clay Co. and after a short time was driven from that county, and then went to Davis County and made animprovement there and built me a house and in 1838 was driven from that county by a mob, who rose up against us as a people, Called Mormons, and then I went to Far West in Caldwell Co. and did not get to stay there long till I was compelled to leave the State by the Exterminating Order of Govener Boggs, and was obliged to suffer all this abuse and loss without any cause, not having offended in any way against the laws of that State, and for which I have never recieved any remuneration, and now appeal to your honorable boddy for redress

Abel Prior

[*Sworn to before C. M. Woods, C.C.C., Adams Co., IL, 8 Jan 1840.*]

RAMSEY, Rachel P.

Damages Sustained on account of By being driven from the State of Missouri A.D. 183[9]

Expen ces of mov ing into the state	$55.00
Loss of Land	65.00
Loss of Time	15.00
Expence of moving out of the State	40.00
	$175.00

Rachel P. Ramsey

[*Sworn to before C. M. Woods, C.C.C., Adams Co., IL, 23 May 1839.*]

RANDALL, James

Illenos Quincy may the th15 1839

A bill of Dameges for Being Driven from the State of Mo By an un lawful Band

first for Being Driven from the State with out compensation $100.00

for propperty Lost in the State	400.00
for mooving from the Stat	50.00

I certify th above acount to Be Just and true a cording to the Best of my Knowledg

James Randall

[Sworn to before C. M. Woods, C.C.C., Adams Co., IL, 15 May 1839.]

RANDALL, MILES

Illenois Quincy May the 13
A bill a gainst the State of Missouri for Debt and Damage ~~against~~ in concequene of the govners Exterminating order

first for mooving in to the State	$100.00
for Loss of property and [d]amage Don in the State By mob	600.00
for mooving from the State loss of propperty and time and Expenc	75.00
	$775.00

I Certify the a bove acount to be Just and true acording to the Best of my Knowledg

Miles Randall

[Sworn to before C. M. Woods, C.C.C., Adams Co., IL, 13 May 1839.]

REDFIELD, David H.

Oct 1833	The State of Missouri To David H Redfield Dr	
	For taring down a Brick Shop and destroying tooles & H[o]ts	$3,000.00
	destroying 10 acers corn in the crib	100.00
	destroying 250 bushel Potatoes 50 cts pr bus	125.00
	Dito 50 bushels Wheat $1.00 pr Bush	50.00
	Destroying 3 acers Oats in ther Stock	25.00
	Destroying Garden Lanse	50.00
	For the loss of 3 years labour $500 pr year	1,500.00

in the fall of 1838	the State taking 1 Bay Horse	125.00
	" " " 2 Bee Hives	6.00
	" " " 2 Pigs	5.00
	" " " 60 chickings [25] cts. each	15.00
	" " " 6 acers corn & etc	60.00
	Thee mooving in & out of the State	100.00
	The amt Five thousand one hundred & fifty one dollars	$5,151.00

Quincy May 14th 1839   David H Redfield

[Sworn to before C. M. Woods, C.C.C., Adams Co., IL, 15 May 1839.]

REED, Delia

This may Certify tha[t] Delia Reed Sustains the Loss of Property in Colwell County State of Missouri I was drove from my land with Seven Small Children had to leave the State and when I left the State I was obliged to leave the most of my Personal property left behind for the want of means to move them away therefore I think I Sustaind the Loss of five hundred dollars

Delia Reed

[Sworn to before A. Monroe, J.P., Hancock Co., IL, 6 Jan 1840.]

REED, Elijah

A bill of Damages sustained by Elijah Reed against the State of Missouri in Consequence of the unlawful Conduct of the Inhabitants thereof & the Unconstitutional Decrees of the Governor

Damage on land	$200.00
Do. Do. on Cows	40.00
Do. Do. on young Stock	12.00
Do. Do. on Mares & Colts	70.00
Do. Do. on Hogs	20.00
Do. Do. on Geese & fowls	7.00
Do. Do. on Sundry articles	20.00
Do. Do. Expence for journey	50.00

Do. Do. being thrown out of business & the
inconveniences & Exposure to the weather in
removeing   500.00
                                                              $919.00

    I leave with your Honerable to Say [what] it shall be

    For my Life being Sought & in Danger & the Loss of my health in
being Exposed to Cold & wet The Circumstances are as follows the mob
Came to my house in Ray County Seeking for me in the time of Excitement
& I was Obliged to flee from my house without having time to take
Clothing or Provision with me & I was Obliged to lay in the fields & woods
being thinly Clothed & having been Sick with the Chill Fever & my family
also for Several Days & th[e]y left without any one to help or take Care
of them & the Mob went to my House Several times Swearing they would
Kill me if they Could find me of which my Family Informed they Finally
got track of me & Pursued me & about two & ahalf miles from home a
Large number of them Surrounded me in the night in a Hazle thicket of
about Five acres but I made my Escape From them & was Obliged to lay
within half a mile of them until the next night being Forty hours without
Food or Drink & Exposed to the Cold which Caused me to take Cold which
Settled on my lungs & I have not been able to labor but little Since & the
mob Set Fire to the Place where they Supposed me to be. In about two
weeks From the time I left I returned home again & one of the Mob James
Snowden Sen by name told me they would have Killed me if they Could
have Found me. this Company was Led by David Snowden James Snowden Jacob Snowden Joseph Ewing. Esqr. Mr. Shaw Thomas Taylor &
others of Ray County who had Previously threatened to Burn our houses
over our heads & Drive us out of the Cou[ntry] after I returned home those
men & others held a meeting & Resolved to Drive me & two others out of
the Country forthwith but Mr. L. B. Fleak a Neighbor of mine Kindly
Interceded For me & my Fam[ily] who were all sick with the Chills &
Fever they were therefore Prevailed upon to let ~~me~~ us Stay untill we were
able to remove but Said we must then Go or Suffer the Consequence

                                       Elijah Reed

    I Certify the within to Be True according to the Best of my
Knowledge

                                       Elijah Reed

[*Sworn to before C. M. Woods, C.C.C., Adams Co., IL, 6 May 1839.*]

REID, Jesse P.

May 6th A.D. 1839 Quincy Adams Co. Ill.

State of Missouri Dr. for expenses of Moving from Illinois to Missouri and being detained on the way by the mob $150.00

for being driven from Ray Co. to Caldwell Co & loss of time $200.00

for being driven out of the State of Missouri loss of time, and expenses $500.00

Jesse P. Reid

I certify this to be a true copy of damages to the best of my knowledge

Jesse P. Reid

[Sworn to before C. M. Woods, C.C.C., Adams Co., IL, 6 May 1839.]

RICH, Charles C.

Illinois May the 7th 1839

A bill of Damages & Debt a gainst the State of Missouri Sustained in Consequence of the Governors Extermnateing order first for preparing and moveing to the State		$200.00
for Loss of time in Consequence of the mob		500.00
for Loss of Crop and Property taken by the mob &c		250.00
for Loss of Sale in Land		1,500.00
for Loss of moveing from the State		1,000.00
	~~$3500.00~~	$3,450.00

I Do Herby Certify that the above account is Just and true according to the Best of my knowledge

Charles C Rich

[Sworn to before C. M. Woods, C.C.C., Adams Co., IL, 7 May 1839.]

RICH, Charles C. [34]

This is to certify that I purchased a bout one hundred and seventy Acres of Land in Caldwell County Missouri part of it of the United States and part of one individual I further testify that I was forced to Leave Said

---

[34] Also found in JH 15 Jan 1840.

Land in Consequence of the Govenors Exterminating order and by the force of arms I further testafy that a bout the last of october 1838 an armed force of two or three thousand men Came into Caldwell County Missouri without any knowledge of the in habitants and Commenced takeing prisioners and also any thing else they chose with out Liberty or askng the owners any questions and piched their tents near far West. I further testify that I was sent with a white flag to transact business withe the a bove Described Army and was met by Captain Samuel Bogart after transacting the business and turning to Go off the said Bogart fired at me when but a few feet Distance

Quincy Adams Co Ills January the 15 1840   Charles C. Rich

[*Sworn to before C. M. Woods, C.C.C., Adams Co., IL, 15 Jan 1840.*]

RICHARDS, Levi[35]

I, Levi Richards, a resident of Quincy, Adams county, Illinois, Practitioner of medicine, Certify, that in the year one thousand eight hundred and thirty eight I was a Citizen of Far West, Caldwell county, Missouri and that in the fall of said year I saw the City invaded by a numerous armed Soldiery, who compelled its inhabitants to surrender give up their firearms & submit to their dictation. They then set a strong guard round the City thereby preventing egress or ingress without special permisson. They then collected the Citizens together upon the public square formed round them a strong guard of soldiers & then at the mouths of their Rifles compeled them to sign what was termed A Deed of Trust thereby depriving them of all their property & Civil Rights. This occupied several days of most inclement weather when they were brought to the same order by Gen. Clarke & I judge some forty or fifty were made special prisoners by him. At this time he delivered his speech to the Mormons, which has been published & which is substantially correct. I was compeled by a company of men armed with rifles to leave my house & go to Capt. Bogarts Camp (he comnanded as I understood a part of the guard which surrounded the City) upon an indirect charge or insinuation,— was detained a prisoner two days,— examined,— & then liberated. I then asked the Clerk of the company who had been my keeper the following questions, which he readily answered in the negative Were those men who massacred the Mormons at Hauns Mills out under the Govenors order or were they

---

[35] Also found in *HC* 4:70–71 and in JH 19 Mar 1840.

Mobbers? A. Mobbers. Are Capt. Guillum (or Gillman) & his company out by legal authority or are they Mobbers? A. Mobbers. Where are those Mobbers now? A. they have joined the Army. This company at the surrender of Far West were painted like Indians. The Army wore a badge of Red. (Blood!!) I saw a large amount of timber & lumber destroyed & used for fuel by the soldiers. the destruction of Cattle, Hogs, &c. seemed to be their sport as their Camp & the fields testified when they withdrew. An excellent Gun was taken from me which I have never seen or heard from since. A gun that was left in my care was taken at the same time which I afterwards found with Wiley E. Williams of Richmond (reputed one of the Govenor's Aids) to obtain which I had to prove property—affirm before a Magistrate—& pay said Williams fifty Cents!! (Carried Over) I was called to extract lead dress the wounds &c. for several persons (Mormons) who were shot in the above siege—two of whom have sin died. Immediately previous to the above transactions & for a long time before the citizens of Caldwell & particularly Far West were called upon to watch for Mobs by day & guard against them by night till it become a burden almost intolerable.

Levi Richards

[Sworn to before C. M. Woods, C.C.C., Adams Co., IL, 19 May 1840.]

RICHARDSON, Ebenezer

Quincy Illinoys May the 16 1839
        Debts and damages aganst state of Missura sir for bing Driven from that state of By orders of the governer

expence of moving into that state By orders of the governor	$100.00
the loss of property in lands and Crops and one rifle and sword	400.00
for the loss of time	200.00
And Being drivin out of the state By orders of the Govanor	300.00

        this may Certify that this is a true Statement of facts Acording to the best of my Knowledg

Ebenezer [C] Richardson

[Sworn to before C. M. Woods, C.C.C., Adams Co., IL, 16 May 1839.]

RICHARDSON, Josiah

Quincy Illinois May 16th 1839
    A bill of damages against the state of Missouri for being driven from that state by the orders of the governor.

Expences in moveing to the state	$100.00
Loss of property in lands and crops and one rifle	400.00
Loss of time	200.00
For being from that state by the orders of the Gov.	300.00

I hereby certify that the above accounts are true and just according to the best of my knowledge

Josiah Richardson

[Sworn to before C. M. Woods, C.C.C., Adams Co., IL, 16 May 1839.]

RIGGS, Burr[36]

I B[urr] Riggs of the town of Quin[c]y and State of Illinois do hereby certify that in the year of 1836 when moving to the State of Missouri with my family & others was met in Ray County in Said State by a Mob of 114 armed men and commanded us not to proced any fur ther but to return or they would take our lives and the Leader Stepped forward and kocked his peace at the Same time we turned around with our team and the mob followed us about Six miles and Left us some time after this I moved to Caldwell County in Said State and purchased about two hundred acres of Land & a[vi···] Lot on which I erected a dwelling home Stable &c and commencd improving my land and had at the time I was drove away about forty acres of Corn vegetable &C and in the year 1838 in the month of November was compelld to Leave my home and possessions in Consequen[ce] of Govoner Boggs exterminati[ng] order without means sufficent to bear my expence out of the State Given under my hand at Quin[c]y Illinois 17th 1840

Burr Riggs

[Sworn to before C. M. Woods, C.C.C., Adams Co., IL, 17 Mar 1840.]

---

[36] Also found in JH 17 Mar 1840.

ROBERTS, Ezekiel

Illenois Quincy May 29th 1839
　　A bill of Damages a ganst the State of Missouri for Being unlawfully Driven from it

first for mooveing to the State	$50.00
for propperty Lost in the State	600.00
for mooveing out of the State	25.00
	$675.00

　　I certify the a bove a count to Be Just and true acording to the best of my knowledg

　　　　　　　　　　　　　　　　　　　Ezekiel Roberts

[Sworn to before C. M. Woods, C.C.C., Adams Co., IL, 29 May 1839.]

ROGERS, Narcissa Ann

May 13th 1829 [*1839*]
　　the State of Missourie to Narcissa Ann Rogers, Dr. Occasioned by the Mob of said State in the years of 1838 and 1829 [*1839*].

to freight and loss of goods	$400.00
to expenses of moving and loss of time	40.00
to suffering and being deprived of ~~citizenship~~ right of citizenship	1,000.00
	$1,440.00

　　　　　　　　　　　　　　　　　　　Narcissa A Rogers

[Sworn to before W. Oglesby, J.P., Adams Co., IL, 13 May 1839.]

ROLFE, Samuel

Clayton Ills. May 10th 1839
　　State of Missouri Dr. To Samuel Rolfe for Losses Sustained by being Driven out of the State one farm worth nine Hundred Dollars
　　Two Town Lots with Two Dwelling Houses on them &c worth five Hundred & fifty Dollars
　　also for haveing to leaveing my work one Hundred miles from home and return home to gard my family from a Lawless Mob one Hundred Dollars

To Two Guns twenty Dollars To one Sword Six Dollars
To Garden sauce & Provisions Con sumed fifty Dollars
To Expences Removeing out of the State one Hundred & fifty
Dollars—Whole amount $1776.00

[*Sworn to before J. Douglas, J.P., Adams Co., IL, 11 May 1839.*]

ROOT, Henry[37]

Quincy Ill. 16th March 1840

This is to certify that I Henry Root am and was a citizen of DeWitt Carroll County Missouri at the time the ~~war~~ persecutin (known by the name of the Mormon war) Commenced and terminated between the Citizens of Said State of Missouri and the Mormons that in the fall of 1838 in the month of September a Mob (under no regular authority) heded by Wm. W. Austin Senr. Consisting of from one hundred to one hundred and fifty Men Came into DeWitt and orderd the Mormons to leave that place within ten days from that time that if they did not leave they would be driven from there by force the mormons did not leave ~~till~~ the appointed time Came and the Mob Came armed and equiped for war the Mormon Citizens petitioned to the Govenor of the State but no relief Came they Sent to the General of that Brigade who orderd the Millitia to repair to DeWitt to disperse the Mob on the arival of the Millitia Brigd. General Parks told me the Mormons had better leave there property and Gow off as his men was prejudiced aganst them and he could do them no good nor relieve them—with that the Mormons left

Henry Root

[*Sworn to before C. M. Woods, C.C.C., Adams Co., IL, 16 May 1840.*]

ROSE, Andrew

The State of Misouri Dr to Andrew Rose for Being Deprived of the Rights of Citizen of the United States

1st Expenses of moveing 12 hundred miles	$400.00
to Loses on Land	1,200.00
to Losses on goods And Chattles	300.00
to Expenses and trouble of moveing	300.00
[*Total*]	$2,200.00

[*Sworn to before A. Enlow, J.P., Adams Co., IL, 13 May 1839.*]

---

[37] Also found in *HC* 4:62–63 and in JH 16 Mar 1840.

ROSE, Ralph

A bill of Damages a gainst the State of Missouri

for mooving to the State	$100.00
for loss of propperty in the State	400.00
for mooveing from the State	50.00
	$550.00

    I [certify] the above acount to Be Just true a cording to the Best of my Knowledg

Ralph Rose

[*Sworn to before C. M. Woods, C.C.C., Adams Co., IL, 20 May 1839.*]

RUST, William W.

Quincy Illinois May 18th 1839

The State of Missouri Dr to Wm. W <u>Rust</u> to Expence of going to that State for to buy land and Settle on it	$100.00
to the Loss of time and Property the year Past	150.00
to Damage in conciquence of being Drove from the State to Illinois	50.00
	$300.00

    I Certify the Above to be true to the best of my Knowlege

Wm. W. Rust

[*Sworn to before C. M. Woods, C.C.C., Adams Co., IL, 18 May 1839.*]

SAGERS, Harrison

Illinois Quincy may the th15 1839
    a bill of Damages against the State of Missouri for being Driven from it

first for mooving into the State	$100.00
for loss of propperty and time in the State in conci[quence] of mob	500.00
for mooving out of the State	100.00

I certify the a bove acount to Be true and Just acording to the Best of my Knowledg

Harrison Sagers

[*Sworn to before C. M. Woods, C.C.C., Adams Co., IL, 15 May 1839.*]

ST. JOHN, Stephen M.

Loss off property which Stephen M St John Receivd By the unlawful acts off the Citizens off State off Missouri total loss one thousand two hundred and sixty dollars

I here Certif that the above is a correct Statement according to the best off my Recolection

Stephen M St John

[*Sworn to before C. M. Woods, C.C.C., Adams Co., IL, 10 May 1839.*]

SANBORN, Enoch S.

Quincy Illenois May 8th 1839.

Enoch S. Sanborns Damages Sustained in Consequence of the Mob or Mobocracy of the State of Mosouri one of the compact of this Union by our Federal Constitution—to being Driven back and not premited to Cross the Grand River in october 1838 the time they the mob Drove the Saints from a place on the other Side of sd. River Caled Dewit and in order to finish my journey I procided on this side of sd. River fifty Miles round and Crosed the River into Livingston County at which place I with my familey and four more waggons with their famil[ys] was Stoped by a Mob Haded by Thomas Ginings who as I was informed had just returned from Dewit with a canon and 25 or 30 men Armed with Rifles and large butcher knives and when they Discoverd us they was in a Grocery So Caled in the Town of Knavesvill and sd. Ginings led them out with the first word God Dam you after hindring us and abuseing us thay turned us off from the Cours we ware persuing which was west to a south Cours and that knight we stopt at Willean Mans in sd. County who told me that the mob had agreed to Drive the Mormons out of that County and then out of Davis County and out of evry County in to Caldwell County and then out of the State. and I found that it was even so for I went to Caldwell County and bought A farm of 125 Acres with a house and 25 acres under improvement two hundred bushells of Corn twenty bushells of potatoes two stacks of hay one plow, and in one wek I was ordred to leave the State by the official orders of Govvernor Boggs and General Clark. and I have Calmly Submitted without gieving a single individual a misleholden warrd

in the State of Illenois I now by Reason of this oppresion am obleaged to Dwell in a tent amongst strangers. for which I Charge the State of Mosouri one thousand nine hundred Dollars Quincy May 8th 1839 Enoch S. Sanborn in the fifty first year of my Age and lately from the State of New York, for the sacred rite as a citizens of the United States I Charge the State of Mosouri one thousan Dollars for Depriveing me of the liberty of purchacing land of the the goverment of the United Sates in the State of Mosouri with the privilge of setle on the Same one thousand Dollars

as above	$1,900.00
Do as above	1,000.00

Enoch S. Sanborn

[*Sworn to before C. M. Woods, C.C.C., Adams Co., IL, 10 May 1839.*]

SANDERS, Moses M.

May the th6 1839
Charge a gainst the State of Missoui

to being Driven from Clay. Co. and lose of property	$100.00
lost on land in Jackson Co.	600.00
on land and other property in Calldwell County	250.00
loss of time ~~of~~ in mooving from the State of Missoui of	100.00

I hereby Certify the above to be atrue account according to the best of my ~~aek~~knowledge

Moses M. Sanders

[*Sworn to before C. M. Woods, C.C.C., Adams Co., IL, 6 May 1839.*]

SESSIONS, Perrigrine

Losses sustained in consequence of oppression in the state of Missouri

To farm and improvements	$1000.00
Loss 4 hundred bushels corn	100.00
Loss on buckwheat	10.00

Loss on pottatoes pumkins and garden	100.00
Loss on hogs	15.00
Loss on 2 stacks of hay	20.00
Loss of time in consequence of oppression	80.00
Expences and time moving out of state and sickness and suferings	500.00
	$1825.00

Caldwell Co state of Missouri

I Perry Green Session do swear that the above account of Losses Sustained by me & my Father David is Just and correct. and that the losses therein mentioned were sustainedby us in Caldwell County State of Missourie during the year A D 1838—

Perrigrine Sessions

[*Sworn to M. M. McGregor, J.P., Hancock Co., IL, 11 May 1839.*]

SHEARER, Daniel

Quincy Ill May th 7th 1839
The State of Missouri To Daniel Shearer Dr.

To mooving from New York to Missouri	$150.00
" do do Missouri to Illinois	50.00
loss on lands	300.00
loss on town property	500.00
in time & months & Board	240.00
for unlawfull & false imprisionment	150.00
do do " " " of my Son N. B. Shearer detain in the jail at Richmond Ray County and one half of the time in the dungeon five months & 24 dayes at $100.00 pr months	585.00
Damiges of Vienna Jakes now my wife in being driven from Jackson County in the State of Missouri & Mooving from the State of Massuhusetts to Missouri	250.00
for being forced out of the State of Missouri Contrary to law to the Constitution of the United States & Justice	1,000.00
1 pr pistols taken from my house by a man Calling himself Colonel Jones	4.50
	$3,129.50

~~Daniel Shearer~~

I herby Certify the above to be a true coppy of the Damiges Sustaind by me in the State of Missourie

Daniel Shearer

[Sworn to before C. M. Woods, C.C.C., Adams Co., IL, 7 May 1839.]

SHEPHERD, Samuel

A Bill of damages Sustained by Samuel Shepherd while a resident of the state of Missouri from the year of our Lord 1833 to the year 1839 by mobs in consequence of not being protected in his rights as a free citizen of these United States also by being Obliged to leave the state by order of Lilburn W Boggs Governor thereof

~~Loss~~ by being Mobbed from Jackson County in 1833

Loss of farm and property estimated at five hundred dollars

By being Obliged to remove from Caldwell loss in farm and other property & expences in removing estimated at Fifteen hundred Dollars

Estimate made out this 9th day of October 1839

[Not sworn.]

SHERMAN, Almon

A Bill of Damage Sustained by Almon Sherman against the State of Missouri in Consequence of the Unlawfull Conduct of the Inhabitants thereof & the Unconstitutional Decres of the Governor Damage on Land	$150.00
Do. Do. on one Town Lot & House	50.00
Do. Do. Personall Property	300.00
Do. Do. for being obliged to remove & the Inconvences & Exposure to weather & Thrown out of Business &c	300.00
Do. Do. Expences for journey	60.00
	$860.00

[Sworn to before C. M. Woods, C.C.C., Adams Co., IL, 6 May 1839.]

SHERMAN, Almon[38]

also in the year A.D. 1836 when journeying in the State into Clay County I was Met by a Mob in Ray County of one Hundred men Led By

---

[38]This petition seems to be a continuation of the one above although they were each sworn to separately.

a Mr. Price who Surrounded My waggon & others who wer in Company with Me & Moving to Clay County & threatened us with Immediate Death if we Did not return Back which we accordingly Did & we were obliged to lay out in the weather which Caused My family to be taken Sick & I lost two Children in Consequence of it also in A.D. 1838 a Company Came to my house & took my arms & ordered me out of my house Forthwith or They would Kill me & I must go with them where they Pleased to take me we according Complied with the Order & we were not Permitted to Live on my Place any more they also Drove off My Cows and I did not get them for a number of weeks ~~they~~

Almon Sherman

I do hereby certify that the within statements are true according to the best of my knowledge

Almon Sherman

[Sworn to before C. M. Woods, C.C.C., Adams Co., IL, 6 May 1839.]

SHIRTLIFF, L. A.

A bill of expences time damages &c occasioned by the inhabitants of Missouri in driveing from that State the Saints of God or people Called mormons

time expencees teams &c in mooving from Kirtland Ohio to Coldwell Co. Missouri with a family of fifteen persons Estimatd at	$546.84
time lost in the war expenses in moveing out of the State arms taken from me property in utensels Lands &c. estimad at	428.00
Damagees exposure to death Sickness by lying on the Cold frozen ground &c &c	1,000.00
Amount Claimd by L. A. Shirtliff	$1,974.84

I here by Certify the above to be true according to the best of my knowledge

L. A. Shirtliff

[Sworn to before C. M. Woods, C.C.C., Adams Co., IL, 18 May 1839.]

SHUMAKER, Jacob

The State of Missouria Dr To Jacob Shumaker To a Bill of damages Viz

	To Expence of moving from othio to Jackson County	
1831	Missouria	$75.00
1833	To Loss of house burnt	100.00
	To one Set of house Loggs and Plank Sufficient for a house	125.00
	To Rails Taken from Land	50.00
	To Destroying timber	50.00
	[*Subtotal*]	$390.00
	To Detaining my Smith tools 9 months and Destroying Part	150.00
	To Loss of Stock	50.00
	To Loss of Book Accounts in Jackson Co	200.00
1839	To loss of Property in Caldwell County	150.00
1833	To Expences for moving from Jackson County to Clay	25.00
	[*Subtotal*]	$575.00
	To Loss time by Sickness occasioned By moving from Jackson To Clay and Doctors Bills for Self & family	300.00
1839	~~to by~~ Expence of moving from Misouria To Illinois occasioned by the Govenors Exterminating order	200.00
	To Loss of Accounts in Clay County and the Surrounding Countys	1,000.00
	[*Subtotal*]	$1,500.00
		$2,465.00

I Do Certify the above bill of accounts to bee Correct according to the best of my Reccollection

Jacob Shumaker

[Sworn to before C. M. Woods, C.C.C., Adams Co., IL, 6 May 1839.]

SHUMAKER, Jacob[39]

Quincy Illinoise Adams County March 18th 1840

I Jacob Shumaker do Certify that I went back to the State of Missouria a bout the first of October Last with the Calculation to live with my familey but finding it impossible as the mob Surounded my house and threatned me with my life Say to the amount of twenty or thirty of them and whilst the ware a quarling a bout me what they Should do an in what way the Should Dispose of me I Crept out of the back window and made my Escape and leaving my familey to their most Scandilous abuses;[40] My Wife and oldest daughter barely Escaping from their unholy designs.— I was thus a second time obliged to leave the State or remain at the risk of my life. The latter alternative I chose. My Loss sustaned by the above mentuned Abuses was not less than three hundred dollars. A Lot of Land Containg about forty acres for which I paid four dollars per Acre situated in Caldwell County was unjustly and unlawfully taken from and is Still retained by some person or persons tome unknown[.] I hereby Certify that the abov is a true Statement

Jacob Shumaker

[Sworn to before W. Tainter, who signed for C. M. Woods, C.C.C., Adams Co., IL, 18 May 1840.]

SLOAN, James

I James Sloan of Quincy, Adams County, Illinois, Dealer, do hereby Certify that I was a resident, and good and lawful Citizen of Davis County in the State of Missouri, in the year of Our Lord One Thousand eight hundred and thirty eight, and at the time the Militia of that State came to that place, under the authority of the exterminating Order of Governor Boggs, that there was a Storehouse with a large quantity of Store Goods and Merchandize therein, to the amount of several hundred Dollars in value, and which was the property of the Members of the Church of latter day Saints (commonly called Mormons,) or some of them, and were purchased for the benefit and advantage of the poor who were of that People, and also that I had a considerable just and lawful Interest in the safekeeping and preservation of said Store, and Goods, and that those in Command over the Militia got into possession of same, and a considerable

---

[39] Also found in *HC* 4:69–70 and in JH 18 Mar 1840.

[40] At this point the handwriting changes. The second hand appears to be W. Tainter's.

quantity in amount and value of said Goods were destroyed and carried away by a great number of said Militia, and that said Militia took possession of said Store and Used same to live in, and this in the presence and View of this Deponent and many other People, and that I was forced and obliged to leave my said residence in compliance, as was alledged of said Order, and for that purpose was handed a written passport or permission to pass from Davis County to Caldwell County, and from thence out of the State, and was also limitted to Ten days to leave that place, that I expended several hundred Dollars in acquiring Property in Davis County, by industry and honesty, and Sale of my moveable Property, all which I have been unjustly, illegally, unlawfully, and most unrighteously driven from, and that I have not at any time, either directly or indirectly, given any offence, reason, or grounds to any Person, or Persons, for such the treatment that I and my Family, (which consisted of four Females besides myself,) have received, that my Life was earnestly sought after, even after the surrender of Arms Arms, and that I was obliged to travel from Davis County in the inclemency of a very severe Winter and Snow Storm, ~~his~~ My Wife walking alongst with ~~him~~ Me from Ten to Fifteen Miles, wet nearly all the time to her Knees, being under the necessity of leaving the remainder of the Family, and Bed and Bedding and other Goods behind ~~him~~ Me, for want of any means, of having any of them conveyed away, although I was possessed of Seven Horses, two Waggons, and much valuable Property on ~~his~~ My coming into that part of the Country, only about Six or Seven Months before, I was also detained a Prisoner for several Hours after the Arms were taken, and also for some Hours the next day, standing upon the Wet Ground, in the open Air, and kept in continual dread of my Life, for many days, and my Life actually threatened by different People. that some of my Goods were carried away by some of the Mob or Militia, from my own dwelling House, and that I believe a Person of the Name of Tarwater is now living upon a Preemption right, which was purchased from him in Davis County, and paid for with my Property. All which I Certify this 17th day of March 1840. Forty.

James Sloan

[*Sworn to before W. Tainter, who signed for C. M. Woods, C.C.C., Adams Co., IL, 17 Mar 1840.*]

SMITH, Elisha

State of Missourie Debtor to Elisha Smith for damages sustained by the inhabitants of the afore said Staet to ~~the~~ wit the following

firstly I moved from the State of Newyork to the State of
    missourie with the expectation of setling considering
    myself to be a free citizan of the United States but was
    deprived of so doing by the inhabitants of the affore
    said State for which I shall charge the inhabitants of
    the same the sume of $10,000.00
this amount is for moveing and being deprived of the
    priviledges afore mentioned
Do. Loss of time 8 months also being driven from the
    state by the inhabitants they receivings their orders
    from the Govornor so to do for which I shall charge
    the sum of   20,000.00
Do. to one spann of horses and waggon and harness the
    waggon was loaded with goods valued to the amount of   350.00
Do. lost of stolen in the time of the trouble by
    Pocketbook with obligations to the amount of   900.00
Do. to moveing from the state of Missourie with myself
    and family allso moveing others that were not able to
    move them selves for which I shall charge the sume of   200.00
Do. to personal abuse that I have recieved in various
    ways namely being thretened to be shot the men
    cocking their guns and swereing by all the oaths that
    could be thought of that I should Di but by the
    overruleing hand of Providence I got away from those
    Mobers the names of some of the men were these
    Solomon Pethero Mitchel Gillum and a man by the
    name of Curl[.] these men were acompaned with
    others to the amount of seventy five ore one hundred
    in number   1,000.00
Do. to being driven throug the inclemency of the wether
    with my family which I have no reason to doubt was
    the occasion of a fit of sickness that my wife has
    experienced by the troubles she has passed through for
    which I shall charge the sum of   500.00

                                                Elisha Smith

    this I certify to be a true statement according to the best of my
Judgement

Quincy Ill. May the 16th 1839   Elisha Smith

[Sworn to before C. M. Woods, C.C.C., Adams Co., IL, 16 May 1839.]

SMITH, Elisha
PATTEN, William W.[41]

This is to certify that I Elisha Smith do Solomly Swear & declare that I am a member of the Church of Jesus Christ of latter day saints commonly called mormons; That I was at the town of Adam-Ondi-Ahman in Davisse County Missouri when an armed force of Mob & Militia in the month of November 1838 entered the Town demanded & took two guns from myself & the armes of the Cityzens Generally, posted their guards round the town & would not let any one to go out without a pass from the General. They quartered the army upon the Cityzens making use of Corn, fodder, beef Cattle, & hogs with out leave or license. that in the ranks with the Militia I saw one hundred or more men with their faces painted in horrid Indian Style and [——— ——— ———] they were known by the name of Cornelius Gilliam's Company, Senator of the State of Missouri,— General Willson commander of the army Stated that he would not put in execution the exterminating part of the goverors order, that his heart Shrunk at the idea, but, that within ten days we must leave Davisse County, for he would no longer defend us from the mob, & if we did not get away in that time the mob would no doubt use us roughly, and gave me & others a pass to to go to Far-West & there winter, and in the Spring all the Mormons Should lieve the State of Missouri

Elisha Smith

This is to certify that I, William W. Patten know the above mentioned particulars are Strictly true, with the execption of the delivery of the two guns named above; and further State that Samuel Music & myself went out of the above named, town to meet the army above named, to acertain what they wanted, and carried a flag with us; and that a flag from the army met us, and informed us that the inhabitants of the town must parade on the Prairie immediately and give up their armes; & if they would do it peaceably no person should be hurt, otherwise measures would be taken to make them do it; that I saw Cornelious Gilliam, Senator of Missouri, at the head of his Indian painted Mob, who were rank & file paraded with the Militia and that General Willson gave me a pass to go to Far West & there winter & in the spring to leave the State

William W Patten

[*Sworn to before D. W. Kilbourn, J.P., Lee Co., IA, 6 Jan 1840.*]

---

[41] Also found in JH 6 Jan 1840.

SMITH, Elizabeth

Illinois adams County may 24: 1839

An account which I Elizebeth Smith hold a gainst the State of Masouri in Concequnce of the governers Exterming orders for time and moving Expence to Missouri	$122.00
to Sale in land	100.00
to lose in grain	87.00
for time and moving Exspenc from Said State	100.00
	$409.00

Elizabeth **X** Smith

[Sworn to before C. M. Woods, C.C.C., Adams Co., IL, 25 May 1839.]

SMITH, Jackson

May 6th 1839
Charge against the State of Missoui

house and land	$100.00
arms & household furniture	25.00
loss of time & mooving	130.00

I here by Certify the above to be true according to the best of my knowledge

Jackson Smith

[Sworn to before C. M. Woods, C.C.C., Adams Co., IL, 6 May 1839.]

SMITH, Jesse

I Jesse Smith do Solomley Swear that in the Year of our Lord 1832 I moved in to the state of missouri and Settled in Jackson County and was Expelled from Said County By A mob that Rose Against the Church of Latter day Saints to my Damage in loss of time and other Damage Sustained five Hundred Dollars in 1838 [&] 9 in Clay and Davis Counties in loss of property By a mob that Rose in Said Counties to my Damage fifteen Hundred Dollars[.] I was ordred and obliged to Give up my arms and leave the state By By Gen. Parks and Wilson

Jesse Smith

[Sworn to before W. Stanley, J.P., Van Buren Co., IA, 13 Mar 1840.]

SMITH, John   *HC*⁴²

Illinois, Columbus, Adams County, March 11, 1840.

I, John Smith, certify that I was a resident in the state of Missouri in 1838, when I was driven from my house, and a pre-emption right, and forbid to stay in the state, [the mob]⁴³ threatening me if I did not go forthwith. I took my family and pursued my journey one hundred miles. In consequence of cold, snow, water and ice at the inclement season in which I was driven, I fell sick, and for four weeks I was unable to travel; during which time I was threatened daily; yet I was so sick it was considered by many that I could not live, and was compelled to start when I was not able to sit up through the day. I landed in Illinois; the long and fatiguing journey, lying out in the cold, open air, proved too much for my companion; it threw her into a violent fever, with which she died. Many others in the company took sick and died with the same hard fare.

JOHN SMITH.

[Sworn to before W. Oglesby, J.P., Adams Co., IL, 11 Mar 1840.]

SMITH, John

State of Illinois adams County March the 12th 1840

this is a true list of the loss of property and time Sustained by me John Smith in the State of Mosourie because I believd and Supported the doctrin of the people called Mormons for Which I was most assuredly compeled to leave the State in the year 1838

Cost of Moveing to the State	$150.00
Cost of Moveing from the State	100.00
loss of time 12 month	200.00
one premtion rite on 160 acre	300.00
to grain and Stock with other amt	250.00
total	$1,000.00

John Smith

[Sworn to before W. Oglesby, J.P., Adams Co., IL, 12 Mar 1840.]

---

⁴² 4:62; also found in JH 11 Mar 1840. Although this petition is not found in the LDS Historical Department, *History of the Church* indicates it was prepared as part of the first appeal (*HC* 4:49).

⁴³ The editorial brackets from *History of the Church* have been maintained.

SMITH, Joseph JSC[44]

Quincy, June 4th, 1839

Bill of Damages against the state of Missouri Recounting the sufferings & losses sustained March 1838 I and my family arrived in Far west Caldwell County after a journey of one thousand miles being 8 weeks on my journey enduring much affliction [in consequence][45] of persecution and expending about two hundred dollars; Soon after my arrival at that place I was informed that a number of men lieing at Daviess County (or the grindstone Forks) had offered the sum of one thousand dollars for my [scalp] persons to whom I was [an] entire Strang[er] & of whom I had no knowledge of [In] order to attain [their End the roads] were frequently [way laid for me] at one time in particular when [watering] my horses in Shoal Creek I distinctly heard 3 or 4 guns snape[d] at me was Credibl[y] informed also that Judge King of the Fifth Judic[ial] Circuit gave incouragement to individuals to Carry into Effect their diabolical designs and has frequently stated that I ought to be beheaded on account of my Religion: In Consequence of such Expressions from Judge King and others in Authority my enemies endeavoured to take Every advantage of me and heaping abuses getting up vexatious law Suits and stirring up the [minds] of the people a gainst me and the people with whom I was connected, altho we had done nothing to deserve such treatment but were busily engaged by our several avocations & desireous to live on peaceable & friendly terms with all men. In consequence of which threats and abuse which I was continually subject to my family were kept in continual state of alarm not knowing what would befall me from day to day, particularly when I went from home; on the Latter part of Sept 1838 I went to the lower part of the County of Caldwell for the purpose of relaying a location for a Town when on my Journey I was ment by one of our Friends with a message from Dwet in Carrol County stateing that our Brethren who had settled in that place were & had for some time been surrounded by a mob who had threatned their lives and had shot Several times at them: Immediately on hearing this strange Intelligence I made preparations to Start in order if possible to ally the feelings of opposition if not to make arrangements with

---

[44] Also found in JH 4 Jun 1839. The original handwritten version of this petition is not found in the same LDS Historical Department which contains the other Missouri petitions, but is found instead in the Historical Department's Joseph Smith Collection.

[45] Parts of this document are illegible on the microfilm copy of the Joseph Smith Collection; however, the same document appears in the Journal History of the Church. Therefore, words and phrases in brackets in this document are substituted from the Journal History.

those individuals of whom we had made purchases and to whom I was responsible and holding for part of the purchase money. I arrived there in the day and found the account which I heard was correct. our people were surrounded by a mob their provisions nearly exhausted messages were immedediately sent to the Governor requesting protection but instead of sending any assistance to the oppressed he stated that the quarrel was between the Mormons and the Mob and that they must fight it out: Being now almost entirely destitute of provisions and having suffered great distress and some of the [brethre]n having died in Consequence of their privations & sufferings and I had then the pain of beholding some of my Fellow creatures perish in a Strange land from the Cruelty of of mob seeing no prospect of relief the Brethren agreed to leave that place and seek a Shelter elsew[h]ere, after having their houses burnt down their cattle driven away and much of their property destroyed, Judge King was also petitioned to afford us some assistance: He sent a company of about 100 men but instead of affording us any relief we were told by General Parks that he could afford none in consequence of the greater part of his Company under these officers Capt Saml Bogart having mutinized about 70 waggons left Dwit for Caldwell and dur[in]g their Journey were continually insulted by the mob who threatened to destroy us and Shot at us in our Journey several of our Friends died and had to be interred without a Coffin & under such Circumstances which were extremely distressing: Immediately on my arrival at Caldwell I was informed by General Donaphan from Clay County that a company of about 100 were marching towards a Settlement of our Brethern in Daviess County and he advised one of the officers that we should immediately go to protect our Brethren in Daviess County (in what he Called Whites town) untill he should get the malitia to put them down immediately a company of malitia to the number of sixty who were going on their rout[e] to that place he ordered back believing as he said that they were not to be depended upon and to use his own language were "damned rotten hearted" Colonel Hinckle aggreable to the advise of General Doniphan a number of our Bretheren Voluntered to go to Daviess to render what assistance they Could My labors having been principally Expended in Daviess County where I intended to take up my residence & having a house in Building, and having other property While I was there a number of the Brethrens Houses were burnt and depredations were continually committed such as driving off Horses Cattle Sheep &c &c Being deprived of Shelter & others having no safety in their houses which were Scattering and <u>laying alarm</u> at the approach of the mob they had to flock togeth[er] their sufferings were very great in consequence of their defenceless situation being exposed to the weather which was Extreemly cold a large Snow Storm having just fallen:

In this state of affairs General Parks arrived at Daviess and was at the House of Colonel Wight [when] the intelligence was brought that the Mob were burning Houses &c and also when women and Children were flocking into the village for safety: Colonal Wight who held a commissioned 59th Regiment under his charge, asked him what steps should be taken He told him that he must immediately call out his men and go and put them down; Immediately preparations were made to practice a force to Quale the mob: As to ascertaining that we were determined to bear such treatment no longer but to make a vigourous Effort to subdue them and likewise being informed of the orders of General Parks broke up their Encampment and fled Some of the inhabitants in the immediate neighborhood who seeing no prospect of driving us by force resorte to stratagem and actually set fire to their own Houses after having removed their property and Effects and then sent sent information to Govenor stating that our Brethren were committing depredations and destroying their property burning houses &c&¶

On the retreat of the mob from Daviess County I retur[ned] home to Caldwell on my arrival there I understood that a mob had commmenced hostilities in the Borders of Caldwell had taken some of our People prisoners burnt some houses and had done considerable damages immediately Captain Patten was ordered out by leutenant Colonel Hinckle to go a gainst them and about day light next morning came up with them: upon the approach of our people they fired upon them and after discharging their pieces fled with great preditation. In this affray Capt Patten fell a victim to that spirit of mobocracy which has prevailed to [*The following sentence breaks up the continuity of the petition, but is correctly placed*] Donophan Brigader General 1st Brigade 3 Division of the missouri malitia Parks Brigader General 2nd Brigade 3 Division of the Missouri malitia such an intent, along with 2 others other were severly wounded: On the day after this affray Capten Patten sent for me to pray for him which request I complied with & then returned to my home There Continued to be great Commotion in the County caused by the Conduct of the mob who were continually burn[ing] Houses Driving off Horses Cattle &c and taking prisoners & threatning death to all the mormons amongst the Cattle driven off were Two cows of mine about the 28th of October a large company of armed Soldars were seen approaching to Far West and Encamped about 1 mile from the Town. The next day I was waited upon by Colonel Hinckle who stated that the officers of the malitia requested an interview with us in order to come to some amicable settlement of the difficulties which then subsisted they the officers not wishing under the present circumstances to carry into Effect the Exterminating orders they had received: I immediately complied with the r[e]quest and in company with M[ess]rs Rigdon Robinson Wight Pratt & [——] Lyman & Hiram Smith my Brother proceeded to meet the officers of the malitia: But instead of treating us with with respect and as persons desiring to accomdate matters we were to our astonishment we were delivered up as prisoners of war and taken into their camp as such It would be in vain for me to give any idea of the Scene which now presented itself in the camp The Horrid yells of more than a thousand infureated beings whose desires was to wreck their vengance upon me and the rest of my Friends was truly awfull and enough to appal the Stoutest heart. In the eveing we had to lye down on the Cold ground surrounded by a Strong guard we petitioned the officers to know why we were thus treated but they utterly refused to hold any Conversation with us: The next day they held a Court Martial upon us and sentenced me with the rest of the prisoners to be shot which sentence was to be carried into Effect on Friday morning in the public Square as they say an Ensample to the rest of the members: but through the Kind providence of God their murderous sentence was not carried into excecution The Malitia then went and selected to my house and drove my Family out of Doors under Sanction of general Clark and Carried away all my property Having oppertunity of speaking to General Wilson and on asking him the Cause of such Strange proceedings told him that I was a Democratt had allways being a supporter of the Constitution he answerd "I know that and that is the reason why I want to Kill you or have you Killed: We were led into Public Square and after Considerable Entreaty we were permitted to see our Family's being attended with a strong guard. I found my Family in Tears Expect that they had Carried into Effect their sentence they clung to my garments with weepng requesting to have an proper interview with my wife & in an ajoining room but was refused when taking my departure from my Family it was almost too painful for me my Child[ren] Clung to me and were thrust away at the point of the swords of the soldery we were then removed to Jackson County under the Care of general Wilson and during our stay in there we had to Sleep on the floor with nothing but a mantle for our Coverings and a Stick of wood for our pillow and had to pay for our own board: While we were in Jackson General Clark with his troops arrived in Caldwell and sent an order for our return holding out the inducement that we were to be reinstated to our former priviledges: but instead of beeing taken to Caldwell we were taken to Richmond w[h]ere we were immured in Prison and bound in Chains. after we were thus situated we were under the Charge of Colonel Price of Chariton County who Suffered us to be abused in Every manner which the people thought propper: our Situation at this time was truly painful: we were taken before the Court of inquiry but in Consequence of the proceedi[ngs] of the mob and there threats we were not able to get such witnesses as would have been servicable Even those we had were abused by the States attorney as the Court and were not permitted to be examined By the Court as the laws direct We were Committed to Liberty Jail and petit[ioned] to Judge Turnham for a writ of Habeas Corpus but on account oweing to the prejudice of the Jailor all Communication was Entirely Cut off however at lengthe we succeeded in getting a petition carryed to the Judge but he neglected to pay any attention to it for Fourteen days and kept us in suspence: he then ordered us to appear before him but he utterly refused to hear any of our witnesses which we had been at great trouble in providing. our Laweys likewise refused to act being afraid of the people: we likewise petitioned to Judge King and other Judges of the Supreme Court but with the same success—they utterly refused us. Our vittleals were of the Coarsest Kind and served up in a manner which was disgusting after bearing up under repeated injuries we were removed to Davies County under a Strong guard We were then arraigned before the grand Jury, who were mostly intoxicated: who indicted me and the the rest of my Companions for Treason we then got a change of venue to Boone County and were on our way to that place on second Evening after our departure our Guards getting intoxicated we thought it a favourable time to Effect our Escape from such men whose aim was only to destroy our lifes and to abuse us in Every manner that wicked men could invent accordingly we took advantage of their Situation and made our Escape and after enduring Considerable Fatigue & sufferig hunger & weariness Expecting that our enemies would be in pirsuit we arrived in the Town of Quincy Illinois amidst the congratulations of our Friends & the Joy of our Family, I have been here for several weeks as it is Known to people in the State of missouri but they Know they had no Justice in their Crusade a g ainst me have not to my Knowledge taken the first Step to have me arrested The Loss of Property which I have sustained is as follows Lossess Sustained in Jackson County, Davies County: Caldwell County in Cluding Lands; Houses; Horses; Harnesses Hogs Cattle Hogs & Books & Store Goods Expences while in Bonds of moneys paid out Expences of moving out of the State & damages sustained by False imprisonments Threatnings [——] Exposures &c &c &c &c &c $100,000

[*Not sworn.*]

SMITH, Samuel

Illenois Quincy May 15th 1839

a bill of Damages against the State Missouri for being Driven from the State

first for mooveing in to the State	$60.00
for loss of propperty in the State	500.00
for mooving out of the State	100.00

I certify the above a count to Be true and Just a cording to the Best of my Knowledg

Samuel Smith

[Sworn to before C. M. Woods, C.C.C., Adams Co., IL, 15 May 1839.]

SMITH, Samuel[46]

Montrose Lee co Iowa Jan 7 ~~1839~~ 1840
I do hereby certify that I Samuel Smith made an improvement and obtained a preemption right upon 160 acres of land in Davis County Mo in 1837 on the first of Nov 1838 I was compelled to leave the county by order of generel Wilson in ten days they took without my concent two horses which has never been returned no remunerated for also destroyed my crop of corn drove off four head of cattle

Samuel Smith

[Sworn to before D. W. Kilbourn, J.P., Lee Co., IA, 7 Jan 1840.]

SMOOT, Abram O.

Abram O. Smoots account against the State of Missouri
Expence & Suffering in travling to that State $100.00
For land lying in that State from which I have been driven by the residents of Sd State   300.00
For time lost in Standing againsts a ruthless Mob in defence of my family & home 180 days at $150 cts. per day with the Expense of each day for myself & horse at 37 1/2 cts.   140.00
as for my Sufference I know not what to Say nature call for a Sum Surfishent to Surport her much ingerd Constitution for years to come but I will limmit her dictations to the limited Sum of   300.00

---

[46] Also found in JH 7 Jan 1840.

For having to leave the State of Missouri with all of my flattering prospects of futer welth & Ease with all the Expence and Sufference that is insedent to Such a removel   500.00

For laying dow my gun & Sword which was worth $35.00 under the orders of Ginarl Lucas which I have never recived again   35.00

For Sickness & doctor bills Surposed to have been caused by Exposure in Sd. troubles   40.00

Total amont $1,415.00

This the 9 of May 1839 Quincy Adams County Ill   A. O. Smoot

I certify the within to be a Just and true a cording to the Best of my knowledg

A. O. Smoot

[Sworn to before C. M. Woods, C.C.C., Adams Co., IL, 15 May 1839.]

SOUTHWORTH, Chester

Loss of Propperty Sustained by going to and from the State of Missouri	$500.00
Propperty lost by Mob	50.00
loss of time	500.00
	$1,050.00

Handcock Co Illinois January 6th 1840   Chester Southworth

[Sworn to before A. Monroe, J.P., Hancock Co., IL, 6 Jan 1840.]

STANTON, Daniel

May the 7—1839 Illenois
      a Bill of Debt and Damages against the state of Missouri sustained By the Gov. Exterminating Order First

Mooving from the State of Ohio to Missouri with a family of 6 Persons Cost of Mooving and time	$200.00
Lost in Jackson County Mo.	200.00
time Lost in Defending my family and Property against a mob	400.20
Loss of Crop Cattle hogs sheep & Horses & waggon	400.74
Loss on Land	200.00
for mooving out of the State	1,000.00
	$2,000.94

I Do Certyfy that the above account is Just and true according to the Best of my Knowedge

Daniel Stanton

[*Sworn to before C. M. Woods, C.C.C., Adams Co., IL, 7 May 1839.*]

STANTON, Daniel[47]

This may Certify that I Daniel Stanton Bought at the Land office at Lexeton Fayett County Missouri Eighty acres of Land Being Sec & SE qrs of NW 1/4 of section 27—O Township No 55 Range 29 the same which I was Oblieged to sell Being Compeld to Leave the state By the gov. order or Be Slain or Exterminated from the Earth a fine steer and also the mob or troops keld and ~~Eat~~ made use of the same worth $15

Quincy January 9th 1840   Daniel Stanton

[*Sworn to before C. M. Woods, C.C.C., Adams Co., IL, 13 Jan 1840.*]

STAVR, Jared

Illenois Quincy May 31st 1839
        a bill of Damage a gainst the State of Missouri for Being unlawfully Driven from it

first for mooveing in to the State
Loss of time expences &c &c $100.00
for propperty Lost in the Stat Loss of time on land &c   700.00
for mooveing out of the State Damage &c   60.00

I certify the a bove acount to Be true and Just a cording to the Best of my Knowledg

Jared Stavr

[*Sworn to before C. M. Woods, C.C.C., Adams Co., IL, 31 May 1839.*]

STEPHENS, Henry

A bill of Damages of property lost by means of a mob in the State of Missouri in the year 1838 by driving me from the State

---

[47] Also found in JH 13 Jan 1840.

Sacrafised by going there in Sale of property	$500.00
expence of moveing there	100.00
loos of time 8 months	240.00
expence of moveing out of the State	30.00
loss of property in the State	30.00
Total	$900.00

Henry Stephens

[Sworn to before A. Monroe, J.P., Hancock Co., IL, 6 Jan 1840.]

STEVENS, Roswell, Jr.

Quincy Illinois May 11 1839
A Bill of Damages and Debt against the State of Missouri

First For Moving to the State	$100.00
Loss on Land	100.00
Loss on property	600.00
Fire arms	25.00
Loss on Grain	50.00
Expences of moving	75.00

I Certify the above account to be Just and true according to the best of my knoledge

Roswell Stevens Jun

[Sworn to before C. M. Woods, C.C.C., Adams Co., IL, 11 May 1839.]

STEVENS, Roswell, Sr.

Illinois Quincy May 11th 1839
A Bill of Damages and Dept against the State of Missouri that acrued in consequence of the Governers Exterminating order

First For moving to the State	$400.00
Loss on Land	950.00
Loss on Property	235.00 225.00
Expences of Moving away	100.00

I Certify the above account to be Just and true according to the best of My knoledge

Roswell Stevens Sen

[*Sworn to before C. M. Woods, C.C.C., Adams Co., IL, 11 May 1839.*]

STEVENSON, Edward

quinsy adams co ill may the 8 1839
a bill of damages against the State of missouri for being expelled from the State by orders of the governor loss of the chanse of 160 acors of land with 5 acors of improvement with corn buckweat potatoes and turnips and others vegatables with a set of house logs $200 loss of time 5 months $75

Edward Stevenson

[*Sworn to before C. M. Woods, C.C.C., Adams Co., IL, 8 May 1839.*]

STEVENSON, Elizabeth

quincy adams co illinois may 8th 1839
a bill of damage sustained against the state of missourie for being expelled from the state by order of the governor loss of lot and house in far west $300.00
and five acres of land within one mile of far west   50.00

Elizabeth Stevenson

[*Sworn to before C. M. Woods, C.C.C., Adams Co., IL, 8 May 1839.*]

STEWART, Urban V.

Account of Damages Sustained by My Self and Family in consequence of being Driven from the State of Missourie by the Governors exterminating order

Loss of land and Crop	$200.00
to 1 yoke Oxen 2 Cows One heifer and Calf	60.00
1 horse Saddle and Blanket	60.00
5 head Sheep and hogs	35.00
1 Rifle	15.00
Debts lost in consequence of Removing	40.00

Expense of Removeing and time lost   <u>100.00</u>
                                                       $510.00

The above is a just estimate according to the best of my knowledge

Urban V Stewart

[Sworn to before C. M. Woods, C.C.C., Adams Co., IL, 11 May 1839.]

STEWART, Urban V.[48]

Montrose Lee Co Iowa Territory Jan 7th 1840

This is to Certify that about the middle of October I was driven by the threats of the Daviess Co Armed force to leave my possessions consisting of a preemption right to a quarter Section of land with 30 Acres under improvement and a good house I went to Diaman and remained untill about the 1st Nov when I was driven from there by an armed force under General Wilson I then went to Far West.

While at Ondi Ahman the Armed force took from me 1 cow & Calf and a yoke of Oxen 1 horse and 5 Sheep they also took from me 15 Hogs[.] While at Far West they took 2 Cows belonging to me And I saw the Soldiery kill the live stock of the Inhabitants without leave or remuneration and burning building timber fences &c

Urban V Stewart

[Sworn to before D. W. Kilbourn, J.P., Lee Co., IA, 7 Jan 1840.]

STEWART, William J.

Accoumpt of Damages Sustained by myself and Family by being Driven out of the State of Missouri by the exterminating order of Govenor Boggs

Loss of Land and Crop	$300.00
1 yoke Oxen and Several hogs	90.00
to fire arms	15.00
to Sundry articles lost	20.00
Loss of time and Removeing out of the State	<u>200.00</u>
	$625.00

---

[48] Also found in *HC* 4:58–59 and in *JH* 7 Jan 1840.

The above is a correct accoumpt according to the best of my judgement

Wm J Stewart

[Sworn to before C. M. Woods, C.C.C., Adams Co., IL, 11 May 1839.]

STILTZ, Levi

Damages against Missouri
Quincy Illenois May 11 A.D. 1839

For moveing into the state	$40.00
For loss of property in lands &c	300.00
Damage by moveing out of the State	100.00

I certify the above to be just and true according to the best of my knowledge

Levi Stiltz

[Sworn to before C. M. Woods, C.C.C., Adams Co., IL, 11 May 1839.]

STODDARD, Sylvester B.

State of Missouri to Sylvester B. Stoddard Dr For damage Sustained in Consequence of Mobs and being driven from the State by Order of the Govenor

To time & expence in moving from Maine to Mo.	$300.00
To loss of two hundred bushels Corn at 25 Cts per bushel	50.00
To potatoes, turnips, Cabbage &C	30.00
To loss of three mo. time in Consequence of mobs at $30 per month	90.00
To loss of time & expence while moving from Daviss to Caldwell Co. & from thence out of the State by Order of the Govenor	75.00
To one Rifle taken by the malitia	10.00
To one Sword	5.00
To loss of money due in consequence of being driven away	14.00
	$574.00

In consequence of being exposed to the inclemency of the weather while moveing. the health of my wife has become very much impaired. so much so that She has not been able to perform any labor for two months. and her condition is such that it is doubtful whether she will ever recover— for which, and being deprived of CitizenShip, I consider of so vast importance that I am not able to set a proper value there on I Shall therefore leave it for an after Consieration

I certify that the above is just and true according to the best of my knowledge

Quincy May 9th 1839   Sylvester B. Stoddard

[Sworn to before C. M. Woods, C.C.C., Adams Co., IL, 10 May 1839.]

STOKER, Eller

Illenois adams County May 1[1]th 1839
    the following is my bill of Damage a gainst missouri in 1838

for loss of Deeded land three hundred Dollar	$300.00
Rifle gun one [and] waggon and set of harness	80.00
Loss of hogs cattle crop of corn seventy five Dollar	75.00
working tools house hold furniture fifteen Dolm	15.00
bees and other vigetables fifteen Dollars	15.00
five months time and moving expence one hund, and fifteen Dollars	115.00
six hundred Dollar total Sum	$600.00

    the above is a correct schedule

                                                            Eller Stoker

[Sworn to before W. Oglesby, J.P., Adams Co., IL, 11 May 1839.]

STOKER, John W.

State of Illenois Adams County May 11th 18[3]9
    the following is my bill of Damage a gainst the State of Missouri by being Driven from my house and home Land and property in the year 1838 and 1839

Loss on Deeded Land in Caldwell county forty five Dollars $45.00

Right for preemption improvement and crop in clinton county 2 hundred 50	250.00
Loss in stock fifty Dollars	50.00
Rifle gun nine Dollars	9.00
two bee hives one cary plough ten Dollars	10.00
mill wheel and irons and whip saw	18.00
Time Lost and Moving Expences one hund	100.00
total sum	$482.00

I certify the a bove to be a true schedule

John W Stoker

[*Sworn to before W. Oglesby, J.P., Adams Co., IL, 11 May 1839.*]

STOKER, Michael

Illenois adams county may 11th 1839
the following is my bill of Damage against State of missouri in 183[8]

viz pre emption Right with improve ment	$100.00
Deeded Land and Rifle gun forty three Doll	43.00
hogs and cattle and house hold furniture and crop of corn and other vegetables seventy five Dollars	75.00
time lost and Moving Expences	100.00
thre hundred and eighteen Dol.Total sum	$318.00

Michael Stoker

[*Sworn to before W. Oglesby, J.P., Adams Co., IL, 11 May 1839.*]

STOUT, Hosea

A bill of damages against the State of Missouri

For moving in the state	$50.00
For the Loss of 200 acres of land	2,000.00
For the Loss of Property	50.00
For the Loss of Time 6 months, 20	120.00
For leaving the State by orders of the Governor	500.00
	$2,720.00

This may certify the above is a correct account according to the best of my knowledge

Hosea Stout

[Sworn to before C. M. Woods, C.C.C., Adams Co., IL, 21 May 1839.]

STUDY, John

Quincy May the 24th 1839

State of Missouri Dr. for damages for moving from ohio to Ray County Missouri	$150.00
for losses in Land stock and household furniture in consequence of having to leave the state by the governors exterminating order	800.00
for loss of citizenship and suffering	550.00

John Study

This may certify that the above bill of damages is true according to the best of my knowledge

John Study

[Sworn to before C. M. Woods, C.C.C., Adams Co., IL, 24 May 1839.]

SUMNER, Jonithan

Illenois Quincy May the 10 1839
a bill of Damage against the State of Missouri

first for mooveing to the State	$300.00
for Being Driven from Jackson, Co to Clay loss of propperty &C &C	1,000.00
from the State and loss of property	1,000.00
	$2,300.00

I certify the above to Be Just and true acording to the Best of my Knowledg

Jonithan Sumner

[Sworn to before C. M. Woods, C.C.C., Adams Co., IL, 10 May 1839.]

SUMNER, Josiah

Illenois Quincy, May th10 1839
    a bill of Damiges and Det against the State of Missouri in conciquence of the Goviners Exterminateing order—

first for mooveing in to th State	$150.00
Being Driven from Jackson County Loss of propperty &C &C	500.00
from clay to Caldwell and Sacrefis of proppert	50.00
from thence out of the State and propperty Lost	1,000.00
	$1,700.00

    I Certify the a bove to Be true and Just acording to the best of my Knowldge

Josiah Sumner

[Sworn to before C. M. Woods, C.C.C., Adams Co., IL, 10 May 1839.]

SUMNER, Nathan

Illeenois Quncy May the 10 1839
    a charg of Dett and Damages a gainst the State of Missouri in concequence of the Governers Exterminnateing order—

for mooveing in to the State	$100.00
for Being Driven from Jackson Co	500.00
for Being Driven from Clay count to Caldwell	300.00
for being Driven from the State Loss of propperty &C &C	500.00
	$1,500.00

    I cert[i]fy the a bove acount to Be true and Just acording to the best of my Knowledg

Nathan Sum[n]er

[Sworn to before C. M. Woods, C.C.C., Adams Co., IL, 10 May 1839.]

TAYLOR, Allen

    State of Mo Dr To Allen Taylor May 8th 1839

Loss Sustaned in Caldwell Co

Expence of moveing to the State	$50.00
Loss on land by Sale & improvements	800.00
Loss on Crops & time	100.00
Expence of moveing out of the State	500.00
	$1,450.00

I hereby Certify the above account to be just and true according to the best of my Knowledge

Allen Taylor

[Sworn to before C. M. Woods, C.C.C., Adams Co., IL, 9 May 1839.]

TAYLOR, Elizabeth

Hancock County Illenois January 6th 1840
A Bill of Damages a gainst the State of Missouri by Elizabeth Taylor in Consequence of the Order of the Govenor to Expell from the State forthwith from the State all people Comonley Called Mormons
for the Loss of property in Clay County on the Sale of Land $100[0] One thousand Dollars
for the Loss of Land in Caldwell County and Other Property One thousand Dollars
for Mooveing from the State of Missouri and Sufferages Five hundred Dollars

Elizabeth Taylor

[Sworn to before T. Crawford, J.P., Hancock Co., IL, 6 Jan 1840.]

TEEPLES, George B.

Quincy Illinois May the 18th 1839
Damages Received in being driven from the state of Missouri

time & Expense of mooving to the state	$100.00
time & loss of property in the state	400.00
time & Expese of mooving from the state	50.00
	$550.00

I Certify the above to be true acording the best of my Knowledge

George B. Teeples

[Sworn to before C. M. Woods, C.C.C., Adams Co., IL, 18 May 1839.]

THOMAS, Daniel S.

In This year of Our Lord 1838 and 1839.
　The State of Missouri To Daniel S. Thomas Dr. as follows (to wit)

To loss in Sale of Land	$250.00
to loss of Corn	50.00
" loss of Fodder	25.00
" loss of Potatoes	10.00
" loss of time	120.00
" Expenses of moveing from the State	60.00
" False imprisionment 18 days	100.00
" loss of wheat	30.00
" being Drove From the State	500.00
	$1,145.00

　　The above losses being Sustained on the account and cosequence of the Govenors exterminating Orders—

Daniel S Thomas

[Sworn to before W. Laughlin, J.P., Adams Co., IL, 11 May 1839.]

THOMPSON, James P.

quincy adams co illinois may 7th 1839
　　a bill of damage sustained against the state of missouri for being expelled from the state by order of the governor

eight acres and a half of corn	$85.00
one cow and calf	25.00
for four months lost time	100.00
and the chance of eighty acres of land with five acres improved and a house on it	100.00
two sheep	8.00
eleven hogs	20.00
	$338.00

James P Thompson

[Sworn to before C. M. Woods, C.C.C., Adams Co., IL, 8 May 1839.]

THOMPSON, Julius

The Loss of time meney by benig Drove from the State of Missouri 1838 & 1839

two days in entering Land	$2.00
and Expences of money	1.50
made prisoner at far West	6.00
one rifle taken	40.00
loss in Land	50.00
Expences of money in moveing from the State	10.95
Expenses of time	26.05
2 days Spent in getting rifle and money paid Out	2.50
Expences & time at Quincy	8.00
loss in the Sale of hogs	13.00
loss in worth of Land	400.00
Expences of Money from Ohio to the State of Missouri	115.00
My time and Team	50.00
	$705.00

Julius Thompson

[Sworn to before C. M. Woods, C.C.C., Adams Co., IL, 23 May 1839.]

THOMPSON, Lewis

Adams County Illinois May 5th 1839
A bill of damages Sustained in the State of Missouri in Consequence of the unlawful proceedings of the inhabitants and the unconstitutional decree of the Governor of Sd State

Losses in Sale of Land	$200.00
Loss of Clothing and Sundry articles	13.00
Loss of four months Labour and expenses in removing from the State and other Losses &c	62.00

I do hereby certify that the above is a true statement according to the best of my judgement

Lewis Thompson

[Sworn to before C. M. Woods, C.C.C., Adams Co., IL, 6 May 1839.]

THOMPSON, Medad

Damage Sustained by me Medad Thompson AD 1839 by being driven from the State of Missouri by a mob that Rose against the Church of latter day Saints in Cattle building and other property
one thousand Dollars

Medad Thompson

[*Sworn to before S. G. Jackson, J.P., Van Buren Co., IA, 12 Mar 1840.*]

THORNTON, Harriet

Hariot Thorton Moved from kirkland Ohio 1836

expences to Colwell County Mo	$200.00
mooved to davis County	
driven from davies County to Calwell Co	
lose of property in davis Co	1,000.00
to 120 acres of land in Colwell	700.00
Driven out of the State with 7 chrelden	1,000.00
lose of time	200.00
	$3,100.00

I certif that the above acount to be trew acording to the best of my knowledge

Harriet Thornton

[*Sworn to before C. M. Woods, C.C.C., Adams Co., IL, 6 May 1839.*]

THORP, John

January 6th 1840 Handcock Co. Illenois
Loss of time and proppity going to and from the State of Missouri
$1000.00

John Thorp

[*Sworn to before A. Monroe, J.P., Hancock Co., IL, 6 Jan 1840.*]

TIDWELL, Absalom

Illenois Quincy May the 11 1839
    a charg a gainst the Staet of Missouri in concequence of the goviners order of Extermination

firrst for mooveing to the State	$100.00
for Loss of propperty and Damag in the State	500.00
for being Driven from the State and loss of propperty	300.00
	$900.00

    I Certify the a bove to Be a Just Estimation a cording to the Best of my knowledg

Absalom Tidwell

[Sworn to before C. M. Woods, C.C.C., Adams Co., IL, 11 May 1839.]

TIPPETS, John W.

April 29th 1839
    A bill of losses in land and other property Received by beeing dispeled from house & home and land and deprved sitizon ship by unreasoneble men and unhalued prinsipals which I obtained lawfully and justly by purchase from govorn ment this loss I consider one hundrend and twenty dolas the suferings & hardships & beeing deprieved of the right of sitizon ship is worthy of notis if I consider my standing Among men of any value and the rights & prvaleges of our liberal government under which we live is of great value and this I consider my right to claim

John W. Tippets

    I certify that the within acount is Just and true acording to the Best of my Knowl[dg]

John W. Tippts

[Sworn to before C. M. Woods, C.C.C., Adams Co., IL, 7 May 1839.]

TOMLINSON, James

May the 10th 1839
    the State of Missouri to James Tomlinson Dr Occaitioned by the Mob in Said State in the year 1838 and 1839

To Cash Land and Debts Standing out	$375.00

To acres of Land in fare west		200.00
To two lots in Dewit		100.00
To expences in moveing from Mosouri to to Illenois		40.00
to Corn and other food		20.00
to one Saddle an bridle		20.00
to one Cow		25.00
to house hold furniture		5.00
to time lost three Month		~~100.00~~
for my Self and Son and wagon and teem and family		200.00
to my Suffering and family		100.00
for Cittison Ship	~~2,200.00~~	2,000.00

James Tomlinson

[*Sworn to before W. Oglesby, J.P., Adams Co., IL, 11 May 1839.*]

TRACY, Moses

May the 5 1839

A bill of loses in land and other property received by being dispeld from house and home and land and deprived of citizenship by unreasonable men and unhlued prinsiple which I obtained lawfully and Justly by puchase from goverment.

and also the expense of moveing out of the State and the Sfferings is of no Small Consequence and also my time from Oct to the month of April is also of Some Consequence, all of these loses and damages which is five hundred dollars, and also being depried of Citizenship[.] this I Consider five hundred dollars[.] this I charge to the State of Mosouri

Moses Tracy

I certify that the above acount is Just and true a ccording to the Best of my knowledg

Moses Tracy

[*Sworn to before C. M. Woods, C.C.C., Adams Co., IL, 7 May 1839.*]

TRYON, Truman

Quincy Ill May 11th A.D. 1839

A list of damages a gainst the State of Missouri for being driven out of the state by a mob

For moveing in to the State	$80.00
Loss of property in lands &C in Jackson Co.	500.00
Loss of property in Clay and Clinton Co.	1,000.00
Loss by being driven out of the state	50.00

I certefy the above to be just and true to the best of my knowledge

Truman Tryon

[Sworn to before C. M. Woods, C.C.C., Adams Co., IL, 11 May 1839.]

TURLEY, Theodore

May 7 1839
State of Mo Dr To Theodore Turley

Loss Sustained in Colwell Co one Blacksmith Shop one GunSmith Shop	$500.00
Loss of 10 acres of Land ~~near Town~~	100.00
Loss of house & Garden well Stable &c &c	300.00
Loss of Town Lot	40.00
Loss of 2 horses Bridle & Sadle &c	150.00
Loss of Harness Taken by men Calling themselves Militia	20.00
Loss of Tools taken by Do.	40.00
Loss Sustained by braking up my Busness	1,000.00
Loss Sustained by Abuse in family & myselfe & Driving from the State 10 pirsons	1,000.00
[Total]	$3,050.00

I hereby certify the above account to be just and true according to the best of my knowledge

Theodore Turley

[Sworn to before C. M. Woods, C.C.C., Adams Co., IL, 7 May 1839.]

TURNER, Benjamin

Illinois qincy May 18th 1839
a bill & damages a gainst the State of Missouri for being Driven from the State

first for Mooving to the State loss of time and expenses	$200.00
loss of land and other property in the State	500.00
for mob Damages	200.00
for moveing out of the State	100.00
	$1,000.00

I Certify the above account to be Just and true according to the best of my knowledge

Benjamin Turner

[Sworn to before C. M. Woods, C.C.C., Adams Co., IL, 18 May 1839.]

TURNER, Cornelius B.

Illinois quincy May 18th 1839
a bill of Damage against the State of Missouri for being Driven from the State Unlawfully

first for moveing in to the State	$100.00
for property lost in the State	200.00
for mob Damages	100.00
for moveing out of the State	100.00
	$500.00

I Certify the above account to be just and true according to the best of my Knowledge

Cornelius B. Turner

[Sworn to before C. M. Woods, C.C.C., Adams Co., IL, 18 May 1839.]

TYLER, Daniel

Quincy Adams Co Ills April 20th 1839
A bill of losses damages &c a gainst the State of Missouri Sustainied by Daniel Tyler

two and a half acres of Sod Corn fifteen Dollars	$15.00
one forth acre of old ground Corn two dollars and fifty Cents	2.50
loss of time and exposure of health two months fifty Dolars	50.00
loss of 5 months time one hundred dollars	100.00
moveing expenses thirty dollars Damages one hundred Dollars	30.00 100.00

to fore hundred and fifty punkins	<u>4.00</u>
	$301.50

I Certify the within to be trui and just a cording to the best of my knowledge.

Daniel Tyler

[Sworn to before C. M. Woods, C.C.C., Adams Co., IL, 11 May 1839.]

VANAUSDALL, William

May the 8 1839
    Wiliam vanausdall left Lauarance County Ohio May 1838
    My famuly Consists of 12

expences to Mo Colwell County	$200.00
i commenst to make a farm in davis Count an the mob drove me fromit damage	400.00
damage Sustain in Colwell County by being dreven from my home and have ing to leave the State and property taken	1,000.00
Lose of time for my Self and famuly	400.00
expences for to get out of the State	<u>100.00</u>
	$2,100.00

i certify that that the above to be just acord to the best of my knowlage

Wm Vanausdall

[Sworn to before C. M. Woods, C.C.C., Adams Co., IL, 8 May 1839.]

VANDYKE, Ferdinand

Ill. 30the 1839
    Loss and damages—which I sustained in being persecuted driven for my religion in the State of Mo.
    would not any more than justify me if I should say the simple sum if five thousand dollars I would not be out of the way—I feel justified in claiming the same—as there is not any law for me in missouri I Beg for redress at the feet of the Cheif of the nation at the general government

Ferdinand Vandyke

[Not sworn.]

VOORHEESE, George Washington

April the 13 1839

George Washington Voorheese his damagees laid in against the state of Missouri for being Driven from Jackson County and not aloud miy Privileges as other Cittizens	$500.00
forbeing driven from Clay County and not aloud the Privileges as other Cittizens of that County	300.00
forbeing driven from Cauld Well County and forthe Loss of property and land	1,000.00
and for false imprisonment and being driven from the state of Missouri	3,000.00

George Washington Voorheese

    I certify the With in to be true and Just according to the Best of my Knowledg

George Washington Voorheese

[Sworn to before C. M. Woods, C.C.C., Adams Co., IL, 10 May 1839.]

VORHEES, Elisha

Illenois Quincy May 28 1839
    A bill of Damage against the State of Missourie for Being Driven out of the State Bey the Govners Order of Extermination

first for mooveing ~~out of~~ to the State	$200.00
Loss of propperty in the State	400.00
for Leaveing the State	1,000.00
	$1,600.00

    I C[er]tify the a bove a count to Be Just and true a cording to the Best of my Knowledg

Elisha vorhees

[Sworn to before C. M. Woods, C.C.C., Adams Co., IL, 28 May 1839.]

WALKER, John

Illenois Quncy May th 13 1839

a bill of Damages a gainst the State of Mo in concequence of Being Drive from th State a cording to the Governors order

first for ~~Being~~ mooving in to the State of Missouri		$375.00
for mooving out of the State Loss of time &c		125.00
	~~$490.00~~	$500.00

I Do certify the a bove a count to Be true and Just a cording to the Best of my Knowledge

John Walker

I was allso wounded By the mob and my life threatend for which money will Not Satisfy me

[Sworn to before C. M. Woods, C.C.C., Adams Co., IL, 13 May 1839.]

WEAVER, Edward

Illinois Qincy may the 20 1839
A Bill of Damage and Debt against the s[t]ate of Missorie by the govener orders

For time and money in moving from the ~~of~~ State of Pensylvania to the State of Missouri	$150.00
time lost in the war	100.00
Loss of prperty and Damage	300.00
time and Expence in Moveing from the state	100.00
[Total]	$650.00

I certify the above acount to be true and corect acording to the best of my knowledge

Edward Weaver

[Sworn to before C. M. Woods, C.C.C., Adams Co., IL, 20 May 1839.]

WELLSON, James

May the 18th 1839
State of Missuria Dr

to 7 Mare [&] pare harnes blind bridle	$80.00
to time lost 5 Months $20 per month	100.00
to 40 acres of val[u]ed at 150.00	150.00
to 200 bushels of Corn 25 Cents Per bushel	50.00

to Pumkins and turnups	20.00
to Expensis	20.00
to Exposeing of My helth and family	40.00
	$440.00

James **X** Wellson

[Sworn to before W. Oglesby, J.P., Adams Co., IL, 18 May 1839.]

WHITING, Charles

May the 10 1839
Damage against the State of Missourie

Expenses in moveing from Ohio to Missourie	$90.00
Three month time lost	60.00
Moveing from Clay to Caldwell Co	30.00
Loss of farming utentials Grain & hay &c	100.00
Eight month time lost	160.00
To moving from Missourie to Illinoise	100.00
Loss on Land	600.00
To being driven from home & exposed to the Cold Snows & rains and haveing to live out of doors for nine weeks & trouble of mind	1,500.00
	$2,640.00

Charles Whiting

[Sworn to before C. M. Woods, C.C.C., Adams Co., IL, 14 May 1839.]

WHITING, Edwin

May the 10 1839
Losses sustained by being driven from the state of Mo

Expence in moveing from Ohio to Mo	$150.00
Eight months lost time	200.00
Loss on one hundred acres of land	1,000.00
Loss on hay grain & farming utentials	50.00

Loss in being drivin from our home our health exposed to
   the cold rain and snow & the expence & trouble of
   moving from Missouri to Illinois   <u>1,500.00</u>
                                     $2,900.00

                                   Edwin Whiting

[Sworn to before C. M. Woods, C.C.C., Adams Co., IL, 14 May 1839.]

WHITING, Elisha

Loss of health property &c by the state of Missouri. in the first place
our family all sick with the chill fever and ague, and at the same time
driven from the County of Clay to Caldwell having to leave shop and tools
and many of our effects with our wheat stacked in the field to the amount
of 20 or 30 bushel damage 500 dollars

~~in second place settled in Caldwell~~ in the next instance bought an
eighty of land in Caldwell County and got a part of it under fence and a
good improvement for the supporting of a family; and then mobbed and
driven from that having to leave farming utentials. a quantity of corn
potatoes and onions; with three bedsteads and a table besides many other
articles two numerous to name damage 2000 dollars

loss of health by being driven from our home being exposed to storms
of every discription and lying in the open air for six or seven weeks ~~three
of us~~ and lying in beds drenched with rain and snow being in the cold
frosty evening air; brought on the ague to myself and wife who was a very
weakly woman and 3 of our children I am still feeble and unable by being
thrown into the rheumatism to do a days work; my wife also afflicted with
the same complaint and not much better damage inestimable

our journey and expenses from Caldwell to Illinois, with the addition
of building a house ~~and~~ clearing and fencing land &c 155 dollars

our journey from Ohio two years before to Missourie for the sake of
settling ourselves for life the expences $185.53cts

May the 10th Town of Lima co. of Adams State of Illinois

                                 Elisha Whiting

[Sworn to before C. M. Woods, C.C.C., Adams Co., IL, 14 May 1839.]

WIGHTMAN, Wilbur

State of Missouri To Wilbur Wightman Dr

1838		
[and]	To 1 yoke of oxen kild by Militia	$60.00
1839	" 1 horse	60.00
	" Expenses moveing from Ohio	100.00
	" loss of Property	[5]00.00
	" los of Labor b[ei]ng a Mechanic by trade	500.00
	by being deprived of citizenship by being driven by a mob (no Charge)	

I do herby Certify that the above bil of Damages and losses were sustained by ben and are Correct acording to the best of my abilities

Wilbur Wightman

[Sworn to before C. M. Woods, C.C.C., Adams Co., IL, 6 May 1839.]

WILBUR, Melvin

The State of Missouri Dr to Melvin Wilbur

March 1st	to moving to wells vill 90 miles	$10.00
	lost time 3 days	3.00
	to provisions	1.75
	to pasage on steamboat to St Lewis	22.50
Apl 4	to Lost time from wells vill to Richmond Landen 22 days	22.00
	to pasage on steamboat up the Missouri	20.00
	to moving from Richmond Landen to Fare west	6.00
	to 50 bushels of Corn 25 per bushel	12.50
Nov. 10	to Lost time from the surender to April 27 a one dollar-per day	208.00
	to one Broad Swoard	6.00
	to moving from Fare west to Quinsey	30.00

Suffered Shameful abuse on bord the Steamer Aslord by some of the Crew Suffered with Sicknes in my family I supose on the ac cound of fatigue &c when sick was thretened of being Mobed Drivin out of of the house before the surender when Sick with the ague my wife was Scared in to fits and how much fatigue we suffered in our way and an other I Cannot tell

I certify the a bove to be correct a cording to the best of my knowledg

May the 6 1839 Quincy Illenois   Melvin Wilbur

[Sworn to before C. M. Woods, C.C.C., Adams Co., IL, 6 May 1839.]

WILLARD, Joseph

The State of Missourie to Joseph Willard Jr Dr. To bill of damages and loss of property in concequence Of having been unconstitutioanally driven from the State bill of damages in movin to and from the State to gether with loss of time five hundred dollars $500.00

For loss of property viz lands stock and produce

For loss of propperty four hundred and fifty dollars   450.00

I certify the above to be a Just and true account according To the best of my knowledge

Joseph Willard

[Sworn to before C. M. Woods, C.C.C., Adams Co., IL, 16 May 1839.]

WILLIAMS, Alexander

Illenois Quincy May th 11 1839
    a bill of Damage a gainst the State of Missouri

first for mooving to the State	$25.00
for Loss of propperty in the State	200.00
for Leaving the state and loss of Loss of propperty	100.00

I certify the above acount to Be true and Just acording to the Best of my Knowledg

Alexander Williams

[Sworn to before C. M. Woods, C.C.C., Adams Co., IL, 11 May 1839.]

WILLIAMS, Frederick G. [49]

I do hereby certify that I was a resident of Caldwell County in the State of Missouri in the year of our Lord 1838, and owned Land to

---

[49] Also found in *HC* 4:69 and in JH 17 Mar 1840.

considerable amount building lots &c in the village of FarWest and in consequence of Mobocracy together with Govoner Boggs exterminating order was compelled to Leave the State under great Sacrifice of real and personal property which has redused and Left myself and family in a state of poverty with a delicate state of health in an advanced stage of life
    furthermore this deponent saith not
    Given under my hand at Quiny Illinois March 17th AD 1840

                          F. G. Williams

[Sworn to before C. M. Woods, C.C.C., Adams Co., IL, 17 Mar 1840.]

WILLIAMS, Samuel

the damages done in davis County State missouri Ad 1838
    By the orders of the governor to one house and lot $50.00
and loss of time and moveing from davis to Caldwell
    County: 90.00
and loss of time in Caldwell County and moveing from that
    to illenois   100.00

    this damag was done for Samuel Williams Ad 1838 and 1839 in the state of missori By Being drove By the mob
    I Certify the a bove to Be Correct acording to the best of m[y] Knowledg

May the 6 1838 Quincy Ilenois   Samuel Williams

[Sworn to before C. M. Woods, C.C.C., Adams Co., IL, 6 May 1839.]

WILLIAMS, Thomas P.

Illenois Quincy may the 15 1839
    a bill of Damage a gainst the State of Missouri fo being Driven from the St

for mooveing in to the State $150.00
for loss of propperty in the State   250.00
for mooving out of the State   150.00
                        $[5]50.00

    I c[er]tify the a bove a count to Be Just and true acording the Best of my Knowledg

                      Thomas P Williams

[Sworn to before C. M. Woods, C.C.C., Adams Co., IL, 15 May 1839.]

WILLSON, Zachariah

Illenois Quincy may 14th 1839
  a bill of Damage against the State of Missouri —

first for mooveing to the State	$50.00
for propperty Lost Damages Don By a Lawles mob	445.00
for haveing to leave the State	150.00
	$645.00

I certify the a bove to Be Just and true acording to the best of my Knowledg

Zachariah Willson

[Sworn to before C. M. Woods, C.C.C., Adams Co., IL, 18 May 1839.]

WILSON, Aron

In the years of Our Lord 1838 & 1839
  State of Missouri To Aron Wilson Dr. as follows To wit

To loss of grain	$125.00
" loss of house hold and kitchan furniture	25.00
" loss of hogs	25.00
" " of Two yoke of work oxen	115.00
" " " One milch cow	25.00
" " " Two horses	112.00
Being false imprisioned Three Days	10.00
To six months lost time	120.00
" Time and expenses in Moveing from the state with large family to find a home in a strange Land	600.00
	$1,157.00

The above losses being sustained on the account and consequence of The Govenor's exterminating Order's

Aron Wilson

[Sworn to before W. Laughlin, J.P., Adams Co., IL, 11 May 1839.]

WILSON, Bradley B.

For losses Sustained in the year of or Lord 1838 and in 1839—

The State of Missouri—To Bradley B. Wilson—Dr.

to money and time expended moveing up to missouri	$150.00
to losses on real estate	600.00
to losses on chattle property	40.00
to loss of time	120.00
to expences time & money moveing to Illenois	100.00
total Amount	$1,010.00

Illenois May 10th 1839   Bradley B. Wilson

I do sirtyfy that the within is a true estatement of facts acording to the best of my knowllege

B. B. Wilson

[*Sworn to before C. M. Woods, C.C.C., Adams Co., IL, 13 May 1839.*]

WILSON, Bushrod W.

For losses Sustained in the year of our Lord 1838 and 1839

The State of Missouri to Bushrod W. Wilson Dr. in Consequence of Govoner Boggs es Decree or Exterminating order

to loss on land	$500.00
to money and time expended in moveing up to missouri	120.00
to loss chattle property	15.00
to loss of time	120.00
to Expences for mooveing to Illenois	60.00
totle amount	$815.00

Illenois may the 10th 1839
$815.00   Bushrod W. Wilson

I do Certify that the above is true according to the best of my knowledge

Bushrod W. Wilson

[*Sworn to before C. M. Woods, C.C.C., Adams Co., IL, 13 May 1839.*]

WILSON, Elijah

Elijah Wilson Mooved from edward County Illi November 1837 to Dave County Mo Dreven from Davis County November 38 to Colwell Co and had to lose all of my effects

Damage sustained	$200.00
Compeled to leave the State with my famaly of 9 in the winter	200.00
expinses by the way	100.00
loose of time ~~November~~ 6 months	180.00
	$[6]80.00

I c[e]rtfy that the above [a]count to be trew acording to the best of my knowleege

Elijah Wilson

[Sworn to before C. M. Woods, C.C.C., Adams Co., IL, 6 May 1839.]

WILSON, George C.

For losses sustained in the year of our Lord 1838 and 1839
The State of Missouri to Geo. C. Wilson— Dr.

to money & time expended in moveing up to Missouri	$200.00
to losses on Real estate	500.00
to losses on chattle property	100.00
for returning to Illenois	100.00
to time lost & expended	150.00
	$1,150.00

all this in Consequence of Governor Boggs's Decree

Illenois May 13th 1839   Geo. C. Wilson

I certify that the above is true accordng to the best of my knowledge

Geo. C. Wilson

[Sworn to before C. M. Woods, C.C.C., Adams Co., IL, 13 May 1839.]

WILSON, Guy C.

A Bill of Losses and damages Sustained By Guy C. Wilson occasiond by an un lawful decree of Governor Boggs of Missouri (Viz)

Loss in the salle of Land ad.	$350.00
Loss of an elegant mare ad.	100.00
Loss of time and money from the Last of September to the first of Aprile	150.00
Expence of Moveing to and from Missouri	175.00
Damage of being de prived of my citizenship and abuces and threats of a lawles Mob	10,000.00

Guy C. Wilson

[Sworn to before C. M. Woods, C.C.C., Adams Co., IL, 15 May 1839.]

WILSON, Henry H.

May 13th 1839

For losses Sustained in the year of our Lord 1838 and 1839 The State of Missouri to Henry H Wilson Dr

to money and time for moveing up to Missouri	$50.00
to loss on real Estate	100.00
to Expences returning to Illenois	20.00
to loss of time	40.00
	$210.00

all this in Consequene of Being Driven from the State by the people

Henry H. Wilson

I Cirtify that the above is a trou Statements of facts according to the best of my memory

Henry H Wilson

[Sworn to before C. M. Woods, C.C.C., Adams Co., IL, 13 May 1839.]

WILSON, Lewis D.

For losses Sustained in the year of our Lord 1838 and 1839
The State of Missouri to Lewis D. Wilson Dr.

to money & time expended in moveing up to Missouri	$200.00
to losses on real estate	800.00
to do on chattle property	200.00
to do of time	120.00
to time & money expended ~~move to Illenois~~ moving to Illenois and Secureing a home	100.00
	$1,420.00

Illenois May 10th 1839
    all in consequense of Govener bogses exterminateing order

Lewis D. Wilson

    I sirtyfy that the above is a true statement of facts according to the best of my judement

Lewis D. Wilson

[Sworn to before C. M. Woods, C.C.C., Adams Co., IL, 13 May 1839.]

WILSON, Whitford G.

Quincy May 14th 1839—
    A List of Losses sustained by Whitford G. Wilson in consequence of an order of Governour Boggs for me to leave the state of Missourie or be put to death. Viz—

Myself wife and team six weks at 3 dollars per day	$126.00
money expended on the way	50.00
expences in hunting and entering 2 hundred acres of land	10.00
To 5 months time lost in consequence of the mob	100.00
To one bay mare taken by Jacson Co mob	60.00
To 1 bridle and halter chain taken by do	4.00
To 1 rifle Gun worth 22 dollars	22.00
To 3 weeks self wife & team laving the stat	60.00
money expended in mooving out of Missourie &C	25.00
Loss in sale of land	540.00
Damage for being deprived of my Liberty	10,000.00

Whitford G Wilson

[Sworn to before C. M. Woods, C.C.C., Adams Co., IL, 15 May 1839.]

WIMMER, Peter

Illinois Adams County March 12th 1840
This certifies that I Peter Wimmer was Driven from the State of Missouri By a lawles mob and Lost the following propperty

first for mooveing to the State	$200.00
for propperty Lost in the State	1,000.00
for mooveing out of the State	150.00
Total	$1,350.00

This certifies the above to Be True and correct a cording to the Best of my knowledg

Peter Wimmer

[Sworn to before W. Oglesby, J.P., Adams Co., IL, 12 Mar 1840.]

WINCHESTER, Stephen

Payson Adams County Illinois May 6th 1839
A bill of losses and damages sustained by the late outrage in the state of Missourie by the order of Gov Boggs

to time and expence in mooveing to Missouri	$250.00
to forty Acres of land in farwest	400.00
to one hundred and twenty Acres of land three and half mils from Farwest with forty Acres improvements and 6 Acres of wheat	600.00
to corn and hogs and other property	100.00
to one cow and two calves	35.00
time and expence of mooveing to Illinois	150.00

I certify the a bove acount to Be true and Just a cording to the Best of my Knowledg

Stephen Winchester

[Sworn to before C. M. Woods, C.C.C., Adams Co., IL, 15 May 1839.]

WINEGAR, Samuel T.

State of Missourie to Samuel T. Winegar Dr. Oct. AD 1838
to Eighty Acres of Land & improvement on the Same

To damage done to ten tun of Hay
To one Waggon
To one Acre of Turnips
To one Cow to one ox yoke
To loss of time 6 months

Samuel T Winegar

State of Illinois County of Adams SS
I William Oglesby A Justice of the peace Within & for the County of Adams aforesaid Do hereby Certify that this day personally apeared before me Samuel T. Winegar and after being Duly Sworn Deposeth & sayeth that the Within Account against the state of Missourie is Just & true to the best of his Knowlege & belief & this Deponent sayeth Not farther

Samuel T **X** Winegar

[*Sworn to before W. Oglesby, J.P., Adams Co., IL, 10 Jan 1840.*]

WINGET, William

May the 11th 1839 Illenois Quinsey
An account against the State of Missouri for debt & Damage Sustained in Consequence of the Exterminating Order

140 Acres of Land	$700.00
Damage	100.00
1 Rifle Gun	20.00
	$820.00

I certify the above to be a Just and a true account according to the best of my Knowledge

William Winget

[*Sworn to before C. M. Woods, C.C.C., Adams Co., IL, 11 May 1839.*]

WIRICK, Jacob

Illenois Quincy may the 11 1839
a bill of Damage a gainst the State of Missourie in conciqunce of the Govenors Exterminateing order —

first for mooveing in to State $150.00

for loss of propperty in the State in land and other
    propperty   3,000.00

for leaving the State propperty Lost in conciquence of
    the Same   <u>150.00</u>

                                                $3,300.00

    I certify the above to be Just and true acording to the Best of my
Knowledg

                                         Jacob Wirick

[Sworn to before C. M. Woods, C.C.C., Adams Co., IL, 11 May 1839.]

WOODLAND, John

May the 10 the 1839
    the State of Misoury Dr to John woodland

to Corn potatoes and hay	$200.00
to loss of time of hands six months	200.00
to loss of team three months	50.00
to loss in moveing	60.00
to hire of hands to send af ter my team	7.00
to one Cow	20.00
to one Gun	20.00
to one plow ~~by~~ for breaking porara	15.00
to hoes and axes	5.00
to loss of improvement	300.00

                          John **X** Woodland

[Sworn to before W. Oglesby, J.P., Adams Co., IL, 11 May 1839.]

WOODLAND, William

    Wiliam Woodland Mooved from Edwards Count Ille Oct 22 1837

expences to Mo	$50.00
Driven from davs to Colwell Damage	250.00
Damaage from colwell out of the State	250.00
expences by the way	50.00
lose of time of myself and famaly of 5	<u>240.00</u>
	$840.00

i certifytify that the above account to be just acording to the best of my jugement

william woodland

[*Sworn to before C. M. Woods, C.C.C., Adams Co., IL, 6 May 1839.*]

YOUNG, Joseph[50]

I Joseph Young of Quincy, Adams County, Illinois, Painter, and Glazier, do hereby Certify that while he I was residing at Hawns Mills, on Shoal Creek, Caldwell County, State of Missouri, together with about twenty Families of my Friends, we were suddenly attacked by about Three hundred of the Citizens of that State, who were mounted upon Horses, armed and equipped, on the thirtieth day of October in the Year of Our Lord One thousand eight hundred and thirty eight, who then and there, being headed or led on by Colonel Jennings of Livingston County, Mister Ashby of Chariton County, and Mister Comstock of Davis County, all in said State, commenced firing upon Men Women and Children promiscuously, and killed to the number of thirteen Persons, whose Corpses or Bodies I assisted in interring upon the following Day, and there were five others who were mortally Wounded, and afterwards Died of their Wounds.

Joseph Young

[*Sworn to before W. Tainter, who signed for C. M. Woods, C.C.C., Adams Co., IL, 17 Mar 1840.*]

YOUNGER, Joseph W.

the State of Missouri indeted to Joseph W Younger in concqunce of the governers ext[urm]minating order and Being drove from the State of Missouri Caldwell County and davis countys in [——] 1838 and 1839

in 1836 I mouved from Band County Illiois to Clay County [——] one hundred dollars and from clay county to caldwell county in July 1836 [I] charge one hundred dollars being compeld to Leve the county of [——] Clay I remand in Caldwell County 2 year in peace But the Last of July 1838 I mouved in to davis County But alas I had peace But a Short time till the mobs Begin to Rage One thousan dollars for Being drove from davis county to Caldwell County for[said] one thousan dollars for being dis armed and compeld to Leve the State the Loss of my perremtions

---

[50]Also found in JH 17 Mar 1840.

Rights five hundred dollars Being cept under gard whil the Land sales at Lexinton was going on for one Bay mare strayd off and having not privelig of [——] hunting after my mare as a Sittison But Leaving my mare in the State as I Supose fifty dollars 2 cows and one calf forty dollars ~~provision one year for my famley one hundred and fifity~~ the exposur of the helth of my wife and children and fright By the mobs one thousan dollasr at Least and no sum wold remunerate them for the desstress and surffering causd By the mobs of missouri as I supose

I certify the abouve a count to Be true and Just ar cording to the Best of my knowlage

Joseph W Younger

[Sworn to before C. M. Woods, C.C.C., Adams Co., IL, 10 May 1839.]

ZABRISKIE, Lewis

A bill of damages that I hold against Missouri

First for moveing to the state of Missouri from Indiana $200.00, Damages for not having the right of setling on Lands in Jackson Co. Mo. $1000.00

For being threatned by a mob in Clay Co. Mo. and had to leave the Co. leaving 40 acres of Land $2000.00

Damages for having to Stand under arms about two weeks against a mob in Coldwell Co. Mo.

and being driven from my Land which was 40 [a]cres not being able to Sell it for its worth $1000.00, loss of sales in property & and property $200.00 Damages,

Damages for being driven from the state of Missouri not having the right as asitizen $5000.00

I was driven from Coldwell Co Missouri in the year 1839

This May the 6th A.D. 1839   Lewis Zabriskie

I certify this to be a true copy of of damages to the best of my knowledge

Lewis Zabriskie

[Sworn to before C. M. Woods, C.C.C., Adams Co., IL, 6 May 1839.]

ZABRISKY, Henry

Abill of damages that I hold against Missouri

First for having to leave Clay Co. Missouri and loss of land 80 acres not having the right of living on the Land. Damages. $2000.00.

For fals Imprisonment and Sufferings $3000.00
For being driven from Coldwell Co. Mo for the loss of Lands and property $2000.00 Damages
for not havin the right as asitizen of Missouri—$3000.00 Damages

This May the 6th AD 1839   Henry Zabrisky

I certify this to be a true copy of damages to the best of my knowlege

Henry Zabrisky

[*Sworn to before C. M. Woods, C.C.C., Adams Co., IL, 6 May 1839.*]

ZIMMES, Catherine

Illinoas Qincey may the 11 1839
a Bill of damage a gainst the state of misuri

for moving in to the State	$100.00
Lost of Land	50.00
Lost of horses	79.00
moving from State of missurie	30.00

I do heerby Certify that the a bove account is Just and true acoordin to the best of my Best of my knoge

Catherine Zimmes

[*Sworn to before C. M. Woods, C.C.C., Adams Co., IL, 11 May 1839.*]

ZIMMES, Lydia

Ilunois Qincey may the 11 1839
a Bill a gainst the state of missurie

for moving in to the state	$50.00
Loss of Land	100.00

I do huerbey Certify that the aBove is a Just and true Bill

Lydia Zimmes

[*Sworn to before C. M. Woods, C.C.C., Adams Co., IL, 11 May 1839.*]

ZUNDEL, Jacob

Illenois Quincy June 3rd 1839
a bill of Damage against the State of Missouri for Bein mobed out of the State

first for mooveing to the State	$150.00
for propperty Lost in the State	700.00
for Leaveing the State Loss on Land Expence of mooveing &c	800.00

I certify the above a count to Be Just and true acording to the Best of my Knowldg

Jacob Zundel

[Sworn to before C. M. Woods, C.C.C., Adams Co., IL, 3 Jun 1839.]

This is to certify to the Barborous Acts of a Cruel Mob Committed on a portion of our Society at Hous Mill of which I was an eye Witness

On the 30 of October 1838 all of a suding the war whoop was heard and an armed force immediately hove in Sight and Commenced firing upon men women and Children our Society called for quearters, but none granted the women and Children fled in every direction nearly frightened out their sensis in this awful Seene of destruction I made out to escape and after a short and Bloody Conflict the mob dispersed not leaving so much as the clothes of the dying and wounded but latterly took their Chothes from of their backs & boots & shoes from their feet also most of their hous furniture and to prove their savage ferocity more clearly they also litearly took a Conn. Sutter and mangled and old Revolutionary Soldier by the none of Beide in Cool Blood, 16 were killed and among the Number killed was my father and two soon dyed of their wounds

January 8th 1840

                                          Maviah her + Bennor
                                                   mark

Sworn to And Subscribeid before me at my office in Adams County Illinois on the 8th day of January AD 1840. Given under my hand And Seal — Josh K Orr Justice of the peace in for Adams Co Illos

MAVIAH BENNOR'S PETITION

In the year of Our Lord 1838. and 1839—
the State of Missouri To Albern Allen Dr—
as follows (to wit)

To loss of time on the account of the Governors Orders
To leave the State — $150. 00
" on account of the Same in Land . —   600. 00
"   "   "   "   in Stock ——   100. 00
"   "   "   "   Beef and Pork —   50. 00
                    Farming Utensils . ——   20. 00
Moving on the account of the Governors
exterminating Orders ————————   400. 00
                                                    $1320. 00

                        Albern Allen

State of Illinois
Adams County { I William Laughlin Justice of the Peace within
                        and for said County, Do certify that this Day
personally came before me Albern Allen and being Duly
Sworn according to law Deposeth and saith that the above
account is Just and correct—
    Given my hand and Seal this 11th day of May AD. 183?
                        William Laughlin
                        J P of A. C.

ALBERN ALLEN'S PETITION

Then personally appeared before me, Samuel Com one of the Justices of the Peace within & for the County of Hancock & State of Illinois, David Dutton, & after being duly sworn, according to law, deposeth & saith that, on the 21st day of October A.D. 1838, he was a citizen of the State of Missouri, residing in Caldwell County on the South West fourth of the North East fourth of Section Number 23, Township 56 and Range 29, and on the day & year aforesaid, & on the ten succeeding days i.e. the first ten days of November A.D. 1838, on the premises aforesaid, certain divisions of the Missouri State Militia, Commanded by Generals Parks, Lucas & Clark, encamped & effected a total destruction of the following articles of property then belonging to me, for which this deponent hath received no compensation whatever. That is to say:—

—	—	11 Hogs	valued at	$40.00
—	—	5 Acres Corn	— —	50.00
—	—	1 2 year old Heifer	— —	10.00
—	—	200 fence Rails	— —	6.00
—	—	— Timber for fuel	— —	25.00
—	—	1 Sword	— — —	8.00
—	—	30 Barn Fowls	— —	5.00
—	—	1 Rifle Gun	— —	15.00
—	—	1 Chopping Axe	— —	2.00

And further this deponent saith not $151.00

State of Illinois }
Hancock County } ss.
                       David Dutton

Sworn to & subscribed before me, at Carthage, Hancock County, State of Illinois, this ninth day of January, eighteen hundred & forty Samuel Comer J.P. of H.C.a.L.S.

DAVID DUTTON'S PETITION

State of Illinois Hancock Co.

I testify that in consequence of a mob arising in
Davis Co. Mo. 1738 was oblige to leave my home and move
to Adam Ondi Ahman in the county aforesaid and to expose
my family with many others, in wet and cold, in a camp
and that the Governor refused to protect us but sent an
armed force to disarm us and they came under the comm
and of Col. Lucas on Gen. marched into our town took possession
of it took our arms then let an other company come
painted black under the command of Cornelus Gillum take our horses abuse our men and then
then sent a strong gard with others and let them plun
der our houses and camps, and that Gen. Wilson
let them come, afterwards, he being sent to guard us
(on the mob) he let them come and take my table
furniture, and told Col. J. Wilson of it but his reply
was, "you mus hook as much from some body els
this I testify that they kild our "cattle" destroyed our
corn and quarter in our private dwellings without
our leave and drove us from the county with only 10 days and forced
us to agree to leave the State, and I say it the fear
of God and that I hold a preemption claim in that county
January 4th AD. 1840   Daniel Cathcart

N.B. they also came into Davis west in 1839 threatend our lives chased us with
knives and parricues from the state witnefs my hand and seal J. Cathcart [seal]

sworn to and subscribed before me this 6th days
of January in the year of our lord one
thousand eight hundred and forty

                        Andrew Monroe J.P.H.C.

January 10th 1840 Aury Brown

This is to certify that I Edward Weever formerly of Coldwell county Missourie do certify that I Entered a certain tract of land in the aforsaid county lying in Section 30 T. 56 North of the base line and west of the fifth principle Meridian Range No 28 containing forty acres was compelled to sacrafise my land and leave the state in consequence of the Governors exterminating orders also had one set of house logs burned up in consequence of the militia who marched on our possessions and encamped therein without liberty. and likewise I saw a pris- oner Shamefully abused who was taking by the Militia

January – 1840

Edward Weever

I Aury Brown a Justice of the peace in an for the county of Pike and State of Illinois do certify that Edward Weever personally appeared before me and affirmed to the truth of This January 10–1840

Aury Brown J P Seal

I David Winter do certify that I bought a certain tract of land in the State of Missourie and county of Coldwell which was entered by Jesse Mann containing 80 acres lying in Section 22 T. 56 R 28 and also another lot containing 40 acres in the aforesaid section which was entered by Henry McHenry, both peaces I had bought and paid 950 dollars for but before the deeds was made out I was compelled to leave the state in consequence of Governor Bogg's Exterminating orders to expell the the church of yesus christ of Latter day saints from the State of Missourie

I was therefore compelled to sell my land for to procure means to leave the state at a reduced price.

and also another piece in the aforesaid section containing 40 acres which was entered by Mr Lyons which I was likewise compelled to sell.

David Winter

a List of Damages that I sustained in Missourie in consequency of Gov Boggs orders to exterminate the mormons

For time lost	$ 52.00
Loss of stock	100.00
Loss on the price of land	700.00
	$ 852.00

I Aury Brown a Justice of the peace in and for Pike Illinois do certify that David Winter personally appeared before me and swore to the above

January 10th 1840 Aury Brown J P Seal

EDWARD WEEVER'S AND DAVID WINTER'S PETITIONS

Handcock Co. and State of Illinois

This may Certify that I Nahum Curtis moved to the State of Missouri in the year 1836 I purchased a farm and resided thereon untill the Autumn of 1838 When the troubles came on between the Inhabitants and the Mormons I went to Farwest my farm and family was ten miles from Farwest — there I was Surrounded by those that call themselves militia Compeld to Sign away my property give up my arms and Compeld to leave the State in the Spring my gun I got Afterwards by paying Six Apteir Cents and Compeld to Swear that I leave the State immediatly My arms was almost ruined by rust and bad usage The destruction of Property while the troops lay in Farwest was great they Killed Cattle hogs and Sheep and wasted and used a large quantity of Corn and after the Troops left the Camp ground they left a large quantity of Meat Some burnt Some mamok overso it was not fit for use — I was Obliged to Sell at great disavantage and leave the State in the winter to the great injury of my health and family — the militia took from me one horse which I never got

Nahum Curtis

sworn to and subscribed before me this 6th — day of January in the year of our lord one thousand eight hundred and forty

Andrew Monroe J P H C

NAHUM CURTIS' PETITION

I Edmund Durphy Jur solemnly declare that sometime in October in year of our Lord One Thousand eight Hundred and thirty eight the Militia under the command of Generals Lucas Wilson & Clark took possession of a house belonging to Uriah B Powell contrary to his wishes likewise that they the said militia burned timber belonging to me that I had moved on to the City of Warsaw for a dwelling House

Edmund Durfee Jr

State of Illinois
McDonough County

I James M Campbell clerk of the County Commissioners Court in and for said County do certify that on this day Edmund Durfee Jr came before me and took and subscribed the above and foregoing affidavit

In Testimony Whereof I have hereunto set my hand and the seal of said Court at Macomb this fourth day of January A D 1840

James M Campbell Clk
By Wm Head Depty

EDMUND DURFEE, JR.'S PETITION

A short time after General Clark came up to Far West he was residing two miles from Far West, when she saw a number of the militia at Mr. Jas Yale's who lived but a short distance from us. we saw them about the house for two days. Saw them shot down one of his hogs. saw them take his corn and believe they destroyed about ten acres. and likewise a small stack of hay. saw them carrying out of Mr Yales house a quantity of furniture. saw them set fire to a large Hay Stack belonging to Mr Mess, which was entirely consumed. Mr Yale, at the time the militia came to his house was absent from home on a journey. we likewise saw some of the troops in possession of Mr Cyrus Daniel's house for several days. saw them take away beds bedding and clothing and almost every thing of value in and about the House. We saw the troops carrying off corn from Mr Mess's who was absent from home

We certify that the above statements are correct, according to our best knowledge and belief.

Samuel Bent

Lettice Bent

Commerce Hancock Co Illinois
Jany 2nd 1840.

I certify that I lived about two miles from Far West in Caldwell County Missouri. Early in November A.D. 1838 a company came to our house and took possession of the same, without any leave whatever as my husband was absent from home, they took several things from the house, destroyed my corn and hay shot our fowls and hogs and took my husbands working tools away

Commerce Hancock Co Illinois
Jany 2. 1840

Hannah Yale

State of Illinois
County of Hancock I do certify that Samuel Bent Lettice Bent and Hannah Yale interrogators officers above did acknowledge the same to be theirs, and likewise were sworn that the facts stated in the above affidavit, were true, before me this 3 day of January A D 1840
Given under my hand and seal the day and year last above

Daniel H Wells seal

Justice of the Peace

SAMUEL AND LETTICE BENT'S
AND HANNAH YALE'S PETITIONS

Part III

The Second Appeal to Congress

Introduction to Part III

In October of 1840, after the unsuccessful first appeal, Church members sustained the Prophet Joseph Smith's proposal that "Elias Higbee and Robert B. Thompson be appointed a committee to obtain redress for the wrongs sustained in Missouri" (*HC* 4:206; JH 5 Oct 1840). Higbee and Thompson drafted a memorial whose substance was much like the first memorial prepared in 1839 by the Prophet, Sidney Rigdon, and Higbee (*HC* 4:237), and on 21 December 1840 this petition, possibly accompanied by some individual claims, was "presented to the House of Representatives . . . referred to the committee of the Judiciary and ordered to be printed" (*HC* 4:250-51; JH 21 Dec 1840). Apparently the petition was printed and circulated within Congress because Mr. Linn of Missouri asked that the legal proceedings held in Missouri also be printed that his state's character might not be impugned (*Congressional Globe* 9:175).

The present location of the Higbee-Thompson memorial is not known. Any individual peitions that may have accompanied it might have been intermixed with the next appeal in the National Archives, for in 1842 Higbee, John Taylor, and Elias Smith wrote another memorial probably to introduce more individual petitions. This final memorial is almost identical to the first memorial and is housed in the National Archives.

For organizational purposes, we have called Part III, which includes all of the individual petitions from the National Archives, most of which are dated 1840, the "Second Appeal." It is not known how or when these individual petitions were sent to Washington. They may have been sent with the Higbee-Thompson memorial in late 1840, they may have been sent with the final memorial in 1842, or some may have been sent with each.

Illinois Representatives John T. Stuart and John D. Reynolds, and Illinois Senator Richard M. Young helped to present the Mormon cause in Congress (Bateman and Selby 446). These attempts failed and the petitions of this second appeal, along with the last memorial, were sent to the National Archives, where they remained until they were discovered in the late 1960s or early 1970s.

Perhaps the petitions were not left in Washington through oversight or neglect but to keep the matter before Congress. It appears that these petitions formed the basis for subsequent efforts made by Orson Pratt, Orson Hyde, Jesse C. Little, and others to place the Mormon cause before the members and the President.

Chapter 5

The Second Memorial

To the Honorable the Senate and House of Representatives of the United States of America in Congress assembled.

Your Memorialists Elias Higbee, John Taylor, and Elias Smith would most respectfully represent, that they have been delegated by their brethen and fellow Citizens the Latter Day Saints, (commonly called Mormons) to prepare, and present to your honorable Bodies a statement of their wrongs, and a prayer for their relief, which they now have the honour to submit to the consideration of the Congress of the United States.

This memorial Showeth: That in the Summer of the year 1831 a portion of the people above named commenced a settlement in the County of Jackson, in the State of Missouri. The individuals making that Settlement had emigrated from almost every State in the Union to that lovely spot in the "Far West" in the hope of improving their condition; of building homes for themselves, and posterity and of erecting Temples, where they and theirs might worship their Creator, according to the dictates of their own consciences. Though they had wandered far from the homes of their childhood, still they had been taught to believe, that a citizen born in any one State in this great Republic might remove to another and enjoy all the rights and immunities guarantied to the citizens of the State of his adoption; that wherever waved the American Flag, beneath its stars and stripes an American citizen might look for protection and Justice—liberty in person, and in conscience. They bought Farms, built houses, erected churches; some tilled the earth, others bought and sold Merchandise and others again toiled in the occupation of the Mechanic. They were industrious and moral; they prospered; and though often persecuted and vilified for their difference in religious opinions from their fellow citizens still they were happy. They saw their society increasing in numbers; their farms teemed with plenty; and they fondly looked forward to the future big with hope. That there was prejudice existing against them they knew; that slanders were propogated against them they deplored: yet they felt that these things were unmerited and unjust; that time and an upright conduct would outgrow them in this enlightened age of the world. While this summer of peace, and happiness, and hope beamed upon them, and shone over the infant Settlement of the "Saints," the dark cloud that bore in its bosom the thunderbolt of its destruction was gathering fast around them, pregnant with prejudice, oppression, and final expulsion or extermination.

On the 20th of July 1833 around their peaceful village, a mob gathered to the surprise and terror of the quiet, unoffending Saints: why, they knew not. They had broken no law; they had harmed no man in deed or thought. Why then were they thus threatened and alarmed? Soon a Committee from the mob called upon the leading saints of the place, and issued forth the mandate, that the Stores, the Printing Office, and the workshops must all be closed; and that forthwith every Mormon must leave the County. The message was so terrible, so unexpected, the "Saints" asked time for deliberation for consultation, which being refused, the Brethren were severally asked "Are you willing to abandon your homes"? The reply was such as became freemen living in a free Country; "we will not go," which determination being made known to the Committee of the mob; one of them replied; "he was sorry as the work of destruction must now begin." No sooner said than done. The Printing Office a two story brick building, was assailed by the mob and torn down, and with all its valuable furniture and materials litterally destroyed. They next proceeded to the principal Store with a like purpose; its owner in part, Mr Gilbert, agreed to close it, and they delayed their purpose of destruction. They then proceeded to the dwelling of Mr Partridge the beloved Bishop of the Church: they dragged him from his family to the Public Square, and when surrounded by hundreds of spectators they partially stripped him of his cloths, and in the most unfeeling manner covered him with Tar and feathers from head to foot. Another by the name of Allen, was treated in a similar manner at the same time. The mob then dispersed with an agreement to meet again on the following tuesday: the above outrages having been committed on Saturday. Tuesday came and with it came the mob, bearing a red flag in token of blood. They proceeded to the houses of Isaac Morley and others of the leading men— seized them, and told them to bid their families farewell as they would never see them again. They were then driven at the point of the bayonet to the Jail, and there amid the jeers and insults of the crowd were thrust into prison, to be kept as hostages and for immolation, in case any of the mob should be killed while depredating upon the persons and property of the Saints. At this awful, and critical juncture, some two or three of the Saints, offered to surrender up themselves as victims if that would satisfy the fury of the mob, and purchase peace, and security for their unoffending brethren their helpless wives, and innocent children. The reply of the mob was—"The Mormons must leave the county en Masse or every man shall be put to death." The Saints terrified and defenceless were in this manner reduced to the necessity of entering into an agreement to leave the County; one half by the first of January; the other half by the first of April next ensuing. This treaty being made and ratified, the mob dispersed. Again for a time the persecuted Saints enjoyed a respite from their relentless persecutors; but their repose was of short duration. Some time in the month of October a meeting was held at Independence at which it was determined to remove the Mormons or die. Inflammatory speeches of the most violent character were made to excite the populace and one of the speakers went so far in his denunciations as to swear "that he would remove the Mormons from the County, if he had to wade to his neck in blood".¶

Up to this time the Mormons had faithfully observed the forced treaty stipulations on their part; and were guilty of no offence against either the laws of the land or of society, but were peacefully following the routine of their daily duties. Shortly after the meeting above referred to, another persecution commenced, with increased sufferings on the part of the devoted Saints: Some of their people were shot at; others were whipped without mercy; their houses assailed with brick bats; the doors broken open and thrown down; their women grossly insulted; and their weeping daughters brutally abused before their mothers' eyes. Thus were they for many days and weeks without offence, and without resistance, by night and by day, harrassed, insulted and oppressed. But there is a point beyond which human endurance ceases to be a virtue—when the worm, if trampled upon, will in the agony of its distress, turn upon its oppressor. A company of about thirty Saints fell in with twice that number of the mob engaged in the destruction of their property, when a battle ensued, in which one mormon was killed, and two or three of the mob. We here regret to say that, acting in concert with the officer who commanded the mob, was Lilbourn Boggs, at that time Lieutenant Governor of the State of Missouri. When the news of this battle was spread abroad, the public mind became much inflamed against our people; the Millitia collected in arms from various quarters, and in great numbers; and being excited to fury by the false accounts which had been circulated against us; they demanded an immediate surrender of all our arms, and gave a peremtory order that we should quit the county without further delay. Compelled by overpowering numbers, the Saints submitted and surrendered up fifty-one guns which have never been returned or accounted for. The next day, parties of the mob went from house to house threatening the women and children with death if they did not immediately leave their homes. Immagination cannot pain nor tongue express, the terror and consternation which now pervaded the community of the Latter Day Saints. The weather was intensely cold; the women and children horror stricken and defenseless, abandoned their homes, and fled for safety in every direction; very many of them without the necessary articles of clothing to protect them from the pitiless storm and piercing cold to which they were exposed. Women gave birth to infants in the woods, and on the bleak bosoms of the praries, houseless and unsheltered; at that critical and trying time without any of the necessaries usual on such occasions; without their husbands, and without Physicians or midwives, or any other assistance except as they could assist each other. One hundred and twenty women and children, for ten successive days with only three or four men to aid them, concealed themselves in the recesses of the Forest, in hourly expectation of Massacre untill they found an opportunity of escaping into Clay County. The society of Latter Day Saints, after these disturbances, removed to the county of Clay, where they were kindly received by their brethren and the inhabitants, who administered to their necessities in the most charitable manner.

In the mean time, the houses of the Saints in Jackson County, which they had abandoned, numbering about two hundred, were burned down, or otherwise demolished by the mob, who destroyed at the same time much of their crops, furniture, and stock. The damage done to the property of the Saints, by the mob, in the county of Jackson, under the circumstances above related, as near as they can ascertain would amount to the sum of one hundred and twenty thousand Dollars. The number of Latter Day Saints thus disfranchised, and driven from their houses and homes in the county of Jackson amounted to about twelve hundred souls. For the property thus destroyed no remuneration has been made. After the expulsion of the Saints from the county of Jackson in the manner above stated, they moved to and settled in the county of Clay. They there purchased farms from some of the citizens, and entered other lands at the land office—wild lands offered for sale by the general Government. The most of them again became freeholders, owning each an eighty-acre tract or more of land. The society now lived peaceably in the county of Clay for about three years, and during all that time increased gradually in numbers by emigration, and in wealth by their industry and diligent attention in their several occupations. After they had resided in that County for the time above mentioned the citizens not connected with their society began to look upon them with suspicion and alarm. Reports were again circulated against them; public meetings were held in the counties of Clay and Jackson, at which violent resolutions were passed against their people, and rumors of mobs began again to spread alarm and dismay among the unoffending saints. At this critical juncture, the saints being desirous of avoiding if possible further conflict with their neighbours and fellow citizens; and anxious to preserve the peace and harmony of the society around them, as well as their own safety; deputed a committee of their leading men to propose terms of peace. An interview took place between them and a committee of citizens not connected with their society; at which it was agreed that the Mormons should leave the county of Clay, and that the citizens of Clay County should purchase their lands. These terms were complied with, and the Saints now removed to, and took up their abode in the county of Caldwell, where they once more reorganized a settlement; but not without very heavy pecuniary losses, and other inconveniences, as the citizens of Clay County never paid them for their lands, with the exception of a very small part of the purchase money to some, while others have not as yet and perhaps never will receive a single farthing. the Saints by this removal, sacrificed much of money and of feeling; but the sacrifice was made upon the altar of duty as Christians, rather than again to afford a pretext for the disturbance of the peace of the community.

Your Memorialists would humbly beg leave here, to give what they believe to be a just, and unvarnished explanation of the causes, which have led to the bitter prejudices, and persecutions against their society as above related; without malice, and without exageration; with the christian desire of rendering fair and impartial justice to all concerned. That there have been some unworthy members among them, they will not deny: but they aver at the same time, that taken as a community, they have been, and are, as moral, as upright, and as observant of the laws of God, and of the land as any body of people in the world, of the same number. Why then this prejudice, and never ending persecution? An answer may readily be found in the following considerations, viz, That they are a body of people distinct from their fellow-citizens in religious opinions, and being most of them from the East, their habits and associations are very dissimilar from those in the West, and withall being sufficiently numerous to make their political and moral power a matter of anxiety and dread to the political and religious parties by which they were surrounded; which prejudice arose, not from what the Saints had done, but from the fear of what they might do, if they should see proper to exercise this power.

In addition to this, the Saints had either purchased of the settlers, the General Government, or held by pre-emption, what were regarded the best lands in that region of the country. The tide of speculation during this period of time ran high; and the cupidity of many was thus unlawfully aroused to possess themselves of these lands and add to their wealth by driving the Saints from the country and taking forcible possession of them; or constraining them to sell, through fear and coercion, at prices merely nominal, and of their own fixing.

After the removal of the Latter Day saints from Clay county, they settled in the county of Caldwell. Your memorialists do not deem it necessary for their purpose to detail the history of the progress of the settlement and anxieties of the Saints from the time they settled in Caldwell county, in the year 1836, untill the fall of the year 1838. They would, however, aver that during all that time they deported themselves as good citizens, obeying the laws of the land, and performing the moral and religious duties enjoined by their faith. That there may have been some faithless ones among them, is very possible; nay, they will not deny but there may have been some who were a scandal to their brethren. But what society, your memorialists would ask, has not some unworthy members in it? Where is the sect, religious, moral, or political—where the community, in which there cannot be found some of its members who trample under foot both the laws of God and of their fellow-man? They sincerely believe that the community of Latter Day Saints have as few such persons as any other association, religious moral or political. Within the above last mentioned period, and under all their difficulties, the Saints continued to increase in wealth and in numbers, untill in the fall of the year 1838 they numbered, as near as they can estimate, about 15,000 souls.

They now held, by purchases from the Government, of the settlers, and by pre-emption, almost all the lands in the county of Caldwell, and a portion of the lands in Davis and Carroll counties. The county of caldwell was settled almost entirely by Latter Day Saints, and they were rapidly filling up the counties of Davies and Carroll. When they first commenced settling in those counties, there were but few settlements, and the lands were for the most part wild and uncultivated. In the fall of 1838, large well improved farms had been made and stocked; lands had risen in value, and, in some instances, had been sold for from $10 to $25 per acre. The improvement and settlement had been such, that it was a common remark that the county of Caldwell would soon be the wealthiest in the state. Thus stood the affairs of the society in the fall of 1838, when the storm of persecution again commenced and raged over their devoted heads. The mob again commenced its devastation, and drove the Saints forth, houseless, homeless, and penniless, upon the charities of the world. This last persecution had its origin at an election which was held in the county of Davis, on the first Monday in August 1838. A Latter Day Saint went to the polls to vote, when one of the mob standing by opposed his voting, contending that a mormon had no more right to vote than a Negro. One angry word brought on another, untill, unfortunately, blows ensued. They are happy, nevertheless, to state that the Latter Day Saint was not the agressor, having acted, as they believe, entirely on the defensive. Others joined in the assault (not one or two, but many) against the Latter Day Saint. His brethren, seeing him thus assailed by numbers, and exposed to great bodily injury interfered to rescue him from this perilous situation;

when others of the mob joined in the affray, being determined, as they said, that the Mormons should not vote. Victory, in this instance, decided on the side of right. Rumor reached the Saints of Caldwell county the next day, that two of their brethren had been Killed in this affray and that a refusal had been made to surrender their bodies for burial. Not knowing at the time that this rumor was without foundation, much excitement prevailed; and several of the Saints started for Davis county with a view of finding, if possible, for their brethren, whom they supposed to have been murdered, a decent burial. They arrived next morning among the citizens, and found great excitement prevailing. They had held a public meeting and resolved to drive all the Mormons from the county. Individuals began again to threaten the Mormons as a body, and to swear that they should all leave the county in three days. The Saints also heard that a large mob was collecting against them, headed by Adam Black, one of the Judges of the county court of Davis county. Under these circumstances, and with a view to allay this excitement, some of the brethren called on Judge Black, and enquired whether the report they had heard was true. Upon his denying the truth of it, they requested him to give that denial in writing, which he freely did; which writing they published, with a view to calm the public mind, and to allay the existing excitement. Having done this, they rested in quiet for some time, hoping these efforts would produce the desired effect. Their surprise, under these circumstances, can be easily imagined, when a short time after this they learned that this same Judge Black had gone before Judge King and made affidavit that he was forced to sign that instrument by an armed band of Mormons and thereupon procured a warrant for the apprehension of Joseph Smith, Junr., and Lyman Wight, which was placed in the hands of the Sheriff to be executed. It was also reported that the accused individuals had refused to be taken, and that an armed party of citizens was collecting to come and take them by force. Your memorialists aver that the Sheriff had never made any effort either to take them or sereve the process; and that Smith and Wight, so far from opposing resistance, did not know that a writ had been issued against them untill they learned that such was the case by the reports above related. In the mean time, the rumour had spread over the whole country that the mormons were compelling individuals to sign certain instruments in writing, that they (the Mormons) were not resisting the process of the law. The public mind had now become much inflamed; and the mob began to collect from all quarters, and in large numbers, with the pretext of assisting the Sheriff to execute the process.¶

And let it be here observed, in passing, that Judge Adam Black had before that time sold the improvements and pre-emption claim on which he then resided to the Latter Day Saints, and had received his pay for the same; that through his instrumentality the Saints were broken up and driven off; and that he now unlawfully retains both their money and improvements. As soon as the report of their intended resistance reached Smith & Wight, they determined immediately to go to the judge who issued the warrant against them, and before the mob proceeded to extremities, submit to the law. They both surrendered themselves, accordingly, to Judge King, who had issued the process: underwent a trial; and no just cause of accusation could be found against them. They hoped that this voluntary submission of theirs to the law, and their successful vindication of themselves against the charges prefferred against them, would allay the excitement of the community. But not so. The long desired opportunity had arrived for consummating the extermination of the Latter Day Saints, or their expulsion from the country, by giving to their persecutions the color and form of legal proceedings; and it could not be forborne. The mobs which had assembled with the pretext of assisting the officers of the law in the execution of their duty, did not disperse after the trial of Smith and Wight, as was expected; but continued embodied in their encampments in the form of a military force, and committing from time to time, one depredation after another upon the property of the Latter Day Saints. The Saints in this extremity appealed to the laws of the land, and to the officers of the law, for protection against their infractions. After much delay, the militia under Generals Atchison, Donaphon, and Parks, were sent to their relief. They arrived on the 13th of September, and encamped between the mob and the Latter Day Saints. These officers made no attempt to disperse the mob, and excused themselves by saying "that the sympathies of their men were in their favor." After remaining in this situation for several days, these officers at length adopted the following expedient of settling the existing difficulties and restoring peace. They mustered the mob, and enrolled them with their troops, and then disbanded the whole together, with orders to return to their several homes. The officers then returned home, with the exception of General Parks, who remained for their protection with his men. The Saints then made an agreement with the citizens of Davis county to buy out their lands and pre-emption rights, and appointed a committee to make the purchases, with instructions to buy untill they purchased to the amount of $25,000. While these purchases were making, some of the settlers were heard to say, "that, as soon as they had sold out to the mormons and received their pay, they would drive them off and keep both land and money." The mob, when disbanded by the generals in Davis county as aforesaid, instead of repairing to their homes as commanded, proceeded in a body to the adjoining county of Carroll, and encamped around a village of the Latter Day Saints called Dewitt. They sent to the county of Jackson and procured a piece of cannon, and invested the village so closely that no person could leave the town in safety: when they did so, they were fired upon by the mob. The horses of the Saints were taken; their cattle and hogs either Killed, or taken and driven away; and the citizens of the village, amounting to about seventy families, reduced to the greatest extremities by sickness and a want of the necessary supplies of food to support exhausted nature.

Thus situated, they applied to Governor Boggs for protection and relief; but neither protection nor relief came. Being thus abandoned to their fate by the executive authority, no alternative was left them but to seek protection by flight, and the abandonment of their homes and houses to the ravages of a mob. Accordingly, on the evening of the 11th of October, 1838, the invested families fled from Dewitt, and made their way to the counties of Davis and Caldwell, leaving many of their effects behind them, in the possession of their besiegers.

Your memorialists will not undertake to draw a picture of the horrors and sufferings of that flight, when shared alike by women and children, as well as men. Let a case or two suffice. One lady, who had given birth to an infant just before the flight commenced, died on the road, and was buried without a coffin; many others were sick from starvation and fatigue, and, being deprived of medical aid and sustenance, died on the road. The remnant of this little band of sufferers arrived in Davis and Caldwell counties at length, and found temporary relief from their troubles among their friends and brethren in these counties; but it was of short duration. After the abandonment of Dewitt, and the flight of the Saints from Carroll county, one Asahel Woods addressed the mob, and advised them to take their cannon and march to the county of Davis, and drive the mormons also from that county, and seize upon their property and lands; saying, by way of encouragement, that the mormons could get no benefit of the law, as they had recently seen that no attention had been paid to their application for protection. They then commenced their march from Carroll to Davis County with their cannon. On their way they seized two of the Latter Day Saints, made them ride on the cannon, and taunted them as they went along with their threats, "that they were going to drive the Mormons from Davis to Caldwell, and from Caldwell to Hell; and that they should find no quarters but at the cannon's mouth." The mob at this time was reported to number about 400 strong. The Saints, in their distresses in pursuance of the laws of Missouri, made application to Judge King, the circuit judge of that circuit, for protection, and for the aid of the officers of the law to protect the magistracy in performance of their duty. Judge King, as they have been informed and believe, made a requisition on Major General Atchison to call out the militia to protect the mormons against the mob. General Atchison thereupon issued orders to Brigadier Generals Parks and

Donaphon. In pursuance of these orders, issued on the 18th of October, 1838, General Donaphon arrived at "Far West," a village of the Latter Day Saints in the county of Caldwell, with a small detachment of militia. After he had been at "Far West" two days only, he disbanded his troops, alleging to the Saints, as his reason for so doing, that his men had feelings in common with the mob, and that he could not rely upon them. In a short time afterwards, General Parks arrived at "Far West"; and also disbanded his detachment. During this period, the mob was slowly making its way from Carroll to Davis county. General Donaphon, while at "Far West," directed the Latter Day Saints to raise a company to protect themselves, telling them that one Cornelius Gilliam was raising a mob to destroy their town; and advised them to place outguards to watch the movements of the mob. He also directed them to raise a company of Latter Day Saints, and send them to Davis county, to aid their brethren there against the like depredations, as a mob was marching down upon them from Carroll county. This the Saints did. They had mustered a company of about sixty men, who had proceeded to Diahman, when General Parks arrived at "Far West," as aforesaid. Having learned that General Donaphon had disbanded his men, he (General Parks) expressed great dissatisfaction that he should have done so. The evening on which General Parks disbanded his men, as before related, he proceeded to Diahman in order to learn what the mob were doing, and; if possible, to protect the Saints. When General Parks arrived in Davis county, he found that the mob had already commenced their work of destruction, which was on the 20th of October, 1838. They commenced by burning the house of a man who had gone to Tennessee on business, and left his wife at home with two small children. When the house was burned down, the wife sought refuge with her children in the hay-mow, and had to walk three miles before she could find a shelter. She carried her two children all that distance, and had to wade Grand River, which was at that time about three feet deep. The mob on the same evening, burnt seven other houses and destroyed all the property of the saints that came in their way. The next morning, Colonel Lyman Wight, an officer of the militia, and a member of the society, inquired of General Parks what was to be done, as he now saw the course the mob was determined to pursue. General Parks replied, that he (Wight) should take a company of men, and, if necessary, give the mob battle, and that he would be responsible for the consequences; saying, they would have no peace with the mob until they had given them a scourging.¶

On the next morning, in obedience to this order, David W. Patten, one of our officers, was dispatched with one hundred men under his command, in the direction of the mob, which was advancing from Carroll county, with orders to protect the citizens from injury, and to collect and bring into "Far West" such of the saints as were scattered through that part of the country; and that, if the mob interfered to prevent the execution of his orders, he should fight them. The company under the command of Patten was the same, in part, that had gone from "Far West," by the order of General Donaphon, to protect the citizens of Davis county. As Patten advanced in the direction of the mob, the retreated before him, leaving their cannon on the way, which fell into the hands of Patten and his men. The mob being thus dispersed, Patten returned with his company to Davis county, and in a few days afterwards came back to "Far West." It was now supposed that all difficulties were at an end, and that the saints would be suffered to rest in peace. But, contrary to this expectation, on the evening of the 23rd of October messengers arrived in "Far West" and informed the Saints that a body of armed men had made its appearance in the south part of the county; and that they were burning houses, destroying property, and threatening the mormons with death "unless they left the county the next morning by 10 o'clock, or renounced their religion." About midnight, another messenger came with news of like import. Patten again collected about sixty men, and proceeded to the scene of the disturbance, to protect, if possible, the lives and property of the Saints from the threatened destruction. On his arrival in the neighbourhood where the first ravages had been committed, he found that the mob had gone to another part of the county, and were continuing to perpetrate acts of plunder and outrage, both against the persons and property of the Saints. He marched a short distance farther, when he unexpectedly came upon the encampment of the mob. The sentinals of the mob instantly fired upon him, and killed one of his men. They continued their fire until Patten ordered a charge, when, after a few fires, the mob were dispersed and fled in all directions. But poor Patten was killed, and one of his men also fell by his side to rise no more. After this fright and the dispersion of the mob, Patten's company again returned to "Far West," but without their leader. The report of these proceedings created much excitement, and the citizens, through false and exagerated reports, were made to believe that the Saints were actually in rebellion against the laws of the country. So cruel and so unprovoked had been the persecutions against them, and those entrusted with the power of the civil and military authority having failed to exercise either for their protection, the Latter Day Saints saw no alternative but that which the law of nature gives—of self defence; and, so far, on this occassion, they exerted it.¶

About this time, the Governor of the State issued the <u>bloody</u> order to General Clark to raise several thousand men, "<u>to march them against the Mormons and drive them from the State, or exterminate them.</u>" Major General Lucas and Brigadier General Wilson collected three or four thousand men, and, with this formidable force, commenced their march against the Mormons, and arrived at "Far West" without molestation, and without seeing an enemy on the way. In their rear marched General Clark with the residue of the army. The Saints were taken by surprise, not having heard of these immense warlike preparations until the enemy was upon them, and, so far from expecting an armed force acting under the State authority against them, they still had hoped that the Governor would, in pity, send a sufficient force in time to protect their lives and property from the ravages of the mob. When this formidable army first made its appearance upon their borders, the Saints, intent on peace, sent a white flag several miles in advance of their village to meet them, to ascertain for what purpose so large an armed force was marching against them, and what the saints were to expect under such appalling circumstances. They gave us no satisfactory answer, but continued their march, without explanation, upon our peaceful village. Immediately on their arrival at "Far West," a man came from their camp bearing a white flag, and demanded the surrender of three persons from the Mormons, before, as he said, "they massacred the rest." These persons refused to go. As soon as this messenger returned back to the camp with our answer, General Donaphon immediately marched his whole brigade upon our village in battle array. The Saints of "Far West" thereupon formed their "forlorn hope" in a line of battle, immediately in front of Donaphon's army. Donaphon, now perceiving that blows were to be received as well as given, and that the fight was no longer on one side only, first ordered a halt, and then commenced a hasty retreat. Fortunately, night came on and separated the parties without collision. On the next day, towards evening, the Saints were officially informed that the Governor had sent this immense force against them, with positive orders "either to exterminate, or drive them from the State." As soon as the Saints learned that this order had the sanction of the Governor of the State, and had been officially promulgated, they determined to make no further resistance in defence of their rights as citizens; but to submit themselves to the authorities of the State, however tyrannical and unjust the exercise of such authority might be. The commanders of the Missouri militia before "Far West" now sent a messenger into the town, requesting an interview at their encampment, with five of the principal persons among the Mormons, pledging their honor for their safe return to the brethren and families on the following morning at eight o'clock. This interview, the Saints supposed, was intended as an overture of peace; and, as a pledge of a safeconduct was given, Lyman Wight, George W. Robinson, Joseph Smith, jr. Parley Pratt, and Sidney Rigdon, started for the camp of the besiegers.

Before they arrived at the camp of the Governor's troops, under this invitation, they were surrounded on all sides by the invading army, and, by an order from General Lucas, placed under a strong guard and marched in triumph into camp; when they were told that they were "prisoners of war." A court-martial was held that night, without a hearing on the part of the delegates of the Latter Day Saints ~~fifty other prisoners of our brethren~~; and, in the absence of all testimony, these men, who had thus trusted their lives to the honor of the Governor's officers, were condemned to be shot next morning. The execution of this bloody sentence was only prevented by the manly protest of General Donaphon. He denounced the act as cold-blooded murder; and immediately withdrew his brigade from the scene where this horrible outrage was to be perpetrated. This noble stand taken by General Donaphon arrested the murder of the prisoners. It is here worthy of remark, (and we repeat it more in sorrow than in anger,) that seventeen preachers of the gospel were on this court martial; and, horrible to relate, were in favor of this merciless sentence. The next morning the prisoners were marched, under a strong guard, to Independence, the seat of justice of Jackson county, where they were detained for a week or two, and then marched to Richmond, where General Clark was encamped with his troops. Here a court of examination was held before judge King, which continued from the 11th to 28th of November; during which time these five prisoners were confined in chains, with about fifty other Mormon prisoners taken at "Far West," and were penned up in an open unfinished court house. In this mock court of enquiry the prisoners were deprived of all testimony, by an armed force stationed at the court-house; they being advised by their attorney not to attempt to bring any persons as witnesses in their behalf, as they would certainly be in danger of either losing their lives, or of being immediately driven from the county. The proceeding was, of course, ex parte, and no witnesses examined, except those against the prisoners; consisting of individuals much prejudiced against the Latter Day Saints. During this investigation, a great many questions were asked relative to our religious opinions. The conclusion of the examining court was, to commit the prisoners once more to jail, on a charge of treason against the state. They do not deem it necessary to detail their sufferings while in prison. The horrors of a gloomy dungeon for four long months, shut up in darkness, exposed to the want of every comfort, and, for much of the time, to the damp and chilling cold of winter, can better be imagined than described. In the following April the prisoners were brought from their prison, and ordered to the county of Davis, for trial. They were there formally indicted for treason, and a change of venue awarded to Boon county. The prisoners were accordingly sent, under an armed escort, to the county of Boon, and, while on their way, suffered to escape; when they fled for safety to the State of Illinois. That they were purposely suffered to escape, cannot be questioned. The truth is, that many of their persecutors, of whom the Governor was most conspicuous at this time, had become ashamed of their conduct against the Latter Day Saints, and resorted to this subterfuge as the best means of getting out of the scrape, by giving the prisoners this opportunity to escape. Is not this fact evidence of the innocence of the Saints, and of the guilt of their accusers and persecutors? But, to return to the military operations of General Lucas before the town of "Far West:" we need only say, that the exterminating order of Governor Boggs was carried into full effect.¶

Immediately after the abovenamed individuals were taken and treated as prisoners of war, all the Saints in "Far West," above five hundred in number, surrendered up their arms to the invaders without further resistance. The Saints now fled in all directions; women and children marked their footsteps on the frozen ground with blood, (it being dead of winter,) as they fled from the State of Missouri, and from the merciless hands of their pursuers. The order of the Governor admitted of no discretion; and all were driven from the State who were not destroyed. Fifteen thousand souls, between the time of the sacking of "Far West" and the following spring, abandoned their homes and property, and fled in terror from the country. The Saints, being thus broken up and ruined, in want of every necessary of life, and with broken and bleeding hearts, sought refuge in the State of Illinois, where most of them now reside. Your memorialists will not trespass further upon your time, by the relation of individual cases of suffering and distress. They would fill volumes; and many of the pages would be stained with the blood of innocent women and children. But what shall they say of the conduct of many of the Missouri militia? Alas! what can be said in extenuation when Humnanity would shudder and hide herself in shame, if one half only of the house burnings, destruction of property, robbery, rapes, and murders, should be told. One instance, only, will they mention, of the many trying scenes of blood and rapine that were then and there transacted. Two hundred of the Governor's militia came suddenly on some families of the saints emigrating to the State of Missouri, who had not yet reached the body of the Society, and were encamped at Haun's-mill, in Caldwell county. The Saints took refuge in an old log house which had been used as a blacksmith shop[.] On seeing the milita approach, they cried for quarter; but in vain. They were instantly fired upon, when eighteen of thei[r] number fell dead upon the spot. Their murderers then advanc[ed] and putting the muzzles of their guns between the logs, fired indiscriminately upon men and children, the living, the dying, and the dead. One little boy, whose father (Warren Smith) had just been killed, cried pitieously to the militia to spare his life. The reply was,

"kill him," "kill him" (with an oath,) "he is the son of a damned Mormon."
He was accordingly shot in the head, and fell dead by the side of his father.
Just before this little boy was shot, an old man by the name of McBride,
a soldier of the Revolution, hearing his cries for mercy, came up and
begged them to spare his life; but, instead of listening to his entreaties,
they hewed him to pieces with an old scythe. They then loaded themselves
with plund[er] and departed from this appalling scene of blood and
carnage[.] Your memorialists have thus, in discharge of the duty confided
to them by their brethren, given a brief outline of the history of their
wrongs and persecutions in missouri; all which they can prove, and aver
to be true. The Latter Day Saints have not provoked these outrages. They
have not either as a body or as individuals, knowingly, violated the laws
of Missouri or of the United States. Their only offence consists of a
difference of religious sentiment; and that they have sometimes, but rarely,
resorted to the laws of self defence. The above statements will show that
the Latter Day Saints have, on all occasions, submitted to the law of the
land, and yielded obedience to its authority in every instance, and often at
the hazard of both life and property

Whenever they have offered resistance to the mob, it was only in self
defence; and not even then, without the authority and sanction of the
officers of the law. And what are the wrongs of which they complain? The
Latter Day Saints, numbering fifteen thousand souls, have been driven
from their homes in Missouri; property to the amount of two millions of
dollars has been taken from them or destroyed; some of their brethren have
been murdered, some wounded, and others beaten with stripes; the chastity
of their wives and daughters inhumanly violated; all driven forth as
wanderers; and many, very many, broken-hearted and penniless. The loss
of property they do not so much deplore, as the mental and bodily
sufferings to which they have been subjected; and, thus far, without
redress. They are human beings, possessed of human feelings and human
sympathies. Their agony of soul for their suffering women and children
was the bitterest drop in the cup of their sorrows.

For these wrongs and sufferings, the Latter Day Saints, as American
citizens, ask, Is there no redress? If so, how and where shall they seek and
obtain it? The constitution you are sworn to support alike guaranties to
every citizen, the humblest in society, the enjoyment of life, liberty, and
property. It promises to all religious freedom; the right to all of worshipping Almighty God, beneath their own vine and fig tree, according to the
dictates of their own consciences. It guaranties alike to all the citizens of
the several States, the right to become citizens of any one of the States,
and to enjoy, upon their removal, all the rights and immunities of the
citizens of the State of their adoption. Yet all these rights and immunities

the Saints have been deprived of. They have, without just cause, without the form of trial, been deprived of life, liberty, and property. They have been persecuted from place to place for their religious opinions; they have been driven from the State of Missouri at the point of the bayonet, and treated worse than a foreign enemy; they have been beaten with stripes as slaves, and threatened with destruction if they should ever venture to return. Those who should have protected them, have become their most relentless persecutors. And what are the Saints to do? It is the theory of our constitution and laws, that, for the violation of every legal right; there is provided a legal remedy. What, then, we would respectfully ask, is the remedy for these violations of right in the persons and property of the Latter Day Saints? Shall they apply to the Legislature of the State of Missouri for redress? They have done so. They have petitioned; and their petitions have been treated with silence and contempt. Shall they apply to the Federal courts in Missouri? They are not permitted to go there; and their juries would be made up of citizens of that State, with all their prejudices against them. But, if they could apply to the courts of Missouri, whom shall they sue? The final order for their expulsion and extermination, it is true, was issued by the Executive of the State. But is he amenable? and, if so, is he not wholly irresponsible, so far as indemnity is concerned? Will not the great mass of our persecutors justify themselves under that order? For ourselves we see no redress, unless it be awarded by the Congress of the United States. And here we make our appeal, as American citizens, as Christians, and as men, believing that the high sense of justice which exists in your honourable bodies will not allow such oppression to be practised upon any portion of the citizens of this vast republic with impunity; but that some measure which your wisdom may dictate may be taken, so that the great body of people who have been thus abused may have redress for the wrongs which they have suffered. And to your decision they look with confidence; hoping it may be such as shall tend to dry up the tear of the widow and orphan, and again place in situations of peace those who have been driven from their homes, and have had to wade through scenes of sorrow and distress.

And your memorialists, as in duty bound, will ever pray &c., &c.

Jany. 10, 1842

Elias Higbee
John Taylor
Elias Smith

[*Not sworn.*]

Chapter 6

Individual Affidavits from the National Archives

A—L

ABBOTT, Lewis

This may go to certify that I moved from Wayland Mass. 1832 to Jackson Co. Missouria. there I perchesd 80 acres of land I remained there untill the mob had driven the largest half of our sosiety out of the Co. where then I was attacked by a company of 40 mobers well armed under the command of Rev Isaac McCoy an Indian Missionary they threaten my life with much violence but left me on condition I would leave the County. Accordingly I move into Clay Co. ~~following~~ 1833. in 1834 I had business to transact with Mr. Dunlap an Indian agent among the Delawers I crost the Missouria River over on to the bank of the Caw River and on my return being disappointed of a Boat I was oblidge to retreat back 7 miles and crose the caw River and pass through the west part of Jackson Co. While I was traveling a few miles from my old place I was discoved by a young man who cared the news into the settlement that there was a mormon on the Pririe four of the men immediately mounted there Horses armd with Clubs they followed me I seeing no possible chance to make my escape I turned to them and plad for mercy a man by the name of Cantral being head one he nocked me down with his club and cut a larg hole in my head the others rode over me and beat me in the most cruel manner I says to Cantral how can it be possible you wish to spill my blood I asked him if I had not always used him as a Neighbor and a friend his answer was I and Jo Smith and all his followers ought to go to Hell likewise he said he had 400 men under his command who were sworn to put every Mormon to death that come within there reach and that I [never] should go a way alive. but as kind providence would have it I was inable to return to my home. The nex year following in August 183[5] I made an attempt to go to Jackson Co on special business old Cantral and Cammil and others leadings mobbers being dead and other having moved I was in hopes of being treated with more humanity but in that I was disappointed after I had crosed the River and traveled a few miles I was met by a man by the name of Linvil who accused me of being a Mormon. I did not deny the charge. After I had traveled about a mile further Linvil overtook me with a number of others they nocked me dow and beat me as they supposed near unto death. but through the mercy of the Lord I was once more enable to return to my family I removed from Clay Co. to what is now Colwald in 1836. There I remaind untill we was driven out by the State mob.

I further testify that I never had eny dispute or misunderstanding with eny Cityerson in Jacson Clay or Colwald Co. to my knowledg In Jacson Co I had 30 Acres under cultivation with Crops of Wheat and Corn which was mostly distroyed by the mob I yet own land there but should not dare to go upon it at the exspence of my life ~~for~~ In Colweld Co I purches'd 50 Acres of land which I paid $150 for that with my House and improvements all that I got for them was 45 dol those sacrifises with many other losses together with mooving out of the State. and being beat at too different times near unto death. All occasioned by a lawles mob without eny provication to my knowledg

I think the State had ought to pay me for my loss $1,500 at least and for my damage a great sum, as money would not hire me to pass through the same scenes again I do hereby certify that the foregoing be true according to the best of my knowledg

Lewis Abbott

[Sworn to before C. M. Woods, C.C.C., Adams Co., IL, 25 Jun 1839.]

ABBOT, Rufus

Handcock Co Ill.

I doe here by testify that while I lived in Jackson Co State of Missouri in 1833 A mob arose ~~in~~ and destroyed our property threatend our lives and whipt and beat a numbers of our people and run us from the county[.] and in clay co I was thretend anumbr of t[i]mes with distruction, and they barbarously murdred my son at Hons mill and drove me from my house and land, and compeld me to leave the state in 1839, this I certefy in the fear of God

Rufus Abbot

[Sworn to before A. Monroe, J.P., Hancock Co., IL, 6 Jan 1840.]

ADAMS, David W.[1]
LEFFINGWELL, William

Pittsfield Jan 22nd 1840

This may Certify that I David W Adams Born in the State of Connecticut and now residing in the State of Illenois that in the fall of the year 1838 remooved to the State of Misourie with my familly Consisting of eight where I had friends and after I go[t] allmost to my journeys end I was anticipating that I should soon embrace the Society of my friends. I was compelld to return back and seek shelter for myself an family the best way I could in the month of December, where I was obligd to sleep with my family in my waggon untill I could build me a house to live in after being deprived of Citizenship and suffering with the inclemency of the weather & the lofs of property I claim damage of the Missourians to the Amount of Four Hundred dollars

David W Adams

Sir please hand thiss over to Joseph Smith & you will oblige your servants

Hon R. M. Yong

David W Adams
Wm. Leffingwell

[*Sworn to before W. H. Boling, C.C.C.C., Pike Co., IL, 22 Jan 1840.*]

ALDRICH, William

Hancock Co Ill. January 6th 1840

This May Cirtefy that In the Month of Sept. AD. 1837 I left Ohio with My Family for upper Mo. We arived in Caldwell Co. Mo in Nov. AD 1837. thence Moved to Daviess Co. Bought an Improvement on a quarter Section Located Myself Dec. 1837 Where I Remained A Citizen untill the fall of AD. 1838 When I was frequently Interrupted By [——] and thretened By armed fourses of men gathered or they sed to Drove us from the Co.

Some time the first of Nov. AD. 1838 When we Received orders from General Wilson that we ware to leave the Co. in ten days it was sed to Be the governers orders Accordingly I left the Co., leaveing My Crops whic

---

[1] This petition was sent to Senator Richard M. Young. Young served as a senator from Illinois during the years 1837-43.

Consisted of Corn 23 acres 100 Bushel, Potatoes several tons Hay Oats and other Produce

I had on the Premesses to lay houses one stable Twenty six acres under fence in too fields under a good state of Cultivation

I also was Intitled too A Preemption on the Quarter Section, Under the act of 1838

I was als deprived of the privelege of Proveing if my Preemption being under the spetial order of General Clark which prohibited us from leaving Farwest in Caldwell Co. I do hereby Certefy that the above improvement part of which I Bought of James Ston the Remainder I made by labouring Eleven Months together with hired help I also Certefy that for the above improvement and Crops I Never have Received on Dollar and was depried the Privelege of going back to Daviess to see to my Bussness and but Compeld to leave the State which I did January AD. 1839 The loss of the Above Property I Value one thousand Dollars

For time and Expenses Moveing too and from five hundred

William Aldrich

[Sworn to before A. Monroe, J.P., Hancock Co., IL, 6 Jan 1840.]

ALEXANDER, H. M.

January 13, 1840

To the honorables Senate and House of Representatives in Congress Assembled at Washington City in the D.C.

I the undersigned by these present Reprisents To Your Honorable Body My Losses & Sufferings that I sustained from the hands of a Mob in the State of Missouri in The Year 1838 . . . and This may Certify while on a Journey To I.a. My family were Left in far west at the Time of the oppression By the Mob they were not Permitted To Leave their Homes To get Bread, and Therefore nearly Perishd for want of food &C. and further say that the Losses which I sustained of Real and personal property To be no Less than 1500 dollars, further was obliged to Leave the State to save my life and was obliged to Leave my family To suffer for about 4 Months

H. M. Alexander

[Sworn to before J. H. Randle, N.P., Madison Co., IL, 13 Jan 1840.]

ALLEN, Albern

State of Illinois Adams County January 7th 1840 SS

This day personally appeard before me Wm. Laughlin Justice of the peace within Said County Albern Allen who Duely Sworn according to Law Deposeth and Saith that he Mooved to Caldwell County Missouri 1836 I entered 2 fortys of which I gave up the Duplicates and the N. E 1/4 of S. W. 1/4 of Section 32 Township No. 56 Range 28 North of the base line and west of the 5th princepal Meridean also the NW. 1/4 of the South E 1/4 of Section 32 Township 56 Range 29 North of the base line of the 5th principal Meridian Also 80 Acres of which my Duplicate will Show Also 40 Acres I gave up my Duplicate and Cannot asertain the numbers which Land I had to leave after bieng taken prissoner and obliged to assine away My right and Compelled to leave the State by the Exterminating Decree of the Governer

Albern Allen

[*Sworn to before W. Laughlin, J.P., Adams Co., IL, 7 Jan 1840.*]

ALLEN, James D.

In the Spring of eighteen hundred and thirty eight I Settled in Randolph County Mo. bought thare 70 acres of land the numbers I do not recollect as the papers are all out of my hands but I paid for the land and had a good title but under the ordrs of the Goven[er] I had to leave the State my loss in So doing ammounted to considerable Say Four hundred Dollars

James D Allen

[*Sworn to before A. Brown, J.P., Pike Co., IL, 10 Jan 1840.*]

ALLRED, Martin C.

State of Illinois Pike County January the 18th AD 1840

A schedule of the Loss of Property time and Citizene ship and imprisonment which Martin C. Allr[ed] Sustained in Missourie By the Exterminating order of the Govenor of the State of Missourie

Taking all to gether I would not of Sufered all these things For less than one thousand Dollars the Number of Acres of Land Entered and owned By Martin C. Allred was one hundred and Twenty as My Duplicates will show or at least I have two of them which I will send you for testimony

Subscribed and Sworn Martin C. Allred

[*Sworn to before W. H. Boling, C.C.C.C., Pike Co., IL, 18 Jan 1840.*]

ALLRED, William

I William Allred and family Left the state of Tenesee & Moved to the State of Missouri in the year 1836 I then Entered in the County of Ray 353 acres of Congress Land I was then obliege to Leave my Land the Same Season the ~~Mormons~~ Church of Jesus Christ of Latterday Saints of which I was a member ware obliege to Leave the Counties of Ray & Clay & Moved to the County of Caldwell I then Entered & bought in Caldwell County 240 acres of Land Lived in peace utill the Summer of 1838 the mob there a rose & Commenced there depridations upon the inhabitants of Caldwell & there was one Continual Scene of war untill Govoner Boggs Issued an Exterminating order the Millitia was then ordered out they encampt near our town we ~~gave~~ ware obliege to give up our guns & took us prisners the Militia quartered in our town & in our houses and stabled there horses in my houses 3 in number they killed our Cattle our hogs & Sheep fed our Corn plunder our houses Stole our propety the Commanding officer Gen. Clark then Cald us together & Selected forty Seven of which I was one they Shut us upin aStorehouse untill the next morning the took us to Richmond in Ray County & Shut us up in an open Corthouse where we Suffered much in hunger & cold we ware then put on trial haveing ben Charged with evry high Crime the trial Continued about fifteen days then they Exhonerated about 23 of which I was one on acount of the order of the Govener I was obliege to Leave the State to Save my life & my family for which I was obliege to Sell part of my Land at any price they please to give. three of my Boys being on ~~were~~ Business were taken by the Militia & kept in there possesion Some few days
the part of my Land that I Sold I was obliege to give up my Duplicates

William Allred

[Sworn to before A. Brown, J.P., Pike Co., IL, 10 Jan 1840.]

ALLRED, William

September the 3rd AD.1839 State of Illinois Pike County
Of Damage sustained By Mr. Wm. Allred by the Mob of the state of Missouri and the Exterminating order of Governor Bogs it is Fourthousand Dollars at a moderate rate.

William Allred

[Sworn to before W. H. Boling, C.C.C.C., Pike Co., IL, 4 Sep 1839.]

BALLARD, Philip

State of Illinois Adams County S.S.

This day personally came before me William Laughlin a Justice of the Peace within Said County, Philip Ballard, being duly sworn Deposeth and saith That he was a Citizen of Missourie in 1834. and that I entered Land in Caldwell County Mo in 1837—and Settled on sd. Land in 1838—The land being the [SE] 1/2 of Section 18 Township 56 North of the base line Range No 27—Containing 80 acres

Philip Ballard

[Sworn to before W. Laughlin, J.P., Adams Co., IL, 7 Jan 1840.]

BARLOW, Lucinda

I hereby certify that in the fall of A. D. 1838, While Genl. Lucus was at Far West Caldwell Co. Mo. with his troops I saw some thirty or forty of the troops go to the house of Mr. Orrin Rockwell whose family was absent from home, and there plundered the house it of vegetables and furniture to the amount of two waggon load. Said Rockwell was a member of the church of Jesus Christ of Latter day saints

Commerce Ill. Jany. 2d 1840   Lucinda Barlow

[Sworn to before D. H. Wells, J.P., Hancock Co., IL, 2 Jan 1840.]

BENNOR, Maviah

This is to certify to the Barbarous Acts of A Cruel Mob Committed on a portion of our Society at Hons Mill of which I was an eye Witness

On the 30 of October 1838 all of A Suding the war whoop was heard and an armed force ameadiately hove in Sight and Comnenced firing upon men women and Children our Society Called for quarters, but none granted the women and Children that fled in every direction nearly frightened out there sensis in this awful Scene of destruction I made out to escape and after a short and Bloody Conflict the mob dispersed not leaving so much as the clothes of the Dying and wounded but littraly took their Clothes from of thir backs & boots & shoes from thire feet also most of thire hous furnitir and to prove their Savage feracity more Clearly they Also literaly took a Corn Cutter and mangled an old gentleman Revolutionary Soldire by the name of McBride Cool Blodd, 16 were killed and

417

among the Number killed was my father and two soon [*sons*] dyed of their wounds

Maviah **X** Bennor

[*Sworn to before J. Orr, J.P., Adams Co., IL, 8 Jan 1840.*]

BENSON, Jerome M.

There personally appeared before me, Samuel Comer one of the Justices of the Peace within & for the County of Hancock & state of Illinois, Jerome M. Benson, & after being duly sworn according to law deposeth & saith that on the 31st day of October A.D. 1838, he was a citizen of the state of Missouri, residing in the County of Caldwell in said state of Missouri, on my own premises viz. the South West fourth of the North East fourth of Section Number 23, Township 56 and Range 29— and on the day & Year aforesaid, & on the ten succeeding days, i. e. the first ten days of November A.D. 1838, on the premises aforesaid, certain divisions of the militia of the said state of Missouri, commanded by Generals Parks, Lucas & Clark, encamped & effected a total destruction of the following articles of property, belonging to me the said Jerome M. Benson, & for which this deponent hath received no compensation whatever—

That is to say		30 acres of Corn—valued at			$300.00
"	"	Timber for fuel	"	"	50.00
"	"	2 Corn Cribs	"	"	30.00
"	"	7 Sheep	"	"	27.00
"	"	1 Colt	"	"	25.00
"	"	1000 fence rails	"	"	20.00
"	"	1 Sword & sabbard	"	"	15.00
"	"	2 Fat Hogs	"	"	12.00
"	"	1 Stable	"	"	10.00
"	"	30 Bushels Potatoes	"	"	10.00
"	"	2 Stacks Oats	"	"	10.00
"	"	50 Barn Fowls "	"	"	6.00
"	"	1 Rifle Pistol	"	"	5.00
"	"	1 3 pail Iron Kettle	"	"	5.00
"	"	1 Chopping Axe	"	"	2.00
"	"	1 Spider & lid	"	"	1.00
					$528.00

And further this deponent saith not—

Jerome M. Benson

[Sworn to before S. Comer, J.P., Hancock Co., IL, 9 Jan 1840.]

BENSON, Mary
DUTTON, Hannah

Also there personally appeared before me, Samuel Comer one of the Justices of the Peace within & for the County of Hancock & state of Illinois Mary Benson, ~~Mary Holden~~ & Hannah Dutton, and, after being duly sworn, according to law, depose &say that they were eye-witnesses of the destruction of the articles of property belonging to Mr Jerome M. Benson, & mentioned by him in the within affidavit and at the time &place mentioned in said affidavit by him subscribed and, to the best of our knowledge said affidavit, contains a true &correct Statement of the losses sustained by Mr Jerome M. Benson in Missouri Caldwell County from the 31st day of October A.D. 1838— to the 10th day of November A.D. 1838 and effected by the agency of the Missouri Militia as stated above by Mr Benson—

Mary Benson
Hannah Dutton

[Sworn to before S. Comer, J.P., Hancock Co., IL, 9 Jan 1840.]

BENT, Samuel & Lettice

A Short time after General Clark came up to Far West We were residing Two miles from Far West, when we saw a number of the malitia at Mr Gad Yale's who lived but a short distance from us. we saw them in about the house for two days. Saw them shoot down one of his hogs, saw them take his corn and belive they destroyed about ten acres, and likewise a small stack of Hay. Saw them carrying out of Mr Yales house a quantity of Furniture. Saw them set fire to a large Hay stack belonging to Mr Moss, which was entirely consumed. Mr Yale, at the time the malitia came to his house was absent from home on a journey. We Likewise saw some of the Troops in possession of Mr Cyrus Daniel's house for several days: saw them take away Beds bedding and clothing and almost every thing of value in and about the House. We saw the troops carrying off corn from Mr

Moss's who was absent from home We hereby certify that the above statements are correct, according to our best knowledge and belief—

Samuel Bent
Lettice Bent

[*Sworn to before D. H. Wells, J.P., Hancock Co., IL, 3 Jan 1840.*]

BEST, Henry

Clifton this twelfth Day of January AD 1840
    To the Honorable the Senate and House of Representatives in Congress Assembled in the City of Washington in the Destrict of Columbia
    I hereby represent to you the Loss that I sustained and the Sufferings I underwent in the State of Misouri because of the Religion of Jesus Christ which I profess and believe I moved into the State of Misouri in the Summer of 1837 and made A preemption right and Commenced to build A House in Davis County whare the Mob Came upon me acting under the Exterminating Order of Govonor Boggs and Drove me of by the forse of Arms and threatened my Life and threw My House into the River took My Gun from Me and Ordered me out of the State on pain of Death to acomplish which I wass obliged to Sacrifise My Stock and then was met by another Mob on the publick High way My Carriage Serched and Robed of All My valuabe papers for all of which Losses and outrage I Can git no redress from the Authorities of the State of Misouri. I Clam Damages to the amount of one thousand Dollars and ask your Honorable Body to award Justice to the opressed and I shall ever pray as in Duty bound &C

Henry Best

[*Sworn to before J. H. Randle, N.P., Madison Co., IL, 13 Jan 1840.*]

BIDWELL, Betsey

State of Illinois Adams Co. Jan 8th 1840
    I Betsey Bidwell do hereby certify that when the Malitia was going to Far West I was about 4 miles from said place at Mr. Morrisses house 3 of the Melitia came there and said now we have got you and ordered us out of the house and then enquired for my husband I then attempted to tell them and one of them put his gun up to his face to take ame and swore that he would blow my brains out if I did not tell the truth they offered maney other abuses to tedious to mention

Betsey Bidwell

I do hereby certify that the above certificate of Betsy Bidwell is correct

Cathrene **X** Morriss

[Sworn to before J. Orr, J.P., Adams Co., IL, 8 Jan 1840.]

BIDWELL, Robert W.

State of Illinois County of Adams Jan 8th 1840
    I Robbert W. Bidwell do hereby certify that I was a citizen of Caldwell Co. Mo. and purchased land in said county but on account of my relegeon being a member of the Church of Jesus Christ of Latter day Saints commonly colled Mormons was compelled to sell my land to raise means to leave the State under the extermiating order of the Govener after I was taken prisoner by the Melitia I was upon the Public square in Far West one of the Melitia struck at me with a butcher knife and swore that he would cut my throat because I would not tell him my name I dodged the blow he then run for his gun I then got out of his way

Robet W Bidwell

[Sworn to before J. Orr, J.P., Adams Co., IL, 8 Jan 1840.]

BOOSINGER, George

State of Illinois Madison County
    This day personally Came before the the undersigned a Justus of the pece in and for Said County of madison George Boosinger who after being Sworn uppon his oath—Says that he did sustain certain damagees by the in habitents of Ray County in the State of missouri during the years of 1836 &—1837 & 1838 & in the fore part of the year of 1839, towit, damages by being
    on Sale of land one thousand dollars and by Sale of Stock & other property one thousand dollars, and by being Compeled to moove one hundred dollars the amount Cared out is $21,000
    Subscribed and Sworn to before me this twentieth day of January A.D. 1840

J. C. Young J.P.

George Boosinger

[Sworn to before J. C. Young, J.P., Madison Co., IL, 20 Jan 1840.]

BOYCE, Peter

I do hereby certify that at a low estimate the damages that I sustained in consequences of Gov. Bogges exterminating orders in Missourie to amount to $100.00

Peter Boyce

[*Sworn to before A. Brown, J.P., Pike Co., IL, 10 Jan 1840.*]

BOZARTH, Squire

I hereby certify that I was born in Kentucky and that I settled in the State of Missouri twenty one years ago where I became a member of the church of Jesus Christ of Latter day Saints some years ago. I continued my residence in Mo. untill I left it last spring in consequence of Governor Boggs' order and the threats of Genl. Clark and others. I know that a large body of armed troops came to Far West about the first of November A.D. 1838, and that they took possession of the town and kept a guard around it for near two weeks and it was with difficulty that I could get out past the guard to go to my family three miles off.

When the arms ware given up by order of Genl. Lucas, I had to give up two rifle guns which cost me seventy five dollars, and two pistols which cost ten dollars. I tried to get them again but did not succceed in obtaining them. A number of companies of troops were stationed in Far West whilst the town was guarded to the great annoyance of the inhabitants. I saw Capt. Bogarts Company which was stationed there burning the house logs which lay there in large quantities. When the troops left there they left the town bare as it were of every movable thing which they could burn. When the troops came to Far West I owned more than fifteen hundred acres of land in Caldwell County and the counties round about. When I sold my land which was at a great sacrifice I had to part with a number of my duplicates, for it is a custom in Missouri for people when they buy land of those who enter it to exact of them their duplicates. I know of no law in the state of Missouri or among any civilized people which would authorize such proceedings as were had by the troops against the Latter day Saints at Far West. Indeed I know that there was no law made by the legislature of the state up to that date authorizing such proceedings. The Legislature had not met for near two years previous, therefore I have had an opportunity to know. I owend one half of a saw and grist mill which I had to leave. I estimate my losses to amount to at least five thousand dollars

Squire Bozarth

[*Sworn to before D. H. Wells, J.P., Hancock Co., IL, 11 Jan 1840.*]

BRACE, Truman

<u>I hereby certify that</u> in the spring of the year A. D. 1832 I moved from the State of Ohio to the State of Missouri and became a resident in Jackson County—In the fall of the ensuing year there began to be Jealousies among the old inhabitants of the County who Soon began to collect in considerable numbers broke in the Houses of the Mormons and threatned their lives and committed a great many outrages One day as I was hauling a load of wood I saw a number of armed men on the prairies When the[y] saw me two of them came up to me. They ordered me to Stop or they would Shoot me. One of them named J Young asked me if I believed the book of Mormon; I told them that "I did" They said that I must leave the County. I told them I had neither team or means to take me and my family away. the said Young then Said he would shoot me and immediately made ready to Carry his threat into execution but the other man persuaded him not to do so. the rest of the Company then rode up I suppose there were about Fifty of them. the said <u>John</u> Young then took an axe gad which I held in my hand and commenced beating me with the same. I suppose I received about fifty strokes after breaking it he got a Raw Hide and Commenced whipping me with it he cut my Hat nearly all to pieces, while he was thus Engaged a man of the name of Jennings came behind me and struck me on the head with a Rifle which nearly knock'd me down; John Young then took an axe from me and going a few steps back threw the axe at me with great force but fortunately it did not hit me; at this time my wife and daughter seeing me thus situated came and entreated the mob to spare my life: I then went to the House and was followed by the mob they came into the House. I sat me down on ~~the~~ a chair when one of them thrust the mussle of the Gun against my neck and thrust me against the wall and then kicked me on the mouth with his foot and cut my lip. this was in my own House—the mob then commenced whipping one of my friends who was in the House of the name of [———] They then took him outside the house while they were doing this I contrived to get away and hide from them. They threatned to take my life so I was obliged to leave the County of Jackson believing my life was in danger; I removed from Jackson to Clay County after the mob had plundered my house and taken some of my property—I then moved into Caldwell County and was there during the disturbances I was taken prisener by the mob who was harrasing our people. Soon after the Malitia came up, I with most of the Citizens of Far West was Compelled to sign

a deed of trust, by order of Generals Clark or Lucus who likewise ordered us to leave the State. I accordingly took my leave of the State and Came to Illinois whare I have resided nearly twelve months.

During the time the Malitia were in Far West I Saw them burning up House logs and saw them Shoot down Hogs and Sheep and Commit depredations on the inhabitants.

Truman Brace

[Sworn to before D. H. Wells, J.P., Hancock Co., IL, 3 Jan 1840.]

BRACKEN, James

State of Illinois Adams County SS January 7th 1840

This day before me William Laughlin a Justice of the peace for said county, personally came James Bracken who being duly sworn according to law deposeth & saith that in the year 1837 & 1838, he was a Citizen in Clinton County, Missouri & made & owned an improvement & house on Congress land in said County of Clinton, & was compelled to leave said improvent & house by orders of GeneralClark pursuant to the exterminating orders of Governor Boggs. & this Deponent further says that at & after leaving said house he suffered a loss of about one hundred barrels of corn & two cows, two yearlings & a Calf, besides different other articles: & he further states that sometime in november 1838, he heard one Richard Welding, a Citizen of Davis County Missouri, under command of Cornelius Gillam, say that he had killed four Mormons & had [——] to do it underhandedly and further this Deponent saith not.

James Bracken

[Sworn to before W. Laughlin, J.P., Adams Co., IL, 7 Jan 1840.]

BRACKEN, Levi

State of Illinois Adams County SS. Jany 7th 1840

This day personally came before me Wm. Laughlin a Justice of the peace within and for Said County—Levi Bracken who being duly sworn according to law deposeth and saith that in the year 1833 he was a citizen of Jackson Cty. State of misourie and there made an improvement on Government Land with an intention of Entering sd. Land But was compelld to leave it on or about the 1st of Nov. of the same year by orders from Col. Pitcher & others in company I then moved to clay Cty. of sd. State mosurie. I there Entered Lands as will be seen by my Duplicates.

And from this I was compelled to leave by a mob of the Citizens of Sd. Clay Cty. I Then moved to Caldwell Cty. Mo. Where I entered Government Land and occupied the Same peacably until in the fall of 1838. I was from this Compelld to leave by the Govenors exterminating Orders, executed by General Clark & others.

Levi Bracken

[Sworn to before W. Laughlin, J.P., Adams Co., IL, 7 Jan 1840.]

BRADY, Lindsey A.

State of Illinois Adams SS County January 7th 1840

This day personally appeared before me Wm. Laughlin a Justice of the peace within Said County Lindsey A Brady who being Duely Sworn according to Law Deposeth and Saith in 1837 He mooved to Missouri and entered one Eighty & forty one being the E 1/2 of the S. W. 1/4 of sextion 7 Township No. 56 Range 25 North of base line and west of the 5th principal meridian. also N. E. 1/4 of the S. W 1/4 of No. 10 Township 55 Range 29 North of the base line and West of the 5th principal Meridian also another forty in Caldwell County the number not Known in Consequence of Having to give up my Duplicate when on the highway was shot at by one & Chased by 5 and made my escape afterwards taken prissoner for One week & was Obliged to leave the state by the exterminating orders of the Governer Damage Estimated at 1000$

Lindsey A X Brady

[Sworn to before W. Laughlin, J.P., Adams Co., IL, 7 Jan 1840.]

BROWN, Alanson

This is to certify to the wrongs and Injuries that I have endurd in the State of Missouri—

in 1834 I Settled in lafaette County Built and made improvements upon Goverment land as was the Costom of the people I then planted a garden and twelve Acres of Corn I was abused and insulted by the inhabitants of the County and my life threatened until I was obliged to leave the Co. I then removed to Clay Co. I there lived untill Compeld to leave by Reason of the treaty which was made bettween our people and the Citizens because they had arisen in arms against us I then Removed to Daviess Co. and purchased, 80, Acres of Goverment land of the United States one Duplicate was taken from me by the Mob I there until the fall of 1838 under Continual threatning of my life if I did not leave the place although in the diferent Counties they repeatedly Said they had nothing against me only for my Religion and they were therefore Determined to drive me from the Country in Consequence of being Continualy harrassed by the Mob I went to Far West Caldwell Co. I was there taken prisioner by General lucas where I was kept for several days During my stay I saw much of the property of the Society Destroyed by the Militia I was then guarded home by order of Gen. Willson I was then ordered out of my house by Gen. Willson I then took my family to Caldwell Co. on my return I found my goods Strewed upon the goods and the soldiers occuping my house in Consequence of this painted armed forse under the Command of Cornelius Gilliam who were Riding through the Country and plundering every Man they Saw of his property I received this pass as it permitted So I did—

January 8th 1840   Alanson Brown

[Sworn to before J. Orr, J.P., Adams Co., IL, 8 Jan 1840.]

BROWN, Mary

State of Illenois Adams County SS
    Personally appeared before me William Laughlin a Justice of the Peace in & for said County Mary Brown being Duly Sworn according to Law Deposeth & Saith that herself with her husband moved into the State of Missouri Carroll County her husband rented a farm for one Year She further States that a boddy of armed men Came to her house (he[r] husband being sick at that time) and ordered the family to leave against the next morning or they Should Suffer the Consequence accordingly the family Departed easterly into the adjoining County and there She States that her husband Died this all happened in the fall of 1838 She States further that She left the State by the exterminating of order of Governor Boggs the Spring following further Deponent Saith not

Mary X Brown

[Sworn to before W. Laughlin, J.P., Adams Co., IL, 8 Jan 1840.]

BURGES, Horace

    This is to Certify to the injuries and Sufferings that I have received in the State of Missourie I arived in Colwel Co. with my fameley in Novem 1837 I bought me a farm and built me a house upon it in October 1838 I went with my fameley to viset my father in law in Daviss while I was in Davis my house was plundered of all that I had whilst I was in Davis General Wilsen came in to Davis, General Wilsen addressed us thus Gentlemen I have an order from the Govoner to exterminate you forthwith; I now take the the responcibilety upon my Self to give you ten days to leave this place; General Wilson gave us a passport saing, we should have protection for ten days; my lands I had to leave; all that I received would not a mount to more than forty dollars. at the same time I valued my lands at $300 dollars undder these imbarisments I had to leave the Stae; my wife was Confined while we ware journeing out of the State

Jan. 8th 1840—   Horace Burges

[Sworn to before J. Orr, J.P., Adams Co., IL, 8 Jan 1840.]

CATHCART, Daniel

State of Illenois Handcock Co
    I testify that in concequence of a mob ariseing in Davis Co. Mo. 1838 I was ablige to leave my home and move to Adam Ondi Ahman in the county a fore said and to expose my family with many others, in wet and cold, in a camp and that the Govenor refused to protect us but sent an armed force to disarm us and they came under the commnd of Col or Gen Lucas marched into our town took possession of it took our arms then let an other company come painted black under command of Cornelus Gillum take our horses abuse our men and then Sent a Strong gard with others and let them plunder our houses and camps, and that Gen. Wilson let them come, afterwards, he being sent to guard us (or the mob) he let them come and take my table furniture, and I told Gen Wilson of it but his reply was, you mus hook as mutch from some body els this I testify that they kild our cattle destroyed our Corn and ~~camped~~ quarterd in our private dwellings without our leave and drove us from the county with only 10 day [notice] and forced us to agree to leave the State, and I say it in the fear of God and that I hold a Premption claim in that county

January 4th A.D. 1840   Daniel Cathcart

    N.B. they also came into Far West in 1839 threatend our lives chased us with knives and forced us from the state witness my hand and Seal

                                                                          D Cathcart

[Sworn to before A. Monroe, J.P., Hancock Co., IL, 6 Jan 1840.]

CHAMBERLIN, Lorenzo D.

Warsaw Hanck County Ill January 5th 1840

This is a list of sufferings that I sufferd in the State of Misouri By the hand of the mob I first was Driven from Jackson Co Mo from my living and all the Joys that this world affords tore Down my fences turnd in their Cattle and hogs and Destroyd my Crops took my house and Caried it of of My land on to theirs and put it up again I lived like the heathen in tents which I Robd my Beds to make the same I then had my family to take care of and Cold winter Comming on I went into Clay Co Mo and there I found some friend I was Robed of my arms 1 gun worth $15 I then Moved into Clinton Co which I had to leave in atoo months through mutch loss of propperty I then went to the village of Diahman thare I was taken prisoner and Robd of my arms one Rifle worth $12 and other arms to the amount of 4 or 5 $4.50 cents and then Compeld to leave the State of misouri in the space of four months I then took what little I had left and started for illinois whare I now am living till further orders

from the time the people of misouri first Began to use their authority[.] they have Ben not less than fifteen hundred dollars danage to me

Lorenzo D. Chamberlin

[*Sworn to before A. Monroe, J.P., Hancock Co., IL, 6 Jan 1840.*]

CHAMBERLIN, Solomon

A Bill of damage

while Suffering as a mormon so cawled in the State of Missouri from the year of december 1831 till the Spring of 1839

I Solomon Chamberlin was driven by a mob from Jackson County and from Clay County from davis County and from Caldwell County and so out of the State and my famuly with me expence in I moved from the State of Newyork with a ton and a half of house furniture which I had nearly all destroyd and wasted by mobs in the above Countys I had I suffered the loss of Seven houses [——] by mobs Some of them they burnt and two or three plantations with the crops on the ground they deprived me of and Said crops and destroyd my fences or removed them on to their own land they Stole two mares from my dore one worth $100—the other worth $75 and one mule worth $75 loss of Cattle hogs: all my farming eutentials and mutch other property by mobs I owned lands but I bought them Secont handed wich is lost nearly all I Claim 15,000$

Solomon Chamberlin

I have Seen mutch of the conduct of the mob while in the State of Missourie I have seen them the mormons drove by the mob into corn fields and hunted as though they had been wolvees and this after they had Surrenderd and given up their arms and at the same time the heads of the mob told me that they did not drive the mormons for any thing they had done but they was afraid they would become more numerous than they and they would put in mormon officers and the sooner they drove them the less they would have to drive I have seen mutch property destroyed and many horses stole and many houses burned by the mob and the malitia quarter upon us and order us out of davis County in 10 days which we had to leave in the time of the great snow storm and many suffered unto death I saw some of the mob by the name of yokeham and kentrail pull down one of the mormon houses and hawl it on to their own premises contrary to the owners mind and with out their leave

I have often had my life threatend and loaded firearms presented and been knocked down by those merceless mob and all without any provocation

Solomon Chamberlin

[Sworn to before T. Crawford, J.P., Hancock Co., IL, 6 Jan 1840.]

CHAPMAN, Amelia

Illenois Sept 30 1839 Quincy

A Bill of Damages a gainst the State of Missourie for Being Driven from the State unlawfully By a mob

first for mooveing to the State	$300.00
for loss of propperty in the State	100.00
for leavin the State	100.00

I certify the a bov a count to be Just and tru a cording to the Bes of my Knowleg

Amelia Chapman
for her husban Absent

[Not sworn.]

CHENEY, Nathan

Hancock Co State of Illenois January 3d 1840

be it known to all whome it may concern that I saw an a[r]med soldire under the command of Gen Lucas come in and encamp on our lands with out our concent in the Town of Adam ondi Ahman and to take possession our houses and took possession of our store and camped in it and Saw them take one hors from Abraham Nelson I saw them kill our stock and plunder our houses and broke open my Chest and took out clothing and plundered my beauro and took me a prisner while labouring in the field and took my Gun from me by force all this was done in the State of Missouri and County of Davis in the fall of Eighteen hundred and thirty eight thay also compell me to leave the s[t]ate and also an anarmed force of Painted men under the command of Cornelius Gillum who was a member of the Legislator of the State afore said went through the Town plundering houses and abuse the inmates of the Same and I give my name and Testimony to that which I have seen and I lie not God bearing witness of it

Nathan Cheney

[*Sworn to before A. Monroe, J.P., Hancock Co., IL, 6 Jan 1840.*]

CHENEY, Nathan

State of Illenois Handcock Co January 3d 1840
    A bill of damage sustained by loss of property in moveing into and from the state of Missouri by being driven out of the state

By moveing into the state lost	$500.00
los of property by the mob 3 Cows	75.00
loss of corops and other property	300.00
loss of time	250.00
loss by having to move out of the state and expence	61.75
Total	$1,186.75

Nathan Cheney

[*Sworn to before A. Monroe, J.P., Hancock Co., IL, 6 Jan 1840.*]

CLAUSON, Moses

    I Moses Clauson & family left the State of Newyork in the Spring of 1836 & moved to the State of Missourie the following Summer & in the month of Dec. 1836 I entered one hundred & twenty acres of Congress Land in the County of Caldwell State of Missouri I then Lived in peace untill the Summer of 1838 the mob then a rose & Commenced there deprodations uppon the in habit[s] of Caldwell & there was one Continuel Scene of war until his Excelency the Govenor of Misso[u]ri Issued an order to Exterminate the ~~Mormons~~ Church of Jesus Christ of [Lat]ter-day

Saints or driv[e] them from the State ~~we ware~~ the Militia was then ordered out to considerable amount they encampd near our town & we ware obliege to give up our guns & took us prisners of war the Militia quartered in our town & in our houses they killed our Cattle our hogs & Sheep fed our Corn plunderd our houses Stole our property ~~killed of the mormons~~ & burned up our timber & fence & our houses the General Mr Clark then Cald ~~the Mormons~~ us together & Selected forty Seven of ~~the mormons~~ us of which I was one we ware then thrust in prison in a Storehouse & kept till Morning then we ware taken to richmond the distine of about 32 miles then thrust in an open Courthouse where we Suferd with hunger & Cold we ware Charged with evry high Crime they then put us on trial & Continued to try us for about fifteen day in Succesion they then liberated about 23 & Continued to try the rest Some few days more thy then liberated five more of which I was a moung the Latter we ware ~~then~~ taken under the Militia order & tried under the Sivil Laws I was obliege to Leave the State I was obliage to Sell my Land at a Low rate haveing been obliage at Some price to raise funds to move with of which I & family Sufferd verry Severly the amount of Loss is $500.00[.] the Land that I entered Lying in Sectians 30 & 31 Township Fifty Six range twenty Eight north of the base Line & west of the fifth principle meridian

Moses Clauson

[*Sworn to before A. Brown, J.P. Pike Co., IL, 10 Jan 1840.*]

COLE, Barnet

The State of Illenois Adams County January 7th 1840

personally appeared before me William Laighlin an acting Justice of the Peace for said County Barnet Cole being Duly Sworn according to law deposeth & saith that he was a Sitizen of Jackson County Missouri in the Year of our Lord 1832–1833 that he Bot land second handed paid for it received no title in Consequence of being Driven from that County by Mob headed by Moses Wilson & Robert Jonson Deponent saith he was Called upon by three armed men in Company to go out a pace with them said they some gentleman wished to see him went with them by Compulson to where there were from forty to fifty men armed one said is this mister Cole the reply was yes by one of the three who Came to the house he was asked do you believe in the book of Mormon yes was the reply made by Deponent they then said God damn him that is enough give it to him took off the Coat and Jaccoat and laid on ten lashes and then told me I mite go holme

Depont. further states that in about five weeks after this there Came a Mob headed by Wilson & Jonson and Came into his house and gave him a second Whiping and ordered him to leave the County or it would be worse for him witness States he went into Clay County and was driven from that by a Mob Composed of the sitizens therof removed into the County of Coldwell entered there 40 acres of land in Township 55 Range 28 Section not known in Consequence of which I gave up the Duplicate further Deponent Saith not except that he left the state in Consequece Boggs exterminating order

Barnet Cole

[Sworn to before W. Laughlin, J.P., Adams Co., IL, 7 Jan 1840.]

COOMBS, Anthony

Clifton the twelfth of January A D 1840

To the Honorable the Senate and House of Representatives in Congress Assembled in the City of Washington Destrict of Columbia

I hereby represent to you My Grievances thinking it My Duty acording to the tenets of My Religion and the Laws of My God (which is not and cannot be Conterary to the Laws of the Land may our Glorious Consitution be prepetuated unimpaired and Handed Down to unborn Generations) to remove to the State of Misouri with my Bretheren I acordingly Sent up My Goods and Chattles by the Hand of A Brother which Consisted of A Chest and A set of Carpenters tools Books and Beding &c worth one Hundred Dollars also I had an Acre Lot in the City Far West Caldwell County worth one Hundred more all of which has been taken from me unlawfully by A Mob acting under the Extermiating Order of Govenor Bogs of Misouri all of which I Submit to your Honorable Body and ask that you in your Wisdom will grant Me redress and I shall ever pray as in duty bound &c

Anthony Coombs

[Sworn to before J. H. Randle, N.P., Madison Co., IL, 13 Jan 1840.]

CORKINS, L.

Handcock Co State of Illenois beit known that I testify that I moved to Jackson County and State of Missouri in the year 1832 and settled in Indipendence and in 1833 a mob arose and demolished a two story brick building belonging to our people ocupied as a dwelling hous and a Printing Office and they broke the Press and strewed the type and paper and Book work in the street and they came and surrounded my house and fastend me in with others and would not suffer us to pass out and afterwods one broke into my house I was a widow and had none to protect me from their insults and I saw one that they had tarred and featherd and we was compeld to leave the county, so I went into clay Co and in 1836 was compeld to leave there I then went to Caldwell co city of Farwest and in 1838 I saw an armed soldiere under the command of Gen. Clark marchd into the city and took our men prisners took there arms, and then selected out fifty or sixty prisners which they took to Richmond and kept them in close confinment for some weks they also took two from my house. they drove off stock, set their sentinels in my house, and burn rails. and frequently during the winter they would come in and threaten our lives and all this with out our leave and we was compeld to leave the State at the perril of our lives in 1839

L[····] Corkins

[Sworn to before A. Monroe, J.P., Hancock Co., IL, 6 Jan 1840.]

CORRILL, John

To the Honorable the Senate and House of Representatives of the United States in Congress Assembled

The petition of Your petitioner respectfully sheweth that Your petitioner emigrated to the county of Jackson in the State of Missouri with his family in the fall of AD 1831, and was then a member of the church of Christ of latter day saints (commonly called Mormons;) about the same time and subsequently many of said society also emigrated to that place, they purchased lands of the United States, built houses, erected a printing office, established a Store and made various other improvements on said land but in the summer and fall of AD 1833 the Citizens of sd County Assembled unlawfully and after much threatning they proceeded violently and with force of Arms to Demolish the printing office and damage much other property, tared & feathered and severely whiped several persons and finally Expelled said society from said county about 1200 in number after taking from them their arms 52 guns or sword & pistol which they agreed to return on their leaving the county but never have done it but proceeded to burn their houses; destroy their fences &c. &c. and with menacing threats prevented them from returning to their possessions. The most of said society removed to Clay county Mo. myself among the rest to which place many others emigrated also from the East and many of said society purchased lands of U.S. and others, built houses and made other improvements on the same; but in the summer 1836 they were unlawfully expelled from said county by many of the Citizens and not permitted to return and peacably enjoy their possessions but by and with the almost universal consent of the citizens of that section of country said society removed to a new and almost entirely unsettled section of that state which has since been organizd into the county of Caldwell, to which place also and to Davis county adjoining many others emigrated from the east, Said society purchased large quantities of land of the United States and others on which they mad extensive and permanent improvements where they remained peacably untill the fall of 1838 when, after being much perplexed and Sorely oppressed by the surrounding Citizens (untill the spirit of Christian forbearance seemingly became exhausted and seemed to give place to that of Desperation) they were expelled from the state of Missouri by the unhallowed Exterminating order of Governor Bogs executed by military force under the command of Generals Lucas, Clark and others, their arms taken from them between 500 & 800 stand, and they forced from their homes and possessions in so short a time that necessity compelled them to leave or otherwise sacrifice them to the great loss and damage of said society and with menacing threats are still prevented from returning to the peacably enjoyment of their possessions, many of said society were detained in prision for several months.

Your petitioner further testifies that he acted as Agent, and entered some 2000 acres of land lying in Caldwell county for, and took Duplicates in the names of Josph Smith Jun, Hirum Smith & Oliver Cowdery, and that the Duplicates for said land were deposited in the office of the Clerk of the county court of Caldwell.

Your petitioner further testifies that he owned land in Caldwell which he was of necessity compelled to sacrifice as well as other property in all as nearly as he can estimate to the amount of $2000—

And further your petitioner is of the opinion and firmly believes that no redress or remuneration can be obtained by the sufferer unless it by gra[n]ted by, or obtain through the intervention of the Sovreignty and General Government of the U.S. Therefor Your petitioner humbly requests Your Honorable body to take this unhappy affair into consideration, cause it to be carefully and thoroughly investigated, restore the unhappy sufferers to and protect them in all their rights of Citizenship, remunerate their losses and properly chastise the guilty and as in duty bound your petitioner will ever pray

Quincy Jan 9 1840   John Corrill

[*Sworn to before C. M. Woods, C.C.C., Adams Co., IL, 10 Jan 1840.*]

CRENSHAW, David

State of Illenois Adams County SS. January 7th 1840
   This day personally appeard before me Wm. Laughlin a Justice of the peace within Said Cty. David Crenshaw who was Duely Sworn according to Law Deposeth and saith In 1839 I was on my way to Far west Got as far as Chariton river Missouri. I returned back in Consequence of a mob In Caldwell, they would not suffer me to remain whire I was in Consequence of my being a mormon & I was told by the Citizens of Chariton Co. that I should leave there or be Killed and in Consequence of the Governers Exterminateing Decree was obliged to Leave the State by Suffering a Considerable Loss.

David **X** Crenshaw

[Sworn to before W. Laughlin, J.P., Adams Co., IL, 7 Jan 1840.]

CRISMON, Charles

   State of Illinois Scott County SS. Charles Chrissman ~~being~~ of Lawfull age being Sworn deposeth &Saith, that himself and family are members of the Church of ~~Christ~~ Jesus Christ Called the "Latter day Saints" and that he is a resident of the State of Missouri, County of Caldwell & City of Far West. & that on or about the Last day of October 1838 or the first day of November in the same year, Himself and family were alarmed alittle before the setting of the sun by the appearance of ~~an armed about~~ several thousand armed men who marched within the Incorporated limits of Said City of Far West aforesaid, & himself ~~& Family~~ was taken a Prisioner of War & after receiving many insults by the Soldiers, was forced to leave the State forthwith with his family greatly to his damage &injury

Charles Crismon

[Sworn to before L. Harlan, C.C.C., Scott Co., IL, 1 Jan 1840.]

CURTIS, Lyman

Warsaw Handcock Co Illenois
   This may Certify that I Lyman Curtis was at Farwest when the mormons Capitulated to the troop of Missouri they took my arms which they took to Richmond thirty miles which only Received on condition of paying Sixty two Cents and Swearing that I would leave the State after Sacrifying the most of my property left the State my wife being in delicate

State of health I arrived in Illinois where I had a Son born Who was taken with fits and Soon died which no doubt was occasioned by the hardship of moving in the midst of winter

While on my farm the Militia Surround my house they said to take me prisioner but I not being at home they Loaded their horses with Sauce and left the plantation

Lyman Curtis

[*Sworn to before A. Monroe, J.P., Hancock Co., IL, 6 Jan 1840.*]

CURTIS, Nahum

Handcock Co and State of Illinois

This may Certify that I Nahum Curtis moved to the State of Missouri in the year 1836 I purchased a farm and resided thereon untill the Autum of 1838 when the troubles came on between the Inhabitants and the Mormons I went to Farwest—my farm and family was ten miles from Farwest there I was Surrounded by those that cald themselves militia compeld to Sign away my property give up my arms and compeld to leave the State in the Spring my gun I got Afterwards by paying Sixteytwo Cents and Compeld to Swear that I leave the State immediately My arms was almost ruined by rust and bad usage the destruction of Property while the troops lay in Farwest was great they Killd Cattle hogs and Sheep and wasted and usd large quantity of corn and after the Troops left the Camp ground they left a large quantity of meat Some burnt Some momock over So it was not fit for use—I was obliged to Sell at great disavantage and leave the State in the winter to the great injury of my health and family— the militia took from me one horse which I never got

Nahum Curtis

[*Sworn to before A. Monroe, J.P., Hancock Co., IL, 6 Jan 1840.*]

CURTIS, Percy

The State of Illenois Adams County SS

Personally appeared before me William Laughlin a Justice of the Peace of said County Purcy Curtis Being Duly Sworn according to Law Deposeth & saith that She moved into the state of Missouri in the month Sept. 1838 Settled in Coldwell County Depont Saith that She lost her husband on the road to Missouri and remained a widow while in that State was Compelled to leave in march 1839 under Circumstances the most distressing in Consequence sickns being Deprived of the necessary means of Comfort being exposed to the inclemency of the weather By Governor Boggses Exterminateing order executed by General Clark & others further Deponent saith not

Percy Curtis

[*Sworn to before W. Laughlin, J.P., Adams Co., IL, 8 Jan 1840.*]

CUTLER, Alpheus

When General Clark and troops were marching to Far West in Caldwell County they stopt at crooked river A number of the troops came up to my house and Barn they took from me a number of Tons of Hay Then came a gain and broke into my stables and took therefrom two horses, they then came into my house and took possession of the same, I told them I had as many in my family as I could take care of and wished them not to come in, they said they did not care for that but rushed-in, they gave me very abusive language and treated me and my family in a very rough manner They threw down my fences and left my fields exposed to the Cattle &c. Some time after they left my house they returned again and demanded a span of Bay Horses, belonging to me. I stood by the stable at the time, I refused to let them go told them that the door was locked and I did not intend to open it that day, They then presented five or Six cock'd Rifles to my breast and told me to take my choice either to open the door so that they could get the Horses or they would take my life. I then unlock'd the Door and they went into the Stable intending to take the Horses. however on account of their rushing in with their arms and the Horses taking fright and snapping at them, they were afraid to take them and exclaimed "Damn the Horses we cannot use them if we were to take them." My son was working in the Yard. they went up to him and told him to do some thing for them, but he said that they must ask his father if they wanted him to do any thing for them, upon which they swore that they would shoot him.

I had Forty acres of land which I purchased from Goverment in Caldwell, and forty acres in Ray County which was entered in the name of another individual. The forty acres in Caldwell I was obliged to sell for Forty Eight dollars in order that I might be able to get away from the state in order to obey the Governer's order—The other forty I Sold for fifty dollars in order to pay some debts I was owing

I hereby certify that the above statements are correct according to the best my Knowledge and belief

Commerce Hancock Co Illinois Jany 2 1840   Alpheus Cutler

I certify that I was present when the Malitia Came to my Father's House and that the foregoing statements are correct according to the best of my Knowledge and belief

Thaddeus Cutler

[*Sworn to before D. H. Wells, J.P., Hancock Co., IL, 3 Jan 1840.*]

DALEY, John

The State of Illenois Adams County SS. January 7th 1840

This day personally Appeard before me Wm. Laughlin a Justice of the peace within Said County. John Daley being Duely Sworn according to Law Deposeth and Saith that In the year 1837 he entered 800 Acres Land at the Land office Lexington as will be Seen by Certain Duplicates in part accompanying this affidavid

John Daley

[*Sworn to before W. Laughlin, J.P., Adams Co., IL, 7 Jan 1840.*]

DAVIS, Daniel C.
HORMUTH, Joseph

This is to certify that I Daniel C. Davis of Lee County, Iowa Territory, do sollomly swear & declare that I am a member of the Church of Jesus Christ of latter day Saints, commonly called Mormons; that I have lived in the State of Missouri more than three years immediately preceding the month of March 1838: that I was at the City of Far-West in the fore part of Nov. 1838 at which time Gen. Lucus of Jackson County Missouri entered the City with a large army, took possession of the City, posted his Centinals to prevent any person from going out, took the armes f[ro]m the inhabitants took Joseph Smith jun., Lyman Wight, Sidney Rigdon, Hyram Smith, George W. Robinson and between forty & Sixty others whom they took to prison in Ray County: that he quatered the army on the inhabitants, fed, waisted & destroyed their corn & forrage, killed Cattle, hogs, sheep &c; burnt rails, building timber & in great quantity without any leave or liberty given by the owners of the same; that, after they had taken the armes of the inhabitants, an order was given by the geniral for all the men in the City to parade on the public square & then Surrounded them with his army and compelled the Cityzens to make to the state of Missouri a deed of trust of their lands to pay the expences of the war; that, he then read Governor Boggs exterminating order given to General Clark to drive the Mormons from the state or exterminate them. General Clark having arrived at Far-West with a large reinforcement [gave] orders for the Cityzens to parade on the public square & made a speach to them aprobating the procedings of General Lucus and declared to the Cityzens that he would not put in rigorous execution the governor's order, but through his mercy the mormons might be permited to Stay till Spring & then leave the state, & never think to ever make another crop in the State of Missouri; that General Clark Esquire quartered his troops on the inhabitants making use of their Corn, fodder, Cattle & hogs &c without leave or license; and I farther State, that in General Lucus troops I saw about two hundred men whose faces were painted black & red in the most horrid Savage Style whose voices corrisponded with their appearance. and was creditably informed that a man by the name of Cornelious Gilliam, a Senator of the State of Missouri, was their commander, which I verily believe.

Daniel C. Davis

This is to certify that I, Joseph Hormuth, am well acquainted with the above written Statements and do Solemly Swear and declare that they are verrily true; further certify that they tare down a house & burnt it for firewood; that, they entered houses, turned women & Children out of doors into the snow bare footed & they was obliged to [wrap] blankets about their feet to keep them from freezing.

Joseph Hormuth

[*Sworn to before D. W. Kilbourn, J.P., Lee Co., IA, 6 Jan 1840.*]

DECKER, Isaac

Deposition of Isaac Decker of Scott County of the State of Illinois taken on the Eighteenth day of January Eighteen hundred and forty, between the hours of ten AM and 6 P.M. at the office of N M Knapp Clerk of the County Commissioners Court of Scott County Illinois, touching the matter of the petition to Congress for relief of the Mormons or Latter day Saints as an indemnity for their Losses by the Citizens of Missouri in the year 1838.

State of Illinois Scott County

Isaac Decker, being Sworn deposeth and Saith that he is now a resident of the County of Scott & State of Illinois, of Lawful age, and that some time in the month of March A.D. Eighteen hundred and thirty Eight, he removed from the State of Ohio, to Davis County in the State of Missouri, with no other intent or purpose than to become a resident Citizen in good faith under the Laws of the Said State of Missouri, And with that intent he purchased a preemption right to Congress Land, of one Benedict Welden, for which he paid the Sum of two hundred and fifty Dollars Lawful money of the United States, in the quiet possession of which this deponent Lived until the following October, and raised on Said Land, Seven acres of Corn, a part of which Crop he gathered and a part of which he left in the field; further that he raised Garden Vegetables of Value twenty five Dollars; and this deponent further says that on or about the twenty Eighth day of October A.D. Eighteen hundred and thirty Eight, he was Surprised in the Lawful possession of his Said premises, by a mob of armed men, Citizens of the State of Missouri, and then and there Surrounded and taken prisoners by Said mob, and Compelled to Surrender his property with force and arms and Compelled to Convey to Said mob his real Estate in trust to Said Mob to defray the Expenses of their unlawful designs, And this deponent further Says that he was Compelled under the order of Governor Bogg of Missouri issued on the twenty Seventh day of October A.D. Eighteen Hundred and thirty Eight, and Communicated by General Clark at Far West on or about the First of November 1838, to leave the State of Missouri under pain of death, In Compliance with which order I he Sought refuge, berift of all my his property in the Said State of Illinois in the Month of Januray A.D. 1839. Suffering the Greatest Extremities from the almost universal prjeudice which Existed against the Sect to which I he belong Ed and further the deponent Saith not.

Isaac Decker

[*Sworn to before E. Sells, J.P., Scott Co., IA, 18 Jan 1840.*]

DEMING, David C.

State of Illinois County of Adams Jan 8th 1840

I David C. Deming do hereby certify that on the 30th Oct 1838 I was on Shoal Creek Caldwell Co. Mo. about 3 oclock P. M. cutting wood and I herd the fireing of guns on the oposite side of the stream about 15 rods from where I was cutting I looked up and beheld a company of armed men surrounding a blacksmithshop in which there was about 30 men belonging to the Church of Jesus Christ of Latter day Saints commonly called Mormons the company was fireing towards the shop one man tried to make his excape from the shop but was shot down by one of the company that was surrounding them I also see a man by the name of David Evins make his excape and as he came running by me I asked him what was going on he said our bretheren were all killed or would be the fireing lasted between

30 and 60 minutes, about 15 minutes after the company was gone I started to the place of action and as I was going by the house of Mr Hawns I foung a man dead by the name of Mr Merrick I then crossed over the stream to the shop and found seven men and one boy dead in the shop and several wounded the next day I help bury 14 of my bretheren that was killed by the said company a few days after 3 or 4 died in consequence of there wounds. On the 3 Nov after there was a company of about 30 men under command of Comstock come to the place where the murder had been committed and incamped Comstock then come to me and told me that Gen. Clark gave him orders to take all the guns that he could find among the Mormons he compelled me to give up 3 guns that belong to my bretheren that had been given me to take care of and this same company under said Comstock committed many other debredations such as taking beehives killing hogs Cattle and taking Corn &C

David C Deming

[Sworn to before J. Orr, J.P., Adams Co., IL, 8 Jan 1840.]

DUDLEY, Moses

State of Illinois Adams County ss January 7, 1840—
This day before me William Laughlin one of the Justices of the peace for said county personally came Moses Dudly who being duly sworn according to law deposeth & saith that in the year of our Lord one thousand eight hundred & thirtyseven & thirtyeight he was a citizen of Caldwell county State of Missouri, & that he made & had an improvement of about three acres of land & a good hewed log house on a Congress lot in Caldwell county state aforesaid. & that he was compelled to sign away & leave said improvement & also to leave said State of Missouri without any compensation or provocation, & this was done by the Militia under command of Generals Lucas & Wilson. and further said deponent saith not.

Moses X Dudley

[Sworn to before W. Laughlin, J.P., Adams Co., IL, 7 Jan 1840.]

DURFEE, Edmund, Jr.

I Edmund Durphy Jun. solemnly declare that sometime in October in Year of our Lord One Thousand eight Hundred And thirty eight the Militia under the command of Generals Lucas Willson & Clark took possesion of a house belonging to Uriah B Powell contrary to his wishes

like me that they the said militia burned [——] timber belonging to me
that I had moved in to the Citty Far West for a dwelling House

Edmund Durfee Jr

*[Sworn to before J. M. Campbell, C.C.C.C., McDonough Co., IL, 4 Jan
1840.]*

DURFEE, Jabis

State of Illinois County of Hancock SS

I Jabis Durfee now living in Hancock County and State aforesaid do
solemnly Swear that I moved into Davies County State of Misouri in
December in the year of 1837 and settled on the North West Quarter of
Section No eighteen in Township fifty eight North and Range—twenty
Seven West. I improved said Quarter by cultivating a portion of the soil
and building a house in which I lived also a mill. I resided on said tract of
land untill October AD. 1838 which—entitled me to a Preemtion right on
said land: according to the laws of the United States: Whereas I was
prevented from proving up said right and entering said tract of land in
consequence of an order from Governor Boggs authorising an armed force
to drive me with others from the State.

State of Illinois County of Hancock   Jabis Durfee

We do solemnly swear that Jabis Durfee whose signature appears
above was entitled to a preemption as above set forth

Perry Durfee
Gilbert Gold Smith

[Sworn to before D. H. Wells, J.P., Hancock Co., IL, 18 Jan 1840.]

DURFEE, Perry

Handcock Co State of Illenois

I do hereby testify that I moved into Jackson Co Mo in the year 1832
and settled my self lived there till 1833 when a mob arose and thretend us
from time to time but in the fall they getherd at Christian Whitmers and
shot at us (we having come to gether to save us from them as the[y] was
continually harrasing of us when they could find one by him self) they
shot at us and kild one and wounded several others and thence we was
requested to lave the county forth with, and I moved to Clay Co when a
body of men collected to gether and burnt up a house belonging to us and

I was frequently threatend, from thence I moved to Davis Co and Staid there till 38 a mob arose and notified us to leave the county and being harrast by them and my life threatend from time to time I for safety moved my Family to Far West and there I Saw an armed Soldiery come in to the town with out our liberty took us prisners searchd our houses plunderd us of what they pleasd, burnd house logs lumber shingles and ralis. also we was compeld at the point of the sword to sign a Deed of trust to defray their expences, they also came afterwards to my own house and took me prisner and caried of my property without my consent. I was prohibited from entering my preemption which I held in Davis Co—and was compeld us to leave the state and they also took Joseph Smith Junr S. Rigdon L. White and fifty or sixty others prisners, and without any tistimony caried them off and confinid them in prison and Joseph Smith Junr. they chaned and kept him with several others in Jail all winter

this 4 day of Jan AD 1840   Perry Durfee

[*Sworn to before A. Monroe, J.P., Hancock Co., IL, 6 Jan 1840.*]

DURFEE, Perry

State of Illinois County of Hancock SS

I Perry Durfee now living in Hancock County and State aforesaid do Solemnly Swear that I moved into Davies County State of Misouri in the month of December in the year 1837 and settled on the South West Quarter of Section No five in Township No fifty eight North and Range No twenty seven West. I improved said Quarter section by cultivating a portion of the soil, and building a house in which I lived. I resided on said tract of land untill October 1838 which residence entitled me to a Pre Emption right on said land according to the law of the United States. Whereas, I was prevented from proving up said Right and entering said tract of land. in consequence of an order from Governor Boggs authorising an Armed force to drive me with others from the State

State of Illinois County of Hancock   Perry Durfee

We Jabis Durfee and Gilbrt Goldsmith do slomnly swear that Perry Durfee whose signature appears above was entilled to a PreEmption as above set forth

Jabis Durfee
Gilbert Gold Smith

[*Sworn to before D. H. Wells, J.P., Hancock Co., IL, 18 Jan 1840.*]

DURFEY, James

State of Illinois County of Adams SS January 8th 1840

And Sayeth that in the month of September eighteen hundred and thirty six removed to the state of Missourie purchaseed Lands in the County of Caldwell of the united States at the Land office at Lexington state of Missourie Lived in the county of Caldwell till the first of November eighteen hundred and thirty eight when I was compeld to leave the state by order of General Lucas or Gener Clarks exterminating order and was compeld by an armd force to leave the state my life being saught for. Also, saw the sitizens of Caldwell County plundered and abused by theinhabitants of the state of Missourie fird on by an armed force several times I savd one man Shot Down exspired in ashort time also two more shot Died in a short after the one the other Died on the spot. Also, was fird on by Samuel Bogard Capttain of the Militia of the State of Missourie being in company with another man while having Corrisspondence with a boddy of armd men by a flag of truce near far West in Caldwell County, &c. And further more this Deponent sayeth not

James Durfey

[Sworn to before J. Orr, J.P., Adams Co., IL, 8 Jan 1840.]

DUTTON, David

Then personally appeared before me, Samuel Comr one of the Justices of the Peace within & for the County of Hancock &state of Illinois, David Dutton, & after being duly sworn, according to law, deposeth &saith that on the 31st day of October A.D. 1838, he was a Citizen of the state of Missouri, residing in Caldwell County on the South West fourth of the North East fourth of Section Number 23, Township 56 and Range 29, and, on the day & year aforesaid, & on the ten succeeding days i. e. the first ten days of November A.D. 1838. on the premises aforesaid certain divisions of the Missouri state Militia, Commanded by Generals Parks, Lucas & Clark, encamped & effected a total destruction of the following articles of property then belonging to me, & for which this deponent hath received no Compensation whatever,

That is to say—

"	" 16 Hogs	valued at		$40.00
"	" 5 Acres Corn	"	"	50.00
"	" 1 2-year old Heifer	"	"	10.00

"	" 300 fence Rails	"	"	6.00
"	" Timber for fuel	"	"	25.00
"	" 1 sword	"	"	3.00
"	" 30 Barn Fowls	"	"	4.00
"	" 1 Rifle Gun	"	"	15.00
"	" 1 Chopping Axe	"	"	2.00
[*Total*]				$151.00

And further this deponent saith not

David Dutton

[*Sworn to before S. Comer, J.P., Hancock Co., IL, 9 Jan 1840.*]

DUTTON, Hannah
BENSON, Mary

Also then personally appeared before me, Samuel Comer, one of the Justices of the Peace within &for the County of Hancock &state of Illinois, Mary Benson, ~~Mary Holden~~ & Hannah Dutton, and, after being duly sworn according to law, depose &say, that they were eyewitnesses of the destruction of the articles of property belonging to Mr David Dutton &mentioned by him in the within affidavit, and at the time &place mentioned in Said affidavit by him subscribed, and to the best of our Knowledge said affidavit Contains a true and correct statement of the losses sustained by Mr David Dutton in Missouri, Caldwell County from the 31st day of October A.D. 1838, to the 10th day of November A.D. 1838, and effected by the agency of the Missouri Militia as stated above by Mr Dutton

Mary Benson
Hannah Dutton

[*Sworn to before S. Comer, J.P., Hancock Co., IL, 9 Jan 1840.*]

EDWARDS, Elisha

State of Illenoise, Gregsville Pike co Jan the 10, 1840
Damage that I have received In Colwel Co Missourie In 1839 damage receivd on land $175 dollars

Buy one gun a rifle taken from me	$20.00
Of Corn and Potatoes	10.00

Beaing confind in prision in Ritchmond Ray county three weaks	100.00
For sundry articles sutch as farming utensils	15.00
Hole amount	$320.00
the Expence of Beeing Compeld to moove out of the State	100.00

Elisha Edwards

[Sworn to before W. H. Boling, C.C.C.C., Pike Co., IL, 10 Jan 1840.]

EDWARDS, Rufus

State of Ilenois Pike County January 10th 1840

Damage sustaind by being drove from my preemtion Right in the State of Masury in the [——] County of Davise $300.00

Together the losse of other property four hundred and fifty bushels of Corn 200.00

Cattle and other property 75.00

Rufus Edwards

[Sworn to before W. H. Boling, C.C.C.C., Pike Co., IL, 11 Jan 1840.]

ELLISON, Isaac

This the 27 of ~~1840~~ January 1840

I a resident of Illinois Pique County hear give and a count of my Self and famley of the Suffrige that we have born by ~~President~~ guverner bogs of mosorie to wit moved thar in the year 1837 and bought eighty acors of congress land I was driven from Colwell conty masouria and sollomly decare of by being fourst right away did [——] me three hundreD dollyars as witnis my hand anD Seald

Isaac Ellison

I being troubbled request to you releaf me and doo cirtyfy that these words are true

Isaac Ellison

I Isaac Ellison doe Salomnly Sware by the Ever living god that the above is a true bill of My Sufrages in the above case so help me god

Isaac Ellison

[Sworn to before D. R. Rogers, J.P., Pike Co., IL, 27 Jan 1840.]

ENGLISH, Lydia B.

In the year of 1832, Myself & husband William Whiting of the church of Jesus Christ of latter day saints moved to Jackson Co Missourie with the addition of eleven families more. we was greatly prospered through our industry for the first year, when insults and threats were becoming very frequent. in october the matter became alarming, a company of the old Settlers of the State met above big blue and were determined that our houses Should be thrown down at night we got the word at sun set, and gathered at different houses for Safety, leaving many alone, when at ten oclock we heard the logs begin to fall from of the buildings. at twelve they got to Peter Whitmers senior where several families had collected and not many rods from the house that we were in. their first attact was to the door and window while some mounted the house and began to throw off the roof while they were throwing stones and clubs in at every chance they could get the women who had crawled into the chamber with their children began to scream & beg for mercey while these barbarous ruffians in the shape of human beings were whipping and hounding their husbands and fathers with clubs and stones. all got from the house and made for the woods[2] as fast as possible, and frightned nearley out of their senses. We being astonished at the horrible noise scarcely knew what to do but in a moment all made for the woods as fast as their feet could carry them. I was then the mother of three children a boy two years old and a pair of twin babes but five weeks old my babes were taken by two young girls. and the boy I took and followed after, but getting sepperated I could find but one of my twins untill morning fortunately the woods was near. we sat down to listen and heard them throw the roof of my house, and chimney down. doors and windows were broken in a chair shop and chairs shared the same fate the same night I heard the roofs of ten buildings, leveled to the ground, no one was killed but some were badly hurt astonishing to think we ware driven from our homes and many were out cold frosty nights in Oct and November with nothing for a shelter but the Starry heavens. but this was not enough to satisfy their vengence. they came the next week with a large company hunting for and shooting at our men: they feeling it their duty to stand in the dfence of us their wives and [——] children, as well at as themselves, returned the fire. My husband [——] received a ball through his foot, which mangled the bones and caused him great distress and it was a great while a healing and I fear his hardships and privations was the cause of his Death which happned the next october the next day

---

[2]See fragment on the next page.

our men went to Independence to try for peace but I believe that the most they obtained was fair promises, and their guns taken from them, which they have never received to this day. the next day after their arms were delivered up the mob marched their band through our settlement enquiring for our fathers, husbands, brothers, and sons and threatning what they would do if they should find them or to us if we would not tell where they were they finally ordered us off in three days or death Should be our portion. what a time of trouble women running in every direction trying to get some one to carry them out of the reach of these deamons of human shape. my husband with many others had fled to Clay Co for their lives as they had been most severly threatned. they as soon as possible sent waggons to carry us awy

widow Lydia B English

[*The above petition is not sworn or dated. However, the following fragment is very similar to the above petition and is sworn and dated, although unsigned. The fragment may have been written at the same time as the petition.*]

woods frightend nearly out of their senses. We being astonis[h] at the horible noise scarely knew what to do but in a minit all made for the woods fast as they could get away. I give my two babes (which was but five weeks old) to two young girls which started. I took my boy two ye[ar] old and followed both did not see but one of then for three hours. Fortunately the woods was nigh, we sat do[wn] to listen I heard them throw the roof of my house an[d] chimney down doors and windows broken in peaces chair shop and chairs had the same fate. I heard the roof pulled from ten buildings that same night no one was killed but badly hurt Astonishing to think we were driven from our houses and homes many of us had to stay out coal from nights in Oct and Nov with no other Shelter than the star[y] heavens. this did not satisfy the mob for they came came the next week with a large company and fired [on] our men, which onely wanted their rights, re[turn] the fire my husband was wounded was ever afflicted with the same ~~untill~~ his death (which was next Oct) Our men went the next day to Indipendence to make peace, if poss[ib]le. Lieut. Boggs had ordered out the Malitia, and demanded their arms, promised peace and safety for three weeks and all their arms when they left the County.

Jan. 8t 1840

[*Sworn to before J. Orr, J.P., Adams Co., IL, 8 Jan 1840.*]

ETTLEMAN, Henry

State of Illinois A Dams County

I Henry Ettleman do Certify that I was Taken prisoner in november A.D 1838 in the State of missouri Caldwell County and Was Compelled to Sign a deed of trust and acknowledge the same to be my free act and Deed and was ordered by General Clark to leave the State forthwith and also was plundered and my horses taken from me by the missourians

and I also owned land the west half of the North East quarter of Section 24 Township 55 and range 29 and also the South East quarter of the north East quarter of Section 15 Township 52 range 26

Henry Ettleman

[*Sworn to before J. Orr, J.P., Adams Co., IL, 8 Jan 1840.*]

ETTLEMAN, Philip

State of illinois Adams county

I do hereby certify that I enterd a tract of land in Ray County misouri north west of southeast quarter section 17 township 52 range 26 and after living on it a while I had to leave it on account of a lawless set of men who came to me and told me that I would have to leave the state and took my horses from me with threatnings and said they would have my land within three days for a trifle

Philip Ettleman

[*Sworn to before J. Orr, J.P., Adams Co., IL, 8 Jan 1840.*]

FERRE, Lodowick H.

State of Ileanois Pike County

I, Lodowick Ferry certify that I was driven from my house and home in the State of Missouri in the winter of 1838 and 1839 out of the State. an sustained the damage of about 1000 dollars occationed by that by ordir of the Governer of said State in connection with others in the mob

Lodowick H Ferre

[*Sworn to before W. H. Boling, C.C.C.C., Pike Co., IL, 14 Jan 1840.*]

FOOT, Reuben

State of Illinois Adams County SS. January 7th 1840

This day personally appeared before me William Laughlin a Justice of the Peace within Said County—Reuben Foot who being duly sworn according to law. Deposeth and saith the he was in the year of our Lord one thousand eight hundred and thirty Seven & eight a Citizen of Caldwell County Missouri. and that [t]he said deponent did at the Land Office in Lexington Fayette Cty. Mo. enter in his own name and for his own use One Eighty acre lot also One Forty acre lot in Township No. 55 North of the base line and west of the fifth principal meridian. Range No. 28. and also by Deed of Conveyance from Timothy B. Foot to said deponent the S. W [1]/4 of the N W. [1]/4 of Section No. Five in Township & Range aforesaid also by Deed of Conveyance from Jacob Stewart The S. E. [1]/4 of the North W [1]/4 of Section Five—Township and Range aforesaid— And that this deponent was in actual and peaceable possession of the lands before discribed, and had in his possession Duplicates of said Entries from the aforesaid Land Office—And That he was by force and arms Compelled to give up said Duplicates to the Citizens of Mosourie. and that without his own free will—was exterminatd from the State of Mosourie and further this deponent saith not.

Reuben Foot

[*Sworn to before W. Laughlin, J.P., Adams Co., IL, 7 Jan 1840.*]

FORD, Jonathan

In the Spring of Eighteen hundred and thirty seven I bought a piece of land in Caldwell county Mo. of Mr. Robin the land being in Section No 22 Township No 56 and Range No 28 this piece of land contained eighty acres which I paid for and Received a lawful title on this land I lived in pice till 1838 when I was ordered to leave thare I complied with the orders with considerable loss of property a list of which follows

Lost on land	$400.00
Personal property	100.00
expence of mooving	100.00

Jonathan X Ford

[*Sworn to before A. Brown, J.P., Pike Co., IL, 10 Jan 1840.*]

FOSDICK, Clarissa

Illenois Quincy Oct the 15 1839
    A Bill of Damage against the State of Missouri for Being Driven from the State and loss of propperty

first for moveing to the State	$200.00
for loss of propperty in the State	500.00
for mooveing from the State	100.00

    I certify the a bove acount to Be true and Just a cording to the Best of my knoweldg

Clarissa Fosdick

[Not sworn.]

FULLER, Catharine

    I hereby certify that my husband and myself settled within about a mile of Haun's mill Coldwell Co. Missouri in the fall of A.D. 1836 where we lived untill the massacre at the mills the 30th of Octr. 1838, at which time and place my husband was killed. About a week after the massacre I was at the mill and saw a large company of our enemies, as I understood, tented there I heard one of them by the name of Comstock say to Sister Merrill who lived in the house with me that if he could get his eye upon her husband he should be a dead man. Companies of from six to ten came to our house enquiring for men and guns a number of times

Catharine Fuller

[Sworn to before D. H. Wells, J.P., Hancock Co., IL, 3 Jan 1840.]

FULLMER, David

    On the twentieth of October Eighteen Hundred and thirty Eight, I was ordered to leave the County of Daviss in the State of Missouri in three days by the Mob under pain of being Burned out I was Just recovering from a long Course of Sickness. I fled to Caldwell County in the Vicinity of Hans Mill. in a fiew days, myself, and the Citizens ware alarmed for our Safty from the fear of Mobs who ware Stroling about the Country. we the Citizens in the Neighborhood Gathered to Hans Mill for the Double purpose of our better Security and Saving the mill from being burned. on the thirteth of the month I hered the report of Several Hundred Guns in the Diriction of Hans Mill. I Soon beheled Several men riding at full Speed having escaped from the mill and informed me ~~that~~ of the <u>Slaughter</u> that had taken place at the mill. in about an hour I repaired to the mill. the Mob was Gon about a Dozen men &Children wounded among the wounded was a woman who was Shot through the hand. there ware fifteen Kiled among whom was a boy who had his brains Shot out. the next day I met at the mill together with Several others to bury them and for the want of Strengh to dig Graves we ware oblijed to throw them into a Dry well. in a fiew days after this the Mob returned and took posesion of the mill and Ground to Suit themselves. for Several weeks together. douring which time they would ride about the neighborhood with their faces painted abousing and insulting the Survivers terrfying our women and Children ordering us off from time to time und[er] pain of extermination & soforth—after thus inhumanly treating us for Several weeks Capt. Cumstock drew his men off [——] and left us to our disconsolate Condition—about the twentieth of November I left the State of Missouri in Consequence of the Order of Gov. Boggs together with the inhumaine treatment of the Citizens of Said State—

I am a Native of Penn. in Eighteen Hundred and thirty five I moved to the State of Ohio where I joined the Church of Jesus Christ of Latter day Saints and in the fall of eighteen Hundred and thirty Seven I moved to the State of Misssouri Caldwell Couty from thense I moved to Daviss County to the place where I was driven out. I now live in Hancock County Illinois

David Fullmer

[*Sworn to before D. H. Wells, J.P., Hancock Co., IL, 3 Jan 1840.*]

GRANGER, Carlos

I hereby certify that I lived in the State of Missouri from the year A.D. 1832 till last winter. I lived in Far West at the time the troops came there about the first of November A.D. 1838. A number of armed companies were stationed in different parts of the town and the town guarded by them a week or ten days, these troops burnt up large quanties of house logs and rails and commit other depredations

They were very saucy threatening and abusing the inhabitants—I saw the Mormons closely guarded on the public square and there compelled to sign a deed of trust as I understood

I am not nor never have been a member of the church of Jesus Christ of Latter day saints called Mormons but I am a friend to equal rights, and I never knew of any law in Mo. or any where else authorising such proceeding as were carried on by those troops at Far West

Carlos Granger

[Sworn to before D. H. Wells, J.P., Hancock Co., IL, 3 Jan 1840.]

GRIFFEN, Loyal C. K.

January 5the 1840 Warsaw Ill

Those are a list of suffering which I sufered by the laws of mobes in the State of Missourie I furst was driven from the county of Jackson at that time I was sick with the feaver not able to rase my head from my pillar I was sent out Into the world to seek friends but they ware hard to find they ware destitute of fealings for sick or well I was taken in to clay count[y] theire I received my health then I moved in to caldwell county which the peopple gave to the church of the laterdaysaints then I was driven into mashure that I did not like nor neather would any other man that thought anything of the laws of his country the laws that Washington planted in the United States of America I was harest around by this mob I was accused of things wrongfuly I was striped of all my property I was striped of that that the laws of my country allowed me to hav and Keep in my possession that was the substance of life that was my fields of provishen my fences throne down to the merces of horces catel and hogs my Riffle gun was taken from me worth 30 dollars and my time lost which was from the time that the mobs comenst until January while I was driven in to the Viledg and their I was surrounded by armed forces garded day and night sum time and I had to live in a campe and their my famaly had to suffer the Cold weather my children sufferd with the want of food and rament for I had not the chanc to go and work for provishon nor clothen for after they gave us the privledg to go to our homes I dare not sho my head for they ware determend to take me their prisner and drag me in to their jale and their take their satisfaction out of me and their reasons for this was because I belonged to the church of the Laterdaysaints this was all of their plea they also brought aletter as they sed ~~from~~ that it was from the guvner of the State and this letter stated that we had to be out of the State by Such times or we should evry sole of us be mad extinct from of the face of the globe or earth from the comensment of this fus to the end of it was as much as 1000 thousand dollars damag to me and my famaly this would not tempt me to go throught the same trubles and loses of time agane so I close my trubles by being a friend to the laws of my country

Loyal C. K. Griffen

[Sworn to before A. Monroe, J.P., Hancock Co., IL, 6 Jan 1840.]

GRIFFEN, Selah J.

Handcock Co and State of Illinois

Selah J Griffen his testamony a gainst the Mob ers of mosurie in Jackson County the mob Commenst thar abuse in 1832 And in 1833 in octobr they begain to whip and Abuse in a shamful Maner tairing down houses Laying our fensses down distroing our crops Driving our woman and childran in to the wilder[ness] thar to suffer the inclemancy of the wether And hunger and thirst plundering our houses And in November they Strip us of guns and Drive us a crost the river in to Clay County the lose of property susstaind in Jackson County $10050 [*150.00*] dollars of book a counts Lost worth 20050 [*250.00*] of Crops and two guns worth 75 dollars hous and Black Smith Shop and tools to the amount of thre hundred Dollars Lost in the hol amounted was Seven hundred And Seventy five dollars is My los Buy the mob

Selah J griffen

In 1836 My family was driven from Clay County to Callwell County my property yet remains In Clay county which is worth three hundred Dollars and i have not had the yous of it Sinse we left Clay county

Selah J Griffin

1838 Callwell the mob begain to drive people from thairr homes to plunder thair houses drive of our stock Lay our fields open and distroy our Crops Taking pris ners without aney athoity Driving abusing in the most shamful Manner Coming in to our houses camping In some Stabeling thair horses in some feeding thairr horses with our grain and hay The troop Came to Calwell took us prisners Disarmed us then thretend us and Said that we must Seign ove[r] all propertys To them or thay wold tak our lives Or imprison us and when we had sinde The deade of trust tha orderd us to leve State or suffer deth i was obliged to leave home which i had paid the govement for Being a Blacksmith i had five hundred dollars of Book a counts taken from me and one Set of Blacksmith toals worth on hundred Forty akers of land in Calwell County The improvements thare or worth fore hundred dollars

Taken from Me Buy the troop 2 riffle guns One of the rifles worthe thirty dollars the Other worthe twenty dollars

Selah J Griffen

[*Sworn to before A. Monroe, J.P., Hancock Co., IL, 6 Jan 1840.*]

GROVER, Thomas

In the year A.D. 1836 I moved from the State of New York to the State of Missouri where I purchased Two hundred and twenty acres of land in the County of Caldwell besides a small lot in Jackson County One hundred and twenty acres of the above I purchased from Government, the remainder from individuals most of the lands were under improvement with good buildings &c &c In the begining of November AD 1838 while I was at home attending to my own concerns an armed force came up to my house one of the men whose name was ――― Baldwin drew a large Bowie Knife and Swore by the "Holy God" that he would cut my head off, this was in consequence of my being a Mormon, However after I had begd for them to spare my Life and he seeing my family in tears; he was softened down and did not put his threats into execution.

The mob obliged me to give up my duplicates which I held for the lands which I had purchased from Goverment.

They destroyed and laid waste ~~your~~ my Corn Fields and would frequently come to my house would give me and my family abusive language and would take what victuals they wanted and Search'd my house for arms at various times

I had frequently to hide from the mob (who I heard had threatned to kill me.) and the weather being very cold, and being continualy harrassed by my Enemies I was taken sick and suffered considerable [―――] After hearing that we were ordered by the Authority of the [――― ――― ―――] State to leave the State of Missouri I made preparations to go. this was in the winter I and my family suffered much. my wife was confined on the road, and suffered every thing but death itself, my children were all sick for several ~~weeks~~ months and our sufferings were extreme, In this manner I was abused and after purchasing lands and improving the same and spending a Considerable sum of money in building &c &c I was driven from my home and was obliged to find a shelter out of the state of Missouri

I certify that the foregoing statements are correct according to the best of my knowledge and belief.

Commerce Hancock Co. Jany 2, <u>1840</u>   Thomas Grover

[Sworn to before D. H. Wells, J.P., Hancock Co., IL, 3 Jan 1840.]

HANCOCK, Solomon

State of Illinois Adams County S.S.

This day personally came before me William Laughlin a Justice of the peace said Cty. Solomon Hancock being duly sworn Deposeth and

Saith that he was a Citizen of Caldwell Cty. Mo. in 1836. and that he sd. deponent entered Government Land at the Land Office Lexington Missouri. and there resided peacable until I was Compelled to leave by the Govenors exterminating orders executed by General Clark and others The Land above refered to will be described by a certain Duplicate accompaning this affidavit also this deponent held by Deed of Conveyance from Roil Ames The NE. 1/4 of SW 1/4 of Section No. Five Township No. 56, Range 29 And further this Deponent saith that he had purchased and paidfor Forty acres of Land lying in Jackson Cty and State of Missouri and being driven as aforesaid was prevented from getting his Deed

Solomon Hancock

[*Sworn to before W. Laughlin, J.P., Adams Co., IL, 7 Jan 1840.*]

HENDERSON, James M.

Handcock Co and State of Illinois January the 3rd 1840

James M Hendersons testimoney and Bill of Damage a gainst the government of Missouri. Commenceing in the faul of 1837 I emigrated from the state of Indiana to Missouri and arivd in farwes Caldwell Co. Mo. and livd there a few Months. I then Moved to ray Co. in the winter of 1838 and livd there about 8 Months which time I maid $40.00 a Month at my trade shoe and boote making.

dureing which time I herd but little else then mob mob mob. yes dam the Mormons we will drive them in the faul. at tenth the Augest Election rold a rould a round and the mob Commencd there fun. I then was forst to leave My home and flee to Caldwell for Protecsion.

My losses sustaind in Ray Co. was $120.00 we soon was serounded on all sides and thretend to sho us no quarters onley at the Canons mouth. during which time we ware not slack in our duties to send Protisions aided by some of the influenshiel men of that upper Cuntry but what was his answer to us he said if you have got into a fus with the mob you must gait out the best way you Can you mus fight your own battles I Can guive you now protectsion atall[.] this was about the first of October 1838[.] there was then ameeteing Cauld of the latter day Saints Conveind in farewest for the Perpose of takeing an expression of the People wether they would stand for there Constitusional rites or not.

we all a greed that we wuld stand for the Constitusion and defend our rits at the expence of life. but what was more supriseing then all the rest was the governers order as extermination which reached farwest in some days after this order reached farewest a bout the 4 or 5 day of Nov but be fore this there was ginerl Lucus of Jackson Co. arivd about the 29th or 30th day of oct. witch also had an order to Eileminate us if we would not Comply with there proposels that was if we would guive up our armes and sign a way all our property to pay the expence of the ware and leave the State forthwith that we Could live otherwise we must Die wich order was a forged one with out Contridiction. to which we Cerrenderd they then marched into our City and begin to plunder our houses insult our women &c they shot our hogs and Cattle to gratify there helish rage a perpose to destroy them and also burn our house logs among home was Capt. S. Bogert, Mathew McGaw, John Craig, Kneel Gillum, Charles Morehead, Leiutenant Cook. About this time there was a Masicree tooke place at Hons Mill were the Mob fell upon a settlement of our people and kild 18. amoung home was one little Boy a bout 8 years old a mong those Merderers ware Anderson Morten, James Blakeley, J Seego, these men I heard say they ware there. Ginerl lucus then took 7 Prisners and started for Jackson Co. names of which is Joseph Smith Jr, Hyrum Smith, Sidney Rigdon, Lyman Weight, Gorge W. Robinson, Amasa Liman, ~~and started for Jackson Co.~~ the next day or 2 ginerl Clarke arivd with 1200–15 hundred men withe the proper order of Extermination from the Gov. tho betwin the time of Lucuss departier and the arivel of Clarke we was Cauld to perrade on the Square where was a strong gard plast a round us and we forst to sign this deede of trust. a mong those of our Entaginest ware Willey Willums, Thomas Berch, Gorge M. Hinkel, the first of importece that was done by Gen. Clarke was to Caul us together again and Celec 50 men of our society and made prisners of them without any proses what ever I was one of the 50. ~~an the next day we~~ amedeintly after this opperation of Clarkes he deliverd to us an adress in wich he stated that if we had not Complide with the treaty proposed by Lucus wich was Equil in athority with him that before that time our Women and Children wuld have ben slain and our housees left in ashes sad thought after some parleamentry remarks said you gentle men are at liberty now to go home to your fameleys to precure wood and food &C but stateed that we neede not expect to see our leaders a gain for there doom is fixed, there dye is Cast, there fait is seald. but stateed to us the prisners: that he would Make Examples of us all. we was kept in Close Confinement that Night. next morning we was drove a way not a loud the priviledg of going to see our fameleys nor even to have brecfast. when the most of our fameleys livd in the City so we arivd at richmond the 3rd day. where we was kept in Close Confinement for a bout 4 weeks dureing the examination. then all that was not liberated Commited to jail or held to Bail. after laying in jail 9 days I guive Bail an got home I then had to Move away from the State

My losses hear was	$275.00
and on the first paig	120.00
for faulse imprisenment	10,000.00
[*Subtotal*]	$10,395.00
to 7 Months lost time $40.00 a month	280.00
	$10,675.00

James M Henderson

[*Sworn to before A. Monroe, J.P., Hancock Co., IL, 6 Jan 1840.*]

HENDRIX, Reuben

January the 22 AD 1840 State of Illinois Pike County five by five township I now give you a true account of what i lost in the missouri I do justly Consider that I have lost 150 Dollars

Reuben Hendrix his hand and Seal

[*Sworn to before D. R. Rogers, J.P., Pike Co., IL, 28 Jan 1840.*]

HENDRIXSON, Jordan P.

State of Illinois Adams County SS.

This day and date afforesaid personally came Jordan P. Hendrxxson who being duly sworn deposeth and saith that he emigrated to misouri in 1837. and in Clinton County Mo. Entered eighty acres of Government Land. And was compelled by the Governor exterminating orders to leave the state

J. P. Hendrixson

[*Sworn to before W. Laughlin, J.P., Adams Co., IL, 7 Jan 1840.*]

HERICK, Phebe

State of Illinois Adams County SS January 7th 1840

This day personally appeared before me William Laughlin a Just[*ice*] of the peace for said County, Phebe Herrick late Phebe Wood being duly Sworn according to law Deposeth and Saith that she was in the year 1838 a citizen of Davis Cty. Mo. and was driven to Farwest Caldwell Cty. Mo. and by being So driven off aforesaid Suffered a loss in house hold furniture & bed and bedding wearing apparel. and in hogs cattle &C to the amt. of

$200. and by being driven from Farwest as aforesaid by the Govenors exterminating orders executed by Gen. Clark and others. Sustained a loss of property to amt. $50

Phebe herick

[Sworn to before W. Laughlin, J.P., Adams Co., IL, 7 Jan 1840.]

HERRICK, Amos F.

State of Illinois Adams County S.S. January 7th, 1840

This day before me William Laughlin one of the Justices of the peace in & for said County, personally came Amos F. Herrick who being Duly sworn according to law deposeth & saith that he was a Citizen of Randolph County, Missouri, from november 1835 to April 1839, & that in november 1835 he did purchase for his own use an improvement of twelve acres of land & house & stable & a preemption right on forty acres of land upon which said improvement was made & paid sixty dollars for the same, said land being in said County of Randolph previously entered by John [G]larkson. And this deponent further says that on the 11th day of July 1836, he did in his own name & for his own use, enter forty acres being north east of the northeast qr. of section no. 28. Township no 54 north of the base line & west of the fifth principal meridian, range no 15. as described in the Duplicate. No 11607: & that in the same year he did purchase for his own use also forty acres, adjoining the other forty on the north, partly improved, with two houses on it, & smoke house & hatter shop: & also that he purchased the northwest quarter of section 13 in township 54 north, Range 16 west, & that he had peaceable possession of the two said forties & lived on them three years, & that in november & December 1837 & 1838 being threatened by Mobbers led on by Daniel Davis & Archibald Rutherford, he sold said lands for less than half their value & left them: & further this deponent saith not.

Amos F Herrick

[Sworn to before W. Laughlin, J.P., Adams Co., IL, 7 Jan 1840.]

HERRICK, Lemuel

In the summer of 1832 I located myself and family in Jackson County Mo. calculating to become a permanent citizen but in that I was dissappointed, for in the fall of 1833 there begun to be quite an excitement with the old settlers about the church to which I belonged which was the church of latter day saints; and soon there was a large mob made their appearance amongst us and began to commit depredations on us.

I saw a man by the name of Robert Johnston who was or had been a member of the assembly; strike Elder Parley P. Pratt, with the breach of his gun which brought him to the ground, and cut a a severe gash in his head, because he contended for the faith and principles of our church. & brother Pratt sought redress at the hand of the authories of the place but could not get a hearing. and had to give it up. In a few days after this there was about sixty armed men with the reverend Mr Isaac McCoy missionary to the indians at their head came into my neighborhood and run of most our men, shooting at some, and whipping others, and swearing that they would kill every Mormon if they was not out of County in three days: They had previous to this taken our guns from us and came to my house for the purpose of searching for guns as they said but they told us that if we was not out of the Co within three days, they would massacree men women and children and leave none alive to carry the news: for they wouldn't have the d——d Mormons in their County, but such a scene of sorrow and confusion I never saw before. Women and children came flocking from every quarter to my house for shelter some screaming & hallooing murder some crying aloud some scared almost into fits others that were sick in beds got up and started for my house and fainted by the way while others had to bring them in their arms. but all this seemed to have no impression on the minds of the mob, but they appeared to be completely hardened to every sense of feeling and mercy. After this company left us I gathered up our beds and bedding with a few articles of household furniture and then took my family consisting of an aged mother wife and ten children and put out for the prarie in the month of November not knowing where we were going or what would become of us. Leaving my farm my buildings crop cattle hogs and fowls, and almost every thing that I possessed to the ravages of the mob. and six week alapsed before I found a shelter to put my head under after I left the mob pillaged my property destroyd my Crop hauld a way my rails and burnt my house and left the place desalate and i never have recievd one cent for the same neither have I ben permitted to return to my land to this day onley at the peril of my life from Jackson Co I got into the county of Clay after much fatiuge and maney hardships with my family thair put up buildings and made another improvement and staid untill the spring of 1837 when I moved with my famaly into Caldwell Co and went to the land office entred Eightyfive acres of land in hopes to lieve thair in peace but in this I was a gane dissapointed but notwithstanding I heard talk of mobs I went to work and my land and put up buildings and opened a farm of a bought thirty acres under good fence and set better then 100—apple trees of the best kind of fruit as I took paines to procure grafts which cost me twenty dollars but I didnot injoy the fruits of my labor long for in the fall of 1838 govener Boggs Extirminating order Came on us and I was compelled to sign a deed of trust and then leave the State at the sacrifise of my land and almost every thing that I possessed in the world I give this in testamoney of things that hapened under my obsirvation in Mosuria this 8th day of Jan 1840

Lemuel Herrick

[*Sworn to before J. Orr, J.P., Adams Co., IL, 8 Jan 1840.*]

HIGBEE, John S.

Quincy March 24 1839:

Johh S. Higbee was Born in the year 1804 in Clermount County State of Ohio late township I lived in that region of Country until I arived to the years of manhood I married and settled mySelf and family in fulton township lewis town hamelton County State of Ohio there I remained until Some Elders came to the town where I resided Calling themselves of the church of Christ of latter day saints they gave out an appointment to hold a meeting I attended after hearing preaching several times I went forward in the ordinances thereof and became a member of that church Comonly Called by the disbeliever the mormon Church my Companion allso Join the same Church by our labour and econmy we had gained a Comfortable home for which we sold for the sum of six hundred dollars and started on the 28 of february 1833 and moved to the west Boundery of the State of missourie to the County of Jackson County where there was a number of members living of the same Church we got to the place we dsighned to go on the first Day of April 1833. here as other citicens I Bought land and allso stock and by my industry I put in a good crop and Built me a good dwelling house and allso other necesary Buildings we lived in this County until about the 7 Day of November but for several weeks Before this it was rumered that the inhabitants of the County, that did not believe as we did threatend to drive us from our lands and homes Contrary to all law Both of God and man we however was unwilling to Believe that any enlighted people could Be so destitute of humanity or feeling for their fellow Beings But to our astonishment and to their shame they commenced their outrages about the 20 20 of July 1833 By gathering to gether and tareing down a printing office belonging to this people a family allso lived in the building in a lower room was orderd forthwith out of their house threatened with immediate death if they refused the[y] allso took the Bishop of the church with an other member and tared and feathered them and abused many others from this time forth they continued to cary their helish desighns into effect they seem to get worse daily and hourly by stoneing our houses whipin some shooting at others runing poles through our windows and at lenth tareing down our Buildings unroofing & so[.] some of our Brothern in trying to rescue others and save their property went to where there was a Banditto of those demons a destroying our corn and allso houses to try to show them the imprepriety of doing as they were But to no purpose for as soon as they was discovered By this lawles Banditto they fired on them Being well armed wounded one man who expired the next day some of our Bretheren having arms they returned the fire and killed two of their number the news of this scurmage was soon carried through the county painted in various forms with many others thing to raise a great excitement of which it had the desired effect november the 5 the Day was set to make a general massecre we however seeing the rage of the people so that something must be done for our safety we agreed to meet togather or the most of the church and go and see these demons and try and have peace restored if possible But all in vain they would not hear our cries nor our petitions nothing but leaveing the County forthwith would appease the wrath of those people in this inclement season of the year not having time to gather our plunder many of us left all and fled for our lives not Being sufered to return to get our property about the sixth of november I started to go to Clay County ~~west~~ north of Jackson with a few of my things I was in company with my father who was about 70 years of age and alls[o] my mother who was about the same age allso my Brothers family with some others my companion at this time was very Dangerisly ill who had Just been confined a few days before she not Being able to set up But to go we must or suffer death immediately the first day we traveled near the ferry on the missourie to clay Co. here we made ourselves as comfortable as we could having left our Bed Beding and household furniture general we had But a few things to put over us here my companion being fatigued with the journey was allmost overcome so that she apeared to lay senseless a part of the night but this was not all for it commenced raining about three o clock in the afternoon it raining all night and part of the time it rained very fast insomuch that it raised the little Broks and rivers Quite high which made it Quite difficult traveling the next day it Being very mudy allso But to my story we had a small shelter for my companion of which one or to did watch her at a time through the nigh[t] whilst the rest clumb a steep hill for about one hundred yards and got under a rock here we sufered until dalight whilst my companion was exposed to the wet Both from rain and from the watter underneath that run under her however we put Brush under her and took care of her the best [way] we could morning came we began to gather up [our] goods to proceed on our Journey our things were all wet my companion takeing fresh cold we allmost gave up all hopes of her recovery she was unable to take care of the child or to give it suck we had to feed it and raiset by hand which was a great truble in the situation we were placed in however we proceded on our Journey Came to the river and crosed over in the afternoon here my compani[on] was not expected to live from one hour to another here we camped again and here we stayed a few days my companion Began to gain in health slowly we at lenth moved up the missourie a few miles wen we got the priveledge of going in astable [——] without doors or chimney in or [clinking] we stayed in until winter was over in the spring we moved again down the river about 8 miles here we lived until the inhabitants of Clay Co. reQuested that we we should allso leave that County and I allso formd resolutions that we should do it we found there was no other alternative But to leave the County of which we did But not without much loss of property and expence we moved to the territory of which was atached to ray County at that time But was soon set of a county which was Called Caldwell County here we Bought land an settled down as other citizens of the united states But not long did we enjoy our priviledgs as free citizens of the united states for mobs arose on every side as it were and killed many of us and drive the Balence from the state I Just mention these last difftly in a slighty manner knowing that I am unable with pen to describe to you the horrers and murders which they performed against this people But knowing that there will be a full account given by those that is more abley to wield the pen

March th24 1839   John S Higbee

[*Not sworn.*]

HILL, Elisha

State of Illenois Handcock Co.

I testify that while I lived in Ray Co and State of missouri a Caucus meeting was hild in the Town of Richmond in 1837 to adapt measures to drive the mormons (so caled) out of the Co. and a committee appointed by Wiley Williams County Clerk consisting of three men to warn them to leave the Co Joseph Ewing David Snowden and Anthony McChristian was the men appointed, which warn us to leave, which we did and I went to Davis Co. at the election in 1838 they commensed depredat[ions] upon us with clubs clapboards loaded whips and knives which caused us to leave the Ground and many of us badly hurt and from that time the mob continued to commit depredations till the malitia was cald or sent out to exterminate us and they came marched into the Town of Adam-ondi-Ahman which we perchased from them the inhabitance of the co and took possestion of the Town took us prisners took our Arms kild hogs cattle &c and wounded many others took possession of our store and also our corn fields and forbid us taking any corn out of the feild and a painted company under the command of Cornelus Guillum amember of the Legeslation who rode through the Town plundering and taking just what they pleasd and abuseing men womin and children and swearing that they would kill Joseph Smith Jr, S. Rigdon and others, and the malitia would not suffer us to leav the town without a pass from Gen Wilson and ten days only given us to leave the Co and in the spring of 1839 to leave the State

Elisha Hill

[Sworn to before A. Monroe, J.P., Hancock Co., IL, 6 Jan 1840.]

HODGES, Curtis, Sr.

A Schedule of the losses of Property and Damages which Curtis Hodges Sen. sustained in the State of Missouri, by the depredations of the mob, and being wounded by the Mob, and being drove out of the state by order of the Govenour of said State, he, not having done any thing contrary to the laws, the Constitution of that State, or of the United States, but in consequence of his Religion All of which was done in the years of our Lord and Savior 1836 and 1838.

1836	Being driven by the mob from Clay County and Total loss of Crop $200	$200.00
1838	[And] 25 acres of improved land 10 per acre	1,400.00
"	115 do not improved	480.00
"	Loss of Crop	1,000.00
"	10 Hogs $3.00 per hog	30.00
"	3 months sickness of a wound inflicted by the mob, and yet a criple	75.00
	having to leave the state precipitately by order of his Excelency, the Govenour, to secure my own life, and the lives of my family, &c. &c. $2000	2,000.00
		$5,185.00

I Curtis Hodges Sen. certify further that I was forsed to sell some of the above named land to get out of the State with my family to save our lives. 100 acres for 29 dollars

Curtis Hogdes Sen

[*Sworn to before W. H. Boling, C.C.C.C., Pike Co., IL, 14 Jan 1840.*]

HOLSCLAW, Elizabeth

Handcock Co and State of Ill.

I herby testefy that when I lived in Jack Son Co and State of Missouri a Mob arose to the number of some hundreds collected in Independense and thew down a two story brick building ocupied as a dweling house and printing office and scaterd the tipe and paper in the street, they also broke open a store and scaterd the goods in the streets and I saw two men that they had tard and fetherd, they also cut open a fether bed in the yard destroyed a barrel of flower Stond houses broke in windows and chased me, fastend our doors Surrounded our house and would not let us pass out, there was 200 of them and there was none with in but widdow women and children aftewards they broke open the door and rushed in with a Dirk knife up on us and at length drove us from the county of Jackson. and when in Caldwell in 1838 an armed soldiery under the command of Gen. Lucas marched on to our premisis without leave, quarterd in our house burnd rails kild stock drive of droves of sheep beloning to our people, in the year of 1839 they came in to the city of Far west and order out our people threatning their lives if they was not gon in three or four days and compeld us to leave the state and I testify this in the fear of God this 4 day of Jan. AD 1840

Elizabeth Holsclaw

[*Sworn to before A. Monroe, J.P., Hancock Co., IL, 6 Jan 1840.*]

HOOPES, Jonathan

Clear crick township Davis County state of Missouri being Driven from my home together with family As I was on my road moving I was taken prisoner by Seventy five armed men the plundered my waggon and swore the shoot me and burn my waggon and all that was in it this was on the tenth day of september 1838 the wanted me to Denounce my religion and move my family from Davis County to levingston County with theirs and fight against my society and then the would protect me after the found that the Could not prevale with me to black my face I them told them that I would suffer Death before I would Join theminany such thing some them Cried out shoot him Dam him shoot em while others Cried let him go we want to have the fun of shooting all the Damed mormons and throwing them in a pile after a bout half a day the let me go tiling me to leave the

County after two or three Days I went to get the ballance of my goods ~~the~~ about 30 or 40 armed men took my family prisoners and sought my life swearing that if the Could see me the would shoot me but by keeping myself hid in the woods I got away from them on the last week of September Thomas N Aubury Stold two of my horses one of them was a stud worth two hundred Dollars the other is worth Seventy Dollar[s] on the seventh of November I was taken prissoner by the malitia Commaned by General wilson and Parks he ordered our guns to be taken from us they took a rifle worth twenty five Dollars there the mob rode on my horses around me I dare not say one word a bout my horses General Wilson told us that we must leave the state forth with or be exterminated he said that was the goverers orders but Gentle men said he I will take it on myself to let you remove out of Davis County in ten Days into Calwell County there to remane Dureing the winter and then you must leave the state he said we kneadd not think to put in a nother Crop if you do the mob will kill you off for we shant Defend you any longer while I was prisoner I hear[d] some of the mob swear that the shot Six mormons as fast as he Could load his gun his name is Wm. Peningston a nother man the name runnels said here is blood on my Shirt bosome thathe go[t] when he was killing a damed mormon

Jonathan Hoopes

N B a on the last february I went to Davis County to try to get my horses but I Could not get them I was attacted by Wm. Boman and Samuel odel the stoned me severly so that I Could scearce get home

[*Sworn to before W. H. Boling, C.C.C.C., Pike Co., IL, 14 Jan 1840.*]

HOOPES, Warner

Mo Davis Co Adamondiamon August

At the election in galiten Wm P[e]niston samuel Black Wilson McKinney with others raised against the Br & said they should not vote calling them thieves robers & liars &c & said they should not vote unless they done it by main strength & when the Br went to vote they ware opposed by the mob these men being at the head of the mob with dirks Clubs & stones & Bro stewart was dirked in the shoulder & others knocked down & we ware all forced from the village with severe threats of our lives & said they would have a mob on us I Warner Hoops immediately went to Richmond in Ray Co & borded with Nicolas Mckinney also with others Wiley Williams & lawyer Burch they ware engag supplying the mob with arms amunition &c & the sheriff of Davis Co Mr Morgan judge King &

others said they ware in hopes that joseph smith jun & Lyman Wight would not be taken & tried acording to law so that they could have the pleasure of taking their scalps & also I was at ameting of the citisens in richmon ray Co in which lawyer Reas made a motion that the citisens should go against the mormons although the mormons had not broken the laws of the land but they should go against them & if the mormons proved to strong for them they would have to be tried their and they would make it as light as possible & on the other hand as heavy as possible on the mormons & I was drove from richmond on account of a false report that I had told the brethren that they had sent arms to the mob they gave me 20 minutes to leave the town in or they would take my life I went to adamondiamon & the mobs came against the Br their & jeneral Wilson & lawyer Davis gave me a writing compelling me to leave the Co. in ten day & the winter to leave the state & also stated that if I would go whare I was not known & renounce my religion I mite live in peace & also that I mite as well do it first as last for I would have to in the end for your leaders say they we intend to put them all to death & also one man by the name of Rogers stated that he had killed one damned old mormon & called him by name McBride & showed the blood on his sword & wished he could get the chance to kill some more damed mormons

Warner Hoopes

[*Sworn to before W. H. Boling, C.C.C.C., Pike Co., IL, 14 Jan 1840.*]

HOUGHTON, Eli

Handcock Co and State of Illenois

I heerby Certify that I Eli Houghton moved to the State of Misouri in 1837 and bought land and Settled on the Same and mid an improved and raised a crop and in the fall of 1838 Some difficilties arose betwen the inhabtans and the mormons & I moved to far-west ten miles for Saifty ~~while~~ where there troops Surrounded us and compeled us to remain in the compas of the town they compeled mee to Sign away my Property gave up my arms and was compeled to leve the State which I did in the Spring ~~middle of the~~ of 1838 after I had moved home from farwest Letumant Lakey took mee prisoner and marched mee to Richman and kept mee two days and then Discharged mee out any charge bing perferd a gainst mee I was left to return with[*out*] any means for my Support

I Sustained a loss of Property to the amount of fourteen hundred Dollars $1400

Eli Houghton

[*Sworn to before A. Monroe, J.P., Hancock Co., IL, 6 Jan 1840.*]

HOUGHTON, James

Handcock Co and State of Illinois

This may Certify that I James Houghton moved to Missouri in the year 1836 I Settled on a piece of Land lived thereon untill of 1838 when there arose a difficulty between the inhabitents of the State of Missouri and the Mormons in the Autum of 1838 I Started for Farwest with a load Corn. I was overtakeen by a Company of men they took me prisioner and kept my horses and waggon in there Service they took me into theer camp there they had prisioners from Seventy to twelve years of age. I was with them two days when I got my discharge by Voliteering to Carry one Cary to his family Said Cary had his head Split open by a Rifle he Lay all the time in an open waggon insensible without any one to aid or assist him he died that night the man that Struk him was not taken into Custody or any notice taken of it the next day I was in Farwest and while there the Militilia tore down my fences distroyd my Corn killd my bees and all of the property they Could Lay theer hands on—they finally Capitulated and they took my Gun and I Signd a deed of Trust and was ordered with the Rest of the Society leftd the State which I did that winter in Cold winter to the great inconvenience of myself and family

I Sustain a loss of to the amount of $1500 in time and property

James Houghton

[Sworn to before A. Monroe, J.P., Hancock Co., IL, 6 Jan 1840.]

HOUGHTON, Ornan

State of Illinois Hancock County

I hereby Certify that I Ornan Houghton moved to the State of Missouri in 1836 I was Compelld to leave Clay County and go and Settle in Colwell County I Settled on land and raisd a Crop and in the Autum of 1838 Some difficulties arose between the Inhabitants and the Mormons I moved to Farwest ten Miles for Security while there troops Surrounded us and Compeld us to remain in the Compass of the town[.] they capitulated at last I Signd away my Property gave up my Arms and was compeld to leave the State which I did in the middle of winter to the great inconvenience of myself and family

After I had moved home again Lieutenant Lakey took me prisioner and marchd me to Richmon and kept me two days and then discharged me with out anny charge being perford against mi I was left to Return with out any means for my Support

I Sustaind a loss of Property to the amount of $800 besides a great exposure of health

Oman Houghton

[Sworn to before A. Monroe, J.P., Hancock Co., IL, 6 Jan 1840.]

HOYT, Mary Ann

State of Illinois Pike County SS

This day personally appeared before me Wm. H. Boling Clerk of the County Commis Court within and for said County and State Mary Ann Hoyt—and after being duly sworn deposeth and saith that in the year of 1835 She moved to the state of Missouri in the County of Caldwell, and that in March 1838 she moved to Davis County in said state, and there Bought a Preemption Right on 160 acris of Land, and from thence was driven to Diaman, and there Remained until the Governor of Missouri Raised the Militia under Command of General Wilson and Gave me his Exterminating order, and thereby Robed me of my Property and Premption Right, which I Consider worth $300.00 and from thence I was driven to the State of Illinois in distressed circumstances where I now Reside a lone widow, with five Children January 14th 1840.

Mary Ann hoyt

[Sworn to before W. H. Boling, C.C.C.C., Pike Co., IL, 14 Jan 1840.]

HULET, Charles

In the year of 1832 I with my family belonging to the church of Jesus Christ of Latter Day Saints made my residence in Jackson Co. Mo. as supposed for life but it seems in this I was mistaken for the old setlers began to be troublesome in a short time and threw down my fences and passed through my field when they saw proper but this I did not considder worth making ~~trouble~~ them trouble about, but in October 1833 things began to wear a more serious aspect the old setlers were much enraged and on the 4th of Nov. following about 80 of the old setlers came upon our brethren and began to commit depredations and I for the defence of myself and brethren with others met them, they fired upon us killed one and wounded anumber, the next day we marched to Independence gave up our guns with the promise of receiving them when out of the Co., for which there was a number days givn but the next day came and a mob with it and we were obliged to skulk in evry direction I with a number of

469

families went south into Vanburen Co. stayed until Jan 1834 we returned although it was a desperate undertaking they soon gathered came upon us took me prisoner and beat my son about cruely and o[*b*]liged us to leave again we then went to Clay C and from there to Caldwell in 1838 a large body of men came upon us with orders to exterminate or drive us from the State they obliged us to sign a deed of trust conveying all our property into there hands they also burned my fence and killed one of my cows and took one gun from me which has never been returned

Ilinois, Adams, County, Jan. 8th 1840   Charles Hulet

[*Sworn to before J. Orr, J.P., Adams Co., IL, 8 Jan 1840.*]

HUMPHREY, Smith

This is to certify that I Smith Humphrey being a member of the Church of Latter day Saints removed with my family to the State of Mo Carroll Co [&] bought a farm near the town of Dewitt in the Summer of 1838 [&] have been eye witness to trans actions of the inhabitance of that country [&] have been made to Suffer by them as follows on the morning of the 19th of August 1838 I being in Dewitt I was returnging home & was met by an armed force of men I suppose nearly one hundred Commanded by Colonel Jones [&] by force took [&] kept me a prisoner about two hours during which time they made many threats against the people called Mormons Such as that they were determined to drive them from that Co I also Saw the Sheriff of said Co. take G. M. Hinkel a prisoner & carry him out of town & said Hinkel returned the same evening & Also about the first of Oct as I was walking out from my house early in the morning I saw that my Stables had been Set on fire by some unknown hand during the night I was met by a party of 12 armed men commanded by Capt Hiram Standly who took me a prisoner back to my own house & there com pelled me to remove my goods from my house by their help in the presence of my self & family Set fire to & burned my two blocks of houses my wife being sick with the ague at the Same time I was then com pelled with my family to move into the town of Dewitt where we remained til about the 11th of Oct where the Church principaly resided & we had to continuly be under arms for our own Safety for the mob were encamped within one mile of town [&] continualy harrased us by night & by day firing at our men where ever they had a chance & they did fire into town [&] on the 11th of Oct we being compeled by force of arms after praying to the Judge [&] the Governor for relief & being denied when we sent by writen petitions [&] by individual mesengers left Dewit for Caldwell Co the people promised to remunerate us for our property but they have not done it many families were sick one woman died on the road I arived in Caldwell Co about the 13th after being there about two weeks I was taken prisoner by a company of several hundred who were under the command of Generals Lucas & Wilson & others of Jackson Co & others & they kept me for about three days [&] threatned of Shooting me during which time they took from me property to the amount of from thirteen to fourteen hundred Dollars braking locks [&] hinges from Chests frightning my family from my house & among the rest took $400.00 in Cash I also heard men that were under the command of General Clark in Farwest threaten individuals that were then under arrest by force of arms with out any legal Civil Process threaten them with imprisionment & punishment if they did not Sign the Deed of Trust So called I also Saw Seciel Wood a noted Cumberland Presbyterian Priest heading a Company of said mob armed about the 18th of Oct. near Dewitt

January 8th 1840   Smith Humphrey

[Sworn to before J. Orr, J.P., Adams Co., IL, 8 Jan 1840.]

HUNTSMAN, Jacob

The State of Illenois Adams County SS January 7th 1840
        this day personally appeared Before me William Laughlin a Justice of the peace within Said County—
        Jacob Huntsman who being duly Sworn according to Law Deposeth & Saith that he was a Sitisen of Coldwell County Missouri in the Year of our Lord 1838 further Deponent Saidth that he had peaceable possesion of a forty acre lot of land Situate in Sd. County the improvement a Cabin & five acres fenced Said Deponent further States that he was Compelled to leave with the receipt of twelve dollars furthr Deponent Saith noth

                                                         Jacob huntsman

[Sworn to before W. Laughlin, J.P., Adams Co., IL, 7 Jan 1840.]

HUSTON, James

State of Illinois Adams County
        I James Huston Do Certify that I was taken Prisnor In November AD 1838 in the State of Missouri Caldwell County and was Compelled to Sign

a Deed of trust and acknolledg the Same to be my free Act and Deed and I was orderd to Leave the State forthwith

and I also oned Land the west half of the South west quarter of Section thirteen Range 29 township 55

James Huston

[Sworn to before J. Orr, J.P., Adams Co., IL, 9 Jan 1840.]

JAMESON, Charles

State of Illinois Madison County

This day personally Came before the undersigned a Justus of the pece in and for said County of Madison Charles Jameson who after being sworn uppon his oath says that he did sustain certain damagees by the in habit[ence] of Culwell County in the state of missouri during the years of 1835 & 1836 & 1837 & 1838. and in the fore part of the year 1839. towit damagees on sale of land and other property and mooving nine hundred and fifty dollars. damagees sustained by being wounded by them and one rifle gun taken at the time of being wounded two hundred and fifty dollars making in all $12.000 [*1,200.00*]

Subscribed and Sworn to before me this twentieth day of January A.D. 1840

J. C. Young J.P. Charles Jameson

[Sworn to before J. C. Young, J.P., Madison Co., IL, 20 Jun 1840.]

JOHNSON, Mahlon

Alton Jany. 13, 1840

To the honorable Senate and House of Representatives in Congress Assembled at the City of Washington and District of Columbia

I the undersigned do by these presents Represent You My Losses And Suffering in the State of Missouri in the Year 1838 by the hands of a mob who pillaged an distroyed my Goods, and Chattels, and drove me and my family from Lands Which I had Entered in that State. And previous To this was driven from Jackson Co my Crop Taken my house Burned &c. in 1833. Also was shot at in my Own house by the Mob and was forsed into Clay County and thene from Clay into Caldwell Co. and from thence To Illinois. This May Certify That—I was at Hawns Mill and one of those who was attacked By A Company of Two Hundred & Sixty Men under the Command of Arthur Cumstock. who fell upon us who were 36 in No.

and killed and wounded 31 of the Company 23 of which are Dead, Then plundered Houses & Drove away Horses Waggons &c Loaded with Goods And this may Certify that the Losses which I sustained To be no Less than Two Thousand Dollars.

Mahlon Johnson

[*Sworn to before J. H. Randle, N.P., Madison Co., IL, 13 Jan 1840.*]

JUDD, Arza, Jr.

Handcock Co and state of Illenois

I doe hereby testify that I moved to Carl Co—State of Missouri in the year 1838 and some time in the fall a mob arose (we haveng perchas[ed] land in that county) and they came a gainst a small branch of the Church and shot at us a number of times, having camped a gainst us for several days and we had to suffer a great deal being exposed to storm and we was oblige to leave there and go to Far West and on the way a woman died in the wagon, and we had to bury her without a coffin, as we was threatend with distruction after we got to Far West several others died in consequense of the exposeure and soon after an armed force ~~came and~~ of 20 or 25 came to my house and orderd us off and said that we should see thunder and lightning at Far West before tomorrow night and in consequence of their threats we had to live in camps during a hard snow storm Soon after this warning by the mob, an armed force under the command of Genl. Clark surrounded us took our arms from us and took us prisners and Genl Clark said that he had orders from Gov. Bogs to exterminate us, but as we had behaved so well he would let us go if we would leave the state, but they compeld me with ~~orders~~ the rest of my brethren to sign a dead of trust at the point of the sword to defray their expences. they burnt house logs lumber rails & I saw them take a cow beas out of a mans inclosure and kill it they also took three yoke of oxen and a wagon from my son a small boy and I was compeld to leave the State and in witness where of I doe here unto set my hand this 6th day of Jan AD. 1840

Arza Judd Jnr.

[*Sworn to before A. Monroe, J.P., Hancock Co., IL, 6 Jan 1840.*]

KELLEY, Moses

State of Illinois Adams County SS January 7th 1840

this day personally appeared before me William Laughlin a Justice of Peace for said County Moses Kelly who being duly Sworn according to law Deposeth & saith that he was a Sitizen of Ray County Missouri in the Year our Lord 1838 that he owned thirty acres of land situate in said County Deponent further saith that he was Compelled to sell to the highest bider & leave the state by order of the Governor further deponent saith that he was at Hons Mill upon Shoal Creek where were Collected several of his Mormon brethren and while there an armed force Came upon us & fired upon which we asked for quarters but they Continued fireing untill there were seventeen or eighteen killed and some eight or ten wounded among the dead was found a man who was literally choped up and was detained Prisioner of war under Captain Comstalk three days women were shot at and abused one woman received a ball through her hand further Deponent saith not

Moses **X** Killey

Moses Kelley against the state of Missouri in bill of Damage Dr. $350.00

Moses **X** Kelley

[*Sworn to before W. Laughlin, J.P., Adams Co., 7 Jan 1840.*]

KENT, H. N.

I Started from the State of Indiania in May Eighteen hundred and thirty seven for the State of Missourie the last of June or first of July bought at the Land office in Lexington Lafayette county Mo. one hundred and thirteen acres of land lieing in Caldwell County Mo. Section No 4 Townsip No 55 in Range No 28 this piece of land I went onto and by my own labours endeauvered to make a comefortable holm for my Self and family but contrary to my expectations after undergoing a considerable Degree of hardship in the fall of the year 1838 was ordered to leave the State which I complied with in febuary 1839 with considerable loss as I was obliged to Sell my property for just what they pleased to give haveing no other means to moove with

Losses damages &C Sustained by the underSigned in the State of Missourie in the fall of 1838 and winter of 1839 under Govener Boggs exterminating order

Loss of time and damages sustained thereby		$150.00
one rifle		6.00
Lost by the sale of land		325.00
do	do hogs	4.00
do	do plow	5.00

do   do corn   25.00
Spent mooving   14.00

                                                H. N. Kent

[*Sworn to before A. Brown, J.P., Pike Co., IL, 10 Jan 1840.*]

KEYES, Perry

State of Illenois County of Adams Jan 8th 1840

    I Perry Keyes do hereby certify that in 1836 in the month of may as my Father was going from the town of Independence to his place of residence a company of about 30 men under command of Moses Wilson attacted him and whipped him most shamefully with there gunns and ramrods and on the 18th gay [*day*] of may I was on the Prairie hunting horses a company of men under command of Controll ~~and they~~ whipped me untill I was scarsely able to stand Controll and one of his men by the name of Yocum held me while one of the others by the name of John Youngs whipped me he gave me 23 lashes with a cowhide and all this for my religeon for I am a member of the church of Jesus Christ of Latter day Saints commonly called Mormons another company also whipped Barnett Cole and Liman Leonard most shamefully and swore that they would kill all the Damned Mormons men women and chrilderen.

    In 1837 I entered me 40 acres of land in Caldwell Co Mo. of government and afterwards ware compelled to leave the State under the exterminating order of Govenor Boggs

                                                Perrey Keyes

[*Sworn to before J. Orr, J.P., Adams Co., IL, 8 Jan 1840.*]

KINGSBURY, Joseph C.

    I hereby Certify That in the fall of the year A.D. 1838 I was residing at Far West Caldwell County Missouri I was there when the Malitia Came up to Far West—Companies of whom were stationed in different parts of the town and the town was strongly guarded by them, they had not been there long before they commensed burning house logs &c &c[.] Four days after the arrival of the Malitia one of the Officers of the name of ——— Bradford (one of the Commissarys I believe) came to my house, and said that he wanted to get a House for the use of the Officers and asked if I would not let them have mine. I told him I could not as three of the Family were sick one of whom was not able to sit up, and only having one room only sixteen feet square. He then said that if I would not suffer them to have the House, that he would suffer the soldiers to come into House and abuse us as they pleased, he then went away—fearing for the safety of my Family from Said threats I was induced to turn out of my home and seek a shelter Elsewere. He then came and took possession of the House without my leave, but fearing the Consequences I was obliged to leave it. I along with the rest of the Citizens were paraded on the public square and compelled to sign a deed of Trust—And to give up our arms which were demand of us—Agreeable to the orders of the Executive of the State I left Missouri for Illinois. my family were sick that I was obliged to stop on the road And our sufferings were extreme.

Joseph C Kingsbury

[*Sworn to before D. H. Wells, J.P., Hancock Co., IL, 3 Jan 1840.*]

KNIGHT, Nathan K.

State of Illinois County of Hancock

Affidavit of Nathan K Knight of Commerce county and State before said taken by me Daniel H. Wells one of the justices of the peace within and for said County said Knight being sworn states under oath About one year ago last July he started from Kirtland Geauga County Ohio for Caldwell County Misouri he arrived in Misouri in Carrol County in the October following while pirsuing his journey through said county of Carrol he was met by an armed force of men he thinks about fifty in number by whom ~~we~~ he was stopped and told he ~~we~~ could not go any farther onward, and demanded ~~our~~ his armes which he gave up into their possession peaceably They then took us back about three miles. they by this time considered his gun of no manner of account and gave it back to him after going back about one mile further at a place called Whitney mill on Shoal creek in said County of Carrol they the said armed force of men stopped with him he was there kept under arrest for the space of four days this company posted men through the country for sentries and then left for the business of holding a caucus or a meeting for the purpose as they told us, to ~~masacre and~~ devise means to masacre and drive the mormons from the county after they had gone he took advantage of that circumstance and maade his escape in order to avoid the sentries he went out in to the praire with no road during his captivity were he was much exposed having no house to go into and one of his children took very sick he died the next morning after he left and was burried in open Praire

the next day he arrived a place called Hons Mill in caldwell County State Of Misouri After suffering much from hunger and the inclimency of the weather he here concluded to stop a short time in order to recruit not only himself and family but his team for they were all very much fatigued. after stoping here two days he thought to prepare to pursue his journey not having yet reached the place of his destination while thus prepareing in order to start early next morning he with others suddenly found himself surrounded by an armed force of about three hundred men on horses the first that he heard was the command to halt and form a line of Battle. they immediately commensed firing as they came into line. these words were often and he distinctly remmembers were frequently repeated by the said armed force of men "kill all" "Spare none" "give no quarters" while some of his friends were crying for quarters he turned his attention to his famly. the women and children who were wholly destitute of any presence of mind and screaming murder &c &c he was trying his utmost exertion to get them away from this horrid masacre. the balls were flying in every direction he turned in order to make a signal for his life and saw many of his friends lay bleeding in their gore. he cried for quarters they replied we have no time to quarter you, but god damn you we will halve you presently. these were the precise words as near as he can remember he was shot through the body and one of his finger was shot off when he fell, they said "they had got the Devil and they would cut him into swine meat" he then tried the utmost exertion in his power and raised to his feet and through their thickest fire made his way several rods over a hill and thus made his escape. his clothing was literally cut to pieces with bullets. they plundered him of property at this time to the amount of about seven [——] dollars. he lay at this place viz Hons Mill six weeks confined to his bed in consequence of his wounds during this time some of those engaged in the proceedings before related came in frequently where he was confined during one of these times one of their number made this expression with an oath, that he shot Mormonism into him and when he should get well he would shoot it out of him again And when he did get able to get about it seemed they designed to put their threats in execution for as he was walking towards the house one ~~evening~~ morning he was shot at, the ball passing through his clothing when the order came for the Mormons to leave the State of Misouri he was brought away by the publick charity of the church he is cripled in all probability for life

Nathan K X Knight

[Sworn to before D. H. Wells, J. P. Hancock Co., IL, 1 Jan 1840.]

LAWSON, John

State of Ill Pike County

I Certify that I John Lawson moved a family to the state of Missouri in the year of 1836 we arived on crooked river on the 14 of July & there was detained about two week on the account of the excitement in Clay & Ray Counties in which tine their was several metings held of the citisens held & desision was that the mormons must leave their counties & also that they ware willing we should settle in calwell Co which we immediately moved the family nane was Murdock I there sold my team waggon & harness for $200.00 to Edward Partridge & let him have $30.00 in money & took a writing for 20 acres of timbered land & alot in farwest & ahouse 16 by 20 fee & returned to the state of New York after [——] family & moved 1837 as far as ohio said Partridge wrote to me [——] house was ready I tarried in ohio till May 1839 & moved to the [——] of Illenois & was informed by Edward Partridge that the mob [——] robed him of all his property & land was uncertain whether he would be able to save any orget any thing for it so that I am depreved of my home & property to the amount of 230 Dollars

John Lawson

[*Sworn to before W. H. Boling, C.C.C.C., Pike Co., IL, 14 Jan 1840.*]

LEANY, Isaac

It is well know that there has bin a great difficulty existing between the Misouriens & the people called Mormons, and I am well aware that there is many false reports respecting the matter, now in circulation, I shall now endeavor to become clear of all prejudice & give to the community a fare account of the barbarous Slaughter that taken place on the 30th day of Oct 1838 at Hawns Mille on Shoal Creek, I was an eye witness to the murder that was thare commited I was one that escaped being murdered or wounded but it was through difficultys, there was but three or four besides myself that Stood to see the result of the matter that escaped being killed or wounded, in order to set forth the matter to the Satisfaction of the inquireing mind I must firs show what gave rise to so horrid a Scene, firstly it was a jealous notion in the Misouriens, that the mormons had some eavl desine in guethering themselves toguether Secondly they thought that the mormons would be apt to all vote the same ticket and many other other notions that ware false & groundless, and when the election came round [——] some of the Misouriens publickly decared that the Mormons Should not be entitled to a vote, for they was not entitled to a vote in jackson county & they Should not be thare, this was in daviss county, the mormons contended that they ware a free people that they Supported the goverment & was in Subjections to the laws of there country & that they had an equal right to vote, this Soon bread a contention between the too partys, & Soon come to blows, it is well known that the Misouriens was the agressers, that they first began to ensult, and also firs began to strike with unlawful weapons, the Misouriens Soon got tyared of there fun for the mormons proved too jolly for them as Soon as the fray was over ~~and~~ the mormons left the ground without voteing in order to keep down fur ther desturbance, this wa at gallington the county Seat of Davess county, the news Soon came to Far West caldwell county that there had bin a fray in gallington with the Mormons & misouriens & that too of the Mormons was killed & also that the Misouriens would not Suffer the mormons to bary there Dead this raised a considerable exitement with the Mormons & about onehundred men went from Fare West to gallington to See ~~about~~ what was going on & to barry the dead and to See if they could not Settle the furse, they found that the report was false about there being any killed, the mormons then endeavored to Settle the mattir without any further desturbance, they went to Adam Black a justice of the peace & ast him if he was willing to Stop the fuss and all live toguether in peace he Said he was, they then ast him to Sign his name to an article that they had drawn to that affect & he refused, they had heard that he had Swore that he would raise a company against them & that they Should not be allowed to live in peace amongst them, so the mormons pressed on Black to Sign his name to the article which was equally as binding on themselves as it was on Black or the Misouriens, he refused to Sign there paper but Said that he would right one him Self & Sign it he acordingly done So, and both partys Signed the article.

It is commonly reported that Joseph Smyth lead this company to Davess county this report is false it is true he went along but not as a leader he went along in order to use his enfluence to kep down further difficultys, but the Misouriens determed to not be at peace with the mormons they noised it a broad that Smyth had brought a great company of men & had compelled Squier black to Sign his name to a certin paper, makeing out that there was Something dreadfull therein contained

Now my friend the truth was but littl regarded by the Misouriens but any thing was Said & done to raise an excitement against the mormons, ther were many things that transpired which I Shalnot mention, because I expect to be breaf in my account & only mention the leadeing items & heads of things that transpired.

We will next notice the Scrape that taken place at Dewit, the Mormons purchassed a town plot in Carroll County at the mouth of grand River 65 miles East of far West & had made a considerable progress in improveing the place the citizens of carroll became displease to See the great emigration from the East to that place So they rose up in open rebellion against the laws of the land & under took to mob the mormons from ther homes & from there land, the mormons was desirous to have the matter farely envestegated & the dificulty Settled without the Shedin of blood they Sent a request to Ketsville Chariton County desireing them to come and See wher the rong laid, they used many efforts to Settle the matter but all in vain. the [——] Misouriens guethered and made there threts until at lenththe militia was Called out, but before this the too pary had a little engagement or rather the Scouters of these too partys got engaged & Some blood was Shed & Some lives was lost, So the militia came and placed them Selvs between the too partys, jeneral Parks was commander the business of the militia was to enquire into the cause to remove the difficulty & put down unlawfull conduct, the fact was easy asertained that the Misourians was in falt, that they reguardless of laws had emboddyed themselves to drive the inocent from there homes the militia new that the Misourians had taken an unlawful Step, but being filled with the Same Spirret, even the Spirrit of mobocracy they was not as reddy to go to work as perhaps they would have bin had they [——] of found the mormons the ones to go to work uppon, and instid of going to work & dispurseing the mob & puting down Such conduck the jeneral came to the mormons [—— —— —— —— —— —— ——] & ~~telling~~ told them that he could not do any thing for them, that it was out of his power to help them ~~that would~~ for Said he if they Should get in an engagement that the greater part of his men would fight against them & that he Should be under the necisity of withdrawing his men amediately to keep them from joining the mob, this was quite encourageing to the mob to See the militia as they was calld So ready to join them, So the mob increased in number verry fast, biding defyance to the law regardless of republickenism trampleing on the libertys our fathers so dearly baught as Soon as the mob thaught there number Sufficint for the mormons they Sent the mormons word that if they was not gone by Such a time which was verry Short that they would come upon them & masacree them, the time rolled round and the mormons was not gone, the mob then Sot an other time which was verry Short for them to be gone in, the mormons Saw that perhaps there was ten to one & that they could not Stay in peace & that if they undertook to sta[y] the result would be evil that there was over [——] by aband of lawless mobs that the result would be in the Sheding of blood, accordingly the time rolled on and the mob came against them & the mormons under took to compermise the matter witth the conditions of the compermise was ~~to~~ that the mormons Should all be gone in the Space of twelve hours with there familys & by complying with these conditions they would not come against them nor molest them any more the mob agreede to pay them for there land which they never done, the mormons bundled up & left there

in the twelve hours being compelled to leave agreat deal of there property
not being able in so Short a time to get teams & to guether there Stock,
there was one poore woman that was Some what afflicted being exposed
in moveing died by the way, the mob being over joyed in the Success that
they had in driveing the mormons the great victory they had gained in
driveing these deluded imposters & false teachers as they called them, that
they guethered themselves toguether to Speak of the noble deed that they
had done it was ajoyful time with them in deed not realizeing the Scandle
& disgrace that they had brought upon themselves & there country & not
realizein that these people had as good a right to by land & Settle on it &
worship god as they pleased so far as they did not enfringe on others rights,
So Some of them not recolecting ther name at presant made a Speech on
the Subject & Said we have gained the victory we have Succeeded in
driveing the mormons from this place, now the land is just comeing in
market in Daviess County & they will go & Settle thare & enter the land
& get Such a hoalt thare that it will be imposile to get them out from there
& now is our time to Stop them So let us take the cannon and follow them
before they get too Strong a holt thare we have helped you drive them from
here now come on boys & help us to drive them from Daviess or they will
take the country in a Short time, So they gueathered up the canon & all
the force that they could & went on to Daviess & located themselves at
mill port they took too of the mormons prisners as they went, this [———]
company was headed by Lawyers & priests there was Sashel Woods a
notible prysbytterian prieast that was a head leader amongst them this man
who professes to be a follower of Christ & one that calls on Sinners to
repent just See what a Sample he has givento the world & his followers,
I Shall more fully treat on the conduct of this man hereafter now my friend
you know that it is commonly reported that the mormons is altoguether in
falt I would have you to clear your Self of prejudice & notice how the
mormons [··]bin treated for these thing is true and this is the way that they
[——— ——— ——— ———] was treated you need not Suppose that because I
am a mormon that I have not told the truth about the matter, & now my
reader this is not all the ill treatment that we the mormons have reseaved,
I did not expect when I commenced wrighting to have wrote So much on
the Subject but Seeing that I could not gave full Satisfaction without first
Showing the leading cause, I only expected to wright a few things, but
Seeing that a few things will not tell the Story I Shall endeavor according
to the best of my understanding to give full Satisfaction, but I am unlurned
& you must excuse my awkerdness & watch for my meaning & not for my
imperfections for I wright this in order that the world may know the truth
of what has taken place in these our days

there is one thing that I forgot to mention which transpired before the mob made there attempt to drive the mormons from Dewit, that is concerning the threats & attempt the mob m[a]de on Daviess county there was about three or four hundred mob came to Davis count & went to driveing off the mormons cattle & hogs & took weguns and many other articles & threatened to masacre them if they did not leave the county the militia was c[a]lled out & the mob was dispersed, they then went amediately to Dewit and as I Stated before that the mormons Sent to Keetsville chariton county to get them to come and investegate the matter, they also Sent to the govenor & the govenors orders was to them you have got your Selves in to difficultys & I cannot help you, you will have to fight your own battle & help your Selves, So we See that the govenor was not reddy to hear the cryes of the inocent but was ready to See the mob plunder & Steal & infringe on the rights of ~~the~~ a people whoos charectors have bin empeached & misrepresented to the world, it is well known that this Same governor was a mob carrector in the jackson county fuss, there was men here from plattsburg & from Davisse & from the different countys round about & they were all engaged in the driveing the mormons from Dewit carroll county, & this is why they could Say to the carroll boys we have helped you now come & help us. Now my fellow travlors to eternity, I have no dout but you have heared the matter in quite a different light, but I expect to Stand before the bare of an impartial god eve the bar of the god of Abraham Isaac & Jacob thare to give an account for the deeds done in the boddy and realizeing this I can clearly & boldly Say that this is the way the mormons has bin treated yea & if this was the worst I Should have but little grouds for complaining to what I have & it is becuse of the religion which they hold too that they are So persecuted the laws of the land guarentees to every man to worship god according to the dictates of there own concience So far as they do not in fringe on other mens rights, & if the mormons has infrom on any ones rights why not take them to the law & punish them according to the crime commited, & if they have stold or robed or murdered punish them & let the inocent go clear, but instid of this the laws of the land was laid down & mob laws ruled & this kind of law wants neither judge nor jewry, but all that the mob laws of Misourie required was to Suspisoion a man to be a mormon & then a pile of black hickrys & this law was put in force against a great many of the mormons & Some that was not mormons, on Suspition fared the Same fate, many of the mormons was cruely whiped there houses burned & there property Stold, & had to put up with many vexations, which I Shall more fully treat on hereafter

As I before Stated the mob guethered there force & there canon and went to mill port & there began to prepare to make an attact on the

mormons in Daviess they increased in number verry fast, they had generally called the mormons cowards because they would Suffer themselves
imposed upon & abused without resenting, now the mob was collecting
dayly at millport & makeing prepareation to burn rob murder & driv the
mormons from Daviess whilst the mob was prepareing themselves with
guns there was a circumstance took place which puts me in mind of an old
Story which I have often heard told upon the mormons, when the mormons
was in jackson county, it was reported that they had a large Stone Fort &
that the mormons was takeing to it a wagon load of coffins which they
Said was to bury there dead in, & the waggon broke down & the coffins
bursted open & they were filled with guns whic[h] they was takeing &
burrying in there fort & in this way there guns was discovered, This report
was false, but this circumstanc which was Similar was true one of the mob
by the name of john comer was takeing a his wagon load of guns to millport
and his wagon broke down & he took out his guns which was in boxes
insted of coffins & drug them into a thicket & hid them & went to get
assistance about fixing his waggon & whilst he was gone Some of the
mormons discovered his loading, & it being in there Settlement got a
company of mormons to watch the wagon & guns until ther owner Should
come & See what was there calculation at lenth there came too men john
comer and a nother man with him, the mormons informed them that they
had found a wagon & Some boxes of guns out in the thicket close by &
that they wanted to get them to hall them to Farewest for them, these men
discovered that the mormons was in earnest they accordingly obeyed there
request the mormons kept these men & guns a few days untin the jineral
came with the militia & they gave up the guns & prisoners to them, there
was 44, united States yawguns there was many that taken place from time
to time which I [——] Shall not mention but leave it for them to Set forth
who are more capeble & who are was eye witnesses to the outrages that
has bin cmmitted

I Shall now prcede to give an account of the bloody but[c]hery that
taken place at a blacksmyth Shop at Hawns mille on Shoal creek on the
30th day of Oct, 1838, the mob party increased from time to time &
committed outrages after outrages until at lenth the mormons not willing
to bare it no longer they Said to the jeneral what must they do was they
not to have no protection must they Stand and See there property Stolen
there familys abused there houses burned there cattle drove off & nothing
to be done for them, then jeneral Donathan Said to them go & defend your
Selves & drive the mob from Daviess county drive them to hell, breathing
out an oath against them. the mormons then went out Supposing that they
was legaly ortherized, & finding that the mob had burned Six or Seven of
there houses & was carying on at a great hand Stealing & driveing off there

Stock So the mormons went to work determed to rout them or dy in the attempt, they Soon got the mob in the notion of leaving Daviess county So a a great portion of them fled in to Livingston a joining county & told that the mormons was burning there houses Steeling & plundering & it was Soon blown to the four winds that the mormons was doing everything that was bad now the citiz of livingston & the mob that had left Daviess began to Steel cattle from the mormons that lived in the neighbourhood of Hawns mille & also to go threw the neighbourhood & take there guns from them, they came twice & drove off cattle & an other time they came & took Several guns they also as we heard Said that they would burn our mill down, & we new that they was not too good to do it, & nowing that it was our only chance to get on going, for we dare not to go to there milles So about thirty of us went to guard them from burning it down & while we was guarding the mill we held a council to now what plan we Should fall upon to accomplish a treaty or to come on Some conditions of peace it was voted that a letter Should be written & Sent to them imediately desireing to k[n]ow what there determinations was, for they had imbod-dyed themselves Several days before we had & we heared thay was comeing on us, we had appointed to take them the letter & just before he Started they came a mesage from them desireing too or three of our leading men to go & meet ~~the~~ too or three of there leading men & see if they compermise the matter, this was the verry thing that we wanted, So in the presance of there mesinger we elected thre men to go compermise with them, we also in the pesance of there mesinger unanimously agreed to abide the treaty that our men Should make with them our thre men then Started fourth with to the place that they desired them to come to & thare they met with twelve or fourtee armed men, So the too partys began to councl the matter & Soon found that the difficulty that was between them was easy removed, that it was in consequence of false reports that had occasioned them to guether themselves to guether, they had heared that the mormons intended to come &C burn dow there houses, they Settled the difficulty without mutch trouble, the Misouriens was not willing to countunance Such conduct as this Steeling party was gilty of, nor be called of that party So they would not associaiat with them, but agreed to use there enfluence to get them to come & compermise with us also & we was useing every effort that lay in our power to get on peasible terms with them when we thought that we had got the difficultys Settled with the greater part of them & was likely to Suceede in geting it[3]

---

[3] At this point the handwriting changes. The following paragraph appears to be written by another person.

About the time that the Church commenced mooving from the State there was a Committe appointed to Receive donations in Cash & property and put into waggans teems &c for the purpose of Removeing the poor they had bin very busily employed for about two months & had got the poor all away except between thirty & forty famulies & arrangements going on as fast as they Could be entered into when out Came from Davise County a Company of men armed with Wm. Bouman at their head Came into Far West and there told their Buisness & there was told by Wm. Slade & a man by the name of Glues neither of them belonging to the Church that the Committe were doing all they could the mormons were ~~doing~~ all of them getting away fast as they could but all would not do they came over to the Committe house & there gave us our orders & that was that we must all be out of the County by the next Fridy night which was giving us Six dayes for to do that—that Requird a month & ~~the~~ then what was to done the Comitte amediately Commenced hiring teems & ~~the~~ Sending the famulies to Ginneyis grove with as little of their affects as they Could get along with & live & amediately there Came in a heyey Rain & fifteen famulies then witheout any manner of a Shelter & Sutch a Storm it was the Creeks Raised So high that they became impasable & the Roads intolerable & ~~the~~ in the attemp to obey the Commands of a mob there was one yoke of oxen drownd & then we had to give up & Run the Risk of their threats but the Lord blocked up their way of Coming to us as well as ours of getting out then the time passed on for about 8 or 10 dayes long & the Committe had got the principle part of the poor out & this Said Bogart [ra]isd a Company of men & came to the Committe house a place this Comitte had to do their Buisness & there they Commenced operations Breaking in the Windows of the houstablees Shacks & evry thing they Could lay their hands on & then there was only two of the Committe left viz Daniel Shearer & Elias Smith & drove them from their Buisness & they were obliged to leave the town & take with them what they Could & leave the Rest of the property ~~to the mob~~ for in the lane of a Coupel of men that had just mooved into the place ~~& what~~ the names of this last mob was Whitiker, Odle, Raglin, Bogart & in the intermediate time between these two mobs there were a number of teems Came up from Illinois for purpose of taking away famullies & while St[a]ying over night there was one for of their horses Stole belonging to a man by the name of Burton & a week after two of our people went back for the purpose of transacting Some bussness & found one of those horses in the possession of a man by the name of Kearns the Very man that we Suspected had Stole the Span & we found afterwards to our Satisfaction that he Kerns had traded the other one away for an indian poney & then Sold the poney to one of our people Sam. Parker

while I was liveing near Hawns mills on Shoal Creek Mo and about
the 25th or 26th of October 1838 I was informed that a company of mob
of twenty in number under Nehemiah Cumstock had been to the mill and
leveled pieces at those present demanding all their guns one man gave up
his rifle another who had his gun in hand refused and started off two of
the mob followed and snaped their guns at him twice or three times each
one of these men I was told was Hiram Cumstock the other name I never
learned though the man whom they were trying to shoot made his ~~of~~ way
off and gave word to the neighbor who met the next day at the mill to hear
the story from the different families who informed us that the mob had
sworn the burning of the neighbourhood and mill with the other hard
threats such as killing Hiram Abbot who would not give up his gun we
also learned that thare was another company of men lying below us at
house of Mr McCrosky & knowing that either of those companies was far
superior to ours in numbers some of the neighbours wanted to leave their
homes and run off but haveing only about seven waggons to twenty three
or four families we had to stay and defend our selves and as I recollect it
was on the twentieighth of the month we concluded to offer them terms
of peace but before our mesengers had started thare came one from the
company below us with a request that we would send three men to the
house of Oliver Walker to make a treaty with three men which they would
send to the same house David Evans Jacob Myers seignior and Anthony
Blackburn was chosen to meet them and on going to Walkers they met ten
men with each a rifle instead of three without arms however peace
prevailed and a treaty was soon made and agreed a pon I suppose to the
satisfaction of both sides and on next day two of our men went back again
those two were Evans and Ames they was told that the other company had
sent a mesenger to Cumstock and his company with word of the treaty
between us and them and also told them that we wanted to treat with them
they said that Cumstocks company was not only mad with us but mad ~~them~~
with them for making any kind of a treaty with us Evans sent them word
that he wanted nothing but peace and would not fight them without
offering them terms of peace I cannot tell whether or not they got the word
or not but well I remember that on the thirtyeth of October about three o
clock in the afternoon Cumstocks whole army of two hundred and fifty
men came a pon us our company was about thirtyseven in number being
joined by a company of families traveling to the other side of that County
and the adjoining Counties stoped thare to get grinding at the mill
Cumstocks company formed a kind of broken line at the distance of about
seventyfive yards situating their horses in front for a kind of breastwork
commenced a fire without passing a word meantime Capt Evans advanced
toward them and called aloud for quarters untill they fired I sppose

between fifty and a hundred rounds with out any answer then we could do nomore than fire afew shots while the women and children made their escape a fire the mob still advancing came within about four or five rods when I made my es cape by flight being shot four times through the body and once across each arm being about the last man off the ground now I am well aware that this is an incredible story to tell that amman being shot four times through body made his escape by flight but I have the scars to show ten in number one ball entering my body through the inside corner of my left shoulder blade came out just below about two and a half or three inches below my collar bone and as far as three inches on the right of the midle of my breast another entered through the muscle under the hind part of my left arm and passed through my body and came out under the middle of my right arm another passed through the my left hip on the inside or through the uper end of my hip bone another through my right hip hit the bone just about the joint glanced out through the skin and rolled down my drawers leg in to my boot these four balls made eight visible wounds with two others one across each arm are all the wounds in my flesh I cannot tell how many bullet holes was in my clothing thare was twentyseven in my shirt but to my story haveing made my own escape and hid my self I listened at them shooting the wounded which could not escape I was informed that one of these murderers followed old father McBride in his retreat and and cut him down with an old sythe while he was pleading for mercy this was seen by Mrs ames and two other ladies who were secreted under the creek bank Waren Smith and his Son was also shot a seccond time being unable to retreat after their first wounds Jacob Fouts and Wm. Champlin feined their selves dead and lay still untill their pockets were robed and after they supposd the wounded all were all dead they robed the houses took the horses from the mill and out of the stables and two waggons from the mill and off they went for the night but on the first or seccond of Nov they returned and camped at the mill robed that plundered the neighbourhood taking off such things as they pleased mob law being established

the in this band of robers murderers and thieves was Wm. Man Esq, N. Cumstock Esq Howard Maupin Jesse Maupin James and Stephan Reynolds called Runnels Hiram Cumstock a young man named Glase Erasmus Severe Jacob Rodgers Robert White George Miller Sardis Smith Elijah Trosper

these men came on painted black trimed of with red rags and ribbands screming like so many demons enough to dis grace a heathen forest much more a land of liberty after some spend in this manner captain went to Richmond to draw pay for his service I was told that instead of pay they gave him a cursing and threatened him with justice throwing the murder and robery in his teeth and orders to return the stolen property [thema] this made Cumstock mad and on his way home he passed the mill and stuck up an advertisement stating that the stolen property should be brought to his house and could be had by paying him for taking care of hit some of the property was got and I have seen some of the horses that was worked [——] ~~to death~~ and rode nearly down but some of the best of them could not be found for asmall reward and one of the mob was going round trying to buy the chance of such they being about the best that was taken

the names of the murdered	wounded
Benjamin Lewis	Tarlton Lewis
John York	Jacob Fouts
John Lee	Jacob Myers
John Byers	Jacob Hawn
Wm Napier	Jacob Potts
Warren Smith	Isaac Leany
Austin Hammer	Wm Yocum
Simon Cox	Nathan Night
Levi Merick	——— Walker
Elias Benner	Charles Jimison
George Richards	Alma Smith a little boy
——— Campbell	Mary Steadwell
Josiah Fuller	Hiram Abbot
Thomas McBride	Charles Merick a boy mortally
Sardis Smith a little boy	wounded

this I will support in any court of justice April the 20 1839 Quincy Illinois

Isaac Leany

[*Not sworn.*]

LEE, Alfred

The State of Illenois Adams County SS Jany 7th 1840

Personally appeared before me William Laughlin a Justice of the Peace in and for said County Alfred Lee being duly Sworn according to law Deposeth and Saith that He was a Sitizen of the State of Missouri in ~~Jackson~~ Clay County in the Year of our Lord 1834 was Driven from that place by a mob Composed of the Sitisens of Sd. Clay County Depont. further Sayeth the he removed to Coldwell County and Came in possession of land as per Duplicat and was Compelled to Sell and leave the State By Governor Boggs Exterminating order executed by General Clark and others further Deponent Saith not

Alfred Lee

[*Sworn to before W. Laughlin, J. P. Adams Co., IL, 7 Jan 1840.*]

LEE, Alfred

The State of Missouri—Dr to Alfred Lee in a bill of Damages Sustained by the extermininating of Goveror Boggs as Stated above $800.00

Alfred Lee

[*Sworn to before W. Laughlin, J.P., Adams Co., IL, 7 Jan 1840.*]

LEE, Eli

State of Illinois Adams County SS

Personally appeared before me Wm. Laughlin a Justice of the peace for said County Ely Lee being Duly sworn according to law Deposeth and Saith that he went into Jackson County Missouri in the Year of our Lord A.D 1833 was driven out the Same Year by the order Colonel Pitcher went into Clay County remained there till 1836 was then driven from thence to Coldwell County by a mob Composed of the Sitizens of that County and was Compilled to leave the state in Consequence Boggs exterminatiing order in AD 1838 Executed General Clark & others further Deponent saith not

Eli Lee

[*Sworn to before W. Laughlin, J.P., Adams Co., IL, 8 Jan 1840.*]

LEE, Eli

The State of Missouri to Eli Lee—Dr in a Bill of Damage to the amt. of $300.00

Eli Lee

[*Sworn to before W. Laughlin, J.P., Adams Co., IL, 8 Jan 1840.*]

LEFFINGWELL, William

Pittsfield Jan 22nd 1840

This is to certify that I Wm. Leffingwell Born & Brought up in the state of Connecticut now residing in the State of Ilinois that in the fall of 1838 removed with my family to the state of Missourie where I had previously paid for Lands I had friends living & after geting prey near my journys end & anticipating that I soon should again embrace my frinds but to my astonishment I was denied the privelige of citizenship on acount of of my religious belief I bing a member of the Church of later-day Saints in consequence of that I was obligd to return back & seek ashelter the best way I could among strangers with a famly of eight souls untill I with my own hands build a cabin suficent to winter in thus you may see that after I had moved along journy I lost the object of of my persuit for the which I claim damage of the Missourians to the amount of five hundred dollars

William Leffingwell

[Sworn to before W. H. Boling, C.C.C.C., Pike Co., IL, 22 Jan 1840.]

LEWIS, Tarlton

I hereby certify that I was born in South Carolina, was raised in Kentucky and lived in Illinois about four years. I then moved into the State of Missouri and settled within about one mile of Haun's Mill Caldwell County in the fall of A. D. 1837. where I lived untill I left the State in consequence of the order of Governor Boggs and the treatment which I received from a merciless band of ruffians

In the fall of A. D. 1838 I frequently heard rumours that mobs were collecting in different parts of the Country around for the purpose of driving the people called Mormons out of the Country. I belonged to that people having joined the Church of Jesus Christ of Latter Day Saints more than two years previous On the 30th of October A. D. 1838 I should judge about thirty five of our society were at Haun's Mill; a large portion of whom were movers who had stopt there in consequence of the threats and abuse which they had received on the road. The first intimation which we had that an Enemy was near us, was Some one cried out that an armed force was coming upon us. I looked and saw a number of armed men rushing out of the woods on Horseback at the distance of of twenty or thirty rods off Their number I judged to be between two hundred and two hundred and fifty. Two of our brethren made signs and cried for quarter, but their entreaties were not heeded The company began to fire upon us instantly, whereupon a number of us took shelter in a Blacksmith Shop which was near at hand. I staid there until six or eight had fallen around me being Shot down by balls, which came through the Cracks. Six of us left the shop about the same time and were the last that left it. we were all either killed or wounded in the attempt to make our Escape I was shot through the shoulder. There were fifteen killed who were buried the next day viz

Elias Brenner	Thomas McBride	———— Campbell
Josiah Fuller	Levi N. Merrick	Warren Smith
John Boyers	John York	and his son Sardius Smith
George Richards	Austin Hammer	William Naper
John Lee		Benj Lewis

There were ten or eleven men two boys and one woman Wounded two of those who were wounded viz Hiram Abbot and Charles Merrick a boy only ten years of age have since, to my knowledge, died of their wounds While I was confined with my wound; companies of Six or Eight came to my house three or four times Enquiring for arms and threatning to take me a prisoner and carry me off. Twice they Examined my wounds to see if I were able to be moved but concluded that I was not.

Tarlton Lewis

[*Sworn to before D. H. Wells, J.P., Hancock Co., IL, 3 Jan 1840.*]

LOVELESS, John

State of Illinois Adams County SS

This day personally Came before me Wm. Laughlin a Justice of the peace in Said County John Loveless being Duely Sworn Deposeth & Saith That In the year 1833 he become a Cittizen of Jackson County Settled on Congress land with The intention of Entering it and was Compelled to Leave there by the Orders of Col. Pitcer in 1836 I mooved To Caldwell and enterd land and Settled on it 80 Acres of which my duplicate will Show I was Taken Prisner on my way To far West by the militia In the month of October or November I was presant at the time That Wm. Cary was Stuck over the head with a Gun by one and of the Militia by the name of Dannohoo Wm. Cary was A prisner at the Time. and at the Same time this Dunnohoo Jurked up a spear and made an attemp to take my Life, And likewise Saw this Dunnohoo brake open several houses while I was a prisner. And I saw them Shoot down Several hogs and Cattle and left them

Lying and I Continued with Them to the Camp and Kept Under Gard for Some days and my mare Saddle and bridle was Taken. after I was Liberated ~~went back and got~~ They gave me my mare without Saddle and bridle they promised If I would ~~go~~ Come back I should have my Saddle & bridle & when on my way back was taken prisner again by John Backster and others and my mare Taken from me and have never Seen her Since when They Took the mare, or at the time they took the mare they presented there Guns to my breast & Swore they would shoot me If I did not Give her up so I dismounted and Gave her up and Finally had To Leave The State by the Exterminateing Decree of The Governer.

John Loveless

[Sworn to before W. Laughlin, J.P., Adams Co., IL, 8 Jan 1840.]

M—Z

McCARL, Jesse

January the 17th Anno Domini one thousand Eight hundred and forty personally came before me Elisha Petty one of the Justices of the peace in and for the County of Pike in the State of Illinois Jesse MC Carl and being Sworn by me Deposeth and Saith that he Suffered loss and Damage in the State of Missouri in the years Anno Domini one thousand Eight hundred and thirty Eight and Nine in Consequnc of the oppression of the Government of that Stat he Saith that he was Born in the State of North Carolina and when Residing in the State of Missouri was Ordered by the Authorties of that State to leave Said State within Six months on pain of Death and he further Saith that he was not accused of any breach of the Laws of Missouri Neither is he Sensible of ever having Broken the Laws of Said State or of the United States and he Saith that in Consequenc of Said illegal and unjust Order he was oliged to Sell his Real and part of his personal property under Value Viz Sixty acres of Land Entered and improved by him Self and for his own use on which he Suffered loss and Damage three hundred Dollars and loss and Damage on personal property including time and expence of leaving Said State two hundred and fifty Dollars total $550.00

Jesse **X** McCarl

[Sworn to before E. Petty, J.P., Pike Co., IL, 17 Jan 1840.]

MCAUL, John M.

The State of Illinois Adams County S.S. January 7th 1840

this day personly appeared before me William Laughlin a Justice of the peace within Said County, John M. Mcall who being duly sworn according to Law, Deposith and saith in 1838 Mooved to Livingston County Missouri. in Consequence of the decree of Gover[ner] was deprived of Cetisenship and Consider myself damaged 200 Dollars

John M. MCaul

[Sworn to before W. Laughlin, J.P., Adams Co., IL, 7 Jan 1840.]

McNELL, Emos

Handcock Co State of Illenois

I doe hereby testify that I moved to Carrol Co Mo not out of any pretence of religion as I did not profes any religion atall and there purchasd farm land for the benefit of my self and family and was sick and in less then two months I was notefied by a mob to leave there, and I went to carlton to get provision for my family was siezed and committed to Jail for an accusation of being friendly to the Mormons where they kept me seven days. and I was taken sick in Jail and sufferd agreat deal and they would not let me out, till I agreed to leave the Sta[te] they then gave me a pass to be out of the Co. in 24 hours or be shot which I did at the loss of my property this I tistefy this 4th day of Jan A D 1840[.] Also loss of property by moveing, purchas, and sicknes, being plunderd, robed and driven, five hundred Dollars

Emos McNell

[Sworn to before A. Monroe, J.P., Hancock Co., IL, 6 Jan 1840.]

MARSH, Eliphaz

Thereby certify that I lived in Davis county Missouri in March 1837 and was entited to a preemption right for eighty ackers of Land on the fourth day of August 183[8] near as I can tell was driven from the bord at election and was not permited to vote on or bout the eight day of Nov was surrounded by a mob or malitia under the command of R. Wilson and compeled to give up my [———— ————] two guns [———— ————] and ordered to leave the county in ten day and in the Spring to leave the state of Missouri

Eliphaz Marsh

[Sworn to before D. H. Wells, J.P., Hancock Co., IL, 10 Jan 1840.]

MARTIN, Moses

Montrose Lee Co Iowa

On the sixeth day of March AD 1840 personaly appeared before me D. W. Kilbourn acting justice of the peace within and for said county Mosess Martin who being duly sworn deposeth and saith, that he lived in Missouri Caldwell Co from the first of Nov 1837 until April 1839 when he was driven from the state by governor Bogg's exterminating orders; that when he came to Missou[ri] he bought forty acres of congress land

and received a duplicate for a deed that he built a house and made improvements on the land. that in the month of Oct 1838 Capt Bogart of Ray Co with a mob of about 60 men fell on the south of Caldwell Co and burned some houses and took some of the citizens prisoners. from this time the citizens of that Co were forced to move their families into Farewest or near there in hopes of protection for their wives and little ones from the civil authority of the state but all in vain for it was one scene of plunder

then some time in Nov an armed force of 4 or 5 thousand encamped within a short distance south of Farwest under the command of generals Lucas Clark Atchison and others they posted their guards about the town then commenced breaking opening houses and plundering the inhabitants at this time he made his escape through the guard and went home that he see armed soldiers quartering ontheinhabitants without their leave that he see them (the soldiers) tare down the fence around corn fields and take corn without leave and left the fence down for the cattle to destroy the remainder that they killed cattle and hogs which belonged to the citizens of that place without remuneration that he also see thim take a waggon and harness from his fathirs door when forbiden to so, that Capt Bogarts company or a part of it came to his hous[e] and took to rifle which were never returned one was Lewis McCrosky another was Wm. Johnson of Ray Co that the mob or militia as they called themselves frequently visited my house in search of me somtimes in the nigt with pistols cocked in their hand examined every bed and avance in the house in search of me and I was obliged to leave my family and all that I had and seek an asylum in a land of strangers through the winter then I returned to family and was obliged to sell my possession and give up my duplicate to enable me to get my family out of the state for I was forced to do so by governor Boggs exterminating orders which caused me to loose much by being forced from my land improvements and other damages which I sustained by being forced away I estimate at five hundred dollars

for which I want redress and further this deponent saith not

Moses Martin

[*Sworn to before D. W. Kilbourn, J.P., Lee Co., IA, 6 Mar 1840.*]

MILES, J. S.

In the year of our Lord 1838 I lived in Daviess County Missouri where I purchased the betterments and rights of the settlers upon two quartir sections of land lying in that county for which I gave upwards of two hundred and fifty dollars both of which were purchased and in my possession before the 18th of June 1838 but in consequence of having to leave the state I have not proved up my claims or sold my possessions.

The same year I purchased a house in Caldwell county Mo. and I took it down and moved the logs into Far West and had partly raised it when the troops arrived there. they were quartered in town and burnt up my logs and boards and also the logs of one hundred houses or more according to my judgement, They also striped the town of rails. These troops came ~~upon~~ to Far West and lived upon us without our consent as far as my knowledge extends. I saw these troops shoot down three large fat hogs and then left them to rot on the ground I saw them lying there a week afterwards. I had two and a half acres of corn which these troops gathered and took away without my consent for which I have never reced any pay ~~for~~

I have never heard of any law in Missouri authorising the calling forth of the militia in the way and manner they came to Far West about the first of Nov. 1838.

In Octr. 1838 just before a number of our people went from Far West to Daviess Co. to assist their brethren there in protecting themselveis against a large mob which rumor said was there, I heard Maj. Genl. Atchison of Clay Co. say to some of the people of Far West to go ahead and drive the mob away and take care of yourselves for it is of no use for me to call out my men as they will all turn against you. Genl. Atchison had previously been to Daviess Co. with a body of troops say from three to five hundred to quell a mob which had collected ~~in Daviess Co.~~ there and threatened our brethren, a portion of these troops were kept in Daviess Co. about three or four weeks after the main body of the mob had dispersed, for fear they would collect again.

I hereby certify that the above statements are correct according to the best of my knowledge and belief

Commerce Hancock Co. Ill. Jany, 2d 1840   J. S. Miles

[*Sworn to before D. H. Wells, J.P., Hancock Co., IL, 3 Jan 1840.*]

MILES, Mary K.

Some time after General Clark came to Caldwell with his troops. I was living about two miles from Far West ~~and~~ near to Mr Gad Yales, a number of General Clarks Troops came to Mr. Yales house and stopt their for about two Days and destroyed considerable property, they tore up both the floors of the House destroyed their poultry and hogs and set fire to [———] a Hay stack I Saw them set fire to the stack which was entirely destroyed, they took what Corn they wanted for their horses from Mr Yale and I believe he had about ten acres distroyed besides a Hay stack, this they did without leave from Mr Yale or any one who had any authority: The Hay stack which they set fire to belonged to Mr. Moss, some of the hogs which they shot down were left ~~down~~ to rot on the ground: I also saw some of the Malitia go into Mr. Syris Daniels house which they plundered. I saw them carry out one Bed, & bedding and some clothing.

I hereby Certify that the above statement is correct according to the best of my knowedge and belief

Commerce Hancock Co Illinois Jany 2 1840   Mary K. Miles

[Sworn to before D. H. Wells, J.P., Hanock Co., IL, 3 Jan 1840.]

MILES, Samuel

State of Missouri to Samuel Miles Dr

To 60 acres of Land @ $20	$1,200.00
To Cow, hogs, & other property taken	100.00
To being driven from Missouri in Jan 1839	100.00

Samuel Miles

[Sworn to before C. M. Woods, C.C.C., Adams Co., IL, 18 (no month given) 1839.]

MILES, Samuel

At Far West in Oct. A. D. 1838 I heard Maj. Genl. Atchison of Clay Co. say to some of the inhabitants of Far West in reference to a mob that was collecting in Daviess Co. Missouri to go against the Latter day Saints in that place, that it was of no use for him to call out his men to put them down for says he they will turn against you therefore you had better take care of yourselves and disperse the mob.

I certify the above to be correct according to the best of my knowledge and belief.

Commerce, Ill. Jany 2d 1840   Samuel Miles

[Sworn to before D. H. Wells, J.P., Hancock Co., IL, 3 Jan 1840.]

MILLS, Alexander

Lima Illinois Adams Co October the 22, AD, 1839
    A Bill and Charge prefered against the State of Missouri for damages
Sustanied by me Alexander Mills while A Citizen of that State in 1838
by reason of the unlawful acts Committed on me and property by the
Authorityes of the State

for the loss of property	$500.00
for the expence of Moving and being driven from the State and being deprived of My Liberty	500.00
Whole Amount	$1,000.00

[*Sworn to before J. Orr, J.P., Adams Co., IL, 8 Jan 1840.*]

MINER, Albert

January 8th 1840
    This is to certify to the wrongs and injuries I received in the State of
Missouri
    I arrived in Caldwell County Sept. 15th 1838 in the month of Oct.
while in my way holm From mils with my team traveling peaceable in the
highway two armed men came to me & told me I must go with them they
took me to the camp of pretended Malitia & Cept. me three days in the
mean time they took from me a fine horse also a [——] & threaten[*ed*]
my lif without cause or provocation

Albert Miner

[*Sworn to before J. Orr, J.P., Adams Co., IL, 8 Jan 1840.*]

MOORE, Andrew

A bill Staiting the loss of property and damagees that I Sustained by
the inhabitence of the State of Missouri, unlawfully. I emagrateed with my
Famaly in the year 1834 from the State of Ohio to the sd State of Missouri
with the expecation of resideing there, which, cost me one hundred dollars
there I bought Land and paid for it in Clay County being compeled to leve
there without any just caus or provication I lost on my land there one
hundred and ten dollars, I remooved from Clay to Caldwell Co damages
for remooveing from Clay to Coldwell one hundred and ten dollars, there
I bought Land and made me afarm there being compeld to leve the State
in 1838 I lost on Land Twelve hundred dollars, on Corn Cattle and other

property two hundred dollars on Hoggs fifty dollars, two Rifle Guns thirty five dollars, one swaord eaight dollars. on 2 Town lots in Farwest one hundred dollars I was Seraunded and takeen and and cept under gard un lawfully six days—damagees twenty dollars loss of time and damagees for remooveing out of the State one thousand dollars, all with out any just caus or provication,

the amount of all the losses and damgees as nigh as I can asertain amounts to two thousand nine hundred and thirty three dollars

Andrew Moore

[Sworn to before J. M. Campbell, C.C.C., McDonough Co., IL, 25 Sep 1839.]

MORLEY, Isaac

Isaac Moreley

This is to Certify to the wrongs and injuris that I have Sustained in the State of Missouri

I moved into Jackson County in, 1831 where I lived in peace, untill, 1833, on the 20 of July, I was called to meet a Committee in Independance, at, A. S. Gilberts Store, composed of Robert Johnson, Moses G. Willson, James Camel, Joel, F. Childs Richard Fristoe, Abner Steeples Jan Johnson, Lewis Franklin, Russel M. Hicks, Samuel, D. Lucas Thomas Willson, James W. Hunter, and Richard Simpson—are the persons that met, A. S. Gilbert, J Corrill, W.W. Phelps, John Whitmer, E. Partridge, and I. Morely They requested us to leave the County forthwith, We told them that we should want a little time to consider upon the matter, they told us that we could have only fifteen minutes, we replyed to them that we could not comply ~~with~~ or consent to their proposals with in that time, one of them observed and said then I am Sorry I think it was Lewis Franklin Said he then, the work of destruction will then Commence Ammeadiately, they went out and Repared to the Court house, in Company I should think with 4 or 5 hundred men, we then returned home, and Shortly after I saw the printing Office leveled to the Ground, in a few days after, I saw a Company passing by my house, towards independance, with a Red Flag hoisted, I was called upon again, with a number of our Society, to meet them again, we then agreed to leave the Country, as individuals, they then promised us protection, on the following terms, that we should use our influence and that one half of our Society Should leave the County, by the first of January next and the Balance by the first of April following, we then attended to our Circular Concerns until about the first of Novem. when they again

499

Commenced to Commit Depredations on us, they Stone in my windows by night with rock exposing the lives of my family, about this time lieutenant Governor Boggs Came to my house and advised me if any of the Citizens Came and Destroyed any of my property by night if he was in my place he would return the Same injuries to them in the Dark, on the 3 of Novem. if I recolect the date news came to Several of us that they (the Mob) were destoying the goods of A. S Gilbert we then Ameadiately repared to the Store and though if posible to Save the property, we there took A Mr. McCartey in the act of plundering the Goods, Several then took him before Esq. Weston and Said they requested a warrent but he would not give them one, they then let McCartey go on the fourth, they took me a prisioner with several others, at evening they took us to the Court house for trial ~~we had Just taken and Sent~~, for arresting McCartey when a party Came in Swearing they would take the lives of the prisioners the Court then ameidiately orderd us to be put into Joal where Lewis Franklin the Jailor turned the key upon us after Consulting upon our Situation, A. S. Gilbert J. Corrill and I Morley requested the priveledge of the Sherriff and Jailor to go and Council with our friends what would be best for us to do they Consented and went with us, and we agreed to leave the County forth with about Eleven O Clock we returned to the prison where we were met with a company of men one of them hailed us Saying who Comes there, the Sheriff answered a friend clothed with Authority, one of them answered Dam you you have no business out with the Prisioners at this time a night and we will Shoot you at the Same time I heard them Cock their guns, I then turnd upon my heal and run a few paces they then fired upon us. Just as the day dawned I went into the house of the Jaylor he asked me how I dared to be there, I told him I was not Sensible of doing any thing wrong, he Said I was in danger I told him I was a prisioner and that if he had any thing to do with me he Could do it he then took me to prision and turned the key upon me, when the Sun was about one hour high in the morning he Came and told us we were at liberty, we then returned home and on the Same day Colonel Pitcher Came out with a pretended Malitia and Compeled our people to deliver up their arms to them, on the 11 I removed my family into Clay County, where we lived until April, 1837. I then removed with my family to Caldwell County, I there purchased two, 80, Acres of Goverment land for my own use also a City lot in far West where I built me a comfortable house and lived in it until 1838, when we received the exterminating orders from Governor Boggs the troops arrived on the Evening of the 30 of October and on the first day of Novem. we were called upon to deliver up our arms on the day we were Called together By order of General Clark Commander in Chief he ordered our people to form a hollow square the General with Several other Officers went into the Square he then Called upon me together with about fifty of my Brethren to walk into the hollow Square General Clark then addressed those who Compased the hollow Square as follows, gentleman you are now at Liberty to go and Settle up your Business and prepare to leave the State and not think to raise another Crop in this County or State and as for those that I have Called into the Square I will make a public example of them, he then told us we were prisioners he Set a Strong guard over us, and placed us in a Store house for the night, the next morning we were taken out and conducted by a strong guard to Richmond to Receive our trial where we weredetained until Novem. 24the, 1838, then I was discharged by Judge King there being no Cause of action found against me all of this abuse and false imprisionment I received without a legal process also I was Commanded to leave the State by order of General Clark

Isaac Morley

[Sworn to before J. Orr, J.P., Adams Co., IL, 9 Jan 1840.]

MORRISON, Arthur

Quincy Illinois January 9th AD 1840

I do hereby Cirtify that I owned a tract of <u>land</u> in Caldwell County Missouri, it being the South 1/2 of the S.W. qu of the S.W. qu of Section 34 township fifty seven N of the base line and W. of the fifth principal Meriden No twenty four, it being Entered by Edward Larkey, and from which I have been driven by the Exterminating order of Governor Boggs, and also owned another tract of land in the same County being the N. W. qu of the N. E. qu of Sec 8, Townsh[ip] fifty six N of the base line and west of the fifth Principal Meriden range No Twenty Nine Containing 40 acres, which I am also deprived of and have been exiled ~~from~~ and driven from the state. I also cirtify that I was present at the reading of the Gover[nor's] order at Far west, by General Lucas, and heard Lucas say that if Joseph Smith Jr. with a number of others was not given up to them, that the city of far-West would be consumed by fire and that it with its contents would soon be in ashes, and General Clark took posession of my storehouse without leave and quartered his ~~men~~ prisoners in it to my annoyance, and that Umbeson Lyons took about 1000 Dollas worth of goods from me by force and for which I have received no compensation, the above is a true statement of facts to the best of my recollection

Arthur Morrison

[Sworn to before C. M. Woods, C.C.C., Adams Co., IL, 9 Jan 1840.]

MUNJAR, Elizabeth C.

State of Illinois Adams County SS January 7th 1840

This day personally appeard before me Wm. Laughlin a Justice of the peace within said county Elizabeth C. Munjar [Duly] Sworn according to Law Deposeth and saith that in the year 1833 she became a Citizen of Jackson Co, Missouri. and was driven from there to Clay County by a Mob. and Suffered Considerable from Exposure & lived in Clay County a short Time & whilst liveing in Clay was sent to liberty on an erand for my mother and on my return Home I was Chased by one of the Male Citizen of Liberty whose name was Wood, who Talked Very insulting to me and was driven from thence to Caldwell sufferd Very Considerable there in the time of the Militia, and finally was obliged by the Exterminating Decree of the Governer to Leave the state.

Elizabeth C. **X** Munjar

[Sworn to before W. Laughlin, J.P., Adams Co., IL, 8 Jan 1840.]

MUNJAR, William

The State of Illinois Adams County SS January 7th 1840

this day personally appear before me William Laughlin a Justice of the peac within Said County, William Munjar, in 1833 bicame a Citizen of Jackson County Missouri I made an Improvement On Government Land & was Compelled to Leave there by The Orders of Col. pitsher went from thence to Clay County And became a [Renter], & then was Compelled to moove from there to Caldwell County Then Settled down on Congress Land and made an Improvement and Kept peacable possession untill the fall 1838 And was Exterminated from the State by the Orders of General Clark and Others on our way from Caldwell to Illinois was Obliged to Leave our waggons and familys and flee to the woods for safety

William Munjar

[Sworn to before W. Laughlin, J.P., Adams Co., IL, 7 Jan 1840.]

MURDOCK, John

This is to certify that I John Murdock being a member of the Church of Crist of Latter day Saints Removed my family to the State of Missouri Shoal Creek afterwards Caldwell Co in the Summer of eighteen hundred & thirty Six & in July the year following I entered forty acres of land the

Duplicate of which I cause to accompany this as proof of the Same the in August or Sep following I entered annother forty in the Same office the No of which I have forgoten & the Duplicate was unlawfully arrested from me & being forced from the State have not had the opportunity of Getting the [con]tent out of the Office. In the Summer of Eighteen hundred & thirty eight I removed to Dewett Carrell Co having previously bought a part of the town platt in company with G M Hinkel. In quite the last part of July 1838 the people of Carroll Co having held a meeting Sent a committee of three men to visit us Abbott Handcock was chief Speaker of the three being a Cumberland Presbyterian Priest also John Smart & another man I do not recollect His name Mr. Handcock ordered Mr. Hinkel & myself & all the Mormons to leave the County by the 7th of August I asked Mr. Hancock by wat authority he did so he said by the authority of Carrell Co. About the 19th of August Pierce Hawley came into Dewett apparrently frightned & Said he had been a prisoner all night by a mob of 60 or 70 who were within 4 miles of town & would be upon us in two hours & his orders was to be out of town in two hours he said but Mr Robert Seelly a friend of ours rode out to see them & learned that the Sheriff of the co was in the company having a Warrent Sworn out by Seciel Wood a cumberland Presbyterian Priest who had sworn the piece against G M Hinkel Mr S—— agreed with the Sheriff to come into town alone & tak Mr. Hinkel & not bring in an army to Scare womin & children. He did so & took Mr. Hinkel before Esq Staton a distance of about 4 or 5 miles & nobody appeared against him he was acquited & returned to his family. Immediately when the Sheriff & Prisoner left town Colonel Jones at the head of I suppose near a hundred armed men entered town accompanied by Seciel Wood & in a verry hostile manner Paraded through town at lea[st] two or three hours threatning men women & children with destruction of person & property if they were not out of the County in ten days & after making a general discharge of their rifles left town hooting & hallowing like wild savages. Again I think it was in the month of Sept Having business into Davis Co as I was riding in a one horse Waggon a Rufus Allen accompanied me we were Surprised & taken prisoners by 22 or 23 armed men Cornelius Gillham being their leader who Stood then elected as a member of the Legislator & after detaining us a half hour or more tantelizing us took a pistol from me & a Rifle from Allen threatning to shoot us & calked & presented their rifles at us but finely let us go this hapned about 5 miles South of Adamonde Ahmin About the first of Oct. we begun to be harrassed by day & by night by Scouting parties of the mob in & about Dewitt firing at [ou]r men in and about town & riding into town making [th]reats of death & destruction against the church. It was said [the]y had gathered Several hundred Strong & encamped within one [mile] of town but [*to*] this I was not an eye wit[ness] but I believe [it] for I heard more than a hundred guns [——] near together likewise many other circumstances causes me to believe it we were harrassed from that time forth til about the 10th or 11th of Oct. On the 19th of August we sent a Petition by P Hawley to Austin A. King the circuit judge for protection but got no answer. Also I think some time in Sept we sent a petition to Lilburn W. Boggs Gov of Mo for releaf & received no answer. Again about the 2nd or 3rd of Oct we sent Mr Calwell in Person to the Gov Soon after when the mob Seemed to be doing all they could against us we Sent Henry Root to Judg King he Sent Genl Park with two hundred men to relieve us he encamped within one mile of town but said he could do nothing for us because of the mob sprit in his men & Some of his officers said so likewise & he withdrew his men about 11th of Oct & we recievd word about the same time that the Gov. would do nothing for us & as we could get no protection from the authorities of the State we were forced to surrender our property our rights & our freedom that our fathers bled for & on the 11th of Oct the Society removed from Dewitt for Caldwell Co the church at this time consisted of forty to fifty families many of them sick & had a cold chilling blast to pass on an open Prary & many in open Waggens one woman died on the way the old man Cross was into town with an armed force before I left town I arived in Caldwell Co near Far West on the 14th of Oct where I remained but a short time til Generals Lucas & Willson of Jackson Co acommpanied by other Genls marched an army of Soldiery to Far West & caused the Church to lay down theer arms & while in this defenceless cituation flung down their fences destroyed their corn Potatoes Ponpians & all kinds of grain & Sauce with Cattle Hogs Sheep & horses to bad to be named they took about 20 acres of corn of Gidean Allen flang down his fence in many places round the corn I sent my boy to put it up I Saw them getting the corn it was in Shockes & many other things I saw too tedious for to name

John Murdock

NB—The Duplicat that I Promised to send accompanying this has got lost so that I cannot send it Lexington Layfayette Co is were the office is that I enterd my land

John Murdock

[*Sworn to before J. Orr, J.P., Adams Co., IL, 10 Jan 1840.*]

MYRICK, Philindia

To the Honourable the Senate And house of Representatives in Congress Assembled At the City of Washington in the District of Columbia January 9th 1840 Heer by represent to you my losdses And troubles that I received under the Exterminateing order Governer Boggs of the State of misourie We moved to the State of missourie in the fall of 1838 we ware stopt by on the way by the mob our waggeon searcht guns taken from us our lives thretened and after keeping us fore days then let us proseed our journey then we went on till we Came to Hawns mills on shole creek in Caldwell CO and a bout the 29th of October thare being several families campt thare the mob came a ponus in the after part of the day with Mr Cumstock at thare hed and commens fireing on helpless men womens and children and thare was fifteen killed and was burried in one hole the next day and others wounded sum mortally and amung whom was my husband ~~instantly killed~~ Levi N. Myrick instantly killed and also a child of mine mortaly woun ded who died about 4 weeks after and the mob took 2 horses 12 sheep 2 guns & sum tools and clothing which was worth no less than three hundred dollars and after all of this I was oblige to get out of the state the best way I Could and now I hav three fatherless Children to main tain with my own hands laber all the above los and agravencies happened because of our Religion so said the mob

Philindia Myrick

[*Sworn to before R. L. Hill, C.C.C. Jersey Co., IL, 10 Jan 1840.*]

NAPER, Reuben

I Certify that I lived near Hauns Mill about three months, On Tuesday the thirtieth day of October being absent from home at the House of Mr Walker, while their a man came up and told us that the mob had come to the Mill and that they had Shown no Quarter, and that they intended to Sweep Shoal Creek. That evening I Started to go to the mill and proceeded Some distance I met Some Families in the Woods who had fled from the Slaughter they persuaded me not to go any further that night. So I Consented to Stay with them. We all Slept in the Woods that night without any beds or any thing to Cover us with excepting two women who had brought Each of them a quilt. The next morning I pursued my Journey and went I got to the Mill I met my Mother and the rest of the family. I asked them if my Father was dead. They told me to go and look into the Shop I immediately went to the Shop and Saw Seven men and one boy lying dead amongst whom was my Father who was shot through the head and through the heart. Three more I found lay dead near the Shop and Several more reached Some houses and Soon afterwards died, in all there were Eighteen killed Sixteen men and two boys.

Witness of Rob B Thompson   Reuben X Naper

[Sworn to before D. H. Wells, J.P., Hancock Co., IL, 3 Jan 1840.]

NAPER, Ruth

I hereby certify that my husband William Naper and myself lived near Haun's mills about three months previous to the massacre at Haun's which was on the 30th of Octr. A. D. 1838

The man we lived with who did not belong to the Church told us the week previous to the massacre that the Mormons would all be killed within a month that there would not be one left a span long in Caldwell Co. in that time. After the massacre was over I went into a certain blacksmith shop where I found my husband dead, he was shot through the breast, there were seven others in the shop dead and dying I did not count those who were dead outside of the shop therefore the whole number killed is unknown to me but I suppose seventeen or eighteen were killed. I judged that there were three at least three hundred of this mob armed force and I heard some of them say that there were over four hundred of them. They came upon us on a sudden for they came rushing out of the woods[.] We had a few days previous moved to within a short distance of Haun's mills. After this company had ceased fireing they sent and you ordered me and other women to leave the houses, which we did and then they plundered them of our efforts.

After a few days there came back a large company of armed men and took possession of Haun's mill and they also crowded into our house and crowded me and my children away from the fire without my consent they lodged there and one night one of them came to my bed and laid his hand upon me which so frightened me that I made quite a noise and crept over the back side of my children, and he offered no further insult at the time. This company camped in the nieghborhood between one and two weeks to our great inconvenience for they took from the brethren grain, cattle, hogs, bee stands, &.C. as free to appearance as though it was they were their own

Commerce Ill. Decr. 2d 1834   Ruth Naper

[Sworn to before D. H. Wells, J.P., Hancock Co., IL, 3 Jan 1840.]

NEWMAN, Elijah

I hereby certify that I settled in the State of Missouri in the year A. D. 1833 and continued my residence there untill last winter

I was living at Far West at the time Genl. Lucus came there with his troops about the first of November 1838. The first day that these troops appeared at Far West they rode up within a short distance of the town where they formed into lines and halted. It was nearly sundown and they soon turned back half a mile or more and encamped for the night. The next day they rode up and formed again as before. Flags of truce were passed back and forward, and I understood the troops[.] requested an interview with some of the leading men of our church at their camp because they wished to make known to them their business those named went out to the troops No sooner had our brethren put themselves into their hands than the troops commenced an awfull yelling and shouting such as I never before heard[.] They made the air ring for miles round and continued to shout and yell for a long time. They demanded our arms ~~were demanded~~ and the next day they were given up. We were kept the most of the day closely guarded in a hollow square while they guarded large bodies of troops say thousands rode through the town in different directions. Guards were placed around the town and a number of companies were stationed in different parts of the town These troops burnt large quantities of house logs. I judged to logs to be sufficent for forty or fifty houses They were houses taken down and moved into town just before the troops came there and the owners had not time to put them up again they were moving in for their safty. I saw the soldiers pull down the body of one house in Far West and burn the logs, they also burnt many rails I was ordered, ~~together~~ with the rest of my brethren that were in town onto the public square where we were closely surrounded by a strong guard and there compelled to sign an instrument of writing said to be a deed of trust, which was to bind us to put all our property into the hands of a committee to be applied in paying the debts of any of the church members and also to pay any damages which the people of Daviess county might claim for any damages they might [———] have sustained by any body and also to defray the expences of calling out the troops. After Genl. Clark arrived and took command we were ordered on to the public square where we were closely guarded in a circle or square with Genl. Clark and a number of other officers in the center—One of them read over a list names and all those who were in the ring whose names were called were ordered forward by Genl. Clark fifty or more of us were called out. we were then marched into a house and closely guarded[.] In a short time Genl. Clark came in and said to us in substance as follows. Your situation I know is an unpleasant one you have been guilty of all manner of crimes and although you may not be more guilty than others who have not been taken yet I intend to make an example of you. The nature and enormeties of your crimes have been such that you are not fit to live among a moral people therefore you shall not be permitted to live in the state. It was a part of the treaty made by Genl. Lucus that the Mormons should leave the state and that was also the Governor's order. In consequence of the present extreme cold weather I will permit them to stay untill the weather becomes warm and if they are not off then I will pledge myself that I will drive them out of the state and if I have to come again I will show them no quarters. The next day we were marched off to Richmond Ray Co. where we were confined a number of days before we had any particular crime alledged against us. The weather was the coldest I ever knew it at that season of the year we had to camp out two nights while upon the road And after we arrived at Richmond we had to lie upon the floor and they did not furnish us with a blanket or any kind of bedding, and we suffered greatly in consequence of the cold. I was kept in custody in Richmond between two and three weeks and then was dismissed by Judge King there haveing been nothing proved against me. I moved out of Mo. in consequence of Governor Boggs' order and the threats of Genl. Clark. My losses I compute at from one hundred and fifty to two hundred dollars

Elijah Newman

[Sworn to before D. H. Wells, J.P., Hancock Co., IL, 3 Jan 1840.]

NISWANGER, William

State of Illinois Adams County SS. January 7, 1840

This day personally appeared before me William Laughlin one of the Justices of the peace in & for said County William Niswanger who being duly sworn according to law deposeth & saith that in the year of our Lord one thousand eight hundred & thirtyseven & thirtyeight he was a citizen of Caldwell county, state of missouri & that he the said deponent did at the land office in Lexington, Fayette Cty. mo. enter forty acres of land in his own name & for his own use, in township 55 Range 28, section 9 southwest of the southwest quarter section Joining the sixteenth section: & that he was taken & put under guard by order of General Lucas, & by order of said Lucas was then compelled to sign away said land or go to prison. & further this Deponent saith not.

William Niswanger

[Sworn to before W. Laughlin, J.P., Adams Co., IL, 7 Jan 1840.]

NORTON, David

January the 22 AD 1840 Township Five by Five Co of Pike State of Illinois

A Statement of los and Dammages done me the undersined David Norton By the athority of Govener Bogs and his asistance of mosoury state I had 200 acres of land and Buildings thare on I had paid government and had government was abelegeed to let my wheat Corn hogs and some of my Cattle to get away [——] not being able to git my money tho I had lent to the missourians to help my self a way and they no now ow me lent money and they in mo and I have been drove [of] from my land and [——] was not allowed to Retirn to it any more and A trifle had to take a trifle for it or loze it all And i Consider that I have Lost 500 Dollars

David **X** Norton his hand and seal

[Sworn to before W. H. Boling, C.C.C.C., Pike Co., IL, 27 Jan 1840.]

OMSTEAD, Harvy

Handcock Co and State of Illenois

I doe here by testify that I emigrated to Jackson Co and State of Missouri in the year 1832 and in 1833 a mob arose and I saw them throw down a two story brick building ocupyed as a private dwelling below and a printing office above and they broke the press Scatterd the type and paper and they tared and fetherd Bishop Patridge and they took me prisner and kept after this they met in council and resol[ve]d to put us out of the County (peaceably if we can, foreceable if we must) they took one prisner and the next morning a company headed by a Baptist Priest came to my house and warnd me to leave the county whic[h] I we did

whil in clay co we was threatend if we did not leave there, and they agread to let us have Caldwell Co I moved from there to Davis Co in 1838 made a claim and intended to enter when it came in market but a mob arose and I was compeld to move to Adam Ondi Ahman and soon after my house was burnt my plows taken my stock distroyed soon after I was cald away on buisness, and when I returnd I found an armed soldiery encamped in the Town under the command of Gen. Wilson and none was allowed to pass out without a pass from him, and then they must be escorted out and ten days was given for all to move out of the county in and we was only permitted to stay till spring and then to leave the State at the perril of our lives which we did Signed this 4 day of Jan A D 1840

Harvy Omstead

[Sworn to before A. Monroe, J.P., Hancock Co., IL, 6 Jan 1840.]

OUTHOUSE, John

State of Illinois County of Adams Jan 8th 1840

I John Outhouse do hereby certify that I was a citizen of Caldwell Co. Mo. and purchased land there to the amount of 80 acres 40 of which I purchased from Government but on account of my religion being a member of the church of Jesus Christ of Latter day Saints commonly called Mormons I was compelled to leave the state under the exterminating order of the Govener of said state

John Outhouse

[Sworn to before J. Orr, J.P., Adams Co., IL, 8 Jan 1840.]

OVERTON, Mahala an

State of Illenois County of Adams Jan 8th 1840

I Mahala ann Overton do hereby certify that in the month of Sept and oct. 1838 I was at Wm Hills Ray Co. Mo. and I herd him say repeatedly that Jo Smith was an imposter and ought to be killed and all the rest of the Mormons for there doctrin was fals and he said that he would kill him as quick as he would a hog and was reagr to go and help drive them out of the State for they was not fit to live on the earth ~~Mr H~~ the said Mr Hill was in Bogart company when they went into Far West to help to perform the act of extemination I also was at Mr Gibson Gates house in clay Co. and a Company of Malitia come and demanded his gunes and Mrs. Gates and sons gave them up for fear of there lives one of the names of the men in the company was Vaun in consequence of our lives being threatened [——] myself and little girl and Mrs Gates and 9 children was compelled to to start to Far West on foot about 30 mils the weather was very cold and we suffered with the cold very much and then was compelled to leave the State under the exterminating order of the Govenor I also had land which I had leave

mahala nn overtonn

[Not sworn.]

PACK, John

State of Ileanis Pike County

I Certifi that I John Pack was Drove from the County of Davis in Mosury to Coldwell County and from Coldwell County Mosury to the State of Ileanois and this by the orders of the govenor of the State of

Mosury I and my Wife was taken prisoners wile travling Seventy five miles from home and received greit a buse I ~~received~~ sustained the loss of upwards of two thousand Dollars in propperty and all this inconsequence of the Governors orders

John Pack

[*Sworn to before W. H. Boling, C.C.C.C., Pike Co., IL, 14 Jan 1840.*]

PAGE, James B. F.

Loss of Propperty by being Driven from State of Mo. It being for Land and Cattle and time $800.00

James B. F. Page

[*Sworn to before A. Monroe, J.P., Hancock Co., IL, 6 Jan 1840.*]

PAGE, James B. F.

I here by testify that in the year 1835 I was Driven from Lafett Co. Mo to Clay Co. by a Mob leaving all of our Crops in Lafett not Receiving any thing for the same, I then was Driven from Clay Co. leaving my House and Land to Colwell Co. in 1837 and in 1838 I past through all the Suferings of leving the State and my House and Land and I saw an armed forse Come in to our Town and surround the plase and was taken prisenor and they took my arms and was not permited to gow of from my one possesion I allso had one youk of Oxen driven of by the armry and further saw my Mother ordered out of her House in Davis Co. Mo. being an old lady of sixty years of of age and was under the necesity of traviling 16 Mills on the Priaria in the snow and at night was under the necessity of lodging in an old Cabin without fire or Clothing and two of her Sons and they Sick with Aqeue and fevor and She was not permited to take any of her House furniture with her nether her Cows or Calvs and then was Driven from the State with the rest of the Inhabitance thus wi Certify being an Eye Witness

James B. F. Page

[*Sworn to before A. Monroe, J.P., Hancock Co., IL, 6 Jan 1840.*]

PALMER, Abraham

Abraham Parmer of Springfield Sangamon County State of Illinois says he is a member of the Church of Latter day Saints commonly called Mormons and that he moved into the State of Missouri in October 1838 and proceeded with his family in a waggon as far as Caldwell County where he arrived two days before the Massacre of the Mormons at Haun's Mill he stopped at a Mr Walkers about four miles from the said Mill where he remained in his waggon with his family in company with six other waggons of his brethren untill after the Massacre The next day after the aforesaid outrage a company of the mob came to him and brethren and said if you will deny your faith you can live with us in peace but if you will not you must leave the Country forthwith on pain of death for we will exterminate all of you that do not deny your faith men women and children. The above proposition was made by a man who had previously assisted in plundering our waggons he called his name Austin and Styled himself Captain of the Livingston County Spies

Abraham Palmer

[Sworn to before J. Adams, J.P., Sangamon Co., IL, 9 Nov 1839.]

PARTRIDGE, Edward

In the year of our Lord 1831 I removed from the State of Ohio to Jackson Co. Missouri. I purchased land and built me a house, near the village of Independence, where I lived a peaceable inhabitant molesting no body.

On the 20th day of July A. D. 1833 George Simpson and two other mobbers entered my house (whilst I was sitting with my wife, who was then quite feeble my youngest child being then about three weeks old,) and compelled me to go with them. soon after leaving my house I was surrounded by about fifty mobbers who escorted me about half a mile to the public square, where I was surrounded by some two or three hundred more.

Russell Hicks Esqr. appeared to be the head man of the mob, he told me that his word was the law of the county, and that I must agree to leave the county or suffer the consequences. I answered that if I must suffer for my religion it was no more than others had done before me—That I was not conscious of having Injured any one in the county therefore I could not consent to leave it. Mr. Hicks then proceeded to strip off my clothes and was disposed to strip them all off—I strongly protested against being stripped naked in the street, when some more humane than the rest interfered and I was permitted to wear my shirt and pantaloons. Tar and feathers were then brought and a man by the name of —— Davies with the help of an other daubed me with tar from the crown of my head to my feet, after which feathers were thrown over me. For this abuse I have never received any satisfaction, although I commenced a suit against some of them for $50,000 damage, and paid my lawyers six hundred dollars to carry it on, I also paid near two hundred dollars to get a change of venue.—My lawyers after getting their pay of me, made a compromise with the defendents, without my consent, and threw my case out of court without giving me any damages by their agreeing to pay the costs, which they never have paid that I know of, and I never could prevail upon my lawyers to collect them for me though they agreed so to do.

Nov. 1833 I was compelled by a mob to leave Jackson county, at which time I held the title to two thousand one hundred and thirty six acres of land all lying in that county and also two villge lots situated in the village of Independence. Such have been the threats of the people of that county that I have never to this day dared to go on to, much less settle upon, my lands there, though I still own some there yet.

From Jackson I moved to Clay county where I lived till the fall of 1836 when I moved my family to what is now Caldwell county there I purchased land and built houses where I lived till last winter when in conformity with the order of Gov. Boggs and the threats of Genl. Clark I moved my family to the State of Illinois, at which time I held the title to forty acres of land in Clay Co. and more than four fifths of the lots in the town of Far West Caldwell Co. which was laid out one mile square and was settleing very rapidly. I had five houses and one barn in the town. I also held eight hundred and sixty eight acres of land in Caldwell county.

The property in Caldwell Co. has sunk to a mere trifle, in consequence of our Church not being protected there.

I give the following for a sample, I bought a house last summer in Far West and gave twelve hundred dollars for it, after I bought it a well was dug and other repairs made amounting to between fifty and a hundred dollars this property has lately been sold by my agent and only brought one hundred dollars—An other house and lot which last summer I would not have been willing to have taken three hundred dollars for has been sold by my agent and brought only thirty dollars, however I cannot think that property there will remain so low long.

Whilst our society lived in Jackson and Clay counties there never was any one of them, to the best of my knowledge, ever convicted of any criminal offence, and a lawsuit of any kind was very rare, although they were accused of mor[e] unlawful things especially in Jackson Co. when at the same time the administration of the laws was in their own hand.

But for the want of any thing legal against us, they proceeded against us illegally, and not only drove us from our lands and homes in Jackson Co. but kept us from them, and this order of things was suffered by the authorities and people of the State to remain year after year untill at last for the want of protection against that spirit of Mobocracy we have been compelled to leave the State.

I lived near three years in Clay Co. within a few miles of the line of Jackson Co., and no man from Jackson Co. or anywhere else brought any law suit of any kind whatever against me during the time.

I feel that the state of Missouri ought to pay an immense sum for damages, for not protecting us in the first place in our rights in Jackson Co., and in the second place in not granting us protection in the State.

Last fall I was taken from my home in Far West Mo. by Genl. Clark, without any civil process, and driven off to Richmond Ray Co. thirty miles, and kept a prisoner between three and four weeks before I was liberated, for which I think the State of Missouri aught to pay me a round sum.

The following charges I make against the state of Missouri for losses sustained, leaving my damages to be computed by others

My losses in Jackson Co. Mo. in stripping my land of timber the destruction of my house, corn, potatoes &.C. &.C.	$15,000.00
My loss in paying lawyers to carry on my suit against certain individuals in Jackson Co. Mo. and costs	950.00
My loss or expected loss on my land, houses, and village lots in Caldwell Co. in consequence of having to leave there	15,500.00
My loss in paying lawyers to defend myself and others who I believe were unlawfully taken before judge King last fall	5,000.00
My loss for time and expences in moving a large family out of the state, sacrifice of furniture &.C. &.C.	400.00
My loss for having taken by the militia a number of guns, pistols and swords	100.00
My loss in the destruction of corn, hay, sheep, and 1 fat horned beast	42.00
	$36,992.00

Quincy Ill. May 15th 1839

I certify that the above statements are correct according to the best of my knowledge and belief.

Edward Partridge

One important item I forgot to mention before the foregoing was testified to, which is as follows, Whilst I was prisoner confined to the town of Far West, I was with the rest of the inhabitants collected within a circle on the public square, and there, surrounded by a strong guard, we were compelled to sign a deed of trust, which deed was designed to put our property into the hands of a committeee, to be disposed of by them to pay all the debts which had been contracted by any and all who belong to the church.— also to pay all damages which might be claimed by the people of Daviess county for any damages they might have sustained from any person whatever. I would remark that all those who did deny the faith were exonerated from signing this deed of trust.

Edward Partridge

[*Sworn to before C. M. Woods, C.C.C., Adams Co., IL, 15 May 1839.*]

PATTEN, Charles W.

January 8t 1840

This is to ceriify that Charles W Patten a member of the church of Christ of Latter Day Saints remooved with my family to Jackson Co, Missourie in the year 1833 expecting to become a permanent setler of that state & County but in that I was disappointed—for I had not remained there but a few days before I hapned into Independance— heard a petition read by Samuel C Owens clerk of said county & after he read the petition he said the Mormons must leave the Co. or deny their religion he was then asked by a gentleman what he had against them why said he we cannot agree & if we do not disperse them & stop the emigration they will sone become so numerous that they will rule the County D——d them they must go, the petition signed by Samuel C Owens contained many heard threatnings & it was not many days untill they put them into practice Some time in Oct. I was present when Robert Johnson struck Parley P Pratt over the head with his gun & knocked him down I herd the blow, but did not see him fall but saw him get up—& saw the blood running. he tryed to get redress by law but could not get a hearig also Moses G Willson came to my house and asked me how long I expected to live there I told him I did not know but I had come there for the purpos of becoming a perminent Setler of that place he told me I had better be gone or quit the Mormons for we are deter-mnined to rid our Cou[nty] of every Mormon you had better be gone and that spedily, This mob continued until at length I was compelled to leave my house & my living & flee for my life & as I was on my way to Clay Co. I was stoped by Thomas Willson & Mr. Cockerill clerk of Moses G Willson & then surrounded by 12 or 13 men well armed. after threatning to let out my hearts blood & crossing some of their Dirks across my breast they let me gow, I saw also many men that was whipped & many houses that was thrown down by this mob I was also presant at the time our <u>arms</u> was demanded by Colonel Pitcher & he promised us protection for a certing length of time by pledging his honor that we should not be harmed & if we was molested he would protect us by the force of arms but to our astonishment the verry next day 60 or 70 men bearing the arms we gave up riding from house to house hunting for men swearing they would kill them if they could find them telling their wives & children if they was not gone in less than 3 days they would massacree all they could find protection was sought for but could not be found

In the year 1838 I bought 80 acres of land in Caldwell Co of government expecting there to enjoy my rights acording to the constitution but in this I was again disappointed for in the year 1838 I was compelled to leave the State by Governor Boggs expelling order & to make a sacrifice of nearly all I possessed also I was compelled to give up my duplicates for the land I had bought with my money which Duplicates call for south east quarter of the south west qr. of township 56 also the N W qr. of the N W qr. Sect, 6 twnship 55 & range 29

Charles W Patten

[*Sworn to before J. Orr, J.P., Adams Co., IL, 8 Jan 1840.*]

PATTEN, John

Personally appeared before me David W. Kilbourn a Justice of the peace of Lee County, Iowa Territory, appointed by the governor of said Territory, John Patten, who after being duely sworn according to law deposeth and sayethe, that he the said Patten is a member of the Church of Jesus Christ of Latter day saints (Ironically called Mormons) that in the month of June 1833 he moved from Greene County, Indiana, into Jackson county, Missourie, and bought a farm with the growing crop; that shortly after the inhabitants of Jackson County began to threaten the Church with destruction if they did not leave the County, stating that they were the first settlers and they would not suffer the Church to settle in the County, assigning as a reason, that our faith on the subject of religion was disgusting, that the Church was made up of yankies, who were of different habits & customs to themselves, that soon the Church would become most numerous and eventually would govern the County, which they were determined not to submit to; & for the purpose of driving the Church from the county they bound themselves in a covenant, pledging "their lives, their fortunes and their sacrid honor to expell the mormons from the County of Jackson peaceably if we can and forceably if we must, (using their own language); to ackomplish which they broke open the church store, scattered the goods in the street, seazed a number of the heads of the Church, demolished a brick building or printing office and threw its contents into the street, tared & feathered the Bishop of the Church, threw down a large number dwelling houses and most unmercifully beat a number of men belonging to the Church; and about the 10th of Nov. 1833 they drove the Church from Jackson County County subjecting it to great losses &c. &c.

My individual loss at this time I estimate at five hundred dollars
$500.00

From Jackson I fled to Clay County, Missourie, and bought a farm of Seventy five acres, and thirty four acres of improvement, hoping to live in peace; but in this I was disappointed; for in 1836 the same mob combination and procedings compelled the Church to leave the County of Clay, again depriving us of the rights of free men & subjecting the Church to great loss of property, afflictions &c, &c

My personal damage in being driven from my home at this time & deprived of the use of my farm untill I was driven from the state, a period of three years I estimate a three thousand dollars—   3,000.00

From Clay County I fled to Caldwell County, Missouri in which County I bought two hundred & thirty acres of land; I moved from Caldwell to Davis County adjoining Caldwell, & thinking that in the wilderness we could live in peace, I selected a valuable seat for mills on unsurveyed government land, built a good log house, planted about sixteen acres of Corn & other vegetables, I had about sixty hogs, a large Prairie plow & three common field plows, a stud horse, 4 neat cattle, together with tools & articles of houshold goods, to numerous to name here, all taken from me by that same Mobocracy or Mob combination, which had operated against the Church from the first. And to cap the climax Lillborn W. Boggs, Governor of Missouri issued his exterminating order, to drive every mormon from the state or exterminate them if Necessary. I estimate my loss of personal property at eight hundred and thirty six dollars at this ant [*amt*]   836.00

The Church received orders from those whom Gov. Boggs sent to exterminate the Mormons, to assemble at Far West in Caldwell county where the church were permited to winter, with express orders not to think of making another Crop in Missourie. My situation at this time was this, to wit; I had & yet have a settlement right in the county of Davise worth five hundred Dollars   500.00

I had two hundred & thirty acres of land in Caldwell County valued at ten Dollars per acre   2300.00
but was oblidged to sell for what I could get, which was about three hundred & ninety five dollars making alloss of one thousand nine hundred & five dollars. I had 75 acres in Clay Co. worth six dollars per acre, for which I got an old horse, thirty seven dollars out of the store & about the same in cash, leaving a balance due me of three hundred dollars   300.00

I have land in Jackson County, which I have not disposed of, & have not the liberty to live upon it. for which privation I charge one thousand dollars   1000.00

Thus I have made a statement of the damage, which according to my knowledge and understanding is strictly true, & I ask the aid of the great and the good to see me & others remunerated for all our privations, I have injured no man, I have transgressed no law of My Country, and I challenge all men to attach any matter of crime to my person. I am fifty two years old, a Physician by profession, but for the Glory of God & the salvation of my soul I chose & yet choose the affliction of the saints in preferance to the honor & glory of the world.

I know that the God of Abraham has commenced a great work in these last days, for which cause those who believe in him & his work suffered the like above mentioned losses & privations I was compelled to leave the State of Missourie or suffer the vengence of the governor and his Mob, for which privation of liberty & all rights of a free man I know not what to demand; but I think that the unadulterated spirit of Liberty will make the extent of the Purse of Missourie this penal sum as a reward for those who have Suffered her unheard of and unexampled cruelties and persecution in moderntimes

I have lived in the state of Missourie nearly six years during which time the Church as a body have been broken up & completely routed three times and deprived of their labor, their property plundered & destroyed, & Subjected to exposure in the most severe winter weather. heavy expenses & every affliction peculiar to the Character of that relentnlys Mob of plunderers, Murderers & perpetrators of almost every outrage, which has had the effect of rendering the Christ Church poor & misserable & particular objects of the pity, comisseration & relief of a good, wise and Patriotic Government: for which purpose I have made the above statement, hoping that the government of my Country will not turn a deaf eare to the cries & entreaties of the much persecuted and afflicted widows & orphans, poor & impoverished Sons and daughters of the patriots of Seventy Six.

John Patten

[Sworn to before D. W. Kilbourn, J.P., Lee Co., IA, 28 Oct 1839.]

PLUMB, Jeremiah

January 13th 1840

To the Honorable Senate and House of Representatives in Congress Assembled at the City of Washington in the district of Columbia—

I the undersignd do By these presents represent To Your Honorable Body My Losses Troubles and sufferings which I sustaned and underwent By the Hands of a Ruthless Mob in the State of Missouri in the Year of our Lord 1838.

By forcibly being driven from my Land and Home in that State. And this is To Petition Your Honorable Body That I may Have Redress of these my Grievances which I Have Sustained By the hand of Law Breakers in Taking from me my Rights which the Constitution of this Republic Guarantees unto all free Born Citizens—Further with Respect to the Conduct of this mob. I have had my Life Threatened And received many Abuses Too numerous To mention And the Loss of Property &C. To be no Less Than 1,000 dollars which I sustained, also my Life was Threatened By William Tailor and a pistal held at my Breast By him. And was obliged to make heavy Exertions To Extricate myself from him This in short is a history of my Grievances and Humbly ask You To Take into Consideration These suffering And by so doing Your Servant will Ever Pray

Jeremiah Plumb

P. S. I the Undersigned Certify in addition That we the people Called Mormons, (after a Conference was held by the principal Men of the Mo. Militia) was forced by the point of the sword To Sign a deed of Trust Signing Away Our Lands; The principal Men Engaged in this Business was Thomas Birch Acting States Attorney for that District also Genl. Clark Commander in General of the Militia also Genl. Saml. D. Lucas of Independence Jackson Co Mo.

Jeremiah Plumb

[Sworn to before J. H. Randle, N.P., Madison Co., IL, 13 Jan 1840.]

PLUMB, Merlin

January 13th 1840

To the Honorable ~~House~~ Senate and House of Representatives in Congress Assembled at the City of Washington in the District of Columbia [I] the undersignd do by these presents Represent To You My Losses Troubles and Sufferings, That I underwent and Recd. from the Hand of a Mob In the State of Missouri in the Year of AD 1838 &C—And this may Certify that I did purchase Improvements and Entd. [———— ————] the E. 1/2 of S. W. 1/4 of Section No. 8 in T. 55 No of Base Line W. of 5 principal M. R. 36 Containing 80 A. Also S. W. 1/4 of N. W. 1/4 of Section 8 T. 55 N. of the Base Line and W. of the 5 principal R. 36 Containing 40 acres @ 1.25 Also N. W. 1/4 of S. W. 1/4 of Section No 8. T. 55 North of the Base Line and W. of the 5 principal Meridian Range No 26 Containing 40 Acres @ $1.25. All the Above Entd. May 29, 1837. and upon which I had 40 Acres Improved and all apparatuses Belonging To a Good farm Thereon, And from which I was forcibly driven By the Hands of a Mob immediately under the apprabation of Governor L. W. Boggs, Acting Governor of the State of Misouri and further Certify that after being forced to leave my Home while on my Road To the State of Illinois I was met By a Mob and our Lives or the Life of Myself and family Threatened our waggons searched and 1 Gun Taken of mine also 3 others from my waggon And Then was ordered To Camp in the Woods and did so until I Got a Chance to Remove. the Commander of this Company was James M Ramsey now acting [————] of the Judges of the Co. C. of Caldwel[*l*] County Missouri. and Certify That The Losses which I Recd. To be no Less Than 2500 Dollars [————] upon my Land Stock &C. which I Left, and further Certify That The whole Loss of property Personal & Real and the loss sustained By Leaving and moving from my Home To be no Less than five <u>Thousand Dollars</u>

Merlin Plumb

[Sworn to before J. H. Randle, N.P., Madison Co., IL, 13 Jan 1840.]

POWELL, Uriah B.

Uriah B. Powell of Springfield Sangamon County and State of Illinois says that he is a member of the Church of Latter Day Saints Commonly known by the name of Mormons and that he has been a resident of Caldwell County Missouri untill he was Obliged to leave in consequence of the exterminating Order of his excellency Governor Lilburn W. Boggs Issued in October 1838 by which he and his brethren were compelled to leave the State on pain of death And that further on the day the arms were given up at Far West in Caldwell County aforesaid which he thinks was about the first day of November in the year aforesaid he had a conversation with a Captain of the Militia who was a citizen of Davies County Missouri and who had been engaged in the Mob in Course of the conversation the said Captain Observed that we (speaking of the mob of Davies County) have burnt houses of our own and the Mormons on the Mormons Credit to accomplish our designs of getting the Mormons out of the State

Uriah B Powell

[*Sworn to before J. Adams, J.P., Sangamon Co., IL, 9 Nov 1839.*]

POWELL, Uriah B.

loss and damage as follows

viz one hundred and ~~sixty~~ twenty one acres
of land in Caldwell Co value to me $2000.00
one House and lot in Far West town   500.00
one horse value   50.00
by Debts standing out on Book Account   256.30
one Rifle value   15.00
loss of time in moving to Missouri from Ohio and back
to Springfield Illinois   100.00
Loss of Citizenship   20,000.00
~~standing as~~ Total sum $22,921.30

the within is strictly true to the best knoledge I posses

Uriah B. Powell

[*Sworn to before J. Adams, J.P., Sangamon Co., IL, 9 Nov 1839.*]

PULSIPHER, Terah

In July 1838 I started from the state of Oh[i]o to Move to the west part of Missouri I arrived in Davies Co. Mo. the fore part of Octbr. folloing with my family Expecting to make it my place of Residence during Life I assisted to pay for a preemtion right and Built a house. soon after Mobs were heard of in various parts Destroying Property Belonging to Mormons About the first of Novbr. I was gathering Corn with 15 or 20 Persons and were taken prisners by aboddy of trops sd. to be sent by the Govornor as soon as the Town was surrounded we were ordered to go to our houses and get our guns if we had any and Come to their Camp and deliver them up we accordingly started for that purpus After going but afew hundred yards from them we were fireed upon by a boddy of men sd. to be Headed by Neal Gillum from Platt Country. but we got our guns and gave them up and then a s[t]rong gard placed over us. in the mean time were in sulted and abused, at the same time aman by the Name of Han[S]ey strove hard to kill one of the prisners an aged man. but was rescued by one of the officers. while I was there under gard my house was robed of the property I brought from Ohio The next morning we were brought before general Wilsons Camp and addresst in the folloing Manner Gentlemen I have an order from the govornor to Exterminate you forth with but I take the responsibility upon my self to give you ten days to Leave this place or we might Expect desruction

This is as near as I can recollect.

Terah Pulsipher

[Sworn to before J. Orr, J.P., Adams Co., IL, 8 Jan 1840].

RAPPLEYE, Tunis

State of Illenois Adams County SS January 7th 1840

This day personally app[eare]d before me Wm. Laughlin a Justice of the peace within Said County Tunis Rappleye who being Duly Sworn according to Law Deposeth and saith he Mooved to Ray County Missouri 1836 personally abused by John Cates & John Bales they Demanded my rifle & I refused & In Consequince of refuseing they threatened My life and I estimated my damage at 150 Dollars

Tunis **X** Rappleye

[Sworn to before W. Laughlin, J.P., Adams Co., IL, 7 Jan 1840.]

REDFIELD, Harlow

Pike Co Illenois January 14 AD 1840

I herby certify that I moved into Missouri in the month of May 1838 Bought a house & Lot in the citty of Farwest & purchased a claim on a quarter of sexion in davis Co with a cabin on it & some improvement I lived in farwest untill febuary 1839 when I was oblieged to leave the state according to his excellency the Govener L W Bogs exterminating order leaving all behind in the hands of my percecutors. I with others was forced to sign a deed of trust at the point of the sword with many others I was deprived contrary to law of citizen ship, the loss of time expense property &c I claim $2000

Harlow Redfield

[Sworn to before W. H. Boling, C.C.C.C., Pike Co., IL, 14 Jan 1840.]

REED, Delia

Handcock Co and State of Illinois
    This may Certify that I Delia Reed moved to Missouri in the year 1836 my husband died Soon after we arrived and left me with Seven Small Children I then moved to Calwell County made an Improvement Continued on Said farm untill the Autum of 1838 when the troubles come on between the Inhabitants and the Mormons I with the rest of our Society was obliged to leave the State—Accordly my family was Scattered and through the Clemency of friends made out to leave the State through the order of the Governor to leave the State I was obliged to Sacrifice the most of my property So that my family become Scattered and I had to gain a daily Pittence among Strangers

Delia Reed

[Sworn to before A. Monroe, J.P., Hancock Co., IL, 6 Jan 1840.]

REED, Elijah

Quincy Illinois January 10th 1840
    This is to Certify that I went from the state of Ohio into the state of Missouri in Nov. 1836 & Stopped in Randolph County until May Following & removed from thence to Ray County & in Oct or Nov 1837 I Entered two Forties of land in Said County at the Lexington office & in the Sumer of 1838 I hired 17 acres of the same Broken up at 3 Dollars Per acre & got out a Set of house logs & some other Improvements intending to Spend my Days there But in October of the Said year During the Excitement or Mormon war as it is Called I was Called uppon By Anderson Martin & Several others of Richmond Ray County & Said if I would give them my gun & Deny my Faith or religion that I should have Protection & if not I Could not be Protected those terms I refused to Comply with I told them my Right of Concience I would Enjoy while I lived & Considerable Conversation Passed & the Same was Proposed again by Mr. Henly & I made the Same reply he then Said by God you Shall not be Protected &

left me in about an hour after there was a Company of men Sent to take me But I kept out of their way & from that time until after the Surrender of the Brethren in Far West the Mob hunted me Constantly the account I have Partially given in my bill of Damages During which time I was Closely Pursued I was at a Br Jimmisons house in a by Place on the 29th of Oct & in the night of of the that day a Company of men Came to the House & Demanded admittence & threatened to Breake Down the Door Mr J got up and opened the Door meantime I hid under the Bed the men Came in and said they were Soldiers & he must go with them his wife asked where they said to the Malitia Camp above Richmond he Dressed himself & he & one of the men went for a horse at the Stable when they had got a little from the house the man Fired a gun & said the D——d rascal had ran from him he then returned to the house & they began to abus[e] Mrs. Jimm[iso]n wanting to sleep with her But she begged & cried For them to Desist & they Did so I lay under the Bed During this time they soon left the house & we supposed they had killed him I lay in the Field the remainder of the night the next Day I went to Caldwell we then learned of the Battle at Hawns Mill the Day Previous & From thence we went to Far West on the third of Nov. I was then taken Sick & was Confined to the house & Consequently Did not hear what General Clark had to Say I then went home in Ray Co a bout 35 miles in a Few Days I had notice by Mr David Snowden who said he was Captain of the men on the Bottom by the authority of the General who had the Command of the men sent to Caldwell & he told me I must leave by Sunday this was on tuesday I accordingly Disposed of my Property as Fast as I could For what I Could get But ~~my~~ one of my Neighbours Iterceded & I got to Stay till my Family was able to Move as they were all Sick with the Chills & Fever & had Been During my absence of 10 Days he Said we had all got to leave the State or Deny our religion law or no law

I accordingly removed to this place in March the Duplicates of my land I have lost or misplacd So that I cannot Find them

Elijah Reed

[*Sworn to before C. M. Woods, C.C.C., Adams Co., IL, 9 Jan 1840.*]

REED, John

Quincy April 21 1839

This May Certify that I John Reed in Consequence of the Late difficulty between a portion of the people of the upper Counties of Missouri and the Church of Lattr day Saints have Suffered the following

Losses Viz in the year 1838 in the month of June I Moved My family to County of Livingston and in the fall was ordered by the Inhabitants to Leave the place in 15 days or be Massacreed I then for My Safty Moved to Davies Co ~~from thence to~~ there Bought the Betterment of 260 acres of Land while I was Making preparration to take possession of the plase the mob tore down the house that I Intended to ocupy and I was Compelled to Live in an uncomfortable Shantee in the Most Severe Cold and Stormy weather from this plase I was ordered by the Malita to go Back to Caldwell Co but in Consequence of having been appointed with Eleven others to Settle with the Inhabitants I Remained in Diahman after ~~the~~ our people had Left and at this time Received great abuse both by threntning my Life and Stealing my property Such as Clothing Houshold stuff tools &c together with one Cow & Calf I in this Situation was obliged in Compliance with the governors orders to Leave the State with but one horse and a Large family on my hands

John Reed Blacksmith

[*Not sworn.*]

RICHARDS, Elisha

To the Honle. The Senate and House of Representatives in Congress Assembled at the City of Washington in the District of Columbia, AD 1840 Here by Represent that I went to the State of Missouri and bought me a house and lot in the City of far west Caldwell Co missouri for which I paid the Sum of $200. likewise ten acres of timber for which I paid $100 and have a warranttee deed of the same Likewise ther lost one waggon worth $60 thirty sheep $90 one cow $20 for which because of the exterminating order of Governor Boggs of missouri is all lost to me

Elisha Richards

[*Sworn to before R. L. Hill, C.C.C., Jersey Co., IL, 10 Jan 1840.*]

ROCKWELL, Oren Porter

Porter Rockwell of Lawful age being duly sworn deposeth and saith that on the 19th day of July 1833 or thereabouts he the deponent resided on the Big Blue River in Jackson County State of Missouri that his father and himself kept a ferry on the said river and that at the time aforesaid he ferried over a company of men on their way to Independence the County seat of Jackson County for the purpose as they said of entering into resolutions to drive the Mormons from the County. deponent also ferried the company on their return home they stated to him the deponent that they had entered into ressolutions to meet on the 20th [Ju··] for the purpose of tearing down the printing Office that belonged to the Mormons. According to Agreement on the 20th July in the Year aforesaid a company of the Mob Crossed the river on their way to Independence on their return as they recrossed the river about sundown of the same day They stated that they had torn down the printing Office Scattered the type broken the press and destroyed the papers and tarred and feathred two men Edward Partridge and Charles Allen both of which were Mormons The Press belonged to W. W. Phelps & Co who also belonged to the Mormon Society They threatned the Mormons saying that they had resolved to drive them out of the County and that if ~~my~~ his father and ~~myself~~ himself would not renounce ~~our~~ their doctrine and religious faith as Mormons ~~we~~ they should share the same fate, refusing to pay unto them their ferriage. The following are some of the names of the persons that ~~I~~ were ferried over the river and stated that they had [~~been~~] entered in to an Agreement to drive the Mormons and had been engaged in the destruction of property as aforesaid —————— McGee & 2 sons Moses Wilson & sons ————— Cockrel ~~Esquire~~ Manship Esq Nimrod Manship Col Bowers Thomas Linville and sons James Linville Samuel Linville ————— Patten Robert Johnson Issac McCoy Missionary of the Indians ————— Cummings indian agent ————— Lovejoy and many others that I do not now reecollect on the 31st day of October A party of the Mob Came to the house of David Whitmer and drew his wife out of the house by the hair of the head and proceeded to throw down the house they then went to other houses throwing them down untill they had demolished ten dwelling houses amidst the shrieks and screams of women and children among those thus thrown down were the dwellings of Stephen Chase George Beebee Hiram Page Peter Witmer They also whipt and beat in a savage manner two of the men ~~in a savage manner~~ namely George Beebe & Hiram Page on saturday night the 2d of November a party of the Mob Called at the house of Orin Rockwell some of whose names were Russel Hicks Attorney at Law Hugh L Brazeale Attorney at Law Moses Wilson Thomas Wilson & two sons of Moses Wilson ————— Cockrel Lewis Franklin Samuel C. Owens Jones H. Flournoy Nimrod Manship Thomas Linville Isaac McCoy ————— Patten Robert Johnson James Linville William Linville ————— Cummings the Indian agent ————— Lovejoy they began making enquiry for deponents father and himself and being answerd that they were not at home began to insult the women the deponents Mother and Sister the said Mob were painted as indians and assuming that character to themselves began abusing and insulting the women [————] ~~Aforesaid~~ some saying that they would tear the house down others said not so let us wait untill we come back they then went to Mr. Pettigrews finding them sick Hugh L Brazeale was Called upon by the Mob as Doctor and desired by them to make examinations to see whether they were sick or not he pronounced them sick and not able to leave their house some said let us tear the house down [——] others said not they passed on and left the house Next house they went to was Noah Johnsons which they threw down and destroyed the most of his property they then proceeded to the house of David Bennetts and dragged himself and family out of the house they then beat and bruised this David Bennett in a most savage and barbarous manner leaving him on the ground for dead they then proceeded to throw down the house and while engaged in this business one of they kept up a continual firing of guns and while throwing down the aforesaid house one of their men was shot through the thigh they immediately then started for for home and while on their way Called at the house of this deponent and threw down his house and destroyed most of the household goods And while destroying some of the goods deponents sister went out and requested that they would be so kind as not to destroy the goods one of the Mob replied if she did not go away he would cut her throat from ear to ear pulling out a knife holding it out towards her After this they threw down a house belonging to David Jones and destroyed his goods.¶

The aforesaid persons on whom these outrages were Committed were all Mormons on the 4th November the Mob Again met at Blue river on Monday and sent Men through the settlement warning the people to leave their houses and lands and leave the County A man by the Name of Overton was deputed as one to do this business he was said to be a member of the baptist Church then threatning the people that if they did not leave immediately A party of men were at the river that would force them to leave or kill them And he was all the man that could keep them off a Many of the Men being absent from home the women and children fled into the woods in every direction upon the receipt of this intelligence. Then this Mob proceeded [there] westward about 2 1/2 miles from Blue river and commenced their depredations again by tearing down fences and turning their horses in to the Mormons Corn fields they went to a house where were a number of women and began to impose upon them one of the women left the house and gave notice to a small company of Mormons about 30 in number who had Collected together for their safty and defence in Case the Mob should attack them who upon hearing of the depredations which the Mob was committing And of the insults given to the women immediately repaired near the place where the Mob had collected and upon coming within about 7 or 8 rods the Mob who was armed and about 60 in number fired upon them the Mormons then returned the fire and there were two of the Mob killed also one Mormon killed by the name of Barber and some wounded on both sides the names of the Mob who were killed were Hugh L. Brazeale and Thomas Linville The said Hugh L Brazeale stated a short time before while in conversation with an old Gentleman in hearing of deponent that he Brazeale would wade to his knees in blood but what he would drive the Mormons from the county if he could get but ten men to follow him. On the 5th day of November 1833 the Arms of the Mormons were demanded by Col Pitcher who it was said had orderd out the Militia (by order of Lieut Gov Boggs as was said) and appointed a committee to receive the arms some of whom were the most actively engaged in the Mob at the time the Printing Office was thrown down namely Henry Chiles Abner Staples and Lewis Franklin. Col Pitcher also stated at the time that if the Mormons would give up their arms they might return to their homes and live in peace Accordingly upwards of about 50 guns were delivered up which have never yet been returnd to the Mormons This Col Pitcher after the guns were given up stated that the Mormons must leave the County forthwith and if they would not go peacably they would be compelled to go at the Muzz[l]e of the gun to He then ordered his rigament several hundred men in to small companies of 15 or 20 in each Company they were marched through the County in every direction threatning the whole Mormon Community with immediate death if they did not forthwith leave the County The Rev. Isaac McCoy was in one of the aforesaid Companies the result of these opperations were that the whole of the aforesaid Community were forced out of the County and in the utmost Confusion had to flee in almost every direction to save their lives sacrifising the most of their property which the Mob either took possession of as their own or destroyed The most of the Mormons took refuge in Clay County at this time where they suffered great inconvenience in Consequence of being robbed of almost all they possessed we they remained their untill the summer of 1836. When public meetings were held and they were desired to leave the County and even Compelled to leave their habitations once more or take up arms against Mobs who were preparing to Come against us them Many at this time had purchased lands in that County and had to remove at a great sacrifice of property from Clay they the Mormons removed to Caldwell and Davies Countys And further this deponent saith that in November of the year of our Lord 1838 he heard certain Men say that They had been in the Mob against the Mormons in Dewitt Carrol County and also in Davies County and in Ray County and that they knew where there were fifteen Mormons put in one hole and Sixteen put into another hole that the Mormons had no knowledge of And Numbers of others through the Country and when interrogated on the subject they replied that replied they were Mormon dogs that had been killed thus comparing Mormon Citizens to dogs. And further this deponent saith that the History of the persecutions narrated By Parley P. Pratt so far as it relates to the robberies Murders imprisonments and all other Matters and things Connected with their abuses and expulsion from the State of Missouri (which is put up and marked document No 2 and now laid on the table by a vote of the Senate) is substantially true to the best of his knowledge.

Oren P. X Rockwell

[Sworn to before B. K. Morsell, J.P.,Washington, D.C., 3 Feb 1840.]

ROCKWELL, Sarah

Commerce Hancock Co Illinois Jany 2 1834

I certify that in the year A.D. 1833 I was residing in the County of Jackson in the State of Missouri In the fall of the same year, an armed force of men Came to our House and beat open the door and Windows, and demanded to know where my husband was, I told them I did not know where he was, they told I must tell them or Else I must be made to suffer. My Son lived in a house opposite, some of the men tore off the roof of his house and then went and took out his goods. I saw them destroy some of the Articles they brought out. Some time after we were obliged to leave that County and suffered a great deal of abuse had to take Shelter in the Woods in order to escape from the Armed force who were pursuing us.

In the Fall of 1838 I was residing in Caldwell County, Missouri about two miles from Far West The Latter part of October the same year I went from home and was absent three weeks. when I returned I found that my house had been plundered of Furniture Bed cloths and Wearing apparel so that I was not able to keep house.

During the time I was absent from home while in ~~Caldwell~~ Clay County at the House of Samuel H Ousley. I was informed that the Malitia had gone on to Far West; and they had left word that the mormons were to be exterminated and had left orders to that Effect. Being informed of this fact and having two of my sons along with me one fourteen years of age and the other Eighteen and Feeling anxous for their safety I advised them to go and hide in the Woods. they had not been gone long before an armed force came to the house, and made inquiry for the Boys, they said that they were going to exterminate the mormons and were going to make Clean Work; Not being able to find my Sons, they took a waggon and span of horses away, which I had brought to Convey me to that place, I then returned home and Found my house as above Stated

Sarah Rockwell

[Sworn to before D. H. Wells, J.P., Hancock Co., IL, 2 Jan 1840.]

ROGERS, Noah

State of Illinois Pike County

This Day personally appeard before me W. H Boling Clerk of the County Coms Court of said Co & state Noah Rogers & after being duly sworn Deposth & says That he Deponant who in the year 1838 moved into Davis Co Mo, & settled on a pece of Land & Cleard twenty Acres Expecting to have a preemption & Corn growing on said twenty acres & was compeld to leave it & from there to Adam ondiaham Whare the People cald Mormmons was compeld to assemble to gether for the Perpose of self Defence & whilst residing at the last named place This Deponant was followed by mobs & divers in dividuals & took from this Deponant a large a mount of Property to the a mount of two hundred Dollars & this Deponant and famley Driven out a bout thirty miles Into Caldwell County In the Month of Nov 1838 Thence Compeld to leave the State & come to [——] Illinois for reffuge and ferther this Deponant ~~saith says not~~ saith not

Noah Rogers

[Sworn to before W. H. Boling, C.C.C.C., Pike Co., IL, 14 Jan 1840.]

ROLLINS, James H.

January 13, 1840—

To the Honorable Senate and House of Representatives in Congress Assembled at the City of Washington in the district of Columbia—

I the undersignd do by these presents represent To Your Honorable body my Losses Sufferings and Troubles which I sustained and underwent by the hands of a Ruthless mob in the State of Missouri upheld and sustained by L. W. Boggs acting Governor of that state in the Year 1838. And this may Certify that on the 6th day of August, 1838. while at an Election held in daviess County Missouri, while we the people Called Mormons were Voting As the Law of our Country dictates and Guarantees unto us that we were hindred from this our privilege By a mob of the people of that County Raising against us and driving us from the polls with Clubs

Raw Hydes &C. [——] Also drove us from the Town and Threatened me If I did not Leave the Town They would Pull down my House over my Head. and which House Contained heavy stones &C &C, and which I was obliged To Leave, and which was mostly distroyed, Also [——] Another Establishment of the same in same County was Broken Open and Liquor & C. Taken Out By the Milita as they Called Themselves under Brgd. Genl. Parks of that Division To a Large amt. and which they Took and made use of &C. Many other Losses ~~To~~ which I suffered which were very grievious To bear of Being driven from Land which I Had Entd. Town Lots &C. And the Loss of which Property Amounting To not less than 3000 Dollars which Loss I sustained By being driven from my Home under The Exterminatig Orders of his Excellency Lilbern W. Boggs. And By this I appeal To Your Honorable Body for redress of the sore Grievances which I And my Brethren have suffered for the Belief of the scriptures of Truth or in other words for our Religion.— And By this I importune at Your feet for Redress &C of My Wrongs And Your Servant will Ever pray—

James H. Rollins

P. S. I The undersigned Certify in addition That We the people Called Mormons after a Conference was held by The principal men of the Mo. Militia, was forced by the Point of the sword To sign a deed of Trust signing away our Lands. The principal man Engaged in this business was Thomas Birch Acting as States Attorney for that district, also Genl. Clark Commander in Chief of the Militia or [——] also Genl. Saml. D. Lucas of Independence Jackson County Mo.

James H. Rollins

[Sworn to before J. H. Randle, N.P., Madison Co., IL, 13 Jan 1840.]

ST. JOHN, Stephen M.

The State of Illenois Adams County

Personally appeared before me William Laughlin a Justice of the Peace for said County Stephen M. St John being Duly Sworn according to Law Deposeth & Saith that he moved into Missouri in the Year of our Lord 1836 Settled in Clay County hired a farm in said County and was Driven away by a Mob made up of the Sitizens of said County went from there to Davis county and settled upon Congress land built upon it improved it & raised a Crop was Driven from it with the loss Crop three horses three Cows & some hogs with household goods farming utensils & one waggon John Legate James Brown & others threatned to take my life

Depont. further States that he left the State by the extermmanating order of Governor Boggs executed by General Clark & Wilson further Depont. saith not

Stephen M. St. John

[Sworn to before W. Laughlin, J.P., Adams Co., IL, 8 Jan 1840.]

SEELY, William

Affidavit of William Seely of Scott County Illinois, taken Jan 20th ~~1838~~ 1840, in relation to the persecutions Sustained by the Mormons or Latter day Saints, in the State of Missouri A.D. 1838,

State of Illinois Scott County S.S.

William Seely of Scott County Illinois, of lawful age, says on oath; that in the Last of March A.D. 1838 he moved with his family to the State of Missouri, and Stopped in Davis County in Said State of Missouri, that in Said County he purchased a pre-Emption right to a tract of Congress Land for which he paid $200.00 and that he accumulated there personal propErty and interest in Crops property in value 250.$ making his property four Hundred and fifty Dollars in value, in the use of which this affiant was using his Endevors to become a resident Citizen of Said Davis County in good faith and due Submission to the Laws of the Said State of ~~Illinois~~ Missouri. And this affiant further says, that on the ~~28~~ 10th day of October A.D. 1838, he was Surprised in the quiet and peaceable possession of the premises he occupied in Said Davis County by an <u>armed mob</u> Composed mostly and as he believes wholly of resident Citizens of Said State of Missouri and Compelled to relinquish all his said property to the plunderers, and make the best of his Escape to Caldwell County in Said State of Missouri with his family. This affiant further Says that on or about day of 24th October he went to Bunkham's Strip a distance of about twelve miles from his Stopping place in Caldwell County, to See one Mr. Pinkham on business; while there he was Surprised & made prisoner by Some armed men. he was Stripped and Searched to see if he had any arms, by which he lost a Jack-knife the only weapon, offensive or defensive which he had about him; the armed men he believes were fifteen in number, two of whom Caught him by the Collar, thrust him out of doors, dragged him over a pannel of fence so vehemently as to do him bodily injury while at the same time a third one facilitated ~~my~~ his Course by the application of his foot to the rear of ~~my~~ his body—When over he was asked if he was a mormon, ~~for~~ to which he replied that he was; this affient further says that he was threatend by his Captors, that "he would never see home again." &c. he was then Compelled to march, and asked where they were taking him? they Said to the rest of their Company. Who, he asked was their Captain? they Said, "Bogart." Affiant arrived in Camp with his Captors and found them about Seventy Strong. Question then arose What Shall we do with the prisoner, many Said at once, "put him to death." Especially was this the Cry of the volunteers who joined Bogart's Company, many of whom were men not Liable to duty by Law but who volunteered to give a martial Covering to the bloody deeds which they sought to perpetrate.

on his arrival at Camp St Cook of Bogarts Company asked who they had got? The Captors Said, "a damned mormon!" Where did you Catch him asked Cook? down to old Pinkhams was the reply of his captors and we'll blow his damned old brains out if he dont leave here before tomorrow morning. Affiant further says next morning after his Capture at daylight, his mormon friends Came down to his rescue, having heard of his Capture. When they approached they were fired upon by Bogart's Company and one man fell. this affiant was then placed on an [——] in front of Bogart's Company So as to be Exposed to the fire of both sides, about 12 feet from Bogarts line. At the word "fire" by Bogart this affiant attempted to Escape but was Shot in the left Shoulder by some one of Bogarts men, which prostrated him to the Earth, and he was supposed to be dead, but his friends took him and Carried him to ~~his place~~ his family, where after four months tedious Confinement he in a measure recoverd of his wounds; when in obedience to the Command of the Executive Gov. Boggs, issued from head Quarters, ordering all Mormons to leave the State, in the month of October 1838, ~~I~~ he left for Illinois in a State of Extreme destitution, deprived of all his property and suffering much from his wound which though measurably restored was yet verey troublesome. This affiant further says that one of his Captors who Considered him so dangerous a man as to justify him in robbing ~~me~~ him and taking ~~my~~ his life, told ~~me~~ him he would give ~~me~~ him forty acres of Land if I would go with him and <u>renounce ~~my~~ his religion,</u> all of which this affiant verifies with his Signature and oath, and further this affiant Says nothing.

Wm Seely

[Sworn to before E. Sells, J.P., Scott Co., IL, 20 Jan 1840.]

SHAW, Elijah, Sr.

Warsaw Hancock County Illinois Jan 6 1840

I do Sertify in the year 1838 November 5th that I was driven from my land by an armed Solgery I went to far west as I got there there was a large body of armed Soldiers inder the Command of general Clark took us prisoers demanded our arms which we gave up me and my son Gave up two guns put us under guard that no Man Should leave that place withou a pass From Some one of there officers by the point of Sword made us Sign to them all our Real and Personal property to defrey the expence of those Armies I heard general Clark Say that we need Not expects to See our leaders again for they Certainly would be put to death the Rest that He had Selected out would not be kiled I Saw Soldiers burn house logs boards, and used Corn Hay and fodder for their horses I heard general Clark also Say that the governors orders was to Exterminate us or dispece us off but on the ACount of our good behavior and the inclemcy of the weather he would let us Stay untill Spring But not put in another Crop

Hancock County illinois January 6 1840   Elijah Shaw Sr

[*Sworn to before A. Monroe, J.P., Hancock Co., IL, 6 Jan 1840.*]

SHAW, Elijah, Sr.

Handcock Co State of Illenois

    My native Country is in the State of new Jersey I emagrated to ohio in 1816 and then Emagrated to missouri in the 1833 landed In Jackson County June 22 I Settled down on Chongress land built ahouse and Cleared Ground Sewed turnip Seed my intention was To enter the land as soon as possible I lade in My winter provission the mob rose and gave orders that we must leave the County or be Masacreed we then left Jackson and went to Rey County by having to leave the County I lost all this property and lived in rey three years and two months thence I move to Caldwe[*ll*] County I enterd the N W qr of the S W qr ⨦ S 21 T 56 R 27 enterd another ~~Joining~~ quarte Joining the S W qr of the N W qr S 21 T 56 R 27 I enterd this land in the year 1837 in the months of may and october My personal property Consisted of a quantity of hogs and Corn Stock fodder buck wheat Seven acres of wheat in the ground Seven bee Stands 20 bushels of potatoes one plow four dozen Chickens one horse beast three Sheep two Calves quantity of Shingles one bull and Estimation of the loss of my property amounts To 2000 dollars also for damadges for being Driven from the Stat for my Self and famly amounts To 8000 dollars hancock County

January 6 1840   Elijah Shaw Sr

[*Sworn to before A. Monroe, J.P., Hancock Co., IL, 6 Jan 1840.*]

SHEARER, Joel

January the ninth ano Domini one thousand Eight hundred and forty personally came Joel Shearer before me Elisha Petty one of the Justices of the peace in and for the County of Pike in the State of Illinois and being by me Sworn Deposeth and Saith that he the Said Shearer Suffered loss and Damage in the State of Missouri in the years ano Domini one thousand eight hundred and thirty eight and nine that he being a Resident of the State of Missouri in Caldwell County was ordered by the Authorities of Said State to leave Said State within Six months on pain of Death and that he Said Shearer was not individually accused of any neither collectively Accused of any misdemeanor against the Laws of Said State and he the Said Shearer further Saith that he is not Concious of ever having offended against the laws of the State of Missouri or these United States and that he is a Natural Born Citizen of the State of New York and being compeled to Sell his Real and part of his personal estate at a Reduced price Viz one hundred and Seventy Acres of Land lying in Caldwell County on which he the Said Shearer Suffered loss according to the best of his kowledge and belief eight hundred Dollars

the above land he Says was Entered and partly improved by himself for his own use

he further Says he thinks he Suffered one hundred and fifty Dollars loss on personal property including time and Expence &C of leaving the State of Missouri

Loss on land	$800.00
Do on personal property	150.00
total	$950.00

Joel Shearer

[*Sworn to before E. Petty, J.P., Pike Co., IL, 9 Jan 1840.*]

SLADE, Benjamin

this I certify that I settled in Jackson County in the year 1831 and Bought Lands & stock, horses cattle hogs &c and in the year 1833 in the month December I was Driven from Jackson county to clay county, Leaving my land, with ten acres of improvement a house & stable and corncrib, six acres of wheat on the ground 2 stacks of wheat 1 stack of Rye 2 stack[s] of oats 5 or [6] tons of hay [—— —— ——] of corn 30 or 40 Barrels of corn 50 or 60 Bushels of potatoes, one hundred Bushels of turnips also 2 horses 7 head of young cattle 6 head of hogs fowls &C Beside som[e] of my house furniture, property and Dama[ges] Estimated at $1000.00

Benjamin Slade

after living in Clay county 3 years I Removed to caldwell county By the Request of the inhabitance of Clay not Suffering so much loss of property But by breaking up and moveing—Damage $100.00

after living in Caldwell county 2 years I was Driven to the state of Illinois leaving 80 acres of land unsold five or six acres under improvement one lot with good Buildings on lying in the town of Farwest which was worth one thousand Dollars Beside Hay corn potatoes one horse 50 Dollars worth of hogs—Besides great Distruction of house furniture [&]c property and Damages   Estimated $2000.00

Illinois April 20 1839   Benjamin Slade

[*Not sworn.*]

SLADE, Benjamin

State of Illinois Pike County Ss

This Day personally appeard before Me W. H. Boling Clerk of the County Coms Court with in & for the County of Pike a foresaid Benjamin Slade and after being duly sworn Deposth & says that he Deponant was Driven from Jackson County Mo. ~~Illenois~~ to Clay County & from thence to Caldwell County Mo. at Which time he Deponant sufferd mutch loss of Property in goods and cloths as well as well as houses & Lands Which Deponant left & from Caldwell County to the State of Illinois all of Which moving was Done at great loss & Expence as well as in danger of the life of this Deponant & family. all Which actings & doings is Conrary to Equity & tends to the Manifest Injury and oppression of this Deponant & farther this Deponant says not

Benjamin Slade

[*Sworn to before W. H. Boling, C.C.C.C., Pike Co., IL, 14 Jan 1840.*]

SLADE, Clark

Personally appeard before me the clerk of Pike Co Illinois, Clarke Slade & deposth & says that While living In Jackson Mo he sufferd mutch a a buce from a lawles banditty that a rose up to persecute him & other in consequence of their theer Religion his life being continually thretened till in the mo[n]th of December 1833 When him self & family & others was compeld to leave theer Homes to seeve theer lives & seek a shelter in some other place I then found a shelter in Clay County for a Short time then a gain compeld to leave & flee to Cald Well County Mo Whare I resided untill the year A D 1838 When the Governor of Mo Issued his order that Men Women & Children belonging to the Church of Latter Day Sinse Should leave the State or be Exterminated General Clark Publicly Declard that he would the Governors Orders Execute In the Month of Febuary 1839 I Clark Slade left Mo to Seek a home in some other State leaving my house & Lands In the hands of my Persecutors & they Pub[···]d my last Cow the Damages of being Driven from the three a bove named Counties & State and loss of Property by means of being driven I estimate at two thosand Dollars & farther the deponant says nothing

Clark Slade

[*Sworn to before W. H. Boling, C.C.C.C., Pike Co., IL, 14 Jan 1840.*]

SLAKER, Coonrad

I do herby certify that at a low estimate the damages that I sustained in Missourie in consequences of Gov. Bogges exterminating order to amount to $100.00

Coonrad Slaker

[*Sworn to before A. Brown, J.P., Pike Co., IL, 10 Jan 1840.*]

SMITH, Alma

I hereby certify that my father stoped at Haun's mill and was living in a tent at the time the massacre took place there. I was in the tent when the company rode up. some of our people hallored to the women and children to leave the tents I run into a blacksmith shop where my father was. I crept under the bellows as also did my brother and an other boy by the name of Charles Merrick I was wounded on the hip, my brother had his brains blown out, and the other boy received three wounds and has since died of them. My mother tells me that I was eight years old last month. I saw some of our enemies pull off my father's boots before he was dead

Alma **X** Smith

[*Sworn to before D. H. Wells, J.P., Hancock Co., IL, 3 Jan 1840.*]

SMITH, Amanda[4]

To whom this may come, I do hereby certify, That my husband Warren Smith, in company with several other families, was moving from Ohio to Missouri, late last fall, We came to Caldwell County [——] Whilst we were traveling, And minding our own business we were stopt by a Mob. they told us that if we went another step they would kill us all. They then took our guns from us. (As we were traveling into a new country we took guns along with us.) They took us back five miles, placed a guard around us, And there kept us three day, then let us go. I thought to myself is this our boasted land of liberty. For Some Said that we must deny our faith or they would kill us, others said we should die at any rate. The names of the Heads of this mob were Thomas O Brion, County Clerk, Jefferson Brion, William [——] Esqr. And James Austin all of Livingston County Mo. After they let us go, we travelled ten miles when we came to a small town, Composed of one grist Mill And One Saw Mill, And eight or ten houses belonging to our Brethren. Here we stopped for the night, when a little before Sunset, a mob of three hundred persons Came upon us. The men hollered for the women and Children to run for the woods, And they ran into an old blacksmith's Shop, for they feared that if we all run together they would rush upon us, And kill the women and Children. The mob fired before we had time to run from our Camp, Our men then took off their hats And swung them round, and Cried, quarter, quarter untill they were Shot down. The mob paid no attention to their cries nor entreaties but fired alternately, I took my little girls (my boys I Could not find) And started for the woods. The mob encir[cled] all sides except towards the brook, I ran down the bank, across the millp[ond] and plank, up the hill into the bushes. The bullets whistled around us all the way like hail, and Cut down the bushes on all sides of us. One girl was wounded by my side and fell over a log, her clothes hung across the logs [and] they Shot at them expecting that they were hitting her, and our people af[ter]wards Cut out of that log twenty bullets. I sat down to witness the dre[d]ful scene. When they had done firing, they began to howl and one woul[d] have thought that all the infernals had came from the ~~infernal~~ lower regi[on] They plundered the principal part of our goods, took our horses and waggon and then ran off howling like Demons. I then Came back to witness [the] awful scene. Oh Horrible! What a sight! My Husband murdered and stript ~~naked~~ before life had entirely gone out of him, And one of my Sons of ~~fourteen~~ ten years old lying lifeless on the ground, And anoth[er] Son badly wounded Seven years old; the ground Covered with the dead. These little

[4] Also found in *HC* 3: 323–25 and in JH 18 Apr 1839.

boys had Crept under the bellows in the Shop. Another boy ten years old had three wounds in him, he lived five weeks and then died. Realize for a moment the Scene. It was sunset, nothi[ng] but horror and distress. The dogs filled with rage, howling ~~of~~ over their dea[d] masters, whilst the Cattle Caught the Scent of innocent blood and bellowed most awfully: A dozen helpless widows, thirty or forty fatherless Children Screaming and groaning for the loss of their husbands and fathers, the groans of the wounded and dying was enough to melt the heart of anything but a Missouri Mob. Fifteen were dead, And ten wounded, or more, two of whom died next day. The women were not able to bury the dead, So they were thrown into a dry well And Covered with dirt. The next day the Mob Came back. They told us, we must leave the State forthwith ~~or leave the State~~ or be killed. It was Cold weather, And they had our teams and Clothes our men all dead or wounded. I told them that they might kill me And My Children in welcome; They Sent to us from time to time, that if we did not leave the State they would come and kill us. We had little prayer meetings, they Said, if we did not stop them they would kill every one of us, man, women and Child. we had Spelling Schools for our little Children. And they Said we must also Stop them. We did our own milling, And got our own wood, no man to help us. I started on the first of Feburary for Illinois, without Money, (mob all the way) drove my own team, Slept out of doors; I had four Small Children, we Suffered hunger, fatigue and cold. And for what? for our religion, Where? In a boasted land of liberty. Deny your faith or die, was the Cry. I will mention Some of the names of the heads of the Mob. Two brothers by the name of Cumstock, William and Benjamin Ashby, Robert White, And one by the name of Rogers who took an old Scythe and Cut an old white headed man all to pieces. I wish further also to State that when the Mob Came there (as I was told by one of them afterwards) their intention was to kill every thing belonging to us that had life, And that after our men were Shot down by them, they went around and Shot all the dead men over again to make sure of their lives. I now leave it with this Honorable Government to Say what my damages may be; or what they would be willing to see their wives and Children Slaughtered for, as I have seen my husband, son & others. I lost in property by the Mob, To goods stolen fifty Dollars, one pocket book and fifty Dollars Cash, notes damage of horses and time, one hundred Dollars one gun ten dollars, In Short my all whole damages are more than the State of Missouri is worth. Written by my own hand in truth and soberness, This eighteenth day of April 1839.

Amanda Smith

[Sworn to before C. M. Woods, C.C.C., Adams Co., IL, 7 May 1839.]

SMITH, John

This is to Certify to the wrongs and injuries that I received in Missourie, I arrived in Far West on the 2nd of October 1838, where I intended to beCome a peasfull inhabitant of that Co; Some of the last days of Oct I was going after ahead of Corn in Company with Wm. Cary; we had a wagon and a Span of horses; we was met by three men that was armed with rifles. they had one prisoner with them; they told us we ware their prisoners Mr Carey asked them by what Arthorety they Should make us, prisoners while we ware peasfully attending to our own Concerns; they gave us Some threats—I told them we ware peacefull and we wished the[m] to use us as priseners; a man by the name of Dunihue told me that I nead not feer you wil make a damd good wagoner for us; but for that damd Sone of a bich directing his words to Mr Carey—all that he is fit for is for Sausage Stuffing; and the quicker he is used for it the bettor; they placed several guns in our wagon we then drove to their Camp a bout thre miles; af ter we came in to their Camp they toock up their guns and fired them of except one which missed fire—they layed it down and left the gun Cocked; this Mr Dunehue came a long and got in to the wagon to hand out the guns he picked up the gun that was Cocked and Said, hear you damd son of a bich; you have Cocked your gun to Shoot us; Cary replied I did not cock it; Said Dunihue, dont you Contradict me you damd Sone of a bich; you by the time the words ware out of his mouth he Struck Mr Carey a full blow with the brich of his gun upon his head, I was Sitting by the Side of Mr Cary upon the Same Seat when he received the fatal blow

Mr Cary pitched for ward and would have falen out of the wagon; but I caught hold of him and raised him in to the wagon; his head was Split open—the Sergon washed his wound and Sowed it up; he was in griat miserey but could not Speak a word; he lived a bout forty four houres and expired—the mob Stole my horse from me the malitia troops that Mr Dunihue belonged to; was under General Lucus; I was compelled to Sine a dead of trust and leave the State

John Smith

[Sworn to before J. Orr, J.P., Adams Co., IL, 8 Jan 1840.]

SNOW, Willard

I hereby certify that I was a permanent Citizen of Caldwell Co Missourie from the fall of 1836 untill the winter of 1839 when I was compelled by an exterminating order of Gov Boggs to leave the State without any civil process ever at any time being attempted to be sustained against me either for debt or crime near the first of Nov 1838 an armed force under command of General Lucas of Jackson co invaded Caldwell and quartered in the vicinity of Far West ordered the arms of the caldwell militia to be delivered into their hands among whome was a company of volunteers who stood as minute men able evry moment to be called upon to defend the frontiers against invasion they took possession of the town making it the head quarters of the army burning building timber boards rails fence &c they burned my siding flooring lumber for my hous & fence round my lot and left it a desolation destroyed my apple trees without leave or remuneration to this day they also plundered and destroyed near one thousand bushels of corn seven stands of honeybees & some farming tools besides other things bing deprived myself of secureing my crop or even putting up the fence after them they ordered all the mormons to leve the state after signing away all their property at the point of the sword & bayonet

Major Gineral Clark soon arrived with his army the officer to whome the order was really given he sanctiond all that Lucas had done and selected about sixty persons and without any legal process marched them off in a drove together like a flock of Sheep to Ray county without their knowing for what we petitioned for relief to the Legislature but to no purpose I therefore was obliged to leave the state leaving my entire property in Caldwell co Missourie I held a deed second handed from the land office of one hundred and twenty five acres of valuable land thirty five acres of improvements good buildings and large stock of cattle hogs sheep &c have suffered much and also my family in consequence of being forsed to leave my home in the winter my wife and young babe [——] fell from the waggon and was nearly killed upon the frozen ground upon her Journey to Illinois the marks of her sufferings she must carry to her grave

Montrose Lee County Iowe Territory Jan 4th 1840   Willard Snow

[Sworn to before D. W. Kilbourn, J.P., Lee Co., IL, 10 Jan 1840.]

SOUTHWORTH, Chester

Illinois Handcock Co Town of Warsaw Jan 6 1840

Be it none to whome it may Conscern that I testify and saw in the State Missouria Colwell Co. Town of Farwest a Large Body of Armed Men Came in to the Town and Demanded of the Inhabitance of that County and Town there Arms and to give them selves up as Priseners of and I saw them lay Dow ther arms the Town was then garded for some Days until General Clark came with a large armey of men and we were then called to gether a gane and Inforsed under the penalty of Imprisenment to sine a Deed of Trust as they caled it depriving us of all our Rights and priviledgs in the state this I state as being the truth I by not this Took plase Nov 1838

Chester Southworth

[*Sworn to before A. Monroe, J.P., Hancock Co., IL, 6 Jan 1840.*]

SQUIER, Charles

Damages Sustain In Consequec of being Driven from Caldwell County Mo in 1838

Fifteen acres of Land and Improvements one hundred and fif ty Dollars 150

one claim In Davis County Contyning two Hundred and forty acres Damage three hundred Dollars 300

Charles Squier

[*Sworn to before W. Frye, C.C.C.C., Calhoun Co., IL, 15 Jan 1840.*]

STANTON, Daniel

I Daniel Stanton testify that on the first of Nov. 1839 the Militia Came to Davis County and Campt. Before my house with an order from gov. Bogg to Exterminate the mormons from the State several of them intruded on my family to wit John Handley James R Handley Calvin Milsap Caleb Samson Benj. Tayler John McCulla and some others and made my Wife and family Cook for them and find the provison without Compensation them and some others opend a trunk and took some sheets Pillow slips and other goods from it and stole a mare and Colt from me and Cow and Calf James Blakely have the Cow & Calf, Nathaniel Blakely Jame Blakely Benj. Tayler Newton Creekmore Wm. Bowman Wm. Peniston Francis Peniston Wm. Mann and Jacob Rogers were in the Battle at hons Mill in Caldwell County Mo. & also heard Jacob Rogers say he hand kild one mormon with his Corn Cutter and he inted to kill ten more Before he stopd. these things I heard them state. this above I Daniel Stanton Certify to Be true according to the Best of my knowledge

Quincy March th 8—1840 Ill.   Daniel Stanton

[*Sworn to before W. Tainter, who signed for C. M. Woods, C.C.C., Adams Co., IL, 18 Mar 1840.*]

STEPHENS, Henry

Handcock Co and State of Illenois

I doe hereby testify that while I was living in Caldwell co and State of Missouri I saw an armed soldirrie marching in Caldwell co and swearing they would kill every Mormon in the State. they came and surrounded us and and took our arms that we had to perform milatory duty and took Joseph Smith Jnr Sidney Rigdon Lyman Wight and fifty or sixty others and drove them off like Sheep for market and swore that Smith, Rigdon, White and others should never return, and this was done with out any legal pretx and they burnt house logs boards rails & without libirty killd Cattle Sheep and hogs. and robd a boy of a good horse and said they would kill all the men Womin and children. took [——] corn and destroyed our property and compeld me to sign a Dead of trus[t] to pay their expences and this they did at the point of the Sword and compeld us to a gree leave the state at the peril of our lives. this I testify that General Clark Said that he had orders from Govened Bogs to exterminate us but as we had behaved ourselves so well, he would let us go with our lives if we would leave the state, this was done in the year one thosand eight hundred and thirty eight

Henry Stephens

[*Sworn to before A. Monroe, J.P., Hancock Co., IL, 6 Jan 1840.*]

STEVENSON, Henry

Mo october 1838

I Herry Stevenson was a moveing my family to the wester[n] part of the state of Mo I was met by a mob in Carl Co which a bused my wife & family with bad language & threatning our live & turned my horses loose from my waggon & gave my feed to their horses & continued it 2 nights we continued our journey in company with Benjamin Hoit the third day after we ware insulted &nd abused we arived at carlton the county seat & their we was met by a sentral man who cocked his gun & damned me to stop or he would blow me through if stept one step further immediately to men rode up armed with swords & pistols & damned me to go on or they would shoot me & drawed their pistols & I told them the other man had swore if I went another step he would shoot me & now said I which shall I obey & they ordered him to shoulder his gun which he did & I proceeded a few rods further & was met by acompany of armed men about 20 that stoped my horses & took possession of my waggon I wanted to know what they intended to do they in quired if I had any arms or amunition & ordered my wife & 2 daughters out of my waggon one of my daughters was sick at the time which excuse they would not receive but said she must get out of the waggon I pled to let her alone but they presented & cocked several guns, & drew knives at me & damned me to speak another word and they would blow me through & dragged my daughter out of the waggon & searched my waggon & throwed my goods in the street & broke a mantle clock & carried of my rifle & amunition & aftr they had searched my waggon & counsel was that I should turn about & go back & not stay within 10m of that place that night or they would massacree us & their was about fifteen armed men followed us about one mile & I also was known to the sufferings of a man by the name of John Gilles that lived in Randolph Co Mo wher[e] I stayed through the winter but durst not let myself be known acitise[n] by the name of Nelson Howard went to said Gillises house & took his Gillises horse & bridle to huntsville & sold the horse for $11.00 he then came home & hired a mob at fifty cents apiece to mob the old man & family away they went on them on sunday evening & shot his dog & went in & drawed the old man out of bed and abused him & brok[e] his clock & carrid of some property & gave him five days to leave the place I saw the broke clock & two of the mob told me they ware hired to go & what they had done I went three or four day after & moved the old man & family by hi[s] request for said he they will kill me & I moved him in the month of dec to acabin with out chimney chink or dob & they destroyed his corn &c

Henry Stevenson

[*Sworn to before W. H. Boling, C.C.C.C., Pike Co., IL, 14 Jan 1840.*]

STILLMAN, Dexter

Deposition of Dexter Stillman of the County of Scott and State of Illinois, in refference to the matter of the Losses Sustained by the Latter day Saints or Mormons in the State of Missouri, A. D. 1838. taken on the 18th day of Jan. 1840,

State of Illinois Scott County SS.

Dexter Stillman, of the County of Scott and State of Illinois, being Sworn Says that he is of Lawful age, and that in the month of June 1838 he left the State of Ohio for the State of Missouri, and that on or about the middle of July A.D. 1838, he arrived at Far West, Caldwell County State of Missouri with the Sole intent of becoming a resident of Sd. State of Missouri in good faith and due submission to the laws of Said State; that to this End he purchasEd a piece of Land, and became a householder in Said County, and was in proper discharge of his duties as a Citizen; and this deponent further says that on or about the first day of November A.D. Eighteen hundred and thirty Eight, he was Surprised in his said premises by a mob of armed men Composed mostly, & he believes wholly of Citizens of the State of Missouri, who then & there Compelled him to Surrender his premises, made him prisoner, and Compelled to themselves a Convey over in trust of his Said real Estate, and by force and arms dispossessed him of his possessions in Said County, Compelling to deliver his arms and become their prisoner; and this affiant further Says that in accordance with the order of Gov. Boggs of the Said State of Missouri isSued from Head Quarters, Oct. 27th A.D. 1838, he was Compell to leave the Said State of Missouri in an Extremity of Suffering destitution under pain of forfeiture of his life, and further the deponent Saith not.

Dexter Stillman

[Sworn to before E. Sells, J.P., Scott Co., IL, 18 Jan 1840.]

STUEART, Nathan

This is to certify to the wrongs and the injuries which I have received in Missouri

In Novem, 1833, I arrived in Jackson County state of Missouri and was Stoped by a man by the name of Davis and Said that they the Citizens of Jackson were determined to drive all of the Mormons from the County, and Said if I attempted to go any farther that they would destroy me and property and the next Morning there Came three Mob men and Mr. Davis began to wring his hands and Cried Saying they will throw down my house and Soon after there Came twelve men to the house of Mr Davis and drove us back ~~Swearing~~ three miles th[r]eatning us and frequently pointing their guns at us Saying if we did not leave forth with they would destroy us and property and at a nother time I was driven from my home and had a gun at the Same time pointed at me and the man Swore he would blow my damed Brains out this was John Hayden in 1838 I with the rest of the Church were Surroundd by an Armed force of about 6 thousand who threatened to Burn the town and destroy both men women and Children without any Reserve I was then taken prisioners and compeled to Sign a deed of trust to pay of the Militia for burning houses pilliageing goods destroying Crops and Stock also for killing some of the Society in the most Savage maner I was also Commanded to leave the state forth with or be exterminated by order of Genral Clark Commander in Chief

Nathan Stueart

[Sworn to before J. Orr, J.P., Adams Co., IL, 8 Jan 1840.]

TAYLOR, Gabriel N.

State of Illinois Hancock County

I tes tify that in Conce quence of a mob in ray county Mo 1838 that I was Compeld to leave my home and fam Ily to save my life they came A company of armd men thretend my life one of them drew A pistol to shute me But did not[.] Af ter this afew days they Came A gane armd and robd me of my rifle gun and pistol At the same time sear chd my house for moneye and thratened mylife as Before at the same time my Self and family was all sick they Com peld me and my family to leave the state fourth with I lost or left my Crops and stock which which Causd my fam Ily to suffer for want of them. But as yet have had none of it returnd

I sus taind a loss of property to the amount of $1500 in time and property

Gabriel N. Taylor

[*Sworn to before A. Monroe, J.P., Hancock Co., IL, on 6 Jan 1840.*]

TEEPLES, George B.

Handcock Co State of Illinois December 1835

I arived at Liberty ~~Misouri~~ Clay County Misouri and in the Summer of 1836 there was A meeting of the mob of Jackson and Clay Counties met at the Cort house in liberty Clay Co and resolved that our peeple Should leve that Co but after proposed that if we would Comply with a propision that they would proscribe that they would Choose a Committe and Survey a Certain Scope of Cuntry or territory and there let us dwell in pease we acordingly Consented to there proposeals and they Chose Judg Camran and neel Gillam and they Chose a Scope of Cuntry now none by the name of Colwell County there we lived in pease for all most two years but the Summer of 1838 the mob Commenced a gain in Davis County at an election in galiton there was a gineral Combat took place in Conse-quence of our peeple voting I was living at that time in Levengston County and I was notified by the mob that they had resolved that there Should not one of our peopls live in that County and that they would give mee four days to leave the County two families of us then moved into Davis County the mob then Commensed taking our horses Cattle and Sheep and taking prisoners of both men and women and Children we then aplied for protection and gineral Atcherson amediate ly Cauled out his malitia and marched for davis Co and took his Stasion near milport for to disperse the mob and did so in part the next that I am an eye witness to was the gathering of the militia against farwest in oct 1838 the day after there Encampment against far west they Presented on or to us an order from the governer that we Should give up our arms to them and deliver up Sertain prisoners and sign away all our property to pay the expenses of the war and leave the State fourthwith or bee Exterminated this we ascerted to we then was Surrounded by a Strong guard on the Square and Compeled to Sign away all of our property then they Selected fifty men which they made prisoners and Marched for richman them Jail

George B Teeples

[*Sworn to before A. Monroe, J.P., Hancock Co., IL, 6 Jan 1840.*]

THOMAS, Daniel S.

The State of Illinois Adams County S.S. January 7th 1840

This day personally appeared before me William Laughlin a Justice of the peace within Said County, Daniel S Thomas who being duely Sworn according to Law Deposeth and Saith, in the year 1837 & 38 A CitiSen of the State of Missouri Held a Claim of 160 Acres on Congress Land with an Improvement of 20 Acres And was Compelled to Lay down my arms & then Taken prisner for Several days In far West and Then was forced off to Richmond Prisson for 16 Days and then was acquited and Then In the Month of Febuary 1839 Had to Leave the State by the Governors decree.

Daniel S Thomas

[*Sworn to before W. Laughlin, J.P., Adams Co., IL, 7 Jan 1840.*]

THOMPSON, Lewis

State of Illinois Adams County SS

This day personally Cam[e] before me William Laughlin a Justice of the peace of Said Cty. Lewis Thompson being duly Sworn deposeth & saith that he was a citizen of Caldwell Co. Mo. in 1838 and that he Sd deponet Entered the S.E. 1/4 N.w. 1/4 and S.W. 1/4 N.E. 1/4 of Section No 20 in Township No fifty six North of the base line and West of the 5th principa[l] Meridian of Range No 27 Containing Eighty acres at the Land office Lexington Missouri and then resided peaceable until I was Compelled to leave the State by the Governors exterminateing orders executed by General Clark and others

Lewis Thompson

The aforesaid Deponent further Says That William J Thompson was a Citizen and in peaceable possession of the SW ———— SW ———— of Section No. 17. Township No. 56. Range No. 27. And was Compelled to leave the Same by Govenors Boggs Exterminat[in]g Orde[rs] exeuted by General Clark & others as will be Seen by the Duplicate to the above land refered to

Lewis Thompson

[*Sworn to before W. Laughlin, J.P., Adams Co., IL, 7 Jan 1840.*]

THORP, John

State of Illinois Handcock Co

I testify that a mob arose in Carl Co State of Missouri headed by Sashel Wood a presbyterian Preacher and marched into the Town of Dewett and fired their their guns and frightend the women this Town belongd to us and they notified us to leave there in ten days. after ten days they [——] came and fired on us. Some time after this they came and made an a tact up on us and after firing some time caralled us so that we could not go out to hunt our cattle without being shot at they kild of our cows and oxen distroyed our corn burnt [—— ——] one house and drove us from the place and we fled to Far West for safety in Caldwell Co and soon after we got there the militia came in and ~~surrounded~~ camped on our land with out liberty and disarmed us and surrounded the city and burnt our house logs fences &c kild sheap cattle and hogs, took oats corn & without liberty and forced us at the point of the sword to sign a dead of trust to defray their expences and compeld us to agree to leave the state but gave us till spring to doe so. after this when going after corn that belonged to our people the mob drove us back and would not suffer us to gather our own corn thus ~~the sun~~ we remaind exposed to the storm till the spring this was in 1838 and in 39 we had to leave the state

John Thorp

[*Sworn to before A. Monroe, J.P., Hancock Co., IL, 6 Jan 1840.*]

TURNER, Lewis

Damages Sustain I in Los of Lands in of Caldwell county Seventy four acres with Improvemens Valued at ten Dollars per acre the Whole a mount Seven hundred and forty Dollars 740

Lewis Turner

[*Sworn to before W. Frye, C.C.C.C., Calhoun Co., IL, 13 Jan 1840.*]

TURNER, Nelson

Alton the thirteenth January AD 1840

To the Honorable the Senate and House of Representatives in Congress Assembled in the City of Washington Destrict of Columbia

I hereby represent to Your Honorable Body My Losses and Sufferings By the hands of the Mob in the state of Missouri And this may Certify That I was Threatened by the mob that they would shoot me whip me &C. And many other sufferings Too numerous to mention And this may Certify that the losses, which I sustained are no Less than 780.00 Dollars by Their driving me from my home &C.

Nelson Turner

[Sworn to before J. H. Randle, N.P., Madison Co., IL, 13 Jan 1840.]

TURNER, William

Being drove from Coldwell Co. Mo. and the damage

1838 Sevnty three Acres of land at ten dollars per acre the loss of Corn wheet potatoes & Hogs Cattle Sheep three Hundred Dollars also the damage & expense of moving in the winter Two Hundred Dollars the whole amount $1330

William Turner

[The following is a land description furnished by William Turner.]

73 acres of Land part of E 1/2 ofthe SE l/4 of Sec 2 T 55. NW 5 pm Range 29. Cont[g] 80 [acres]

[73 acres of land part of] NE 1/4 of NE 1/4 of Sect 11. T 55. N.W 5 pm. R 29. 40 [acres]

[73 acres of land part of] SE 1/4 " NW 1/4 " " 12. T 55 N.W 5 pm. [R] 29. 40

belonged to the aforesaid Wm Turner.

74 acres ofthe foregoing Tracts belonged to the aforesaid Lewis Turner.

[7]0 acres ofthe above Tracts belonged to the aforesaid Charles Squires

5 " ofanother tract bought by Said Squires of Martin Alred belonged to Said Charles Squires

The enclosed duplicates will Show as to Turner's enteries at the Land Office at Lexington

[Sworn to before W. Frye, C.C.C.C., Calhoun Co., IL, 13 Jan 1840.]

TYLER, Elisabeth

Illenois Quncy Sept 30th 1839
    A bill of Damages for Being Driven from the State of Missouri by a mob—

first for mooving to the State	$500.00
for propperty Lost in the State	100.00
for leaving the State	100.00

    I certify the abov a count to Be true and Just acording to the Best of my knowledg

Elisabeth Tyler

[*Not sworn.*]

WALKER, John R.

Alton January 13, 1840
    To the Honorable House of the Senate & Representatives in Congress Assembled at the City of Washington And District of Columbia
    I the undersigned do by these presents represent To You my Losses and Sufferings in the State of Missouri in the Year 183[8]. &C by the Hands of a mob who pillaged and destroyed my Goods &C. &C. in Jackson and Caldwell Countys and Which Losses I Certify To be no Less than Five Hundred Dollars further that I suffered many Injuries from this mob By Breaking in my Windows By Thrusting Long Poles Through at My family and Driving them from their Habitation.

John R. Walker

[*Sworn to before J. H. Randle, N.P., Madison Co., IL, 13 Jan 1840.*]

WALKER, William C.

Alton January 13, 18[40]
    To the honorable Senate and House of Representatives in Congress Assembled at the City of Washington District of Columbia
    I The Undersigned do by these presents Represent To You my Losses And Suffering in the State of Missouri in the Year 1838 By the Hands of the Mob in that State who Distroyed and pillaged My Goods & Chattels and drove me and my family from my home. And do Certify my Loss of property To be no Less than Six Hundred Dollars

Wm C. Walker

[*Sworn to before J. H. Randle, N.P., Madison Co., IL, 13 Jan 1840.*]

WEEVER, Edward

This is to certify that I Edward Weever formoly of Coldwell County Missourie do certify that I Entered a certain tract of land in the aforsaid county lying in Section 30 T 56 North of the base line and west of the fifth principle meredian Range No 28 containing forty acre[s] was compelled to Sacrafise my land and leave the State in consequen[ce] of the Governors exterminating orders allso I had one Set of house logs burned up in consequence of the militia who marched on our posessions and encamped there without liberty. And likewise I saw a prisener Shamefully abused who was taking by the militia January—1840

Edward Weever

[Sworn to before A. Brown, J.P., Pike Co., IL, 10 Jan 1840.]

WELCH, John

Alton Ill. January 13, 1840

To the honorable Senate and House of Reprsentatives in Congress Assembled at Washington City District of Columbia

I the undersigned do Hereby Certify to You my Losses, Sufferings &C. in the state of missouri By the Hands of a Mob By driving me from my home and depriving me from the comforts of Life And do by these presents Certify the Losses which I have Sustained To be no Less than five Hundred Dollars; And further Certify that I was Threatened To be shot and was obliged To Leave all and flee to save my Life

John Welch

[Sworn to before J. H. Randle, N.P., Madison Co., IL, 13 Jan 1840.]

WHILOCK, Andrew

State of Illenois Pike County

This Day personally appeard before me W. H. Boling Clerk of the Couty Com. Court Andrew Whillock and after being duly sworn Deposth & says that in the Fall of 1835 This Deponant moovd to Clay Co Mo & on or a bout July following ther was some Difficulty a Rose Con[ce]rning the Mormons that this Deponant Caulds him self a Mormon that in consequence of his religious belief Deponant was for[ce]d to leave the County of Clay & seek reffuge in Cald Well County Mo, That Deponant thinks that he must of lost five hun hundred dollars. That in C[l]ay County this Deponant had forty acres of Land that will more fully appear from a certiffed of the register heare with fild & also In Cald Well 80 Acres both of whitch Places this Deponant & family have been Driven form & farther this Deponant says not

Andrew Whilock

[*Sworn to before W. H. Boling, C.C.C.C., Adams Co., IL, 14 Jan 1840.*]

WHITING, Elisha

In the year of our Lord 1837

I Elisha Whiting of the Church of Jesus Christ of latter day Saints, moved my family into the State of Missouri, Clay County for the purpose of making a permanent settlemen[t] I soon purchased an improved farm & moved my family consisting of a wife and 5 children onto the same. in a few months 6 out of the 7 were taken sick a part of them were put into a waggon on a bed and moved to Caldwell Co myself being left, and soon taken sick and in a few days a mob threatened to come upon and drive me from my home not withstanding my sickness. [—— —— ——] ~~gave me~~ but through the kindness of a neighbor who informed me of the plot, and offered me an asylum under his roof which I accepted and escaped from their snare. I had preveiously purchased an 80 of goverment land in the county of Caldwell for which I had paid my money. my family then there and not hearing what had be[c]ome of me Sent one of my sons to learn: he found me very low. but put me into his waggon on a bed and carried me to Caldwell: where I lay sick for many months two of my sons together with a son in law: had also bought of government and paid their money for the same; consisting of 300 and 20 acres. and there we thought surely to settle ourselves in peace as the authorities of the County of Clay, had promised us protection: but in this we were mistaken for not many days after our move a ruthless act of barbarians, living in the State of Mo. and even claiming to be the free born sons of America marched their thousands of deamons into the County and there threatened to extirminate or drive us from our lands and home and we being insufficient to meet so large a band of ruffians, were obliged to submit: and for a trifling Sum to Sign away our duplicates and then to cap the climax driven in the month of March through cold storms of Snow and rain, having to make our beds on the cold wet ground which when we arose in the morning we often found drenched with water and then obliged to load our wet bedding into the waggon and move slowly forward[5] but after all our sufferings we finally

---

[5]The last part of this petition was written twice, once without the date and once without the signature. The two have been combined.

reached a friendly and hospitable people in the State of Illinois for whose friendly feelings, our hearts ought ever to flow with gratitude. and we are now here without a foot of land that we can call our own.

January 8t 1840   Elisha Whiting

[*Sworn to before J. Orr, J.P., Adams Co., IL, 8 Jan 1840.*]

WILSON, Bradley B.

January 7th 1840 The state of Illenois Adams County SS

this day personally appeared before me William Laughlin a Justice of the Peace within said County

Bradley B. Wilson who being Duly sworn according to Law deposeth and saith that he was a sitizen of Ray County Missouri in the year A.D 1838 and that he entered at the Land office in Lexington Layfayett County one hundred & twenty acres of land situate in Ray County Township No 54 that he had possession of the same and lived upon it that he was forced to leave the same and also the State by the authorities of the state of Missouri this Deponent further states that he was passing along the Road and was shot at chased vigerously by a party of perhaps 8 or 10 men and was Detained as Prisoner of war under General Lucas three days Contrary to law further Deponent saith not

Bradey B. Wilson

[*Sworn to before W. Laughlin, J.P., Adams Co., IL, 7 Jan 1840.*]

WILSON, Eleanor

The State of Illenois Adams County SS

Personally appeared before me William Laughlin a Justice of the Peace in and for said County Eleanor Wilson being duly Sworn according to law Deposeth & Saith that She moved into Missouri in 1836 and Settled in Davis County in 1837 upon Congress land and gained a preemption improved & raised a Crop & had it Secured was driven by the mob from it lost Crop one Cow & some hogs and all her chickens sauce &C She States further that She had another house built and was driven from it by the mob in the dead of winter under the most distressing Circumstances occasioned from Sickness & other Deprivation and lastly left the State from Boggs exterminating order

Eleanor **X** Wilson

[*Sworn to before W. Laughlin, J.P., Adams Co., IL, 8 Jan 1840.*]

WILSON, George C.

The State of Illenois Adams County SS Jany. 7th 1840

this day personally appeared before me William Lawlin a Justice of the Peace in and for said County Geo. C. Wilson who being duly Sworn according to Law Deposeth & saith that he moved into the state of Missouri in Oct. 1837 in Ray County and entered ~~five~~ one 80 & three 40 acre lots of land at the land office at Lexington Layfayett County for my own use and made it my holm while I lived in the State Deponent saith further that he was Compelled to leave the State and ~~my~~ his holm by Governor Boggs Exterminating order executed by General Clark & others he further said he was kept in Prision three days lay on the ground Sick further Deponent saith not

George C. Wilson

[*Sworn to before W. Laughlin, J.P., Adams Co., IL, 7 Jan 1840.*]

WILSON, Lewis D.

I hereby certify that I purchased from Congress Two hundred and forty acres of land lying in Caldwell County and State of Missouri and Was compelled to leave the same on a c count of the order of the executive of the State.

When the Malitia came to Far West they took from me a valuable Horse which broke up my team I made extertions to obtain it again but without success. I was obliged to part with my land (in order to make up my team and for means to get me conveyed out of the State) for one sixth of the value. I had consequently to part with the duplicates I had for the same

Lewis D. Wilson

[*Sworn to before D. H. Wells, J.P., Hancock Co., IL, 3 Jan 1840.*]

WILSON, Polly

A Bill of damage

I Polly Wilson A Widow and a mormon so cauld great has been my sufferings on the accoun of mobs while in the state of Mosouri which was a number of years I was driven from Jacson County and from Clay County and from davis County and from Caldwell County and thence out of the state without any provocation except the name mormon $1000

Polly X Wilson

Hancock County Illinois State

This day personally appeared before me the the under Signed an acting justice of of the peace within & for Said County polly Wilson and filed the following affidavit

I polly Wilon Do Solomnly Swear that the above Statements as I veriably believe are true

Polly X Wilson

[Sworn to before T. Crawford, J.P., Hancock Co., IL, 6 Jan 1840.]

WILSON, William

Morgan County State of Illinois SS

Personally appeared before me Ja A Graves an actting justice of the peace in and for the county of Morgan aforesaid Willian Wilson and on oath says he blongs to the Church of Jesus Christ of latter day saints, and in the summer of 1838 he went into the state of Missouri and purchased a house and lot in a small town Called Dewett in Carrol County in the state of Missourie aforesaid, he further says he obtoined a deed of said lot which he now holds but in consequence of the difficulties which took place between the missourians and the latter day saints soon after, and the threats of the missourians to drive the saints from that place he has never ventured to go to get his deed recorded this lot he values one hundred dollars[.] This deponant further says that in the early part of the difficulties aforesaid he left the state of Missouri and returned to his family in the state of Ohio and in consequence of the peremtory order of the executive of the state of Missouri for all the latter day saints to leave the state of Missouri he has never been permitted to come into possession of the property he left in the state of Missouri which consisted of the lot before mentioned and one cow worth twenty dollars also one rifle gun worth ten dollars and also one hundred dollars worth of goods which he shiped in Ohio for Richmond in the state of Missouri where they did not arrive untill after he left the state of Missourie[.] This deponant further says that in consequence of the [de]rangement of his business it is at least one hundred dollars damage to him this together with other losses So Sustained by by said deponant he says amount to three hundred and thirty dollars he therefore prays the interposition of Congress to aid and assist him in obtaining redress for his losses and injuries so sustained all of which are by said deponant respectfully submitted

William Wilson

[Sworn to before J. A. Graves, J.P., Morgan Co., IL, 24 Jan 1840.]

WINTER, David

I David Winter do certify that I bought a certain tract of land in the State of Missourie and county of Coldwell which was entered by Jesse Mann containing 80 acres lying in Section 22. T. 56. R 28 and allso another lot containing 40 acres in the aforesaid section which was entered by Henry McHenry both peaces I had bought and paid 950 dollars for but before the deeds was made out I was compelled to leave the state in comsequence of Governors Bogg's Exterminating orders to expell the ~~Mormons~~ the Church of Jesus Christ of Latterday Saints from the state of Missourie

I was therefore compelled to sell my land for ~~no~~ to pro cure means to leave the state at ~~the~~ a reduced price

and allso another piece in the afforesaid section containg 40 acres which was entered by Mr. Lyons which I was likewise compelled to sell

David Winter

a List of bamages that I sustained in Missourie in consequences of Gov. Boggs orders to exterminate the mormons

For time lost	$52.00
Loss of stock	100.00
loss on the price of land	700.00
	$852.00

[*Sworn to before A. Brown, J.P., Pike Co., IL, 10 Jan 1840.*]

WOOD, Gideon D.

The State of Illinois Adams County SS. January 7th 1840

this day personaly appeared Before me Wm. Laughlin a Justice of the peace within Said County. Giddion D. Wood Mooved to Missouri Caldwell County 1838 and perchased an Improved farm being Compelled to leave it by the exterminating orders of the Governer. and Consider my Loss at Least 1000 Dollars

Gideon D. Wood

[*Sworn to before W. Laughlin, J.P., Adams Co., IL, 7 Jan 1840.*]

WOOD, Hannah

State of Illinois Adams County SS. January 7th 1840

This day personally appeared before me Wm. Laughlin a Justice of the peace within Said County Hannah Wood who being Duely Sworn according to Law. Deposeth and Saith, She being a neighbour of Mr John Daley Saw the Militia take of his propperty as much as 200 Bushels of Oats She likewise Saw them take off his hogs which were fated. She did not See them Kill but one threw Down his fences let in Cattle which Distroyed his Corn distroyed one beehive

Hannah Wood

[*Sworn to before W. Laughlin, J.P., Adams Co., IL, 7 Jan 1840.*]

WOODLAND, William

State of Illinois Adams County SS January 7th 1840

This day personally appeared before me Wm. Laughlin a Justice of the peace for said County Wm. Woodland being duly sworn according to Law. Deposeth and Saith, in the year of 1837 he became a Citizen of Davis Co. Missouri in September Settled on Congress land made an improvment of about 5 Acres raised a good Crop of Corn and placed it in shocks and was driven from my home and lost my Crop & hogs. I was on the place long enough to gain a preemption, after I was taken prisener by the militia [——] & my Gun Taken from me a man by the name of John Handley who punched me and struck me over the Head with his Gun and Had to leave the state by the Exterminatig Decree of the Governer

Wm X Woodland

[*Sworn to before W. Laughlin, J.P., Adams Co., IL, 8 Jan 1840.*]

WORTHINGTON, James

The State of Illinois Adams County SS

Before me William Laughlin one of the Justices of the peace for said County, personly came James Worthington who being duly sworn according Law deposeth & saith that he is the true owner of the Southwest quarter of the southwest quarter of section sixteen in Township 55, Range 28, in the County of Caldwell & State of Missouri, which forty acres of land the militia under command of Generals Lucas & Willson Compelled him to assign away by a Deed of trust running to the State of Missouri, sometime in the month of october or november in the year 1838: And this Deponent further states that previous to this he was chased by four of said militia & when they could not get him they fired four guns at him, & about three or four days afterwards he was taken prisioner by said militia who kept him a prisioner about six or seven days, & after he was released they hunted & chased him about twelve days: & that afterwards said militia compelled him to leave said land without any compensation: & that they also compelled him & his family to leave the said State of Missouri, & that he was a Citizen of said state in the year aforesaid: & further this deponent saith not.

James Worthington

[*Sworn to before W. Laughlin, J.P., Adams Co., IL, 7 Jan 1840.*]

YALE, Hannah

I certify that I lived about two miles from Far West in Caldwell County Missouri. Early in November A.D. 1838 A company came to our house and took possession of the same, without any leave whatever as my husband was absent from home, they took several things from the house destroyed my corn and hay Shot our fowls and hogs and took my husbands working tools away

Commerce Hancock Co Illinois Jany. 2, 1840   Hannah Yale

[*Sworn to before D. H. Wells, J.P., Hancock Co., IL, 3 Jan 1840.*]

YORK, Hannah

January 22 1840 Township of five five pike County
I the under sind have imbrased the truth as is in Jesus christ being 55 years of age and my Companion being 59 years of age 3 years a go with 2 Children a boy of 14 years of age and a helpless Criple girle moved in to Colwell County State of missouri and Entered us forty acres of land I Bilt a hous one stable smoke house crib hog pen & a bout 10 acres under cultivation for our fa[m]ley in hopse of spending our days with title property But alas our corn is gone wheat is gone our hay is gone our Cow is gone yea and my Companion is John york wase kild at the masacred by the mob at h[aun]s mill and I the wife of John york and have bin with my two helpless Children have a Blige to leave the state of missoury and now have know other sorse than present my case to the powers that be thus in Consequence of Govener Bogs of Misoury his and with his asisters given

at Clark I am Left to move ~~and~~ [—— —— ——] and is this beeing to all
to whare it may Come A true Statement of the fact of the above word of
Is my hand and Seal

Hannah **X** York

I have suffered the loss of $250
I Hannah york Doe Solomnly Sware by the Ever living god that the
be fore Mentioned is a true bill of My Suffrages in the before Mentioned
Case so help Me god

hannah **X** york

[*Sworn to before D. R. Rogers, J.P., Pike Co., IL, 27 Jan 1840.*]

YOUNG, Phineas H.

Deposition of Phinehas H. Young of Scott County Illinois, in relation
to the Losses of the MorMons in the State of Missouri in 1838, taken this
18th day of Jan 1840 in Said County Scott

State of Illinois Scott County SS.
Phinehas H Young of Said County of Scott of Lawful age, being
Sworn deposeth and Saith, that on or about the twenty fith day of august
AD Eighteen Hundred and thirty Seven he arrived at Far West, Caldwell
County State of Missouri With the intent to become a Citizen of Said State,
in good faith and due Submission to the Laws of Said State of Missouri;
and further, that he purChased on Good Consideration one hundred and
Sixty acres of Land in Said State; also three pre-emption rights, to
Congress Lands for all of which he paid the Sum of five hundrd and Eighty
five dollars, and that by other Lawful means he then accumulated personal
property in value five hundred dollars; And this deponent further says that
on or about the 28th day of October AD 1838, having been previously
threatened, he was Surprised in the peaceable possession of his Said
premises, by a Mob of Armed Men, Citizens of the State of Missouri, who
then and there Compelled him <u>Vi Et Annus</u> to deliver up his Said premises
and property to the aforsaid Mob of Armed men under pain of having his
dwelling burnt and his family massacred, and that he was Compelled to
leave the State of Missouri by order of Gov. Boggs issued on the 27th of
October A.D. 1838 from Head Quarters ~~at far West~~ Jefferson City, under
pain of death which order he obeyed in the greatest Extremity of Suffering
and this utmost State of d[essittution] And further the deponent saith not.

Phineas H. Young

[*Sworn to before E. Sells, J.P., Scott Co., IL, 18 Jan 1840.*]

Part IV

The Appeal en Masse

Introduction to Part IV

In 1844 Church leaders submitted at least three documents to Congress: a memorial asking that Nauvoo be made a territory of the federal government, an appeal to settle land in the Oregon Territory, and a memorial applying to Congress for redress for sufferings in Missouri (*HC* 6:131; Hyde, 11 June 1844; *Congressional Globe* 13:605).

Rather than submitting individual petitions, Church leaders sent a single petition in the final appeal. It was 50 feet long and rolled up like a scroll. After a brief, four-page introduction summarizing the sufferings of the Latter-day Saints in Missouri, 3,419 people signed their names. Some signed the petition more than once. Not all of the signers had been in Missouri, but signed the petition in support of those who had suffered there.

The scroll petition was prepared in the late fall of 1843 in Nauvoo (*HC* 6:88). Unlike most of the individual petitions, it was not notarized or sworn to before legal authorities. The Nauvoo City Council voted that Orson Pratt should "present the Memorial and Ordinance to Congress" (*HC* 6:124). Two other emissaries, Apostles John E. Page and Orson Hyde, helped Pratt present the Mormon cause in Washington during the winter and spring of 1844 (Page; *HC* 6:286).

Once again Church leaders secured the help of Illinois congressmen such as Senator James Semple, who previously had helped the Mormons (*Congressional Globe* 13:497, 13:605, 13:694). Of the ten representatives Illinois had in the House at this time (Bateman and Selby 446), it is most likely that Church leaders solicited help from John T. Stuart, Stephen A. Douglas, and John Wentworth. These three men were previously acquainted with the Saints (*HC* 4:356–57, 535–36; Wentworth). This time, however, the Saints did not have the help of their former advocate, Richard M. Young for by 1844, he was no longer in the Senate.

This scroll appeal fared no better than the others. On 9 June 1844, Orson Hyde wrote to Joseph Smith that Congress had rejected their plea to present the petition (Hyde). Still, Hyde had not given up, and he appealed directly to President John Tyler. In a letter dated 11 June 1844, he reported that President Tyler spent a "good deal of time with [me]" and "was very frank . . . but seemed to feel that I should be satisfied with a few words because of the press of business." Continuing, Hyde explained, "We are now thrown back upon our own resources. We have tried every department of government to obtain our rights, but we cannot find them" (Hyde).

Chapter 7

The Scroll Petition

To the honorable the Senate and house of Representatives of the United States, in Congress assembled

The Memorial of the undersigned Inhabitants of Hancock County in the State of Illinois respectfully sheweth:

That they belong to the Society of Latter Day Saints, commonly called Mormons, that a portion of our people commenced settling in Jackson County Missouri, in the Summer of 1831, where they purchased Lands and settled upon them with the intention and expectation of becoming permanent Citizens in Common with others.

From a very early period after the Settlement began, a very unfriendly feeling was manifested by the neighboring people; and as the Society increased, this unfriendly Spirit also increased, until it degenerated into a cruel and unrelenting persecution and the Society was at last compelled to leave the County. An Account of these unprovoked persecutions has been published to the world; yet we deem it not improper to embody a few of the most prominent items in this memorial and lay them before your honorable body.

On the 20th of July 1833 a mob collected at Independence, a deputation or Committee from which, called upon a few members of our Church there, and stated to them that the Store, Printing Office, and all Mechanic Shops belonging to our people must be closed forthwith, and the Society leave the County immediately. These Conditions were so unexpected and so hard, that a short time was asked for consider on the subject Before an Answer could be given, which was refused, and when some of our men answered that they could not consent to comply with such propositions, the work of destruction commenced. The Printing Office, a valuable two story brick building, was destroyed by the Mob, and with it much valuable property; they next went to the Store for the same purpose, but one of the Owners thereof, agreeing to close it, they abandoned their design. A series of outrages was then commenced by the mob upon individual members of our Society; Bishop Patridge was dragged from his house and family, where he was first partially stripped of his clothes and then tarred and feathered from head to foot. A man by the name of Allan was also tarred at the same time. Three days afterwards the Mob assembled in great numbers, bearing a red flag, and proclaiming that, unless the Society would leave "en masse," every man of them should be killed. Being in a defenceless situation, to avoid a general massacre, a treaty was entered into and ratified, by which it was agreed that one half of the Society should leave the County by the first of January, and the remainder by the first of April following. In October, while our people were gathering their crops and otherwise preparing to fulfil their part of the treaty, the mob again collected without any provocation, shot at some of our people, whipped others, threw down their houses, and committed many other depredations; the Members of the Society were for some time harassed, both day and night, their houses assailed and broken open, and their Women and Children insulted and abused. The Store house of A. S. Gilbert & Co. was broken open, ransacked, and some of the goods strewed in the Streets. These repeated assaults so aroused the indignant feelings of our people that a small party thereof on one occasion, when wantonly abused, resisted the mob, a conflict ensued, in which one of our people and some two or three of their assailants were killed. This unfortunate affair raised the whole County in guns, and we were required forthwith to Surrender our arms and leave the County. Fifty one Guns were given up, which have never been returned or paid for to this day. Parties of the Mob from 30 to 70 in number [——] the Country in evry direction, threatning and abusing Women and Children, until they were forced; first to take shelter in the woods and prairies at a very inclement Season of the year, and finally to make their escape to Clay County, where the people permitted them to take refuge for a time.

After the Society had left Jackson County, their buildings amounting to about two hundred, were either burned or otherwise destroyed, with a great portion of their Crops, as well as furniture, stock &c for which they have not as yet received any renumeration. The Society remained in Clay County; nearly three years, when in compliance with the demands of the Citizens there, it was determined to remove to that Section of Country, known afterwards as Caldwell County. In order to secure our people from molestation, the members of the Society bought out most of the former Inhabitants of what is now Caldwell County. and also entered much of the wild land, then belonging to the United States in that Section of Country, fondly hoping that as we were American Citizens, obeying the laws, and assisting to support the government, we would be protected in the use of homes which we had honestly purchased from the general government and fully paid for. Here we were permitted to enjoy peace for a Season, but as our Society increased in numbers, and settlements were made in Davies and Carrol Counties, unfounded jealousies sprung up among our neighbors, and the spirit of the Mob was soon manifested again. The people of our Church who had located themselves at DeWit, were compelled by the Mob to leave the place, notwithstanding the Militia were called out for their protection. From DeWit the mob went to Davies County, and while on their way took some of our people prisoners and greatly abused and mistreated them. Our people had been driven by force from Jackson County; they had been compelled to leave Clay County and sell their lands there, for which they have never been paid; they had finally settled in Caldwell County where they had purchased and paid for nearly all the Government land within its limits, in order to secure homes where they could live and worship in peace, but even here they were soon followed by the mob. The Society remained in Caldwell from 1836 until the fall of 1838, and during that time had acquired, by purchase from the Government, the Settlers, and preemptions, almost all the lands in the County of Caldwell, and a portion of those in Davies and Carrol Counties. Those Counties when our people first commenced their Settlements were for the most part wild and uncultivated, and they had converted them into large and well improved farms. well stocked. Lands had risen in value from ten to 25 dollars per acre, and those Counties were rapidly advancing in Cultivation and wealth. In August 1838 a riot commenced growing out of the attempt of a member of the Society to vote, which resulted in creating great excitement and many scenes of lawless outrage. A large mob under the conduct of Cornelius Gilliam came into the vicinity of Far West, drove off our Stock and abused our people, another party came into Caldwell County took away our horses and cattle, burnt our houses, and ordered the inhabitants to leave their homes immediately. By orders of Brigadier General Donnovan and Colonel Hinkle a company of about 60 men went to disperse this mob under the command of David W. Patten. A conflict ensued in which Captain Patten and two of his men were killed and others wounded. A mob party from two to three hundred in number, many of whom are supposed to have come from Chariton, fell on our people and notwithstanding they begged for quarters shot down and killed Eighteen, as they would so many Wild Beasts.

They were finally compelled to fly from those Counties; and on the 11th of October 1838, they sought safety by that means, with their families, leaving many of their effects behind that they had previously applied to the constituted authorities of Missouri for protection but in vain. The Society were pursued by the Mob, Conflicts ensued, deaths occurred on each side, and finally a force was organized under the authority of the Governor of the State of Missouri, with orders to drive us from the State, or exterminate us. Abandoned and attacked by those to whom we had looked for protection, we determined to make no further resistance but submit to the authorities of the State, and yield to our fate however hard it might be. Several members of the Society were arrested and imprisoned on a charge of treason against the State; and the rest amounting to above 14,000 Souls, fled into the other states, principally into Illinois, where they now reside.

Your Memorialists would further state, that they have heretofore petitioned your Honorable Body praying redress for the injuries set forth in this memorial but the Committee to whom our petition was referred, reported, in substance, that the general government had no power in the case; and that we must look for relief to the Courts and the Legislature of Missouri. In reply, your Memorialists would beg leave to state that they have repeatedly applied to the authorities of Missouri in vain. that though they are American Citizens, at all times ready to obey the laws and support the institutions of the Country, none of us would dare enter Missouri for any such purpose, or for any purpose whatever. Our property was seized by the Mob, or lawlessly confiscated by the State, and we were forced at the point of the Bayonet to sign Deeds of Trust relinquishing our property but the exterminating order of the Governor of Missouri is still in force and we dare not return to claim our just rights—the Widows and Orphans of those slain, who could legally sign no deeds of Trust, dare not return to claim the Inheritance left them by their Murdered Parents.

It is true the Constitution of the United States gives to us in Common with all other Native or adopted Citizens, the right to enter and settle in Missouri, but an executive order has been issued to exterminate us if we enter the State, and that part of the Constitution becomes a nullity so far as we are concerned.

Had any foreign State or power committed a similar ourtrage upon us, we cannot for a moment doubt that the strong arm of the general government would have been stretched out to redress [——] our wrongs, and we flatter ourselves that the same power will either redress our grievances or shield us from harm in our efforts to regain our lost property, which we fairly purchased from the general government.

Finally your Memorialists, pray your Honorable Body to take their wrongs into consideration, receive testimony in the case, and grant such relief as by the Constitution and Laws you may have power to give.

And your Memorialists will every pray &c.

Nauvoo, Illinois, November 28th 1843.

Joseph Smith Mayor	Hyrum Smith Counsellor
Daniel H. Wells	Brigham Young Counsellor
Orson Spencer	John Taylor
Geo. W. Harris	Orson Pratt

Geor A Smith
Saml. Bennett
H G Sherwood City Marshal
Willard Richards Recorder
H. G. Sherwood city marshal
Edw. [Hunter]
Ann Hunter
Edward Hunter Jr.
[Margaret] Calhoon
J. D. Parker
David L Rising
Lousia C Rising
Abel Butterfield
Caroline Butterfield
Silas Nowell
Nancy Nowell
Zina D Jacobs
Henry B Jacobs
Francis Welch
James Barnes
Wm Parshall
A. M. Parshall
Elijah Malin
Catherine Malin
Sarah Malin
Eliza Ann Malin
Samuel Malin
Albert Petty
Charles Bird
Mary Ann Bird
R. A. Russell
Margaret B. Russell
Margaret P Downing
[Thomazin] D. Woodward
Sarah D Foster
Addison Greene
Amanda Greene
Nathen K Knight

Benjm. Warrington
W. W. Phelps
Daniel Spencer
Heber C. Kimball
Orson Hyde
John A. Forgeus
David Brinton
Robert Maxton
James Downing
John F Renault
Matilda Streeper
Martha A Reanault
Wm. A Gheen
Margrat Sutherland
Nancey Sutherland
Margret Johnson
Augustus Stafford
Martha Stafford
Charlotte Barnes
Wm. C Patten
Ann Patten
Allis Walworth
William Walworth
Catherine Barker
Thomas Barker
Alfred Pew
Elizabeth Pew
Catharine Pettey
Wm. [——]
O M Deuel
William Allen
Maria Wills
Margret Wells
James [——]
Rob[·] W. Bidwell
Elizebath Bidwell
[George] Babcock
Amada Babcock

Naomia Knight
Hannah Mar[s]h
William Jones
Elisabeth Jones
Catharine A Jones
Mary E Jones
Willaim Jones Jur
Charlote Jones
Mercy Jones
Anna [melrih] Jones
Sarah metilda Jones
Warren Markham
Ira Hillman
Elisabeth Corbridg
Mary Corbridg
James Corbrdg
Silvia Mory
George Morey
J W Johnson
Elizabeth Johnson
Orson Pratt
Andrew Cahoon
Sarah M. Pratt
Lydia A Bates
Graham Coltrin
John Coltrin
Henry G Coltrin
Alpha C Davis
Benjamin Davis
Mary Brown
A M B Perry
Minerva A. Reed
Samuel Bell
John Halladay
Emily Halladay
Thomas Dollinger
Eliza Dolinger
J T D Turnbull

Eliphaz Marsh
John M. Bernhisel M.D.
Constantia E Hutchinson
Margaret Copeland
John Eagle
Suson Eagle
E. D. Woolley
S. A. Woolley
Mary Woolley
Samuel Wooley
Ellen Wilding
Rachel Wolley
John Woolly
Franklin Woolley
Susanna Yarman
J. S. Sparks
Alles Heap
Sarah Stanford
Edward Stanford
Nanncy W Ott
Fred Ott
Jacob K. Butterfield
Alexander Walker
Lorenzo Wells
Louis Walker
Louisa Butterfield
Jammina Bell
Uriah B Johnson
Simon Mcintier
Isabella Mcintier
Josh Billington
Martha Billington
Eliza Billington
Peter Mattice
Chas. A. Foster
Abele Lamb
Almira Lamb
Ann Martin

Lorindia Turnbull
Abm. Palmer
P D Palmer
John Laird
Marion Laird
Robt. D Foster
Sarah Foster
Hannah Mail
Edward Pugh
John Procter Sen
Jane Procter
Thomas Procter
Samuel Hodge
Theo. J. T. [F]oster
David Fullmer
Rhoda Ann Fullmer
Hannah M. Boynton
Abram D Boynton
Wm. Milam
Elizabeth Milam
Thomas Sanders
Mary Thompson
Augustine [Z]ory
Moses Olmstead
Almira Olmstead
Joseph S Scofield
Claressa A Scofield
Hiram Mace
Elizabeth Mace
Henry E Lamoreaux
Harriet Lamomoreax
John Haven
Judith T Haven
Maria S. Haven
H. P. Murray
Lorensa Murray
Thomas Jones
Mary Jones

William [Haines]
Philip Smith
Sarah Smith
James Hawkins
John Parry
Ann Parry
Henry Nelson
Isaac Nelson
Thomas Nelson
Betcy Nelson
James Jepson
Eleanor Jepson
Thomas Corbitt
Ann Corbitt
Mary Corbitt
James Jarret
Mary Jarret
Joseph Barron
Wm. Box
Jane Brown
Joseph Bostock
Ann Bostock
James Gorden
Mary Gorden
John Murdock
Electa Murdock
Arthur Roscow
Emma Roscow
Ann Thompson
Daniel Burch jr
Ann Burch
Daniel Burch sen
Jesse Higgins
Susan Higgins
Nathanl Higgins
Maryann Higgins
Newel Knight
Lydia Knight

Samuel West
Margaret West
Ralph Thompson
Levi W Hancock
Moses Mecham
James Goff
Robert Campbell
Susanna Campbell
Jesse Lambson
Ruth Lambson
Nilson Lambson
Loisa Lampson
Mary Jane Robbins
Loisance Baluy
Alfred Lambson
Charles Robinis
Charles Ivins
Elizabeth L Ivins
William N S Ivins
Mary S Ivins
James Ivins
Mary S Ivins
Robert Ivins
Garret C. Ivins
Jacob C Ivins
Mary Ann Ivins
Rachel R Ivins
Brigham Young
Mary A Young
Joseph A Young
Brigham A Young
Elizabeth Young
Vilate Young
Mary A Young
Jany Muray
Haritt Cook
John Harrington
Martha Harrington

Truman Gillitt
Fidilia Gillett
Roxsina Repsher
Edward T Repsher
Mary [Puegh]
Elizebath Davis
Pensifor L Maxton
John Binley
Mary Maxton
Ann Riley
George Washington Boyde
Lewius N Scovil
Lucy Scovil
Joel F. Scovil
Lucy L. Scovil
Sariah Scovil
Samuel Rolfe
L B Stoddard
Wm. E Horner
Abraham Hoover
J. D. Parker
J. J. Jackson
John A. Forgeus
E. Robinson
Angeline E. Robinson
Rosannah Forgeus
Hunting Johnson
Jemima Johnson
A B. Williams
Lucy Ann Munjar
Marcellus L. Bates
Wm. M Allred
R. A. Allred
Orissa A. Allred
Julia A. Bates
Horace Roberts
Harriett Roberts
Margaret Wilcocks

Richard Garstang
Sarah Garstang
James Procter
Ietis Proctor
William Hartley
Heber Hartley
Joseph A. Kelling
Elizabeth Kelling
Dionitia Plum
Nelson McCarty
Mary Jane McCarty
Delilah Morace
Vina Holaster
Almira Babbit
Phebe Graves
Elisa A Graves
lydia Hadlock
Emily Hadlock
J. F. Weld
A. M. Harding
K. O. Harding
Sisson Chase
Dorothy Chase
Lucinda Chase
John P Greene
Elisa M Greene
Jacob Zundel
Sarah Zundel
John Zundel
Christina Zundel
F H Maesar
Magdalin Maeser
N. N. Davis
Thomas Richmond
Sarah Richmond
Jonathan H Hale
Olive B. Hale
Olive A. Montgomery

Mariah Burgess
Harrison W. H. Sagers
Andrew J. Clothier
Alzina M. Easton
Amy Clothier
Samuel Musick
Elizabeth Musick
Gehial Hildreth
Elizabeth Rowe
Louisa Hildreth
Samuel Simpson
Eleanor Simpson
Joseph Horne
Mary T Horne
Edmund J Carbine
Mary Adelia Carbine
Adelia Carbine
William Van Orden
Julia Ann Van Orden
Charlotte A Van Orden
Peter E Van Orden
Everette Van Orden
William Carline
Mary H Van Orden
Arvet L L Hale
Rachel J S Hale
David Candlands
David D. Yearsley
Mary Ann Yearsley
Leonora Amy
Dustin Amy
James A Banister
Leonard Soby
Helen Soby
Asahel A. Lathrop
Jeone Lathrop
Wm. M Powers
Mary A Powers

Samuel Bent
Lettice Bent
George Wm. Fowler
Stephen Wilkinson
Hannah Wilkinson
James Moses
Eliza Moses
James [Mcdagh]
John Wat[ers]
W. H. J. Marr
S. M. Marr
John M Finch
George W. Crouse
Catherine E. Crouse
Jacob Shumaker
Nancy Shumaker
Alonzo W. Whitney
Gustavus Williams
Maria H Williams
Geo. P. Stiles
Edw. Johnson
David Stoker
John Stoker
John McDaniels
A. C. Hodges
Rebecca Hodges
Catharine Rhoads
Hannah Worthen
Thomas Speirs
Mary Speirs
James Rodeback
Phebe Rodeback
James Standing
Sarah Gibbs
Nancy M Cahoon
Charles R Dana
Margaret Dana
Samuel Williams

Roswell Ferre
Issack Harriman
J Asahel Howe
Fanny Howe
Samuel M. Howe
Fanny J. Howe
Susan E. Howe
Amos Davis
E. M. Davis
P. S. Cahoon
Louisa Cahoon
Juliaett Bowen
Alpheus Cutler
Lois Cutler
R Cahoon
Thirza Cahoon
Henry HoagLand
Emely S HoagLand
Gustavus Hills
Elisabeth A Hills
Docia Houston
Isaac Houston
Jane M. Houston
Samuel Miles jr
Joseph Hartshorne
Fanny Hartshorne
Thomas M Harrell
Asher Baldwin
Jane Baldwin
Rosannah Beecher
Eli Houghton
Deborah Houghton
Jacob Zundel
Sarah Zundel
Zepheniah Warren
Cornelia Ann Warren
Samuel Wood
Sally Wood

Ruth Williams
[Pegus] Raymond
Rebecka Raymond
[Peaus] A Raymond
Samuel Miles
Prudence Miles
Wm. H. Woodbury
Clarissa H Woodbury
John W. Bell
Ann Bell
R. D. Sprague
Louisa M Sprague
Polly Deuel
John S. Twiss
Charles A. Adams
Ezra [Faitoute]
Moses Adams
Edward Miller
Clarissa Miller
Joseph W Pierce
Amanda M Pierce
Daniel Hill
Elizabeth Hill
Rebecca White
Wm. White
Malinda White
Shadrach Driggs
Elisa Driggs
Hannah Kempton
John Kempton
Miriam T Kempton
Levi Loveland
Hannah Loveland
Daniel Dye
Ann Dye
Isaac Ashton
Edward Martin
Alice Martin

Olive Smith
Ann B Bowermaster
Martha Orsen
Henry Boley
Barbary Boley
Sarah Ann Smith
Henry Boley jr
Sophia Botsford
Jabez Botsford
Thomas Johnson
Patience Johnson
William Ralphs
Elizabeth Ralphs
George Wardle
Fanny Wardle
Francis [Fob]
Cynthia [Fob]
Elijah N. Truman
Roxana Truman
john Hill
Margrat Hill
Samuel White
Rebecca White
Richard Kempton
Hiram Kempton
Caroline Kempton
Zebedee Coltrin
Mary Coltrin
Chloe Thayer
Elizabeth M Wight
Elizabeth Ann Thayer
Simeon Thayer
Joseph Godfry
Eliza Godfry
Abigail Ashton
Henry White
Sarah Buckwa[··]
Meriness Loveland

William Pitt
Caroline Pitt
Mary Pitt
Ellen S Edwards
Rchard Barlow
Jacob Foutz
Margaret Foutz
John Stevens
Elizabeth Stevens
Increase Van Deusen
Maria Van Dusen
James Smithis
Ann Smithis
Wm. Smith
Hanah Smith
Samuel G. Smith
John P. Smith
Andw. W Smith
Wealthy Pratt
John Worthen
Geo. P. Stiles
Archibald Patten
Numan Blodget
Elizabeth G. Blodget
Simeon Carter
Lydia Carter
William Player
Zillah Player
James Grocott
Ann Grocott
Zillah Player Jun
Charles Player
William Player
Charles C Rich
Sarah D Rich
Geo. W. Pitkin
Amanda Pitkin
John H Tippets

Reuby Loveland
Samuel Oliver Holmes
Eliza Holmes
Eliza Barlow
Eli Colby
Susan Colby
Ruben C. Spaulding
Mariah Spaulding
William Jenkins
Eliza Jenkins
Charles [Sazram]
Maria [Sazram]
Joseph Fisher
Evelina Fisher
John P[r]ince
Mary Prince
Maria L Brown
Samuel Brown
John [C]utler
Sophia J Stiles
Perces Stiles
Charles Hubbard
Mary Ann Hubbard
Jesse Baker
Sally Baker
Andrew Moore
Rebecca Moore
Amanda J Moore
Mary Moore
Robert C Moore
Charles Hales
Julia Ann Hales
Laura Pitkin
Abigail Pitkin
John McIlwrick
May McIlwrick
Benjm. T. Mitchell
Lavina Mitchell

Caroline Tippets
Zadock Parker
Mariam Parker
Andrew Brim
Vanness Brim
Alfred Brim
Wm. [Syum]
Charles Rodaback
J. Finch
Lewis D Wilson
Nancy Wilson
Tanner C Green
Adolphia Young
Rhoda Young
Elisha Edwards
Mariah E Edwards
Urial Driggs
Hannah Driggs
Urben V Stewart
Lydia Stewart
Joel Judd
Phebe Judd
Nelson Judd
Evi Judd
Thomas Judd
[Terricy] Judd
Mary Judd
Ira Hinkley
Thomas Pearson
Catherine Pearson
Chancy Gaylord
Mary E Gaylord
Stephen Winchester, sen
Nancy Winchester, sen
Alexander C Winchester
Nancy M. Winchester
Thos S. Edwards sr
Elizabeth Edwards

Jonathan Taylor
Martha Boley
Prudance Van Hining
Benjm. R. Bentley
Rhoda Ann Bentley
Wm. L Thompson
Abraham Washburn
James Washburn
John E Royce
Kezia Royce
Mary Ann Merrill
Rosilla Gren
Nancy Fluno
Lorenzo Driggs
Wm. J Stewart
Sarah Stewart
Levi Stewart
Melinda Stewart
Chancy Nobles
Anjaline Nobles
Hiram Dayton
Permilia Dayton
Permelia M Dayton
Ann Dayton
Hiram Dayton jr
Benjamin Brown
Sarah Brown
Lorenzo Brown
Frances [Crosb··n]
Benjm. Winchester
Mary H. M. Winchester
Stephen Winchester Jr
George McKinzie
Elizabeth McKinzie
Barnet Cole
Phebe Cole
Lucinda E Cole
Mary Ann Cole

p.m. Edwards
wm. H. Edwards
Thos S Edwards jun
Melvin Ross
Rebecca Ross
George Scholes
Mariah [*or Maviah*] Scholes
Stephen Hales
Mary Ann Hales
John Ellis
Harriett Ellis
Job C Barnum
Marcia Barnum
Sarah Silsby
Hosea Stout
Louisa Stout
W. H. Stout
Henry Harriman
Clarrissa Harriman
Albert Banat
Mary Banta
Euphma Jackson
Charity J Banta
Samuel H Banta
William L Banta
Hannah A Banta
Thomas Dobson
Sarah Dobson
Benjamin Jones
Anna Jones
Ezra T. Benson
Pamelin A. Benson
Adaline B. Andrus
Thomas Carrico
Betsey Carrico
Joseph Hutchinson
Mary Hutchinson
Peter Maughan

James B Cole
Reuben Atwood
Lucy Atwood
John Winings
Hesekiah Peck
Martha Peck
Mary A Peck
Matthew Peck
Geroge Hales
Sarah Ann Hales
Daniel Pierson
Julia Pierson
Harmon A Pierson
Ebenezar Pierson
George Woodward
Joseph Thompson
Isabella Thompson
John Evans
Mary Evans
Frederick Cook
Sarah Elizabeth Cook
Nelson Turner
Lucinda Turner
John Peart
Nicholas Robson
Mary Thompson
John Pack
Julia Pack
Phylote Pack
John Alston
Ann Alston
Ga[·] Ritchie
Christeeny Ritchie
Briggs Alden
Lydia Alden
Franklin Bevier
Abraham Hoagland
Margaret Hoagland

M. A. Maughan
John Craig
Elenor Craig
Mary Greenwell
Henery Landers
Elenor Landers
Ralph Thompson
Ann Thompson
John Maughan
Agnes Maughan
John Landers
Margart Landers
Richard Bentley
Richard Benson
Elizabeth Bentley
Jacob Peart
Phebe Peart
Armstead Meoffett
Enoch Burns
Daniel Hendrix
Jonas Killmer
C. W. Hunt
[Henry Pearmain]
William Niswanger
George Morriss
David Lewis
Briggs Malin
Lewis Stead
Thomas Bishop
Mary Parsons
William Parsons
Richc. Worthen
Wm Worthen
Samuel Worthen
Mary Worthen
John Alleman
Christeanna Alleman
Wooren Smith

Allen Taylor
Sarah L Taylor
Joseph Egbert
Mary C Egbert
Elizabeth Taylor
Joseph Taylor
P G Taylor
Sarah Parker
Silas W Condit
Julia Ann Condit
Josiah Butterfield
Margaret Butterfield
Stephen Hales jr
Ecerline Hales
John Wootton
Ann Wootton
Ann Wootton jr
Elizabeth J Burns
Isaac Matteson
Louisa M Hendrix
Lucinda [Jaguns]
[Thebe A. Peatmain]
Nancy Shoemaker
Eunice Barter
Agnes Nightengale
Julia [——]
Maria [Moriss]
Mary Ann Wilkennr
Mary Call
Betsy Turner
Carilha Leewis
James Beavan
Hannah Beavan
Mary Ann Beavan
Hannah Maria Beavan
Elizabeth Spotswood
Lucy Spotswood
Mary Ann [Kenam]

Orson Spencer
Catharine C. Spencer
Augustin Spencer
James Hendrix
William Hendrix
Sarah Lancaster
Sarah Lancaster jun
Wm. W Rust
Welthy Rust
William Swett
Lucy Swett
Harley Mowry
Evaline Bollin
Nancy Walker
Howard Egan
Tamson Egan
Samuel Thompson
Freenan Nickerson
Huldah Nickerson
Mary Thompson
Caroline Bullard
M Jordan
C A Harper
Lavine Harper
Aaron Smith
Amy A Smith
Lewis Robison
Wm. Casper
Wm. R Helm
Elizabeth Helm
Stephen Perry
Rhoby Perry
Jesiah H Perry
Asa Barton
Mary Barton
Salley Ann L Brooker
Jacob Huntsman
Catherine Huntsman

Caroline Steed
Margarett [C]utler
Amanda Smith
Henrietta Whitney
Tina Conner
W. J. Conner Esqr
Drusila Hendrix
Elizabeth M Hendrix
P. P. Pratt
William D. Pratt
Newel Knight
Chancy Park
Orson Pratt
Sarah Higbee
A J Higbee
Merlin Plumb
Jesse [K.] Nichols
Caroline Nichols
Sarah Parker
William Mendenhall
Sarak L. Mendenhall
Saml. G. Hagg
Harriette Hagg
Jerome O. Hagg
Henry a Buckwalter
Emlly Buckwalter
Phebe Danfielde
Levi Fafield
Amy Fafield
C. M. Robison
Ira N Spaulding
Ann Elisa Spaulding
Wm. H Perry
Susan Perry
Sally S Perry
John Barton
Sally Barton
Wm Barton

Luman H Calkins

Mahetable Calkins

Edmund Fisher

Cornelia J. Fisher

Asenath Sherman

King Fisher

Sally Fisher

James Wareham

Harriett Wareham

Martin H Peck

Edwin Peck

Asahel A Lathrop

Charles W Brewster

John Brewster

Allen Weeaks

E J Sabin

Alexander Hill

Daniel S Cahoon

John Huse

Thomas Winkless

George Callam

[Andrew] Lamoreaux

James Leithead

John Harvey

Mary Anne Reece

Thomas Reece

George C. Wilson

Lewis K Wilson

James M Butler

Edmund B Butler

Lorenzo D Butler

Milton Callam

John P. Herr

Seth Dodge

Augustus Dodge

John H Powers

Solon Powers

Aron Powers

Matilda Barton

Julia Barton

Alvin Horr

Sarah Horr

Moses Daley

Rufus Fisher

Almira Daley

Olive Fisher

Eliphalet Boynton

Susan Boynton

Joseph Peck

Amos Fuller

Jove Lathrop

Hannah Clark

Lydia C Brenster

Sarah J Weaks

Mary Ann Sabin

Agness Hill

Jane Cahoon

Mary Spencer

Antoinett Spencer

Esther Huse

Mary Winkless

Deborah Leithead

Electa Lamoreaux

Elizabeth Wilson

Mary Wilson

Charily Butler

Surretta Callum

Margaret Herr

Melissa Dodge

Lovina Dodge

Sally Dodge

Martha Jane Powers

Sarah Powers

Martha Powers

Abigail D Hovey

Jane Galann

Orlando D Hovey
Guy C Wilson
Willim Yoom
Ormond Butler
David Moor
John Wood
John Henderson
Betsey Jane Henderson
William Meeks
Mary Mitchell
Johnson Bentley
William Parks
John M King
William S Batchlor
Enoch M King
Francis Jolly
Henry Jolly
Daniel Allan
Robert Telford
John Telford
Alvira Young
George B. Hicks
Noah Hubbard
John Winn
William Edwards
Robert Booth
Joseph Booth
John Newhem
Charles Smith
Eleaezer King
Arza Judd
William Edwards
John Hardman
William Gare
Charlotte Curtis
Abel Owen
Betsey Owen
Rhoda Richards

Elizabeth Wilson
Susan Yocom
Huldah Butler
Rose Wood
Lewis Eager
Mary Eager
Eleazar King Jr
Mary C King
John M MCaul
Elizabeth MCaul
Elizabeth Weeks
Abigail Bentley
Milesant Parks
Fanny Parks
Sally D King
Huldah H Batchlor
Mary King
Francis G Polly
Mary Ann Allen
Harriet O Taggart
Jane Telford
Lucretia Young
Martha Hicks
Cinthy Hubbard
Christiana Winn
Ann Booth
Elisabeth Edwards
Sary Ann Needhem
Elizabeth Smith
Nancy King
Mary Gardner
Sarah Jolley
Louis Judd
Susannah C Boyce
Mary Ann Edwards
Mary Hardman
Elizabeth Gore
Lyman Curtis

Levi Richards
Nahum Curtis
Delia Curtis
Sally an Reed
George Curtis
Moses Curtis
Peter W Cownover
Daniel D. Hunt
SuSan hunt
SuSan P. hunt
John A Hunt
James W Hunt
Levi B Hunt
John C West
Thomas J Brandon Junr
T J Brandon Sergnr
Abigal Brandon
Leah Brandon
M B Weltose
Sarah Stepehinson
Isaac S. Welton
Samuel N. Welton
Sarah J. Moon
Welthy R. Welton
Keziah Welton
John G Luce
Eli Tibbets
Harriet Luce
Ruth Tibbets
Andrew Hall
Charles Hall
Sarah j Hall
John Pea
John Lovel
Ann Lovel
Henry Payne
Mary Payne
Peter Joseph Fory

Bartholomew Mahoney
Mary ann Mahoney
Sarah ann Smith
Calvin Reed
Mary Reed
Aurelia Curtis
Sarah Perry
Napolean Perry
Malatiah Luce
Elizbth Pea
Jane F Pea
Hugh Lytle
Ebenezer Hanks
Horace B Skinner
Cyrus Winget
Elennor Skinner
Mary A [Hamman]
Christena Lytle
Mary jane Lytle
Aron H Cownover
Abram G Cownover
Charles W. Cownover
Eveline Cownover
Samuel Field
Thomas Gray
Alvah Alexander
Phebe Alexander
Saml H Alexandr
Walter Crane
Jane Crane
John Barton
Susanah Barton
John Edger
Ann Edger
John Robinson
An Robinson
Mary Ann Barton
Elizabeth Barton

Elizabeth Fory
Rebecca Highi[beger]
Prisciler Snider
Levi Thornton
Elizabeth Thornton
Elizabeth Foutz
Francille Durfey
Miriam Durfey
John D Chase
Prissillar Chase
Nahum Ward
Sally Ward
Wm. Stanley
Julia A Stanley
Joseph Young
Jane A Young
Joseph Murdock
Eunice Murdock
Jerusha Seabury
Wesley H Seabury
Sally Murdock
Wm. Seabury
Loisa Seabury
John Murdock
S L. Forgeus
Elizabeth Forgeus
Eliza Priser
Josephus Hatch
Henry Moulton
Wm. F. Cahoon
James H Rollins
[Charles F ——]
Samuel S [Hucher]
Thomas Miller
William Jenkins
Peter Sheffield
John G Sheffield
Sarah Sheffield

Catherine Barton
Chandler Holbrook
Unice Holbrock
Dwight Harding
Phebe Harding
Malenda Hatch
Mary R Hatch
Jerm. Hatch
Elizabeth Hatch
Nancy Walker
Martha Maulton
Hannah Holbrook
Joseph Holbook
John Frohock
John Cokine
Mary Cokine
Dexter Stillman
Barbara Stillman
Stephen Alden
Nancy Alden
Nancy S. Tracy
Sarah Perkins
Susannah Miller
Mary Jankins
Ann Rowberry
Mary Williams
Anna B Fordham
Jane Denison
Susan Sheffield
Ann C Busby
Emily F Spencer
Evelina M Harman
Aurela Harman
Edna S Harman
Sarah Speir
Mary Ann Nicherson
Flora Drake
Sophrana Drake

George Sheffield
Henry Denison
James W Denison
Hiram Spencer
Clauduis P Spencerr
A Daniel Spencer
Lyman Hinman esqr
Thos Jaup
Edward Gardner
John Twentyman
U C Nickerson
John Wheeler
Owen Cole
Phinehas Richards
Franklin D. Richards
Samuel W. Richards
Joseph W. Richards
Henry P. Richards
Edson Barney
Horace Fish
Charles Leavitt
Phebe Leavitt
Jermiah Leavitt
Leonard Hill
John Dalton
Harry Dalton
Eupheamia Bouck
Eliza Bouck
Margaret Bouck
Johnathan L Harvey
[Ta··] Harvey
Lew is Harvey
Elis abeth Harvey
Alfred Harvey
William Carson
Currilla Carson
Alisabeth frampton
Lu Ledda Braden

Wealthy Richards
Jane Richards
Mariah W. Richards
Leillis Barney
Huldah Cole
Sarah Fish
Mary Brown
Rebecka Dalten
Benjamin Covey
Almra Covey
Archibald Hill
Isabela Hill
Agnes Richards
John Richards
John A Bouck
Henson Walker
Thomas Heap
~~Thomas~~
Eli Bennitt
george H Smith
Sarah Smith
Hannah smith
Arel j Smith
Eden Smith
Henry W willson
Matilda k wilson
Lucinda J wilson
Malicia wilson
Margaret Wilson
Miles Wilson
Sarah West
Lucinda Jackman
Betsey Parsons
Emma S Parsons
Caroline Parsons
Uriah Roundy
Polly Roundy
fennet Roundy

Eleanor Braden
thomas M bennett
Margart bennett
Mary wilson
Mary Bennett
Marin da Bennett
Malicia Bennett
Elizabeth Smith
William Wheetley
Moroni Parsons
Lucinda Kinyon
Farnum Kinyon
Caleb C Baldwin
Eliza Baldwin
Green W Allred
David H Allred
Barton B Allred
Isaac N Allred
Sally Alred
Mary ann Fisher
John R Fisher
William L allred
Andew F allred
Joseph Thompson
Thomas C. Ivie
John P Peart
Nichlos Robson
Robert Thompson
Jacob Peart
Phoebe Peart
Jacob Peart Junr
Ezekiel Peck
Evoline Peck
Electy Peck
A. H. Lewius
Thomas Wheetly
Sarah Hall
Richard Hewitt

Charles Butler
Mary Midleton
William Midleton
Charles F Midleton
Thomas Butler
Luvisa Butler
Isaac Herrin
Cornelius Hendrickson
William Hendrickson
James Hendrickson
Nicholus Hendrickson
Elizabeth Hendrickson
Ma[rg]aret Hendricksn
Sophronia Hendrickson
Lucinda Hendricksone
Thomas B Foy
Catharine Foy
Elizabeth Foy
Susan Foy
Perry Durfee Sen
Perry Durfe Junr
Jane Durfee
Elisabeth Durfee
Fredrick Levi
Henry Suit
Phebeann Suit
Sarah Shelley
Joseph Shelley
Lorenzo D. Allen
Sinthy Allen
Mary Parsons
Thorit Parsons
Susann Adams
Hariat Newbuury
Caroline Weeks
William Weeks
Eliza Perry
Melissa Jane Bigler

E B Hewitt
Sophia Hewitt
Jarusha Hewitt
Julian Levi
Jediah Wheetley
Orson B. Adams
Jeremiah Robey
Ruth Robey
~~Ru~~ Stephen Sitz
Fanny Sitz
William A Sitz
John Fair child
Timothy B. Foot
Jane Ann Foot
Reuben R Foot
Wm. Foot
Loisa Hgginbotham
William Niswanger
Mayry Niswanger
Ellin Niswanger
Sphoenss [Hicky]
Wm. Finch
John [Hicky]
Ramson Hickey
Duncan McArthur
Susan McArthur
Sally McArthur
Henry McArthur
Olive Case
Horac M Alexander
Nancy Alexander
Howard Coray
M. J. Coray
Mary Ann Knowlton
Hannah Markham
Warren Markham
Wm. Whiting Markham
P Fairchild

~~G S B Liyns~~
~~Sarah~~ Lyons
Ausker F Lyons
Amanda F Lyons
Caleb W Lyons
Benjman Chapman
Jane Chapman
Allice Chapman
C M Chapman
Nancy Fleming
Sarah Ann Fleming
Thaddeus E Fleming
Josiah W Fleming
Sussanah Bigler
Blackferd Bigler
Isaac Chase
Phebe Chase
Clarissa Chase
Desdemona Gleason
Rhoda Chase
George Chase
Louisa Chase
John S Gleason
Polly Dosman
Frances M Stillman
Charles Stillman
Isaac Russell
[—— ——]
Elizabeth Porter
Lydia A Porter
[A⋯] Dolten
Rachel Drollinger
Amos [Louis]
Mary [Louis]
Edmund Nelson
Jane Nelson
Price Nelson
Elisabeth Nelson

Betsy Fairchild
Elisha Averett
William Averett
Ben
Truman Gilbert
Mary Gordon
Lany Gilbert
Joseph Dobson
Henry Oaks
Prudence Oaks
Thomas M. Taggart
Phillis M Taggart
Mary Shaw
Mahlon Johnson
Maryan Johnson
Wm. Johnson
Susany Hamblin
Nancy Johnson
Charles Dolten
Mary E Dolten
Lorezno Clark
Juliann Clark
Mary Green
J. S. Woodard
Emily Woodard
W Fossett
Maleby Fossett
Sarah Moore
Calvin Moore
Nancy Moore
Joseph W. Moore
Hannah Henderson
William Myers
John Fox
Jacob E Terry
Maria Terry
Elizabeth Kirby
John D. Lee

Martha Nelson
Rhoda Nelson
Hiram Nelson
Wiliam Nelson
Mary Nelson
Thos. Nelson
Matthew Mansfield
Angeline Jackman
Bohan Clark
Hiram C. Jacobs
Caroline Jacobs
Thos. Gordon
Jacob Hamblin
Ann Bosley
Horace Rockwell
Ruth Stoddard
Mary Rockwell
Georg Mills
Anna [Purtn··y]
Enos M Nall
thirsy M Nall
Jane Judd
Jonathan O Duke
Mary Duke
James Duke
Sarah Duke
Thomas Boardman
Jane Boardman
Hannah Henderson
Noah Packard
Sophia Packard
Noah Packard Jn
Orin Packard
Henry Packard
Sophia A Packard
Morgan M Thomas
Milan Packard
[—— ——]

Aggeathann Lee
James Pace
Lucinda Pace
Esther S Pratt
Elisa A Tyler
James H P Tyler
Hiram F Dayton
Charles Huelet
Margaret Huelt
Anna M Hulet
David Pratt
Electa Hillman
Silas Hillman
Davi Wood
Catherine Wood
Sarah ann Wood
Amandah Wood
Edmund Bosley
George C Bosley
Mary Bosley
Milton [Store]
Margret [Store]
Chandler Rogers
Amanda Rogers
Rogrs
R. M. Rogers
Mark Rogers
Sarah Rogers
Samuel H Rogers
Amos D Rogers
H. B. M. Jolley
Brittanna E Jolley
Eda Rogers
Washington B Rogers
Samuel A. [P.] Kelsey
Jannet Kelsey
Thomas M Kelsey
Elisabeth M King

[James D. ——]
Altamira Gaylord
Jean Naymen
Lanson Colby
Ransford Colby
Samuel Henderson
Nathan A West
Whitford G Wilson
Nathan Cheney
King Follet
Eliza A Cheney
Elizabeth Henderson
Louisa Follett
Adaline Louisa West
Mary Wilson
John Winn
Christiana Winn
Martha Boley
Elizabeth Caly
John Wickel
Richard Wickel
Laman Wickel
Homer Wickel
Eliabeth Wickel
Thos. G Fisher
David Jones
Mercy Jones
Moses Jones
Ameleia Jones
[Zenoses] Jones
Elisabeth Jones
Joseph Jones
franklin green
Abigail Thorne
Esther Russell
Henry Russell
Margaret Ault
Richard Ault

Synthia Hamp[shiar]
David Clough
Betsey Clough
William Earl se
Jacob Earl
John Earl
William Earl Jr
Samiel F M Fritnell
John A Hicks
Samuel Steele
Alvira Steele
John gaylorde
John Gaylord
Joanna Gaylord
Wm H [Reddan]
Henry Thos. Powell
Elizabeth Powell
Thomas Holt
Sarah Holt
Rodney R. Smith
Susan Smith
William A Empey
Mary Ann Empey
Maneroy Empey
Nelson Empey
Emma Empey
John Blezard
Sarah Blezard
Hiram Kimball
Sarah M Kimball
Jane Himir
John Himir
Marthy Himir
Nansy Himir
Samuel Himir
Jane Himer
W. W. Edwards
Lujia Edwards

John R Blanchard
Mary E Blanchard
Polly Phelps
Morgan Phelps
Poly Perry
P M Perry
Huldh Nickerson
Arthur Morrison
E P Ann Morrison
Sabray Vorhees
William Morrison
Nancy D Andrews
Margret f V Andrews
John f M andrews
Abigail Andrews
Orange Warner
Thomas R Kinng
Delilah Warner
Matilda King
Jane Roberon
Charles Allen
Davis McOlney
Lucy Olney
Harriet B [Lowe]
Esther Morton
Lydia M Smith
Lydia Braden
Lucretia Gaylord
Emeline Hays
Sarah D Smith
Sarus Boise
Sophronia Norris
Lucy Hodges
Luzette Hodges
Lydia Hodges
Melinda Lewis
Harriett Dille
Roxey Keller

Joseph Edwards

James Edwards

M. E. Lott

J N Murphy

Sary Ann Murphy

Joseph F Palmer

James L Nurse

Nowell [Nurse]

Moses Smith

Croley P Smith

George W Taggart

patrick Norris

Hyrum Curtis

Samuel Reed

E C Ho[d]ges

Stephen Hodges

Tarlton Lewis

David Dille

Alva Keller

Richard Clark

Thomas Horton

George Spilsbury

Philip Greene

Boda Green

Ann Dutoon

Jane Green

Elisabeth Green

Thomas Peterson

Stephen M Farnsworth

Alexander Hay

John Ballantyne

Andrew Ballantyne

William Ballantyne

William Steed

Henry Steed

John Reed

Nathaniel Loree

Nathan Steel

Elizabath Clark

Elizabeth Madison

Hannah Horton

Fanny Spilsbury

William Green

Harriett Green

John Dutson

Jane Dutson

Jane Green

Julia Ann Farnsworth

Jennet Hay

Jennet Ballantyne

Helen Ballantyne

Hannh Steed

Sarah Steed

Rebecka Reed

Lydia Reed

M Amanda M Hartson

Lydia L Losee

Maryann Steebel

Eliza [P]itcher

Harriett Clark

Elizabeth Burn

Lucinda Barlow

Julia A Shumway

Phebe Beebe

Elizabeth B Hyde

Harriet Nurse

Mary H Palmer

Elizabeth M[cnill]

Elizabath Withnall

Mary Withnall

Margarett Carter

Matilda Hook

Elizabeth Lamb

Polly Bend

Abiah Porter

Mary Grow

Samuel Fowler
Thomas Pitcher
Walter Clark
Watson Barlow
Charles Shumway
Isaac Beebe
Milton Beebe
William Hyde
Levi Grandy
Silas Wilcox
E H Allan
Sarah Allen
John F Ford
R H Withnall
John Withnall
Thomas Carter
Charles Carter
Aaron Hook
Benjamin R Lamb
James C Consten
Jared Porter
John Meilihe
Abraham Pound
Michael Katz
Henry Grow
Ethan Barrows
John Parkes
Samuel White
Amy C Kent
Carlos Granger
Salmon Warner
Isaiah Williams
Daniel D Williams
Gilbert B Williams
Francis E Williams
Norman S Williams
James Cummings
William Aldridge

Catherine Katz
Lorena Barrows
Ellen Parker
Morgan L Gardner
Nancy M Gardner
Mary H [White]
Lydia B Kent
Sarah Granger
Rebeca Warner
Lucy Williams
Susannah Cumming
Hannbal Mathe[ws]
Elizabeth Mathews
B. Brassell
Priscilla Mathews
Elizabeth Brassell
Sophiah Aldredg
Hannah Gardner
Malla Knight
hanah Mcbride
Rebecca Mcbride
Ann Cross
Susan Thomas
Hannah A Bibble
Susan M. Moore
Charles A. Chase
Susan G. Chase
Lucina Johnson
Harriet Stanley
Eliza Burr
Jane Choppall
[Manurfy] Durffey
Clarrissa Haight
Ann Dutson
Emeline Coling
Moriah M Green
Ann Erskine
Rachel Worthington

William Gardner
John Knight
Amos McBride
Richard Moyle
Nathaniel Thomas
Philo Dibble
[H]arvey [S]tanley
James Barr
Richard Chppall
Cecilia Durphey
David F Haight
John Wilkie
Cathren Wilkie
John Cording
Epha[rim L Evan]
Peter Erskine
A C Mont
Justin J Merrill
P C Merrill
Cyrena Merrill
Commilla Merrill
James Willcox
Joseph Harwood
Joseph Owens
George D Van Beck
William W Lane
James Eastman
Franklin Eastman
Seth Cook
William Cook
Christy Ann Mills
James Newberry
Philander Colton
Charles Price
John Topham
John Topham
William Topham
Jeremiah Curtis

James Worthington
Elizabeth Mclean
[——] Wells phares Wells
Sarah Wilcox
Catherine Harwood
Elizabeth Owens
Adaline E Van Beck
Norton Jacob
Emily Jacob
Mariah Lane
Clarisa Eastman
W[····] W[·····]
Sarah Cook
Freeborn B Smith
Nancy Smith
Fidelia Colton
Nancy Newberry
Louisa Newbery
Polly M Colton
Lucy Ann Merrill
Jane Price
Jane Green
James Topham
Elisha Marriott
Hannah Topham
Elizabeth Weeks
Abigail Shelton
Nancy Stewart
Rhoda Pearson
Lurania P Eggleston
Melissa Stewart
Losana Newan
Margrett Mace
Caroline F Butler
Asseneath Miller
[Amnillra] Miller
Mary Miller
Hannah Huntsman

Ruth Curtis
Eliza Curtis
P Meecks
Sarah Meecks
Stephen Shelton
John Stewart
E J [Wenress]
Elias F. Pearson
Ephrarim Pearson
Henry Pearson
Samuel Eggleston
Joshua Stewart
Elijah Newan
Wandle Moore
John L Butler
Willard Miller
Bethuel Miller
James W Huntsman
Welcom Chapman
William Wordsworth
Eliphalet Bristol
William Hallim
Charles Steelar
Robert Porter
John M Burk
A S Stanley
Miles Romney
Richard Riley
Elizabeth Riley
Susannah Riley
Ruth Riley
John Riley
Elizabeth Riley
Nancy Riley
Hugh Riding
Johnson F Lane
Francis B[i]rch
John Chase

Amelia Chapman
Ann Wordsworth
Sally Plumb
Rena Bristol
Esther Hallim
Sarah Hallim
Elisa A Haight
Isaac P Haight
Caleb Haight
Kesiah Burk
Philinda Stanley
Elizabeth S[t]andley
Elizabeth Romney
Margarett Riding
Metilda Lane
Francis [Daley]
Elizabeth Burch
Liley jenkins
Mary Cheese
Margriet Cheese
Cathrine Bird
Mary Robey
Evan Evans
Elizabeth Evans
Charles S. Peterson
Ann B Peterson
Jonah R Ball
Sophronia Ball
Tryphena Anderson
Editha M. Anderson
Josef Mount
Elizabeth Mount
Ann Right
Hery [Swink]
Annah [Swink]
David H Redfield
Fanney M Redfield
Peris Atherton

Thomas Bird
John Robey
William Robey
Stephen Chase
Orryanna Chase
Aza Adams
Sabina Adams
Alonzo LeBaron
Clorisa LeBaron
Hugh Herringshaw
Edward Thompson
Julia Thompson
John Maybury
Mary Maybury
Gab[ri]el Mayby
Joseph Maybury
David Maybury
Thomas Maybury
May Maibury
Joseph [H]atting
Marquis Hatting
Margrat [Sh]ifflin [*or Phipplin*]
Maryann [Sh]ifflin [*or Phipplin*]
John Mackleey
Betsey Mackleey
Joseph W Coolidge
Elizabeth Coolidge
[Summer] Pinkham
[Offin] G Hare
Wm. N. [Lisrich]
Margaret Stewart
Robert B Stewart
James Brinkerhoff
Sally Ann Brinkerhoff
Wm. Huntington
Lydia Huntington
Eliza M. Partridge
John Burghurdt

Titus Bettings
Diantha Bettings
Eunce Billing
O. P. Rockwell
Luana H Rockwell
William Felshaw
Mary H Felshaw
James M Chadwick
Elizabeth B Chadwick
Alanson Ripley
Sarah Ripley
Aidah Clemnt
Samuerl D Billings
Lucy Ann Billings
Alvah L Tippets
Vernon H. Bruce
Bejami Bruce
Alexr. Mullinder
Sarah Mullinder
Dan Foster
Rachel Foster
Wm. Foster
Marther A Hovey
Ann D Smith
Magerett Hardman
Polly Chidester
Mary Ainscough
Mary Southworth
Elizabath Garlick
Hannah Garlick
Mary Garlick
Tatitha camy Garlick
Nancy Breger
Ezra Strong
Christian Beard
Eunice B Shirtliff
Maria Kimpton
[Lodemia] Barnets

Ellen Burghurdt
Joseph G Hovey
John Pye Smith
Richard Hurdman
John M. Chidester
William Ainscough
Chester Southworth
Stephan Byington
Andrew Creger
Lymon A Shirtliff
George Davis
Ann Davis
Horace Evans
Candace Evans
Olliva Evans
Lydia Evans
Emily Evans
Samuel [Vernets]
John Morrison
Henry Davis
David Burrows
William Burrows
Henry Banta
Abraham Banta
Leambird Banta
Elisha H Groves
W J Peden
Lewis Booth
Edwin Booth
Eliza Booth
Joseph Parker
Robert Parker
Madison D Hambleton
W James Whitehead
John Anderson
James Jefts
George Whitley
David Study

Sarah Morrison
Rachael Davis
Sarah Burrows
Charity Banta
Dian Banta
Charety Banta
Eliza Banta
Mary Roundtree
Lucy Groves
Doritha Childs
A Potter
Anna Gifford
Lucy Parker
Chelnicia Hambleton
Jane Whitehead
G Y. Potter
[——] Allen
Emily Potter
Mary Ann Allen
Smtha Shirtliff
Lydia Anderson
Ann Davis
John Pollard
William Pollard
Jacob S. Wigle
Jefferson King
Henry Kingsley
Ezra Kingsley
David Evans
Wm. Mcgah[an]
Coleman Boren
James T. Baldwin
David Penroe
Stephen M St John
Ezra Chase
Eli H Chase
Almon Newell
Lewis Thompson

Abraham Hunsaker
Charles Davis
Henry W. Briggs
John Davis
Horace B. Owens
J. T. Packer
[·]isal Bradford
John M Ewell
Nathan W Packer
Thomas M Ewell
William Watkins Sen.
William Watkins Jun.
P. Ewell
Joseph H Champlin
[James] Shaur
Samuel Smith
Henry Sprague
John Field
Samuel Merrils
Jesse McCarl
Austin S. Merrill
Ithamer Sprague
Martin Potter
Daniel Smith
Anthony J Stratton
Martin Wood
Oliver Stratton
J M Stewart
Daniel Smith
James B. Boren
Allabama Boren
Thomas J. Fisher
Ezra Kingsley
Almon Sherman
William C. Macintush
Daniel Fisher
Thaddeus Cutler
Philena Gibbs

Robert W[···]
Alonzo Rhoades
humphrey Mcgaham
Martin Littlewood
John Muir
G W Mikesell
Ruben middleton
Joseph B Peck
Francis Hornes
John Woodland
J A MikeSell
isaac H Stevison
John Conyers
J. C. Owens
[J] Sanderson
Philip Ballard
John Jameson
Elisha Hill
John [Boame]
Christopher Smith
Sarah Boame
Porter P Gibbs
Mary Boame
Eliza L Christie
Hyriam Boman
William Bateman
Sarah Bateman
Emma Bastman
Ellis Eames
Olive Eames
Harriet Eames
Abigail Eames
Ann Stedwell
Mary Eames···
S A [Caster]
Alvira L. Parrish
Amy ann Graves
Thomas Parker

Denisa Gibbs
Delila Moris
Qubaet Morris
G M Christie
Joseph Bateman
John Willson Sen.
John Willson Jun.
Margaret Willson
Elizabeth Willson
Ansel M Eames
Edson J Eames
Benjamin Eames
D L Carter
Wm. R. Parrish
John Graves
Elizabeth Graves
Emeline Kesler
Oliver C Graves
George Chapman
George W Parrish
Abigail A Parrish
Sarah Hancock
T S Smithwick
Jonas G. Gibbs
Esther Brown
John M. Wooly
Mary Walters
William Jackson
Ann E Raper
Garrett L Groesbeck
Henry Whitny
Robert Walker
B. F. Brown
Thomas Booth
Levi Moffet
Mary Abbott
Mary Austin
Sally Putnam

Welb Graves
William Burman
Suanna Burman
John Farnsworth
James H Neely
David Jackson
Martin Jackson
Hannah Willard
Elizabeth Brotherson
Isac Walker
Mary Pincock
Ruth Walker
Solomon Tindall
Mary Mosteler
Mary Bateman
Wm. Springsteen
Andrew Springsteen
Jas. Springsteen
Martha Steen
Nancy Richarson
A D Whitney
Maroni Broden
Joseph D Alford
Robert Orton
Frederich Kesley
Emeline Kesley
Maryett Kesley
Antynette Kesley
[—— ——]
John W lasly
Elizabeth laslay
lucinda Stoker
William Duncan
Amy Duncan
Absolum Tidwell
Elizabeth Tidwell
Ranson Tidwell
Thomas Tidwell

Rhoda ann Whitney
James Bateman
Thos. Bateman Sen
Franklin Brown
Roynez Moffet
Antoinette Moffet
Mari Lacharite
Almira Fisher
Andrew Goodwin
Ester Frost
Alvira Frost
Elisa Daily
Elisabeth White
Woods Burdno
Wilson Porter
Ellen Wemar
Edward Daily
Jas. Duncan
Sally Duncan
Malinda Duncan
Susan Duncan
M W Lasley
Beverly Boran
A D. Boran
Adaline Boran
Mary Boran
Marcus Lemmons
Hiram Clark
Stephen Johnson
John Wimer
Elizabeth Wimer
Montazuma Archer
John Frost
Hiram Frost
Ann Hess
Elizabeth Hess
Sarah Hess
Peter Nichol

Patsy Tidwell
David Winter
Sarah Winter
Francis Beckstead
Mary Beckstead
Chester Loveland
Fanny Loveland
Cyril Call
Lucinda Call
Mary Call
Sarah Call
Malissa Call
Samantha Willey
Jacob Hess
John W Crary
Nancy Crarey
John Crandel
Magdalene Crandel
Abner Frost
Margaret Frost
Saprony Overton
Joshua Helser
Margaret Helser
John Hess
Mary Johnson
Polly Smith
Nephi Loveless
James Clenger
John Dayley
Catherine Warren
John Archy
Mary Archy
Ebonade Archy
Cleopatre Archy
Elles Stoker
Mary Stoker
Catharine Stoker
Chareles Kenedy

John W. Pickett
Rhoda Winegar
Ann Winegar
Stephen Winegar
Sarah Phelps
Lucinda Cunningham
James A Cunningham
James Warren
Frederick D. Winegar
Lodema Wingar
Henry Munro
Lovina Munro
F M Vanleuven
Lydia Vanleuven
Joseph Fletcher
Pamelia Fletcher
John Vanleuven
Fanny Vanleuven
Cornelius Vanleuven
Lovina Vanleuven
Benjamin Vanleuven
Catharine Vanleuven
Ransom Vanleuven
Lucinda Vanleuven
Louisa Vanleuven
Dianah Vanleuven
Mary Ann Vanleuven
Labey Vanleuven
Alfred Draper
Poly Draper
Willis Banks
Andrew Cunningham
Evaline Banks
Jacob Waggal
James Warren
[—— —— ——]
[—— —— ——]
[—— —— ——]

Alvira Kenedy
Alexander M Shoemaker
Margaret Shoemaker
Daniel Smith
Mahala Porter
John G. Wilkins
Nancy Wilkins
John Loveless
Sarah Loveless
Jas. Loveless
Jos. Loveless
Elizabeth Waymer
Orlincy Crandel
Thomas Hess
Jacob Stoker
Catharine Stoker
Parry Proter
Sally Porter
Nancy Wood
Lorenso Carpenter
John Stoker
John Wood
William Porter
William Bett
Elizabeth Birdeno
William Moony
Elizabeth Mony
Betsy Bett
Peter Wimer
Betsy [G]olson
Sarah Stoker
Eliza Jane Grayham
Robert Grayham
Ann Isabella Grayham
George Grayham
Sarah Rawlins
M. J. Rawlins
Geo. Graybill

Cyrus Sanford
Benjamin Johnson
Lorina Johnson
Michael Stoker
Martha Stoker
Gabrael Stoker
John O. Johnson
Sarah Crandle
Sarah Williams
Moriah Vaniel
Sarah Newman
William Stoker
Almira Stoker
Samuel D Stoker
William Stoker
John Phelps
Mary Phelps
Sarah Phelps
Phebe Phelps
Alma Phelps
Jno. Smith
Sarah Smith
Henry Smith
Hannah Smith
Elizabeth Smith
Stephen Smith
James Walker
Elizabeth Walker
Jos. Smith
Rhoda A Smith
James W. Walker
John Walker
Mary Graybill
William Graybill
Adam Graybill
Sidney R Graybill
Levi Graybill
Patience Graybill

Mary Graybill
John Stoker
Jane Stoker
Hannah Graybill
C. M. Rawlins
Hyrum Stoker
Alma Stoker
Franklin Stoker
C. Lewis
Isabel Lewis
Warren Jones
Julian Hudson
Jacob Wigle
Franklin Stoker
Alma Stoker
M. A. Lewis
Mary Wigle
Sintha Wigle
George Grayham
Mary Grayham
Margaret Lewis
James Tomlinson
Sarah Tomlinson
John P. Wigle
Hannah Wigle
James B Tomlinson
Elizabeth B Tomlinson
Mary A Tomlinson
A. T. Tomlinson
A B Tomlinson
Saml. T. Winegar
Franklin Chapman
Elisha Richards
Truman Richards
James Surnington
James Surnington Jr
Lorence Lake
Jonathon Right

John Lovel
Ann Lovel
George Lovel
Abigail Graybill
Edmant Lovel
James Grayham
Mary Grayham
Joseph Smith
James Rawlin
geo Parker
J. Carpenter
Wm. Willson
Welliton Willson
Jacob Chapman
Sidny Chapman
Howard Smith
~~Frank~~ John Vance
D W Murn Vance
David Orton
Amby Page
Thomas [Deborst]
Joshuay Noleman
Wm. Jackson
J. shelton
Jamese Horton
James Johnson
James Henry
John Earl
Curtis Rogers
Harvy Downy
Isaac Cleavland
Charles Coneley
Bradford Springer
J [Ausbit]
Montey Green
[Elanson ——]
James S. Holman
Charles Crismon

John Bairytor
John Presley
Munra Crosier
Eboneser Page
Eli Dehort
John tery
Harry Parks
F Guinor
Wesley Horton
Samuel [Reel]
Asa C Earl
Isaac Rogars
Isaac Sheen
David Labaran
Alexander Brin
Samuel McConnel
Zebulon Springer
Joseph [——]
William Perkins
John Smith
Daniel D Clark
John Brown
Jerome Benson
Hanz Morse
Isaac Clark
David Humphry
James Keeler
John Fife
John Vanhouten
Thos. P Kerr
Geo. W Baxter
Hirum M Burnham
Nelson Burnham
Rufus Forbush
Loren Forbush
Otis Shumway
Lanson Shumway
David Dutton

Justus Morse
John Crosby
Elijah B. Gaylord
John L Smith
William Johnston
Wm L Perkins
John Wardle
George F. Kerr
Simons P Bexter
Wm. E Bexter
David Holemons
John B Wilson
Harvy Burnham
John Lindsey
Rufus ForBush Jr
Sanford Forbush
Aurora Shumway
R B Dutton
Ezra Duton
Thomas Callister
Thos. Kelly
Jacob Wetherbee
James Crookston
R C Wetherbee
William J. Phelps
Ute Perkins
Wm. S Durfee
Frederick L. Galay
Absalome Perkins
David M Perkins
Jesse Johnston
Octary Purcet
Paul Purcet
J. E. Johnson
Alson Allen
Benj. Andrews
Jos. Parker
Josh. Parker

Ozias Kilburn
Almond W Babet
Ezekiel Johnson
David Kemp
Bobard Cruxton
Wm. G Perkins
Ute Perkins
Peter Boyce
Edmond Durfee Jr
Schuyler M. Horton
Levi Perkins
Georg [Preston]
John Shepby
Elijah Elmer
Tomas Dungan
[A ——]
Jno Allen
A Stevens
T Naves
N Wall
Chs Thompson
J Quayle
Matthis Cowley
Jonathan Newman
Franklin Taylor
Cyrus Ellsworth
Wm. Willis
Jno. Evans
Chs Spry
[Valentine] Purdam
Geo Brown
C. C Downey
Jno DawSon
Watson Faburn
Geo N Johnson
A. H. Perkins
Reuben Perkins
S. Carpenter

B. F. JohnSon

J. H. JohnSon

William AngeS

John Fife

John Auges

JameS Fife

Isaac Y Vance

Martin Lawphere

Ira Babbat

Norman Taylor

Joseph Keucham

William Jackson

Taylor Jackson

WN Yager

John Coffern

Geo EurnS

Abm Jackson

Stephen PearSonS

Chs. Warden

Robert A Jackson

Isaac Yager

Orrin Page

Joseph Jackson

Seymor Page

Wm. Mcleary

S W Condit

J Condit

E Larky

Alanson Shumay

Martin White

James Gibson

E. D. White

G G Johnston

Jesse Johnston

David White

Nathan Frampton

John Niggs

M Carpenter

Benj. Benson

Alfred Benson

Silas Green

Noah Green

Guy Green

John Jelly

John Wakely

David Dutton

Matthew Smith

W. Wade

F. Eaton

Lyman Eaton

Erastus Weghtun

J Hatch

Benj Peck

John Larker

Thoret Peck

J McFate

R Nall

J W Wood

A. Tadlock

F Beach

N T Brown

Sidney Chapman

H. Downey

Reuben Napier

W. P Willson

J Thompkins

John N Cowley

Alphus Johnson

Daily Carpenter

Wm. Savage

Lorenzo Young

Levi Knight

Thomas Tarbut

Charles Cowley

P. D. Bailey

Andrew Smith

Robert Bliss
Sixtus Johnson
Isaac Peck
Joseph Peck
David MDonough
Wm. Johnston
John Myers
Timothy Terry
Emery Dutton
Lawford Larkey
N Mason
Geo Willson
N Thompkins
William Young
C. Houghton
C. G. Fletcher
Jos. E. Fletcher
Rachael Fletcher
Jno. Fletcher
Hazen Kimball
James S. Kimball
Jno. B. Kimball
Ruhama Kimball
Solomon P. McIntosh
Sidney Knowlton
Ephraim Knowlton
Harriet Knowlton
[Mary Ann] Knowlton
William Coray
Gerge Coray
Martha J Coray
Mary Ett Coray
Polly Coray
Burrier Griffin
Sally A. Griffin
Thos. Hayse
Lovina Hays
Catharin Spears

Thomas Henry Bullock
Charles Richard Bullock
Pamela Bullock
Sarah Ann Nixon
Jennetta Richards
Heber John Richards
Rhoda Ann Richards
E [Mathew] Miels
B Adrian Jr Miels
Mashala Dudley
Sarah Jane Martin
Mary Willson
Thomas G Wilson
Malen Wilson
Stratton Thornton
Horace Thornton
Hariet Thornton
Jefferson Hunt
Celia Hunt
Gilbert Hunt
Nancy Hunt
Marshel Hunt
John Hunt
Josheph Hunt
[H········] Hunt
July Hunt
Hariet Hunt
selvester Wilson
Elisabeth Wilson
Elijah N. Wilson Jr
Dimon Fierson
Jasper Dudley
Johnthon Cox
emley Cox
Indina f. Cox
Eivn obanion
George obanion
Mary Jane obanion

Geo. Knowlton
Quincy Knowlton
Jas. Shepherd
Emily Shepherd
Catharin Shepherd
Hanna Akis
Patty Akis
Betsy Akis
David Miller
Henry Miller
Rebecca Miller
Susan Miller
[L]ehigh Miller
Peter Miller
Jacob Caswell
Abagail A. Caswell
Calvin Beebe
Submit R Beebe
Agaried Tullbe
Ansen Tullbe
Percis Tippets
Harriet A Pelles
John Cram
Rebekah Cram
Henry Cram
[Loreno] Cram
Jacob Degraw
Sophia Degraw
Rebecca Degraw
John Cleminson
Lydia Cleminson
Laura S Cleminson
Ebeneser Kerr
Jane Kerr
Mariah Mich
Albert Mich
William Brown
Lurinda H. Brown

John obanion
James obanion
Jaspher obanion
Nathan Miles
Sallyann Miles
James Woodland
Catharine Woodland
[unez] A mosher
William Woodland
Elisabeth Rose
Orson H Rose
[Ann V.] Rose
Aley G Rose
Marthy Rose
Dolly [Hed···]
Louisa [——]
Sariah [Cheney]
Mary [—— Cheny]
Francis [Brown]
Ezekiel [Brown]
Isaac L. [Brown]
Suzannah Brown
Joseph Brown
William N Tubbs
Henry Brooke
John Brooke
Robert A Brooke
July A Brooke
Hariet Brooke
[Calvin mills]
Erastus Snow
Sarah L. Snow
Cordelia Morley
Ira Willsey
Rebeca E King
Horace Rawson
Elizabeth Rawson
Matilty Chase

James Dudley
Mary Dudley
Moses Dudley
Sarah Dudley
Joseph Dudley
Sarah Dudley
Sintan Dudley
Rubian Dudley
Jesey Dudley
Mark Dudley
Salvester Dudley
Joseph ephfrom Dudley
John G Dudley
Louisa Thornton
Mehetable Thornton
Calista Thornton
Stephen Thornton
Charlotte Thornton
Elijah Wilson
Martha Wilson
Irwn R Wilson
Alpherd Wilson
Milton [Lanicky] ~~wilson~~
Elenor Wilson
Sarah Wilson
Melvina Wilson
Martha J Dudley
Sarah ann Dudley
Granbury Wilson
A[bram] Miles
Eliza Miles
Franklin Miels
Phebe H hancock
Mary Brown
Isaac Hancock
Solomon Hancock Jun
Alta Hancok
Abraham Rose

Obiedience Boss
Henry Boss
Caroline Allen
Willis Boss
Lucy Allen
Nancy Boss
Caroline E Pellsey
Olivee Rawson
Daniel Rawson
Polly Boss
Candelia Allen
John Boss
Solomon Boss
Anna E Pellsey
Samantha Rawson
William Rawson
Sariah Rawson
Jabis Durfee
Emily [Bragg]
Benjamin [Bragg] Jr
Nancy J putnam
Chloe Rawson
Arther Rawson
Therissa Morley
[Isaac Mortinson]
John Edmiston
Martha Snow
Eliaza Gardner
Amy gardner
Walter E Gardner
Nancey W Gardner
Henry F. Gardner
Wilber J Earl
Silvester H Earl
Lois C Earl
Wilber J Earl
[Elaine] Earl
Eleanor Willson

Katharine Rose
Adaline Rose
Wm. W Rose
Wm. Harris
Mary Harris
John [B······]
John [Grant]
David Garner
Samuel Alger
Alexander [Sh······]
Mary Brown
Daniel Brown
Charles B Hancock
[Huck] Alger
Electa Miles
Joseph B. Noble
Mary A. Noble
Susan Noble
Joseph H. Noble
Edward A. Noble
Louisa [Beman]
Isaac Morley
Gardner Snow
James C. Snow
Eliza A Snow
J. C. Snow
Artimesia Snow
Sarah J. Snow
John C. Snow
Carlos Z. Snow
Eliza A Snow
Lewis Whiting
Elisha Whiting
Philena Cove
Mary Child
[Ezlion] Child
Ann Cox
Lucy D Allen

H. H. Hays
[Elizaier] Hays
Alma Hays
Sarah E Hays
John Brown
Erastus H. Rudd
Elisa W Rudd
Alta E. Rudd
Ira F Rudd
John Huston
George Hancock
Ruth Tyler
P. C. Tyler
Orville L. Cox
Gaine Durfee
Willim S Durfee
Benjamin Bragg
Abram Durfee
Hannah Bragg
William H. Clawson
Moses Clauson
Fredck W Cox jr
Ruffus Vaughn
Walace Clauson
Loiza Jane Cox
George Clauson
John Israel
Moroni Clauson
Amos Cox
Chases T Cox
Amelia Cox
Wm. A Cox
Phebe Jane Losee
Jemima Losee
David Losee
Lydda Losee
Rebeca Losee
Sarah Losee

Mary J King
Benjamine R Wescott
Jane Wescott
Lane A King
Mary Durfee
Enoch E King
Augustus [Bragg]
Shephor Hutchings
Marcellus [Broigg]
Lucinda Hutchings
Plina Hutchings
Nefi Durfee
Lucy Morley
George Snow
Mary Snow
Sarah S. Snow
Elisabeth C. Snow
Betsy E Markham
Mary Gardner
william woodland
Solomon Hancock Sen
David Tyler
Daniel Stanton
Clarinda Stanton
Daniel W. Stanton
Constanza C. Stanton
Thomas Hancock sen
Amy Hancock
Wm. Mooney
David Mooney
Marilda Moony
Eliza A Mooney
John G. Lofton
Gemila Lofton
Mildred H Lofton
Thomas D Lofton
Solon P Bassett
Clarinda An Bassett

Lydia Losee
[Matilda] Losee
David garner
fredrick grner
Jan garner
Thomas King
Emeline Cox
~~Lev~~ Eliza Cox
george E King
Asy garner
Eunice Clauson
Cornelia Clauson
Wm. E King
Jane Clauson
Levina Jane Cox
Susan M. Cox
Mary Mimerly
James Israel Sen.
James Woodward
Jeremiah Mitchel
Philip Garner
~~Hiram Halletts~~
Mary Allen
henry garnr
Hiram Hallett
Joseph G Alben
Polly Garner
Sary garner
Sally Whiting
Parthine King
Devey King
Henry Ettleman
Christina Ettleman
Syilvester Whiting
George King
Moroni Ettleman
Henry J Ettleman
Thomas King Jr

Sandra C. Bassett
Melinda E. Stanton
Harriet L Stanton
Caroline A Stanton
Nancy Koyl Jane Ko[···]
Edward Koyl Harie[·]
Koyle Mary Koyl
John Koyl
Eluvia P. Cox
Adelia B. Cox
Mara X Horne
Catharine Brooke
Jolly King
Cornelia Leavitt
Hannah B. Merriam
Lorett [Kent]
Lucia Leavitt
Jemima Lindsey
Elizabeth Whiting
Abaigail L Leavitt
Eliza R. Snow
Dolly Daniels
Sarah Weston
Lucy McKown
Elizabath McKown
Rawana McKown
Marcellus McKown jr
Susan Ann Brunell
Elizabeth Brunell
Joseph Bunell
Margarette Brunell
Laureign Brunell
Jasinth M Brunell
Mary Bragg
Benja R Hall
Mehetabel Hall
Horrace L Hall
Dorothy M Hall

Isaac H. Lowse
Jane Whiting
Asher King
Samuel Ettleman
Nancy J Rillsey
Abraham Israel
Elijah Israel
Almon Whiting
Joel King
Marian Ettleman
Edsen Winters
Stratton Vradenburg
Sabina Vradenburg
William Vradenburg
James Vradenburg
Phenius Vradenburg
Ebenezer Clauson
Luther Vradenburg
Anna E Vradenburg
Sarah Lamoreaux
Abagaile Lamoreaux
David Rirlock
Amos Scott
Lydia Scott
Hiram A Scott
Richard Scott
Mahittablle O. Daniels
Luthrea B Daniels
Nancy C Naughn
Henry Boss
Willis Boss
Nancey Boss
[Nely] Boss
John Boss
F[··] Boss
Thomas Bullock
Henrietta Bullock
A. A. Smith

Mary H Hall
Catharine Hall
Louisa M Hall
Wiliam H Hall
Amanda Clauson
Edwin Cox
Hiliam Cox
Elizabeth Israel
James Israel Jr
Caroline E Israel
Clark Hallett
Phebe Hallett
Louwisa P. Hallett
Thacker C. Hallett
Marcelus McKown
Orin McKown
Lorenzo Snow
William C Perry
Eliza B Perry
Wm. A Lindsey
Jemima Lindsey
Abraham Losee
Mary Losee
Enoch King
Sarah King
Betsey Snow
N. H Jennings
Cornelia Jennings
Rueben Daniels
F W Cox
Moses Clauson
Dominicus Carter
Edman Durfee
Stephen Jackson
David B Lamoreaux
Berton B Scott
Henry Deam
Elizabeth Deam

William Rowley
George Cannon
Nehemiah Hartley
Margrett Hartley
Philip Smith
Hirum Watts
John Ogden
Joseph Moffet
Eliza Chapman
Julia Moffet
George Chapman
Elisabeth Moffit
[Rawfene] Roff
Sylvester Chapman
Mary Conner
Ellis Schofield
Ellen Schofield
Elias Smith
Washington Peck
Margaret Groesbeck
Ruth Butterfield
Emerson Butterfield
Mary Rigby
Jane Pincock
John Pincock Junr
Thomas Bateman sen
Mary Bateman
J. M Alford
Richard Bradshaw
William Bradshaw
Samuel Bateman
Joseph B. Austin
Peter Armstrong
Ann Armstrong
J L Bateman
William Winterbottom
Mary Winterbottom
Margaret Winterton sen

Sarah E Deam
Cathrine A Deam
Isaac M Deam
Saml Blair
Catharine Blair
Mary Elizabeth Blair
Enoch King jr.
Phillip Ettleman
James Dunn
Elizabeth Dunn
Susana Dunn
Patience Ozgood
Jane Mitchiel
Prody Blanchard
William Whighting
Isaiah Jackson
James L Knapp
Mary A Lamoreux
John Lamoreaux
Lydia S Scott
Amos B Scott
Caleb Scott
Wm. Daniels
Noble N. Daniels
Polly Vaughn
Hannah York
Asa York
Julia A. York
James S. York
A. M. York Jr.
Arlytte Carter
Lucinda Carter
John Deam
Elisabeth Deam
L. O. Littlefield
A. C. Brewer
W. Leyland
John Greenhow

Margaret Winterbottom Jun
H S Parrish
Mary J Moor
George A Moor
Margaret Bateman
Wm. R Parrish
Rachel Steen
Adaline Melical
Sophia Lansdell
R. H. Watts
Wm Bradshaw
Ellen Bradshaw
Ann Bradshaw
John Bradshaw
Jane Rigby
John Pincock Sen
James Southern
Mary Bowan
Margaret Bateman
Joseph Bateman
Elizabeth Bateman
Frederic Mills
Mercy Groesbeck
Henry Groesbeck
Franklin Watts
Bernice Monroe
Roger Orton
Peirpont Orton
Elisabeth Richarson
Sylva Richardson
Jack Orton
Clarisa Orton
Amos Orton

Ann Smith
Wm. Whit Smith
Alex Brown
Margaro Groobek
John Gressmen
Ann Elisabeth Roper
Mariah groosbeck
Alvin C. Graves
Orrin D Farrin
Daniel Brown Jun
Ann Brown
Cholott Walker
Jas. Brown Senr.
Mary Parmer
Effelender Gressmen
William Brown
John Walker
Nancy Brown
C L Whitny
J. S. Brown
Amer S Walker
Ellen Walker
Jacob J Abbott
Ann Austin
Anna Bateman
Lucinda Moffet
James Brown Sen
John Bullard
Joseph H Botherson
Luman Gibbs
[Fenley] Jackson
John Groesbeck
Amos Jackson
Sophia Lansdale
John M Brown
Asher Gressman
Delia Groesbeck
Jones [Putman]

Eliza H Brotherton
Eliza Watts
Isaac Butterfield
John Butterfield
James Howard
Mary Howard
C. C. Fisher
Mary A. Fisher
Elisabeth Foster
Martha Jane Rigbey
James Pincock
Harriet Bateman
Grace Bradshaw
William Black Sen.
William Black Jun
Joseph Black
Jane Black
George Black
Sophia Munroe
Julia H. Neely
Eliza Jackson
Jane Lanasdell
Rossannah Alford
Henry Melimicul
J O Hillman
Charlott Pincock
Tyrus C Moore
James C Orten
Emilse Hopner
James Neely
Ellen Neely
Baldwin Watts
Samuel L Sprague
Mary Sprague
Elizabeth Watts
James Rigby
Martha Anne Abbott
Thomas Bateman Jun

Part V

Other Petitions

Introduction to Part V

The petitions that constitute Part V are those which do not logically belong in earlier parts. Chapter 8 consists of sworn, legal testimony given before the Municipal Court of Nauvoo in 1843. Prominent Church leaders in an effort to protect Joseph Smith, who was then being accused of treason and threatened with extradition by Missouri officials (*HC* 3:403). Their testimonies tell of the harassment of Latter-day Saints by both local and state leaders in Missouri. Even though they do not specifically request redress, these documents tell the same story of abuse as many other petitions.

Also included in this part are individual petitions which were never presented to the federal government. Most of these were written in 1845, suggesting that the Saints intended to make yet another appeal. These petitions are similar to the individual petitions prepared earlier.

The last chapter of this section contains undated petitions. Many of these may have gone to Washington with one of the appeals—their content is similar to the petitions dated 1839 and 1840. However, since they are undated it seemed imprudent to designate them as a formal part of any appeal.

Chapter 8

Testimonies Given before the Municipal Court of Nauvoo

SMITH, Hyrum HC[1]

Hyrum Smith sworn, said that the defendant now in court is his brother, and that his name is not Joseph Smith, Jun., but Joseph Smith, Sen., and has been for more than two years past. I have been acquainted with him ever since he was born, which was thirty-seven years in December last; and I have not been absent from him at any one time not even for the space of six months, since his birth, to my recollection, and have been intimately acquainted with all his sayings, doings, business transactions and movements, as much as any one man could be acquainted with another man's business, up to the present time, and do know that he has not committed treason against any state in the Union, by any overt act, or by levying war, or by aiding, abetting or assisting an enemy in any state in the Union; and that the said Joseph Smith, Sen., has not committed treason in the state of Missouri, or violated any law or rule of said state; I being personally acquainted with the transactions and doings of said Smith whilst he resided in said state, which was for about six months in the year 1838; I being also a resident in said state during the same period of time; and I do know that said Joseph Smith, Sen., never was subject to military duty in any state, neither was he in the State of Missouri, he being exempt by the amputation or extraction of a bone from his leg, and by having a license to preach the Gospel, or being, in other words, a minister of the Gospel; and I do know that said Smith never bore arms, as a military man, in any capacity whatever, whilst in the state of Missouri, or previous to that time; neither has he given any orders or assumed any command in any capacity whatever. But I do know that whilst he was in the state of

---

[1] 3:404–24; also found in JH 1 Jul 1843.

Missouri, the people commonly called "Mormons" were threatened with violence and extermination; and on or about the first Monday in August, 1838, at the election in Gallatin, the county seat in Daviess county, the citizens who were commonly called "Mormons" were forbidden to exercise the rights of franchise; and from that circumstance an affray commenced and a fight ensued among the citizens of that place; and from that time a mob commenced gathering in that county, threatening the extermination of the "Mormons." The said Smith and myself, upon hearing the mobs were collecting together, and that they also murdered two of the citizens of the same place, [Gallatin][2] and would not suffer them to be buried, the said Smith and myself went over to Daviess county to learn the particulars of the affray; but upon our arrival at Diahman we learned that none was killed, but several were wounded. We tarried all night at Colonel Lyman Wight's. The next morning, the weather being very warm, and having been very dry, for some time previously, the springs and wells in the region were dried up. On mounting our horses to return, we rode up to Mr. Black's who was then an acting justice of the peace, to obtain some water for ourselves and horses. Some few of the citizens accompanied us there; and, after obtaining water, Mr. Black was asked by said Joseph Smith, Sen., if he would use his influence to see that the laws were faithfully executed, and to put down mob violence; and he gave us a paper written by his own hand, stating that he would do so. He [Joseph Smith, Sen.] also requested him to call together the most influential men of the county on the next day, that we might have an interview with them. To this he acquiesced, and, accordingly, the next day they assembled at the house of Colonel Wight, and entered into a mutual covenant of peace to put down mob violence and protect each other in the enjoyment of their rights. After this, we all parted with the best of feelings, and each man returned to his own home.

This mutual agreement of peace, however, did not last long; for, but a few days afterwards, the mob began to collect again, until several hundreds rendezvoused at Millport, a few miles distant from Diahman. They immediately commenced making aggressions upon the citizens called "Mormons," taking away their hogs and cattle and threatening them with extermination or utter extinction, saying that they had a cannon, and there should be no compromise only at its mouth. They frequently took men, women and children prisoners, whipping them and lacerating their bodies with hickory withes, and tying them to trees and depriving them of food until they were compelled to gnaw the bark from the trees to which

---

[2]The editorial brackets from *History of the Church* have been maintained.

they were bound, in order to sustain life; treating them in the most cruel manner they could invent or think of, and doing everything they could to excite the indignation of the "Mormon" people to rescue them, in order that they might make that a pretext for an accusation for the breach of the law, and that they might the better excite the prejudice of the populace, and thereby get aid and assistance to carry out their hellish purposes of extermination.

Immediately on the authentication of these facts, messengers were despatched from Far West to Austin A. King, judge of the fifth judicial district of the state of Missouri, and also to Major-General Atchison, commander-in-chief of that division, and Brigadier-General Doniphan, giving them information of the existing facts, and demanding immediate assistance.

General Atchison returned with the messengers, and went immediately to Diahman, and from thence to Millport, and he found that the facts were true as reported to him—that the citizens of that county were assembled together in a hostile attitude, to the number of two or three hundred men, threatening the utter extermination of the "Mormons." He at once returned to Clay county, and ordered out a sufficient military force to quell the mob.

Immediately after, they were dispersed, and the army returned. The mob commenced collecting again soon after. We again applied for military aid, when General Doniphan came out with a force of sixty armed men to Far West; but they were in such a state of insubordination that he said he could not control them, and it was thought advisable by Col. Hinkle, Mr. Rigdon and others, that they should return home. General Doniphan ordered Colonel Hinkle to call out the militia of Caldwell and defend the town against the mob; for, said he, you have great reason to be alarmed. He said Neil Gillium, from the Platte country, had come down with two hundred armed men, and had taken up their station at Hunter's Mill, a place distant about seventeen or eighteen miles northwest of the town of Far West, and also that an armed force had collected again at Millport, in Daviess county, consisting of several hundred men; and that another armed force had collected at De Witt, in Carroll county, about fifty miles southeast of Far West, where about seventy families of the "Mormon" people had settled upon the banks of the Missouri river, at a little town called De Witt.

Immediately, whilst he was yet talking, a messenger came in from De Witt, stating that three or four hundred men had assembled together at that place, armed *cap-a-pie*, and that they had threatened the utter extinction of the citizens of De Witt, if they did not leave the place immediately;

and that they had also surrounded the town and cut off all supplies of food, so that many of the inhabitants were suffering from hunger.

General Doniphan seemed to be very much alarmed, and appeared to be willing to do all he could to assist and to relieve the sufferings of the "Mormon" people. He advised that a petition be gotten up at once and sent to the Governor. A petition was accordingly prepared, and a messenger despatched to the governor, and another petition was sent to Judge King.

The "Mormon" people throughout the country were in a great state of alarm and also in great distress. They saw themselves completely surrounded by armed forces on the north, and on the northwest and on the south. Bogart, who was a Methodist preacher and a captain over a militia company of fifty soldiers, but who had added to this number out of the surrounding counties about one hundred more, which made his force about one hundred and fifty strong, was stationed at Crooked creek, sending out his scouting parties, taking men, women and children prisoners, driving off cattle, hogs and horses, entering into every house on Log and Long creeks, rifling their houses of their most precious articles, such as money, bedding and clothing, taking all their old muskets and their rifles, or military implements, threatening the people with instant death, if they did not deliver up all their precious things and enter into a covenant to leave the state or go into the city of Far West by the next morning, saying that they "calculated to drive the people into Far West, and then drive them to hell." Gillium also was doing the same on the northwest side of Far West; and Sashiel Woods, a Presbyterian minister, was the leader of the mob in Daviess county; and a very noted man of the same society was the leader of the mob in Carroll county. And they were also sending out their scouting parties, robbing and pillaging houses, driving away hogs, horses and cattle, taking men, women and children and carrying them off, threatening their lives, and subjecting them to all manner of abuses that they could invent or think of.

Under this state of alarm, excitement and distress, the messengers returned from the governor and from the other authorities, bringing the startling news that the "Mormons" could have no assistance. They stated that the governor said the "Mormons" had got into a difficulty with the citizens, and they might fight it out, for all he cared. He could not render them any assistance.

The people of De Wit were obliged to leave their homes and go into Far West, but did not do so until after many of them had starved to death for want of proper sustenance, and several died on the road there, and were buried by the wayside, without a coffin or a funeral ceremony; and the distress, sufferings, and privations of the people cannot be expressed.

All the scattered families of the "Mormon" people, with but few exceptions, in all the counties, except Daviess, were driven into Far West.

This only increased their distress, for many thousands who were driven there had no habitations or houses to shelter them, and were huddled together, some in tents and others under blankets, while others had no shelter from the inclemency of the weather. Nearly two months the people had been in this awful state of consternation; many of them had been killed, whilst others had been whipped until they had to swathe up their bowels to prevent them from falling out.

About this time General Parks came out from Richmond, Ray county. He was one of the commissioned officers sent out at the time the mob was first quelled, and went out to Diahman. My brother, Joseph Smith, Sen., and I went out at the same time.

On the evening that General Parks arrived at Diahman, the wife of my brother, the late Don Carlos Smith, came into Colonel Wight's about 11 o'clock at night, bringing her two children along with her, one about two and a half years old, the other a babe in her arms.

She came on foot, a distance of three miles, and waded Grand river. The water was then waist deep, and the snow three inches deep. She stated that a party of the mob—a gang of ruffians—had turned her out of doors and taken her household goods, and had burnt up her house, and she had escaped by the skin of her teeth. Her husband at that time was in Tennessee, [on a mission] and she was living alone.

This cruel transaction excited the feelings of the people of Diahman, especially of Colonel Wight and he asked General Parks in my hearing *how long we had got to suffer such base treatment*. General Parks said he did not know how long.

Colonel Wight then asked him what should be done? General Parks told him "he should take a company of men, well armed, and go and disperse the mob wherever he should find any collected together, and take away their arms." Colonel Wight did so precisely according to the orders of General Parks. And my brother, Joseph Smith, Sen., made no order about it.

And after Col. Wight had dispersed the mob, and put a stop to their burning houses belonging to the "Mormon" people, and turning women and children out of doors, which they had done up to that time to the number of eight or ten houses, which houses were consumed to ashes. After being cut short in their intended designs, the mob started up a new plan. They went to work and moved their families out of the county and set fire to their houses; and not being able to incense the "Mormons" to commit crimes, they had recourse to this stratagem to set their houses on fire, and send runners into all the counties adjacent to declare to the people that the "Mormons" had burnt up their houses and destroyed their fields; and if the people would not believe them, they would tell them to go and see if what they had said was not true.

Many people came to see. They saw the houses burning; and, being filled with prejudice, they could not be made to believe but that the "Mormons" set them on fire; which deed was most diabolical and of the blackest kind; for indeed the "Mormons" did not set them on fire, nor meddle with their houses or their fields.

And the houses that were burnt, had all been previously purchased by the "Mormons" of the people, together with the pre-emption rights and the corn in the fields, and paid for in money, and with wagons and horses, and with other property, about two weeks before; but they had not taken possession of the premises. This wicked transaction was for the purpose of clandestinely exciting the minds of a prejudiced populace and the executive, that they might get an order that they could the more easily carry out their hellish purposes, in expulsion, or extermination, or utter extinction of the "Mormon" people.

After witnessing the distressed situation of the people in Diahman, my brother, Joseph Smith, Sen., and myself returned to the city of Far West, and immediately dispatched a messenger, with written documents, to General Atchison, stating the facts as they did then exist, praying for assistance, if possible, and requesting the editor of the *Far West* to insert the same in his newspaper. But he utterly refused to do so.

We still believed that we should get assistance from the Governor, and again petitioned him, praying for assistance, setting forth our distressed situation. And in the meantime the presiding judge of the county court issued orders, upon affidavits made to him by the citizens, to the sheriff of the county, to order out the militia of the county to stand in constant readiness, night and day, to prevent the citizens from being massacred, which fearful situation they were in every moment.

Everything was very portentous and alarming. Notwithstanding all this, there was a ray of hope yet existing in the minds of the people that the governor would render us assistance; and whilst the people were waiting anxiously for deliverance—men, women, and children frightened, praying, and weeping, we beheld at a distance, crossing the prairies and approaching the town, a large army in military array, brandishing their glittering swords in the sunshine; and we could not but feel joyful for a moment, thinking that probably the governor had sent an armed force to our relief, notwithstanding the awful forebodings that pervaded our breasts.

But, to our great surprise, when the army arrived, they came up and formed a line in double file within one-half mile on the south of the city of Far West, and despatched three messengers with a white flag to the city. They were met by Captain Morey, with a few other individuals, whose names I do not now recollect. I was myself standing close by, and could very distinctly hear every word they said.

Being filled with anxiety, I rushed forward to the spot, expecting to hear good news. But, alas! and heart-thrilling to every soul that heard them, they demanded three persons to be brought out of the city before they should massacre the rest.

The names of the persons they demanded were Adam Lightner, John Cleminson, and his wife. Immediately the three persons were brought forth to hold an interview with the officers who had made the demand, and the officers told them they had now a chance to save their lives, for they intended to destroy the people and lay the city in ashes. They replied to the officers, if the people must be destroyed and the city burned to ashes, they would remain in the city and die with them.

The officers immediately returned, and the army retreated and encamped about a mile and a half from the city.

A messenger was at once dispatched with a white flag from the colonel of the militia of Far West, requesting an interview with General Atchison and General Doniphan; but as the messenger approached the camp, he was shot at by Bogart, the Methodist preacher.

The name of the messenger was Charles C. Rich, who is now Brigadier-General in the Nauvoo Legion. However, he gained permission to see General Doniphan; he also requested an interview with General Atchison.

General Doniphan said that General Atchison had been dismounted a few miles back, by a special order of the Governor, and had been sent back to Liberty, Clay county. He also stated that the reason was, that he (Atchison) was too merciful unto the "Mormons," and Boggs would not let him have the command, but had given it to General Lucas, who was from Jackson county, and whose heart had become hardened by his former acts of rapine and bloodshed, he being one of the leaders in murdering, driving, and plundering the "Mormon" people in that county, and burning some two or three hundred of their houses, in the years 1833 and 1834.

Mr. Rich requested General Doniphan to spare the people, and not suffer them to be massacred until the next morning, it then being evening. He coolly agreed that he would not, and also said that he had not as yet received the Governor's order, but expected it every hour, and should not make any further move until he had received it; but he would not make any promises so far as regarded Neil Gillium's army, it having arrived a few minutes previously and joined the main body of the army, he [Gillium] knowing well at what hour to form a junction with the main body.

Mr. Rich then returned to the city, giving this information. The Colonel [G. M. Hinkle] immediately dispatched a second messenger with a white flag, to request another interview with General Doniphan, in order to touch his sympathy and compassion, and, if it were possible for him to use his best endeavors to preserve the lives of the people.

On the return of this messenger, we learned that several persons had been killed by some of the soldiers who were under the command of General Lucas.

One Mr. Carey had his brains knocked out by the breech of a gun, and he lay bleeding several hours; but his family were not permitted to approach him, nor any one else allowed to administer relief to him whilst he lay upon the ground in the agonies of death.

Mr. Carey had just arrived in the country, from the State of Ohio, only a few hours previous to the arrival of the army. He had a family, consisting of a wife and several small children. He was buried by Lucius N. Scovil, who is now [1843] the senior Warden of the Nauvoo [Masonic] Lodge.

Another man, of the name of John Tanner, was knocked on the head at the same time, and his skull laid bare to the width of a man's hand; and he lay, to all appearances, in the agonies of death for several hours; but by the permission of General Doniphan, his friends brought him out of the camp; and with good nursing, he slowly recovered, and is now living.

There was another man, whose name is Powell, who was beat on the head with the breech of a gun until his skull was fractured, and his brains ran out in two or three places. He is now alive and resides in this [Hancock] county, but has lost the use of his senses. Several persons of his family were also left for dead, but have since recovered.

These acts of barbarity were also committed by the soldiers under the command of General Lucas, previous to having received the Governor's order of extermination.

It was on the evening of the 30th October, according to the best of my recollections, that the army arrived at Far West, the sun about half-an-hour high. In a few moments afterwards, Cornelius Gillium arrived with his army and formed a junction.

This Gillium had been stationed at Hunter's Mills for about two months previous to that time, committing depredations upon the inhabitants, capturing men, women, and children carrying them off as prisoners and lacerating their bodies with hickory withes.

The army of Gillium were painted like Indians: some, more conspicuous than others, were designated by red spots; and he also was painted in a similar manner with red spots marked on his face, and styled himself the "DELAWARE CHIEF." They would whoop and halloo, and yell as nearly like Indians as they could, and continued to do so all that night.

In the morning, early, the colonel of militia [G. M. Hinkle] sent a messenger into the camp with a white flag, to have another interview with General Doniphan. On his return, he informed us that the governor's order had arrived.

General Doniphan said that the order of the governor was, to exterminate the Mormons, by God; but *he* would be *damned* if *he* obeyed *that order*, but General Lucas might do what he pleased.

We immediately learned from General Doniphan, that "the Governor's order that had arrived was only a copy of the original, and that the original order was in the hands of Major-General Clark, who was on his way to Far West with an additional army of 6,000 men."

Immediately after this, there came into the city a messenger from Haun's Mills, bringing the intelligence of an awful massacre of the people who were residing in that place, and that a force of two or three hundred detached from the main body of the army, under the superior command of Colonel Ashley, but under the immediate command of Captain Nehemiah Comstock, who, the day previous, had promised them peace and protection; but on receiving a copy of the Governor's order "to *exterminate or to expel*" from the hands of Colonel Ashley, he returned upon them the following day and surprised and massacred nearly the whole population of the place, and then came on to the town of Far West, and entered into conjunction with the main body of the army.

The messenger informed us that he himself, with a few others, fled into the thickets, which preserved them from the massacre; and on the following morning they returned and collected the dead bodies of the people, and cast them into a well; and there were upwards of 20 who were dead or mortally wounded; and there are several of the wounded now [1843] living in this city [Nauvoo].

One, of the name of Yocum, has lately had his leg amputated, in consequence of wounds he then received. He had a ball shot through his head, which entered near his eye and came out at the back part of his head, and another ball passed through one of his arms.

The army, during all the while they had been encamped at Far West, continued to lay waste fields of corn, making hogs, sheep, and cattle common plunder, and shooting them down for sport.

One man shot a cow and took a strip of her skin, the width of his hand, from her head to her tail, and tied it around a tree to slip his halter into to tie his horse with.

The city was surrounded with a strong guard; and no man, woman or child was permitted to go out or to come in, under penalty of death. Many of the citizens were shot at in attempting to go out to obtain sustenance for themselves and families.

There was one field fenced in, consisting of 1,200 acres, mostly covered with corn. It was entirely laid waste by the hands of the army. The next day after the arrival of the army, towards evening, Colonel Hinkle came up from the camp, requesting to see my brother Joseph, Parley P. Pratt, Sidney Rigdon, Lyman Wight, and George W. Robinson, stating that the officers of the army wanted a mutual consultation with those men; Hinkle also assured them that these generals—Doniphan, Lucas, Wilson, and Graham—(however, General Graham is an honorable exception; he did all he could to preserve the lives of the people, contrary to the order of the governor);—had pledged their sacred honor that they should not be abused or insulted, but should be guarded back in safety in the morning, or as soon as the consultation was over.

My brother Joseph replied that he did not know what good he could do in any consultation, as he was only a private individual. However, he said he was always willing to do all the good he could, and would obey every law of the land, and then leave the event with God.

They immediately started with Colonel Hinkle to go down into the camp. As they were going down, about half way to the camp, they met General Lucas with a phalanx of men, with a wing to the right and to the left, and a four-pounder [cannon] in the center. They supposed he was coming with this strong force to guard them into the camp in safety; but, to their surprise, when they came up to General Lucas, he ordered his men to surround them, and Hinkle stepped up to the general and said, "These are the prisoners I agreed to deliver up." General Lucas drew his sword and said, "Gentlemen, you are my prisoners," and about that time the main army were on their march to meet them.

They came up in two divisions, and opened to the right and left, and my brother and his friends were marched down through their lines, with a strong guard in front, and the cannon in the rear, to the camp, amidst the whoopings, howlings, yellings, and shoutings of the army, which were so horrid and terrific that it frightened the inhabitants of the city.

It is impossible to describe the feelings of horror and distress of the people.

After being thus betrayed, they [the prisoners] were placed under a strong guard of thirty men, armed *cap-a-pie*, who were relieved every two hours. They were compelled to lie on the cold ground that night, and were told in plain language that they need never to expect their liberties again. So far for their honor pledged! However, this was as much as could be expected from a mob under the garb of military and executive authority in the state of Missouri.

On the next day, the soldiers were permitted to patrol the streets, of Far West to abuse and insult the people at their leisure, and enter into houses and pillage them, and ravish the women, taking away every gun and every other kind of arms or military implements. About twelve o'clock on that day, Colonel Hinkle came to my house with an armed force, opened the door, and called me out of doors and delivered me up as a prisoner unto that force. They surrounded me and commanded me to march into the camp. I told them that I could not go; my family were sick, and I was sick myself, and could not leave home. They said they did not care for that—I must and should go. I asked when they would permit me to return. They made me no answer, but forced me along with the point of the bayonent into the camp, and put me under the same guard with my brother Joseph; and within about half an hour afterwards, Amasa Lyman was also brought and placed under the same guard. There we were compelled to stay all that night and lie on the ground. But some time in the same night, Colonel Hinkle came to me and told me that he had been pleading my case before the court-martial, but he was afraid he would not succeed.

He said there was a court-martial then in session, consisting of thirteen or fourteen officers; Circuit Judge Austin A. King, and Mr. Birch, district attorney; also Sashiel Woods, Presbyterian priest, and about twenty other priests of the different religious denominations in that country. He said they were determined to shoot us on the next morning in the public square in Far West. I made him no reply.

On the next morning, about sunrise, General Doniphan ordered his brigade to take up the line of march and leave the camp. He came to us where we were under guard, to shake hands with us, and bid us farewell. His first salutation was, "By God, you have been sentenced by the court-martial to be shot this morning; but I will be damned if I will have any of the honor of it, or any of the disgrace of it; therefore I have ordered my brigade to take up the line of march and to leave the camp, for I consider it to be cold-blooded murder, and I bid you farewell;" and he went away.

This movement of Colonel Doniphan made considerable excitement in the army, and there was considerable whisperings amongst the officers. We listened very attentively, and frequently heard it mentioned by the guard that "the damned Mormons would not be shot this time."

In a few moments the guard was relieved by a new set. One of those new guards said that "the damned Mormons would not be shot this time," for the movement of General Doniphan had frustrated the whole plan, and that the officers had called another court-martial, and had ordered us to be taken to Jackson county, and there to be executed; and in a few moments two large wagons drove up, and we were ordered to get into them; and while we were getting into them, there came up four or five men armed with guns, who drew up and snapped their guns at us, in order to kill us; some flashed in the pan, and others only snapped, but none of their guns went off. They were immediately arrested by several officers, and their guns taken from them, and the drivers drove off.

We requested General Lucas to let us go to our houses and get some clothing. In order to do this, we had to be driven up into the city. It was with much difficulty that we could get his permission to go and see our families and get some clothing; but, after considerable consultation, we were permitted to go under a strong guard of five or six men to each of us, and we were not permitted to speak to any one of our families, under the pain of death. The guard that went with me ordered my wife to get me some clothes immediately, within two minutes; and if she did not do it, I should go off without them.

I was obliged to submit to their tyrannical orders, however painful it was, with my wife and children clinging to my arms and to the skirts of my garments, and was not permitted to utter to them a word of consolation, and in a moment was hurried away from them at the point of the bayonet.

We were hurried back into the wagons and ordered into them, all in about the same space of time. In the meanwhile our father and mother and sisters had forced their way to the wagons to get permission to see us, but were forbidden to speak to us; and they [the guard] immediately drove off for Jackson county. We traveled about twelve miles that evening, and encamped for the night.

The same strong guard was kept around us, and were relieved every two hours, and we were permitted to sleep on the ground. The nights were then cold, with considerable snow on the ground; and for want of covering and clothing, we suffered extremely with the cold. That night was the commencement of a fit of sickness, from which I have not wholly recovered unto this day, in consequence of my exposure to the inclemency of the weather.

Our provision was fresh beef roasted in the fire on a stick, the army having no bread, in consequence of the want of mills to grind the grain.

In the morning, at the dawn of day, we were forced on our journey, and were exhibited to the inhabitants along the road, the same as they exhibit a caravan of elephants and camels. We were examined from head to foot by men, women and children, only I believe they did not make us open our mouths to look at our teeth. This treatment was continued incessantly until we arrived at Independence, in Jackson county.

After our arrival at Independence, we were driven all through the town for inspection, and then we were ordered into an old log house, and there kept under guard as usual, until supper, which was served up to us as we sat upon the floor, or on billets of wood, and we were compelled to stay in that house all that night and the next day.

They continued to exhibit us to the public, by letting the people come in and examine us, and then go away and give place for others, alternately, all that day and the next night. But on the morning of the following day, we were all permitted to go to the tavern to eat and to sleep; but afterward they made us pay our own expenses for board, lodging, and attendance, and for which they made a most exorbitant charge.

We remained in the tavern about two days and two nights, when an officer arrived with authority from General Clark to take us back to Richmond, Ray county, where the general had arrived with his army to await our arrival. But on the morning of our start for Richmond, we were informed, by General Wilson, that it was expected by the soldiers that we would be hung up by the necks on the road, while on the march to that place, and that it was prevented by a demand made for us by General Clark, who had the command in consequence of seniority; and that it was his prerogative to execute us himself; and he should give us up into the hands of the officer, who would take us to General Clark, and he might do with us as he pleased.

During our stay at Independence, the officers informed us that there were eight or ten horses in that place belonging to the Mormon people, which had been stolen by the soldiers, and that we might have two of them to ride upon, if we would cause them to be sent back to the owners after our arrival at Richmond.

We accepted them, and they were ridden to Richmond, and the owners came there and got them.

We started in the morning under our new officer, Colonel Price, of Keytsville, Chariton county, with several other men to guard us.

We arrived there on Friday evening, the 9th day of November, and were thrust into an old log house, with a strong guard placed over us.

After we had been there for the space of half an hour, there came in a man who was said to have some notoriety in the penitentiary, bringing in his hands a quantity of chains and padlocks. He said he was commanded by General Clark to put us in chains.

Immediately the soldiers rose up, and pointing their guns at us, placed their thumb on the cock, and their finger on the trigger; and the state's prison-keeper went to work, putting a chain around the leg of each man, and fastening it on with a padlock, until we were all chained together—seven of us.

In a few moments General Clark came in. We requested to know of him what was the cause of all this harsh and cruel treatment. He refused to give us any information at that time, but said he would in a few days;

so we were compelled to continue in that situation camping on the floor, all chained together, without any chance or means to be made comfortable, having to eat our victuals as it was served up to us, using our fingers and teeth instead of knives and forks.

Whilst we were in this situation, a young man of the name of Jedediah M. Grant, brother-in-law to my brother William Smith, came to see us, and put up at the tavern where General Clark made his quarters. He happened to come in time to see General Clark make choice of his men to shoot us on Monday morning, the 12th day of November. He saw them make choice of their rifles, and load them with two balls in each; and after they had prepared their guns, General Clark saluted them by saying, *"Gentlemen, you shall have the honor of shooting the Mormon leaders on Monday morning at eight o'clock!"*

But in consequence of the influence of our friend, the inhuman general was intimidated, so that he dared not carry his murderous designs into execution, and sent a messenger immediately to Fort Leavenworth to obtain the military code of laws. After the messenger's return the general was employed nearly a whole week examining the laws; so Monday passed away without our being shot. However, it seemed like foolishness to me that so great a man as General Clark pretended to be should have to search the military law to find out whether preachers of the Gospel, who never did military duty, could be subject to court-martial.

However, the general seemed to learn that fact after searching the military code, and came into the old log cabin where we were under guard and in chains, and told us he had concluded to deliver us over to the civil authorities as persons guilty of "treason, murder, arson, larceny, theft, and stealing." The poor deluded general did not know the difference between theft, larceny, and stealing.

Accordingly, we were handed over to the pretended civil authorities, and the next morning our chains were taken off, and we were guarded to the court-house, where there was a pretended court in session, Austin A. King being the judge, and Mr. Birch the district attorney—the two extremely and very honorable gentlemen who sat on the court-martial when we were sentenced to be shot!

Witnesses were called up and sworn at the point of the bayonet; and if they would not swear to the things they were told to do, they were threatened with instant death; and I do know positively that the evidence given in by those men whilst under duress was false.

This state of things continued twelve or fourteen days; and after that time, we were ordered by the judge to introduce some rebutting evidence—saying that, if we did not do it, we should be thrust into prison.

I could hardly understand what the judge meant, for I considered we were in prison already, and could not think of anything but the persecutions of the days of Nero, knowing that it was a religious persecution, and the court an inquisition. However, we gave him the names of forty persons who were acquainted with all the persecutions and sufferings of the people.

The judge made out a subpoena and inserted the names of those men, and caused it to be placed in the hands of Bogart, the notorious Methodist minister; and he took fifty armed soldiers and started for Far West. I saw the subpoenas given to him and his company, when they started.

In the course of a few days they returned with almost all those forty men whose names were inserted in the subpoenas, and thrust them into jail, and we were not permitted to bring one of them before the court. But the judge turned upon us with an air of indignation and said, "Gentlemen, you must get your witnesses, or you shall be committed to jail immediately; for we are not going to hold the court open on expense much longer for you anyhow."

We felt very much distressed and oppressed at that time. Colonel Wight said, "What shall we do? Our witnesses are all thrust into prison, and probably will be; and we have no power to do anything. Of course, we must submit to this tyranny and oppression: we cannot help ourselves."

Several others made similar expressions in the agony of their souls; but my brother Joseph did not say anything, he being sick at that time with the toothache and pain in his face, in consequence of a severe cold brought on by being exposed to the severity of the weather.

However, it was considered best by General Doniphan and lawyer Rees that we should try to get some witnesses before the pretended court.

Accordingly, I gave the names of about twenty other persons. The Judge inserted them in a subpoena, and caused it to be placed into the hands of Bogart, the Methodist priest; and he again started off with his fifty soldiers to take those men prisoners, as he had done the forty others.

The Judge sat and laughed at the good opportunity of getting the names, that they might the more easily capture them, and so bring them down to be thrust into prison, in order to prevent us from getting the truth before the pretended court, of which he was the chief inquisitor or conspirator. Bogart returned from his second expedition with one witness only, whom he also thrust into prison.

The people at Far West had learned the intrigue, and had left the state, having been made acquainted with the treatment of the former witnesses.

But we, on learning that we could not obtain witnesses, whilst privately consulting with each other what we should do, discovered a Mr.

Allen standing by the window on the outside of the house. We beckoned to him as though we would have him come in. He immediately came in.

At that time Judge King retorted upon us again, saying, "Gentlemen, are you not going to introduce some witnesses?"—also saying it was the last day he should hold court open for us; and that if we did not rebutt the testimony that had been given against us, he should have to commit us to jail.

I had then got Mr. Allen into the house and before the court (so called). I told the Judge we had one witness, if he would be so good as to put him under oath. He seemed unwilling to do so; but after a few moments consultation, the State's Attorney arose and said he should object to that witness being sworn, and that he should object to that witness giving in his evidence at all, stating that this was not a court to try the case, but only a court of investigation on the part of the state.

Upon this, General Doniphan arose and said, "He would be ———— ———— if the witness should not be sworn, and that it was a damned shame that these defendants should be treated in this manner,—that they could not be permitted to get one witness before the court, whilst all their witnesses, even forty at a time, have been taken by force of arms and thrust into that damned 'bull pen,' in order to prevent them from giving their testimony."

After Doniphan sat down, the Judge permitted the witness to be sworn and enter upon his testimony, but as soon as he began to speak, a man by the name of Cook, who was a brother-in-law to priest Bogart, the Methodist, and who was a lieutenant, [in the state militia] and whose duty at that time was to superintend the guard, stepped in before the pretended court, and took him by the nape of his neck and jammed his head down under the pole, or log of wood, that was around the place where the inquisition was sitting to keep the bystanders from intruding upon the majesty of the inquisitors, and jammed him along to the door, and kicked him out of doors. He instantly turned to some soldiers who were standing by him, and said to them, "Go and shoot him, damn him; shoot him, damn him."

The soldiers ran after the man to shoot him. He fled for his life, and with great difficulty made his escape. The pretended court immediately arose, and we were ordered to be carried to Liberty, Clay county, and there to be thrust into jail. We endeavored to find out for what cause; but all we could learn was, that it was because we were "Mormons."

The next morning a large wagon drove up to the door, and a blacksmith came into the house with some chains and handcuffs. He said his orders were from the Judge to handcuff us and chain us together. He informed us that the Judge had made out a mittimus and sentenced us to jail for treason. He also said the Judge had done this that we might not get bail. He also said the Judge declared his intention to keep us in jail until all the "Mormons" were driven out of the state. He also said that the Judge had further declared that if he let us out before the "Mormons" had left the state, we would not let them leave, and there would be another damned fuss kicked up. I also heard the Judge say, whilst he was sitting in his pretended court, that there was no law for us, nor for the "Mormons" in the state of Missouri; that he had sworn to see them exterminated and to see the Governor's order executed to the very letter; and that he would do so. However, the blacksmith proceeded and put the irons upon us, and we were ordered into the wagon, and they drove off for Clay county. As we journeyed along on the road, we were exhibited to the inhabitants, and this course was adopted all the way, thus making a public exhibition of us, until we arrived at Liberty, Clay county.

There we were thrust into prison again, and locked up, and were held there in close confinement for the space of six months; and our place of lodging [bed] was the square side of a hewed white oak log, and our food was anything but good and decent. Poison was administered to us three or four times. The effect it had upon our system was, that it vomited us almost to death; and then we would lie some two or three days in a torpid, stupid state, not even caring or wishing for life,—the poison being administered in too large doses, or it would inevitably have proved fatal, had not the power of Jehovah interposed in our behalf, to save us from their wicked purpose.

We were also subjected to the necessity of eating human flesh for the space of five days or go without food, except a little coffee or a little corn-bread. The latter I chose in preference to the former. We none of us partook of the flesh, except Lyman Wight. We also heard the guard which was placed over us making sport of us, saying they had fed us on "Mormon" beef. I have described the appearance of this flesh to several experienced physicians and they have decided that it was human flesh. We learned afterwards, by one of the guard, that it was supposed that that act of savage cannibalism in feeding us with human flesh would be considered a popular deed of notoriety: but the people, on learning that it would not take, tried to keep it secret; but the fact was noised abroad before they took that precaution.

Whilst we were incarcerated in prison we petitioned the Supreme Court of the state of Missouri for [a writ of] habeas corpus twice but were refused both times by Judge Reynolds, who is now [1843] the Governor of that state. We also petitioned one of the county Judges for a writ of habeas corpus, which was granted in about three weeks afterwards, but were not permitted to have any trial. We were only taken out of jail and kept out for a few hours, and then remanded back again.

In the course of three or four days after that time, Judge Turnham came into the jail in the evening, and said he had permitted Mr. Rigdon to get bail, but said he had to do it in the night, and had also to get away in the night and unknown to any of the citizens, or they would kill him; for they had sworn to kill him, if they could find him. And as to the rest of us, he dared not let us go, for fear of his own life as well as ours. He said it was damned hard to be confined under such circumstances, for he knew we were innocent men; and he said *the people also knew it*; and that it was only a persecution, and treachery, and the scenes of Jackson county acted over again, for fear that we should become too numerous in that upper country. He said that the plan was concocted from the governor down to the lowest judge and that damned Baptist priest, Riley, who was riding into town every day to watch the people, stirring up the minds of the people against us all he could, exciting them and stirring up their religious prejudices against us, for fear they would let us go. Mr. Rigdon, however, got bail and made his escape into Illinois.

The jailer, Samuel Tillery, Esq., told us also that the whole plan was concocted by the governor down to the lowest judge in that upper country early in the previous spring, and that the plan was more fully carried out at the time that General Atchison went down to Jefferson city with Generals Wilson, Lucas, and Gillium, the self-styled Delaware Chief. This was sometime in the month of September, when the mob were collected at De Witt, in Carroll county. He also told us that the governor was now ashamed enough of the whole transaction, and would be glad to set us at liberty, if he dared do it. "But," said he, "you need not be concerned, for the governor has laid a plan for your release." He also said that Squire Birch, the state's attorney, was appointed to be circuit judge on the circuit passing through Daviess county, and that he (Birch) was instructed to fix the papers, so that we should be sure to be clear from any incumbrance in a very short time.

Some time in April we were taken to Daviess county, as they said, to have a trial. But when we arrived at that place, instead of finding a court or jury, we found another inquisition; and Birch, who was the district attorney, the same man who had been one of the court-martial when we were sentenced to death, was now the circuit judge of that pretended court; and the grand jury that were empannelled were all at the massacre at Haun's Mills and lively actors in that awful, solemn, disgraceful, cool-blooded murder; and all the pretense they made of excuse was, they had done it because the governor ordered them to do it.

The same men sat as a jury in the day time, and were placed over us as a guard in the night time. They tantalized us and boasted of their great achievments at Haun's Mills and at other places, telling us how many houses they had burned, and how many sheep, cattle, and hogs they had driven off belonging to the "Mormons," and how many rapes they had committed, and what squealing and kicking there was among the d——b——s, saying that they lashed one woman upon one of the damned "Mormon" meeting benches, tying her hands and her feet fast, and sixteen of them abused her as much as they had a mind to, and then left her bound and exposed in that distressed condition. These fiends of the lower regions boasted of these acts of barbarity, and tantalized our feelings with them for ten days. We had heard of these acts of cruelty previous to this time, but we were slow to believe that such acts had been perpetrated. The lady who was the subject of this brutality did not recover her health to be able to help herself for more than three months afterwards.

This grand jury constantly celebrated their achievements with grog and glass in hand, like the Indian warriors at their war dances, singing and telling each other of their exploits in murdering the "Mormons," in plundering their houses and carrying off their property. At the end of every song they would bring in the chorus, "G—— d——, G—— d——, G—— d——, Jesus Christ, G—— d—— the Presbyterians, G—— d—— the Baptists, G—— d—— the Methodists," reitering one sect after another in the same manner, until they came to the "Mormons." To them it was, G—— d—— the G—— d—— Mormons, we have sent them to hell." Then they would slap their hands and shout, Hosanna! Hosanna! Glory to God! and fall down on their backs and kick with their feet a few moments. Then they would pretend to have swooned away into a glorious trance, in order to imitate some of the transactions at camp meetings. Then they would pretend to come out of the trance, and would shout and again slap their hands and jump up, while one would take a bottle of whisky and a tumbler, and turn it out full of whisky, and pour down each other's necks, crying, "Damn it, take it; you must take it!" And if anyone refused to drink the whisky, others would clinch him and hold him, whilst another poured it down his neck; and what did not go down the inside went down the outside. This is a part of the farce acted out by the grand jury of Daviess county, whilst they stood over us as guards for ten nights successively. And all this in the presence of the *great Judge Birch*, who had previously said, in our hearing, that there was no law for the "Mormons" in the state of Missouri. His brother was there acting as district attorney in that circuit, and, if anything, was a greater ruffian than the judge.

After all their ten days of drunkenness, we were informed that we were indicted for *"treason, murder, arson, larceny, theft, and stealing."*

We asked for a change of venue from that county to Marion county; they would not grant it; but they gave us a change of venue from Daviess to Boone county, and a mittimus was made out by Judge Birch, without date, name, or place.

They fitted us out with a two-horse wagon, and horses, and four men, besides the sheriff, to be our guard. There were five of us. We started from Gallatin in the afternoon, the sun about two hours high, and went as far as Diahman that evening and stayed till morning. There we bought two horses of the guard, and paid for one of them in clothing, which we had with us; and for the other we gave our note.

We went down that day as far as Judge Morin's—a distance of some four or five miles. There we stayed until the next morning, when we started on our journey to Boone county, and traveled on the road about twenty miles distance. There we bought a jug of whisky, with which we treated the company; and while there the sheriff showed us the mittimus before referred to, without date or signature, and said that Judge Birch told him never to carry us to Boone county, and never to show the mittimus; and, said he, I shall take a good drink of grog and go to bed, and you may do as you have a mind to.

Three others of the guard drank pretty freely of whisky, sweetened with honey. They also went to bed, and were soon asleep, and the other guard went along with us, and helped to saddle the horses.

Two of us mounted the horses, and the other three started on foot, and we took our change of venue for the state of Illinois, and in the course of nine or ten days arrived safe at Quincy, Adams county, where we found our families in a state of poverty, although in good health, they having been driven out of the state previously by the murderous militia, under the exterminating order of the executive of Missouri; and now [1843] the people of that state, a portion of them, would be glad to make the people of this state [Illinois] believe that my brother Joseph had committed treason, for the purpose of keeping up their murderous and hellish persecution; and they seem to be unrelenting and thirsting for the blood of innocence; for I do know most positively that my brother Joseph has not committed treason, nor violated one solitary item of law or rule in the state of Missouri.

But I do know that the "Mormon" people, *en masse*, were driven out of that state, after being robbed of all they had; and they barely escaped with their lives, as also my brother Joseph, who barely escaped with his life. His family also were robbed of all they had, and barely escaped with the skin of their teeth, and all this in consequence of the exterminating order of Governor Boggs, the same being sanctioned by the legislature of the state.

And I do know, so does this court, and every rational man who is acquainted with the circumstances, and every man who shall hereafter become acquainted with the particulars thereof, will know that Governor Boggs and Generals Clark, Lucas, Wilson, and Gillium, also Austin A. King, have committed treason upon the citizens of Missouri, and did violate the Constitution of the United States, and also the constitution and laws of the state of Missouri, and did exile and expel, at the point of the bayonet, some twelve or fourteen thousand inhabitants from the state, and did murder a large number of men, women and children in cold blood, and in the most horrid and cruel manner possible; and the whole of it was caused by religious bigotry and persecution, because the "Mormons" dared to worship Almighty God according to the dictates of their own consciences, and agreeable to His divine will as revealed in the scriptures of eternal truth, and had turned away from following the vain traditions of their fathers, and would not worship according to the dogmas and commandments of those men who preach for hire and divine for money, and teach for doctrine the precepts of men; the Saints expecting that the Constitution of the United States would have protected them therein.

But notwithstanding the "Mormon" people had purchased upwards of *two hundred thousand dollars' worth of land*, most of which was entered and paid for at the land office of the United States, in the state of Missouri; and although the President of the United States has been made acquainted with these facts and the particulars of our persecutions and oppressions, by petition to him and to Congress, yet they have not even attempted to restore the "Mormons" to their rights, or given any assurance that we may hereafter expect redress from them. And I do also know most positively and assuredly that my brother Joseph Smith, Sen., has not been in the state of Missouri since the spring of the year 1839. And further this deponent saith not.

[Signed] HYRUM SMITH.

[Sworn to before the Municipal Court, Nauvoo, IL, 1 Jul 1843.]

PRATT, Parley P. *HC*[3]

Parley P. Pratt, sworn, says that he fully concurs in the testimony of the preceding witness, so far as he is acquainted with the same; and that Joseph Smith has not been known as Joseph Smith, Jun., for the time stated by Hyrum Smith. He was an eye-witness of most of the scenes testified to

---

[3] 3:424–32; also found in JH 1 Jul 1843.

by said Hyrum Smith, during the persecutions of our people in Missouri. That during the latter part of summer and fall of the year 1838, there were large bodies of the mob assembled in various places for the avowed object of driving, robbing, plundering, killing, and exterminating the "Mormons," and they actually committed many murders and other depredations, as related by the preceding witness.

The Governor was frequently petitioned, as also the other authorities, for redress and protection. At length, Austin A. King, the Judge of the Circuit court of the Fifth Judicial District, ordered out somewhere near a thousand men, for the avowed purpose of quelling the mob and protecting the "Mormons." These being under arms for several weeks, did in some measure prevent the mob's proceedings for some time. After which, Judge King withdrew the force, refusing to put the State to further expense for our protection without orders from the Governor.

The mobs then again collected in great numbers, in Carroll, Daviess, and Caldwell counties, and expressed their determination to drive the "Mormons" from the State or kill them. They did actually drive them from De Witt, firing upon some, and taking other prisoners.

They turned a man by the name of Smith Humphrey and family out of doors, when sick, and plundered his house and burned it before his eyes. They also plundered the citizens generally, taking their lands, houses, and property.

Those whose lives were spared, precipitately fled to Far West in the utmost distress and consternation. Some of them actually died on the way, through exposure, suffering and destitution. Other parties of the mob were plundering and burning houses in Daviess county, and another party of the mob were ravaging the south part of Caldwell county in a similar manner.

The Governor was again and again petitioned for redress and protection, but utterly refused to render us any assistance whatever. Under these painful and distressing circumstances, we had the advice of Generals Atchison, Doniphan and Parks to call out the militia of Caldwell and Daviess counties, which was mostly composed of "Mormons" and to make a general defense.

The presiding Judge of Caldwell county, Elias Higbee, gave orders to the sheriff of said county to call out the militia. They were called out under the command of Colonel Hinkle, who held a commission from the Governor, and was the highest military officer in the county. This force effectually dispersed the mob in several places, and a portion of them were so organized in the city of Far West, that they could assemble themselves upon the shortest notice, and were frequently ordered to assemble in the public square of said city, in cases of emergency.

These proceedings against the mob being misrepresented by designing men, both to the Governor and other authorities and people of the State, caused great excitement against the "Mormons." Many tried to have it understood that the "Mormons" were in open rebellion, and making war upon the State.

With these pretenses, Governor Boggs issued the following:—

Exterminating Order.

HEADQUARTERS OF THE MILITIA,
CITY OF JEFFERSON, OCTOBER 27, 1838.

Gen. John B. Clark.

SIR:—Since the order of the morning to you, directing you to come with 400 mounted men to be raised within your division, I have received, by Amos Rees, Esq., of Ray county, and Wiley C. Williams, Esq., one of my aides, information of the most appalling character, which entirely changes the face of things, and places the "Mormons" in the attitude of an open and avowed defiance of the laws, and of having made war upon the people of this State.

Your orders are, therefore, to hasten your operations with all possible speed. The "Mormons" must be treated as enemies, and must be exterminated or driven from the State, if necessary, for the public peace.

Their outrages are beyond all descriptions. If you can increase your force, you are authorized to do so to any extent you may consider necessary. I have just issued orders to Major-General Willock, of Marion county, to raise 500 men, and to march them to the northern part of Daviess [county],[4] and there unite with General Doniphan, of Clay, who has been ordered with 500 men to proceed to the same point for the purpose of intercepting the retreat of the "Mormons" to the north. They have been directed to communicate with you by express. You can also communicate with them, if you find it necessary.

Instead, therefore, of proceeding as at first directed, to reinstate the citizens of Daviess, in their homes, you will proceed immediately to Richmond, and there operate against the "Mormons."

Brigadier General Parks, of Ray, has been ordered to have 400 of his brigade in readiness to join you at Richmond. The whole force will be placed under your command.

I am very respectfully your ob't Serv't

L. W. BOGGS,
COMMANDER-IN-CHIEF.

---

[4]The editorial brackets from *History of the Church* have been maintained.

In the meantime Major-General Lucas and Brigadier-General Wilson, both of Jackson county, (who had, five years previously, assisted in driving about 1,200 "Mormon" citizens from that county, besides burning 203 houses, and assisted in murdering several, and plundering the rest), raised forces to the amount of several thousand men, and appeared before the city of Far West in Battle array.

A few of the militia then paraded in front of the city, which caused the cowardly assailants to come to a halt at about a mile distant, in full view of the town.

A messenger arrived from them and demanded three persons before they massacred the rest and laid the town in ashes. The names of the persons demanded were Adam Lightner, John Clemenson, and his wife. They gave no information who this army were, nor by what authority they came; neither had we at that time any knowledge of the governor's order, nor any of these movements, the mail having been designedly stopped by our enemies for three weeks previously. We had supposed, on their first appearance, that they were friendly troops sent for our protection; but on receiving this alarming information of their wicked intentions, we were much surprised, and sent a messenger with a white flag to inquire of them who they were, and what they wanted of us, and by whose authority they came.

This flag was fired upon by Captain Bogart, the Methodist priest, who afterwards told me the same with his own mouth. After several attempts, however, we got an interview, by which we learned who they were, and that they pretended to have been sent by the governor to exterminate our people.

Upon learning this fact no resistance was offered to their will or wishes. They demanded the arms of the militia, and forcibly took them away. They requested that Mr. Joseph Smith and other leaders of the Church should come into their camp for consultation, giving them a sacred promise of protection and safe return. Accordingly, Messrs. Joseph Smith, Sidney Rigdon, Lyman Wight, George W. Robinson, and myself started in company with Colonel Hinkle to their camp when we were soon abruptly met by General Lucas with several hundred of his soldiers, in a hostile manner, who immediately surrounded us, and set up the most hideous yells that might have been supposed to have proceeded from the mouths of demons, and marched us as prisoners within their lines.

There we were detained for two days and nights, and had to sleep on the ground, in the cold month of November, in the midst of rain and mud, and were continually surrounded with a strong guard, whose mouths were filled with cursing and bitterness, blackguardism and blasphemy—who offered us every abuse and insult in their power, both by night and day;

and many individuals of the army cocked their rifles and, taking deadly aim at our heads, swore they would shoot us.

While under these circumstances, our ears were continually shocked with the relation of the horrid deeds they had committed and which they boasted of. They related the circumstance in detail of having, the previous day, disarmed a certain man in his own house, and took him prisoner, and afterwards *beat out his brains with his own gun,* in presence of their officers. They told of other individuals lying here and there in the brush, whom they had shot down without resistance, and who were lying unburied for the hogs to feed upon.

They also named one or two individual females of our society, whom they had forcibly bound, and twenty or thirty of them, one after another, committed rape upon them. One of these females was a daughter of a respectable family with whom I have been long acquainted, and with whom I have since conversed and learned that it was truly the case. Delicacy at present forbids my mentioning the names. I also heard several of the soldiers acknowledge and boast of having stolen money in one place, clothing and bedding in another, and horses in another, whilst corn, pork, and beef were taken by the whole army to support the men and horses; and in many cases cattle, hogs, and sheep were shot down, and only a small portion of them used—the rest left to waste. Of these crimes, of which the soldiers boasted, the general officers freely conversed and corroborated the same. And even General Doniphan, who professed to be opposed to such proceedings, acknowledged the truth of them, and gave us several particulars in detail.

I believe the name of the man whose brains they knocked out was Carey, Another individual had his money chest broken open and several hundred dollars in specie taken out. He was the same Smith Humphrey whose house the mob burned at De Witt.

After the "Mormons" were all disarmed, General Lucas gave a compulsory order for men, women, and children to leave the state forthwith, without any exceptions, counting it a mercy to spare their lives on these conditions. Whilst these things were proceeding, instead of releasing us from confinement, Hyrum Smith and Amasa Lyman were forcibly added to our number as prisoners; and under a large military escort, commanded by General Wilson before mentioned, we were all marched to Jackson county, a distance of between fifty and sixty miles, leaving our families and our friends at the mob's mercy, in a destitute condition, to prepare for a journey of more than two hundred miles, at the approach of winter, without our protection, and every moment exposed to robbery, ravishment, and other insults, their personal property robbed and their houses and lands already wrested from them.

We were exhibited like a caravan of wild animals on the way and in the streets of Independence, and were also kept prisoners for a show for several days.

In the meantime, General Clark had been sent by Governor Boggs with an additional force of 6,000 men from the lower country, to join General Lucas in his operations against the "Mormons." He soon arrived before Far West with his army, and confirmed all Lucas had done, and highly commended them for their virtue, forbearance, and other deeds in *bringing about so peaceable and amicable an adjustment of affairs.* He kept up the same scene of ravage, plunder, ravishment, and depredation, for the support and enrichment of his army, even burning the houses and fences for fuel.

He also insisted that every man, woman, and child of the "Mormon" society should leave the state, except such as he detained as prisoners, stating that *the governor had sent him to exterminate them,* but that *he* would, as a *mercy, spare* their *lives,* and gave them until the first of April following to get out of the state.

He also compelled them, at the point of the bayonet, to sign a deed of trust of all their real estate, to defray the expenses of what *he* called *"The Mormon War."*

After arranging all these matters to *his* satisfaction, he returned to Richmond, thirty miles distant, taking about sixty men, heads of families, with him, and marching them through a severe snowstorm on foot, as prisoners, leaving their families in a perishing condition.

Having established his headquarters at Richmond, Ray county, he sent to General Lucas and demanded us to be given up to him. We were accordingly transported some thirty or forty miles, delivered over to him, and put in close confinement in chains, under a strong guard.

At length we obtained an interview with him, and inquired why we were detained as prisoners. I said to him, "Sir, we have now been prisoners, under the most aggravating circumstances, for two or three weeks, during which time we have received no information as to why we are prisoners, or for what object, and no writ has been served upon us. We are not detained by the civil law; and as ministers of the Gospel in time of peace, *who never bear arms,* we cannot be considered prisoners of war, especially as there has been no war; and from present appearances, we can hardly be considered prisoners of hope. Why, then, these bonds?" Said he, "You were taken to be tried." "Tried by what authority?" said I. "By court-martial," replied he. "By court-martial?" said I. "Yes," said he. "How," said I, "can men who are not military men, but ministers of the Gospel, be tried by court-martial in this country, where every man has a right to be tried by a jury?" He replied, it was according to the treaty with General Lucas, on the part of the state of Missouri, and Colonel Hinkle, the commanding officer of the fortress of Far West, on the part of the "Mormons," and in accordance with the governor's order. "And," said he, "I approve of all that Lucas has done, and am determined to see it fulfilled." Said I, "Colonel Hinkle was but a colonel of the Caldwell county militia, and commissioned by the governor, and the 'Mormons' had no fortress, but were, in common with others, citizens of Missouri; and therefore we recognize no authority in Colonel Hinkle to sell our liberties or make treaties for us."

Several days afterwards, General Clark again entered our prison, and said he had concluded to deliver us over to the civil authorities. Accordingly, we were soon brought before Austin A. King, judge of the Fifth Judicial Circuit, where an examination was commenced, and witnesses sworn, at the point of the bayonet, and threatened on pain of death, if they did not swear to that which would suit the court.

During this examination, I heard Judge King ask one of the witnesses, who was a "Mormon," if he and his friends intended to live on their lands any longer than April, and to plant crops? Witness replied, "Why not?" The judge replied, "If you once think to plant crops or to occupy your lands any longer than the first of April, the citizens will be upon you; they will kill you every one—men, women and children, and leave you to manure the ground without a burial. They have been mercifully withheld from doing this on the present occasion, but will not be restrained for the future."

On examining a "Mormon" witness, for the purpose of substantiating the charge of treason against Mr. Joseph Smith, he questioned him concerning our religious faith:—1st. Do the Mormons send missionaries to foreign nations? The witness answered in the affirmative. 2nd. Do the Mormons believe in a certain passage in the Book of Daniel (naming the passage) which reads as follows:—"And the kingdom and dominion, and the greatness of the kingdom under the whole heaven, shall be given to the people of the Saints of the Most High, whose kingdom is an everlasting kingdom, and all dominions shall serve and obey him?" (Dan. 7:27.) On being answered in the affirmative, the judge ordered the scribe to put it down as a strong point for treason; but this was *too* much for even a Missouri lawyer to bear. He remonstrated against such a course of procedure, but in vain. Said he, "Judge, you had better make the Bible treason."

After an examination of this kind for many days, some were set at liberty, others [were] admitted to bail, and themselves and [those who went their] bail [were] expelled from the state forthwith, with the rest of the "Mormon" citizens, and Joseph Smith, Hyrum Smith, Sidney Rigdon, Lyman Wight, and others, were committed to the Clay county jail for further trial. Two or three others and myself were put into the jail at Ray county for the same purpose.

The "Mormon" people now began to leave the state, agreeably to the exterminating order of Governor Boggs. Ten or twelve thousand left the state during the winter, and fled to the state of Illinois.

A small number of the widows and the poor, together with my family and some of the friends of the other prisoners, still lingered in Far West, when a small band of armed men entered the town and committed many depredations and threatened life; and swore that if my wife and children, and others whom they named, were not out of the state in so many days, they would kill them, as the time now drew near for the completion of the exterminating order of Governor Boggs.

Accordingly, my wife and children and others left the state as best they could, wandered to the state of Illinois, there to get a living among strangers, without a husband, father or protector. Myself and party still remained in prison, after all the other "Mormons" had left the state; and even Mr. Smith and his party had escaped.

In June, by change of venue, we were removed from Ray county to Columbia, Boone county, upwards of one hundred miles towards the state of Illinois; and by our request a special court was called for final trial. But notwithstanding we were removed more than one hundred miles from the scenes of the depredations of the mob, yet such was the fact, that neither our friends nor witnesses dare come into that state to attend our trial, as they had been banished from the state by the governor's order of extermination, executed to the very letter by the principal officers of the state, civil and military.

On these grounds, and having had all these opportunities to know, I testify that neither Mr. Smith nor any other "Mormon" has the least prospect for justice, or to receive a fair and impartial trial in the state of Missouri.

If tried at all, they must be tried by authorities who have trampled all law under their feet, and who have assisted in committing murder, robbery, treason, arson, rape, burglary and felony, and who have made a law of banishment, contrary to the laws of all nations, and executed this barbarous law with the utmost rigor and severity.

Therefore, Mr. Smith, and the "Mormons" generally, having suffered without regard to law, having been expelled from the state, Missouri has no further claims whatever upon any of them.

I furthermore testify that the authorities of other states who would assist Missouri to wreak further vengeance upon any individual of the persecuted "Mormons," are either ignorantly or willfully aiding and abetting in all these crimes.

Cross-examined he stated that he was very intimate with Mr. Smith all the time he resided in the state of Missouri, and was with him almost daily; and that he knows positively that Mr. Smith held no office, either civil or military, either real or pretended, in that state; and that he never bore arms or did military duty, not even in self-defense; but that he was a peaceable, law-abiding and faithful citizen, and a preacher of the Gospel, and exhorted all the citizens to be peaceable, long-suffering and slow to act even in self-defense.

He further stated that there was no fortress in Far West, but a temporary fence made of rails, house logs, floor planks, wagons, carts, etc., hastily thrown together, after being told by General Lucas that they were to be massacred the following morning, and the town burnt to ashes, without giving any information by what authority. And he further states that he only escaped himself from that state by walking out of the jail when the door was open to put in food, and came out in obedience to the governor's order of banishment, and to fulfill the same.

PARLEY P. PRATT.

[Sworn to before the Municipal Court, Nauvoo, IL, 1 Jul 1843.]

PITKIN, George W. *HC*[5]

George W. Pitkin sworn. Says that he concurs with the preceding witnesses, Hyrum Smith and Parley P. Pratt, in all the facts with which he is acquainted; that in the summer of 1838 he was elected Sheriff of the county of Caldwell and State of Missouri. That in the fall of the same year, while the county was threatened and infested with mobs, he received an order from Judge Higbee, the presiding Judge of said county, to call out the Militia, and he executed the same.

The said order was presented by Joseph Smith, Sen., who showed the witness a letter from General Atchison, giving such advice as was necessary for the protection of the citizens of said county. Reports of the mobs destroying property were daily received. Has no knowledge that Joseph Smith was concerned in organizing or commanding said Militia in any capacity whatever.

About this time he received information that about forty or fifty "Yauger rifles" and a quantity of ammunition were being conveyed through Caldwell to Daviess county, for the use of the mob, upon which he deputized William Allred to go with a company of men and intercept

---

[5] 3:432–33; also found in JH 1 Jul 1843.

them, if possible. He did so, and brought the said arms and ammunition into Far West, which were afterwards delivered up to the order of Austin A. King, Judge of the Fifth, Circuit in Missouri.

It was generally understood at that time that said arms had been stolen by Neil Gillum and his company of volunteers, who had been upon a six months' tour of service in the war between the United States and the Florida Indians. They were supposed to have been taken from the Fort at Tampa Bay, and brought to Richmond, Clay county, and that Captain Pollard or some other person loaned them to the mob.

He further says that whilst in office as Sheriff, he was forcibly and illegally compelled by Lieutenant Cook, the son-in-law or brother-in-law of Bogart, the Methodist priest, to start for Richmond; and when he demanded of him by what authority he acted, he was shown a bowie-knife and a brace of pistols; and when he asked what they wanted of him, he said they would let him know when he got to Richmond. Many of the citizens of Caldwell county were taken in the same manner, without any legal process whatever, and thrust into prison.

GEORGE W. PITKIN.

[*Sworn to before the Municipal Court, Nauvoo, IL, 1 Jul 1843.*]

YOUNG, Brigham   *HC*[6]

Brigham Young sworn. Says that so far as he was acquainted with the facts stated by the previous witnesses, he concurs with them, and that he accompanied Mr. Joseph Smith, Sen., into the State of Missouri, and arrived at Far West on the 14th day of March, 1838, and was neighbor to Mr. Smith until he was taken by Governor Boggs' Militia a prisoner of war, as they said, and that he was knowing to his character whilst in the State of Missouri; and that he, Mr. Smith, was in no way connected with the Militia of that state, neither did he bear arms at all, nor give advice, but was a peaceable, law-abiding, good citizen, and a true Republican in every sense of the word.

He was with Mr. Smith a great share of the time, until driven out of Missouri by an armed force, under the exterminating order of Governor Boggs.

He heard the most of Mr. Smith's public addresses, and never did he hear him give advice or encourage anything contrary to the laws of the State of Missouri; but, to the contrary, always instructing the people to be

---

[6] 3:433–37; also found in JH 1 Jul 1843.

peaceable, quiet, and law-abiding; and if necessity should compel them to withstand their enemies, by whom they were daily threatened in mobs at various points, that they, the "Mormons," should attend to their business strictly, and not regard reports; and if the mob did come upon them, to contend with them by the strong arm of the law; and if that should fail, our only relief would be self-defense; and be sure and act only upon the defensive. And there were no operations against the mob by the Militia of Caldwell county, only by the advice of Generals Atchison, Doniphan, and Parks.

At the time that the army came in sight of Far West, he observed their approach, and thought some of the Militia of the state had come to the relief of the citizens; but, to his great surprise, he found that they were come to strengthen the hands of the mobs that were around and which immediately joined the army.

A part of these mobs were painted like Indians; and Gillum, their leader, was also painted in a similar manner, and styled himself the "Delaware Chief;" and afterwards he and the rest of the mob claimed and obtained pay as Militia from the state for all the time they were engaged as a mob, as will be seen by reference to the acts of the Legislature.

That there were "Mormon" citizens wounded and murdered by the army under the command of General Lucas; and he verily believes that several women were ravished to death by the soldiery of Lucas and Clark.

He also stated that he saw Joseph Smith, Sidney Rigdon, Parley P. Pratt, Lyman Wight, and George W. Robinson delivered up by Colonel Hinkle to General Lucas, but expected that they would have returned to the city that evening or the next morning, according to agreement, and the pledge of the sacred honor of the officers that they should be allowed to do so; but they did not return at all.

The next morning, General Lucas demanded and took away the arms of the Militia of Caldwell county, (which arms have never been returned), assuring them that they should be protected. But as soon as they obtained possession of the arms, they commenced their ravages by plundering the citizens of their bedding, clothing, money, wearing apparel, and every-thing of value they could lay their hands upon; and also attempting to violate the chastity of the women in sight of their husbands and friends, under the pretence of hunting for prisoners and arms.

The soldiers shot down our oxen, cows, hogs, and fowls at our own doors, taking part away and leaving the rest to rot in the streets. The soldiers also turned their horses into our fields of corn.

Here the witness was shown General Clark's speech, which is as follows, viz.:—

"Gentlemen,—You, whose names are not attached to this list of names, will now have the privilege of going to your fields, and of providing corn, wood, etc., for your families.

"Those that are now taken will go from this to prison, be tried, and receive the due demerit of their crimes; but you (except such as charges may hereafter be preferred against,) are at liberty as soon as the troops are removed that now guard the place, which I shall cause to be done immediately.

"It now devolves upon you to fulfill the treaty that you have entered into, the leading items of which I shall now lay before you.

"The first requires that your leading men be given up to be tried according to law. This you have complied with. The second is, that you deliver up your arms. This has also been attended to. The third stipulation is, that you sign over your properties to defray the expenses that have been incurred on your account. This you have also done.

"Another article yet remains for you to comply with, and that is, that you leave the State forthwith. And whatever may be your feelings concerning this, or whatever your innocence is, it is nothing to me.

"General Lucas (whose military rank is equal with mine,) has made this treaty with you. I approve of it. I should have done the same, had I been here, and am therefore determined to see it executed.

"The character of this state has suffered almost beyond redemption, from the character, conduct, and influence that you have exerted; and we deem it an act of justice to restore her character by every proper means.

"The order of the Governor to me was, that you should be exterminated, and not allowed to remain in the state. And had not your leaders been given up and the terms of the treaty complied with before this time, your families would have been *destroyed* and your houses in *ashes*.

"There is a discretionary power vested in my hands, which, considering your circumstances, I shall exercise for a season. You are indebted to me for this clemency.

"I do not say that you shall go now, but you must not think of staying here another season, or of putting in crops; for the moment you do this, the citizens will be upon you. And if I am called here again, in case of non-compliance with the treaty made, do not think that I shall act as I have done now.

"You need not expect any mercy, but *extermination*; for I am determined the Governor's order shall be executed.

"As for your leaders, do not think—do not imagine for a moment— do not let it enter into your minds that they will be delivered and restored to you again; for their *fate* is fixed—the DIE is cast—their doom is *sealed*.

"I am sorry, gentlemen, to see so many apparently intelligent men found in the situation that you are; and oh! if I could invoke that great Spirit of the unknown God to rest upon and deliver you from that awful chain of superstition and liberate you from those fetters of fanaticism with which you are bound—that you no longer do homage to a man! I would advise you to scatter abroad, and never again organize yourselves with Bishops, Priests, etc., lest you excite the jealousies of the people and subject yourselves to the same calamities that have now come upon you.

"You have always been the aggressors. You have brought upon yourselves these difficulties by being disaffected, and not being subject to rule. And my advice is, that you become as other citizens, lest by a recurrence of these events you bring upon yourselves irretrievable ruin."

When asked by the Court if it was correct, and after reading it, he [Brigham Young][7] replied:—

Yes, as far as it goes; for, continued he, I was present when that speech was delivered, and when fifty-seven of our brethren were betrayed into the hands of our enemies, as prisoners, which was done at the instigation of our open and avowed enemies, such as William E. M'Lellin and others, and the treachery of Colonel Hinkle. In addition to the speech referred to, General Clark said that we must not be seen as many as five together. If you are, said he, the citizens will be upon you and destroy you, but flee immediately out of the state. There was no alternative for them but to flee; that they need not expect any redress, for there was none for them.

With respect to the treaty, the witness further says that there never was any treaty proposed or entered into on the part of the "Mormons," or even thought of. As to the leaders being given up, there was no such contract entered into or thought of by the "Mormons," or any one called a "Mormon," except by Colonel Hinkle. And with respect to the trial of the prisoners at Richmond, I do not consider that tribunal a legal court, but an inquisition, for the following reasons: That Mr. Smith was not allowed any evidence whatever on his part; for the conduct of the Court, as well as the Judge's own words, affirmed that there was no law for "Mormons" in the state of Missouri. He also knew that when Mr. Smith left the state of Missouri, he did not flee from justice, for the plain reason that the officers and the people manifested by their works and their words that there was *no law nor justice* for the people called "Mormons." And further, he knows that Mr. Smith has ever been a strong advocate for the laws and constitutions of his country, and that there was no act of his life

---

[7] The editorial brackets from *History of the Church* have been maintained.

while in the state of Missouri, according to his knowledge, that could be implied or construed in any way whatever to prove him a fugitive from justice, or that he has been guilty of "murder, treason, arson, larceny, theft, and stealing,"—the crimes he was charged with by General Clark, when he delivered him over to the civil authorities; and he supposes that the learned General did not know but that there was a difference between "larceny, theft, and stealing."

The witness also says that they compelled the brethren to sign away their property by executing a Deed of Trust at the point of the bayonet; and that Judge Cameron stood and saw the "Mormons" sign away their property; and then he and others would run and kick up their heels, and said they were glad of it, and "we have nothing to trouble us now." This Judge also said, "G—— d—— them, see how well they feel now." General Clark also said he had authority to make what treaties he pleased, and the Governor would sanction it.

The witness also stated that he never transgressed any of the laws of Missouri, and he never knew a Latter-day Saint break a law while there. He also said that if they would search the records of Clay, Caldwell, or Daviess counties, they could not find one record of crime against a Latter-day Saint, or even in Jackson county, so far as witness knew.

BRIGHAM YOUNG.

[Sworn to before the Municipal Court, Nauvoo, IL, 1 Jul 1843.]

WIGHT, Lyman   *HC*[8]

Lyman Wight sworn, saith that he has been acquainted with Joseph Smith, Sen., for the last twelve years, and that he removed to the state of Missouri in the year 1831, when the Church of Jesus Christ of Latter-day Saints was organized agreeable to the law of the land. No particular difficulty took place until after some hundreds had assembled in that land who believed in the Book of Mormon and revelations which were given through said Joseph Smith, Sen. After nearly two years of peace had elapsed, a strong prejudice among the various sects arose, declaring that Joseph Smith was a false prophet, and ought to die; and I heard hundreds say they had never known the man; but, if they could come across him, they would kill him as soon as they would a rattlesnake. Frequently heard them say of those who believed in the doctrine he promulgated, that, if they did not renounce it, they would exterminate or drive them from the

---

[8] 3:437–49; also found in JH 1 Jul 1843.

county in which they lived. On inquiring of them if they had any prejudice against us, they said "No: but Joe Smith ought to die; and if ever he comes to this county we will kill him, G—— d—— him."

Matters went on thus until some time in the summer of 1833, when mobs assembled in considerable bodies, frequently visiting private houses, threatening the inmates with death and destruction instantly, if they did not renounce Joe Smith as a prophet, and the Book of Mormon. Sometime towards the last of the summer of 1833, they commenced their operations of mobocracy. On account of their priests, by uniting in their prejudices against Joseph Smith, Sen., as I believe, gangs of them thirty to sixty, visited the house of George Bebee, called him out of his house at the hour of midnight, with many guns and pistols pointed at his breast, beat him most inhumanly with clubs and whips; and the same night or night afterwards, this gang unroofed thirteen houses in what was called the Whitmer Branch of the Church in Jackson county. These scenes of mobocracy continued to exist with unabated fury.

Mobs went from house to house, thrusting poles and rails in at the windows and doors of the houses of the Saints, tearing down a number of houses, turning hogs and horses into corn fields, and burning fences. Some time in the month of October they broke into the store of A. S. Gilbert & Co., and I marched up with thirty or forty men to witness the scene, and found a man by the name of McCarty, brickbatting the store door with all fury, the silks, calicos, and other fine goods entwined about his feet, reaching within the door of the store-house. McCarty was arrested and taken before Squire Weston; and although seven persons testified against him, he was acquitted without delay. The next day the witnesses were taken before the same man for false imprisonment, and by the testimony of this one burglar were found guilty and committed to jail.

This so exasperated my feelings that I went with 200 men to inquire into the affair, when I was promptly met by the colonel of the militia, who stated to me that the whole had been a religious farce, and had grown out of a prejudice they had imbibed against said Joseph Smith—a man with whom they were not acquainted. I here agreed that the Church would give up their arms, provided the said Colonel Pitcher would take the arms from the mob. To this the colonel cheerfully agreed, and pledged his honor with that of Lieutenant-Governor Boggs, Samuel C. Owen, and others. This treaty entered into, we returned home, resting assured on their honor that we should not be farther molested. But this solemn contract was violated in every sense of the word.

The arms of the mob were never taken away, and the majority of the militia, to my certain knowledge, were engaged the next day with the mob, (Colonel Pitcher and Boggs not excepted), going from house to house in gangs from sixty to seventy in number, threatening the lives of women and children, if they did not leave forthwith. In this diabolical scene men were chased from their houses and homes without any preparation for themselves or families. I was chased by one of these gangs across an open prairie five miles, without being overtaken, and lay three weeks in the woods, and was three days and three nights without food.

In the meantime my wife and three small children, in a skiff, passed down Big Blue river, a distance of fourteen miles, and crossed over the Missouri river, and there borrowed a rag carpet of one of her friends and made a tent of the same, which was the only shield from the inclemency of the weather during the three weeks of my expulsion from home. Having found my family in this situation, and making some inquiry, I was informed I had been hunted throughout Jackson, Lafayette, and Clay counties, and also the Indian Territory. Having made the inquiry of my family why it was they had so much against me, the answer was, "He believes in Joe Smith and the Book of Mormon, G—— d—— him; and we believe Joe Smith to be a ——— rascal!"

Here, on the banks of the Missouri river, were eight families, exiled from plenteous homes, without one particle of provisions or any other means under the heavens to get any, only by hunting in the forest.

I here built a camp, twelve feet square, against a sycamore log, in which my wife bore me a fine son on the 27th of December. The camp having neither chimney nor floor, nor covering sufficient to shield them from the inclemency of the weather, rendered it intolerable.

In this doleful condition I left my family for the express purpose of making an appeal to the American people to know something of the toleration of such vile and inhuman conduct, and traveled one thousand and three hundred miles through the interior of the United States, and was frequently answered, "that such conduct was not justifiable in a Republican government; yet we feel to say that we fear that Joe Smith is a very bad man, and circumstances alter cases. We would not wish to prejudice a man, but in some circumstances the voice of the people ought to rule."

The most of these expressions were from professors of religion; and in the aforesaid persecution, I saw one hundred and ninety women and children driven thirty miles across the prairie, with three decrepit men only in their company, in the month of November, the ground thinly crusted with sleet; and I could easily follow on their trail by the *blood that flowed from their lacerated feet* on the stubble of the burnt prairie!

This company, not knowing the situation of the country or the extent of Jackson County, built quite a number of cabins, that proved to be in the borders of Jackson county. The mob, infuriated at this, rushed on them in the month of January, 1834, burned these scanty cabins, and scattered the inhabitants to the four winds; from which cause many were taken suddenly ill, and of this illness died. In the meantime, they burned two hundred and three houses and one grist mill, these being the only residences of the Saints in Jackson county.

The most part of one thousand and two hundred Saints who resided in Jackson county, made their escape to Clay county. I would here remark that among one of the companies that went to Clay county was a woman named Sarah Ann Higbee, who had been sick of chills and fever for many months, and another of the name of Keziah Higbee, who, under the most delicate circumstances, lay on the banks of the river, without shelter, during one of the most stormy nights I ever witnessed, while torrents of rain poured down during the whole night, and streams of the smallest size were magnified into rivers. The former was carried across the river, apparently a lifeless corpse. The latter was delivered of a fine son on the banks, within twenty minutes after being carried across the river, under the open conopy of heaven; and from which cause I have every reason to believe she died a premature death.

The only consolation they received from the mob, under these circumstances, was, "G—— d—— you, do you believe in Joe Smith now?" During this whole time, the said Joseph Smith, Sen., lived in Ohio, in the town of Kirtland, according to the best of my knowledge and belief, a distance of eleven hundred miles from Jackson county, and I think that the Church in Missouri had but little correspondence with him during that time.

We now found ourselves mostly in Clay county—some in negro cabins, some in gentlemen's kitchens, some in old cabins that had been out of use for years, and others in the open air, without anything to shelter them from the dreary storms of a cold and severe winter.

Thus, like men of servitude, we went to work to obtain a scanty living among the inhabitants of Clay county. Every advantage which could be taken of a people under these circumstances was not neglected by the people of Clay county. A great degree of friendship prevailed between the Saints and the people, under these circumstances, for the space of two years, when the Saints commenced purchasing some small possessions for themselves. This, together with the immigration, created a jealousy on the part of the old citizens that we were to be their servants no longer.

This raised an apparent indignation, and the first thing expressed in this excitement was, "You believe too much in Joe Smith." Consequently, they commenced catching the Saints in the streets, whipping some of them until their bowels gushed out, and leaving others for dead in the streets.

This so exasperated the Saints that they mutually agreed with the citizens of Clay county that they would purchase an entire new county north of Ray and cornering on Clay. There being not more than forty or fifty inhabitants in this new county, they freely sold out their possessions to the Saints, who immediately set in to enter the entire county from the general government.

The county having been settled, the governor issued an order for the organization of the county and of a regiment of militia; and an election being called for a colonel of said regiment, I was elected unanimously, receiving 236 votes in August, 1837; we then organized with subaltern officers, according to the statutes of the state, and received legal and lawful commissions from Governor Boggs for the same.

I think, some time in the latter part of the winter, said Joseph Smith moved to the district of country the Saints had purchased, and he settled down like other citizens of a new county, and was appoined the first Elder in the Church of Jesus Christ of Latter-day Saints, holding no office in the county, either civil or military. I declare that I never knew said Joseph Smith to dictate, by his influence or otherwise, any of the officers, either civil or military; he himself being exempt from military duty from the amputation, from his leg, of a part of a bone, on account of a fever sore.

I removed from Caldwell to Daviess county, purchased a pre-emption right, for which I gave seven hundred and fifty dollars, gained another by the side thereof, put in a large crop, and became acquainted with the citizens of Daviess, who appeared very friendly.

In the month of June or July there was a town laid off, partly on my pre-emption and partly on lands belonging to government. The immigration commenced flowing to this newly laid off town very rapidly. This excited a prejudice in the minds of some of the old citizens, who were an ignorant set, and not very far advanced before the aborigines of the country in civilization or cultivated minds. They feared that this rapid tide of immigration should deprive them of office, of which they were dear lovers. This was more plainly exhibited at the August election in the year 1838. The old settlers then swore that not one "Mormon" should vote at that election; accordingly they commenced operations by fist and skull. This terminated in the loss of some teeth, some flesh, and some blood. The combat being very strongly contested on both sides, many Mormons were deprived of their votes, and I was followed to the polls by three ruffians with stones in their hands, swearing they would kill me if I voted.

A false rumor was immediately sent to Far West, such as that two or three "Mormons" were killed and were not suffered to be buried. The next day a considerable number of the Saints came out to my house. Said Joseph Smith came with them. He inquired of me concerning the difficulty. The answer was, political difficulties. He then asked if there was anything serious. The answer was, No, I think not. We then all mounted our horses and rode on to the prairie, a short distance from my house, to a cool spring near the house of Esquire Black, where the greater number stopped for refreshments, whilst a few waited on Esquire Black. He was interrogated to know whether he justified the course of conduct at the late election, or not. He said he did not, and was willing to give his protest in writing; which he did, and also desired that there should be a public meeting called; which, I think, was done on the next day.

Said Joseph Smith was not addressed on the subject, but I was, who, in behalf of the Saints, entered into an agreement with the other citizens of the county that we would live in peace, enjoying those blessings fought for by our forefathers. But while some of their leading men were entering into this contract, others were raising mobs; and in a short time the mob increased to two hundred and five, rank and file, and they encamped within six miles of Adam-ondi-Ahman.

In the meantime, Joseph Smith and those who came with him from Far West returned to their homes in peace, suspecting nothing. But I, seeing the rage of the mob and their full determination to drive the Church from Daviess county, sent to General Atchison (major-general of the division in which we lived). He immediately sent Brigadier General Doniphan with between two and three hundred men. General Doniphan moved his troops near the mob force, and came up and conversed with me on the subject. After conversing some time on the subject, Major Hughes came and informed General Doniphan that his men were mutinying, and the mob were determined to fall on the Saints in Adam-ondi-Ahman. Having a colonel's commission under Doniphan I was commanded to call out my troops forthwith, and, to use Doniphan's own language, "kill every G—— d—— mobocrat you can find in the county, or make them prisoners; and if they come upon you give them hell." He then returned to his troops and gave them an address, stating the interview he had with me; and he also said to the mob, that if they were so disposed, they could go on with their measures; that he considered that Colonel Wight, with the militia under his command all sufficient to quell every G—— d—— mobocrat in the county; and if they did not feel disposed so to do, to go home or G—— d—— them, he would kill every one of them. The mob then dispersed.

During these movements, neither Joseph Smith nor any of those of Far West were at Adam-ondi-Ahman, only those who were settlers and legal citizens of the place.

The mob again assembled and went to De Witt, Carroll county, there being a small branch of the Church at that place. But of the transactions at this place I have no personal knowledge. They succeded in driving the Church twice from that place, some to the east and some to the west. This increased their ardor, and, with redoubled forces from several counties of the state, they returned to Daviess county to renew the attack. Many wanton attacks and violations of the rights of citizens took place at this time from the hands of this hellish band.

Believing forbearance no longer to be a virtue I again sent to the Major-General for military aid, who ordered out Brigadier-General Parks. Parks came part of the way, but fearing his men would mutiny and join the mob, he came on ahead and conversed with me a considerable time.

The night previous to his arrival, the wife of Don Carlos Smith was driven from her house by this ruthless mob, and came into Adam-ondi-Ahman—a distance of three miles, carrying her two children on her hips, one of which was then rising of two years old, the other six or eight months old, the snow being over shoemouth deep, and she having to wade Grand river, which was at this time waist deep. The mob burnt the house and everything they had in it. General Parks passing the ruins thereof seemed fired with indignation at their hellish conduct and said he had hitherto thought it imprudent to call upon the militia under my command, in consequence of popular opinion; but he now considered it no more than justice that I should have command of my own troops, and said to me, "I therefore command you forthwith to raise your companies immediately, and take such course as you may deem best in order to disperse the mob from this county."

I then called out sixty men, and placed them under the command of Captain David W. Patten, and I also took about the same number. Captain Patten was ordered to Gallatin, where a party of the mob was located, and I went to Millport where another party was located. Captain Patten and I formed the troops under our command and General Parks addressed them as follows:

"Gentlemen, I deplore your situation. I regret that transactions of this nature should have transpired in our once happy state. Your condition is certainly not an enviable one, surrounded by mobs on one side and popular opinion and prejudice on the other. Gladly would I fly to your relief with my troops, but I fear it would be worse for you. Most of them have relations living in this county, and will not fight against them.

"One of my principal captains (namely Samuel Bogart) and his men have already mutinied and have refused to obey my command.

"I can only say to you, gentlemen, follow the command of Colonel Wight, whom I have commanded to disperse all mobs found in Daviess county, or to make them prisoners and bring them before the civil authorities forthwith.

"I wish to be distinctly understood that Colonel Wight is vested with power and authority from me to disperse from your midst all who may be found on the side of mobocracy in the county of Daviess.

"I deeply regret, gentlemen, (knowing as I do, the vigilance and perseverance of Colonel Wight in the cause of freedom and rights of man) that I could not even be a soldier under his command in quelling the hellish outrages I have witnessed.

"In conclusion, gentlemen, be vigilant, and persevere, and allay every excitement of mobocracy. I have visited your place frequently, find you to be an industrious and thriving people, willing to abide the laws of the land; and I deeply regret that you could not live in peace and enjoy the privileges of freedom. I shall now, gentlemen, return and dismiss my troops, and put Captain Bogart under arrest, leave the sole charge with Colonel Wight, whom I deem sufficiently qualified to perform according to law, in all military operations necessary."

Captain Patten then went to Gallatin. When coming in sight of Gallatin, he discovered about one hundred of the mob holding some of the Saints in bondage, and tantalizing others in the most scandalous manner. At the sight of Captain Patten and company the mob took fright and such was their hurry to get away, some cut their bridle reins, and some pulled the bridles from their horses' heads and went off with all speed.

I went to Millport, and on my way discovered the inhabitants had become enraged at the orders of Generals Doniphan and Parks, and that they had sworn vengeance, not only against the Church, but also against the two generals, together with General Atchison; and to carry out their plans, they entered into one of the most diabolical schemes ever entered into by man, and these hellish schemes were ingeniously carried out.

Namely, by loading their families and goods in covered wagons, setting fire to their houses, moving into the midst of the mob, and crying out, "The Mormons have driven us and burnt our houses." In this situation I found the country between my house and Millport, and also found Millport evacuated and burnt.

Runners were immediately sent to the governor with the news that the "Mormons" were killing and burning everything before them, and that great fears were entertained that they would reach Jefferson City before the runners could bring the news.

This was not known by the Church of Latter-day Saints until two thousand two hundred of the militia had arrived within half a mile of Far West; and they then supposed the militia to be a mob.

I was sent for from Adam-ondi-Ahman to Far West; reached there, the sun about one hour high, in the morning of the 29th of October, 1838; called upon Joseph Smith, and inquired the cause of the great uproar. He declared he did not know, but feared the mob had increased their numbers, and were endeavoring to destroy us.

I inquired of him if he had had any conversation with any one concerning the matter. He said he had not, as he was only a private citizen of the county—that he did not interfere with any such matters.

He told me there had been an order, either from General Atchison or Doniphan, to the sheriff to call out the militia in order to quell the riots, and to go to him; he could give me any information on this subject. On inquiring for the sheriff, I found him not. That between three and four p.m. George M. Hinkle, colonel of the militia in that place, called on me, in company with Joseph Smith, and said Hinkle said he had been in the camp in order to learn the intention of the same. He said they greatly desired to see Joseph Smith, Lyman Wight, Sidney Rigdon, Parley P. Pratt, and George W. Robinson.

Joseph Smith first inquired why they should desire to see him, as he held no office, either civil or military. I next inquired why it was they should desire to see a man out of his own county.

Colonel Hinkle here observed, There is no time for controversy. If you go not into the camp immediately, they are determined to come upon Far West before the setting of the sun; and said they did not consider us as military leaders, but religious leaders. He said that if the aforesaid persons went into the camp, they would be liberated that night or very early next morning; that there should be no harm done.

We consulted together and agreed to go down. On going about half the distance from the camp, I observed it would be well for Generals Lucas, Doniphan and others, to meet us, and not have us go in so large a crowd of soldiers. Accordingly, the generals moved onwards, followed by fifty artillerymen, with a four-pounder. The whole twenty-two hundred moved in steady pace on the right and left, keeping about even with the former.

General Lucas approached the aforesaid designated persons with a vile, base and treacherous look in his countenance. I shook hands with him and saluted him thus: "We understand, general, you wish to confer with us a few moments. Will not tomorrow morning do as well."

At this moment George M. Hinkle spake and said, "Here, general are the prisoners I agreed to deliver to you." General Lucas then brandished his sword with a most hideous look and said, "You are my prisoners, and there is no time for talking at the present. You will march into the camp."

At this moment I believe that there were five hundred guns cocked, and not less than twenty caps bursted; and more hideous yells were never heard, even if the description of the yells of the damned in hell is true, as given by the modern sects of the day.

The aforesaid designated persons were then introduced into the midst of twenty-two hundred mob militia. They then called out a guard of ninety men, placing thirty around the prisoners, who were on duty two hours and off four. The prisoners were placed on the ground, with nothing to cover them but the heavens, and they were over-shadowed by clouds that moistened them before morning.

Sidney Rigdon, who was of a delicate constitution, received a slight shock of apoplectic fits, which excited great laughter and much ridicule in the guard and mob militia. Thus the prisoners spent a doleful night in the midst of a prejudiced and diabolical community.

Next day Hyrum Smith and Amasa Lyman were dragged from their families and brought prisoners into the camp, they alleging no other reason for taking Hyrum Smith than that he was a brother to Joe Smith the Prophet, and one of his counselors as President of the Church.

The prisoners spent this day as comfortably as could be expected under the existing circumstances. Night came on, and under the dark shadows of the night, General Wilson, subaltern of General Lucas, took me on one side and said; "We do not wish to hurt you nor kill you, neither shall you be, by G——; but we have one thing against you, and that is, you are too friendly to Joe Smith, and we believe him to be a G—— d—— rascal, and, Wight, you know all about his character." I said, "I do, sir." "Will you swear all you know concerning him?" said Wilson. "I will, sir" was the answer I gave. "Give us the outlines," said Wilson. I then told Wilson I believed said Joseph Smith to be the most philanthropic man he ever saw, and possessed of the most pure and republican principles—a friend to mankind, a maker of peace; "and sir, had it not been that I had given heed to his counsel, I would have given you hell before this time, with all your mob forces."

He then observed, "Wight, I fear your life is in danger, for there is no end to the prejudice against Joe Smith." "Kill and be damned sir," was my answer. He answered and said "There is to be a court-martial held this night; and will you attend, sir." "I will not, unless compelled by force," was my reply.

He returned about eleven o'clock that night, and took me aside and said: "I regret to tell you your die is cast; your doom is fixed; you are sentenced to be shot tomorrow morning on the public square in Far West, at eight o'clock." I answered, "Shoot, and be damned."

"We were in hopes," said he, "you would come out against Joe Smith; but as you have not, you will have to share the same fate with him." I answered "You may thank Joe Smith that you are not in hell this night; for, had it not been for him, I would have put you there." Somewhere about this time General Doniphan came up, and said to me, "Colonel the decision is a d—— hard one, and I have washed my hands against such cool and deliberate murder." He further told me that General Graham and several others (names not recollected) were with him in the decision and opposed it with all their power; and he should move his soldiers away by daylight in the morning, that they should not witness a heartless murder. "Colonel, I wish you well."

I then returned to my fellow-prisoners, to spend another night on the cold, damp earth, and the canopy of heaven to cover us. The night again proved a damp one.

At the removal of General Doniphan's part of the army, the camp was thrown into the utmost confusion and consternation. General Lucas, fearing the consequence of such hasty and inconsiderate measures, revoked the decree of shooting the prisoners, and determined to take them to Jackson county. Consequently, he delivered the prisoners over to General Wilson, ordering him to see them safe to Independence, Jackson county.

About the hour the prisoners were to have been shot on the public square in Far West, they were exhibited in a wagon in the town, all of them having families there but myself; and it would have broken the heart of any person possessing an ordinary share of humanity to have seen the separation. The aged father and mother of Joseph Smith were not permitted to see his face, but to reach their hands through the cover of the wagon, and thus take leave of him. When passing his own house, he was taken out of the wagon and permitted to go into the house, but not without a strong guard, and not permitted to speak with his family but in the presence of his guard; and his eldest son, Joseph, about six or eight years old, hanging to the tail of his coat, crying, "Father, is the mob going to kill you?" The guard said to him, "You d—— little brat, go back; you will see your father no more."

The prisoners then set out for Jackson county, accompanied by Generals Lucas and Wilson, and about three hundred troops for a guard. We remained in Jackson county three or four days and nights, during most of which time the prisoners were treated in a gentlemanly manner and boarded at a hotel, for which they had afterwards, when confined in Liberty jail, to pay the most extravagant price, or have their property, if any they had, attached for the same.

At this time General Clark had arrived at Richmond, and, by orders from the Governor, took on himself the command of the whole of the militia, notwithstanding General Atchison's commission was the oldest; but he was supposed to be too friendly to the "Mormons," and therefore dismounted; and General Clark sanctioned the measures of General Lucas, however cruel, and said he should have done the same, had he been there himself.

Accordingly, he remanded the prisoners from Jackson county, and they were taken and escorted by a strong guard to Richmond; threatened several times on the way with violence and death. They were met five miles before they reached Richmond by about one hundred armed men; and when they arrived in town, they were thrust into an old cabin under a strong guard. I was informed by one of the guards that, two nights previous to their arrival, General Clark held a court-martial, and the prisoners were again sentenced to be shot; but he being a little doubtful of his authority, sent immediately to Fort Leavenworth for the military law and a decision from the United States' officers, where he was duly informed that any such proceedings would be a cool-blooded and heartless murder. On the arrival of the prisoners at Richmond, Joseph Smith and myself sent for General Clark, to be informed by him what crimes were alleged against us. He came in and said he would see us again in a few minutes. Shortly he returned and said he would inform us of the crimes alleged against us by the state of Missouri.

"Gentlemen, you are charged with treason, murder, arson, burglary, larceny, theft, and stealing, and various other charges too tedious to mention at this time;" and he immediately left the room. In about twenty minutes, there came in a strong guard, together with the keeper of the penitentiary of the state, who brought with him three common trace chains, noozed together by putting the small end through the ring, and commenced chaining us up, one by one, and fastening us with padlocks about two feet apart.

In this uncomfortable situation the prisoners remained fifteen days, and in this situation General Clark delivered us to the professed civil authorities of the state, without any legal process being served on us at all during the whole time we were kept in chains, with nothing but *ex parte* evidence, and that given either by the vilest apostates or by the mob who had committed murder in the state of Missouri. Notwithstanding all this *ex parte* evidence, Judge King did inform our lawyer, ten days previous to the termination of the trial, whom he should commit and whom he should not; and I heard Judge King say on his bench, in the presence of hundreds of witnesses, that there was no law for the "Mormons," and they need not expect any. Said he, "If the Governor's exterminating order had been directed to me, I would have seen it fulfilled to the very letter ere this time."

After a tedious trial of fifteen days, with no other witnesses but *ex parte* ones, the witnesses for the prisoners were either kicked out of doors or put on trial themselves. The prisoners were now committed to Liberty jail, under the care and direction of Samuel Tillery, jailer. Here we were received with a shout of indignation and scorn by the prejudiced populace.

Prisoners were here thrust into jail without a regular mittimus, the jailer having to send for one some days after. The mercies of the jailer were intolerable, feeding us with a scanty allowance on the dregs of coffee and tea from his own table, and fetching the provisions in a basket, without being cleaned, on which the chickens had roosted the night before. Five days he fed the prisoners on human flesh, and from extreme hunger I was compelled to eat it. In this situation we were kept until about the month of April, when we were remanded to Daviess county for trial before the grand jury. We were kept under the most loathsome and despotic guard they could produce in that county of lawless mobs. After six or eight days, the grand jury (most of whom, by-the-bye, were so drunk that they had to be carried out and into their rooms as though they were lifeless,) formed a fictitious indictment, which was sanctioned by Judge Birch, who was the State's Attorney under Judge King at our *ex parte* trial, and who at that time stated that the "Mormons" ought to be hung without judge or jury. He, the said Judge, made out a mittimus, without day or date, ordering the Sheriff to take us to Columbia. The Sheriff selected four men to guard five of us.

We then took a circuitous route, crossing prairies sixteen miles without houses; and after traveling three days, the Sheriff and I were together by ourselves five miles from any of the rest of the company for sixteen miles at a stretch. The Sheriff here observed to me that he wished to God he was at home, and your friends and you also. The Sheriff then showed me the mittimus, and he found it had neither day nor date to it, and said the inhabitants of Daviess county would be surprised that the prisoners had not left them sooner; and, said he, "By G——, I shall not go much further."

We were then near Yellow Creek, and there were no houses nearer than sixteen miles one way, and eleven another way, except right on the creek. Here a part of the guard took a spree, while the balance helped us to mount our horses, which we purchased of them, and for which they were paid. Here we took a change of venue, and went to Quincy without difficulty, where we found our families, who had been driven out of the State under the exterminating order of Governor Boggs. I never knew of Joseph Smith's holding any office, civil or military, or using any undue influence in religious matters during the whole time of which I have been speaking.

LYMAN WIGHT.

[*Sworn to before the Municipal Court of Nauvoo, IL on 1 Jul 1843.*]

RIGDON, Sidney   HC[9]

Sidney Rigdon sworn, says I arrived in Far West, Caldwell county, Missouri, on the 4th of April, 1838, and enjoyed peace and quietness, in common with the rest of the citizens, until the August following, when great excitement was created by the office-seekers. Attempts were made to prevent the citizens of Daviess from voting. Soon after the election, which took place in the early part of August, the citizens of Caldwell were threatened with violence from those of Daviess county and other counties adjacent to Caldwell.

This, the August of 1838, I may date as the time of the beginning of all the troubles of our people in Caldwell county and in all the counties in the state where our people were living. We had lived in peace from the April previous until this time; but from this time till we were all out of the state, it was one scene of violence following another in quick succession.

There were at this time settlements in Clay, Ray, Carroll, Caldwell, and Daviess counties, as well as some families living in other counties. A simultaneous movement was made in all the counties and in every part of the state, where settlements were made, this soon became violent; and threatenings were heard from every quarter. Public meetings were held, and the most inflammatory speeches made, and resolutions passed, which denounced all the "Mormons" in the most bitter and rancorous manner. These resolutions were published in the papers, and the most extensive circulation given to them that the press of the country was capable of giving.

The first regular mob that assembled was in Daviess county, and their efforts were directed against the settlements made in that county, declaring their determination to drive out of the county all the citizens who were of our religion, and that indiscriminately, without regard to anything else but their religion.

The only evidence necessary to dispossess any individual or family, or all the evidence required, would be that they were "Mormons," as we were called, or rather that they were of the "Mormon" religion. This was considered of itself crime enough to cause any individual or family to be driven from their homes, and their property made common plunder. Resolutions to this effect were made at public meetings held for the purpose, and made public through the papers of the state, in the face of all law and all authority.

---

[9] 3:449–66; also found in JH 1 Jul 1843.

I will now give a history of the settlement in Carroll county. In the preceding April, as myself and family were on our way to Far West, we put up at a house in Carroll county, on a stream called Turkey Creek, to tarry for the night. Soon after we stopped, a young man came riding up, who also stopped and stayed through the night. Hearing my name mentioned, he introduced himself to me as Henry Root; said he lived in that county at a little town called De Witt, on the Missouri river, and had been at Far West to get some of those who were coming into that place to form a settlement at De Witt. Speaking highly of the advantages of the situation, and soliciting my interference in his behalf to obtain a number of families to commence at that place, as he was a large proprietor in the town plat, he offered a liberal share in all the profits which might arise from the sale of property there to those who would aid him in getting the place settled. In the morning we proceeded on our journey.

Some few weeks after my arrival, the said Henry Root, in company with a man by the name of David Thomas, came to Far West on the same business; and after much solicitation on their part, it was agreed that a settlement should be made in that place; and in the July following the first families removed there, and the settlement soon increased, until in the October following it consisted of some seventy families. By this time a regular mob had collected, strongly armed, and had obtained possession of a cannon, and stationed themselves a mile or two from the town. The citizens, being nearly all new comers, had to live in their tents and wagons, and were exerting themselves to the uttermost to get houses for the approaching winter. The mob commenced committing their depredations on the citizens, by not suffering them to procure the materials for building, keeping them shut up in the town, not allowing them to go out to get provisions, driving off their cattle, and preventing the owners from going in search of them. In this way the citizens were driven to the greatest extremities, actually suffering for food and every comfort of life; in consequence of which, there was much sickness, and many died. Females gave birth to children, without a house to shelter them; and in consequence of the exposure, many suffered great afflictions, and many died.

Hearing of their great sufferings, a number of the men of Far West determined on going to see what was doing there. Accordingly we started, eluded the vigilance of the mob, and, notwithstanding they had sentinels placed on all the principal roads, to prevent relief from being sent to the citizens, we safely arrived in De Witt, and found the people as above stated.

During the time we were there, every effort that could be was made to get the authorities of the county to interfere and scatter the mob. The judge of the circuit court was petitioned, but without success; and after that, the governor of the state, who returned for answer that the citizens of De Witt had got into a difficulty with the surrounding country, and they might get out of it, for he would have nothing to do with it; or this was the answer the messenger brought, when he returned.

The messenger was a Mr. Caldwell, who owned a ferry on Grand river, about three miles from De Witt, and was an old settler in the place.

The citizens were completely besieged by the mob: no man was at liberty to go out, nor any to come in. The extremities to which the people were driven were very great, suffering with much sickness, without shelter, and deprived of all aid, either medical or any other kind, and being without food or the privilege of getting it, and betrayed by every man who made the least pretension to friendship; a notable instance of which I will here give as a sample of many others of a similar kind.

There was neither bread nor flour to be had in the place. A steamboat landed there, and application was made to get flour; but the captain said there was none on board.

A man then offered his services to get flour for the place, knowing, he said, where there was a quantity. Money was given to him for that purpose. He got on the boat and went off, and that was the last we heard of the man or the money. This was a man who had been frequently in De Witt during the siege, and professed great friendship.

In this time of extremity, a man who had a short time before moved into De Witt, bringing with him a fine yoke of cattle, started out to hunt his cattle, in order to butcher them, to keep the citizens from actual starvation; but before he got far from the town, he was fired upon by the mob, and narrowly escaped with his life, and had to return; or, at least, such was his report when returned.

Being now completely enclosed on every side, we could plainly see many men on the opposite side of the river, and it was supposed that they were there to prevent the citizens from crossing; and, indeed, a small craft crossed from them, and three men in it, who said that that was the object for which they had assembled.

At this critical moment, with death staring us in the face, in its worst form, cut off from all communication with the surrounding country, and all our provisions exhausted, we were sustained as the children of Israel in the desert, only by different animals,—they by quails, and we by cattle and hogs, which came walking into the camp; for such it truly was, as the people were living in tents and wagons, not being privileged with building houses.

What was to be done in this extremity? Why, recourse was had to the only means of subsistence left, and that was to butcher the cattle and hogs which came into the place, without asking who was the owner, or without knowing; and what to me is remarkable is, that a sufficient number of animals came into the camp to sustain life during the time in which the citizens were besieged by the mob. This, indeed, was but coarse living; but such as it was, it sustained life.

From this circumstance the cry went out that the citizens of De Witt were thieves and plunderers, and were stealing cattle and hogs. During this time, the mob of Carroll county said that all they wanted was that the citizens of De Witt should leave Carroll county and go to Caldwell and Daviess counties.

The citizens, finding that they must leave De Witt or eventually starve, finally agreed to leave; and accordingly preparations were made, and De Witt was vacated.

The first evening after we left, we put up for the night in a grove of timber. Soon after our arrival in the grove, a female who a short time before had given birth to a child, in consequence of exposure, died.

A grave was dug in the grove, and the next morning the body was deposited in it without a coffin, and the company proceeded on their journey, part of them going to Daviess county, and part into Caldwell. This was in the month of October, 1838.

In a short time after their arrival in Daviess and Caldwell counties, messengers arrived, informing the new citizens of Caldwell and Daviess that the mob, with their cannon, was marching to Daviess county, threatening death to the citizens, or else that they should all leave Daviess county. This caused other efforts to be made to get the authorities to interfere. I wrote two memorials, one to the governor and one to Austin A. King, circuit judge, imploring their assistance and intervention to protect the citizens of Daviess against the threatened violence of the mob.

These memorials were accompanied with affidavits, which could leave no doubt on the mind of the governor or judge that the citizens before mentioned were in imminent danger.

At this time things began to assume an alarming aspect both to the citizens of Daviess and Caldwell counties. Mobs were forming all around the country, declaring that they would drive the people out of the state.

This made our appeals to the authorities more deeply solicitous as the danger increased, and very soon after this the mobs commenced their depredations, which was a general system of plunder, tearing down fences, exposing all within the field to destruction, and driving off every animal they could find.

Some time previous to this, in consequence of the threatenings which were made by mobs, or those who were being formed into mobs, and the abuses committed by them on the persons and property of the citizens, an association was formed, called the Danite Band.

This, as far as I was acquainted with it, (not being myself one of the number, neither was Joseph Smith, Sen.,) was for mutual protection against the bands that were forming and threatened to be formed for the professed object of committing violence on the property and persons of the citizens of Daviess and Caldwell counties. They had certain signs and words by which they could know one another, either by day or night. They were bound to keep these signs and words secret, so that no other person or persons than themselves could know them. When any of these persons were assailed by any lawless band, he would make it known to others, who would flee to his relief at the risk of life.

In this way they sought to defend each other's lives and property; but they were strictly enjoined not to touch any person, only those who were engaged in acts of violence against the persons or property of one of their own number, or one of those whose life and property they had bound themselves to defend.

This organization was in existence when the mobs commenced their most violent attempts upon the citizens of the before-mentioned counties; and from this association arose all the horror afterwards expressed by the mob at some secret clan known as Danites.

The efforts made to get the authorities to interfere at this time was attended with some success. The militia was ordered out under the command of Major-General Atchison of Clay county, Brigadier-Generals Doniphan of Clay, and Parks of Ray county, who marched their troops to Daviess county, where they found a large mob; and General Atchison said, in my presence, that he took the following singular method to disperse them.

He organized them with his troops as part of the militia called out to suppress and arrest the mob. After having thus organized them, he discharged them and all the rest of the troops, as having no further need for their services, and all returned home.

This, however, only seemed to give the mob more courage to increase their exertion with redoubled vigor. They boasted, after that, that the authorities would not punish them, and they would do as they pleased.

In a very short time their efforts were renewed with a determination not to cease until they had driven the citizens of Caldwell, and such of the citizens of Daviess as they had marked out as victims, from the state.

A man by the name of Cornelius Gillum, who resided in Clay county, and formerly sheriff of said county, organized a band, who painted themselves like Indians, and had a place of rendezvous at Hunter's Mills, on a stream called Grindstone. I think it was in Clinton county, the county west of Caldwell, and between it and the west line of the state.

From this place they would sally out and commit their depredations. Efforts were again made to get the authorities to put a stop to these renewed outrages, and again General Doniphan and General Parks were called out with such portions of their respective brigades as they might deem necessary to suppress the mob, or rather mobs, for by this time there were a number of them.

General Doniphan came to Far West; and, while there, recommended to the authorities of Caldwell to have the militia of said county called out as a necessary measure of defense, assuring us that Gillum had a large mob on Grindstone Creek, and his object was to make a descent upon Far West, burn the town and kill or disperse the inhabitants; and that it was very necessary that an effective force should be ready to oppose him, or he would accomplish his object.

The militia were accordingly called out. He also said that there had better be a strong force sent to Daviess county to guard the citizens there. He recommended that, to avoid any difficulties which might arise, they had better go in very small parties without arms, so that no legal advantage could be taken of them. I will here give a short account of the courts and internal affairs of Missouri, for the information of those who are not acquainted with the same.

Missouri has three courts of law peculiar to that state—the supreme court, the circuit court, and the county court; the two former about the same as in many other states of the Union. The county court is composed of three judges, elected by the people of the respective counties. This court is in some respects like the court of probate in Illinois, or the surrogate's court of New York; but the powers of this court are more extensive than the courts of Illinois or New York.

The judges (or any one of them of the county court of Missouri) have the power of issuing habeas corpus in all cases where arrests are made within the county where they preside. They have also all power of justices of the peace in civil as well as criminal cases. For instance, a warrant may be obtained from one of these judges by affidavit, and a person arrested under such warrant.

From another of these judges, a habeas corpus may issue, and the person arrested be ordered before him, and the character of the arrest be inquired into; and if, in the opinion of the judge, the person ought not to be holden by virtue of said process, he has power to discharge him. They are considered conservators of the peace, and act as such.

In the internal regulations of the affairs of Missouri, the counties in some respects are nearly as independent of each other as the several states of the Union. No considerable number of men armed can pass out of one county into or through another county, without first obtaining the permission of the judges of the county court, or some one of them; otherwise they are liable to be arrested by the order of said judges; and if in their judgment they ought not thus to pass, they are ordered back from whence they came; and, in case of refusal, are subject to be arrested or even shot down in case of resistance.

The judges of the county court (or any one of them) have the power to call out the militia of said county, upon affidavit being made to them for that purpose by any of the citizens of said county, showing it just, in the judgment of such judge or judges, why said militia should be called out to defend any portion of the citizens of said county.

The following is the course of procedure: Affidavit is made before one or any number of the judges, setting forth that the county (or any particular portion of it) is either invaded or threatened with invasion by some unlawful assembly, whereby the liberties, lives, or property of the citizens may be unlawfully taken.

When such affidavit is made to any one of the judges, or all of them, it is the duty of him or them before whom such affidavit is made to issue an order to the sheriff of the county, to make requisition upon the commanding officer of the militia of said county to have immediately put under military order such portion of the militia under his command as may be necessary for the defense of the citizens of said county.

In this way the militia of any county may be called out at any time deemed necessary by the county judges, independently of any other civil authority of the state.

In case that the militia of the county is insufficient to quell the rioters and secure the citizens against the invaders, then recourse can be had to the judge of the circuit court, who has the same power over the militia of his judicial district as the county judges have over the militia of the county. And in case of insufficiency in the militia of the judicial district of the circuit judge, recourse can be had to the Governor of the state, and all the militia of the state called out; and if this should fail, then the Governor can call on the President of the United States.

I have given this explanation of the internal regulation of the affairs of Missouri, in order that the court may clearly understand what I have before said on this subject, and what I may hereafter say on it.

It was in view of this order of things that General Doniphan, who is a lawyer of some celebrity in Missouri, gave the recommendation he did at Far West, when passing into Daviess county with his troops, for the defense of the citizens of said county.

It was in consequence of this that he said that those of Caldwell county who went into Daviess county should go in small parties and unarmed; in which condition they were not subject to any arrest from any authority whatever.

In obedience to these recommendations the militia of Caldwell county was called out, affidavits having been made to one of the judges of the county, setting forth the danger which it was believed the citizens were in from a large marauding party assembled under the command of one Cornelius Gillum, on a stream called Grindstone.

When affidavit was made to this effect, the judge issued his order to the sheriff of the county, and the sheriff to the commanding officer, who was Colonel George M. Hinkle; and thus were the militia of the county of Caldwell put under orders.

General Doniphan, however, instead of going into Daviess county, soon after he left Far West returned to Clay county with all his troops, giving as his reason the mutinous character of his troops, who he believed would join the mob, instead of acting against them, and that he had not power to restrain them.

In a day or two afterwards, General Parks, of Ray county, also came to Far West, and said that he had sent on a number of troops to Daviess county, to act in concert with General Doniphan. He also made the same complaint concerning the troops that Doniphan had, doubting greatly whether they would render any service to those in Daviess, who were threatened with violence by the mobs assembling; but on hearing that Doniphan, instead of going to Daviess county, had returned to Clay, followed his example and ordered his troops back to Ray county; and thus were the citizens of Caldwell county and those of Daviess county, who were marked out as victims by the mob, left to defend themselves the best way they could.

What I have here stated in relation to Generals Doniphan and Parks, was learned in conversations had between myself and them, about which I cannot be mistaken, unless my memory has betrayed me.

The militia of the county of Caldwell were now all under requisition, armed and equipped according to law. The mob, after all the authority of the state had been recalled except from the force of Caldwell county, commenced the work of destruction in earnest, showing a determination to accomplish their object.

Far West, where I resided, which was the shire town of Caldwell county, was placed under the charge of a captain by the name of John Killian, who made my house his headquarters. Other portions of the troops were distributed in different portions of the county, wherever danger was apprehended. In consequence of Captain Killian making my house his headquarters, I was put in possession of all that was going on, as all intelligence in relation to the operations of the mob was communicated to him. Intelligence was received daily of depredations being committed not only against the property of the citizens, but their persons; many of whom, when attending to their business, would be surprised and taken by marauding parties, tied up, and whipped in a most desperate manner.

Such outrages were common during the progress of these extraordinary scenes, and all kinds of depredations were committed. Men driving their teams to and from the mills where they got their grinding done, would be surprised and taken, their persons abused, and their teams, wagons and loading all taken as booty by the plunderers. Fields were thrown open, and all within exposed to the destruction of such animals as chose to enter. Cattle, horses, hogs and sheep were driven off, and a general system of plunder and destruction of all kinds of property carried on, to the great annoyance of the citizens of Caldwell and that portion of the citizens of Daviess marked as victims by the mob.

One afternoon a messenger arrived at Far West calling for help, saying that a banditti had crossed the south line of Caldwell and were engaged in threatening the citizens with death, if they did not leave their homes and go out of the state within a very short time—the time not precisely recollected; but I think it was the next day by ten o'clock, but of this I am not certain. He said they were setting fire to the prairies, in view of burning houses and desolating farms; that they had set fire to a wagon loaded with goods, and they were all consumed; that they had also set fire to a house, and when he left it was burning down.

Such was the situation of affairs at Far West at that time, that Captain Killian could not spare any of his forces, as an attack was hourly expected at Far West.

The messenger went off, and I heard no more about it till some time the night following, when I was awakened from sleep by the voice of some man apparently giving command to a military body. Being somewhat unwell, I did not get up. Some time after I got up in the morning the sheriff of the county stopped at the door and said that David W. Patten had had a battle with the mob last night at Crooked River, and that several were killed and a number wounded; that Patten was among the number of the wounded, and his wound supposed to be mortal. After I had taken breakfast, another gentleman called, giving me the same account, and asking me if I would not take my horse and ride out with him and see what was done. I agreed to do so, and we started, and after going three or four miles, met a company coming into Far West. We turned and went back with them.

The mob proved to be that headed by the Reverend Samuel Bogart, a Methodist preacher; and the battle was called the Bogart Battle. After this battle there was a short season of quiet; the mobs disappeared, and the militia returned to Far West, though they were not discharged, but remained under orders until it should be known how the matter would turn.

In the space of a few days, it was said that a large body of armed men were entering the south part of Caldwell county. The county court ordered the militia to go and inquire what was their object in thus coming into the county without permission.

The militia started as commanded, and little or no information was received at Far West about their movements until late the next afternoon, when a large army was descried making their way towards Far West. Far West being an elevated situation, the army was discovered while a number of miles from the place.

Their object was entirely unknown to the citizens as far as I had any knowledge on the subject; and every man I heard speak of their object expressed as great ignorance as myself. They reached a small stream on the south side of the town, which was studded with timber on its banks, and for perhaps from half a mile to a mile on the south side of the stream, an hour before sundown.

There the main body halted; and soon after a detachment under the command of Brigadier-General Doniphan, marched towards the town in line of battle. This body was preceded probably three-fourths of a mile in advance of them by a man carrying a white flag, who approached within a few rods of the eastern boundary of the town and demanded three persons who were in the town, to be sent to their camp; after which, the whole town, he said, would be massacred. When the persons who were inquired for were informed, they refused to go, determined to share the common fate of the citizens. One of those persons did not belong to the Church of Latter-day Saints. His name is Adam Lightner, a merchant in that city.

The white flag returned to the camp. To the force of General Doniphan was opposed the small force of Caldwell militia, under Colonel Hinkle, who also marched in line of battle to the southern line of the town. The whole force of Colonel Hinkle did not exceed three hundred men; that of Doniphan perhaps three times that number. I was in no way connected with the militia, being over age, neither was Joseph Smith, Sen.

I went into the line formed by Colonel Hinkle, though unarmed, and stood among the rest to await the result, and had a full view of both forces. The armies were within rifle shot of each other.

About the setting of the sun, Doniphan ordered his army to return to the camp at the creek. They wheeled and marched off. After they had retired a consultation was held as to what was best to do. By what authority the army was there, no one could tell, as far as I knew. It was agreed to build, through the night, a sort of fortification, and, if we must fight, sell our lives as dearly as we could. Accordingly, all hands went to work; rails, house-logs and wagons were all put in requisition, and the south line of the town as well secured as could be done by the men and means, and the short time allowed; we expected an attack in the morning.

The morning at length came, and that day passed away, and still nothing was done but plundering the cornfields, shooting cattle and hogs, stealing horses and robbing houses, and carrying off potatoes, turnips, and all such things as the army of General Lucas could get, for such they proved to be; for the main body was commanded by Samuel D. Lucas, a deacon in the Presbyterian church. The next day came, and then it was ascertained that they were there by order of the governor.

A demand was made for Joseph Smith, Sen., Lyman Wight, George W. Robinson, Parley P. Pratt and myself to go into their camp. With this command we instantly complied, and accordingly started.

When we came in sight of their camp, the whole army was on parade marching towards the town. We approached and met them, and were informed by Lucas that we were prisoners of war. A scene followed that would defy any mortal to describe; a howling was set up that would put anything I ever heard before or since at defiance. I thought at the time it had no parallel except it might be the perdition of ungodly men. They had a cannon.

I could distinctly hear the guns as the locks were sprung, which appeared, from the sound, to be in every part of the army. General Doniphan came riding up where we were, and swore by his Maker that he would hew the first man down that cocked a gun. One or two other officers on horseback also rode up, ordering those who had cocked their guns to uncock them, or they would be hewed down with their swords. We ware conducted into their camp and made to lie on the ground through the night.

This was late in October. We were kept here for two days and two nights. It commenced raining and snowing until we were completely drenched; and being compelled to lie on the ground, which had become very wet, the water was running around us and under us. What consultation the officers and others had in relation to the disposition that was to be made of us, I am entirely indebted to the report made to me by General Doniphan, as none of us was put on any trial.

General Doniphan gave an account, of which the following is the substance, as far as my memory serves me: That they held a court-martial and sentenced us to be shot at eight o'clock the next morning, after the court-martial was holden, in the public square in the presence of our families; that this court-martial was composed of seventeen preachers and some of the principal officers of the army. Samuel D. Lucas presided. Doniphan arose and said that neither himself nor his brigade should have any hand in the shooting, that it was nothing short of cold-blooded murder;

and left the court-martial and ordered his brigade to prepare and march off the ground. This was probably the reason why they did not carry the decision of the court-martial into effect. It was finally agreed that we should be carried into Jackson county. Accordingly, on the third day after our arrest, the army was all paraded; we were put into wagons and taken into the town, our families having heard that we were to be brought to town that morning to be shot. When we arrived a scene ensued such as might be expected under the circumstances.

I was permitted to go alone with my family into the house. There I found my family so completely plundered of all kinds of food, that they had nothing to eat but parched corn, which they ground with a handmill and thus were they sustaining life.

I soon pacified my family and allayed their feelings by assuring them that the ruffians dared not kill me. I gave them strong assurances that they dared not do it, and that I would return to them again. After this interview I took my leave of them and returned to the wagons, got in, and we were all started off to Jackson county.

Before we reached the Missouri river, a man came riding along the line apparently in great haste. I did not know his business. When we got to the river, Lucas came to me and told me that he wanted us to hurry, as Jacob Stolling had arrived from Far West with a message from General John C. Clark, ordering him to return with us to Far West, as he was there with a large army. He said he would not comply with the demand, but did not know but Clark might send an army to take us by force. We were hurried over the river as fast as possible, with as many of Lucas' army as could be sent over at one time, and sent hastily on, and thus we were taken to Independence, the shire town of Jackson county, and put into an old house, and a strong guard placed over us.

In a day or two they relaxed their severity. We were taken to the best tavern in town, and there boarded and treated with kindness. We were permitted to go and come at our pleasure without any guard. After some days Colonel Sterling G. Price arrived from Clark's army with a demand to have us taken to Richmond, Ray county. It was difficult to get a guard to go with us. Indeed, we solicited them to send one with us, and finally got a few men to go, and we started. After we had crossed the Missouri, on our way to Richmond, we met a number of very rough-looking fellows, and as rough-acting as they were looking. They threatened our lives. We solicited our guard to send to Richmond for a stronger force to guard us there, as we considered our lives in danger. Sterling G. Price met us with a strong force, and conducted us to Richmond, where we were put in close confinement.

One thing I will here mention, which I forgot. While we were at Independence, I was introduced to Burrell Hicks, a lawyer of some note in the country. In speaking on the subject of our arrest and being torn from our families, he said he presumed it was another Jackson county scrape. He said the Mormons had been driven from that county and that without any offense on their part. He said he knew all about it; they were driven off because the people feared their political influence. And what was said about the Mormons was only to justify the mob in the eyes of the world for the course they had taken. He said this was another scrape of the same kind.

This Burrell Hicks, by his own confession, was one of the principal leaders in the Jackson county mob.

After this digression, I will resume. The same day that we arrived at Richmond, Price came into the place where we were, with a number of armed men, who immediately on entering the room cocked their guns; another followed with chains in his hands, and we were ordered to be chained together. A strong guard was placed in and around the house, and thus we were secured. The next day General Clark came in, and we were introduced to him. The awkward manner in which he entered and his apparent embarrassment were such as to force a smile from me.

He was then asked for what he had thus cast us into prison? To this question he could not or did not give a direct answer. He said he would let us know in a few days; and after a few more awkward and uncouth movements he withdrew. After he went out, I asked some of the guard what was the matter with General Clark, that made him appear so ridiculous? They said he was near-sighted. I replied that I was mistaken if he were not as near-witted as he was near-sighted.

We were now left with our guards, without knowing for what we had been arrested, as no civil process had issued against us. For what followed until General Clark came in again to tell us that we were to be delivered into the hands of the civil authorities, I am entirely indebted to what I heard the guards say. I heard them say that General Clark had promised them before leaving Coles county, that they should have the privilege of shooting Joseph Smith, Jun., and myself; and that General Clark was engaged in searching the military law to find authority for so doing, but found it difficult, as we were not military men and did not belong to the militia; but he had sent to Fort Levenworth for the military code of law, to find law to justify him in shooting us.

I must here again digress to relate a circumstance which I forgot in its place. I had heard that Clark had given a military order to some persons who had applied to him for it, to go to my house and take such goods as they claimed. The goods claimed were goods sold by the sheriff of Caldwell county on an execution, which I had purchased at the sale.

The man against whom the execution was issued availed himself of that time of trouble to go and take the goods wherever he could find them.

I asked General Clark if he had given any such authority. He said that an application had been made to him for such an order, but he said, "Your lady wrote me a letter requesting me not to do it, telling me that the goods had been purchased at the sheriff's sale; and I would not grant the order."

I did not, at the time, suppose that Clark in this had barefacedly lied; but the sequel proved he had; for, some time afterwards, behold there comes a man to Richmond with the order, and showed it to me, signed by Clark. The man said he had been at our house and taken all the goods he could find. So much for a lawyer, a Methodist, and a very pious man at that time in religion, and a major-general of Missouri.

During the time that Clark was examining the military law, there was something took place which may be proper to relate in this place. I heard a plan laying among a number of those who belonged to Clark's army, and some of them officers of high rank, to go to Far West and commit violence on the persons of Joseph Smith, Sen's wife and my wife and daughter.

This gave me some uneasiness. I got an opportunity to send my family word of their design and to make such arrangements as they could to guard against their vile purpose. The time at last arrived, and the party started for Far West. I waited with painful anxiety for their return. After a number of days, they returned. I listened to all they said, to find out, if possible, what they had done. One night—I think the very night after their return—I heard them relating to some of those who had not been with them the events of their adventure. Inquiry was made about their success in the particular object of their visit to Far West. The substance of what they said in answer was that they had passed and repassed both houses, and saw the females; but there were so many men about the town, that they dare not venture, for fear of being detected; and their numbers were not sufficient to acomplish anything, if they made the attempt; and they came off without trying.

No civil process of any kind had been issued against us. We were then held in duress, without knowing what for or what charges were to be preferred against us. At last, after long suspense, General Clark came into the prison, presenting himself about as awkwardly as at the first, and informed us that we would be put into the hands of the civil authorities. He said he did not know precisely what crimes would be charged against us, but they would be within the range of treason, murder, burglary, arson, larceny, theft, and stealing. Here, again, another smile was forced, and I could not refrain from smiling at the expense of this would-be great man, in whom, he said, "the faith of Missouri was pledged." After long and awful suspense, the notable Austin A. King, judge of the circuit court, took the seat, and we were ordered before him for trial; Thomas Birch, Esq., prosecuting attorney. All things being arranged, the trial opened. No papers were read to us, no charges of any kind preferred, nor did we know against what we had to plead. Our crimes had yet to be found out.

At the commencement we requested that we might be tried separately; but this was refused, and we were all put on our trial together. Witnesses appeared, and the swearing commenced. It was so plainly manifested by the judge that he wanted the witnesses to prove us guilty of treason, that no person could avoid seeing it. The same feelings were also visible in the state's attorney. Judge King made an observation something to this effect, as he was giving directions to the scribe who was employed to write down the testimony, that he wanted all the testimony directed to certain points. Being taken sick at an early stage of the trial, I had not the opportunity of hearing but a small part of the testimony when it was delivered before the court.

During the progress of the trial, after the adjournment of the court in the evening, our lawyers would come into the prison, and there the matters would be talked over.

The propriety of our sending for witnesses was also discussed. Our attorneys said that they would recommend us not to introduce any evidence at that trial. Doniphan said it would avail us nothing, for the judge would put us in prison, if a cohort of angels were to come and swear we were innocent. And besides that, he said that if we were to give the court the names of our witnesses, there was a band there ready to go, and they would go and drive them out of the country, or arrest them and have them cast into prison, or else kill them, to prevent them from swearing. It was finally concluded to let the matter be so for the present.

During the progress of the trial, and while I was lying sick in prison, I had an opportunity of hearing a great deal said by those who would come in. The subject was the all-absorbing one. I heard them say that we must be put to death—that the character of the state required it; the state must justify herself in the course she had taken, and nothing but punishing us with death could save the credit of the state; and it must therefore be done.

I heard a party of them, one night, telling about some female whose person they had violated; and this language was used by one of them: "The d—— b——, how she yelled!" Who this person was, I did not know; but before I got out of prison I heard that a widow, whose husband had died some few months before, with consumption, had been brutally violated by a gang of them, and died in their hands, leaving three little children, in whose presence the scene of brutality took place.

After I got out of prison and had arrived in Quincy, Illinois, I met a strange man in the street who inquired of me respecting a circumstance of this kind, saying that he had heard of it, and was on his way going to Missouri to get the children if he could find them. He said the woman thus murdered was his sister, or his wife's sister, I am not positive which. The man was in great agitation. What success he had, I know not.

The trial at last ended, and Lyman Wight, Joseph Smith, Sen., Hyrum Smith, Caleb Baldwin, Alexander McRae, and myself were sent to jail in the village of Liberty, Clay county, Missouri.

We were kept there from three to four months; after which time we were brought out on habeas corpus before one of the county judges. During the hearing under the habeas corpus, I had, for the first time, an opportunity of hearing the evidence, as it was all written and read before the court.

It appeared from the evidence that they attempted to prove us guilty of treason in consequence of the militia of Caldwell county being under arms at the time that General Lucas' army came to Far West. This calling out of the militia was what they founded the charge of treason upon, an account of which I have given above. The charge of murder was founded on the fact that a man of their number, they said, had been killed in the Bogart battle.

The other charges were founded on things which took place in Daviess county. As I was not in Daviess county at that time, I cannot testify anything about them.

A few words about this written testimony:

I do not now recollect one single point about which testimony was given, with which I was acquainted, but was misrepresented, nor one solitary witness whose testimony was there written, that did not swear falsely; and in many instances I cannot see how it could avoid being intentional on the part of those who testified, for all of them did swear to things that I am satisfied they knew to be false at the time, and it would be hard to persuade me to the contrary. There were things there said so utterly without foundation in truth—so much so, that the persons swearing must at the time of swearing have known it. The best construction I can ever put upon it is that they swore things to be true which they did not know to be so; and this, to me, is wilful perjury.

This trial lasted for a long time, the result of which was that I was ordered to be discharged from prison, and the rest remanded back. But I was told by those who professed to be my friends that it would not do for me to go out of the jail at that time, as the mob were watching and would most certainly take my life; and when I got out, that I must leave the state, for the mob, availing themselves of the exterminating order of Governor Boggs, would, if I were found in the state, surely take my life; that I had no way to escape them but to flee with all speed from the state. It was some ten days after this before I dared leave the jail. At last, the evening came in which I was to leave the jail. Every preparation was made that could be made for my escape. There was a carriage ready to take me in and carry me off with all speed. A pilot was ready—one who was well acquainted with the country—to pilot me through the country, so that I might not go on any of the public roads. My wife came to the jail to accompany me, of whose society I had been deprived for four months. Just at dark, the sheriff and jailer came to the jail with our supper. I sat down and ate. There were a number watching. After I had supped, I whispered to the jailer to blow out all the candles but one, and step away from the door with that one. All this was done. The sheriff then took me by the arm, and an apparent scuffle ensued,—so much so, that those who were watching did not know who it was the sheriff was scuffling with. The sheriff kept pushing me towards the door, and I apparently resisting until we reached the door, which was quickly opened, and we both reached the street. He took me by the hand and bade me farewell, telling me to make my escape, which I did with all possible speed. The night was dark. After I had gone probably one hundred rods, I heard some person coming after me. I drew a pistol and cocked it, determined not to be taken alive. When the person approaching me spoke, I knew his voice, and he speedily came to me. In a few moments I heard a horse coming. I again sprung my pistol cock. Again a voice saluted my ears that I was acquainted with. The man came speedily up and said he had come to pilot me through the country. I now recollected I had left my wife in jail. I mentioned it to them, and one of them returned, and the other and myself pursued our journey as swiftly as we could. After I had gone about three miles, my wife overtook me in a carriage, into which I got and rode all night. It was an open carriage, and in the month of February, 1839. We got to the house of an acquaintance just as day appeared. There I put up until the next morning, when I started again and reached a place called Tenney's Grove; and, to my great surprise, I here found my family, and was again united with them, after an absence of four months, under the most painful circumstances. From thence I made my way to Illinois, where I now am. My wife, after I left her, went directly to Far West and got my family under way, and all unexpectedly met at Tenney's Grove.

SIDNEY RIGDON.

[*Sworn to before the Municipal Court, Nauvoo, IL, 1 Jul 1843.*]

Chapter 9

Later Petitions

ALDRIDGE, Sophia   SL

March 5th 1845
    to Sophia Aldridge the widow of Uzzial Stevens Uzzial Stevenses losses persecutions exterminations &c in Missouri
       The loss of Property in Jackson co Lands Privations ~~and~~ driven &c
                                       $3,000.00
    from Clay co driven losses of Houses and land Persecution and Privations &c
                                         3,000.00
       Extermiation of his widow from the state and &c   3,000.00
       Total $9,000.00
       Interest from 1833 to the time paid at 10 [per] Cent
       Sophia Stevens now married to William Aldridge

                                     Sophia Aldridge

[*Not sworn.*]

ALDRIDGE, William   SL

Nauvoo March 5th 1845
    ~~From 18~~ William Aldridges grievances in Missouri ~~From 1833 to~~ first the Loss of Property in Jackson co and extermination &c
                                         $3,000.00
    Driven from Clay co to caldwell co Difficulties & persecutions
                                       2,000.00.
    As a freeborn american citizen having fought for my liberty in the last War with Great Britain as a bold soldier and then to be exterminated from the state of Missouri from Caldwell co privations losses lands persecutions &c   10,000.00
    Total $15,000.00

Interest from 1833 to the time it shall be paid at 10 [per] Cent

William Aldridge

[*Not sworn.*]

BALDWIN, Caleb et al.   JH[1]

State of Illinois, Hancock county. SS.

Personally appeared before Ebenezer Robinson, a notary public within and for said county, the undersigned citizens of said county, who being first severally duly sworn according to law upon said oath, depose and say that the said affiants were citizens and residents of Caldwell county, and the adjoining counties in the State of Missouri during the years A.D. 1837, 1838, and a part of A.D. 1839; that said affiants were personally conversant with, and sufferers in the scenes and troubles usually denominated the Mormon war in Missouri. That Governor Boggs, the acting executive officer of said State, together with Major General Atchison and Brigadier General Doniphan, and also the authorities of the counties within which the Mormons resided, repeatedly by direct and public orders and threats, commanded every Mormon in the State, Joseph Smith their leader included, to leave the State on peril of being exterminated; that the arrest of said Smith in the month of November, A.D. 1838, was made without authority, color or pretended sanction of law; said arrest having been made by a mob, by which said Smith, among others, was condemned to be shot; but which said sentence was finally revoked, said mob resolving itself into a pretended court of justice without the pretended sanction of law, then and there made out the charges and procured the pretended conviction for the same which are mentioned in the indictment against the said Smith, by virtue of which he, said Smith, on the requisition of the executive of Missouri, has been recently arrested by the order of His Excellency Thomas Ford, Governor of the State of Illinois.

Said affiants further state that they were imprisoned with the said Joseph Smith, when they and the said Smith were delivered into the hands of a guard to be conducted out of the State of Missouri, and by said guard by the order and direction of the authorities of said counties, where said Mormons were arrested and confined, and by order of the Governor of the State of Missouri, were set at large, with directions to leave the State

---

[1] 7 Jul 1843.

without delay. That said Joseph Smith and said affiants were compelled to leave the State for the reasons above mentioned, and would not, and did not leave said State for any other cause or reason than that they were ordered and driven from the State of Missouri by the Governor and citizens thereof, and further say not

CALEB BALDWIN,
LYMAN WIGHT,
P. P. PRATT,
HYRUM SMITH,
JAMES SLOAN,
ALEXANDER MCRAE,
DIMICK B. HUNINGTON.

[*Sworn to before E. Robinson, N.P., Hancock Co., IL, 7 Jul 1843.*]

BALDWIN, Caleb,
RIPLEY, Alanson
SMITH, Joseph, Jr.   JSC[2]

State of Illisnois Hancock County
    Personally came before Ebenezer Robinson a notary public in and for said County Caleb Baldwin who being sworn says that after the arrests of himself and others as mentioned in the fore-going affidavit he went to Judge Austin A. King and asked Judge King to grant him a fair trial at law saying that with the result of such a trial he would be satisfied—but Judge King answerd that "there was no law for the Mormons"—that "they must be exterminated"—that the prisoners, this deponent Smith and others, must die but that same people, as women and children, would have the privilege of leaving the State but there was no hope for them He told Judge King that his family composed of helpless females had been plundered and driven out into the prairie and asked Judge King what he should do. to which Judge King answered that if he would renounce his religion and forsake Smith he would be released and protected. that the same offer was made to the other prisoners all of whom however refused to do so and were in reply told that they would be put to death. Alanson Ripley being in like manner sworn says that the same offer was made to him by Mr Birch the prosecuting attorney, that if he would forsake the mormons he should be released and Restored to his home and suffer to remain; to which he

---

[2] Also found in JH 7 Jul 1843.

returned an answer similar to that of Mr Baldwin—Joseph Smith being in like manner Sworn says, that he and Mr Baldwin were chained togeather at the time of the conversation above recited by Mr Baldwin, which conversation he heard and which is correctly stated above, but that no such offer was made to him it being understood as certain that he was to be shot

Joseph Smith
Caleb Baldwin
Alanson Ripley.

[*Sworn to before E. Robinson, N.P., Hancock Co., IL, 7 Jul 1843.*]

CALL, Anson   SL

Losses in Missouri in Caldwell & Clinton and Ray counties.
Lands & goods in clinton county 10,000 ten thousand dolls,
In Land & goods in caldwell 5000, five Thousand dolls
property in Ray 500 five hundred dolls,

Nauvoo, Febr 20, 1845   Anson Call

[*Not sworn.*]

CHAPMAN, Welcome and Susan A.   SL

City of Joseph May 25, 1845
    Loss sustained by the inhabitent of Missourie during the oppressi[on] of the Laterday Saints Suffered from the above named inhabitents in the Latter end of the year Eigteen hundred and thirty Eight

One broad cloth coat	$12.00
one pernell vest	3.00
Three wollen carsey Blankets	12.00
One calico bed quilt	3.00
Four cotton and wool blankets	8.00
Two woollen bed Blankets	2.50
One lennen Sheat	1.00
one razer	0.75
Two tin pales	0.50
one shoe hammer	0.75
Calf skin	20.00
For sundries	2.75
Fouling gun	9.00

For loss of time Distress of famely trouble of removing <u>450.00</u>

$507.25

Welcome Chapman
Susan A Chapman

[*Not sworn.*]

FOOT, T. B.   SL

Bill of damages sustaned in the State of Missourie in consequenc Boggs ext[ermin]ating order

loss in land	$650.00
Crop	80.00
Stock	50.00
time and expences	300.00

Nauvoo Feb. 13th 1845   T B Foot

[*Not sworn.*]

HOLBROOK, Hannah   SL

I hereby certify that I Hannah Holbrook which was Hannah Flint in Missouri was through the general persecutions in Davis and Caldwell counties that I sustained losses of the following kind viz. in Clinton county of a claim of lands of 100 acres situated on Grand river of the choicest Lands in that section of country, worth $500 and Also 80 acres in Ray county of Deeded Lands worth $1,000 and also many other Losses of different kinds

Nauvoo Feb. 19— 1845—   Hannah Holbrook

[*Not sworn.*]

MACKLEY, John   SL

January 22ond 1845
This is a true list of property lost by the Subscriber in the State of Mousourie by the Mob in 1838 & 39

One Farm worth Five hundred Dollars

One rifle gun Fifteen Dollars
7 head of hogs ten dollars
the lose of time fore hundred and Sevinty five dollers

John Mackley

[*Not sworn.*]

PRINDLE, Roswell   SL

State of Missouri Dr To Roswell Prindle.

To driving & mobbing from Jackson Co. Mo. 1834	$500.00
To mobbing in Clay Co. & loss of 40 acres of land 1837	500.00
To mobbing in Caldwell in 1838 loss of 138 acres Land	1,500.00
To loss of 160 acres of Land in Clinton Co	1,500.00
To driving from the state by Gov Boggs exterminating order & exposure consequent theron entirely destroying his health	1,000.00
	$5,000.00

Nauvoo March 19 1845.   Roswell Prindle

[*Not sworn.*]

RISHARDS, Phinehas   SL

Amount of property ~~destroyed~~ sacrafised in the Missouri persecution.
State of Missouri to Phinehas Rishards Dr

to nineteen volumn Books	$27.00
to Manuscrips & pamphlets	7.00
Carpenter tools	9.50
Tainer tools	59.87
Missolanious articles	122.72
to ploom Milatary	2.50
to Clothing and shoes	30.00
to pemil brushes &c	2.49
	$261.08

Nauvoo January 1st 1844
furnished by request.

[*Not sworn.*]

TELFORD, John   SL

Nauvoo January 29th 1845
    State of Misouri to John Telford Dr

to a house, hay, and other property, left in concequence of being driven by a mob from the county of Carrol, in September 1838	200.00
to loss of time and traveling expences from Carrol to Howard	50.00
to loss of time ocasioned by sickness brought on by exposure	50.00
to a Doctor bill november 1838	50.00
to traveling expences and loss of time when driven by a mob from Howard County Nov 9th 1838	50.00
to building a house, making rails, fencing and other improvements Done on a farm in Monroe County which I was oblidged to leave in complyance with the order of Governer Boggs on the 8th of April 1839	200.00
to traveling expences and loss of time in leaving the state of Misouri in the Spring of 1839	100.00
to damagages in concequence of being drven from the State	1,000.00
	$1,700.00

                                                    John Telford

[Sworn to before W. Richards, City Recorder, Nauvoo, IL, 27 Jan 1845.]

TIPPETS, John W.   SL

Nauvoo Hancock Co Ill Febuary the 21 1845
    Bill of the loss of property in Misouri by lawless moroders also unhumanly dispeled from the state while under the aflictions of a fit of sickness and deprived of all the rights of men which I claim as my Just and lawful right to geather with the loss of property loss in lumber property and crops and in neat stock five hundred dolars also the losses and drivings of Caroline Pew from Jackson County to Illinois who is now my wif five hundred dolars

                                                    John [W] Tippets

[Not sworn.]

Chapter 10

Undated Petitions

ANONYMOUS   SL

A Bill of Damagees Susstaind by the Jackson County Mob of Missoury 1833

Five years I was Deprived of the youse of my Farm
1200 feet of Sqare Timber Stolen
02 thousand ~~feet of Square~~ of Shingle
40 Perch of Stone Laid in the Wall in Lime Morter
4 Window frames & one Door frame all of Oak Plank
Diggin the Suller 28 feet by the 20
2500 or 3000 Rails
Also the Land Strip of All the Best Timber on 100 Hundred
    Acres
the Loss of 1 Cow & Caff 6 Hoogs

Moveing from Jac to Clay	$10.00
Moveing from Clay to Collwell	70.00
Lost two Cows in Consiquence of Moveing	50.00
Mooveing from Colwell to ~~Missoury~~ Illinois	420.00
Deprived of Working at my Mecanical Buiziness 6 years	800.00

[*Not sworn.*]

ALDRIDGE, James H.   SL

A bill of Damages a ganst the State of Missouri in the year 1833 in behalf of James H Aldridge in Jackson County for Los of Lands Personal property and the los of time	$700.00
for false imprisonment for the suposed murder of Brazill and Linvill	4,500.00
For the Los of Property in Clay County	300.00

For the Los of Lands town Lot stock Crops Time and
   Expulsion from the state and County of Cowell ~~County~~   6,000.00

   With intrust from Date at 12 per sent Jackson County Independance
Missouri November 5the 1833

                                    James H. Aldridge

[*Not sworn.*]

ALLEN, Gideon   SL

Gideon Allen loss of property be being driven out of Missouri
The amount lost $900

[*Not sworn.*]

ALVORD, T.   HC[1]

   I removed my family from the state of Michigan to Clay county,
Missouri, in the year 1835, where I lived in peace with the people, on my
own land, eighteen months or more, when the people began to be excited
in consequence of the emigration of our people to that county. The
excitement became so great that I was obliged to sell my place at half price,
and removed to the county of Caldwell, where I purchased me a farm, and
settled my family, and made a good improvement, and was in a good
situation to support my family, and there lived in peace with the people
until the summer and fall of 1838, when the mob began to rise, and we
were obliged to fly to arms in self defense; but notwithstanding our
exertion, they murdered and massacred many of our people. We applied
to the governor for assistance, and his reply to us was, "If you have got
into a scrape with the mob, you must fight it out yourselves, for I cannot
help you." The mob still increased, until I was obliged to remove my
family to Far West, and there remained, surrounded with mobs of murderers, until General Clark arrived with his army, with the governor's
exterminating order. Then we were all taken prisoners; our arms taken
away; they then treated us with all the cruelty they were masters of, and
took possession of whatever they pleased, burnt timber, and laid waste
town and country.

---

   [1] 4:57; also found in JH 6 Jan 1840. Although this petition is undated, *History of the
Church* indicates it was prepared as part of the first appeal (*HC* 4:49).

I heard General Clark say, that he would execute the Governor's order; "but [said he][2] notwithstanding, I will vary so much as to give some lenity for the removal of this people, and you must leave the state immediately, for you need not expect to raise another crop here." Those who were not taken to prison, were permitted to return to their homes to make preparations to leave the state. Finding I had no safety for myself and family in Missouri, I fled to Illinois for safety.

T. ALVORD.

[Sworn to before D. W. Kilbourn, J.P., Lee Co., IA.]

AVERETT, Elijah   SL

State of misouri debter to Elijah Averett fourteen hundred 65 dollas
A list of propperty stolen by the mob of misouri

in the year 1838 november one gun	$15.00
twenty barrels of corn and seven head of Sheep	50.00
one improvement	100.00
expences by moveing	100.00
damages done by moveing and loss of time	1,200.00
	$1,465.00

[Not sworn.]

CLEMENTS, Albert   SL

State of Missouria [Dr.] To Albert Clements

To Claim on Land	$400.00
To Grain Stock Furniture	400.00

[Not sworn.]

COLE, Barnet   NA

Barnet Cole—Against the State of Missour in a bill of Damage received by being driven from Jackson County	$500.00
Damage Recd. in Coldwell Co	1000.00

[Not sworn.]

---

[2]The editorial brackets from *History of the Church* have been maintained.

DUNN, James   SL

damiges done by the State of [Misouri] September
taken by aparty of Ruffins on the Hiway while travling to the far west
and Compeld to Ride the thare God which I Call Canon for the Space of
5 days damiges 200

    to 1 gunn 25 dollars & to 1 sword 20
    to lost time 7 months at 20 dolars
    2010 dito to family 100 dolares

                           James Dunn

[*Not sworn.*]

FOUTZ, Jacob   SL

Ashort S[*k*]etch Conserning my dificulty and loses in missuri i lost
at lest fife hundred dollars besides being shot i was at the murders sene at
hons mill in Colvell County the reasen that ve was thare is this thare was
a mob of about twenty or twenty fife men came thare stolde horses and
catel and took guns and thretend to burn our gritmill as i was informd ve
then concludid to gether at the said mill to prevent them from robing us
ve like vice getherd thare about thirty six armd men on our one [*own*] land
and in our one [*own*] county tht then came apone us with uperts of too
hundred men armd and [unexpecit] ve pled for q[a]ters but thare was none
grantit tha commenceit the bludycein ~~of~~ sum of our men runavy and wen
the others vare kild and vaundid tha came round a blacksmith shop that ve
had got in i then saw that the idea was to cil us all for tha run thare guns
in thru the cracks and shot the voundid i being Shot in the thi could not git
a vay i laid on my fais and pertenit to be ded that came in and i heird sum
pleiding for thare lives a mung us a litil boy pled also tha replide that he
must dy tht he woold be a mormn after awile i heird the guns craking i had
to doo as the ded don in part one of them came and put his arm under me
hunting for pistels and one swor it was too bad to take ded mens buts but
i must have them and after tha had us all kild as tha supposd and then wente
to pludering the ded and houses and robd the pure wi[*d*]ows of thare horses
and wagons beding and Clothing after kiling thare husbands there was
severel newcomer tha took thare wagons and temes and put on the stolen
prperty and hollerd hurraw boys lets git out of this plase tha then left in
an our or too the poor vides and childron came [~~and the~~] veping for the los
of thare husband and fath thers thare was none left to bery the ded only
wimen and a few sick and crpelt men tha put the ded in a vell that was part
dug the mob came back in a fue dys and took persestion of the mill staid

8 or ten days during this time tha and thare horses lived on our grain and meit and drove of ou catel and vente frum hous to hous with thare guns and thare faises blackend thretning if ve did not leve tha kild men and boys after ve vare priseners and boastit of it in public and remaind unpon ishit

Jacob Foutz

[Not sworn.]

GREEN, Harvey   SL

State of Mo. to Hervey Green Dr To losses Sustained in Jackson County Mo. by being driven from Said place, with loss of Houses, lands & grain to the amount of one thousand dollars; also by being driven from Caldwell County Mo. to the amount of twenty five hundred dollars

Harvey Green

[Not sworn.]

HALE, Jonathan H.   SL

Account of property lost and Damage sustaind by Jonathan Hale the subscriber in consequence of Governor Boggs Exterminat[ing] law in the state of Missouri in AD 1838

by being Driven from the state with a helpless Family	$500.00
by property left behind and not daring to take away without endangering life	500.00
by loss of Citizenship	20,000.00
	$21,000.00

J. H. Hale

[Not sworn.]

HUNTINGTON, Dimick B.   SL

Memorandum of Property Destroyed in Missouri

Notes & accounts	$2,000.00
House stable Lot &c with one acre of Land	500.00
One Cow	15.00

Three Bedsteads iron ware chains &c. &c.	35.00
Five City Lots one acre each	500.00
One acre of timber	10.00
Damages By Being driven out	2,000.00
[*Total*]	$5,150.00

Dimick B Huntington Complainant

[*Not sworn.*]

JACKMAN, Levi   SL

State of Missouri Dr. to Levi Jackman

1833	To being driven from Jackson County the loss of property, loss of time and expence of mooving, and bein deprived of the rights of citizen ship in Said County	1,000.00
1836	To being driven from Clay County, the loss of property, time and expence of mooving and being deprived of the rights of Citezenship in Said County	200.00
1839	To being driven from Caldwell County, to loss of property by being obliged to dispose of it under value, and having to leve some unsolde, to loss of time of my son who had to escape for his life, the loss of a lot and buildings in the City of Far West the loss of one rifle gun taken from the Smiths Shop, and time and expence of removing to the State of Illenois, and the loss of citzenship	2,000.00
		$3,200.00

The above is a low etemate of my damage and loss of property—

As it respects my knowlede of the abuse inflicted on us from the time we went to Jackson County untill this presant season would be enough to fill a vollum, But Sufise it to Say that I have Seen houes torn down which was don in the nite by the hands of the mob while wmen and children fled into the woods to save thar lives, I have seen the distruction of the Printing Office, I have seen them discharge the guns at our people by which means some ware kiled and many wounded. I have sean women and children who had ben driven by the mob, fleaing befor[e] them into the woods to prserve thar lives whose husbands had ben driven from there imbraces, I have sean inesant men draged off to prisen without eaven telling them what charge they had a gainst them, and many such things I have ben eye witness to, and I have a number of times I have ben under the necesity of leving my house in the night and takeing shelte in the woods to save my life and that too when I was sick and sood in nead of a bed. a man by the name Samuel Hill threned to kill me without the least provocation, and in short our Sufferings were grate in the extreem, and I bair this testemonie against the people of the upper countyes of Missouri, with the exceptions of a fue individeles they boath by word and actions bid a bolde defiance to the Constitution of the united states and all order of governmant excepin a mob law which they make from time to time to suit there own condition

Levi Jackman

[*Not sworn.*]

KELSEY, Samuel A. P. SL

the State of mos Dr to Samuel A. P. Kelsey for losis in Said State in the year 1839 Feb the 15

forty acres land sexion 34 tonship 37 raing 29	
one farm worth	$1,000.00
Cloth	8.00
Sacrifis of Sundry things	100.00
the exspince of moving and trubel	200.00
Suffering in sickness and other ways	200.00
	$1,508.00

[*Not sworn.*]

LEE, John D. SL

State of Missouri D: To John D. Lee.

1838			
May		Loss of 49 Head of Cattle in Davies Co.	$800.00
	"	Farm	1,000.00
Nov.	"	Lot in Diahman & House	1,000.00
	"	Cattle & Hogs	100.00

"	Horse Shot by the mob	100.00
"	Waggon & Harness & Horse	250.00
"	Money—Cash	100.00
"	Arms 100 Clothing 50	150.00
"	Time in being driven from place to place 1 year	500.00
		$4,000.00

[Not sworn.]

LEMMON, Peter   SL

This is to Certify that I Peter Lemmon have lost in Consequen[*ce*] of Governour Boggs Exterminating Law in Missouri and a ruthless Mob under the protection of the Law special, contrary to the Laws of then U. States the following Property &c

(Viz) eight months time value to mi	$400.00
" one gun value " "	15.00
blades of Corn " " "	3.50
Loss of Corn " " "	75.00
Thirty Hogs value	150.00
one Farm with its improvment	500.00
Loss of Citizenship	30000.00
Total	$31,143.50

The within named is a true statement of my losses while in Missouri to the best of my knowledge with the exception of my value of the loss of Citizenship as an american ~~of there~~ Money never can repay for the loss of my right as an American Citizen however the value placed here in this Memorial is for the purpose of recove[ring] Damage from there Mobocrats as money is the only damage within the reach of the arm of the Law a let any one of your Honourable body say what you would value your Citizenship at or what would you give in exchange for your Citizenship and I will abide the decision

Peter Lemmon

[Not sworn.]

LEONARD, Lyman   SL

State of Missouri To Lyman Leonard Dr.

To loss and damage by being driven from house and land in Jacson
Cou in Nov 1833 by mob violance one thousand dollars $1000.00

To being beat and whipt untill life was almost extinct loss and
damage sustained theirby five thousand dollars   5000.00

Clay Co. March 1837 by being compel to leave house and farme loss
and damage one thousand dollars   1000.00

Caldwell Co. March 1839 by being Compeled to leave by Govr
Boggs exterminateing order one thousand five hundred dollars. 1500.00

Sum total $8500.00

[*Not sworn.*]

LEWIS, David   SL

Bill of an accounts against the state of Missouri for the years of 1838
and 1839

State of Missouri Debt to David Lewis for Eighty two Acres of Land house and betterments	$500.00
Do to corn and potatoes	50.00
Do to one cow	10.00
Do to Two guns 20 Dollars each	40.00
Do to one powder horn 50 cts, and 1/2 lb. of powder 25	0.75
Do to Shooting five Bullet holes threw my close whils they was on me five thousand Dollars each hole	
Do to false imprinment	1,000.00
Do to Driveing me and family from the State	5,000.00
Do to expenses of traviling to and fro on that acount	200.00
Do to Defamation of carecter	2,000.00

[*Not sworn.*]

MACKLEY, Sarah   SL

State of Missoura Dr. To Sarah Mackley widow of Jeramiah Mc

To Claim on land	$[7]00.00
To graine Stock Furniture	[7]00.00

[*Not sworn.*]

MOORE, Andrew   NA

A bil showing the los of property money damages I recieved by a lawles mob in the state of Missouri

I left Ohio in the yeare 1834 expence of mooveing	$75.00
settled in Clay County— being compeled to leve sd county in the year 1836 by the mob I lost on land in sd county	255.00
purchest land in Coldwell County expence of moveing from Clay to Coldwell County	150.00
los of property Cattle Hoogs &c	112.00
in the year 1838 the mobe commened a gane being compeld to leve the state lost on land	1,300.00
two rifles guns and one sword	40.00
two Town lots in farwest	275.00
houshold furniture and farming utential	85.00
on Cattle hoggs corn whete and other property	550.00
Cash expences to prepare for mooveing	40.00
Six monthes los of time and famaly	150.00
expence of mooveing out of the state with a large famaly without any just caus or provication	75.00
	$3,107.00

I sertify the a bove to be a trew account

Andrew Moore

[*Not sworn.*]

NELSON, Abraham   SL

Mis Soury losses of missoury

Land 160 Acres At thare [——] va[*l*]ue ATion fore thousand Dallars	$4,000.00
Corn crop	200.00
Hgs	60.00
Cattle	
Sheep	60.00

loss of lib erty five hundred [——] Dalars ..... <u>500.00</u>

$[4],820.00

Abraham Nelson

[*Not sworn.*]

NELSON, Edmund   SL

Edmund Nelsons loses in Messoury
land and crop $4000
horsees Cattle and sheep and hogs $1000
loss of liberty five hundred thousand Dollars

EDmund Nelson

[*Not sworn.*]

NEWBERRY, James   SL

the Acts of James Newbury in far West Mo. At the time of the S[*t*]ate
distress at the time of the Expulsion of the Mormons from that State

Pait P H Bunett for Lawyers fees		$820.00
he having Receiveed back to himself	[*subtracted*]	375.00
the balance he Gives to the Church freely	[*Subtotal*]	$445.00
also the Amount of $80.00 worth of Provisions pd L.Whites		
family 33 Whilst ~~in~~ he was in prison making in the hole		525.00
the history of this I wish mite be put on Record in the		
Church history		<u>33.00</u>
		$558.00

James Newbury

[*Not sworn.*]

PEA, John   SL

damage for los of timber that is timber Cut off by the militia in misouri Caldwell Co 40 Acres hogs kild bees destroid also Compeld to leve my house and land to gather with a large frame Smith Shop of two forges the loss of which to me is astamated low at fifteen thousand dollars

John Pea

[*Not sworn.*]

PETTEGREW, David   SL

State of Missouri Dr to David Pettegrew for Damages and loss of property by being driven from Jackson County to Clay County and from Clay to Caldwell and from Caldwell out of the state in to Illianois

Dr to Damages sustaind by being [d]riven from my home in Jackson County by a mob headed by Thomas Willson and the burning of my ~~and~~ house and the loss of property plundered $5,000.00

to the loss of my crop and stock   500.00

to one Rifle Gun taken by the mob   32.00

to the suffering of my self and family in Jackson on the account of being Driven to vanburin and from vanburen to Clay   2,000.00

to being Driven from Clay to Caldwell and the loss of property
                                                            1,000.00

to being falsely imprisened by Gen. Clark by Order of the Govener 34 days without a process   2,000.00

to being forsed to sign a Deed of trust and being forsed to leave house and land and the loss of property and being Deprived of sitizonship and forsed to leave the state and the suffering of my family   25,000.00
                                                          $35,532.00

The History of my sufferings I have handed over to sidney previous to his leaveing this place

David pettegrew

I certify the above a count to be true a cording to the Best of m[y] knowledg

David Pettegrew

[*Sworn to before C. M. Woods, C.C.C., Adams Co., IL.*]

PETTEGREW, David   NA

I David Pettegrew moved to Jackson in the fall of 1832 and purchaced a Quarter sec. of land and settled my family and made an improvement of a house and 12 or fifteen acres under good fence and rased a good crop and was in a comfortabl[e] sittuation to live some time in the spring or summer of 1833 the sittisons began to thretton us with mobs and some time about the last of June or first July thare was a ~~petition~~ paper got up for signers to drive the mormons from Jackson County they be came more and more enraged till I think the 22d of July when the printing Office was torn down some tard and feathered &c they still continued their depredations till in Oct. when a mob came to my house in the night of between 50 and a hundred men headed by brazill Moses willson Luis franklyn and burst Open my door and cried how many mormans have you got here I told ~~him~~ them we ware sick to come in and light a candle and see which was done by brazill he then came to the bed and felt the potts of my self and wife and pronoinced us sick the cry was made to tare down the house which was forbidden to be done that night by brazill but threttoned us with amediate destruction if we did leave the county forthwith they still continued there violence untill the fore part of Nov. when a mob of forty or fifty armed men full of violence and fury headed by Thomas Willson drove us men wimen and Children out of our houses saying if we ware found thare that night our noses should smell hell we being sick was forsed to leave all and, put out on foot with 7 or 8 men and 60 or 70 wimen and childred in to the wide spread prarie to face the cold winds having the Earth for our bed and the canapies of heaven for our covring not knowing whare to go with six of my childr[en] bare footed with their feet bleeding by occasion of the stubs on the burnt praries we steared our course south towards vanburin County the third night we came to a ledge of rocks whare we had shelter and staid two or three days till we had Eaten up our scanty allowance of provisons while we lay in this situation thare came two men to us and advised us to go with them to big crick 12 or 15 miles which we complied with as we had a few waggons in company I got my children or the sickest of them in to the waggons not expecting they would live till night but we made our way through whare we found provisions and shelter for a few weeks in which time Solomon Hancock Gipson Gates David Jones and my self made our way back to our places and found our houses plundered of our beds and beding and Cloathing and many other things among the rest was about ten Dollars worth of leather I had perchaced for my childrens shoes we succeded geting a way a few loads of corn but ware forbidden taking any more under the penalties of death we succeded in geting three of my Cows but thare bags ware spoiled and in a few weeks after this I had to leve my family and make my Escape to clay County being forced out by John Cornet and others but I sucseeded in giting my family a way in a few weeks after which my house and many others ware burned we livd in clay County a bout three years but ware often times threatned by mobs untill some time the last of June or first of July in 1836 the excitement run so high that we had to leave clay and settle in an attached part of Ray County after words struck of in to Calwell County whare ~~we~~ I purchased 64 1/2 acres of land built me a house and stable and made an improvement of 30 acres whare I lived in peace till some time in august 1838 when we began to be thretned with mobs I among the rest stood in my own defence untill Farwest was given up which was on the last of Oct I after being forced to give up my arms was taken prisner with about 60 others and marched to Richmond in Ray County whare we ware kept in close confinement and under a strong guard whare ~~we~~ I was kept for 34 or 35 days being chargeed with arson burglary and larsonry all the proof they had was that I was seen in Davis County I was bailed out under five hundred Dollars bondse then returned to my family whare I laid about a month when they found their procedings ware illegal and I found my bail was retieecd and that we ware likely to be taken again I left my family and made my Escape for Quincy Illianois ~~whare~~ my family are yet left behind and are not able to move without a grait sacrifice

David Pettegrew

NB. the mob in Jackson said if we ware permited to settle in the county we would soon become more numerous than them selves and would soon put in their officers

[*Not sworn.*]

PETTEGREW, David   NA

Inaddtion to what I have written thare has a few things occurd to my mind which I shall [re]late when; I was in vanburin County d[esti]tute of [provissions] in a thinly inhabited place and being sick and not able to work we suffered much for the want of provissions and had it not ben for Brother Gipson Gates we must have perished he brought us provissions and administered to our wants while he was at my house thare came a mob at my house the snow being werry Deep called me to the door John Cornet who appeared to be the head of the mob told us they had suffered much on the account of you mormans and we believe you are a grand set of tories connected with the british and you must leave immediately or your blood shall run my wife standing in the door said will you drive us out now in this deep snow with all these bare footed Children when you have plundered our hous and even the leather that was provided for these childrens shoes he then replied not to day but dont let many warm days pass over your heads I then askd him whare we should go he said out of the state broth Gates replied that it was rather a hard case he (Cornet) then replied oald man if you Open your head I will mark it as flat as a flounder he went with his abuses awhile and left but advised me to sell my lands in Jackson and said I never should possess it I left my family in a suffering condition and went to Clay whare I had to make [toils] to procure provissions for my family whare we had not the privilige of voting we livd in som[e] degree of peace till the time the camp [ro]se up and now will relate a conversation [th]at took place between Judge Elisha Camron and myself as I met him in the road he said its terrible time oald man the Mail Carrier Eat breckfast at my house this morning and said he came by an army of mormans this side of richmond and they are twleve hundred strong in Jackson and they have four cannon and recruits are coming in from other counties continually for Gods sake dont take your family over thare to be cut all to peices I replied that we had ben Driven from our homes without a cause and robd of our property and we had as lives Di now as any other time unless we can have our rights and I calculate to go over and he said he did not dis pute all this but you cant git your rights in any of these upper counties

David Pettegrew

[*Not sworn.*]

PETTEY, Albert   SL

A List of property lost by Albert Pettey in Caldwell County State of Missouri 1838 by mob Violence

40 Acres timber Land lying on Plumb creek 1 1/2 miles West of Far West 20 dollars per Acre	$800.00
32 1/2 Acres Land adjoining the S. W. corner of City Farwest 50 dollars per Acre	1,625.00
2 City Lots in Far West improved & not imp.	400.00
To Black smith tools & stock of iron	100.00
To Gunsmith tools	25.00
To one rifle gun & brace pistols & sword	25.00
To Book accounts lost in consequence of having To leave the state	500.00
To household furniture	50.00
To being deprived of citizenship with out a Just case	2,000.00

Albert Pettey

[*Not sworn.*]

PICKARD, Jane   SL

State of Mo to Jane Pickard Dr To losses Sustained in Jackson County Mo by being driven from Said place with loss of lands, houses &

grain to the amount of one thousand Dollars, also to losses Sustained in Caldwell County Mo. in lands, houses & grain to the amount of one thousand five hundred dollars

Jane Pickard

[*Not sworn.*]

REDFIELD, Harlow et al. NA

To the Honorble the Senate & House of of Representatives of the United States In Congres Assembleed

Your Petitioners Honrbly Complaning Wants Respectfully Represent that your under signd Petitioners ware Those unfortunate People Caled Mormons, that your Petitioners attempted to settle in Mo. that your Petitioners was taught to be leave that in a free & In Depen ant Government All People had a Right to Worship Acording to the Dictates of their Own Conshensh—But to the great surprise of your Petitioners—The gentle men of Mo. objected to this course of conduct & be came considerablely Refraclentory And Through the a gency of Executive patronage & fisical force Suseded in making the State of Mo So In con venient that your Petitioners had to leave the State of Mo. At a great Sacrifise & whilst in the State a fore said Some of your Petitions Property was taken from them & Some of their men & Connections Kild & wounded Wharefour for the Reasons that ~~the~~ your Pettitioners have been So Shamefully treate your Pettioners Would Respecfully Pray that your Honorable Body Would take the Subject under consederation & We plege our Selvs to prove all we allege & more if requ[este]d & your Petitioners as in duty bound Will ever pray &c

Harlow Redfield
John Pack
John Lawson
Lodowick H Ferre
Noah Rogers
Curtis Hodges Sen
Henry Stevenson
William Marks
Jonathan Hoopes

[*Not sworn.*]

RICH, Charles C.   SL

A sketch that I was an eye witness to in the State of Missourie Charles C. Rich on the 24th of october 1838 Messengers Come into Farwest stating that the mob was on Log creek burning houses and Loaded waggons and threatening the lives of the people those was a few men Sent out to ascertain the movements of the mob these men returned a bout eleven O Clock at night Stateing that thare had been considerable Damage Done and also that they had taken three of the Brethren prisoners and intended to kill them that night the trumpet was Sounded and men com together and prepard for to march in haste in persuit of the mob that we might Deliver our Brethren out of their hands we raised all the men we Could till we got to Braggs on Logg Creek where we organised them in to ~~three divisions The first Division in~~ a Company and found we had a bout Seventy five men David W Patten was first in Command and Charles C Rich Second and James Durfee third we proceeded on towards Crooked River and when we Came in a bout one mile of Fields we Dismounted and Hiched our Horses to a fence leaveing four or five men to watch them D W Patten took the first Division of the Company and kept on the road Charles C Rich took the Second Division and went Round on the east side of Fields Farm James Durfee to the third Division and went through the field we expected to find the mob Quartered at his Field house but found they were not thare we then formed our Company and marched towards the Crossing of Crooked river. we had not gone but a few rods when on top of the Hill near one Quarter of a mile from the Camp of the mob we was hailed and fired upon by one of the mob guard who Shot young Obanion wh[o] reeled out of the Compay and fell mortally Wounded Patten ordered a Charge and we marched Down the Hill on a fast trot when we got within a bout fifty yards of the camp we formed a line the mob had formed under a bank Behind the Camps which was west of us and as Day was just makeing its appearance it was Still Dark to look to the west so that we Could not see them Very plain this was the morning of the 25th the mob fired a broad side at us three or four of our men fell D. W. Patten ordered our men to fire which they Did we recieved an other fire from the mob we fired a gain and Commenced Crying the watch word (which was (God and Liberty) D. W. Patten ordered a Charge which was immediately obeyed and we routed what had not fled and we Came in Collision with our Swords one of the men that fled from behind a tree who was persued by D W Patten whirled and Shot him he Instantly fell mortally wound haveing received a large Ball in his Bowels in a few moments the ground was Cleared and and on finding D W Patten mortally Wounded Charles C Rich Took Command and gatherd up the Wounded ~~Patten~~ and made them as Comfortable as posible took the horses of the mob about seventy in Number Camps and baggage and returned to our horses here we ministered what we Could to the wounded Sent a messenger to Far west, took our horses and Continued our journey towards Farwest near Log Creek we was met By sister Patten, President Joseph and Hyrum Smith and Lyman Wight and [——] we left Br Patten at Log Creek he was moved to Goose Creek and Died that evening also Br Obanion Br Gideon Carter was Left Dead on the Ground Supposeing him to be one of the enemy but was after brought a way

I will also relate on other circumstance that occured in Far west after the troops or mob militia arrived two of them was taken prisioner they was kept at my house it was though Best to release them I was sent with a white flag to communicate with Said Militia on the 31 of october 1838. I was met by Capt Bogard the prisoners went with me to join the militia after a little Conersation and his threating the city with Destruction he told these men to pass on after which I wheeled my horse to ride off I was fired upon by Cap Bogard when only about twenty feet Distant I attempt to return the fire but he flid

Charles C. Rich

after Joseph and others was given up to the mob I was warned by the Spirit of God to flee into the willderness north or my life would be taken before the Sitting of the next sun I Started to Se Br Hyrum Smith to get Council Met Br Brigham Young he asked me whare I was going I told him the perticulars he told me he had been to see Br Hyrum and said Br Hyrum said I must flee north into the willderness and take all that I Could find of the Brethren that was in the Crooked river Battle accordingly about ~~that 12 oclock th night gave~~ 12 O clock that night we left Farwest and next morning a bout sunrise we crossd Grand river a bout 2 miles above Diomman being the first Day of November we sent some to Diommon to get some provisions the rest of us went up Hicky Creek a bout ten miles and camped there we organised ourselves into a Company thare was about 26 after we all collected and I was appointed Captain of Said Company 2 Day we traveled and Camped on Big Creek Send men Back to get news and provisions 3 Day we moved and camped on Sugar Creek and learned that Diomman was taken and that the forces was in persuit of us 4 Day we Set out for Iowa thrugh the willderness Snowed that night and turned Cold and Snowy it was eleven Days and a half before we reached the white Settlements on the Desmoine River During our Journey we had but little to eat and [our] horses nothing only what they Could gather from under the Snow we crossed the missippi at Quincy where we found friends and was kindly recieved

~~Charles C. Rich~~

[*Not sworn.*]

RIGDON, Sidney
SMITH, Joseph Jr.
HIGBEE, Elias   JSC[3]

Therefore The undersignd who are chosen by the Church of Latter day Saints to represent to the President and Congress of the United States of America the Cruel Outrages and injustice inflicted upon the said Church by the Citizens of the State of Missouri and also their Suffering Condition in Consequence thereof Do hereby for and in behalf of the said Church Petition his Excellency the President and also the Honorable the Senate and house of Representatives of the United States of America in Congress Assembled that they cause to be made a full and complete restoration of all the rights and priveleges which we have been and now are deprived of that we may enjoy all the rights and priveleges guarranted to us (in common with other Citizens of the United States of America) by the Constitution thereof And not only do we Ask to be reinstated to enjoy and be protected in the peaceable possession of our Lands purchased of the United States in the State of Missouri but we also Ask for a Just remuneration of damages which we have Sustained by being deprived of the right of Citizenship Contrary to the Constitution and Laws of the United States of America And your Petitioners in behalf of the said Church as in duty bound will every pray

Sidney Rigdon
Joseph Smith Jr
Elias Higbee

[*Not sworn.*]

---

[3] Even though this letter is not sworn or dated, it was probably written in 1839 and sent with Joseph Smith to Washington, D.C., as part of the first appeal.

RIPLEY, A.   SL

I Certify that I was expelled from the State of missori by Order of the exe[ci]tive, and that My individual damages I estimate at one thousand dollars

A Ripley

[*Not sworn.*]

ROBERTSON, Nichols   SL

This is to certify that I was Driven from Missouri and was Robed of my Goods and my Wife went to Davis County and found some of my Goods in the Possession of Henry Auberry ~~Rob~~ My Bill of Damage for loss of Property loss of liberty and being Driven out of the State in the winter ten thousand Dollars

Nichols Robertson

[*Not sworn.*]

ROCKWOOD, A. P.   SL

Quincey Ill
    State of Missouri to AP Rockwood Dr

March 1839	to Damage sustained by being thrown out of businss	$300.00
" "	" Loss by Damage on goods	400.00
" "	" lost of removing out of the State	100.00
" "	" Damage sustained by the Exposier and imparing the helth of myself & Famaly	6,000.00
	to Damage sustained by Deffermation of Character	5,000.00
	1 Rifle— $25, 1 Soard 5,	30.00
		$11,830.00

[*Not sworn.*]

SHAW, Elijah   SL

this is to certify that I was Driven out of Jackson Co. Missouri in 1833 and lossed all of my Provision and Improvements and was Driven in the winter and also ordered to Leave Ray Co and then Driven from Caldwell Co had to leave my home and property and flee to Illinois for Safety while liveing in ray Co I my life was threatened by a Mr. Johnson and Drake a bill of Damage for being Drove from my home and property life in Danger loss of liberty &c.
ten thousand Dollars

                                                    Elijah Shaw

[*Not sworn.*]

SLOAN, James   *HC*⁴

James Sloan made affidavit at Quincy, that the officers of the militia under the exterminating order of Governor Boggs in Missouri in 1838, took possession, carried off and destroyed a store of goods, of several hundred dollars' value, belonging to the people called "Mormons," in Daviess county; that his life was threatened, his property taken, and he was obliged to flee the state with his family, greatly to his disadvantage.

[*Not sworn.*]

SMITH, Hyrum   *HC*⁵

I left Kirtland, Ohio, in the spring of 1838, having the charge of a family of ten individuals; the weather was very unfavorable, and the roads worse than I had ever seen, which materially increased my expenses, on account of such long delays upon the road. However, after suffering many privations, I reached my destination in safety, and intended to make my permanent residence in the state of Missouri. I sent on by water all my household furniture and a number of farming implements, amounting to several hundred dollars, having made purchases of lands of several hundreds of acres, upon which I intended to settle.

---

⁴4:69. Although this petition is undated, *History of the Church* indicates that it was prepared as part of the first appeal (*HC* 4:49).

⁵3:373–74; also found in JH 4 Jun 1839. Although this petition is undated, *History of the Church* indicates that it was prepared as part of the first appeal (*HC* 3:368).

In the meantime, I took a house in Far West, until I could make further arrangements. I had not been there but a few weeks, before the report of mobs, whose intention was to drive us from our homes, was heard from every quarter. I thought that the reports were false, inasmuch as I know that as a people we had done nothing to merit any such treatment as was threatened. However, at length, from false and wicked reports, circulated for the worst of purposes, the inhabitants of the upper counties of Missouri commenced hostilities, threatened to burn our dwellings, and even menaced the lives of our people, if we did not move away; and afterwards, horrid to relate, they put their threats into execution.

Our people endeavored to calm the fury of our enemies, but in vain; for they carried on their depredations to a greater extent than ever, until most of our people who lived in places at a distance from the towns had collected together, so that they might be the better able to escape from the fury of our enemies, and be in better condition to defend their lives and the little property they had been able to save. It is probable that our persecutors might have been deterred from their purposes, had not wicked and shameful reports been sent to the Governor of the state, who ordered out a very large force to exterminate us. When they arrived at Far West, we were told what were their orders. However, they did not fall upon us, but took several of my friends and made them prisoners; and the day after, a company of the militia came to my house and ordered me to go with them into the camp. My family at that time particularly needed my assistance, being much afflicted. I told them my situation, but remonstrance was in vain, and I was hurried into the camp, and was subject to the most cruel treatment.

Along with the rest of the prisoners, I was ordered to be shot; but it was providentially overruled. We were then ordered to Jackson county, where our bitterest persecutors resided. Before we started, after much entreaty, I was privileged to visit my family, accompanied with a strong guard. I had only time to get a change of linen, &c., and was hurried to where the teams were waiting to convey us to the city of Independence, in Jackson county. While there I was subjected to continued insult from the people who visited us. I had likewise to lie on the floor, and had to cover myself with my mantle; after remaining there for some time we were ordered to Richmond, in Ray county, where our enemies expected to shoot us; but finding no law to support them in carrying into effect so strange an act, we were delivered up to the civil law. As soon as we were so, we were thrust into a dungeon, and our legs were chained together. In this situation we remained until called before the court, who ordered us to be sent to Liberty in Clay county, where I was confined for more than four months, and endured almost everything but death, from the nauseous cell, and the wretched food we were obliged to eat.

In the meantime, my family were suffering every privation. Our enemies carried off nearly everything of value, until my family were left almost destitute. My wife had been but recently confined and had to suffer more than tongue can describe; and then in common with the rest of the people, had to move, in the month of February, a distance of two hundred miles, in order to escape further persecutions and injury.

Since I have obtained my liberty, I feel my body broken down and my health very much impaired, from the fatigue and afflictions which I have undergone, so that I have not been able to perform any labor since I have escaped from my oppressors. The loss of property which I sustained in the state of Missouri would amount to several thousand dollars; and one hundred thousand dollars would be no consideration for what I have suffered from privations—from my life being continually sought—and all the accumulated sufferings I have been subjected to.

HYRUM SMITH

[*Not sworn.*]

SMITH, John   *HC*[6]

Lee County, Iowa Territory.

This day personally appeared before me, D. W. Kilbourn, an acting Justice of the Peace in and for said county, John Smith, and after having been duly sworn, desposeth and saith, "That in the months of October and November, 1838, I resided in the town of Adam-ondi-Ahman. Daviess county, Missouri, and whilst being peaceably engaged in the ordinary vocations of life, that in the early part of November my house was entered by a body of armed men painted after the manner or customs of the Indians of North America, and proceeded to search my house for fire arms, stating that they understood the Mormons knew how to hide their guns, and in their search of a bed in which lay an aged, sick female, they threw [her][7] to and fro in a very rough manner, without regard to humanity or decency. Finding no arms, they went off without further violence.

"Shortly after this above described outrage, there was a number of armed men, say about twenty, rode into my yard and inquired for horses

---

[6] 4:59–60; also found in JH 7 Jan 1840. Although this petition is undated, *History of the Church* indicates that it was prepared as part of the first appeal (*HC* 4:49).

[7] The editorial brackets from *History of the Church* have been maintained.

which they said they had lost, and stated, under confirmation of an oath, that they would have the heads of twenty 'Mormons,' if they did not find their horses. These last were painted in like manner as the first. These transactions took place when the citizens of the village and its vicinity were engaged in a peaceable manner in the ordinary pursuits of life."

This deponent further saith, "That the mob took possession of a store of dry goods belonging to the Church of Latter-day Saints, over which they placed a guard. I went into the store to get some articles to distribute to the suffering poor, and the officer who had the charge of the store ordered me out peremptorily, stating it was too cold to wait on me, that I must come the next morning; and returning the next morning, I found the store almost entirely stripped of its contents. Thereupon we as a Church were ordered to depart the county and state, under the pains and penalty of death or a total extermination of our society. Having no alternative, (having my wagon stolen), I was compelled to abandon my property, except a few movables which I got off with in the best way that I could, and on receiving a permit or pass which is hereto appended. I then proceeded to depart the state.

"'I permit John Smith to remove from Daviess to Caldwell county, there remain during the winter, or remove out of the state unmolested.

"'Daviess county, November 9th, 1838.

"'R. Wilson, Brigadier-General. By F. G. Cochnu.'

"I accordingly left the state in the month of February following in a destitute condition."

JOHN SMITH.

[Sworn to before D. W. Kilbourn, J. P., Lee Co., IA]

SNOW, Willard   NA

I landed in Caldwell County the first of Jany 1836 (soon after the church was driven from Clay) as we lived there and been an eye witness to the most of the scenes that have transpired relative to the mormon people (so called) untill the last of Jan. 1839. During this period I shall give a short detail of facts relative to this affair some of which might contribute to raise the excitement of the people and if considered of any servise they are at your disposal. and first there appeared an existing principle riceted in the mind of the sitizens of those upper counties of Mo that the mormons should not have the privilege of settling unmolested in any other county but Caldwell for as early as the next July & August 1837 severel of the Mormons had bought preemption rights in the county of Davis and many settled there which caused great excitement and the sitizens of Davis may

if not all united in the disapproving the measure & entered into a negotia-
tion to drive the mormons from the county among the principle leading
characters of this gang was Mr Adam Black Wm. Peniston & Mr Boman
who visited many of the mormon peoples dwelling ordering them to leave
the county some came to caldwell for fear of their threats others determined thy would not obey their mandates. By some means however the
cloud passed over and the mormon people continued to emigrate to both
Davis and Caldwell to some considerable extent untill about the first of
August 1838 at the election in Davis where hostilities were again recom-
menced upon the Mormons some of which were knocked down with clubs
and others dirked and the rest left the town and returned home at the same
time news were received at farwest that severel of the mormons lay dead
on the field in galerton who were not permitted to be buried therefore
several sitizens of Caldwell fourthwith repaired to Adammondiahman a
small town upon grand river settled principly by the mormons and there
in counsel with severel of the principle men of that place agreed to visit
the principle officers of ~~galiten~~ Davis county to know whether thy were
disposed to join a mob or whether thy were disposed to enforse the sivil
law according to their oath of office among these were Adam Black one
of the Justises of the county who Stated for the satisfaction of the mormon
people by a written document of his own composition that he had not nor
would not Join himself to any mob but would administer the sivil law
according to his oath of offise also the Sherif Mr Morgan with severel
other of the most sivil men in the county met a committy on the part of the
mormons and mutually agreed to endeavour to suppress all mobing and
live by the law of the land but the spirit of mobing could not easily be
suppressed longer Adam Blacks testimony soon appeared in the Richmond
paper stating that he under the threat of death had been compelled by an
armed forse of the mormons to sign an article that now free man ought to
sign Wm. Penderston Weldon and others faned the flame and sounded
the alarm of mob Ray county assembled and appointed a committee to
investigate the subject and Soon about three hundred had collected at
galerton and mill port to drive the mormons out of the county when they
the called on mormons Major generel Acherson and Donaphan who
marched in to davis with about 600 troops and so far affected a settlement
as to disprse the most of the mob others stoped their hostility for the present
and once more it would seem that they might live in the county whill all
this was transpiring a settlement was commenced at Dewitt in Carrol
County where the Sitizens of that place collected and passed resolutions
to drive them from that county they were ordered out of the place several
times but did not go till a number arrived from Canada to seek them a
location when the mob arose called on Jackson Ray and Davis and drove

them from that place burning buildings and destroying property they also took their Cannon and marched back to Davis and the day following something near one hundred mounted men traveled throu Farwest going to Davis commanded by Wm A Dunn to suppres insurrection information was also received that the mob were determined to drive the mormons from Davis these men ~~were~~ went as far as Raglins and [——] returned the mormons now collected in Adammondiahma[n] determined to defend them selves against mobs who soon commenced to burn and destroy property they were however routed their cannon taken by D W Patten and dispersed without the shedding of blood the people at Ray county soon collected a gang and commenced taking prisoners and ordering off the sitizens of Caldwell when Capt Patten volunteered to disperse them which he done but lost his life in an engagement on th banks of Crooked river with two or three others one week from this an army appeared at Farwest of five thousand or nearly that under the command of General Lucas and others from Jackson county to still the Mormons and here for the first time it was made known that the governor had ordered the Mormons to be removed fourthwith from the state and even to be exterminated if nescessisary for the publick peace they took Farwest and th[e] sitizens of Caldwell as prisoners of war took their guns from them and at the point of the sword and bayonnet compelled to sign an article or deed of trust in which all their propirty both personal and real was to be given up to be disposed of by certinan sitizens of caldwell ray or Davis other than the mormons and after secureing the prisoners and sending Joseph Smith Jr and others to Jackson marched on to Davis gave the mormons ten days to lave the county men women and children, took their arms and returned to Caldwell took about fifty selected prisoners and marched them to Richmond to be tried for crimes of great magnitude¶

In the mean time general Clark had arrived with another dettchment who also took part in the affair by sanctioning all that had been done and added more than S D Lucas had done the terms of general Lucas and his army were that the mormons to avoid extermination should give up their arms sign away their property and fourthwith be guarded by the militia out of the State when Clark came he done away what they called the treaty by refusing to guard them out of the State but ordered them to leave or be exterminated his last official orders given publickly in Farwest I will coppy a few items. After ordering them the mormons all out upon the Square guarded by his own troops he thus addressed them gentlemen you whose names are attached to this list of names when they are called over march in front and after about sixty or seventy were named over they were marched into the house & a strong guard set over them And now the rest of you gentlemen it only remains with you to fulfil on your part the stipulations all ready entered into with ginerel Lucas who is equal in authority with myself evry article contained in the treaty you will be required to fulfil a part of which has already been complied with (such as delivering up your leaders laying down your arms giving yourselves up as prisoners) but a very important part yet remains to be fulfilled which is for you to leave the state the governor has left his order discretionary with me either to remove you fourthwith from the state or exterminate you and I have pledged my honour to the Executive of State to see his order faithfully fulfilled and I am determined to carry it through. had I am glad you have thus far complied with the order had you not have done so you must and would have been exterminated now this is the grounds on which the treaty was made it now only remains to fill en the time of your removal. The power is invested in me to forse you out at this inclement season but as you have thus complied with the requirements offered & your Savility toward me I do not feel disposed now to compel you to go till spring but gentlemen you must not think of planting or putting in another crop in this state if you do the sitizens will be upon you neither of embodying yourselves in your metings for if this comes to my ears I shall consider it a violation of the treaty and shall be under the painful necessity of returning with these same troops & if So there will be no other alternative but extermination for if you violate any article in the stipulation there will be no confidence on which to rest another treaty. I have not time now neither do I intend to investigate this matter to know who is right or who is rong suffise it to say I have my orders from the Executive of State and the power is in our own hands and we will put it in execution what ever your feelings have been and still are it all matters nothing to me And concerning your being guarded out of the State by the militia of the state there can be no necesity of that only not go in a body or large bodies together for if you do you cannot get out of five much more out of the state before you will meet with trouble let each one go as fast as he can get ready one here and another there and from this time form characters for themselves only let them not take any arms or weapons of any kind and no one will trouble them the sitizens will not molest them they never have molested you They never will molest you untill you first [——— ———] you have always been first the aggressors and it has been proven in many instances that we cannot live with you the State cannot enjoy peace while you remain in it. And your new form of goverment gentlemen the laws of this land must be supported they shall be supported you must not think of becoming free and independant of this goverment; oh that I could invoke the Spirit of the unknown god upon you (who appear to be inteligent men) that you might be delivered from this awful delusion into which you have been lead that you may never cause any other people such trouble as you have caused us. you are now permitted to go to your homes and provide for the wants and necessities of your families all except these whome I have taken out of your number and such others as may be hereafter arested whome I intend to take to Richmond and there make a publick example of them. And concerning Smith and Rigdon & others your leaders whome we have got do not flatter yourselves that they will ever be given up again do not let it once enter your heart for their die is cast their doom fixed and their fate is sealed. This short address be it remembered was delivered to a people who have been mobed out of Jackson forsed to leave Clay driven from Carrol rooted out of Davis and last of all commanded to give up their pleasant possessions in Caldwell and leave the State or be exterminated by its authority their property has been plundered their cattle killed their provisions distroyed and their dwellings burned down and yet it would appear from the above addres that they had always been the aggressors nor is this all while six or eight thousand troops lay in caldwell & the sitizens of Farwes guarded as prisoners in these circumstances they suffered another mob of near three hundred to collect from Livingston and Davis and paint themselves and on the east part of caldwell and murder (within sixteen miles of Farwes) seventeen of the mormon people shooting the wounded men over again after they had fallen cutting them down with old swords or scythes swearing they should have no quarters but would only halve them not even spearing women & children out of about thirty seventeen were draged and thrown into an old well togither few only escaped to tell the news some of which were shot through the body no les than four times and yet the government we are told must be supported and its law Shall be put in execution.

Willard Snow

[*Not sworn.*]

STEWART, Levi   SL

State of Missouri Dr. To Levi Stewart

1838	Loss of Two Farms in Davies Co. 280 acres &	
June	improvements	$2000.00
	" 30 head of Horses, Cattle, & c	500.00
	" Household Furniture	100.00
Nov.	Loss of Lot in Diahman	500.00
	" Far West	200.00
	[*Subtotal*]	$3,300.00

one years loss of time in being driven by a
relentless mob

500.00
$3,800.00

Loss of arms 50.00 Cash 100.00

[*Not sworn.*]

THOMPSON, Lewis   NA

Adams County State of Illinois Sept. 3rd [*18*]39
    Bill of damages Against the State of Missouri For the unlawful
proceedings of the inhabitants and the unconstitutional decree of the
Governor of Sd. State. During the past winter & fall And up to the present
time

Loss in Sale of Land	$186.00
Loss of time	40.00
Loss of Sundry articles taken Feloniously	15.00
Expenses in removing & Loss of Corn potatoes &c	16.00
	$257.00

    The above Mentioned Losses were Sustained in the State of Missouri
by Me

Lewis Thompson

[*Not sworn.*]

WILBER, Benjamin S.   SL

    Account of property lost and damage sustained by Benjamin S.
Wilber the subcriber in consequence of being driven from the state of
Missouri by governor Boggs Exterminating law

Viz Expenses	$000.00
by moving to and loss of time	150.50
by moving from and loss of time	300.00
by loss of five Horses harness and waggon	900.00
by loss of Cattle	140.00
by loss of Citizenship	20,000.00
The sum total	$21,490.50

The above is a just and honest estimate of my losses according to the best of my Judgment and Knowledg

B. S. Wilber

[*Not sworn.*]

WILLIS, William W.   SL

A Bill of Damages and Loss of property by William W Willis in the State of Missouri in conseqenence of the Orders of the govornar Orders to Expell from the State all People Comanley Called Mormons
for the Loss on the Sale of 80 Acres of Land Four hundred Dollars
for the Loss of other Property fifty Dollars
for the Expences of Mooveing fom the State and Sufferng Two hundred Dollars

W. W. Willis

[*Sworn to before Thomas Crawford, J.P., Hancock Co., IL.*]

YOUNG, Joseph & Jane A.   NA[8]

The following is a short history of my travels to the state of Missouri and of a bloody tragedy acted at Haunn's mills on Shoal creek Oct 30th 1838 On the sixth day of July last I started with my family from Kirtland Ohio for the State of Missouri The county of Caldwell in the upper part of the state being the place of my destination

On the thirteenth of Oct I crossed the Mississippi at Louisianna at which place I heard vaguereports of the disturbances in the upper country but nothing that could be relied upon I continued my course westward till I cross'd Grand River at a place called Comptons ferry, at which place I heard for the first time that if I proceeded any further on my journey I would be in danger of being stopped by a body of armed men. I was not willing however, while treading my native soil, and breathing republican air to abandon my object. which was to locate myself and family in a fine healthy country, where we could enjoy the society of our friends and connections.

---

[8] Also found in *HC* 3:183–86. The account found in *History of the Church* differs slightly from the one above. Besides a few differences in the wording, Jane Young did not sign the petition, and it was sworn to before C. M. Woods, C.C.C., Adams Co., IL, 4 Jun 1839.

Consequently I prosecuted my journey, till I came to Whitneys mills situated on Shoal creek in the eastern part of Caldwell county. After crossing the creek, and going about three miles, we met a party of the mob, about forty in number, armed with rifles and mounted on horses ~~back~~ who informed us that we could go no farther west, threatning us with instant death if we proceeded any further I asked them the reason of this prohibition to which they replied that we were mormons, and that every one who adhered to our religious faith would have to leave the State in ten days or renounce their religion. Accordindly they drove us back to the mills above mentioned. Here we tarried three days, and on Fryday the twenty sixth we recrossed the creek and following up its banks, we succeeded in eluding the mob, for the time being and gained the residence of a friend in Myer's settlement. On Sunday 28th of Oct. we arriv[ed] about ~~twelve oclock~~ at noon at Haunns Mills; where we found a number of our friends, collected together who were holding a council; and deliberating on the best course for them to pursue. to defend themselves against the mob who were collecting in the neighbor hood under the command of Col. Jennings of Livingston ~~and Mr. Ashby of Ca a member of the State Legislature~~, and threatning them with house burning and killing. The decision of the council was that our friends there should place themselves in an attitude of self defence. Accordingly about twenty eight of our men armed themselves and were in constant readiness for an attack of any small body of men that ~~should~~ might come upon them The same evening for some cause best known to themselves, the~~y~~ mob sent one of their number to enter into a treaty with our friends, which was accepted of on the condition of mutual forbearance on both sides and that each party as far as their influence extended should exert themselves to prevent any further hostilities upon either party. At this time however there was another mob collecting on Grand River, at William Manns who were threatning us. consequently we remained under arms on monday the twenty ninth which passed away without ~~any~~ molestation from any quarter. On tuesday the thirtieth ~~of Oct~~ that bloody tragedy was acted the scenes of which I shall never forget. More than three fourths of the day had passed in tranquillity, as smiling as the preceeding one I think there was no individual of our company that was apprised of the sudden, and awful fate that hung over our heads, like an overwhelming torrent, which was to change the prospects, the feelings and circumstances of about thirty families. The banks of Shoal creek on either side teemed with children sporting and playing, while their mothers were engaged in domestick imployments and their fathers employed in guarding the mills and other property while others were engaged in gathering in their crops for their winters consumption. The weather was very pleasant; the sun shone clear; all was tranquil and no one espressed any apprehensions of the awful crisis that was near us even at our doors

It was about four o clock; while sitting in my cabbin with my babe in my arms, and my wife standing by my side The door being open I cast my eyes on the opposite bank of Shoal creek, and saw a large company of armed men on horses directing their course towards the mills with all possible speed As they anvanced through the scattering trees that stood on the edge of the prairie, they seemed to form themselves into a three square position forming a vanguard in front. At this moment David Evans seeing the superiority of their numbers (there being two hundred and forty of them according to their own account) swung his hat and cried for peace. This not being heeded they continued to advance and their leader Mr Comstock fired a gun, which was followed, by a solemn pause of ten or twelve seconds, when all at once they dis charged about one hundred refiles aiming at a blacksmiths shop into which our friends had fled for safety. and charging up to the shop the cracks of which between the logs were sufficently large to enable them to aim directly at the bodies of those who had there fled for refuge from the fire of their murderers

There were several families tented in the rear of the shop. whos lives were exposed, and amidst a shower of bullets fled to the woods in different directions After standing and gazing on this bloody scene for a few minutes and finding myself in the utmost danger. the bullets having reached the house where I was living I committed my family to the protection of Heaven & leaving the house on the opposite side I took a path which led up the hill folloing in the trail of three of my brethren that had fled from the shop[.] While ascending the hill we were discovered by the mob who immediatly fired at us and continued so to do till we reached the summit ~~of the hill~~[.] In desending the hill I secreted myself in a thicket of bushes where I lay till eight oclock in the evening at which time I heard a female voice calling my name in an under tone, telling me that the mob had gone and there was no danger. I immediately left the thicket and went to the house of Benjamin Lewis where I found my family (who had fled there) in safety and two of my ~~brethren~~ friends mortally wounded one of whom died before morning

Here we passed that painful night in deep and awful reflections on the scenes of the preceeding evening. After day light appeared some four or five men with myself who had escaped with our lives from the horrid massacre, repaired as soon as possible to the mills to learn the condition of our friends whose fate, we had but too truly anticipated

When we arrived at the house of Mr Haunn we found Mr. Merricks body lying in rear of the house. Mr. McBride's in front litterally mangled from head to foot. We were informed by Miss Rebecca Judd who was an eye witness that he was shot with his own gun after he had given it up, and then was cut to pieces with an old corn cutter by a Mr Rogers of Daviess county, who keeps a ferry on Grand river and who has since repeatedly boasted of this act of savage barbarity. Mr Yorks body we found in the house and after viewing these corpses we immediately went to the black-smiths shop where we found nine of our friends, eight of whom were already dead the other Mr Cox of Indiana struggling in the agonies of death and soon expired.—We immediately prepared and carried them to a place of interment This last office of kindness due to the relics of departed friends was not attended, with the customary ceremonies [nor] decency, for we were in jeopardy every moment expecting to be fired on by the mob who we supposed were lying in ambush waiting for the first opportunity to dispatch the remaining few who were providentially preserved from the slaughter the preceeding day. However we accomplished without moles-tation this painful task. The place of burying was a vault in the ground formerly intended for a well, into which we threw the bodies of our friends promisocously Among those slain I will mention Sardius Smith son of Warren Smith about nine years old who through fear had crawled under the bellowses in the shop where he remained till the massacre was over. when he was discoverd by a Mr Glaze of Carroll county, who presented his rifle near the boys head and litterly blowed off the upper part of it. Mr. Stanley of Carroll, told me afterwards that Glaze boasted of this deed all over the country. The number killed and mortally wounded in this wanton slaughter was eighteen or nineteen whose names, as far as I recollect were as follows Thomas McBride, Levi Merrick, Elias Benner Josiah Fuller, Benjamin Lewis, Alexander Campbell, Warren Smith, Sardius Smith, George Richards, Mr. Napier, Mr. Harmer, Mr Cox, Mr Abbot, Mr York, William Merrick[9] a boy 8 or 9 years old, and three or four more whose names I do not recollect as they were strangers to me. Among the wounded who recovered were Isaac Laney, who had six balls shot through him two through his body one through each arm and the other two through his hips. Nathan K. Knight shot through the body; Mr Yokum who was severly wounded besides being shot through the head. Jacob Myers, ———— Myers, Tarlton Liwis, Mr Haunn and several others. Miss Mary Stedwell while fleeing was shot through her hand and fainting fell over a log into which they shot upwards of twenty balls

To finish their work of destruction this band of murderers composed of men from Daviess, Livingston, Ray, Caldwell, and Carroll Counties led

---

[9] The boy Young refers to here is Charles Merrick according to other accounts of the Haun's Mill massacre.

by some of the principal men of that section of the upper country proceeded to rob the houses wagons and tents of bedding and clothing, drove
off horses and wagons, leaving widows and orphans destitute of the
necessaries of life and even stripped the clothing from the bodies of the
slain

According to their own account they fired seven round in this awful
massacre making upwards of fifteen hundred shots at a little Company of
men of about thirty in number

I certify the above to be a true statement of facts relative to the above
mentioned massacre according to my best recollections

Joseph Young
Jane A Young

[*Not sworn.*]

Part VI

Related Documents

Introduction to Part VI

Part VI is comprised of miscellaneous documents which are found among the petitions in the National Archives or the LDS Historical Department.

Item one is a letter that was printed in the *Latter Day Saints' Messenger and Advocate Extra*. It was addressed to nine men in Clay County, Missouri, thanking them for their help in trying to mediate the differences between the Saints and the citizens of Clay County. The article also attempts to discount many of the accusations that had been made against the Mormons who were then living in Missouri.

The second document is an incomplete letter written to Colonel Price. Presumably, this is Colonel Sterling Price, who opposed the Mormons and served in the state militia that effected the surrender of Far West in 1838. This document tries to give perspective to the events at the Gallatin election by describing the political tension that led to the riot on election day.

The third document, written by Sidney Rigdon, is a letter to Felix Grundy, Attorney General for President Martin Van Buren. Rigdon wrote for advice on how the Saints might obtain recourse for the wrongs they had suffered. He must have written the letter while confined to prison in Liberty, Missouri, since it is dated 23 February 1839.

The next document is a letter Anson Call wrote to Sidney Rigdon. It is essentially a petition and even includes a bill of damages. However, it has been placed in this chapter since it is in letter format and was not sworn to before a county official.

Items five and six are endorsements signed by Church leaders recommending Joseph Smith. The first sustains him as presiding elder of the Church, and the second authorizes him to manage and transact all business for the Church before Congress and the President of the United States.

Next is a letter from Edward Partridge to Joseph Smith and Elias Higbee, who were then in Washington, D.C., detailing the land that Partridge lost in Jackson County.

The eighth document is a letter from Robert Lucas, governor of Iowa Territory, to A. Riply, who had asked Lucas for a statement of his opinion of the Mormons—Lucas replied that the Mormons were good citizens. This letter was presumably going to be used in the Church's appeal to Congress for remuneration.

The ninth document, a letter from four citizens of Pittsfield to Illinois Senator Richard M. Young, is a letter of reference for the whole Mormon society. It expresses support for the Mormons' attempts to gain redress, and requests Young's help in this cause.

Document ten is a list of landholdings signed by Joseph Smith, Sidney Rigdon, and Elias Higbee. They certify that they hold land duplicates for lands that were purchased in Missouri by members of the Church.

The eleventh and twelfth documents are much like petitions, but are actually letters to Willard Richards, the Nauvoo Historian. Richards was collecting information regarding the Saints' experiences in Missouri. The eleventh document is written by Isaac Higbee; the twelfth is probably written by Levi Hancock.

Documents thirteen through sixteen are accounts written by William Bowman, John Brassfield, and Adam Black concerning conversations they had with James B. Turner. It is ironic that these documents are filed with the petitions in the National Archives, for all four men were enemies of the Saints. In addition to these four accounts there is a remnant of a similar fifth account, not included because it is so fragmentary that it is almost meaningless. These documents probably were submitted to Congress as part of an 1841 Missouri response to the Mormon accusations.

The final documents are the permits to travel. After the Saints had surrendered to the Missouri State Militia, they were told to leave the state. However, they were apparently under the duress of obtaining permission from militia officers to travel. Several petitioners mentioned receiving permits to travel, and four included a copy of their permits with their petitions. Included here are passes for Nathan Baldwin, Alvin Hor, David Lewis, and Eliphaz Marsh.

Chapter 11

Letters, Permits to Travel, and Other Documents

Latter Day Saints' Messenger and Advocate Extra   NA

Kirtland, Geauga County, Ohio, JULY 25, 1836.
To John Thornton, Esq., Peter Rogers, Esq., Andrew Robertson, Esq., James T. V. Thompson, Esq., Col. William T. Wood, Doct Woodson J. Moss, James M. Hughs, Esq., David R. Atchison, Esq. and A. W. Doniphan, Esq.
GENTLEMEN,—

We have just perused, with feelings of deep interest, an article in the "Far West," printed at Liberty, Clay County, Mo. containing the proceedings of a public meeting of the citizens of said county, upon the subject of an excitement now prevailing among you occasioned, either from false reports against the church of Latter Day Saints, or from the fact, that said church is dangerous to the welfare of your country, and will, if suffered among you, cause the ties of peace and friendship, so desirable among all men, to be burst asunder, and bring war and desolation upon your now pleasant homes.

Under existing circumstances, while rumor is afloat with her accustomed cunning, and while public opinion is fast setting, like a flood-tide against the members of said church, we cannot but admire the candor with which your preamble and resolutions were clothed, as presented to the meeting of the citizens of Clay county, on the 29th of June last. Though, as you expressed in your report to said meeting—"We do not contend that we have the least right, under the constitution and laws of the country, to expel them by force,"—yet communities may be, at times, unexpectedly thrown into a situation, when wisdom, prudence, and that first item in nature's law, SELF-DEFENCE, would dictate that the responsible and influential part should step forward and guide the public mind in a course to save difficulty, preserve rights, and spare the innocent blood from staining that soil so dearly purchased with the fortunes and lives of our fathers. And as you have come forward as "mediators," to prevent the effusion of blood, and save disasters consequent upon civil war, we take this opportunity to present to you, though strangers, and through you, if you wish, to the people of Clay county, our heart-felt gratitude for every kindness rendered our friends in affliction, when driven from their peaceful homes, and to yourselves, al[—— —— —— ——] [in] the present excited state of your community. But, in doing this, justice to ourselves, as communicants of that church to which our friends belong, and duty towards them as acquaintances and former fellow citizens, require us to say something to exonerate them from the foul charges brought against them, to deprive them of their constitutional privileges, and drive them from the face of society:

They have been charged, in consequence of the whims and vain notions of some few uninformed, with claiming that upper country, and that ere long they were to possess it, at all hazards, and in defiance of all consequences.—This is unjust and far from a foundation, in truth. A thing not expected, not looked for, not desired by this society, as a people, and where the idea could have originated is unknown to us—We do not, neither did we ever insinuate a thing of this kind, or hear it from the leading men of the society, now in your country. There is nothing in all our religious faith to warrant it, but on the contrary, the most strict injunctions to live in obedience to the laws, and follow peace with all men. And we doubt not, but a recurrence to the Jackson county difficulties, with our friends, will fully satisfy you, that at least, heretofore, such has been the course followed by them. That instead of fighting for their own rights, they have sacrificed them for a season, to wait the redress guaranteed in the law, and so anxiously looked for at a time distant from this. We have been, & are still, clearly under the conviction, that had our friends been disposed, they might have maintained their possessions in Jackson county. They might have resorted to the same barbarous means with their neighbors, throwing down dwellings, threatening lives, driving innocent women and children from their homes, and thereby have annoyed their enemies equally, at least—But, this to their credit, and which must ever remain upon the pages of time, to their honor, they did not. They had possessions, they had homes, they had sacred rights, and more still, they had helpless harmless innocence, with an approving conscience that they had violated no law of their country or their God, to urge them forward—But, to show to all that they were willing to forego these for the peace of their country, they tamely submitted, and have since been wanderers among strangers, (though hospitable,) without homes. We think these sufficient reasons, to show to your patriotic minds, that our friends, instead of having a wish to expel a community by force of arms, would suffer their rights to be taken from them before shedding blood.

Another charge brought against our friends is that of being dangerous in societies "where slavery is tolerated and practiced." Without occupying time here, we refer you to the April (1836) No. of the "Latter Day Saints' Messenger and Advocate," printed at this place, a copy of which we forward to each of you. From the length of time which has transpired since its publication, you can easily see, that it was put forth for no other reason than to correct the public mind generally, without a reference or expectation of an excitement of the nature of the one now in your country. Why we refer you to this publication, particularly, is because many of our friends who are now at the west, were in this place when this paper made its appearance, and from personal observation gave it their decided approbation, and expressed those sentiments to be their own, in the fullest particular.

Another charge of great magnitude is brought against our friends in the west—of "keeping up a constant communication with the Indian tribes on our frontier, with declaring, even from the pulpit, that the Indians are a part of God's chosen people, and are destined, by heaven, to inherit this land, in common with themselves." We know of nothing, under the present aspect of our Indian relations, calculated to rouse the fears of the people of the Upper Missouri, more than a combination or influence of this nature; and we cannot look upon it other than one of the most subtle purposes of those whose feelings are embittered against our friends, to turn the eye of suspicion upon them from every man who is acquainted with the barbarous cruelty of rude savages. Since a rumor was afloat that the Western Indians were showing signs of war, we have received frequent private letters from our friends, who have not only expressed fears for their own safety, in case the Indians should break out, but a decided determination to be among the first to repel any invasion, and defend the frontier from all hostilities. We mention the last fact, because it was wholly uncalled for on our part, and came previous to any excitement on the part of the people of Clay county, against our friends, and must definitively show, that this charge is also untrue.

Another charge against our friends, and one that is urged as a reason why they must immediately leave the county of Clay, is, that they are making or are like to, the same "their permanent home, the center and general rendezvous of their people." We have never understood such to be the purpose, wish or design of this society; but on the contrary, have ever supposed, that those who resided in Clay county, only designed it as a temporary residence, until the law and authority of our country should put them in the quiet possession of their homes in Jackson county. And such as had not possessions there, could purchase to the entire satisfaction and interest of the people of Jackson county.

Having partially mentioned the leading objections urged against our friends, we would here add, that it has not been done with a view on our part, to dissuade you from acting in strict conformity with your preamble and resolutions, offered to the people of Clay county, on the 29th ult. but from a sense of duty to a people embarrassed, persecuted and afflicted. For you are aware, gentlemen, that in times of excitement, virtues are transformed into vices, acts, which in other cases, and under other circumstances, would be considered upright and honorable, interpreted contrary from their real intent, and made objectional and criminal; and from whom could we look for forbearance and compassion with confidence and assurance, more than from those whose bosoms are warmed with those pure principles of patriotism with which you have been guided in the present instance, to secure the peace of your county, and save a persecuted people from further violence, and destruction?

It is said that our friends are poor; that they have but little or nothing to bind their feelings or wishes to Clay county, and that in consequence, have a less claim upon that county. We do not deny the fact, that our friends are poor; but their persecutions have helped to render them so. While other men were peacefully following their avocations, and extending their interest, they have been deprived of the right of citizenship, prevented from enjoying their own, charged with violating the sacred principles of our constitution and laws; made to feel the keenest aspersions of the tongue of slander, waded through all but death, and, are now suffering under calumnies calculated to excite the indignation and hatred of every people among whom they may dwell, thereby exposing them to destruction and inevitable ruin!

If a people, a community, or a society, can accumulate wealth, increase in worldly fortune, improve in science and arts, rise to eminence in the eyes of the public, surmount these difficulties, so much as to bid defiance to poverty and wretchedness, it must be a new creation, a race of beings super-human. But in all their poverty and want, we have yet to learn, for the first time, that our friends are not industrious, and temperate, and wherein they have not always been the *last* to retaliate or resent an injury, and the *first* to overlook and forgive. We do not urge that there are not exceptions to be found: all communities, all societies and associations, are cumbered with disorderly and less virtuous members—members who violate in a greater or less degree the principles of the same. But this can be no just criterion by which to judge a whole society. And further still, where a people are laboring under constant fear of being dispossessed, very little inducement is held out to excite them to be industrious.

We think, gentlemen, that we have pursued this subject far enough, and we here express to you, as we have in a letter accompanying this, to our friends, our decided disapprobation to the idea of shedding blood, if any other course can be followed to avoid it; in which case, and which alone, we have urged upon our friends to desist, only in *extreme* cases of self-defence; and in this case not to *give* the offence or provoke their fellow men to acts of violence,—which we have no doubt they will observe, as they ever have. For you may rest assured, gentlemen, that we would be the last to advise our friends to shed the blood of men, or commit one act to endanger the public peace.

We have no doubt but our friends will leave your county, sooner or later,—they have not only signified the same to us, but we have advised them so to do, as fast as they can without incurring too much loss. It may be said that they have but *little* to lose if they lose the whole. But if they have but *little, that little is their all*, and the imperious demands of the helpless, urge them to make a prudent disposal of the same. And we are highly pleased with a proposition in your preamble, suffering them to remain peaceably till a disposition can be made of their land, &c. which it suffered, our fears are at once hushed, and we have every reason to believe, that during the remaining part of the residence of our friends in your county, the same feelings of friendship and kindness will continue to exist, that have heretofore, and that when they leave you, you will have no reflection of sorrow to cast, that they have been sojourners among you.

To what distance or place they will remove, we are unable to say: in this they must be dictated with judgment and prudence. They may explore the Territory of Wisconsin—they may remove there, or they may stop on the other side—of this we are unable to say; but be they where they will, we have this gratifying reflection, that they have never been the first, in an unjust manner, to violate the laws, injure their fellow men, or disturb the tranquility and peace under which any part of our country has heretofore reposed. And we cannot but believe, that ere long the public mind must undergo a change, when it will appear to the satisfaction of all that this people have been illy treated and abused without cause, and when, as justice would demand, those who have been the instigators of their sufferings will be regarded as their true characters demand.

Though our religious principles are before the world, ready for the investigation of all men, yet we are aware that the sole foundation of all the persecution against our friends, has arisen in consequence of the calumnies and misconstructions without foundation in truth, or righteous-ness, in common with all other religious societies, at their first commencement; and should Providence order that we rise not as others before us, to respectability and esteem, but be trodden down by the ruthless hand of extermination, *posterity* will do us the justice, when our per-secutors are equally low in the dust, with ourselves, to hand down to succeeding generations, the virtuous acts and forbearance of a people, who sacrificed their reputation for their religion, and their earthly fortunes and happiness, to preserve peace, and save this land from being further drenched in blood.

We have no doubt but your very seasonable mediation, in the time of so great an excitement, will accomplish your most sanguine desire, in preventing further disorder; and we hope, gentlemen, that while you reflect upon the fact, that the citizens of Clay county are *urgent* for our friends to leave you, that you will also bear in mind, that by their complying with your request to leave, is surrendering some of the dearest rights and first, among those inherent principles, guaranteed in the constitution of our country; and that human nature can be driven to a certain extent, when it will yield no farther. Therefore, while our friends *suffer* so much, and forego so many sacred rights, we sincerely hope, and we have every reason to expect it, that a suitable forbearance may be shown by the people of Clay, which if done, the cloud that has been obscuring your horizon, will disperse, and you be left to enjoy peace, harmony and prosperity.

With sentiments of esteem and profound respect, we are, gentlemen, your obedient servants.

> SIDNEY RIGDON,
> JOSEPH SMITH, Jr.
> O. COWDERY,
> F.G. WILLIAMS,
> HYRUM SMITH.

Letter to Sterling Price[1]   NA

Far West 8th Septr. 1838
Col. Price
Dear Sir

As a duty which I owe to the Church of Latter Day Saints, commonly called Mormons, and also to the public generally; I take the liberty of addressing this communication to you, and through you to the publick, in order that the publick mind may be disabused in relation to the affray which took place on the 6th of August last in Davie's County at the

---

[1] Col. Sterling Price was one of the principle mobbers. He guarded the prisoners from Jackson County to Richmond and was responsible for the conduct of the guard during the prisoners' trial before Austin A. King during November 1838 (*HC* 3:205, 208, 327, 372). This letter is incomplete, but identifies the political fervor existing in Caldwell County as the initial cause of the violence that erupted in 1838.

Election: together with the cause of the great excitement which has grown out of it.

I think Sir, that when the whole surface of this matter comes to be laid before you, You will agree with me, that it is one of those strange political, manouveres which occasionally occur (though I am happy to say but rarely) in times of high political feeling. As proof of the great excitement which prevailed in Davies County at and immediately preceding the day of Election, Judge Morin, our Senator elect, when conversing with myself on the affairs of the election declared that such was the excited state of publick feeling, that if he should lose his election; he did not know but that he would have to leave his present place of residence. I merely mention this to let you see how exceedingly high political feeling ran.

So great being the desires of the political parties to effect their object, as well as th[e] Candidates to obtain their election, You may well suppose that there would be great exertions made to enlist the Mormons, as they called them, in their favour: each Candidate in his turn using all the means in his pow[er] to obtain this object, Calculating with certainty that the ones who obtained their suffrage would be elected, as they comprised about one third of the Voters in the County. Proposals were made to Mr. Wight at one time or other by all the Candidates to obtain his influence, believing that such was his influence among the members of the Church to which he belongs that they woul[d] be easily persuaded by him to vote for the Candidates for whom he himself would vote. And among the rest, Col. Penningston made application for his share of Mr. Wights influence. The Col. was a Candidate for the house of Representatives and in order more fully to obtain his object he proposed to Mr. Wight if he would give him ~~all the aid he could~~ his influence; he in turn would give him all the aid he could to have him elected Assessor. Mr. Wight knew that Mr. Penningston previous to this time had been a great enemy to himself as well as to the Society to which he belongs, and took the liberty of enquiring concerning his former prejudices against the society, And as he had previously engaged in a <u>mob</u> to drive the Mormons out of the County; Mr. Wight desired to know what they might expect from him in time to come. Mr. P. said that he never designed to drive them out of the County that if he could not scare them so as to cause them to leave, he intended to let them alone. He further stated that he had been deceived by false reports and that he was now convinced that the Mormons were not such a peopl[e] as they had been represented to be, but were good citizens, with many other sayings which were favorable to the society.

But Sir, all this flattery and expression of good will could not prevail against Mr. Wights inflexable democracy. He was a Democrat and there was no compromise which could be made, which would cause hi[m] to sacrifice his political creed, nor could the promise of office have the least effect with him. If he could not get office without supporting men whose political ~~creed~~ sentiments he considered incorrect, he would not have it atall, and gave Mr. P. to understand positively that he need not expect to receive any assistance from him, but on the contrary, he would use his influence against him. Mr. P. was the whig Candidiate.

Perhaps it would not be amiss to let you know something of Mr. Wights political feelings as a democrat. He is one of the Old School. Uncompromising in his political creed. As an instance of his inflexibility. Mr. Awberry of Davie's County who was a candidate for sheriff had been Mr. Wights personal friend, as also a friend to the society to which he belongs, and had lifted his voice against a Mob which had been raised in that county against the Latter Day Saints, at the time they first began to settle in that county: But notwithstanding the personal friendship which existed between them, and the former kindness of Mr. Awberry, Mr. Wight would not vote for him because he was of a different political creed from himself. He was willing to perform any office of kindness to Mr. A. but he would not do it at the expence of his political faith, He was willing to do anything in accordance to it, but nothing against it. This determined and unchangeable course of Mr. W. brought the indignation of his political opponents on his head. Fearing that his influence would be fatal to their election, plans were accordingly laid to put a final end to his influence if possible and prohibit those of the society from voting at the election. Threats were issued to this effect in order, no doubt, to intimidate them, so that they would not go to the election Previous to this time, Mr. Wight and the persons now engaged in issuing these threats were on terms of friendship, and the friendship was only broken by Mr. Wights determination to maintain his own political creed at all hazards, and support those and those only, who were of the same political faith with himself.

Threats of personal violence were made concerning Mr. Wight. Mr. Bowman had sworn that he would cut his throat. These things were going on sometime before the election. I was at the house of Mr. Wight several times during this political campaign, though I did not suppose that it would terminate in any thing serious, But in this I have been disappointed.

Before the day of election came, feelings, if we may judge from sayings, ran high, and threatnings were made, but to what extent I am not able to say, but sufficiently to create considerable animoSity. The whole of this difficulty originated about the election; for before the electioneering campaign commenced, as far as I have know[led]ge there were no difficulties existing whatever, And the difficulties existing were purely political in their character. Religion had nothing to do with it on either side. It was fears entertained about the final issue of the election. Mr.

Penningston and his friends became convinced that they had nothing to hope from the Mormons, as they called them, but all to fear and they supposed the dye was cast with Mr. P. if the Mormons voted. These are facts, Sir, I think that cannot be contradicted in truth. So Stood the affairs up until the day of election arrived.

I wish you, Dear Sir, particularly to mark, that during all this time there was nothing thought about raising the Indians, about enlisting the Negroes or about abolitionism. These were all creatures of a more modern date

Letter from Sidney Rigdon to Felix Grundy[2]   NA

Quincy Ill. Febr 23 1839
Hon. Felix Grundy
Dear Sir:

I take the liberty of addressing on a subject of great importance of which you have no doubt heard as the publick papers generally have been giving publicity to it: I mean the affairs of the Mormons so called in Missouri I am one of that number who has been driven by violence from my home after being held in prison for near four months and all my property distroyed. My object in writing to you is to assertain if recourse can be had to the federal and whether or no we can enter suit in the court not only against individuals inhabitants of Missouri but against the state also for the unconstitutional acts of the executive of said state as well as the refusal of the leguslature to prohibit the execution of the executive order which was to drive us from the state and confiscate our property for no other cause than because we refused to tamely to submit to be desolated by a banditta of lawless marauders led on by a few persecuting priests I will be able to lay before the court the most satisfactory evidence of the violence and lawless outrages of the people of Upper Missouri as also the abusive tyring of the governer and the legislative acquiesenc in those those tyranical and unconstitutional measures which has been the ruin of many hundred families as well as the death of many persons not even children excepted who have been inhumanly butchered

I wish to know Sir if suits can be entered in the federal to recover damages for the distruction of property and the driving of families from their homes. As also whether criminal prosecutions can be entered against the murderers

---

[2]This letter was written while Rigdon was in Liberty Jail where he and others had been confined since the end of November 1838 (*HC* 3:212, 264). Felix Grundy was Attorney General for President Martin Van Buren, 1838-40 (Crutchfield 43).

who without cause indiscriminately murdered men women and children and eludes justice by driving from the state all those who are acquainted with their iniquity so as to be witnesses against them and so many of of the authorities of the state identified with these barbarities that it is impossable to have law executed

All these things I can prove most clearly to the fullest satisfacction of any court.

I also wish to know if the persons who are now in prison in missouri cannot be taken out of their hands and taken to the federal court for trial or else released by that court As it is openly declared in missouri that if any court or jury will clear them that not only the persons cleared but the court or jury doing it shall be instantly murdered.

There are in addition to all this a multitude of persons holden under heavey bonds among whom is myself to appear before the courts in Missouri whose sittings commences in March who have been driven out of the state and dare not return knowing that they will be instantly put to death if they attempt to return.

Your council in all these matters is solicited with as little delay as possable you will observe Sir that we are out of the state and dare not return.

Should you council to enter suits in the federal court please such instruction as you may think as to the manner of proceeding I will comply and will repair immediately on the receipt of a letter from you to the city of Washington and proceed forthwith to commence opperations. I have the honor to be Sir yours respectfully

Sidney Rigdon

Letter from Anson Call to Sidney Rigdon   SL

Feb 24th 1839[3]

[Mis]ter S. Rigdon I under stand that the [Broth]eren are requested to make out a bill [of] damageres and loses that we have sustaned by the Missori mob and grieveances when [I] [th]ink of the sufferanges of many many of [our] Brotheren I think at times I ought to [——] silant but I will give a short history [A]t the commencement of the Mormon difficulty I lived in Clinton Co. I ~~was~~ left Clinton and removed ~~to~~ in Davis Co. here I remained un till we ware all driven out [I] then went to Ray Co. to harvest a field of Corn that I rased there I was taken by a mob of ten men I was

---

[3]In this letter, one edge of the paper is torn. Brackets indicate a conjectural reading where it was torn.

searched they found I had know weapons they then drew their knives and swor they would kill me for i was a mormon they beat me with with there flat hand and then struck me in the fase with their knives time affter time I made my ascape from them a bout dark they per sude me but in vane I then re turned to Clinton Co. to attend to my bisness there I found a family in my House he said there was no law for the mormons and bat me severely with a club I was glad to git a way a live and and leave my farm and other proprty

I will give a statement of my damages two Preemption rights one for my Father and one for my self and secured 800 acres of timbered land and all pade for worth 300 hundred dollars each $600.00

Property left on farm and damage of moving from Clinton	150.00
Corn lost in Ray Co. fifteen acres	150.00
pade 560 dollars for land in Caldwell Co. ~~not sold~~ no value recd	560.00
pade 220 dollars for land in Ray Co. no value recd	220.00
200 hundred dollars totl gods stolen	200.00
Notes and acconts lost	440.00
	$2,320.00

Seven months lost time self and [Family]
Moving from Missorei to Illenois [———]

Total [———]

Missouri Marine Co.
Sidney Rigdon   Anson [Call]

[*Not sworn.*]

Endorsement of Joseph Smith   NA

At a public Meeting of the branch of the Church of latter day Saints, held in the City of Quincy: Illinois, on the 20th Day of October 1839. the expression of the Church was called for, concerning the standing and Fellowship of Joseph Smith Junior, in said Church. there are present about One Hundred Members composed of the High Council, High Priests, Elders, Priests, Teachers, Deacons, and lay Members, who gave their unanimous Voice, that he be considered the presiding Elder, over said Church, and have ever considered him as such since the rise of the Church, uncriminated of any Crime whereby he might be amenable to the Laws of the Land, and as such they recommend him, to all whom this may Come.

Reynolds Cahoon   James Sloan

Presiding Elder of the Meeting   Clerk

Endorsement of Joseph Smith   NA

To all persons whom this may concern—Or to whom it may appear—This is to certify that we the Subscribers hereof who are a Council in and for the Church of Jesus Christ of Latter Day saints—chosen & appointed by the Said Church to transact certain church business relative to the concerns of the said church as aforesaid do hereby Reccommend Joseph Smith Jun the bearer hereof to be a true & trusty man who we consider worthy of our best Confidence & trust as a man of integrity truth and Sobriety—and think him Entitled to general Esteem from all with whom he is acquainted—We feel it to be our priviledge & pleasure to intrust to his care the care and management & transacting for us the said Church any and all business & matters that may be needed to be done and performed with his Excellency the President as also the Congress of the United States of America in representing to ~~them~~ him his Excellency & then the Congress the abuse wrongs—Sufferings & Exitement from our homes & from the State of Missouri by the people thereof

Commerce Hancock Co Ill—Oct 27th 1839

Geo. W. Harris
Samuel Bent
Henry G Sherwod   David Dort
David Fullmer   Seymour Brunson
Alpheus Cutler   Levi Jackman
Wm Huntington
Thomas Grover
Newel Knight
Don C. Smith

We the undersigned do cordially Join in the above sentiment

Edward Partridge   Bishops
Alanson Ripley   of said
Vinson Knight   Church
Newel K. Whitney

Letter from Edward Partridge to Elias Higbee and Joseph Smith, Jr.   NA

Commerce Ill. Jany. 3d 1840

Dear brethren

The following is a list of land patents held by me for land in Jackson county Mo. which being heavy we think best not to send, but to send you the list of them so that you can go to the recorder's office of land patents and get him to certify that such patents are recorded in his office

This we conceive to be the cheapest and safest way their weight is about eight ounces

Certificate No. 3172 dated March 8th 1834—Recorded in Volume 6 page 180—Exd

Certificate No. 1871—Dated Decr. 5th 1833—Recorded in Vol. 6 page 446—Exd

Certificate No. 1872—Dated Decr. 5th 1833—Recorded [in] Vol. 6 page 447— Exd

Certificate No. 1873—Dated Decr. 5th 1833—Recorded in Vol. 6 page 448—Exd.

Certificate No. 14—Dated March 8th 1834—Recorded in Vol. 6 page 471—Exd.

Certificate No. 1961—dated Decr. 5th 1833—Recorded in Vol. 7 page 37—Exd

Certificate No. 1962—dated Decr. 5th 1833—Recorded in Vol. 7 page 38—Exd

Certificate No. 2317—dated January 20th 1834 Recorded in Vol. 7. page 387—Exd

Certificate No. 26—Dated March 8th 1834—Recorded in [V]ol. 8. page 483 Exd.

Certificate No. 27—Dated March 8th 1834—Recorded [in] Vol. 8. page 484—Exd.

Certificate No. 34—Dated Sept. 12th 1835 Recorded Vol. probably 6 or 8 the figure is so obscured that it is difficult to tell what it is. Page 491 Exd.

Certificate No. 3172—dated Nov. 4th 1835— Recorded in Vol. 9 page 272—Exd

~~What the Exd. means I do not know but it is on the patents and I do not know but that it may be of use~~

~~I remain yours in the bonds of the everlasting Covenant~~

~~J. Smith Jun.~~   ~~Edward Partridge~~
Elias Higbee

Letter from Robert Lucas[4] to A. Riply   NA

Coppy of Gov Lucas's letter dated Jan 4th 1840.

Sir you informed me that a Committee of Mormons are about to apply to Congress of the United States for an investigation on the cause of their expulsion from the State of Missouri and to ask of the General Government remuneration for the losses sustained by them in consequence of such expulsion and ask of me to state my opinion of the character and general conduct of these people while they resided in the State of Ohio: and also the conduct and general report of those who have settled in the territory of Iowa since their expulsion from the State of Mo.—

In compliance with your request I will state that I have had but little personal acquaintance with them. I know that there was a community of them in the north part of the State of Ohio and while I resided in the state they were generally considered an industrious inofensive people And I have no reccollection of ever having heard in that State of their being Charged with violating the laws of the Country.

Since their expulsion from Missouri a portion of them about one hundred families have Settled in Lee County Iowa Territory, and are generally considered industrious, inofensive and worthy citizens. very respectfully yours

A. Riply   Robert Lucas
                                                        Gov. of Iowa Ter.

Letter from Citizens of Pittsfield
to Richard M. Young[5]   NA

Pittsfield Jan 18th 1840
To the Hon R M Young

Sir We have been informed that A certain portion of our Citizens known as Mormons or latter day Saints are at this time petitioning Congress for a redress of the Grievances which they have sustained at the hands of our neighbors the Missourians. you no doubt have seen the newspaper Statements concerning them which are in some cases contradictory from our knowledge of many of them from a residence of twelve

---

[4]Robert Lucas was Governor of the Territory of Iowa from 1838 to 1841 (Tuttle 674–76).

[5]Richard M. Young served as a U.S. Senator from Illinois from 1837 until 1843 (*Historical Encyclopedia of Illinois* 603–04).

months among us we are enabled to State that their conduct has been unimpeachable. they are industrioustions and inoffencive Citizens, as any society that we have among us, and we hope that they may remain among us as long as they demean themselves as they have done. It is but seldom that we find a body of men among whom there are not some who are a disgrace to their society but among the mormons of this County we have known of no disorderly conduct. We therefore take the liberty of request-ing you to use your influence to procure for them whatsoever redress you may think they deserve. from the affidavits which they have transmitted to you or other members of our Congress, there can be but little doubt that they have been maltreated and we consider our duty as persons desiring the preservation of equal rights and religious toleration to ask their protection your obedient servants

> D.H. Gilmer
> James C Clark
> Daniel B Bush
> J Paullin

List of Land Holdings NA

Washington City January 20th 1840

We the Undersigned do hereby Certify that we hold at this time Land Duplicates belonging to our brethren purchased of the U S in the State of Missouri and frwarded to us by our brethren to present as testimony to show that we still are in possession lawfully of the same but compelled by the Exterminating order of Gov Lilbourn Boggs of Missouri to leave the same in the hands of the mob the following is a true list of the Numbers of the duplicates now in our possession at this time and which will be presented to Committe if requird as testimony

No 8482 Held by George W Harris
No 9779 Held by Squire Bosworth
No 680   "   "   "   "
No 9780   "   "   "   "
No 9987   "   "   "   "
No 8421   "   "   "   "
No 9986   "   "   "   "
No 10606 "   "   "   "
No 9782   "   "   "   "
No 10106 "   "   "   "
No 8420   "   "   "   "
No 10723 Held by James Goff

No 11834 Held by John Rowley
No. 10394 Held by Edward Partridge
No 10031   " "   "   "
No 11221   " "   "   "
No 9415   " "   "   "
No 9157   " "   "   "
No 8675   " "   "   "
No 9269 Held by Chandler Holbrook
No 9156 Held by Charles W Hubbard
No 10813 " " Wilson Vanderliss
No 8976   " " Gad Yale
No 10161 " " Samuel Miles
No 9374   " " John Fausett
No 10663 " " Samuel Rolfe
No 10992 " " Samuel Miles

The within is a list of the land duplicates in our hand as being a part of the many belonging to the people that was driven from Missouri by Gov Bogg Exterminating Order

~~Joseph Smith Jr.~~
~~Sidney Rigdon~~
~~Elias Higbee~~

The undersignd also have in ther possession vouchers setting forth thier Claims, from the individuals who have suffered being Notes Book accounts and instruments truly setting foth thier lawful claim the[y] will be presentd to the Committe if required at any time.

Joseph Smith Jr
Sidney Rigdon
Elias Higbee

[*Not sworn.*]

Letter from Isaac Higbee to Willard Richards   NA

To the Nauvoo historian Willard Richards sir

I understand that you wish to have the facts in relation to the loss of property and suffering of the saints in Missouri I will therefore give you a few items in relation to some of my suffering and losses in Missouri for you to dispose of as you may think proper I imbraced the gospel at Cincinnati about the first of June 1832 I removed with my family to Jackson county Missouri in April 1833 I entered 80 acres of land in Missouri which I since gave to the church laid out money to improve the land by making a farm and building a good house raised a crop and got things around me comfortable

In october 1833 we ware driven out of the county by mob violence and our house burned and property destroyed on the 9th of November we crossed the Missouri River into Clay county and that night in a tent in the woods my wife was delivered of a ~~boy~~ son several familyes of us had to live in camps all winter not being able to find houses on the first of september 1836 we removed to Caldwell County where I again bought land built a house and made a farm oct. the 24th I was in the crooked river battle. The 31st day of october 1838 when the army of Missouri came against us to execute the governors exterminating order I with some of my bretheren not willing to fall into the hands of a ruthless mob made our escape to Quincy Illinois to prevent being insulted and mobed by them we passed through a part of the country not inhabited and suffered much with cold and hunger. My real loss of property only would be about one thousand dollars But the damages Sustained besides my trouble sickness and death in my family in consequence of exposure &etc would be more than five thousand dollars

Isaac Higbee

Letter to Willard Richards[6]   SL

Doct Richerds <u>sir</u> I understand of you are Calculating to record the losses of individual property lost in the state of Missouri that it may be had in rememberance herafter—If it is the case you may record mine I consider I have lost at three different—once among those who first went to that state for when money was called for to purchass in jackson when all things was considered common stock I layed down three hundread dollars at one time at an other sixteen that there might be money to purchess lands in jackson and lands was bought for the saints and I should have had an inheritance if the mob had not drove the saints I done it for good and lost my money at an other time I put my hand in my pocket and pulled out my hand full of silver money and gave it to Joseph the prophet all I had save fifty cents I reserved to myself Joseph told I should be rewarded in Zion which I should have bin as sure as the Lord lives if the mob had not have drove us I then would not impose so much upon the man of God as to ask him for any thing and at many other times I have gave money in small peaces believeing I should be rewarded when the inheritances ~~was~~ should be got off to the saints all of this loss has bin caused

---

[6] This letter is presumably written by Levi Hancock, for the following is written at the bottom: "The Losses of Levi W. Hancock in the State of Missouri."

(save fifty dollars I had payed back to me) by Missouri mob which makes about three hundread dollars

The next loss was in Coldwell County I purched forty acors of land with in three miles of the temple ground in the City of farwest I payed fifty one dollars for it built a shop and house of logs had cleared two lots out and fenced them as good a lot of hogs as I wanted say forty and in the best place I could be for any trad a streem of water with the best of a water mill—seet and for small macheenry a laythe for turning and it was so nere the lawn I have thought I would not take a thousand dollars for it—the next was a lot of land in farwest Citty ten acors I payed a horse I gave one hundread dollars for and a harness new [twelve] and mad the runing geers to a two horse wagon

also I made one payment on a City lot on one of the greate streets closs to the temple I had in my power to have payed for the whole lot and not to have felt it als[o] I had an acor I in the vilag of Independance I gave the Bishop to pay the Lawyer to plead Joseph Smiths and the others cause which he never did all of this property I have left in Missouri which I will asure you I prised (with the timber I had for my house all hewed and sash made chaires table bedstids work bench turning laythe plank and shingle corn destroyed) at not less than fifteen hundread makeing twenty five hundread in Coldwell and not less than a thousand in Jackson And the hardships the hardships of my famelys deprivations for the want of some of this property to make them comfortable is more than the property it self and yet doct I feel as ever to do the works of Christ as I shall be directed by the twelve as much so as when the Prophet was a live you may think I prise my property high but I think I have not high enough but I will be satisfied at this

Account[7] of William Bowman[8]   NA

this is to certify that James B Turner wrote apiece of writing about the mormons that was stuck up in millport last Summer but the precise

---

[7]The following four accounts, found together in the National Archives, are written by three men concerning conversations they had had with James B. Turner. Turner, along with 41 others, appeared in court before Judge Austin A. King in November 1838. Turner was a witness against the heads of the Church who were imprisoned in Richmond (*HC* 3:209–10). Also found with these accounts is a two-line fragment of a fifth account, author unknown, which has not been included here.

[8]William Bowman was a member of the guard overseeing Joseph Smith and other Church leaders during their trial before Judge Austin A. King in April 1839 (*HC* 3:309). Bowman had earlier sworn that he would "never eat or drink" until he had murdered Smith (*HC* 3:306).

time I cant Recollect & I will State to the people how the conversation Took place betwen me and Turner

my self and Turner was setting in the Grocerry at millport. Says I to Turner what is to be done about these mormons comeing in to this county so fast for days I the are Settling over on honey creek the other Side of Grand River verry fast. I further observd that there ought to be some means Taken to prevent them forom comeing over on this Side of Grand River

then Turner spoke up and Said there ought then he named to me lets go out and Talk Some about it and after we Got out Turner stated to me that he was verry anxious that there should some corse be taken to prevent them from Taking the county for be cause said he I doant want to Raise my family among a Set of mormons

and he further stated that his feelings was to of went with us boys To of seed the mormons but my Reason was what I told you some Time Back

then I ast him if it would not be best to stick up a notice Requesting the mormons not to come over on this side of the River in the bounds of Daviess County

Turners Reply was I think it would then says I to Turner will you wright the notice Turners Reply was yes for I can change my hand so much that people cant Tell who wrote it then I cald John Brassfield and he come to us then Turner said Get me some pen ink & paper I went and done so

then my self Turner and brassfield went round the house on the west side and we all squatted down together and Turner again named about changeing his hand for some people would make Remarks if the knew who doneit[.] then he proceded To wright the notice and after he had Got ~~To Gether~~ it wrote he Red it ove[r] to my self and Brassfield as near in these words as I Recollect

Notice

is here by Given by Request of aportion of the citizens on the north side of Grand River any mormon that comes on this side of Grand River will be [start] and drove back no mormon that settle on this Side of Grand River if the do the may abide by the concequence Turner red the notice Over to me and Brassfield in these words as near as I can Recollect and as we Turnd the corner of the house gowing in Turner says dam them I think this will scare them[.] I stuck the notice up but did not Read it that day but the ~~next day or the following I~~ next day or the day following I did and there was a mis take and in the place of it being put mormon it was put morgans to which John Brassfield will Testify at any day that Turner acknoledge to him next day that it ought to of been mormons in the place of morgans these words I am willing to Testify at any Time to the best of my Recollection

747

the above is the coppy of Bowmans certificate To which he is willing to sware at any Time

Account of John Brassfield[9]   NA

this is to certify that I have herd Bowmans certificate Red over concerning the chat that took place betwen my self Turner & bowman When Turner wrote the notice Turner acknowledged to me next day that it ought to of been mormons in the place of morgans and from this Time Bowman cald me up to them I Tistify to the same of Bowmans to the Best of my Recollectioun and also I was setting squatted down by Turner when he wrote the notice

and he red it over to me & Bowman I p[re]sumd that James B Turner cannot deny these facts and if Requested I am willing to Testify the same in any place to the Best of my Recolection

the above is a coppy of Brassfieolds certificate to Which if cald on he will Testify any day

Account of William Bowman   NA

This is to certify the conversation that took place between me and James B Turner before the mob party went to see the mormons Last Summer

me and Turner was coming a long the road Last one day Just below whare Turner now Lives

I ast Turner if he was not gowing with us to find the mormons and his Reply was no for says he I in tend to Run for clerk here next year and if I do it will Effect something in my Election against me[.] & for that Reason I shal not Gow but I am Just as anxious to have the mormons drove out of this county as you or any other man for I doant want to Raise my fam ily among Such people this is the place Turner had Refferance to in that other place ~~When he~~ that his cause was what I told you some Time back these words I am willing to state before any man on any place in this county, when Requested

---

[9] John Brassfield guarded Joseph Smith and others when they were arrested and tried before Judge King (*HC* 3:309).

Account of Adam Black[10]   NA

This is to certify some Time ~~Last~~ Summer in conversation with James B Turner concerning these people cald mormons I Said to him that we concluded to gow and See these people and Request them to Leave this county peacibley and I would like for you to gow ~~a long~~ with us and his Reply was about to this amt he would Like to gow but he was a new Commer here and I daoant think it would be proper for me to do So

As I Exspect to Run for clerk it mite make some thing against my Election but I am opposed to them as much as any now he observd that he was opposed to Raising his family among then and I Replide to him he was Excusible says I for I doant want no man to Gow that doant feel willing

Given under my hand this the 27 July 1838

the above is a coppy of Adam Black Esq certificate.

Nathan Baldwin's Permit to Travel   SL

I Permit Nathan B. Waldwin to remove from Daviess to Caldwell County there to remain dering the winter or to pass out of the State

Nov. 12th 1838   R Wilson Brig Gen
                                        By F G Cocknee aid

Alvin Hor's Permit to Travel   NA

I permit Alvin Hor to remove from Daviss to Caldwell County there to remain during the winter

Nov 9th 1838   R Wilson Brig Gen
                                        Com

David Lewis's Permit to Travel   JSC

November 13 1838 this is to certify that David Lewis a Mormon is permitted to travel and pass through the State of Missouri in an Eastward direction unmolested during good behavior

                                        Nehemiah Cumstock
                                        Captain of the Militia

---

[10] Adam Black, justice of the peace and judge elect for Daviess Co. (*HC* 3:59), was a mob leader (*HC* 3:71).

Eliphaz Marsh's Permit to Travel NA

I permit Eliphaz Marsh to remove from Daviess to Caldwell County there to remain during the winter or to pass out of the state

Nov 9th 1838   R Wilson Brig Gen
                                            cmp.

APPENDIX

Adams, James — was a justice of the peace in Sangamon County from 1823 until 1843 (Bateman, Newton, and Paul Shelby, eds. *Historical Encyclopedia of Illinois* [Chicago: Munsell, 1899], 10-11).

Boling, William H. — was a clerk of the county commissioner's court from 1838 to 1843 (Grantee Grantor Records 17:440-41; *History of Pike County* [Chicago: Chapman, 1880], 871).

Brown, Aury — as justice of the peace performed twenty-six marriages from 17 May 1839 to 11 Nov 1846 (Marriage records, Pike Co., IL).

Bush, Daniel B. — lived in Pike County from 1836-44 and was an active justice of the peace beginning in 1838 (Grantee Grantor Records, Pike Co., IL, 1836-45; Marriage records, Pike Co., IL).

Campbell, James Morrison — was appointed clerk of the circuit court by Governor John Reynolds in 1831. He also served as clerk of the county commissioners court (*History of McDonough County* Springfield: Continental, 1885, 277).

Clark, Jones — was a treasurer in Pike County from 1839-43 (*History of Pike County* [Chicago: Chapman, 1880], 872). He notarized the petitions as a clerk of the circuit court.

Comer, Samuel — acted as a justice of the peace during the years 1839 to 1843 (Grantee Grantor Records, Carthage, IL: Hancock County Courthouse, 1839-43).

Crawford, Thomas — was a justice of the peace in Hancock County during the early 1840s (Grantee Grantor Records, Carthage, IL: Hancock County Courthouse).

Douglas, Joseph — made nine land transactions in Adams County from 1837 to 1841 (Grantee Grantor Index 1, Adams Co., IL.) as a justice of the peace. He performed marriages from 8 Apr 1841 through 25 Aug 1842 (Marriage records vol. 1, Adams Co., IL: 1825-90).

Enlow, Amos — served as a justice of the peace in Adams County, IL, beginning in 1838 (Marriage records vol. 1. Adams Co., IL; Grantee Grantor Records 1840-42, 674).

Frye, William — lived in Calhoun County from 1825 until his death in 1854. He served as clerk of the county commissioner's court from 1829 until 1843 (Grantee Grantor Records, Calhoun Co., IL; see also County Commissioner's Record Books A and B).

Graves, James A. — lived in Morgan County, Illinois from 1831-46 and served as a justice of the peace during much of that time (Grantee Grantor Records; Marriage records, Morgan Co., IL).

Harlan, Levi — was the first clerk of the circuit court (*Scott County Bicentennial Book* [IL: Bluff & Winchester, 1976], 23).

Hill, Robert L. — served as clerk of the circuit court for Jersey County, IL from 1840 through 1851 (Grantee Grantor Records, Jersey Co., IL).

Holton, John H. — was the county recorder from 1839 to 1846 (Wilcox, David F. *Quincy and Adams County, History and Representative Men* [Chicago: Lewis, 1919], 129) and also a notary public (Grantee Grantor Records 6:552).

Humphrys, Richard — made land transactions using his seal as a notary public 1840-47 (Grantee Grantor Index, Van Buren Co., IA: 1837-52).

Jackson, Samuel G. — a justice of the peace, was in Van Buren County, Iowa, from October 1840 until December 1849 (Grantee Grantor Index, Van Buren Co., IA: 1837-52; see also Marriage records, Van Buren Co., IA: 1838-40).

Johnson, John — notarized Parley P. Pratt's pamphlet. His office is not known.

Kilbourn, David W. — was a justice of the peace in Lee County during 1838-44 (*HC* 4:50, 416-417, 444; see also Grantee Grantor Records, Keokuk, IA: Lee County Courthouse).

Kimball, Hasen — performed two marriages in Hancock County, IL, between 1837 and 1846. Each time he signed as a justice of the peace (Marriage records, Hancock Co., IL: 1836-46).

Laughlin, William — lived in Adams County from 1837 to 1844. (Grantee Grantor Records, Adams Co., IL). As a justice of the peace he performed forty marriages between 16 Feb 1836 and 26 June 1845 (Marriage records, Adams Co., IL: 1825-90).

McGregor, Malcom M. — served as a justice of the peace from 14 March 1839 until his death in Jan 1842 (Grantee Grantor Records, Carthage, Hancock, IL).

Martin, Philip W. — entered fifteen land transactions between 1833 and 1842 (Grantee Grantor Index vol. 1, Adams Co., IL). Acting as a justice of the peace he performed six marriages between 9 Oct 1835 and 8 Sept 1842 (Marriage records, Adams Co., 1825-90).

Monroe, Andrew — was an acting justice of the peace in Hancock County, Illinois, between 1839 and 1842 (Marriage records, Carthage, IL: Hancock County Courthouse, 1839-43).

Morsell, B. K. — was a justice of the peace for District of Columbia, Washington, D. C. as evidenced by his signature on Porter Rockwell's petition.

Oglesby, William — justice of the peace, used his office and seal to officially record land transactions from 1837 to 1841 (Grantee Grantor Index vol. 1, Adams Co., IL). As a justice of the peace he performed twenty-four marriages from 1838 to 1842 (Marriage records vol. 1, Adams Co., IL: 1825-90).

Orr, Joseph — built the first store in Lima, Illinois, in 1833 (Wilcox, David F. *Quincy and Adams County, History and Representative Men* [Chicago: Lewis, 1919], 633). He acted as a justice of the peace from 1837 to 1848 (Marriage records, Adams Co., IL: 1825-90).

Petty, Elisha — lived in Pike County, Illinois, 1826-43. As a justice of the peace he performed thirteen marriages between the years 1837 and 1842 (Marriage records, Pike Co., IL; Grantee Grantor Records, Pike Co., IL: 1826-43).

Prentis, Daniel — served as justice of the peace for Hancock County, Illinois (see Marriage records).

Randle, John H. — apparently lived in Madison County during the years 1812-40 (Grantee Grantor Records, Madison Co., IL). As a justice of the peace he performed marriages between 21 Sept 1839 and 18 Dec 1845 (Marriage records, Madison Co., IL: 1813-71), but signed petitions as a notary public.

Rew, Horatio G. — settled in Morgan County in 1831. As a justice of the peace he performed twelve marriages from 1 Feb 1839 to 4 Dec 1842 (Grantee Grantor Records, Morgan Co., IL: 1831-42; see also Marriage records vol. 13, Morgan Co., IL: 1837-61).

Richards, Willard — was appointed general Church recorder on 30 July 1843 and had been a member of the Nauvoo City Council since 30 Oct 1841, during which he served as a recorder and minute keeper (*HC* 4:442; 5:522; *Latter-day Saint Biographical Encyclopedia* 1:53-56).

Robinson, Ebenezar — was a notary public in Hancock County, Illinois, on 7 July 1843 (Marriage records, Hancock Co., 1840).

Rogers, David R. — made land transactions in Pike County, Illinois from 1837 through 1846 (Grantee Grantor Records, Pike Co., IL). Acting as a justice of the peace, he performed twenty marriages during the years 1837-46 (Marriage records, Pike Co., IL).

Sells, Elijah — was appointed a Petit Juror 3 Apr 1839 (*Scott County Bicentennial Book* [IL: Bluff and Winchester, 1976], 22). Acting as a justice of the peace, he also performed marriages in Scott County from 1839 to 1841 (Scott County Marriage Record Book, Early Period, 1839-74).

Shafer, Abraham — was a justice of the peace in Clay County (*HC* 2:454; 3:281) who helped the Mormons while they were in Missouri.

Smith, Abram — was a justice of the peace in Hancock County during the years 1839-43. He died in 1843 (Grantee Grantor Records, Carthage, Hancock Co., IL: 1839-43).

Stanley, Wilson justice of the peace, made land transactions in Van Buren County, Iowa, from 1839 to 1843 (Grantee Grantor Index, Van Buren Co., IA: 1837-52; see also Marriage records, Van Buren Co., 1839-40).

Wells, Daniel Hammar — was an acting justice of the peace in Hancock County, Illinois, from Sept 1838 through 1846 (Marriage records, Carthage, Hancock Co., IL).

Woods, Carlo M. — acted as clerk of the circuit court for Adams County, Illinois, from 5 Dec 1838 through 21 Feb 1842 (Chancery record, Adams Co., IL, Book D:79, 205; Book 5:159, 184).

Young, John C. — actively purchased and sold land from 1833 to 1850 in Madison County (Grantee Grantor Records, Madison Co., IL: 1812-56). Acting as a justice of the peace he performed marriages from 26 Sept 1839 through 18 Dec 1845 (Marriage records, Madison Co., IL: 1813-71).

BIBLIOGRAPHY

Allen, James B. and Glen M. Leonard. *The Story of the Latter-day Saints.* Salt Lake City: Deseret Book, 1976.

Bateman, Newton and Paul Selby, eds. *Historical Encyclopedia of Illinois.* Chicago: Munsell Publishing Co., 1899.

Bushman, Richard. "Mormon Persecutions in Missouri, 1833." *BYU Studies (Aut 1960) 3:11–20.*

The Congressional Globe. Blair & Rives, ed. Washington: Printed at the Globe Office, 1844.

Crutchfield, James A. *The Tennessee Almanac.* Nashville: Rutledge Hill, 1986.

Grant, Roger H. "Missouri's Uptopian Communities." *Missouri Historical Review* (Oct 1971) 66:22–23.

History of the Church. 7 vols. Salt Lake City: Deseret Book, 1980.

Hyde, Orson. Letter to Joseph Smith. 9 June 1844. Joseph Smith Papers, 1827–44. LDS Historical Department, Salt Lake City.

————. Letter to Joseph Smith. 11 June 1844. Joseph Smith Papers, 1827–44. LDS Historical Department, Salt Lake City.

Jenson, Andrew. *The Latter Day Saint Biographical Encyclopedia.* 4 vols. Salt Lake City: The Andrew Jenson History Company, Publishers, 1901.

Jessee, Dean C. "The Original Book of Mormon Manuscripts." *BYU Studies (Spr 1970) 10:259–78.*

Journal History of the Church. LDS Church Archives.

Page, John E. Letter to Joseph Smith. 1 March 1844. Joseph Smith Papers, 1827–44. LDS Historical Department, Salt Lake City.

Richards, Paul C. "Missouri Persecutions: Petitions for Redress." *BYU Studies (Sum 1973) 13:520–43.*

Times and Seasons. Nauvoo, Illinois (1841–44).

Tuttle, Charles R. *An Illustrated History of the State of Iowa.* Chicago: Richard S. Peale and Company, 1876.

Wentworth, John. Letter to Joseph Smith. 25 May 1844. Joseph Smith Papers, 1827–44. LDS Historical Department, Salt Lake City.

INTRODUCTION TO INDEXES

Three indexes cover the broad indexing requirements of this book. The Author Index lists every individual who wrote or signed a document found in this book, petition or not. The Missouri Place Index lists places of geographical significance in Missouri, from creek to city. The General Index handles all other matters not covered by the first two indexes. This includes signers of the scroll petition, individuals who are mentioned in petitions, officials who notarized petitions, place names not in Missouri, and major events, like the Haun's Mill massacre.

For the most part, this index is not interpretive. It simply lists the page numbers where certain names or terms occur. For example, the entry from Caldwell County, Missouri, lists numerous page numbers; however, these page numbers do not necessarily indicate an in-depth discussion of Caldwell County, they only indicate that Caldwell County is mentioned at least once on all of the listed page numbers.

For the convenience of the reader, the index does include some uncontroversial interpretations. For example, well-known historical figures are indexed by their full names even if only a last name was mentioned. this was done as long as there was enough information to clearly identify a specific person. Thus some of the page numbers listed under Lilburn Boggs might refer to the word *Governor*. Well-known historical events have been handled the same way: a mention of the conflict at the Daviess County election is included under Gallatin election.

Perhaps the most difficult problem in indexing this book has been how to handle the variant spellings found throughout the petitions. Early in the indexing process, we decided to include all of the variant spellings of names and places in the index. However, as the project progressed, we decided to include alternate spellings only for a person's name and only when a spelling was so unusual that a reader might not recognize the reference on the cited page number. The final signature of each petition was our guide for the spelling of authors' names. The most common variant was our guide for the spelling of names mentioned in the petitions. We occasionally turned to an outside source, like the *History of the Church* to find the most acceptable variant.

What all this means is that our readers need to be open-minded about spelling. If the spelling expected is not in the index, try a variant.

We did not index general references to Missouri or Illinois, nor did we index proper nouns used figuratively. We did not index mention of a person unless at least one of their proper names was used.

The Editors

AUTHOR INDEX

A

Abbot, Rufus, 121, 412
Abbott, Lewis, 411–412
Adams, Arza, 121–122
Adams, David W., 413
Aldrich, William, 413–414
Aldridge, James H., 691–692
Aldridge, Sophia (*formerly Sophia Stephens*), 683
Aldridge, William, 683–684
Alexander, H. M., 414
Alexander, Randolph, 122
Alleman, John, 122
Allen, Albern, xxix, 123, 414–415
Allen, Anna, 123
Allen, Elihu, 123–124
Allen, Gideon, 692
Allen, James D., 415
Allen, Joseph S., 124
Allen, Nelson, 124–125
Allen, Rufus, 125
Allred, James, 300–302
Allred, Martin C., 300-302, 415
Allred, Reuben W., 125–126
Allred, William, 416
Alred, Isac, 126
Alvord, T., 692–693
Annis, John C., 126–127
Anonymous, 691
Archer, John, 127
Averett, Elijah, 693
Avery, Daniel, 127–128

B

Babcock, Dolphus, 128–129

Badlam, Alexander, 129
Baggs, Cinthia, *also spelled Cinhiy*, 129–130
Bagley, Eli, 130
Baker, Jesse, 130
Baldwin, Caleb, 130–131, 684–686
Baldwin, Nathan B., 131–132
Ballard, Philip, 132, 417
Barlow, Lucinda, 417
Bates, Archibald, 133
Batson, William, 133
Beebe, Calvin, 133–135
Behunin, Isaac, 135
Behymer, Jonethan, 136
Benner, Christiana, xxxiii, 136
Benner, Henry, 136–137
Bennet, David, 137
Bennor, Maviah, 417–418
Benson, Jerome M., 418–419
Benson, Mary, 419, 445
Bent, Lettice, 419–420
Bent, Samuel, 419–420, 740
Bernell, Jacinth, *also spelled Brunell*, 137–138
Best, Henry, 420
Bett, Henry H., 138
Bidwell, Betsey, 420–421
Bidwell, Robert W., 138–139, 421
Billings, Titus, 139–140
Bingham, James R., 140–141
Bird, Benjamin F., 141–142
Bird, Phineas R., 142
Birdeno, Zebiah, 142–143
Black, Adam 749
Blackman, Stephen, xxvii, 143
Blood, Roswell, 143

Y

Z

MISSOURI PLACE INDEX

A

Adam-ondi-Ahman, MO, xxvii, 17, 24, 26, 77, 112, 147, 159, 175, 222, 226, 294, 299, 303, 313, 343, 356, 404, 427–429, 463, 466–467, 469, 503, 509, 525, 530, 620–621, 623–624, 638, 657–659, 697, 708, 713, 715–716, 718

Arrow Rock, MO, 97

B

Big Blue River, 133, 447, 525, 654

Big Creek, 708

Big Creek, MO, 703

Blue River, 315, 527

Boone Co., MO, 93, 115–116, 349–350, 407, 638. *See also* Columbia, MO

Bunkham's Strip, MO, xxxii, 532

C

Caldwell Co., MO, xix, xxix–xxx, xxxii, 12, 14, 16–17, 21, 24–28, 32, 36, 39, 52, 73, 75–78, 80, 83, 90, 107–109, 111, 124, 126–127, 129–130, 132–134, 138, 140, 144, 146, 148–150, 152, 155, 161–163, 170–172, 174–175, 177, 180, 184–187, 191, 193–197, 199, 201, 204, 206, 208, 210–215, 219, 222, 224–226, 228–232, 234–235, 240–241, 245–248, 251, 253–257, 265, 279, 281, 286, 291–294, 296–299, 302, 305, 308, 310–313, 316–320, 325, 327–330, 334–341, 346–350, 357–358, 361–362, 365, 368, 370–371, 373–374, 376–377, 380, 385–388, 399–401, 403–404, 412–413, 415–419, 421– 423, 425–426, 428, 430, 432–437, 441, 444–446, 449–456, 460, 462–463, 465–466, 468–473, 475–476, 478, 488–489, 491, 494–496, 498, 500– 502, 504, 506, 508–514, 516–518, 520, 523–525, 528–530, 532, 534–538, 540–543, 546–552, 554, 556–558, 566–567, 640, 647–648, 652, 656, 665, 668–674, 678, 680, 683–684, 686– 688, 691–693, 695–696, 699–703, 705–706, 711, 714–718, 720–721, 723, 739, 745– 746, 749–750. *See also* Far West, MO; Haun's Mill, MO

Carroll Co., MO, xix, xxix, 16, 31, 38, 75, 81–82, 108, 111–113, 237, 400, 402–404, 426, 470, 473, 476, 479, 494, 503, 543, 548, 566–567, 622, 640, 665–666, 668, 689, 717–718, 723. *See also* Carrollton, MO; DeWitt, MO

Carrollton, MO, 237, 494, 543.

Caw (Kaw) River, 411

D

GENERAL INDEX

A

Abbot, Hiram, 32, 268, 320, 486, 488, 491, 723
Abbott, Jacob J., 613
Abbott, Martha Anne, 614
Abbott, Mary, 598
Adams, Aza, 595
Adams, Charles A., 575
Adams, James, J.P. for Sangamon Co., IL, 512, 521, 751
Adams, Moses, 575
Adams, Orson B., 587
Adams, Sabina, 595
Adams, Susann, 586
Ainscough, Mary, 595
Ainscough, William, 596
Akis, Betsy, 606
Akis, Hanna, 606
Akis, Patty, 606
Alben, Joseph G., 609
Alden, Briggs, 578
Alden, Lydia, 578
Alden, Nancy, 584
Alden, Stephen, 584
Aldredg, Sophiah, 592
Aldridge, William, 592
Alexander, Alvah, 583
Alexander, Horac M., 587
Alexander, Nancy, 587
Alexander, Phebe, 583
Alexandr, Samuel H., 583
Alford, J. M., 611
Alford, Joseph D., 598
Alford, Rossannah, 614
Alger, Huck, 608

Alger, Samuel, 608
Allan, Daniel, 582
Allan, E. H., 592
Alleman, Christeanna, 579
Alleman, John, 579
Allen, 315, 596, 634
Allen, Alson, 603
Allen, Candelia, 607
Allen, Caroline, 607
Allen, Charles, 15, 64, 104, 396, 526, 565, 590
Allen, General, 210
Allen, Gidean, 504
Allen, Isaac, 209
Allen, James, 139, 217
Allen, Jno., 603
Allen, John, 209
Allen, Lorenzo D., 586
Allen, Lucy, 607
Allen, Lucy D., 608
Allen, Mary, 609
Allen, Mary Ann, 582, 596
Allen, N., 55–57
Allen, Rufus, 503
Allen, Sarah, 592
Allen, Sinthy, 586
Allen, William, 569
Allred, Andew F., 586
Allred, Barton B., 586
Allred, David H., 586
Allred, Green W., 586
Allred, Isaac N., 586
Allred, Orissa A., 572
Allred, R. A., 572
Allred, William, 647
Allred, William L., 586

Blackburn, Anthony, 267, 486
Blair, Catharine, 612
Blair, Mary Elizabeth, 612
Blair, Samuel, 612
Blakely, Nathaniel, 542
Blakely, James, 457, 542
Blanchard, John R., 590
Blanchard, Mary E., 590
Blanchard, Prody, 612
Blezard, John, 590
Blezard, Sarah, 590
Bliss, Robert, 605
Blodget, Elizabeth G., 576
Blodget, Numan, 576
Boame, John, 597
Boame, Mary, 597
Boame, Sarah, 597
Boardman, Jane, 588
Boardman, Thomas, 588
Bogart battle, 43, 92, 673, 680. *See also* Crooked River, battle of
Bogart, Samuel, *also spelled Bogard*, xxxii, 17–18, 27–28, 79–80, 92, 96, 128, 179, 209, 220, 280, 328, 347, 422, 444, 457, 485, 495, 510, 533, 622, 625, 633–634, 642, 648, 658–659, 673, 708
Boggs, Lilburn W., xvii, xxv, 9, 14, 23, 26, 32, 34, 64, 69, 73, 76, 80, 82, 92, 105, 111, 114, 116, 121, 132, 139, 167, 170, 179, 203, 209, 262, 293, 316, 332, 347–348, 397, 403, 406, 408, 427, 446, 448, 470, 482, 500, 504, 509, 517–518, 520–521, 528, 530, 558, 622, 624–625, 636, 639–642, 644, 652–653, 656, 667–668, 684, 692, 712, 737
Boise, Sarus, 590

Boley, Barbary, 575
Boley, Henry, 575
Boley, Henry, Jr., 575
Boley, Martha, 577, 589
Boling, William H., C.C.C.C. for Pike Co., IL, 302, 413, 415–416, 446, 449, 465–467, 469, 478, 490, 509, 511, 523, 530, 536–537, 544, 552, 751
Bollin, Evaline, 580
Boman, Hyriam, 597
Booth, Ann, 582
Booth, Edwin, 596
Booth, Eliza, 596
Booth, Joseph, 582
Booth, Lewis, 596
Booth, Robert, 582
Booth, Thomas, 598
Boran, A. D., 599
Boran, Adaline, 599
Boran, Beverly, 599
Boran, Mary, 599
Boren, Allabama, 597
Boren, Coleman, 596
Boren, James B., 597
Bosley, Ann, 588
Bosley, Edmund, 589
Bosley, George C., 589
Bosley, Mary, 589
Boss, F., 610
Boss, Henry, 607, 610
Boss, John, 607, 610
Boss, Nancey, 610
Boss, Nancy, 607
Boss, Nely, 610
Boss, Obiedience, 607
Boss, Polly, 607
Boss, Solomon, 607
Boss, Willis, 607, 610
Bostock, Ann, 571
Bostock, Joseph, 571
Bosworth, Squire, 743

Botherson, Joseph H., 613
Botsford, Jabez, 575
Botsford, Sophia, 575
Bouck, Eliza, 585
Bouck, Eupheamia, 585
Bouck, John A., 585
Bouck, Margaret, 585
Bowan, Mary, 612
Bowen, Juliaett, 574
Bowermaster, Ann B., 575
Bowers, Colonel, 526
Bowman, 715, 736
Bowman, William, 466, 485, 542,
    728, 748
Box, William, 571
Boyce, Peter, 603
Boyce, Susannah C., 582
Boyde, George Washington, 572
Boynton, Abram D., 571
Boynton, Eliphalet, 581
Boynton, Hannah M., 571
Boynton, Susan, 581
Brace, 273
Braden, Eleanor, 586
Braden, Lu Ledda, 585
Braden, Lydia, 590
Bradford, 475, 597
Bradshaw, Ann, 612
Bradshaw, Ellen, 612
Bradshaw, Grace, 614
Bradshaw, John, 612
Bradshaw, Richard, 611
Bradshaw, William, 611–612
Brady, 316
Bragg, 707
Bragg, Augustus, 609
Bragg, Benjamin, 608
Bragg, Benjamin, Jr., 607
Bragg, Emily, 607
Bragg, Hannah, 608
Bragg, Mary, 610
Brandon, Abigal, 583

Brandon, Leah, 583
Brandon, T. J., 583
Brandon, Thomas J., Jr., 583
Brassell, B., 592
Brassell, Elizabeth, 592
Brassfield, John, 728, 747
Brazeale, Hugh L., *also spelled*
    Brazill, Braseal, Brazil,
    Brizeale, 22, 63, 68, 254, 316,
    526–528, 691, 703
Breger, Nancy, 595
Brenster, Lydia C., 581
Brewer, A. C., 612
Brewer, Wiley, 275–276
Brewster, Charles W., 581
Brewster, John, 581
Briggs, Henry W., 597
Brim, Alfred, 577
Brim, Andrew, 577
Brim, Vanness, 577
Brin, Alexander, 602
Brinkerhoff, James, 595
Brinkerhoff, Sally Ann, 595
Brinton, David, 569
Brion, Jefferson, 538
Bristol, Eliphalet, 594
Bristol, Rena, 594
Broden, Maroni, 598
Broigg, Marcellus, 609
Bronson, Major, 33
Brooke, Catharine, 610
Brooke, Hariet, 606
Brooke, Henry, 606
Brooke, John, 606
Brooke, July A., 606
Brooke, Robert A., 606
Brooker, Salley Ann L., 580
Brotherson, Elizabeth, 598
Brotherton, Eliza H., 614
Brown, Alex, 613
Brown, Ann, 613

Davis, Henry, 596
Davis, John, 597
Davis, N. N., 573
Davis, Rachael, 596
Dawson, Jno., 603
Dayley, John, 599
Dayton, Ann, 577
Dayton, Hiram, 577
Dayton, Hiram F., 589
Dayton, Hiram, Jr., 577
Dayton, Permelia M., 577
Dayton, Permilia, 577
Deam, Cathrine A., 612
Deam, Elisabeth, 612
Deam, Elizabeth, 611
Deam, Henry, 611
Deam, Isaac M., 612
Deam, John, 612
Deam, Sarah E., 612
Deborst, Thomas, 602
Degraw, Jacob, 606
Degraw, Rebecca, 606
Degraw, Sophia, 606
Dehort, Eli, 602
Delaware Indians, 411
Democratic Association, 3, 10,
    12–13
Denison, Henry, 585
Denison, James W., 585
Denison, Jane, 584
Des Moines River, 708
Detroit River, 250
Deuel, O. M., 569
Deuel, Polly, 575
Dibble, Philo, 593
Dille, David, 591
Dille, Harriett, 590
Dobson, Joseph, 588
Dobson, Sarah, 578
Dobson, Thomas, 578
Dodge, Augustus, 581
Dodge, Lovina, 581

Dodge, Melissa, 581
Dodge, Sally, 581
Dodge, Seth, 581
Dolinger, Eliza, 570
Dollinger, Thomas, 570
Dolten, A., 587
Dolten, Charles, 588
Dolten, Mary E., 588
Donihue, *also spelled Dunnohoo,
    Dunehue, Dannhohoo*, 157,
    279, 491, 540
Doniphan, Alexander W., *also
    spelled Donnovan*, 25–26, 32–
    34, 38–39, 47, 75, 83, 110,
    112–115, 347–348, 402, 404–
    407, 483, 567, 621–622, 625–
    629, 633–634, 640–641, 643,
    649, 657, 659–662, 669–672,
    674–675, 679, 684, 715, 729
Dosman, Polly, 587
Douglas, Joseph, J.P. for Adams
    Co., IL, 142, 218–219, 332, 751
Douglas, Stephen A., 563
Downey, C. C., 603
Downey, H., 604
Downing, James, 569
Downing, Margaret P., 569
Downy, Harvy, 602
Drake, 711
Drake, Flora, 584
Drake, Sophrana, 584
Draper, Alfred, 600
Draper, Poly, 600
Driggs, Elisa, 575
Driggs, Hannah, 577
Driggs, Lorenzo, 577
Driggs, Shadrach, 575
Driggs, Urial, 577
Drollinger, Rachel, 587
Dudley, James, 607
Dudley, Jasper, 605
Dudley, Jesey, 607

E

F

Fletcher, Rachael, 605
Flint, Hannah. *See* Holbrook, Hannah
Florida, Tampa Bay, 648
Florida Indians, 648
Flornay, John H., 63
Flournoy, Jones H., 526
Fluno, Nancy, 577
Fob, Cynthia, 575
Fob, Francis, 575
Follett, King, 95, 201, 589
Follett, Louisa, 589
Foot, Jane Ann, 587
Foot, Reuben R., 587
Foot, Timothy B., 450, 587
Foot, William, 587
Forbush, Loren, 602
Forbush, Rufus, 602
Forbush, Rufus, Jr., 603
Forbush, Sanford, 603
Ford, John F., 592
Ford, Thomas, 684
Fordham, Anna B., 584
Forgeus, Elizabeth, 584
Forgeus, John A., 569, 572
Forgeus, Rosannah, 572
Forgeus, S. L., 584
Fort Leavenworth, 247, 632, 663, 677
Fory, Elizabeth, 584
Fory, Peter Joseph, 583
Fossett, Maleby, 588
Fossett, W., 588
Foster, Charles. A., 570
Foster, Dan, 595
Foster, Elisabeth, 614
Foster, Rachel, 595
Foster, Robert, xxi, 101
Foster, Robert D., 571
Foster, Sarah, 571
Foster, Sarah D., 569

Foster, Theo. J. T., 571
Foster, William, 595
Foutz, Elizabeth, 584
Foutz, Jacob, 267, 277, 320, 487–488, 576
Foutz, Margaret, 576
Fowler, George William, 574
Fowler, Samuel, 592
Fox, John, 588
Foy, Catharine, 586
Foy, Elizabeth, 586
Foy, Susan, 586
Foy, Thomas B., 586
Frampton, Alisabeth, 585
Frampton, David, Jr., 209
Frampton, Nathan, 604
Frampton, Samuel, 209
Frampton, Willim, 209
Franklin, 139
Franklin, Lewis, 63, 69, 316, 499–500, 526, 528, 703
Fristoe, Richard, 499
Fritnell, Samiel F. M., 590
Frohock, John, 584
Frost, Abner, 599
Frost, Alvira, 599
Frost, Ester, 599
Frost, Hiram, 599
Frost, John, 599
Frost, Margaret, 599
Frye, William, C.C.C.C. for Calhoun Co., IL, 542, 548–549, 752
Fuller, Amos, 581
Fuller, Josiah, 31, 268, 320, 488, 491, 723
Fullmer, David, 571
Fullmer, Rhoda Ann, 571

G

Galann, Jane, 581

H

Hubbard, Cinthy, 582
Hubbard, Mary Ann, 576
Hubbard, Noah, 582
Hubble, Johanathan, 209
Hucher, Samuel S., 584
Hudson, Julian, 601
Huelet, Charles, xxix, 589
Huelt, Margaret, 589
Huggins, 96
Hughs, James M., 729
Hughs, Major, 657
Hulet, Anna M., 589
Humphrey, Smith, 75, 228, 640, 643
Humphry, David, 602
Humphrys, Richard, N.P. for Van Buren Co., IA, 171, 752
Hunsaker, Abraham, 597
Hunt, C. W., 579
Hunt, Celia, 605
Hunt, Daniel D., 583
Hunt, Gilbert, 605
Hunt, H., 605
Hunt, Hariet, 605
Hunt, James W., 583
Hunt, Jefferson, 605
Hunt, John, 605
Hunt, John A., 583
Hunt, Josheph, 605
Hunt, July, 605
Hunt, Levi B., 583
Hunt, Marshel, 605
Hunt, Nancy, 605
Hunt, Susan, 583
Hunt, Susan P., 583
Hunter, Ann, 569
Hunter, Edw., 569
Hunter, Edward, Jr., 569
Hunter, James W., 499
Huntington, Lydia, 595
Huntington, William, 41, 44, 48, 595

Huntsman, Catherine, 580
Huntsman, Hannah, 593
Huntsman, Jacob, 580
Huntsman, James W., 594
Hurdman, Richard, 596
Huse, Esther, 581
Huse, John, 581
Huston, John, 608
Hutchings, Lucinda, 609
Hutchings, Plina, 609
Hutchings, Shephor, 609
Hutchinson, Constantia E., 570
Hutchinson, Joseph, 578
Hutchinson, Mary, 578
Hyde, Elizabeth B., 591
Hyde, Orson, xxii, 393, 563, 569
Hyde, William, 592

I

Illinois
  Scott Co., 532
  Adams Co., 204. *See also* Columbus, IL; Quincy, IL
  Band Co., 386
  Columbus, 222. *See also* Adams Co., IL
  Commerce, 476. *See also* Nauvoo, IL; Hancock Co., IL
  Cook Co., 296
  Edwards Co., 380, 385
  Hancock Co., 224, 255, 442–443, 452, 565. *See also* Commerce, IL; Nauvoo, IL
  Nauvoo, 101–102, 563, 627
  Pike Co., 300, 446
  Pittsfield, 728, 742
  Quincy, 3, 6, 8, 10–12, 53, 57, 95, 101, 172, 179, 187, 257, 328, 330, 340, 349–350,

K

M

McDaniels, John, 574
McEe, 183
MDonough, David, 605
M'Dowell, Doctor, 56
Mace, Elizabeth, 571
Mace, Hiram, 571
Mace, Margrett, 593
McFate, J., 604
McGaham, Humphrey, 597
McGahan, William, 596
McGaw, Mathew, 457
McGee, 526
McGee, James, 254
McGregor, Malcolm M., J.P. for
    Hancock Co., IL, 281, 336, 753
McHenry, Henry, 556
McIlwrick, John, 576
McIlwrick, May, 576
McIntier, Isabella, 570
McIntier, Simon, 570
McIntosh, Solomon P., 605
MacIntush, William C., 597
McKinney, Nicolas, 466
McKinney, Wilson, 466
McKinzie, Elizabeth, 577
McKinzie, George, 577
Mackleey, Betsey, 595
Mackleey, John, 595
Mackley, Jeremiah, 699
McKown, Elizabath, 610
McKown, Lucy, 610
McKown, Marcellus, Jr., 610
McKown, Marcelus, 611
McKown, Orin, 611
McKown, Rawana, 610
McLean, Elizabeth, 593
McLeary, William, 604
McLellin, William E., *also spelled*
    M'Lellin, 83, 651
MNall, Enos, 588
MNall, Thirsy, 588
McNill, Elizabeth, 591

McOlney, Davis, 590
McRae, Alexander, *also spelled*
    McRay, 33, 36, 45–46, 92, 149,
    680
Madison, Elizabeth, 591
Maesar, F. H., 573
Maeser, Magdalin, 573
Mahoney, Bartholomew, 583
Mahoney, Mary Ann, 583
Maibury, May, 595
Mail, Hannah, 571
Maine, 357
Malin, Briggs, 579
Malin, Catherine, 569
Malin, Elijah, 569
Malin, Eliza Ann, 569
Malin, Samuel, 569
Malin, Sarah, 569
Mann, Jesse, 556
Mann, William, *also spelled*
    Wilean, 29, 208, 268, 334, 487,
    542, 721
Mansfield, Matthew, 588
Manship, 526
Manship, Nimrod, 526
Mar, John, 209
Markham, Betsy E., 609
Markham, Hannah, 587
Markham, Warren, 570, 587
Markham, William Whiting, 587
Marr, S. M., 574
Marr, W. H. J., 574
Marriott, Elisha, 593
Marsh, 66–67
Marsh, Eliphaz, 570, 728, 750
Marsh, Hannah, 570
Martin, Alice, 575
Martin, Anderson, 523
Martin, Ann, 570
Martin, Edward, 575
Martin, Philip W., J.P. for Adams
    Co., IL, 204, 753

N

O

P

Q

R

S

Y